Mexican Phoenix
Our Lady of Guadalupe: Image and Tradition across Five Centuries

In 1999 Our Lady of Guadalupe was proclaimed patron saint of the Americas by Pope John Paul II. How did a sixteenth-century Mexican painting of the Virgin Mary attract such an unprecedented honour?

Across the centuries the enigmatic power of this image has aroused fervent devotion in Mexico: it served as the banner of the rebellion against Spanish rule and, despite scepticism and anti-clericalism, still remains a potent symbol of the modern nation. But devotion was also sustained by the tradition that in 1531 Mary appeared to a poor Indian named Juan Diego and miraculously imprinted her likeness on his cape. From the start this narrative was inspired by a scriptural theology in which Juan Diego figured as another Moses and the Virgin's image as the Mexican Ark of the Covenant.

The purpose of this book is to trace the intellectual origins, the sudden efflorescence and the adamantine resilience of the tradition of Our Lady of Guadalupe. It is a story that will fascinate anyone concerned with the history of religion and its symbols.

DAVID BRADING is Professor of Mexican History, University of Cambridge. His previous books include *Miners and Merchants in Bourbon Mexico 1763–1810* (1971), which was awarded the prestigious Bolton Prize, *Haciendas and Ranchos in the Mexican Bajío* (1978), *Caudillo and Peasant in the Mexican Revolution* (ed., 1980), *Prophecy and Myth in Mexican History* (1984), *The Origins of Mexican Nationalism* (1985), *The First America* (1991) and *Church and State in Bourbon Mexico* (1994). Professor Brading taught at the University of California, Berkeley, and at Yale University before returning to Cambridge.

Our Lady of Guadalupe

MEXICAN PHOENIX

OUR LADY OF GUADALUPE:
IMAGE AND TRADITION
ACROSS FIVE CENTURIES

D. A. BRADING

CAMBRIDGE
UNIVERSITY PRESS

PUBLISHED BY THE PRESS SYNDICATE OF THE UNIVERSITY OF CAMBRIDGE
The Pitt Building, Trumpington Street, Cambridge, United Kingdom

CAMBRIDGE UNIVERSITY PRESS
The Edinburgh Building, Cambridge CB2 2RU, UK
40 West 20th Street, New York NY 10011–4211, USA
10 Stamford Road, Oakleigh, VIC 3166, Australia
Ruiz de Alarcón 13, 28014 Madrid, Spain
Dock House, The Waterfront, Cape Town 8001, South Africa

http://www.cambridge.org

First published 2001

Printed in the United Kingdom at the University Press, Cambridge

Typeface 10.5/14pt Minion   [GC]

A catalogue record for this book is available from the British Library

Library of Congress Cataloguing in Publication data
Brading, D. A.
   Mexican Phoenix: Our Lady of Guadalupe: image and tradition across five centuries / D. A. Brading.
      p.   cm.
   Includes bibliographical references and index.
   ISBN 0 521 80131 1
   1. Guadalupe, Our Lady of.   2. Mary, Blessed Virgin, Saint – Apparitions and
miracles – Mexico.   3. Mexico – Religious life and customs.   I. Title.

BT660.G8 B67 2001
232.91′7′097253–dc21   00–063061
ISBN 0 521 80131 1 hardback

For Celia Wu

And there appeared a great sign in heaven; a woman clothed with the sun, and the moon under her feet, and upon her head a crown of twelve stars; and she being with child cried, travailing in birth, and pained to be delivered . . . And to the woman were given two wings of a great eagle, that she might fly into the wilderness . . .
And I, John, saw the holy city, new Jerusalem, coming down from God out of heaven, prepared as a bride adorned for her husband.

REVELATION 12.1–2, 14; 21.2

The day in which the Virgin of Tepeyac is not adored in this land, it is certain that there shall have disappeared, not only Mexican nationality, but also the very memory of the dwellers of Mexico today . . . In the last extreme, in the most desperate cases, the cult of the Mexican Virgin is the only bond that unites them.

IGNACIO MANUEL ALTAMIRANO, *The Feast of Guadalupe*

Contents

Illustrations

Preface

In 1993 I returned to Mexico and there, in the idyllic surroundings of the Centre for the Study of the History of Mexico at Condumex, I immersed myself in reading a profusion of baroque sermons preached in honour of Our Lady of Guadalupe. So enthused was I by these panegyrics that I persuaded Condumex to publish in facsimile form *Seven Guadalupan Sermons 1709–1765* as their book for that year. In *The First America* (1991), I had already included a chapter on the Virgin entitled 'Mexican Phoenix'. Inspired by Francisco de la Maza's classic work, *Mexican Guadalupanism* (1952), I there emphasized the patriotic motivation of Miguel Sánchez, the first chronicler of the Virgin Mary's apparitions to Juan Diego, even if it was obvious that he was also a profound theologian. What the sermons revealed was the extent to which preachers drew on the Greek Fathers of the Church to elaborate a neo-platonic theology of the Mexican image. Here was the starting point of my research and the explanation of why this book begins in the ancient rather than in the New World.

Distracted by a vain attempt to define the relation between patriotism and nationalism, I did not begin to write this general account of the Guadalupe tradition until 1996. By then I had already delved into the extensive works of Clemente de Jesús Mungía, the nineteenth-century bishop of Michoacán, and, much earlier, in *The Origins of Mexican Nationalism*, first published in Spanish in 1973, had described the idiosyncratic intervention of Servando de Mier, the insurgent ideologue. What soon became clear was that in almost every generation since the middle years of the seventeenth century something of note or interest had been written about the Virgin of Tepeyac. The materials for a study of the cult and tradition of the Guadalupe are abundant but heterogeneous. They range from weighty treatises, polemical disquisitions and critical pamphlets to panegyrical sermons, illustrated albums and detailed descriptions of public celebrations, not to mention pastoral letters, papal pronouncements and iconographical assessments. The causes and occasions of these publications were diverse. But it should be noted that devotion to the Virgin has played a major role in Mexican history, be it in the achievement of independence or as a symbol of the Church's resistance to political intervention. On another plane, the historical credibility of the apparition narrative has been a source of contention since the beginning of the nineteenth century. To trace the development of the tradition of Our Lady of Guadalupe is thus no easy task, since it is imperative to eschew any diversion into general history or embroilment in partisan polemic.

A word about method and terminology may prove helpful. The introduction provides a conspectus of the subjects covered in the chapters which follow. The order is essentially chronological, starting in the seventeenth century and reaching the present day. The last chapter offers a brief theological interpretation of the image and its tradition. Generally, but not invariably, sources are discussed, not when they were written but when they were published; thus the 1556 *Statements* are examined in chapter 11, since they were not printed and analysed until the 1880s. This method thus allows readers to observe the gradual growth in knowledge of the cult's origins and how the discovery of early documents affected the tradition. As regards terminology, I follow Mexican usage and at times refer to the image as 'the Guadalupe', which is to say, *la guadalupana*. To render my account more readable, I have translated all book titles into English, albeit retaining their original titles in the notes and bibliography.

In the research and writing of this book I have incurred many debts. Without the invaluable, pioneering works of Francisco de la Maza and Edmundo O'Gorman my interest in this theme would never have been aroused or indeed sustained. An understanding of the historical and theological significance of holy images came from reading Peter Brown, Jaroslav Pelikan and Hans Belting. Like all students of the Guadalupe, I have benefited from *Testimonios históricos guadalupanos* (1982), a comprehensive collection of sources expertly edited by Ernesto de la Torre Villar and Ramiro Navarro de Anda. At Condumex I wish to thank Julio Gutiérrez Trujillo, the president of the Consultative Council, and especially Manuel Ramos Medina, the director, who welcomed me as the first visiting scholar and encouraged me to make Condumex my base of research in Mexico. I am grateful to the staff of that Centre, and in particular to José Gutiérrez, who found many a book that I had been unable to trace. Fausto Zerón Medina first alerted me to the significance of both Clemente de Jesús Munguía and the 1895 coronation and thereafter assisted me by comment and through the supply of valuable source material. Guillermo Tovar de Teresa was remarkably generous, both with rare books and in good counsel. Ramón Mujica Pinilla told me about Blessed Amadeus of Portugal. Peter Burke offered a prompt, instructive assessment of the completed text, and so incisive were the generous comments of Eric Van Young that I reframed an entire chapter and transposed another. As regards the illustrations, I am greatly indebted to Jaime Cuadriello, who helped me understand the iconography of the Virgin and then obtained the photographs of the images which adorn this book. In that task he was assisted by the interim rector of the Basílica of St Mary of Guadalupe, Mons. Antonio Macedo Tenllado, by the director of the Basilica's Museum, Jorge Guadarrama, and by Eumelia Hernández, head of the photographic section of the Instituto de Investigaciones Estéticas of the National Autonomous University of Mexico. For other materials, comments and assistance I thank Clara García Ayluardo, Susan Deans-Smith, Edmund Hill, OP, Marta Eugenia García Ugarte, Manuel Olimón Nolasco, Enrique Florescano, Aidan Nichols, OP, José Luis Neyra, Julie Coimbra and Alejandro González Acosta. It should be emphasized, however, that I alone am responsible for the opinions and interpretation advanced in this book.

It was the award of a Leverhulme Research Fellowship which allowed me to undertake research in Mexico during 1993. A subsequent visit in 1996 was made possible by my appointment as Julio Cortázar Visiting Professor at the University of Guadalajara. Without two terms of sabbatical leave from the University of Cambridge I could not have completed the book. Margaret Rankine typed the manuscript, corrected my errors, and generally encouraged me. At the Cambridge University Press, William Davies, as always, offered a generous welcome to the typescript and urged me to find illustrations. Permission to reproduce from paintings and books in their possession was granted by the Museo de la Basílica de Guadalupe, the Instituto de Investigaciones Estéticas, the Instituto de Antropología e Historia, the Museo Nacional de Arte, the Museo Nacional de Historia, the Centro de Estudios de Historia de Mexico, Condumex, the Archivo Casasús, the Centro de Cultura Casa Lamm, the Biblioteca Nacional, the José Luis Neyra Collection, the Ramón Cuadriello Collection, and in Madrid the Biblioteca Nacional. To conclude, at all moments during both the research and the writing of this book, I enjoyed the unstinting support of my wife, Celia Wu, and I dedicate the book to her, not least for her good sense in choosing to enter the world on the feast day of Our Lady of Guadalupe.

Introduction

In 1557 an Englishman in Mexico, Robert Tomson, was arrested on charges of heresy. Over conversation at dinner, he had declared that in England the monasteries had been dissolved and that 'the images that were in their churches and other places were taken away and used no more', since their veneration was 'contrary to the express commandment of Almighty God, Thou shalt not make to thy selfe any graven image'. A Spaniard present replied that everyone knew that such images were not to be worshipped; but justified their presence in churches by asserting that 'they were books for the simple people, to make them understand the glory of the saints in heaven'. He further defended praying for the intercession of saints by the analogy of a royal court where it was always better to approach the king through the mediation of a favourite. To counter these arguments, Tomson simply appealed to scripture, where God, acting through the prophets and evangelists, encouraged all sinners to repent and seek his mercy. Had not Christ said: 'Come unto me all ye who labour and are over laden, and I will refresh you'? Angered by this response, a 'villanous Portugal' exclaimed: 'Basta ser Inglés para saber todo esto y más', which was to say, 'It is enough to be an Englishman to know all this and more.'[1] To punish his Protestant iconoclasm, Tomson was arrested and sent to Spain.

Only a year before this dangerous conversation, in September 1556, the Franciscan provincial in Mexico had bluntly criticized the archbishop, Alonso de Montúfar, for preaching a sermon in which he had commended devotion to *Our Lady of Guadalupe*, a painting of the Virgin Mary venerated in a chapel at Tepeyac, just outside the city. In their mission to the Indians of New Spain the Franciscans had taught the natives to worship God in heaven and not to adore images made from wood and stone. But the archbishop had now referred to certain miracles which had been performed at Tepeyac. There was thus the danger that the Indians might imagine that a mere painting had some divine power and hence return to idolatry. Although all record of this dispute disappeared from sight, not to enter the public domain until the 1880s, its occurrence indicated the tensions that surrounded the cult of holy images in sixteenth-century Mexico. Indeed, some twenty years later, Bernardino de Sahagún, the most renowned of the Franciscans who studied Nahua language and religion, complained that the cult of Guadalupe afforded Indians a subterfuge for idolatry, since prior to the Spanish conquest they had come on pilgrimage from afar to worship Tonantzin, the mother of the gods, at her temple in Tepeyac, and continued to arrive at the Christian chapel to pray to that goddess since in Nahuatl the Virgin was also addressed as Tonantzin.[2]

It was another Englishman, Miles Philips, who wrote one of the earliest descriptions of the chapel at Tepeyac. A member of the expedition led by John Hawkins, in 1568 he was captured and taken to Mexico City, where before entry he saw:

> a very faire church, called our Ladyes church, in which there is an image of our Lady of silver and gilt, being as high, and as large as a tall woman, in which church, and before this image, there are as many lamps of silver as there be dayes in the yeere, which upon high dayes are all lighted. Whensoever any Spaniards passe by this church, although they be on horse backe, they will alight, and come into the church, and kneele before the image, and pray to our Lady to defend them from all evil; so that whether he be horseman or footman he will not passe by, but first goe into the Church, and pray as aforesayd, which if they doe not, they thinke and believe that they shall never prosper: which image they call in the Spanish tongue, Nuestra sennora de Guadalupe. At this place there are certain cold baths, which arise, springing up as though the water did seeth: the water whereof is somewhat brackish in taste, but very good for any that have any sore or wound, to wash themselves wherewith, for as they say, it healeth many: and every yeere once upon our Lady day the people used to repaire thither to offer, and to pray in that Church before the image, and they say that our Lady of Guadalupe doeth worke a number of miracles. About this Church there is not any towne of Spaniards that is inhabited, but certaine Indians doe dwell there in houses of their own countrey building.

Situated at the foot of a hill, the chapel marked the beginning of a causeway across the marshy lake into the island city of Mexico, and hence attracted the devotion of travellers. As a Protestant, Philips was more impressed by a silver statue recently donated by a wealthy silver miner, Alonso de Villaseca, than by the simple painting of the Virgin which adorned the sanctuary.[3] It was from the 'brackish' spring water that subsequent miracles were to come.

When Archbishop Montúfar encouraged devotion to Our Lady of Guadalupe, he cited as comparable cases the veneration of images of the Virgin in the cathedral at Seville, at Zaragoza and Montserrat, and at Loreto in Italy. In so doing, he implicitly rejected the Franciscan vision of their mission as a revival of primitive Christianity, a Church stripped of medieval abuse and complication. Instead, he proposed that the clergy should promote devotions which aroused popular fervour in Europe. And what better way was there to attract Indians than to create sanctuaries to house images endowed with the power of performing miracles? In Europe such sanctuaries were visited by countless pilgrims. It was before Our Lady of Montserrat that in 1522 St Ignatius Loyola spent a night's vigil before renouncing all worldly ambition by adopting pilgrim garb and becoming a hermit. So too, in 1581 the French humanist, Michel de Montaigne, spent three days at the Holy House of Loreto, where he offered a silver votive tablet and confessed that he had been deeply impressed by the sanctuary's 'show of religion'. As late as the eighteenth century, Benedict-Joseph Labre (1748–83), a flea-bitten pilgrim, visited all the principal images in Western Europe before settling in Rome.[4] As we shall see, during the colonial period the Church in New Spain created an entire network of sanctuaries which attracted pilgrims seeking spiritual comfort and cures of their ills, and thus emulated the Spanish pattern of devotion.

In Europe, most of the famous holy images derived from the late Middle Ages, even if pious legend often claimed that they had been carved or painted by St Luke. But the greatest of these figures had a miraculous origin ascribed to them. The Holy House of Loreto had been brought by angels from Nazareth, where it had served as the dwelling of the Holy Family. The wooden image of Our Lady of Pilar at Zaragoza had been left by the Virgin Mary herself, when she appeared to St James the Apostle during his mission to Spain. Obviously, the more impressive the spiritual credentials, the more elaborate was the cult which developed across the centuries. Moreover, in Spain, virtually all the leading images became the symbols of civic or provincial identity and thus attracted patriotic sentiment. In 1641 the Virgin of Pilar was acclaimed as patron of the city of Zaragoza, only then, in 1678, for the Cortes of Aragon to name her as patron of that kingdom. So significant had the cult become that, in 1681, work began on the construction of a new cathedral to house the image, a grandiose building which took a century to complete. It was in this period that sanctuaries vied to obtain distinctions from Rome. As far as can be ascertained, Our Lady of Loreto was the first of these holy figures to be 'canonized', which was to say, that in 1699 this Virgin was given a feast day with her own mass and office. Less than a generation later, in 1723, the Virgin of Pilar was similarly honoured, with her feast celebrated on 12 October.[5]

The New World was not slow to imitate Europe. Although it has been argued that the Renaissance robbed sacred art of its numinous quality by imposing the primacy of aesthetic values, in Spanish America any number of holy images, some imported from Spain, others made locally, aroused fervent devotion.[6] An intimation of the spiritual power of such figures can be observed in Peru, when in 1593 there arrived at the port of Callao a life-sized crucifix, a replica of the Christ of Burgos. The image was escorted by Augustinian friars in public procession to Lima, its progress accompanied by salvoes of cannon-fire and excited crowds thronging the streets. Once it was installed in the conventual church, the friars celebrated mass graced with the presence of the viceroy, judges of the high court and other dignitaries, many of whom promptly enrolled in the confraternities raised to support the cult.[7] In 1574, the city council of Mexico named Our Lady of Los Remedios as its patron, a small saddle image which had been brought over by a conqueror, lost during battle, and then, thanks to an apparition of the Virgin Mary, discovered by an Indian. Only two years later the figure was carried in procession from its sanctuary just outside the city and placed in the cathedral to pray for the Virgin's help in the great plague that then afflicted the Indians. On a less dramatic occasion, in 1595 the image was brought to the cathedral to intercede for the arrival of the seasonal rains. So effective was its intercession that in the two following centuries the Virgin of Los Remedios was regularly carried through the streets with the aim of hastening the seasonal rainfall. In the course of the seventeenth century virtually every city in Spanish America came to possess its own patron saint, and every province a sanctuary with a miraculous image.

One of the most curious features of Catholic theology in this epoch was the divorce between devotion and doctrine. Confronted with the challenge of Protestant iconoclasm and charges of idolatry, the Council of Trent denied that holy images possessed any divine power and insisted that all the veneration paid to them was transferred to their heavenly originals. But during the sixteenth century there were any number of Latin editions of the works of the Greek Fathers of the Church, and not least among them, the treatises of St John Damascene and St Theodore of Studios, which defended the veneration of icons from the attacks of the iconoclasts of the seventh century. As we shall see, these Eastern theologians were keenly read in New Spain and their neoplatonic doctrines applied to celebrate the cult of Marian images. In effect, the absence of any positive Catholic theology on this devotion drove preachers and chroniclers to draw on the tradition of the Orthodox Church.

What Mexican chronicles reveal, however, is that there was indeed a Catholic doctrine of miraculous Marian images, but that it was to be found in a controversial, prophetic work, the *New Apocalypse*, written in Latin by Joannes Menesius da Silva (1431–82), a Franciscan visionary and reformer better known as Blessed Amadeus of Portugal. Widely known for his prediction of the imminent advent of an angelic pope and defence of Mary's Immaculate Conception, Amadeus also revealed that the Virgin had declared that to the end of the world she would be bodily present in those images through which she performed miracles; present in much the same way as Christ in the Eucharist.[8] Although Amadeus was denounced for heresy, in Spain the Franciscans defended his reputation and published commentaries on his revelations. In seventeenth-century Mexico both Franciscans and Jesuits accepted the doctrine that Mary was present in her sanctuaries where miracles were performed. And indeed, several Jesuit preachers applied the doctrine of transubstantiation to the image of Guadalupe, arguing that its paints and colours had been miraculously transfigured into the likeness of Mary, wherein she was perpetually present. Not for nothing were the sanctuaries which housed these cult images defined as spiritual fortresses, where the faithful were protected from demonic assault by the real presence of the Mother of God.[9]

The application of such a doctrine was in part anticipated by Miguel Sánchez (1596?–1674) in his *Image of the Virgin Mary, Mother of Guadalupe* (1648), in which he informed his enthralled compatriots that the Mexican Virgin was a faithful copy made by miracle of the image of Mary seen by St John the Evangelist and described in chapter 12 of his Apocalypse. This was but prelude to a densely argued text in which Sánchez deployed all the resources of scriptural typology to magnify the Guadalupe, so that figures such as the burning bush and the Ark of the Covenant, which had been applied to Mary since the early Church, were taken as specific references to the Virgin of Tepeyac. At the same time, Sánchez provided the first published account of the Virgin's apparition to a poor Indian, Juan Diego, and the miraculous imprinting of her likeness on his cape. Here too, typology was invoked to elucidate the significance of these events, since the Indian figured as both the St James of Mexico, its San Diego, and more important, its Moses who brought the Guadalupe, the Mexican Ark of the Covenant, to Tepeyac, which by turns was described as the Mexican Sinai and Zion. A disciple of St Augustine, Sánchez was animated as much by patriotic as by religious sentiment, and his whole concern was to demonstrate that the Mexican Church owed its foundation to the direct intervention of the Mother of God, who thereby declared herself the special patron and mother of the Mexican people.[10]

The arguments of Miguel Sánchez can only be understood within the context of an hispanic culture where the Catholic monarchy of the Habsburgs was seen as chosen by divine providence to defend the Catholic faith from both Muslims and Protestants. Charles V was hailed as another David and Philip II as a second Solomon, especially since the latter's convent palace at Escorial was seen as the building which most resembled the Temple at Jerusalem. Moreover, the early Franciscans in Mexico had interpreted the conversion of the Indians both as a revival of the primitive Church and as divine compensation to the Church for the Reformation, since in precisely the same years when the rich, arrogant nations of Northern Europe fell into heresy, the poor, humble peoples of New Spain entered the fold. Confronted with such a powerful theological justification of the Catholic monarchy's dominion, the creole clergy embraced Sánchez' revelations as the means of providing their *patria* with an autonomous spiritual foundation. It was not the case that his book created the devotion to the Guadalupe, since, already in 1622, a handsome new sanctuary had been built to replace the chapel raised by Montúfar. Its importance lay in providing the theological rationale for the cult.

Such was the explosion of fervour that in 1695–1709 a majestic new church was constructed at Tepeyac, an edifice which in scale and splendour rivalled all but the greatest cathedrals of New Spain. In many provincial cities subordinate sanctuaries dedicated to the Guadalupe were built, usually situated *extra muros* at some distance from the city, in replication of the relation of Tepeyac and the capital. The next development occurred in 1737, when Mexico City was devastated by an epidemic which drove thousands to an early grave. With no material remedy of any avail, the city council joined with the cathedral chapter to proclaim Our Lady of Guadalupe as the capital's principal patron. Other cities followed suit and in 1746 the image was acclaimed as the patron of the entire kingdom of New Spain. The euphoria of the creole elite which these events occasioned reached new heights when in 1754 Benedict XIV not merely confirmed the Virgin of Tepeyac as patron, but also endowed her with a feast on 12 December with its own mass and office. Since only Our Lady of Pilar had obtained a similar honour within the hispanic world, the Mexican Virgin could now claim to rival the most celebrated Marian images in Europe. In a sermon preached in 1748 on the last days of the world, Francisco Javier Carranza declared that although Anti-Christ would seize power in Europe in that epoch, in America Our Lady of Guadalupe would preserve the Catholic faith and thus ensure that both the pope and the king of Spain would flee to Mexico, thereby converting the city into the capital of a new, universal Catholic monarchy.

It was in the sermons preached in honour of the Guadalupe in the period 1661–1767 that creole orators drew especially on the Greek Fathers to exalt the 'Mexican Phoenix'. What was the Guadalupe but 'a portrait image of the idea of God', which was to say, a faithful likeness of Mary which the Almighty had conceived from all eternity? From this startling claim it was but a short step to assert that the Guadalupe was a portrait of the Virgin as she appeared in the flesh, but whereas the image of Mary which appeared in Palestine was present only for a few years, by contrast, her image in Mexico was destined to remain for ever. In the sermons preached before the assembled dignitaries in the sanctuary at Tepeyac, learned canons and Jesuits scaled the neo-platonic chain of images in audacious metaphors which trembled on the limits of orthodoxy, all designed to exalt the singular Providence which distinguished their country.

If the Mexican Church proved successful in obtaining Rome's approval of their national cult, it was in part because in the late seventeenth century a circle of learned clerics had laboured to substantiate Sánchez' revelations by obtaining juridical statements about the origin of Juan Diego and the antiquity of the tradition of the Virgin's apparitions. In their search for historical evidence they were immeasurably assisted by a simple but moving account of the apparitions written in Nahuatl, the principal native language of central Mexico, and published in 1649 by the chaplain at Tepeyac. It was soon accepted that this text derived from a manuscript written in the sixteenth century by Antonio Valeriano, a disciple of the Franciscans. A Spanish translation of this account, modified to suit contemporary taste, was printed and enjoyed considerable circulation. Here were grounds enough for Rome to approve the tradition. It was left to the eighteenth century, when talented artists competed to copy the Guadalupe, to scrutinize the image and conclude that its incomparable beauty derived from a combination of painting techniques that could be described as miraculous.

In the very years when devotion to the Mexican Virgin appeared to command universal assent, in Europe the cult of holy images was dismissed as idolatrous or superstitious. Many of the philosophers of the Enlightenment were deists who rejected and ridiculed the Christian faith. The Scots thinker, David Hume, defined miracles as an impossibility, an affront to the laws of Nature, and wrote a natural history of religion in which he portrayed the Catholic cult of saints as a popular revival of pagan polytheism.[11] Equally important, orthodox Church historians deployed their erudition to demonstrate the falsity of many pious legends. So too, Benito Jerónimo Feijoo, a respected Benedictine abbot, questioned the value of pilgrimage, criticized the expectation of miraculous cures, and roundly condemned any number of 'vulgar errors' which afflicted the populace of eighteenth-century Spain. In effect, both historical criticism and scientific method were invoked to undermine the religious culture of baroque Catholicism. It was in 1794 that the chief cosmographer of the Indies, Juan Bautista Muñoz, presented a memoir to the Royal Academy of History in Madrid, in which he cited Sahagún's early criticism of the Guadalupe cult and concluded that the apparition narrative had no reliable historical foundation. Only published in 1817, this brief memoir was to be echoed by Mexican scholars later in the century.

A further portent of the change in the climate of opinion was afforded by a sermon preached by Servando de Mier, a creole Dominican, at Tepeyac in 1794, where he scandalized the congregation by asserting that not merely had St Thomas the Apostle preached the gospel in Mexico, but he had also left the image of Guadalupe inscribed on his cape, which thus had been venerated centuries before the Spaniards arrived in the New World. With this ingenious theory, Mier sought to by-pass contemporary doubts and to provide the Mexican Church with an apostolic foundation equal to that of St James in Spain. By this time news of the French Revolution had reached Mexico and inflamed men's minds in diverse ways. Many young creoles were stirred by the spectacle of Napoleon's conquests and the example of the United States, and hence silently espoused the cause of independence. Among devout priests, however, Carranza's prophecy was recalled and cited in sermons, so that as the Church in Europe suffered expropriation and the closure of monasteries, in Mexico expectations grew that the New Spain was destined to become a Catholic bulwark, the refuge for both the pope and the king of Spain.

It was in 1810 that Miguel Hidalgo, the parish priest of Dolores, called out the rural masses in rebellion against Spanish rule. By then French troops had already invaded the Peninsula, imposed Joseph Bonaparte on the Spanish throne, and launched an attack on the Church. The secular spirit of this era was best expressed when the image of Our Lady of Loreto was seized and despatched to Paris for deposit in the National Library as 'a celebrated monument of ignorance and the most absurd superstition'.[12]

So too, Pius VII was taken to France and obliged to witness Napoleon's coronation as emperor of the French. But in Spain, resistance to the French invasion was nowhere more intense than in Zaragoza, where friars and priests played a leading role during the siege of that city, when the populace chanted: 'the Virgin of Pilar says she does not want to be French, she wants to be Captain of the Aragonese people'.[13] Much the same patriotic spirit animated the Mexican insurgents, since for their banner Hidalgo gave them a copy of the Virgin of Tepeyac, so that they marched to the cry of 'Long Live Our Lady of Guadalupe.' The patron of New Spain was thus transformed into the symbol and flag of an insurgent nation engaged in civil war to achieve independence. Not all creoles favoured the rebels, and indeed the propertied classes supported the creation of a royalist army capable of containing popular depredations. In the event, Mexico obtained its freedom in 1821, when Agustín de Iturbide, a royalist colonel, launched a military rebellion against the anti-clerical measures of the Spanish Cortes. His seizure of power was hailed by preachers who thanked Our Lady of Guadalupe for uniting the Mexicans in pursuit of independence and who expressed their confidence that she would preserve their Church from the revolutionary excesses of Europe.

When Iturbide's short-lived empire was replaced by a federal republic, clerical apprehensions were soon aroused by the emergence of Liberal politicians intent on seizure of Church wealth. For their part, the clergy declared that the Mexican State had not inherited the patronage rights of the Spanish crown, so that until a concordat was agreed with Rome the government had no right to meddle in the nomination of bishops and canons. To strengthen their case, many priests now adopted an ultra-montane theology, in which the papacy was defined as an absolute monarchy with powers of intervention throughout the Church. It was a theology that was to culminate in the proclamation of papal infallibility in 1870. Before then, however, the Mexican Church had suffered the onslaught of the Liberal Reform of the 1850s. In successive blows, the radical government expropriated all Church property, stripped the clergy of their legal privilege, dissolved the monasteries, secularized education, and finally separated Church and State. These measures were vehemently condemned by the bishops, who openly supported the conservative generals who opposed the Liberals. The result was a bitter civil war. The anguish experienced by the clergy during this conflict was nowhere more powerfully expressed than in the two sermons preached at Tepeyac in 1859–60 by Clemente de Jesús Munguía, the intransigent bishop of Michoacán.

When the bishops were expelled from Mexico they took refuge in Rome, where they were welcomed by Pius IX. It was then that Archbishop Pelagio Antonio de Labastida joined with the pope to plan the reinvigoration of the Mexican Church through the creation of new dioceses. Thanks to their residence in the Vatican the Mexican bishops became fully conscious of belonging to a universal Church and thereafter chose to despatch their most promising young priests to complete their education in Rome. So too, it was during their time in Europe that they took cognizance of the sudden emergence of Lourdes as the leading Marian sanctuary and were able to observe how the French hierarchy took advantage of the railway system and the printing press to organize national pilgrimages and popularize the cult. If the papacy constituted the principle of authority on which their Church rested, it was Catholic France which offered Mexican bishops a living example of a renewal which encompassed both theology and devotion.[14]

During the long years when Mexico was ruled by Porfirio Díaz, 1876–1911, the Church slowly rebuilt its institutions and sought to re-establish its public influence. Inspired by the example of Lourdes, the bishops obtained permission from the papacy to crown the image of Guadalupe. In 1895 the entire month of October was given over to celebration as diocesan pilgrimages arrived at Tepeyac to hear mass and listen to sermons. The director of the project, José Antonio Plancarte, sent invitations to bishops across North America and the Caribbean, so that on 12 October, when the coronation was staged, twenty-two Mexican archbishops and bishops were joined by fourteen prelates from the United States and another three from Quebec, Havana and Panama. The album which commemorated the celebrations not merely offered a description of events, but also printed the texts of the sermons which were preached during the month. As was to be expected, the neo-platonic theology and sacramental pretensions of the baroque epoch had long since been abandoned; but by contrast the scriptural figures first advanced by Miguel Sánchez still attracted many orators. The spirit of the occasion was best expressed by the bishop of Colima, when he exclaimed that he had come to Tepeyac, 'the Mexican Zion', to scrutinize in the tablets of its laws the destiny of his country. So also, the renovated sanctuary was compared to the Temple at Jerusalem and the image of Guadalupe to the Ark of the Covenant. But preachers also asserted that the foundation of Mexico could be dated from the apparition of the Virgin Mary at Tepeyac, since she had then liberated its people from the bondage of idolatry and tyranny. Equally important, they saluted the Virgin as the foundress of the new, mestizo nation, since in her sanctuary she had reconciled Spaniards and Indians, uniting them in common devotion and faith. In this emphasis on the social role of the Guadalupe these preachers in part echoed the affirmations of Manuel Ignacio Altamirano, a radical who admitted that, for the Mexicans, 'in the last extreme, in the most desperate cases, the cult of the Mexican Virgin is the only bond which unites them'.

The revival of the Church was nowhere more manifest than in the flood of publications dealing with Our Lady of Guadalupe during the 1880s. Several of these treatises aimed to interpret the sixteenth-century chronicles and documents that had been recently printed for the first time. Some were merely panegyrical, designed to promote devotion. But there was also a great deal of controversy. In particular, the discovery and publication of the 1556 manuscript dealing with the dispute between Archbishop

Montúfar and the Franciscan provincial caused a stir, since here could be found the attribution of the Guadalupe image to an Indian artist named Marcos. Alarm in clerical circles deepened when it became known that Joaquín García Icazbalceta, Mexico's most respected historian, had concluded that the apparition narrative had been first recorded by Sánchez 116 years after the event, and that the universal silence of sixteenth-century chroniclers about the miracle meant that the tradition had no historical credibility. The fury of the 'apparitionists' knew no bounds and they savagely attacked not merely García Icazbalceta, a devout and conservative Catholic, but also the very Franciscans who had founded the Mexican Church for their silence or hostility to the Guadalupe cult. Yet further controversy was occasioned when it was found that the golden crown which had adorned the Virgin in her image since time immemorial had been silently erased.

The outbreak of the Mexican Revolution in 1910 unleashed a wave of anticlericalism that eventually threatened to destroy the achievements of the late nineteenth century. Bishops were expelled from the country, priests persecuted and churches confiscated. The 1917 Constitution denied the Church all legal personality and forbade ministers of religion to intervene in education or politics. But, when the revolutionary State sought to curtail the number of priests and places of worship, the bishops placed the republic under interdict. In 1926–9 there ensued a bitter civil war in which the Catholic peasantry, especially in western Mexico, fought the federal army to a standstill. Rebel banners consisted of the figure of the Guadalupe under which was inscribed the slogan, *Viva Cristo Rey*, 'Long live Christ the King.' It was from the ranks of Cristero clerics that there emerged the campaign to beatify Juan Diego, thus offering the faithful a loyal Indian hero to offset the revolutionary nationalist emphasis on the pre-hispanic civilization and the contemporary native peasantry. When Church and State effected a silent reconciliation after the Second World War, the way was opened for the construction of a vast new basilica at Tepeyac, its cost in part covered by government subsidy, which was consecrated in 1976. With the arrival of John Paul II in 1979, Mexico assumed a new importance within the general scheme of the Catholic Church, and in 1990 its Church was rewarded with the beatification of Juan Diego.

During the twentieth century the previous debate over the 'historicity' of the apparitions continued unabated and new sources were periodically discovered, only later to be found wanting. But a new, theological emphasis became evident when the *Nican mopohua*, the Nahuatl text of the apparition narrative, became the object of sustained meditation. The effect of the Theology of Liberation, not to mention the Second Vatican Council, was to concentrate attention on the pastoral character of the dialogues between the Virgin and Juan Diego. By the 1990s, various translations in different languages had been made and the text was now seen to be, in some ill-defined sense, 'inspired', and thus constituted a Mexican gospel. If the 'option for the poor' led Mexican commentators to dismiss Sánchez as the exponent of baroque conceits, North American scholars not merely restated the sceptical approach of Muñoz and García Icazbalceta, but also demonstrated the textual dependence of the *Nican mopohua* on the Spanish account provided by Sánchez. None of these scholarly discoveries and controversies, however, had much effect on the faith of the Mexican people, and in 1999 that faith was further honoured by John Paul II when he proclaimed the Mexican Virgin to be the patron of the entire American hemisphere. The Holy See thus implicitly designated the Guadalupe as the premier Marian image within the Catholic Church, since, be it in theological significance or in geographical extension, where could her equal be found?

The purpose of this book is thus to illumine the sudden efflorescence and the adamantine resilience of the tradition of Our Lady of Guadalupe. If Miguel Sánchez did not initiate the devotion, he certainly determined the manner in which the image was exalted and justified. To understand the doctrinal matrix in which the tradition emerged, it is necessary to return to Byzantium, St Augustine and Habsburg Spain. However, even in Sánchez' lifetime, a sustained campaign was launched to subvert his authority by attributing the tradition to Indian manuscript sources. Much of the controversy which has haunted the cult in the past two centuries has been focused on the credibility of that attribution. For all that, the triumphant survival of devotion to Our Lady of Guadalupe, encountered at all levels of Mexican society, demonstrates the enduring spiritual power of this image and its tradition.

Some caveats are in order. The cult and tradition of the Guadalupe developed within the context of the universal Catholic Church, and to isolate the image from the history of that Church is to run the risk of distortion. In particular, readers unfamiliar with Catholicism should remember that, for the Church at large, Our Lady of Guadalupe is simply a Mexican representation of the Virgin Mary, Mother of God, and that in her sanctuary the faithful attend the same Eucharistic service, hear the same scriptural readings and receive the same communion as can be found in any other Catholic church throughout the world. On the other hand, the changes in the way the Virgin has been presented and interpreted reflect the equally profound changes wrought in Mexican society across the centuries. It is no coincidence that the clerics who sought to establish the Guadalupe tradition upon the basis of Indian sources equally strove to identify pre-hispanic civilization as the classical antiquity of their country. Indeed, the manner in which the native past has been conceived bears an intimate, albeit variable, relation to the way in which the Virgin's role in Mexican history has been presented.

The most important caveat remains. This book concentrates on doctrine, history and ceremony. It does not pretend to trace the development of the cult of the Guadalupe either as regards its geographical diffusion or its social and ethnic penetration. Obviously, devotions only grow in strength when they are actively received by the faithful. Bishops and priests can preach; but over time it is the laity who decide the success or failure of any given devotion. Much has been made of the pre-hispanic roots of native participation in the cult of Guadalupe; but little evidence has survived of the perdurability of any pre-hispanic image of Tonantzin in native minds and hearts. In any case, from the start the devotion was as much creole as Indian and it was clearly the creole clergy who were chiefly responsible for its diffusion across the vast territories of New Spain. There was, of course, also the role of Mexican women in the reception and transmission of the devotion, a role which this book utterly neglects, but which is central to any understanding of how Our Lady of Guadalupe came to be regarded and cherished as the mother of the Mexican people.

In a celebrated essay, Henry Adams, the New England historian, penned an eloquent contrast between the spiritual power exerted by the Virgin Mary in medieval France and the dynamo, the electrical power which drove the industrial civilization of the United States. In that contrast he marvelled at the power of women in the Middle Ages, be it in religion or literature, only to lament the absence of that power in the United States at the beginning of the twentieth century.[15] He added: 'An American Virgin would never dare command; an American Venus would never dare exist.' Since his day, thanks to Hollywood, any number of American women may have claimed the title of American Venus. But where is the American Virgin? Like most of his compatriots in that era, Henry Adams knew little about Mexico. Yet in Mexico both the insurgents of 1810 and the Zapatistas of 1910, not to mention the Cristeros, marched under the banner of the Guadalupe, and in the present day millions of pilgrims visit its sanctuary each year. What is the source and nature of the power of this image? Oddly enough, at the doctrinal level, the contemporary Catholic Church has little to say about such matters. In the concluding chapter some rudimentary reflections concerning the spiritual power of holy images are advanced, albeit as much written to elicit theological debate as to answer the question.

1

Image and typology

I

At the beginning of the fourth century, when Constantine the Great embraced Christianity as his imperial religion, his sister asked Bishop Eusebius of Caesarea, the church historian, to give her a likeness of Christ. But he refused, explaining that since Christ was both God and man it was impossible to represent him. In this opinion Eusebius echoed St Clement of Alexandria and Origen, whose insistence that the words of scripture were but outward signs of profound spiritual doctrine led them to scorn any attempt to paint, carve or sculpt figures of Christ or the Holy Trinity. With the spectacle of idolatry still enacted in all the temples about them, how could they approve the veneration of images?[1] In his passionate manner, the North African apologist, Tertullian, condemned all makers of images, no matter what their purpose, and compared these artists to actors and harlots, since to represent was to deceive, its evil purpose being to arouse the passions and incite spectators to idolatry or sin.[2] In these denunciations Christian theologians drew upon the Old Testament and in particular upon the Book of Exodus, where the ten commandments given to Israel began by stating:

> I am the Lord thy God, who have brought thee out of the land of Egypt, out of the house of bondage. Thou shalt have no other gods before me. Thou shalt not make unto thee any graven image, or any likeness of anything that is in the heavens above, or that is in the earth beneath, or that is in the water under the earth; thou shalt not bow down thyself to them, nor serve them.

In the Book of Deuteronomy, Moses reminded Israel that on Mount Horeb or Sinai, God had spoken in the midst of fire, so that only his voice could be heard, without any form or likeness being seen.[3] Thereafter, throughout the Old Testament, the worship of man-made images was mocked and condemned as sinful folly. So too, in his Letter to the Romans, St Paul continued this denunciation of idolatry when he condemned the Greeks, since 'professing themselves to be wise, they became fools, and changed the glory of the incorruptible God into an image made like to corruptible man, and to the birds, and four-footed things and creeping things'.[4] As heir to the Judaic dispensation, early Christians suffered martyrdom rather than worship or pay honour to Roman and Greek gods. And indeed, when the divinity of the emperors was proclaimed, many refused to offer the incense demanded by this civic cult and gladly went to their death.

It was thus not until the sixth and seventh centuries that the Christian Church began actively to promote the cult of the holy images, albeit in the form of painting rather that of sculpture or carving. This veneration had its roots in various practices. In the catacombs, Christians commemorated the dead by leaving votive tablets on which at times the departed were depicted as praying to Christ and the saints. The tombs of martyrs were especially venerated, and eventually these saints were represented. Equally important, the Eastern empire continued the Roman practice of a public display of statues and paintings of the emperors, who as Christians, were obviously no longer adored, but whose likeness was still accorded all due honour.[5] This practice was justified by Christian theologians, since as St Basil the Great argued, 'the honour given to the image is transferred to its prototype'. The reasoning behind this famous judgement was spelt out by St Athanasius when he declared: 'in the image of the emperor is appearance and form, and in the emperor is the appearance which is in the image . . . whoever venerates the image venerates the emperor in it, for the image is his form and appearance'.[6] Obviously, here were reasons enough to defend the veneration of paintings of Christ and his saints.

At much the same time there emerged the pious tradition that Christ himself had imprinted his likeness on a cloth sent to Agbar, king of Edessa, and that during his Passion a likeness remained imprinted on the towel offered to him by St Veronica. Then again, certain icons of the Virgin Mary were thought to have been painted by St Luke during her lifetime, albeit in idealized form, when she was invariably represented as a young woman with the Christ child in her arms.[7] These originals of Christ and Mary were soon copied and the copies equally became the objects of veneration. It was not long before certain icons had the power of performing miracles ascribed to them, usually by curing their devotees of their illnesses and other infirmities. Once this became widely known, these icons became cult images, which is to say, they attracted pilgrims and were accorded especial devotion with, at times, confraternities formed in their honour. From this it was but a short step for icons to be acclaimed as the patrons of cities, especially since it had become the practice to dedicate churches to the Virgin Mary or to other saints. During Christian festivities such icons were at times carried through the streets of the cities they protected by their presence. Indeed, when the armies of the Byzantine empire sallied forth to do battle with the forces of Islam, they were accompanied by holy images.[8]

With the accession of the Isaurian dynasty in the eighth century, however, the emperors led a fierce campaign to eradicate all forms of sacred representation. Leo III (717–41) not only decreed the destruction of all icons, but also had mosaics in churches which depicted Christ, Mary and the angels replaced by simple crosses. His successor, Constantine V, justified the campaign by affirming that 'anyone who makes an icon of Christ has failed to penetrate to the depths of the dogma of the inseparable union of the natures of Christ', which was to say, that if Christ was indeed the second Person of the Holy Trinity, then it was both impossible and offensive to encompass his divinity in any likeness made of wood and paint.[9] When a change of ruler brought about a return to traditional practice, the Seventh General Church Council, held at Nicaea in 787, strongly approved of the cult of icons:

> like the figure of the honoured and life-giving cross, the revered and holy images, whether painted or made of mosaic or of other suitable material, are to be exposed in the holy churches of God, on sacred instruments and vestments, on walls and panels, in houses and by public ways; these are the images of our Lord, God and saviour, Jesus Christ, and of our Lady without blemish, the holy God-bearer, and of the revered angels and of any of the saintly holy men. The more frequently they are seen in representational art, the more are those who see them drawn to remember and long for those who serve as models, and to pay these images the tribute of salutation and respectful veneration. Certainly this is not the full adoration in accordance with our faith, which is properly paid only to the divine nature, but it resembles that given to the figure of the honoured and life-giving cross, and also to the holy books of the gospels and to other sacred cult objects. Further, people are drawn to honour these images with the offering of incense and lights, as was piously established by ancient custom. Indeed, the honour paid to an image traverses it, reaching the model; and he who venerates the image, venerates the person represented in that image.[10]

Although the iconoclastic fury was to return to haunt the Eastern empire, the decrees of Nicaea were accepted across the Christian world and constituted, so to say, the theological charter for the veneration of holy images in both the Latin and Greek Churches.

The most powerful defence of icons was mounted by St John Damascene (675–749), a Syrian theologian who ended his days in a monastery situated close to Jerusalem, then under Muslim rule. From this vantage point, he protested against emperors meddling in doctrinal matters, which were the province of apostles, prophets and bishops. In his treatise *On Holy Images*, he cited God's commandment against idolatry in Exodus, only then to note that God had also instructed Moses to construct the Ark or tabernacle of the Covenant to house the tablets of the Law brought down from Mount Sinai. But this ark, upon which a gold mercy seat or throne was to be placed, was flanked and overshadowed by two golden cherubs. When Solomon built the Temple at Jerusalem, the ark and mercy seat were placed in the inner sanctuary, the Holy of Holies, with the two cherubim still guarding it. Similar figures, together with those of lions and bulls, decorated the temple walls. It followed, so St John argued, that although the Law condemned the worship of material objects as idolatry, it did not forbid the representation of angels with gold and silver despite their spiritual nature.[11] Moreover, although Moses did not describe God save by fire and word, the prophet Isaiah saw God apparently seated on his throne, albeit obscured by the wings of six seraphim. Such was the Jewish veneration for the material symbols of their religion that, as the author of the Letter to the Hebrews recalled, the Tables of the Law, Aaron's miraculous rod, and a jar of manna collected in the desert were preserved in the Temple's inner sanctuary.[12] And indeed, in their synagogues the Jews continued to venerate the scrolls of the Law, the Torah, which were kept in a sacred ark or tabernacle.[13]

The emphasis on material signs was also justified by human psychology: 'since we are fashioned of both soul and body, and our souls are not naked spirits, but are covered, as it were, with a fleshly veil, it is impossible for us to think without using physical images'. Moreover, of all senses, so St John affirmed, sight was the noblest and that which most illuminated the soul. Writing at a time when books were read aloud rather than silently, he added: 'What the book is to the literate, the image is to the illiterate. Just as words speak to the ear, so the image speaks to the sight; it brings us understanding.'[14] But to deny icons was not merely to hinder devotion and understanding; more gravely, it was to deny the Incarnation of Christ. By their blasphemous destruction of holy images, the iconoclasts denied the doctrine of the Council of Chalcedon (450) that Jesus Christ was 'one person with two natures', true God and true man. As St John explained, 'I worship Him who clothed himself in the royal purple of my flesh . . . the flesh assumed by Him becomes divine and endures after its assumption.' If Christ was fully human, then he could be materially represented and these images demanded veneration, since 'I do not worship matter; I worship the Creator of matter who took flesh.' At the same time, St John agreed with the iconoclasts that to portray the Almighty, to confine the uncircumscribed Godhead within an icon frame, would be an act of idolatry: 'If we attempted to make an image of the invisible God, this would be sinful indeed', an opinion which prevented Orthodox painters from depicting the Trinity save under the form of the three angels who visited Abraham.[15]

Not content with mere defence, St John drew upon neo-platonic philosophy to frame a theology of holy images. His starting point was the principle that if 'an image is a likeness . . . showing in itself what it depicts', it also 'reveals or makes perceptible those things which are hidden'. Which was to say, that since artists had an idea of their painting before sitting down to work, the painting possessed within itself something of that idea. And although there was a difference between a natural and an artificial image, nevertheless, a logical relation existed between a son's likeness to his father and a portrait's likeness to the artist's model. If these premises be granted, then it was possible to construct what has been called 'The Great Chain of Images', which descended all the way from the Trinity to the lowliest icon.[16] As St John explained, with the Holy Trinity, 'the Son of the Father is the first natural image of the invisible God'. But the Trinity, which dwelt in eternity, possessed 'images and figures of things He has yet to do, and the purpose of each of them were called predeterminations by holy Dionysius'. The third class of image was mankind, since as Scripture declared, man was made in the image and likeness of God. The fourth category of images was the descriptions of natural phenomena in the Bible, such as the sun, light and mountains, which could be interpreted as symbols of God and his power. There followed the fifth class, which consisted of the prefigurations of persons and events of Christian revelation which were found in the Old Testament. Finally, the sixth class comprised the material remembrances of past events, be they the words of scripture, icons, or objects such as Aaron's rod or the jar of manna. In all these categories of images, the divine power was in some measure revealed and, if the Holy Spirit dwelt within the saints, who were Christ's friends, so also he stayed close to their images and tombs. Thus it was not merely Christ's images which were to be venerated, but also the likenesses of his Mother, the saints and the angels. What could be more moving than the story of St John Chrysostom, who, in reading St Paul's epistles, had an icon of the apostle before him and who took the icon into his hands when he conversed with his beloved master?[17]

The implications of this neo-platonic theology of holy images were explored by St Theodore of Studios (759–826), a monk of Constantinople, who sought to counter the iconoclastic charge that a true image should have the same essence as its prototype. Which was to say, that whereas Christ was the natural image of his Mother, sharing the same human essence or nature, by contrast, an icon of Christ was his artificial image, its essence as a material object being radically different. To venerate such an object was to be guilty of idolatry. In response to these objections, Theodore reiterated the arguments of St John Damascene, but then drew a scholastic contrast between essence or nature on the one hand and likeness or form on the other. An icon was like the shadow of its heavenly prototype, or, to change the metaphor, it resembled a likeness stamped in wax: and thus in both cases its existence depended on the prototype. He affirmed that 'Christ is the prototype of his image . . . the artificial image is the same as its archetype in likeness, but different in essence . . . It is not the essence of the image we venerate, but the form of the prototype which is stamped upon it . . . the image has one form with its prototype; therefore they have one veneration.'[18] It thus followed that 'although two in nature, the prototype and image are one in hypostatic likeness' and hence icons should command the same veneration as that accorded to Christ or Mary. These were indeed bold conclusions.

With such powerful theological defence, it was no wonder that the veneration of icons was restored across the Orthodox world. However, the iconoclastic campaign led to a strict regulation of the cult of images. Henceforth, in virtually all Greek churches Christ was depicted either in mosaic or painting as Pantocrater, the ruler of the universe, his image dominating the sanctuary from the high walls of the dome. So too, Mary was invariably portrayed as Theotokos, the Mother of God, with the Christ child in her arms, often accompanied by angels or saints, and located in the apse. It later became the practice to hang icons on the chancel screen which shielded the sanctuary from the faithful, and to carry these images in procession during the liturgy. At the same time individual images once more came to be venerated for the miracles they performed or for the protection they afforded, and hence attracted pilgrims and devotion. Moreover, despite the strict control exercised over the subject matter of icons, regional schools differed in their portrayal and during the eleventh century a new style arose which sought to arouse devotion through the illusion of life.[19] Scenes from the life of the Virgin and Christ thus came to depict their love and suffering. When the famous Mandylion image of Christ was brought from Edessa to Constantinople in 944, it was acclaimed as 'a second Ark of the Covenant'.[20]

Although St John Damascene was the last Greek Father to be honoured by the Latin Church with his own feast day, his abstruse theology of holy images was not adopted in the West. Instead, Rome chose to stress the didactic and devotional value of church paintings. Pope Gregory the Great reiterated the common view that 'the picture is for the simple man what writing is for those who can read'. In effect, an icon or mosaic was defined as a representation, the purpose of which was to assist the imagination and stir the devotion of worshippers whose minds should be firmly fixed on the heavenly originals of the paintings they saw.[21] For all that, in Rome a much-venerated icon was thought to be the likeness of Christ that had been imprinted on St Veronica's towel, and the ancient icon of Mary kept in the church of St Maria Maggiore was reckoned to have been painted by St Luke. Both of these images were carried through the streets in processions and became the objects of fervent cults. Moreover, with the tragic capture of Constantinople in 1206, many icons were seized and brought back to Italy, where later they were also attributed to St Luke.[22] Where the West came to differ from the East was in the construction of elaborate altarpieces in which painters vied to demonstrate their skill in portraying the suffering humanity of Christ and the Virgin.

In the Latin Church, however, it was the relics of martyrs and confessors which most attracted popular devotion. In the closing pages of the *City of God*, St Augustine (354–430) marvelled at the miraculous cures wrought at the tombs of martyrs in North Africa.[23] Quick to avert charges of idolatry, he defended this new cult by arguing that whereas pagans had erected temples to honour the cures performed by their idols, Christians had built memorial shrines in which the normal liturgy was performed, all prayer thus directed to Christ and the Trinity, with the martyrs merely named rather than being directly invoked. It was thus in the fifth and sixth centuries that the cult of saints extended across the Western provinces of the former Roman empire, generally centred on the relics which were deposited in splendid shrines, often built by local bishops and at times housed within their cathedrals. Although the souls of martyrs and confessors were obviously in heaven, their bones were thought to possess a numinous power, a heavenly indwelling presence, which could cast out devils and heal the sick. Their tombs attracted numerous pilgrims; their lives and sufferings became the subject of pious biography, and the miracles enacted at their shrines were faithfully recorded. Martyred saints were adopted by cities as their patrons, and the celebration of their feast days became annual expressions of collective solidarity. These patrons were seen by the populace as heavenly guardians, whose protection was ensured by the presence of their relics. As was the case with icons, there was thus a general craving for the divine truths of Christianity to be firmly rooted in a tangible, material presence.[24]

Whereas these early cults were usually confined to a particular city and its province, by contrast, in ninth-century Spain the discovery of the tomb of St James at Compostela led to that apostle's being proclaimed patron of Spain. Since at this time most of the Peninsula was occupied by Muslim rulers, his protection became all important, especially when it was affirmed that the saint had intervened at the battle of Clavijo, an action which soon led to his being dubbed the 'Moorslayer', and thus invariably portrayed on horseback, sword in hand. So powerful was the cult that Muslims compared the sanctuary to the Kaaba at Mecca and, although in 997 the caliph Almansor burnt the church at Compostela to the ground and carried off its bells, he left the tomb untouched. For their part, many Christians confused St James the son of Zebedee with St James the 'brother' of Christ and first bishop of Jerusalem. In any case, it was alleged that the saint had come to Spain to preach the gospel shortly after Christ's death and, although he returned to Palestine where he was martyred, his remains were brought back to Compostela.[25] With such a lineage, it was small wonder that the relics of Santiago Matamoros came to attract pilgrims not merely from Spain but from across Europe.

At some point, possibly in the tenth century, the cult of images was transformed when relics of martyrs and saints were deposited in cavities within wooden statues, which were then covered in gold foil and decorated with jewels. Among the first of these reliquary statues was the bejewelled figure of St Faith, venerated at Conques in France, which attracted pilgrims from afar and wrought many miraculous cures.[26] Obviously, relics continued to be worshipped, and both the bones of St Thomas à Becket, the martyred archbishop of Canterbury, and the bones of St Francis interred in Assisi attracted pilgrims in their thousands. But once reliquaries were shaped as images it was but a short step for statues and crucifixes to become objects of devotion in their own right. By the close of the Middle Ages, each country possessed shrines of images, mainly statues but including some paintings, which had become famous for their thaumaturgic powers and which thus generated devotion which raised them far above the level of mere representations.[27] By this time, many of these shrines were managed by the religious orders who derived both prestige and handsome donations from the presence of these miraculous images. Unlike its Eastern counterpart, the Latin Church failed to exercise any rigorous control over the manner in which holy images were manufactured, and oddities abounded. Nowhere was this more the case than at Compostela, where the figure of Santiago placed above his tomb had movable limbs and a sword attached, which on one occasion was used to knight a king of Castile.[28]

It was during the Middle Ages that the Eucharist also became an object of devotion. In 1215 the papacy formally defined the doctrine of the Real Presence, which was to say, that at mass the bread and wine were transformed by the words of consecration into the true body and blood of Christ. This definition was followed by the introduction of the feast of Corpus Christi in 1264 and again in 1317. By then members of the religious Orders, especially the Dominicans, were actively promoting the cult and the feast, for which St Thomas Aquinas composed prayers. By the fourteenth century the Eucharist was exhibited as a circular host, set in a jewelled silver or golden monstrance, often decorated with the rays of the sun, and placed on altars for worship or carried in processions. It later became common for churches to install tabernacles at the centre of their altars, where the communion hosts could be deposited. The permanent presence of the Eucharist in churches thus confirmed the sacred character of these buildings. In many ways, the tabernacle was the Christian version of the Ark of the Covenant, but whereas in Jewish synagogues the ark contained the scrolls of the Law, the Christian equivalent housed the sacramental sign of Christ's Real Presence.[29] Although the cult of the Eucharist sprang from the same desire for physical manifestation of the divine which had inspired devotion to icons, relics and statues, it differed in that devotion concentrated on a sign rather than an image and was derived directly from the central liturgy of the Church.

II

The first Christians affirmed that Jesus Christ came to fulfil scriptural prophecy. Both the gospels and the epistles interpreted his mission as Saviour by citing biblical precedent. He was thus defined as a second Adam sent to liberate humanity from the effects of man's first sin and as a Moses come to lead the new Israel out of Egypt. He was both the Suffering Servant of Isaiah and a Messiah of the house of David. The comparison with Moses, however, was transformed when Christ was defined as the Paschal Lamb, offered up in sacrifice so as to initiate a universal exodus. Thereafter, he was described both as high priest and as sacrificial victim. Far from mere metaphor, these titles derived from a mode of theological reasoning later known as typology. Its premise was that Old Testament events could be interpreted as types or figures of New Testament events, the relation defined as prophecy and fulfilment. At its most profound level, typology was based on biblical history and thus established a living relation between the two Testaments. To assert that Christ was a second Moses not merely implied an exodus, but also promised a revelation which completed God's prior revelation on Mount Sinai.[30]

With the inclusion of the Book of the Apocalypse in the New Testament, the intellectual reach of typological reasoning was projected onto the Christian future. Obviously, both the gospels and St Paul had preached the Parousia, the Second Coming of Christ, when he would reign in glory amidst the general resurrection of the saints. But in the last book of the Christian Bible this eschatological expectation was grounded in the apocalyptic visions of Daniel, Ezekiel, Isaiah and Zechariah. Christ was depicted as both a Davidic Messiah and as Paschal Lamb leading the new Israel into spiritual battle against Satan. In effect, typology became the basis of a theology of history in which Israel's ancient enemies, Babel, Sodom, Tyre and Babylon were invoked as figures of the Roman empire which was currently persecuting and martyring countless Christians. But despite the terrifying strength of Satan, manifest variously as a seven-headed dragon and as the harlot of Babylon seated on a beast, final victory for the new Israel was assured. The Parousia was seen as a new Jerusalem, a city constituted by the army of martyred saints, a city with twelve gates symbolic of the twelve tribes and apostles, a city which was both temple and spouse of the Lamb. In this revelation the Jewish apocalyptic tradition was renewed and given Christian significance and, although its vivid imagery was to yield diverse interpretations, its unmistakable message was that the epoch stretching from Christ's Resurrection until his Second Coming was to be distinguished by bitter conflict between Babylon and Jerusalem.[31]

In the Eastern Church, however, the typological reasoning of the Apocalypse failed to capture the attention of theologians who were more concerned to discern the spiritual meaning of scripture by applying criteria taken from Platonic philosophy. It was typical of their approach that St John Damascene should have included biblical types within his Great Chain of Images, placing them between those images in scripture which denoted Divine Power and icons and other sacred objects. The examples of types that he mentioned were of such material objects as the Brazen Serpent made by Moses and the Ark of the Covenant, the one taken as referring to Christ and the other to Mary.[32] By and large, Greek theologians more employed allegory, which is to say, moral or spiritual interpretation than genuine typology. Indeed, in his *Ecclesiastical History*, Eusebius of Caesarea (c. 260–c. 340) declared that the first patriarchs had possessed the one true religion, worshipping God and adhering to the dictates of natural morality. By contrast, the Mosaic dispensation sprang from the need to restrain the

Jews from idolatry by severe punishments. The value of the Old Testament chiefly consisted in its prophecy of Christ, whose Incarnation fulfilled the promise inherent in God's creation, and this marked a renewal of patriarchal religion. The conversion of Constantine and the establishment of a Christian empire was hence interpreted as the fulfilment of biblical prophecies to Abraham that in his seed all nations would be blessed, all human history and Christ's Incarnation thus reaching their culmination.[33]

All this was a far cry from St Augustine (354–430), who, in his short treatise *On Catechizing the Uninstructed*, followed the first apostles in giving neophytes an outline of biblical history, pausing at each stage from Adam to Moses, to explain its Christian signficance.[34] It was in his *City of God*, however, that St Augustine drew upon Revelation, St Paul and the apocalyptic books of the Old Testament to frame a dualistic vision of history. The typological basis of his theology of history was elucidated when he wrote: 'In the Old Testament the New lies hid; in the New Testament the meaning of the Old becomes clear.'[35] He thus read scripture not merely to note historical events, 'but events with prophetic meaning'. Thus Noah's ark was taken as a figure of the Christian Church, the sure refuge in the universal wreckage of humanity, and, more pointedly, the quarrel between Esau and Jacob over Isaac's birthright was taken as the type of Christians supplanting the Jews. But such interpretations were but incidental to his transformation of the obscure eschatological prophecies of the Apocalypse into a fully developed providential history of the cosmic conflict between Jerusalem and Babylon, the heavenly and earthly cities. He boldly identified the sequence of empires described in the Bible – Assyria, Babylon, Persia and Macedon – as embodiments of the earthly city and hence all dominated by pride and lust for dominion. Nor did he shrink from affirming that 'the city of Rome was founded to be a kind of second Babylon'.[36] By contrast, the biblical patriarchs and prophets, not to omit King David, represented the self-sacrificing virtues of those dominated by love of God. The strength of this typology was further illustrated when St Augustine depicted the City of God as wandering through the world in perpetual pilgrimage, like Israel in the desert, dependent on God for its survival. It followed that he did not endorse the Eusebian glorification of the Christian empire, since he asserted that all exercise of political power was tainted by its origin in the earthly city and hence accompanied by 'painful necessities' far removed from the impulses of Christian love. At the same time, he sought to defuse apocalyptic expectations by insisting that all the prophecies concerning the Messiah and the kingdom of God had been fulfilled with Christ's Incarnation, Passion and Resurrection. Dividing the history of the world into seven ages in imitation of the seven days of creation, he declared that Christ had inaugurated the sixth age, the equivalent to the fifth monarchy of Daniel, and that it would last until Christ's Second Coming.[37]

It was in the late twelfth century that the full implications of typological interpretation were explored anew by Joachim di Fiore (c. 1135–1202), a Cistercian abbot of

Calabria, who argued that the history of Israel offered a complete prefiguration of Christian history, with each sequence divided into seven ages. He revised St Augustine's chronology by declaring that the sixth and penultimate age was only about to begin, and was to be an epoch of unparalleled conflict and expansion of the Christian faith, marked both by the appearance of Anti-Christ and by the preaching of two new orders of spiritual men. Superimposed upon this traditional scheme of seven ages was a grand Trinitarian sequence in which the first stage was the Mosaic dispensation presided over by God the Father, followed by the second stage initiated by Christ, but which was to make way for the third stage of the Holy Spirit, soon to begin during the turmoil of the sixth age. What was important here was not so much the details of Joachim's complex schemes, which were illustrated in diagrammatic 'figures' included in his texts, but rather his intellectual premise and method. In essence, he affirmed that contemporary events possessed an inner spiritual significance and that it was possible to discern their meaning by typological exegesis of Old Testament figures and events.[38] It was a method which derived from St Augustine, but which broke with the African Saint by its application to contemporary events and the immediate future. As such, it obviously had political potential and indeed was soon applied for the magnification of both kings and popes.

The tendency to confer theological significance upon contemporary events was strengthened by the charismatic personality of St Francis of Assisi and the sudden emergence of the mendicant orders. By precept and example St Francis inspired thousands of Christians to abandon all worldly entanglements and to embrace 'Our Lady Poverty' as their social ideal. As pilgrims and mendicants, the early friars embodied St Augustine's vision of the City of God as a band of travellers forever strangers in the earthly city. Moreover, when it became known that St Francis had experienced the divine infliction of stigmata on his suffering body, he was venerated as a second Christ. After his canonization the church at Assisi was decorated with the famous paintings by Giotto, which depict the principal moments of his life, including the miracles he had wrought. It was St Bonaventure, the Franciscan Order's leading theologian and master-general, who identified St Francis as the angel of the apocalypse who opened the seal of the sixth age, thus clearly placing the saint within the general frame of Joachite prophecy.[39] In later years the Spiritual branch of the Order was to claim that St Francis had inaugurated the third stage, that of the Holy Spirit.

By the fifteenth century, Western Europe was torn asunder by warfare, the plague, and a schism caused by rival claimants to the papacy. These events generated a widespread sense of crisis which was often accompanied by a craving for radical renewal. Joachite prophecy often took a political form, with the advent of a world emperor or an angelic pope canvassed as heaven's solution for current ills. At the same time, the growing power of the Ottoman Turks, which was to lead to the fall of Constantinople in 1454, was interpreted as a sign of the Anti-Christ. In a treatise on the papal schism,

St Vicente Ferrer (1350–1413), a Valencian Dominican, cited the Book of Daniel's vision of four beasts threatening Israel as a prefiguration of the four schisms which had afflicted the Christian Church, identifying them successively as the Jews, the Saracens under Mahomet, the Greeks at Constantinople who denied the pope's authority, and lastly, the rival claimants to the papacy. In 1398 Ferrer was granted a vision of Christ flanked by St Francis and St Dominic, in which he was charged with the task of preaching repentance and preparing the faithful for the end of the world. He spent the remainder of his life in missions, forming confraternities and encouraging his followers to practise self-flagellation as their penitence. Towards the end of his life he wrote to Benedict XIII asserting that if the preaching of St Francis and St Dominic had achieved spiritual renewal, the Orders they founded had fallen into decay, leaving Christendom in ruin, so that the advent of Anti-Christ and the end of the world could soon be expected.[40] As can be seen, the application of Joachim di Fiore's method, which is to say, the interpretation of contemporary events by scriptural figures, could lead to radically different conclusions.

III

In his defence of holy images, St John Damascene affirmed that in addition to scripture the Church drew on the unwritten tradition which was manifest in its liturgy. There was, for example, no scriptural instruction on how baptism was to be administered or as to the form of the Eucharistic celebration. So also, nowhere was there any reference to the Trinity in the New Testament, or any definition of Christ as 'one person with two natures'.[41] If such considerations were advanced to justify veneration of icons, how much more could they have been cited concerning the deep veneration of the Virgin Mary that then characterized the Christian Church. In this case, there was indeed scriptural justification. At the Annunciation the angel Gabriel told Mary that: 'The Holy Spirit shall come upon thee, and the power of the Highest shall overshadow thee: therefore that which is to be born of thee shall be called holy, Son of God.' There was here a possible reference to the Book of Exodus, where we read that the cloud, symbol of God, covered the Ark of the Covenant with its shadow and 'the glory of the Lord filled the tabernacle'. So also, when Mary went to the hills of Judah to visit her cousin Elizabeth, she was greeted as another Ruth, which was to say, bearing the child of the house of David. Her reply, later known as the Magnificat, was a highly wrought text, filled with echoes of the Old Testament, in part based on the song of Hannah, the once barren mother who was to bear the prophet and high priest Samuel, but also on reminiscences of the prophetess Judith and the general tendency of prophets to address Israel as a woman.[42]

In the first instance, devotion to Mary derived from her role in the scheme of salvation. It was in the second century that St Irenaeus (c. 130–c. 200), bishop of Lyons, developed the implications of St Paul's definition of Christ as the second Adam so as to include Mary:

> for Adam had necessarily to be restored to Christ, that mortality be absorbed in immortality, and Eve in Mary, that a virgin become the advocate of a virgin, should undo and destroy virginal disobedience by virginal obedience.[43]

Once Mary was thus identified as the second Eve, then obviously the way was open for devotion to grow and scripture to be ransacked to celebrate her as both Virgin and Mother. Generally described as sinless, she was soon thought to have been taken up to heaven after her death by Christ. But her most glorious title derived from the exigencies of the bitter theological disputes that centred on the precise terms in which Christ could be defined as both God and man. It was in order to defend the doctrine of the Council of Ephesus (431) that Mary was audaciously acclaimed as the Mother of God, in Greek, Theotokos, and in Latin, Deipara.[44] Henceforth, there could be no doubting her central role in the economy of salvation.

Like other theologians, St Augustine interpreted Mary's role as analogous to that of the Church and, indeed, saw her as the prototype of the Church. In her reply to the angel Gabriel: 'Behold the handmaiden of the Lord: be it done to me according to thy word', Mary had acted, so to say, as the first Christian. Moreover, St Augustine asserted that the Church was also the mother of Christ, which was to say, that through the actions of its members it brought forth Christ into the world, much as Mary had given birth to Christ in the flesh. Both Mary and the Church were virgins, in their essence uncorrupted by sin, and both the Church and Mary were animated by the Holy Spirit.[45] At much the same time as St Augustine, in the fifth century, Mary was also identified as the Woman of the Apocalypse. For in the antithesis of Jerusalem and Babylon, the role of the Church, the new Israel, was presented in chapter 12 under the symbolic form of a woman with child threatened by Satan:

> And there appeared a great sign in heaven; a woman clothed with the sun, and the moon under her feet, and upon her head a crown with twelve stars: and she being with child cried, travailing in birth, and pained to be delivered. And there appeared another sign in heaven; and behold a great red dragon, having seven heads and ten horns, and seven crowns upon his heads . . . And there was war in heaven: Michael and his angels fought against the dragon; and the dragon fought and his angels prevailed not . . . And when the dragon saw that he was cast unto the earth, he persecuted the woman which brought forth the man child. And to the woman were given two wings of a great eagle, that she might fly into the wilderness.[46]

Although the woman was generally identified as the type or figure of the Church, as both the new Israel and the new Jerusalem, some theologians also came to identify her as the Virgin Mary. In a text later ascribed to St Augustine, a contemporary of the African Saint wrote:

> In the Apocalypse of John the Apostle it is written, that the dragon stood before the Woman who was ready to be delivered, that, when she should be delivered, he might devour her. Now none of you is ignorant that the dragon is the devil, and that by the woman is signified the Virgin Mary, who, herself all-pure, gave birth to our Head all-pure; who also in her own person showed forth a figure of the holy Church. For just as she, in giving birth to her Son, still remained a virgin, so too does the Church in all time give birth to His members without losing her virginity.[47]

One consequence of this identification was that Mary was seen both as a protagonist in the perennial war of Jerusalem and Babylon and as sign and symbol of the Church. All these scriptural titles of Mary could be thus cited as referring to the Church, so that devotion to Mary also entailed devotion to the Church, which was to say, to use the terms of a later period, the mystical body of Christ.

In the Eastern Church it was no coincidence that the chief advocates of the cult of images were those theologians who also exalted devotion to the Mother of God. In his sermons on the Assumption of Mary, St John Damascene affirmed that 'she found an abyss of grace which kept her double virginity undefiled, her virginal soul no less spotless than her body'. He taught the doctrine of the Greek Church that after Mary had been placed in her tomb by the apostles, where she lay for three days, Christ himself descended to raise her up to heaven, body and soul. Here was a doctrine, the Dormition, which was to be commemorated in countless icons and was to form a principal feast in church liturgy. But St John Damascene also applied to Mary any number of scriptural types or figures, in which holy objects of the Old Testament were all seen as prefigurations of Mary's role:

> Thou art the royal throne which angels surround, seeing upon it their very King and Lord. Thou art a spiritual Eden, holier and diviner than Eden of old. That Eden was the abode of the mortal Adam, whilst the Lord came down from heaven to dwell in thee. The ark foreshadowed thee who kept the seed of the new world. Thou didst bring forth Christ, the salvation of the world, who destroyed sin and its angry waves. The burning bush was a figure of thee, and the Tables of the Law, and the ark of the testament. The golden urn and candelabra, the table and the flowering rod of Aaron were significant types of thee.[48]

Obviously, what this plethora of symbols had in common was that all referred to Mary's maternal role in bringing Christ into the world. Other figures not mentioned in this passage were the ladder seen by Jacob in Bethlehem and the closed door of the

Plate 1   St Luke painting the Virgin Mary

Temple seen by Ezekiel. But of these figures, the most commonly repeated and the most powerful was the acclamation of Mary as the new Ark of the Covenant, with Christ in her womb as the equivalent of the Tables of Law. But she was also commonly described as the burning bush seen by Moses on Mount Horeb, since God appeared and spoke in the midst of fire without consuming the bush. Finally, the symbol of Aaron's calling as high priest had been that his rod alone among the rods of the tribes of Israel had flowered, a figure in which Mary was the rod and Christ the flower.

Here is no place to describe the ever-growing devotion to the Virgin Mary which characterized medieval civilization and which was expressed in countless prayers, poems, paintings and treatises. What requires emphasis, however, is that in the late Middle Ages particular images of Mary, mainly statues but including some paintings, became the objects of intense devotion and were venerated for the miracles performed in their sanctuaries. If some of these cult images were attributed to St Luke, others were thought to possess a miraculous, even a heavenly origin. Among the most spectacular of these Marian devotions was the Holy House of Loreto, a small chapel no more than thirty-one feet long and thirteen wide, built of rough stone and brick, which was assumed to be the self-same house in Nazareth where Mary was born and where the Annunciation and Conception of Jesus occurred. According to later accounts it was in 1291 that an angelic host had transported the house from Nazareth, first to Tersato in Dalmatia and then to Loreto, situated close to the Adriatic Sea at Ancona. Although there is evidence of devotion to a smoke-blackened image within this chapel since the twelfth and thirteenth centuries, it was only after the publication in 1472 of the narrative of its miraculous origin that it was recognized as the premier Marian shrine in Italy. In 1507 Pope Julius II placed the sanctuary under papal jurisdiction and thereafter commissioned leading artists to 'clothe' the chapel in a classical marble frame, decorated with skilfully wrought reliefs depicting the Virgin's life and accompanied by figures of sybils and prophets. In this Renaissance form the Santa Casa of Loreto was to attract countless pilgrims during the ensuing centuries, the devotion vigorously promoted by the Jesuits who established a college in the town.[49]

Theological justification for the cult of Marian images was provided by Blessed Amadeus of Portugal (Joannes Menesius da Silva, 1431–82), a Franciscan visionary and founder of a reformed congregation of his Order in Italy. In his *New Apocalypse*, he revealed that the archangel Gabriel had confirmed to him the doctrine of Mary's Immaculate Conception, thereby affording heavenly approbation for a dogma already sustained by Duns Scotus and other Franciscans. But it was his prophecy of the imminent advent of an angelic pope which attracted influential interest, since he foresaw that this pope would unite the Eastern and Latin Churches and inaugurate a new, transfigured epoch in the history of Christendom. It was in his eighth and last 'rapture' that Amadeus portrayed Mary informing the apostles that she would be 'bodily present' in her holy images until the end of the world, her presence made manifest by the miracles she would perform through them. Although Amadeus' writings were condemned as heretical or misguided by orthodox theologians, in Spain several Franciscans defended him, and St Peter of Alcántara sponsored the publication of an extended commentary on his work, thereby diffusing knowledge of revelations which hitherto had been known only to those who had access to manuscript copies.[50]

IV

Late medieval devotional excesses provoked the sharp criticism of Christian humanists such as Desiderius Erasmus (1466/9–1536), who condemned the popular practice of praying to individual saints for particular assistance, arguing that such forms of piety were 'not a great deal different from the superstitions of the ancients'. It was not so much the practices in themselves as the attitudes which inspired them that he condemned, since all devotion should be directed towards Christ, through whom men were led to God, abandoning material things in favour of the spiritual world. He asserted: 'Charity does not consist in many visits to churches, in many prostrations before the statues of saints, in the lighting of candles.' Instead of such practices, one should imitate the virtues of the saints and seek God in prayer. So also, 'when you venerate the image of Christ in the paintings and other works of art that portray him, think how much more you ought to revere that portrait of His Mind that the inspiration of the Holy Spirit has placed in Holy Writ'. In effect, Erasmus advocated a simplified, evangelical Christianity which would replace the complications of scholastic theology and popular devotions with a religion based on scripture and the teachings of the early Fathers. Although later condemned by the Counter-Reformation popes, the writings of Erasmus offered a model of Christian humanism that was destined to emerge again in Catholic circles in the late eighteenth century.[51]

With the Reformation, the cult of images was brought to an end in all parts of Europe where the new Churches prevailed. Protestantism was a religion of the word, be it heard as scripture, sermon or hymn, so that the ear and its apprehension, which Greek theologians had thought inferior to the eye and its vision, now gained primacy of esteem. In the event, the Reformation was fired by a 'revolutionary iconoclasm', in which mobs invaded churches and smashed images, altars and windows. The Mosaic injunction against idols was taken literally and church walls, once covered with scenes taken from the Bible, were whitewashed, and decorated only with the inscription of scriptural texts. Henceforth, there was to be no further practice of pilgrimage, no invocation of saints and their images, no more prayers to the Virgin Mary, and no more miracle-mongering and apparitions. Equally important, the Reformers condemned the whole system of allegorical exegesis of the Bible and sought to bring in a literal reading of scripture. However, although Luther at first doubted whether the Book of the Apocalypse was canonical, the exigencies of Church politics soon led him to accept a revised form of typology in which the papacy was denounced as the Harlot of Babylon and as Anti-Christ. The Augustinian antithesis of Jerusalem and Babylon was adopted to express the difference between Protestantism and Catholicism. Indeed, Luther and other Reformers were persuaded that the end of the world was imminent and that the epoch in which they lived was to be characterized by the final battle between the new Israel and Anti-Christ. Among the more radical Protestants, such as the Anabaptists, the Joachite doctrine that the Age of the Holy Spirit had arrived or was about to arrive enjoyed wide circulation.[52] In effect, the more Protestants relied on the Bible as their religious mainstay, the more inclined were they to accept the projection of typological interpretation into the present and the future.

The reaction of the Catholic Church to this assault was slow and hesitant. But at session 25 of the Council of Trent (1545–63), the traditional veneration of holy images was reaffirmed, albeit together with a warning against superstition and a demand for careful regulation by bishops of all cults of images and relics. The precise wording of the decree reflected traditional doctrine:

> And they must also teach that images of Christ, the virgin mother of God and the other saints should be set up and kept, particularly in churches, and that due honour and reverence is owed to them, not because some divinity or power is believed to lie in them as reason for the cult, or because anything is to be expected from them, or because confidence should be placed in images as was done by pagans of old; but because the honour showed to them is referred to the original which they represent: thus, through the images which we kiss and before which we uncover our heads and go down on our knees, we give adoration to Christ and veneration to the saints, whose likeness they bear. And this has been approved by the decrees of councils, especially the second council of Nicaea, against the iconoclasts.

As can be observed, the classic defence of St Basil the Great was here incorporated into the governing statutes of the Counter-Reformation Church.[53] What has been less observed is that the works of St John Damascene and, to a lesser extent, St Theodore of Studios were repeatedly printed in Latin editions in the sixteenth and seventeenth centuries.[54] The effect of their influence was to modify the simple Tridentine doctrine of holy images as mere representations of heavenly originals.

The Council of Trent also reaffirmed the doctrine of the Real Presence of Christ in the Eucharist, stating that:

> After the consecration of the bread and wine, our lord Jesus Christ, true God and true man, is truly, really and substantially contained in the propitious sacrament of the holy eucharist under the appearance of those things which are perceptible to the senses.

It followed from this doctrine, which was best called transubstantiation, that all Christians should 'reverently express for this holy sacrament the worship of adoration which is due to the true God'. Thus, whereas images were to be honoured and venerated, the Eucharist was to be adored. And the Council commended the feast of Corpus Christi in which the Eucharist was carried in public procession through the streets.[55] It was thus destined to figure in the post-Tridentine calendar as a major feast, second only to the celebrations of Holy Week, and marked by processions in which all the institutions of the Church, the religious orders, the chapters of canons, and the confraternities, paraded through the streets.

The only typological theme which can be found in the Tridentine decrees arose from the Council's insistence that, contrary to the Protestant affirmation, Christ instituted the Eucharist as a rite of sacrifice:

> For after celebrating the old passover which the whole people of the children of Israel offered in memory of their departure from Egypt, he instituted a new passover, namely the offering of himself by the church through its priests under visible signs, in memory of his own passage from this world to the Father, when he redeemed us by the shedding of his blood, rescued us from the power of darkness and transferred us to his kingdom.

This was prefaced by the citation of the Letter to the Hebrews, where Christ was defined as a high priest of the order of Melchisedech, whose bloody sacrifice on the cross should be represented in the manner of the Last Supper.[56]

To counter the Protestant tenet that their church was a new Israel liberated from a Babylonian captivity, the Catholic Church resolutely defended the institutions and practices of medieval religion. But it also sought to deploy the intellectual and aesthetic achievements of the Italian Renaissance to strengthen its prestige. Even before the Reformation, Julius II had not only covered the Holy House of Loreto with marble walls, but also initiated the destruction of St Peter's, a basilica which had been funded by Constantine the Great, in order to replace it with the majestic edifice designed by Bramante. Thereafter, all the resources of Renaissance architecture, painting and sculpture, later to be transmuted into mannerist and baroque styles, were employed to build and renovate churches across Catholic Europe. If Protestantism was a religion of the word, Catholicism remained, or became, a religion of the image. But there was a price to be paid for the adoption of this classical culture. Renaissance art, so it has been argued, robbed holy images of their religious power, since they became mere objects of aesthetic enjoyment. Virgins painted by Raphael or Murillo were admired for their beauty; they rarely induced prayer.[57] So too, in reaction to the Protestant emphasis on scripture, theologians presented the Catholic religion as the fulfilment of all humanity's quest to attain knowledge of the Godhead. Typology was abandoned in favour of allegory, with the religion of antiquity, be it of Greece or Egypt, scoured for symbolic anticipations of Christian revelation.

Nowhere were the cultural trends which determined the religious destiny of the Catholic Church in this epoch more apparent than in the Company of Jesus. Its founder, St Ignatius Loyola (1491–1556), drew upon late medieval spirituality to devise his *Spiritual Exercises*, where in good Spanish fashion he enjoined the initiate to enlist in the service of Christ, the lord of the universe, in much the same spirit as a loyal subject might follow his king into battle against the infidel. But he was then called upon to picture in his mind's eye 'a vast plain embracing the whole region of Jerusalem, where the supreme Captain-General of the good is Christ our Lord: and another plain, in the region of Babylon, where the chief of the enemy is Lucifer'. In this grand Augustinian figure of the Two Cities, the battle was fought between 'the two standards', signifying the opposing values of riches, honour and pride as against poverty, shame and humility. In his 'Rules for thinking with the Church', St Ignatius also exhorted his Jesuit followers to maintain the devotional practices of medieval Catholicism by encouraging veneration of saints' relics, candles and holy images, the frequent hearing of mass and reception of communion, and the practice of pilgrimage.[58]

In the seventeenth century, however, Jesuits such as Athanasius Kircher (1601–80) sought to reconcile neo-platonic, Hermetic speculation with scientific research so as to frame a cosmological synthesis in which the Catholic religion would be defined as the fulfilment of the entire philosophical and theological quest of humanity. The spirit of that enterprise was expressed in the declaration that 'there is no doubt that not only the prophets, apostles and other holy men of God, but also the Gentile poets, priests and prophets were inspired by this divine *numen* (the Holy Spirit) and made prophets of the birth of the Eternal Word in the flesh'.[59] In effect, complex Alexandrine allegory replaced any simple reliance on scriptural typology. Moreover, when the Jesuits came to defend the cult of images against Protestant attack, they had recourse to the works of St John Damascene, St Theodore of Studios and St Basil the Great. Although they followed St Ignatius in actively promoting devotion to these images as a medieval legacy, they also magnified and interpreted this cult by appeal to the neo-platonic theology of Eastern Church Fathers. Here is a theme we shall explore in Mexico.

2

Myth and history

I

In his *Spanish Polity* (1619) Juan de Salazar, a Benedictine abbot, emphasized 'the almost complete similarity' of the Hebrew and Spanish peoples, concluding that 'in the law of grace the Spanish people is God's favourite and is the one which has especially succeeded to the place held by the chosen people in the time of the written law'. Had not the Moorish captivity reduced the Spaniards to a captivity which closely resembled that suffered by the Israelites in Egypt? Was not King Pelayo another Moses and El Cid a veritable Samson? This typological similitude reached its inevitable climax when Salazar saluted Charles V as a second David and Philip II as another Solomon who followed his exemplar's policy, 'even in the distinguished and marvellous edifice of San Lorenzo el Real, which he built in El Escorial, in imitation of the Temple built by Solomon in Jerusalem'.[1] Unlike the Jews, however, who had so often fallen into idolatry, the Spaniards had never betrayed their Catholic faith. A defender of the authenticity of Santiago's mission to Spain, Salazar affirmed that, together with the Virgin Mary and an image of the cross, St James had appeared in the sky to assist the Spaniards against the Moors in the great battle of Las Navas de Tolosa.

Here is no place to dwell on Salazar's sustained eulogy of the Catholic monarchy, which, at the time he wrote, comprised the three crowns of Aragon, Castile and Portugal, not to mention their vast overseas possessions and other states such as Milan and the Low Countries. What other monarchy could boast of such captains at war as Hernán Cortés and Gonzalo Fernández de Córdoba, of such riches as were produced by the American mines, of the great learning of its universities, of the wisdom and justice of its courts, the valour and power of its armies and navy, and the sanctity of its clergy? And what kings could rival St Ferdinand, who had defeated the Moors, or indeed Philip III, who had so recently cleansed his kingdom of Moriscos and dedicated Spain to the Immaculate Conception of Mary? All this was but prelude to Salazar's citation of the prophecies in the Book of Daniel, which he interpreted as foretelling the current struggle between the Ottoman Turks and the House of Habsburg, which in turn exemplified the age-long conflict between Babylon and Jerusalem. Since the Ottomans obviously figured here as Anti-Christ, it was clear that hostilities would culminate in the reconquest of the Holy Land, the defeat of the Turks and the extinction of Islam, events which astrologers calculated would be realized by the year 1661. But, whereas St Vicente Ferrer had applied Daniel's prophecies to signify the end of the world, Salazar concluded that these events would entail Spain's becoming 'the seat and chair of the universal monarchy, which (as can be seen from Daniel) all nations shall have to obey'.[2]

This providential vision of the Spanish monarchy can be traced to the middle decades of the fifteenth century when patriotic chroniclers hailed the kings of Castile as chosen by the Almighty to take the lead in the perennial war against Islam. The fall of Granada in 1492 fuelled a mood of messianic expectation that infected Spain as much as other countries in Western Europe at the close of the Middle Ages. With the accession of Charles V in 1517 to the thrones of Castile and Aragon, Spain became the centre of a vast Habsburg patrimony that encompassed the Low Countries, Austria, Bohemia, Milan and Naples. Small wonder that, on becoming Holy Roman Emperor, Charles was saluted as another Caesar and a second Charlemagne, chosen by Providence to reunite Christendom, defeat the Ottoman Turks and reconquer Jerusalem, thereby establishing the long-awaited world monarchy.[3] All these fervid hopes, more medieval than modern, were given eloquent expression by Hernando de Acuña in a poem addressed to the emperor on the eve of his expedition to Tunis.

> Sire, now approaches, or already has arrived
> The glorious age when heaven will proclaim
> One pastor, and a single flock
> By fortune for your times reserved . . .
> And now, for its solace, announces to the world
> One monarch, one empire and one sword.
> Already the orb of earth in part now experiences
> And everywhere awaits your empire
> Conquered by you in just war.[4]

In the 1520s Charles V defeated the king of France in the struggle for mastery in Italy, and then led the successful defence of Vienna against the Turkish onslaught of Suleiman the Great. It was in his long reign that Hernán Cortés conquered Mexico and Francisco Pizarro laid waste the Inca realm, thereby laying the foundations of a vast Spanish empire in the New World. The chronicler of their exploits, Francisco López de Gómara (1511–c. 1566), a humanist educated in Italy, did not hesitate to affirm that 'the greatest event since the creation of the world, apart from the incarnation of He who created it, is the discovery of the Indies which is thus called the New

World'. God had chosen the Spaniards and their king to subjugate these vast territories so that their inhabitants might be brought into the fold of the Catholic Church. In a formal eulogy of his nation, Gómara pronounced: 'never at any time did a king or people move or subject so much in so short a time as we did . . . as much in warfare and exploration as in preaching the gospel and the conversion of idolaters'.[5]

The succession from Charles V (1517–54) to Philip II (1554–98) marked the transition from a warrior king who led his armies across Europe, to a sedentary monarch eventually resident in the Escorial, a majestic edifice that served as palace, monastery, church and dynastic sepulchre. That the façade of the church which dominated the Escorial was adorned with statues of David and Solomon, flanked on either side by their regal descendants, Jehosa and Hezekiah and Josiah and Manasseh, demonstrated where Salazar in part had drawn his typological inspiration. A later commentator, Bishop Juan de Caramuel Lobkowitz (1607–80), affirmed not only that God Almighty was the architect of Solomon's Temple but that, of all modern edifices built since the revival of European architecture by Bramante in Italy, the Escorial alone rivalled the Temple in conception and grandeur.[6] Philip II's own fascination with the comparison was demonstrated when he funded the publication of *In Ezechielem Explanationes* (1596–1610), a profusely illustrated three-volume commentary on the prophet Ezekiel's vision of the Temple and city of Jerusalem. Its Jesuit authors, Jerónimo de Prado and Juan Bautista Villalpando, not merely took the prophet's measures as providing the correct proportions of Solomon's Temple, but also affirmed that those proportions exhibited 'the origin and source of all architectural rules'. Yet more important, they insisted that the Temple was the material incarnation of the Church and symbol and prelude of the new Jerusalem envisioned in the Apocalypse.[7]

In this context it should be noted that Philip II's private rooms in the Escorial immediately overlooked the church's high altar and that his chapel was situated at its side, so that he passed his days within the inner sanctum, the Holy of Holies, where the Eucharist was perpetually reserved in the tabernacle. From his cell-like apartment, daily communing with the Almighty, the king governed an empire which spanned the globe.[8] It was a spectacle that irresistibly evokes Eusebius of Caesarea's panegyric of Constantine the Great, wherein that emperor was depicted as a philosopher-king who had mastered his passions, an intermediary between heaven and earth, dwelling in his palace in communion with his divine original.[9] Not for nothing did Juan de Palafox y Mendoza, bishop of Puebla (1639–54) and Visitor General of New Spain, exclaim that 'royal palaces are the heart of this world, where ambition and human power are most at play, where all that is high, great and sovereign in the temporal sphere is to be found'. But he also commended King David for bringing the Ark of the Covenant to his new capital at Jerusalem, thereby contriving to endow his office with the blessing of heaven. So also, Palafox counselled that the diverse kingdoms and states of the

Spanish monarchy should be bound together by insistence on the king's religious character and role.[10]

The quasi-sacral character of the Spanish monarchy, reminiscent of the Byzantine empire, was provided with a theological rationale by a Dominican mythographer, Juan de la Puente, who published an extraordinary work in which he not merely traced the travels and settlements of the sons of Noah but also plotted the itineraries of the apostles. *Conformity of the Two Catholic Monarchies, that of the Roman Church and that of the Spanish Empire, and Defence of the Precedence of the Catholic Kings of Spain over all the Kings of the World* (1612) was dedicated to Philip III, 'Lord Emperor of the Spains, Lord of the Greatest Monarchy that men have had since the creation of the world', and sought to demonstrate the apostolic foundation of the Spanish Church. The widely canvassed mission of St James was fully expounded, only to be topped by the arrival of both St Peter and St Paul, thereby demonstrating the equality of the Spanish Church with its Roman counterpart. So also, Puente surmised that St Thomas may well have visited America and preached the gospel all the way from Mexico to Brazil, albeit without leaving much trace owing to the inconstant nature of the Indians and the determining influence of the heavenly constellations that governed the destiny of the New World. In a notable aside, when discussing the fate of the Jews and their diaspora, Puente observed that 'the natural love that a man has for his country is born of the stars, which engender us and preserve us in our first years'.[11]

Within the majestic ambit of the Catholic monarchy, urban and provincial patriotism continued to thrive and, although the authorities embellished their cities with civic edifices built in classical style, the medieval cult of miraculous images continued unabated. All the major regions and leading cities of Spain possessed images of Mary or of Christ which attracted pilgrims and whose sanctuaries were lined with testimonies of the miraculous cures they had wrought. Equally important, new images appeared which exhibited all the plastic possibilities of Renaissance art, albeit transformed by mannerism and the baroque, to stir emotion and capture the hearts of the faithful. In Seville, for example, it was during the late sixteenth and seventeenth centuries that the confraternities commissioned the images of Christ in his Passion and of his sorrowing Mother which to this day are carried through the streets of the city during Holy Week. These powerful images can certainly be esteemed as artistic masterpieces; but their purpose was to evoke intense devotion. In the hispanic world, therefore, the adoption of Renaissance style did not impede the creation of new cult figures, albeit generally more as statues than as paintings.[12]

No matter how impressive the ability of Spanish artists to stir devotion, most of the cult images which effected miracles were medieval in origin. By far the most important Marian shrine in the kingdom of Castile was that of our Lady of Guadalupe, an image reputed to have been carved by St Luke and later given by Pope Gregory the

Great to San Leandro, the archbishop of Seville. When that city was taken by the
Moors, a group of clerics escaped northwards, carrying the image, which they later
interred in the hills near the river of Guadalupe in Extremadura. At the beginning of
the fourteenth century, so it was alleged, the Virgin Mary appeared to a poor herdsman who had lost his cow, and commanded him to tell the priests to come and dig
at the place where she had appeared. Sure enough, the image was found and a small
chapel built to house it. By 1326 pilgrims began to arrive and, from 1340 onwards, King
Alfonso XI took an active interest in enlarging the church. It was in 1386 that the shrine
was entrusted to the Jeronymites, an Order of monks with close association with the
royal dynasty of Castile.[13] From that point this wooden statue of the Virgin Mary
seated and with the Christ child in her arms became the object of a cult which by the
sixteenth century had developed any number of subordinate chapels scattered across
the domains of the Castilian crown, in which copies of the image were venerated. By
this time the Jeronymites had enlarged their monastery to house over a hundred
monks and had constructed ample rooms for royal visitors, not to mention the hospice for the pilgrims who sought the Virgin's assistance. Since many of the first conquerors of the New World came from Extremadura, it was only to be expected that on
return to Spain they should visit the sanctuary to offer thanks and proffer donations.[14]
In all this, Guadalupe was not unusual, since all the chief regions of the Peninsula possessed images which were adopted as their patrons and whose cults served to articulate
urban and provincial identity.

The fusion of patriotism and religion can be best observed in the twin treatises
on the sanctuary of Our Lady of Pilar and the excellencies of the city of Zaragoza
published in 1616 by Diego Murillo, a Franciscan chronicler. To start with, he cited
Hiercoles as saying that 'the *patria* is a God and the first and principal parent' for
its citizens, so that the obligation to serve one's country 'is so old that it starts
with nature and is more compelling . . . than that which we owe to the parents who
bore us'. With such sentiments it was not surprising that he celebrated 'the greatness
of the renowned city of Zaragoza, my *patria*, to which I owe life, education, good
formation . . . and the very being that I have'. In good humanist fashion he described
the impressive array of churches, palaces, colleges and convents which dominated the
city. So too, he was at pains to deploy the categories of Aristotle's *Politics* to define
Aragon's constitution as essentially mixed, comprising the elements of monarchy,
aristocracy and democracy. But as befitted a patriotic Franciscan, he vigorously defended the Spanish tradition of St James preaching the gospel in the Peninsula.[15] The
doubts that had been entertained by as eminent a figure as Cardinal Bellarmine had
been allayed by the old chronicles discovered by Fray Jerónimo Román de la Higuera
and by the inscribed lead tablets found in Montesacro in Granada.[16] In any case, there
existed a strong tradition, handed down across the generations, that St James, the
son of Zebedee, had arrived with disciples and had appointed bishops in Zaragoza

Adevocion del Señor D. Bernardo Iráquez del Baua Capitan de Corazas. Alcalde Maior dèz
Cas Potosi. y Teniente de Capitan General delas tropas.

Plate 2   Juan Correa, *Our Lady of Pilar with Santiago at Zaragoza*

and Compostela before returning to Palestine, where he suffered martyrdom. So soon after the Saviour's death had this mission occurred that it could be said that Christ 'entrusted the Church to St Peter, his Mother to St John, and Spain to St James: the three most beloved things'.[17]

But Murillo's chief purpose was to justify the cult of Our Lady of Pilar. Like Jacob at Bethel, who had seen angels ascending a ladder to heaven, so too at Zaragoza St James had a vision of the Virgin Mary in which he heard celestial music and saw her standing on a column of jasper. She said to him: 'I, son Diego, am your protector . . . build me a church in my name . . . I shall work wonderful signs, especially to help those who in their necessity come to this place.' On departing, the Virgin left a small wooden image of herself, crowned and with the child Jesus in her arms, standing on a jasper column, and promised St James that 'until the end of the world I shall preserve this pillar in the place where it now is'.[18] But although the image had been secretly preserved during the Moorish occupation, Murillo confessed that nothing remained of the first sanctuary and that after the reconquest of Zaragoza there had been many disputes between the cathedral and the holy chapel, so that the sumptuous edifice, replete with a chapter of canons, which now housed the chapel and its precious image only dated from 1515.

The theological implications of this narrative were all important. At a time when the apostles still celebrated the Eucharist in private houses, St James, whom Murillo accounted second only to St Peter, had raised a chapel which could claim to have been the very first church ever built in the world and had founded a bishopric which was subsequent only to the sees at Jerusalem and Antioch. Equally important, it was at Zaragoza that the first holy image had been presented to the faithful for their venera-tion. The only other images that could parallel its heavenly provenance were the St Veronica preserved in St Peter's, the Holy Shroud in Turin and the likeness of Christ sent to Edessa. There were also certain portraits of Mary painted by St Luke. But the only Marian sanctuary which Murillo admitted as being possibly superior to the chapel at Zaragoza was the Holy House in Loreto, since not merely did it have a statue which might have been carved by St Luke but, more importantly, it enclosed the house wherein the sublime mystery of the Incarnation had been enacted. For all that, it had been at Zaragoza that 'there thus began the holy use of images so agreeable to God'. Careful to note that the Council of Trent had taught that the purpose of images was to awaken devotion to their heavenly originals through lively representation, Murillo admitted that it would be idolatrous to esteem one image over another. However, in the case of Zaragoza, it had been the Virgin herself who had given the image and thus introduced its cult. In all this, Murillo cited St John Damascene as claiming that images had been venerated since the first days of the Church and insisted that: 'God is accustomed to work through images, which are also books and preach silently to us and at times with greater effect than writings.'[19]

Such was the power of Our Lady of Pilar that during the seventeenth and eighteenth centuries the sanctuary at Zaragoza was enlarged and embellished to the point where it rivalled most cathedrals, its majestic frame dominated by a central dome and a high tower at each corner. Devotion to the image was confirmed by the appearance of the *Mystical City of God* (1680), a life of the Virgin Mary written by Sor María de Jesús de Agreda, a Franciscan nun and the most celebrated visionary of her time. For here all the elements of the traditional narrative were reiterated, albeit with the addition that St James was related to the Virgin and hence all the more beloved. In this account Mary came to Zaragoza assisted by a thousand angels, and on endowing the chapel built by St James with her image, she promised that 'it shall last with the Holy Faith until the end of the world'. Blessed with what was the first image of the 'evangelical law', Spain was distinguished and magnified among the nations by its devotion to the Mother of God and in return had been rewarded more than other kingdoms by the apparition of so many images dedicated to her cult.[20]

Sor María de Agreda's endorsement was all the more valuable since her narrative purported to have been dictated by the Virgin Mary herself. This claim was rejected by the Roman Inquisition, which condemned the book. But Sor María was protected by the Franciscan Order and by Philip IV, who corresponded with her and indeed in 1643 visited her convent, when he was counselled by her to pray for assistance in the chapel of Pilar. Her ecclesiastical superior, the bishop of Tarazona, defended the nun's book on the grounds that its contents accorded with Church doctrine and scripture and was written by a person of proven virtue. The Church had always accepted the private revelations made to saints such as St Catherine of Siena, St Brigid of Sweden and St Hildegard of Bingen. Although no-one was obliged to accept these revelations, for his part, the bishop concluded that 'in these writings of Mother María de Jesús, we find the royal seal of God's Majesty'.[21] So too, her confessor and biographer, Fr José Jiménez Samaniego, argued that the Church was sustained by the 'perpetual assistance of the Holy Spirit', by the doctrines of scripture and the Church Fathers, and by the discernment of spirits conducted by learned men. In the case of Sor María, the king had commanded a junta of theologians to consider the nun's writings and they had found nothing contrary to Catholic teaching in her work. Although some theologians denied the possibility of any 'new divine revelation', others, most notably St Bonaventure, argued that God had the power to reveal hidden truths to the Church. Moreover, from the Old Testament until recent times, there had appeared an entire line of inspired women, several of whose visions had been approved by successive popes. For all these reasons, so Samaniego concluded, the *Mystical City of God* carried the seal of heavenly approbation.[22] In effect, the Virgin Mary had chosen Spain and its Catholic monarchy for her especial protection and through her revelation had confirmed both the providential election of the monarchy as the chief defender of the Church and the enduring value of her miraculous images.

II

The first general chronicler of the Indies, Gonzalo Fernández de Oviedo (1478–1557), recounted that during the great siege of Mexico-Tenochtitlan some Spaniards claimed that they had seen Santiago appear mounted on a white horse, and others asserted that at one desperate moment the Virgin Mary had cast dust in the eyes of the Indians. Oviedo admitted that many would say about such miracles: 'well, I did not see it; it is superfluous or a waste of time to tell such stories'. And yet, if demons and false gods had intervened in human history, why should not God and his saints help the faithful in times of need?[23] Although this part of Oviedo's chronicle was not published in the sixteenth century, nevertheless, in his *History of the Conquest of Mexico* (1552) Francisco López de Gómara equally insisted that the apostle Santiago had intervened to assist the Spaniards in battle. So also, he related that Cortés placed an image of the Virgin Mary on the altar of the great pyramid temple in Mexico-Tenochtitlan and that when the Indians tried to remove it they were unable to do so. In the subsequent fighting, so he related, the Indians were stunned to see 'fighting for the Spaniards St Mary and Santiago on a white horse, and the Indians said that the horse wounded and killed as many with its mouth and hoofs as did the horseman with the sword, and that the woman of the altar cast dust in their faces and blinded them'.[24] In effect, just as Santiago and the Virgin had appeared in the sky to help the Spaniards defeat the Moors during the great battles of the Reconquest, so in Mexico the apparition of the same heavenly powers had disheartened the Indians and brought victory to Hernán Cortés and his band of conquerors.

When Juan de Torquemada (1562?–1624), the Franciscan chronicler, described the conquest of Mexico in his *Monarchy of the Indies* (1615), he preferred to invoke scriptural typology rather than miraculous apparitions to interpret events. If like earlier historians he compared the fall of Tenochtitlan to the siege of Jerusalem, he chose to define Cortés as a veritable Gideon, chosen by God to lead his small band of followers to victory over vast native hordes. But he also drew on the millennial expectations of Fr Toribio de Benavente alias Motolinia, one of the first Franciscans to arrive in Mexico, to present the conquest as a grand exodus, in which the natives of New Spain sallied forth from the Egypt of idolatry to enter the promised land of the Christian Church.[25] In effect, he wrote more to celebrate the foundation of a new church than to praise the conquerors. However, he also followed Fr Jerónimo de Mendieta, on whose *Church History of the Indies* (1596) he drew extensively, to salute Cortés as another Moses who had liberated the peoples of Anáhuac from the Devil's dominion and contrasted his role to that of Martin Luther, who, in the same year of 1519, had led the nations of Northern Europe into heresy. In any case, the greatest act of Cortés, so these Franciscans all affirmed, was not his military triumph but rather his splendid act of humility, when in 1524 he knelt in the dust before the assembled nobility, both Spanish and Indian, to kiss the hand of Fr Martín de Valencia, leader of the twelve friars who had walked barefoot from Veracruz to Mexico City.[26]

The purpose of the *Monarchy of the Indies*, a three-volume work densely printed in double columns, was to defend the native peoples of Mexico from European disparagement and to celebrate their conversion by the Franciscans. A keen student of Nahuatl and a skilled interpreter of the pictographic codices in which the Aztecs preserved records of their history, Torquemada drew on the enquiries of two generations of mendicant chroniclers. But amidst the vast range of material which he incorporated into his work, often without much modification, there can be discerned the influence of St Augustine's *City of God*. On describing the journey of the Aztecs from the northern steppe-lands to the Valley of Mexico, Torquemada identified their tribal god, Huitzilopochtli, as Satan in person, who guided his new-found chosen people by means of oracles and omens. Throughout this narrative, the Mexica were repeatedly compared to the Israelites in the desert, albeit with Satan rather than Jehovah as their master. It followed that it was the Aztecs rather than the Toltecs or Chichimecas who were held responsible for introducing the practice of human sacrifice into Anáhuac. In his description of Mexico-Tenochtitlan, Torquemada emphasized the grandeur of the island city, which possessed over 60,000 dwellings, all dominated by the great temple of Huitzilopochtli, which soared over the central sacred compound where another forty temples were to be found.[27] In all this, the Franciscan depicted the Aztec empire as a glittering Babylon, the horrific scale of its idolatry and human sacrifice proof enough of the Devil's dominion.

The third volume of the chronicle was devoted to a detailed description of the conversion of the natives of Mexico and the foundation of the new church. Since Torquemada incorporated entire chapters of Mendieta, who in turn had taken material from Motolinia, he transmitted the spirit of exultation and hope which animated these early accounts. After a brief moment of coldness, no doubt occasioned by the destruction of their temples and gods, the Indians had flocked to hear the mendicants and had collaborated enthusiastically in building a vast array of churches and convents. So also, the friars assembled the children of the nobility in their convents to instruct them both in Spanish and in Christian doctrine so they could thereafter serve as interpreters and intermediaries. Moreover, to attract their new converts, the Franciscans exploited all the resources of the Catholic liturgy, seeking to replace the pagan cycle of feasts with the Christian calendar. As Torquemada later commented, since the Indians 'by their very nature are so addicted to the rites of religion', it was necessary to gratify their tastes by the construction of great churches adorned with rich altarpieces and paintings. Indeed, so successful was this strategy of conversion that by the early seventeenth century, the Holy Week ceremonies in Mexico City were distinguished by several thousand natives carrying crucifixes through the streets. By then, the great seven-naved church of San José, which formed part of the great

Franciscan convent in the capital, served as the starting point of these parades, its altars offering a permanent shrine for the images most venerated by the Indians.[28]

Although the mendicants generally resettled the native population and built new towns, in certain places they replaced existing temples by Christian churches, especially in the cases of sites which attracted pilgrimage. As Torquemada explained:

> In this New Spain these gentile Indians had three places, in which they honoured three different gods and celebrated them with feasts. One of them is situated in the skirts of the Sierra Grande, which is called, of Tlaxcala, and which the ancients called (and these now call) Matlalcueye. In this place they held a feast to the goddess called Toci, which is to say, Our Grandmother. Another place to the East of this . . . is called Tianquizmanalco, which is to say, a flattened place, or made by hand, for markets and fairs. In this place they held a feast to a god they called Telpuchtli, which is to say, Young Man. And in the other, which is a league from this city of Mexico, to the North, they held a feast to another goddess, called Tonan, which is to say, Our Mother. This devotion to gods prevailed when our friars came to the land and to these feasts there came great numbers of people from many leagues about, and especially to that of Tianquizmanalco, to which they came in pilgrimage from Guatemala, which is 300 leagues, and other more distant parts, to offer gifts and presents.

On these sites, the mendicants built churches, so Torquemada explained, replacing Toci with a church dedicated to St Anne, the grandmother of Christ. At Tianquizmanalco they built a house in honour of St John the Baptist, and so also a chapel 'in Tonantzin, close to Mexico, to the Most Sacred Virgin, who is Our Lady and Mother', which was to say, at Tepeyac. In all three places they celebrated feasts to which many people came, especially to that of St John the Baptist, albeit not on the previous scale, since the Indian population had declined and those who remained were overworked or had other devotions. When Torquemada wrote these lines, he resided in the Franciscan convent at Tlatelolco, not far from the chapel at Tepeyac dedicated to Our Lady of Guadalupe and which had been in existence since at least 1556. But at no point in his voluminous work did he make the slightest reference to the image and its cult.[29]

From their first arrival, so Mendieta observed, the Franciscans assembled children in their convent for instruction in Christian doctrine and Spanish. Thereafter, they relied on their assistance to the point where 'children were the masters of the evangelists, children also the preachers and children the agents of the destruction of idolatry'. Equally important, it was native painters and sculptors taught by Pedro de Gante, a Flemish lay-brother, who were responsible for adorning the mendicant churches with their gilded retables and the numerous pictures which covered their walls. But the most talented of these young disciples were educated at the college of Santa Cruz Tlatelolco, founded by the Franciscans in 1536, where pupils learnt Latin and the elements of theology and philosophy so as to prepare them for the priesthood. In the event, these students were soon found to be more apt for marriage than for celibacy, and most returned to their homes, where they soon emerged as leaders of their communities. But a small number taught at the college and assisted the mendicants in translating sermons, sacred drama and scriptural texts into Nahuatl. It was at Santa Cruz that Bernardino de Sahagún lectured and encountered the disciples who enabled him to compose his *General History of the Things of New Spain*, an encyclopedic, bilingual survey of pre-hispanic religion, culture and language. So dramatic was the rhythmical prose employed to describe native reactions to the Spanish occupation and siege of Mexico-Tenochtitlan that doubts must remain as to whether Sahagún was the sole author or whether his native collaborators were active in its composition. For their part, the Franciscans freely acknowledged their debt to these Nahua intellectuals, and indeed in his *Sermons in the Mexican Language* (1606), Fray Juan Bautista not merely thanked Antonio Valeriano, the Indian governor of San Juan Tenochtitlan, for his assistance, but also printed a letter written in Latin by this former professor at Tlatelolco. So too, Torquemada described Valeriano as his master in Nahuatl and claimed that he had translated Cato into that language. In effect, the sustained collaboration of the mendicants and the native elite led to the emergence of a considerable body of writings in literary Nahuatl, in which pre-hispanic songs were preserved alongside sermons and historical accounts.[30]

The *Monarchy of the Indies* was written by a Spaniard who confessed that Mexico was not his *patria*, albeit asserting that 'although it is not mine, at least I take it as my own, through having been raised in it'. Since it transmitted the vision of the first two generations of mendicants who had laboured to comprehend native culture and create a new church in Mexico, its vision was retrospective, not to say archaic, and as such it did not address the tensions that haunted the Mexican Church at the time it was published. Moreover, it was animated by an Augustinian dualism in which, if Mexico-Tenochtitlan figured as another Babylon where the altars of Huitzilopochtli were stained by a holocaust of human sacrifice, the hispanic city was now a new Jerusalem where in forty churches and chapels the Lamb of God, Jesus Christ, was daily offered in the sacrifice of over six hundred masses. For the pious mind it was an enthralling contrast. But the characterization of Cortés as another Moses did not always attract Spaniards born in Mexico, who had become all too aware of the loss of life and destruction caused by the conquest. Moreover, the triumphalism of the 'spiritual conquest' equally disturbed those priests who now sought to encounter an autonomous, spiritual foundation for their Mexican Church. Nor were all American Spaniards so persuaded of the diabolic character of Aztec society. In consequence, Torquemada's great chronicle eventually came to be regarded with suspicion, even though it was not until the eighteenth century that its account of ancient Mexico was rewritten and Satan finally expelled from the historical record.[31]

Clear testimony of the rivalries and conflicts which divided the Mexican Church in the first decades of the seventeenth century was presented in the *Chronicle of the Order of St Augustine in New Spain* (1624), written by Juan de Grijalva (1580–1638), a native of Colima, who magnified the contribution of the Augustinian friars to the conversion of the Indians in order to defend their retention of the vast parishes or *doctrinas* that they still administered. For by then the bishops had launched a campaign to transfer all parishes into the care of the secular clergy or, at the least, to subject the mendicants to regular visitations. It was to emphasize the achievements of his Order that Grijalva described the life of Fr Alonso de la Veracruz, four times provincial and a learned theologian who had been chiefly responsible for ensuring that, unlike their coun-terparts in Peru, the natives of New Spain were admitted to the Eucharist. But he lamented that the heroic labours of the first missionaries were passing into oblivion: no friar had been canonized, no tomb housing their relics attracted popular devotion, and for the most part their writings mouldered in manuscript. Much the same point had been made by Torquemada when he equally lamented that Martín de Valencia's earthly remains had been lost and that no miracles were associated with his name, wrought either in his lifetime or at his tomb. But if Torquemada attributed the absence of miracles to the direct intervention of the Holy Spirit, who had moved the Indians to accept the gospel without external marvels, by contrast Grijalva argued that whereas the primitive Church had required miracles because the apostles were poor, ignorant men who had to deal with the pride and learning of the Romans and Jews, by contrast in America 'the preacher was in all things superior to the Indians' and hence stood in no need of spiritual wonders.[32]

Where Grijalva most differed from Torquemada was in his frank reference to the rivalry between European and American Spaniards. In this context it should be noted that as early as 1574 Jerónimo de Mendieta had warned that of the Spaniards born in the Indies, few were fit to become priests since 'the greater part take the nature and customs of the Indians, as they are born in the same climate and reared among them'. Much the same point was made by the celebrated Franciscan chronicler, Bernardino de Sahagún, who also blamed the climate and heavenly constellations, observing that 'those who are born here [are] very similar in character to the Indians, in aspect they appear Spaniards and in their condition they are not', adding that they were 'intoler-able to govern and most difficult to save'.[33] Despite these opinions, creoles flooded into the religious orders, with the result that in the opening decades of the seventeenth century virtually every mendicant province in New Spain was torn asunder by bitter partisan conflict which centred on the elections of candidates to high office as priors and provincials. It was in this context that Grijalva reproached those Spaniards who came to Mexico to seek their fortune and to enjoy its honours, only then to slander the character and good name of its inhabitants, pining for return to the Peninsula. Of his own 'nation', which was to say, the Spaniards born in Mexico, he wrote: 'generally speaking their wits are so lively that at eleven or twelve the boys read, write, count, know Latin and make verses like the famous men of Italy; at fourteen or fifteen they graduate in arts'. The University of Mexico, where both the faculty and the students were mainly creole, could figure among the most illustrious in Europe. And yet, so he exclaimed:

> despite so much experience, they still ask us, who are born in this land, whether we speak Castilian or Indian. The Church is filled with creole bishops and prebends, the religious orders with prelates, the high courts with judges, the provinces with governors, all creoles, who govern with great judgement and head, and despite it all, they doubt whether we are capable.[34]

In these indignant affirmations, written by a chronicler who had fought within his own Order to obtain the election of creoles to high office, we can observe the bitter resentment of American Spaniards who sought access to the governance of their country, be it in Church or State.

It was also Grijalva who testified that by the early seventeenth century the Mexican Church was characterized by a fervent cult of holy images, cults which united Indians and Spaniards, clergy and people, the elite and the masses. As regards the natives, Grijalva justified the splendid churches built by the Augustinians as necessary to impress upon the Indians the authority of their new religion. Around these imposing edifices they had concentrated the native population, providing each family with a house and with ample water from public fountains. So too, they had organized the Indians into confraternities devoted to the Virgin Mary and the Blessed Souls in Purgatory, and promoted a great reverence for the cross and the Eucharist. The churches were filled with images and richly decorated altars, and each possessed an organ, a choir and expert instrumentalists. Each town and each district within these towns possessed patron saints, whose images were paraded through the streets on their feast days, during Holy Week and on Corpus Christi. Indeed, Grijalva commented that the Indians 'were extreme in the cult and reverence of images', since each family had erected an altar in their house on which they placed a crucifix, and various figures of the Virgin Mary and the saints.[35]

It was in the cult of holy images that the creole hunger for miracles was finally satisfied. By this time all the great mendicant priories of Mexico City possessed images, usually of the Virgin Mary or of Christ, which had come to attract intense devotion and to whose intercession miracles were attributed. Where Grijalva sounded an entirely new note, as compared to Torquemada, was in his report of the extraordinary case of the image of Our Lady of Los Remedios, which by the time he wrote was housed in a rich sanctuary close to the capital. For here was the image which Cortés had placed on the altar of the great temple of Mexico-Tenochtitlan, but which had been thereafter taken out and buried by a faithful conqueror during the *noche triste*. Some years after the conquest the Virgin Mary appeared to an Indian nobleman, known as don Juan, to inform him of the whereabouts of the image and that she wished to have a chapel built in her honour. Once the sanctuary was built, the image soon attracted pilgrims and miracles were attributed to its power. The result was that the city council declared Our Lady of Los Remedios patron of the capital, and on three separate occasions the image was brought in grand procession from Tlacopan to the cathedral so as to obtain its assistance, first against the plague and then against the droughts that threatened agriculture. Although Grijalva inserted this account largely to suggest that the Virgin performed her miracles by using an Augustinian belt, nevertheless, his ready acceptance of the Virgin's apparitions, both during the conquest and afterwards to don Juan, attested to a decisive change in the attitude of the ecclesiastical elite of Mexico to apparitions, miracles and holy images.[36] In part, that change derived from the quest of American Spaniards to encounter the means of endowing their Church with spiritual foundations other than the conquest and the mendicant mission.

II

In his *History... of the Holy Image of Our Lady of Los Remedios* (1621), Luis de Cisneros, a Mercedarian friar and professor of theology in the University of Mexico, averred that this small statue had been brought to Mexico by Juan Rodríguez de Villasuerte, a conqueror, and that Hernán Cortés had placed it on the altar of the great pyramid temple dedicated to Huitzilopochtli. Such was the power inherent in the image that when the Indians sought to remove it from the temple, it resisted all their attempts. But as the Spaniards fled Tenochtitlan during the *noche triste*, they took the figure and placed it on the altar of a temple at Otoncalpulco, a hill not far from the city. During this retreat, an Indian nobleman, later known as don Juan, saw the Apostle Santiago and the Virgin Mary appear in the sky to assist the Spaniards, and witnessed the Virgin casting dust in the eyes of the Indians. It was some fifteen or twenty years after these dramatic events that don Juan saw the Virgin 'in resplendent and beautiful figure', dressed as Our Lady of Los Remedios, and recognized her as the heavenly woman who had helped the Spaniards. She informed him of the whereabouts of her image, which was hidden in a dense wood under a great maguey cactus which had grown through the steps of the temple at Otoncalpulco. He kept the image in his cottage for another twelve years until, when news of its existence became public, the chancellor of the cathedral chapter, Alvaro Tremiño (who left Mexico in 1553), ordered him first to erect an altar in his house and then to place the image in the hermitage of San Juan.[37]

At this point, when Juan was injured by a pillar falling on him, he went to the chapel at Tepeyac to pray to Our Lady of Guadalupe to help him. But in her sanctuary the Virgin reproached him, saying:

> Does it seem good to you what you have done to me, that you have thrown me out of your house? Are you so annoyed with my company? And now that you have thrown me out, why did you not put me back in the place where you found me?

Cured by the Virgin, Juan returned to his village at Totoltepec, and built a chapel for Our Lady of Los Remedios at the foot of the old temple. Thereafter, devotion to the image mounted steadily, and on 30 April 1574 the city council of Mexico, noting that the Franciscans in the convent at Tlacopan took little interest in the cult, appointed García de Albornoz, a councillor, to take charge of the chapel. Within a year he built a new sanctuary, formed a confraternity headed by three noblemen and three merchants, and obtained licences from the viceroy and the archbishop for the council to name the image as the patron of Mexico City, fixing its feast on the Sunday within the Octave of the Assumption of Mary.[38]

In framing this account, Cisneros confessed that it had caused him immense toil to discover any information about the image, adding:

> I cannot but blame my *patria* . . . for having so neglected to provide an account . . . of the beginning and origin of this holy image, of its visits, and of the overflowing graces that all kinds of people at all times have received from its generous hands, of which there hardly remains a trace of ascertained and established truth.[39]

His chief written sources were the standard chronicles of the Spanish conquest, material about the cult in the city archives, and certain elderly Indians, most notably doña Anna, the daughter of don Juan, a woman of about seventy. So also he had consulted 'the most elderly and most trustworthy witnesses' in the hispanic community, but concluded that 'all who live in this city know that there is no more proof of the origin of this holy image than some common rumours or statements'. As a native of Mexico City, he himself had visited the sanctuary over the past forty years.[40] Oddly enough, he did not include as a source the pictorial evidence that existed in the sanctuary. Yet in 1595 the current chaplain, Dr José López, had commissioned artists to cover the walls with scenes depicting the miracles performed by the Virgin, each accompanied by explanatory verses. On one side of the sanctuary there were scenes of the Virgin's apparition during the conquest, of don Juan finding the image, of his miraculous cure after a pillar had fallen on him, of the Manila galleon saved at sea, and of a four-year-old child saved on a runaway mule. On the other side were paintings of Cortés replacing idols with the holy image in the great temple, of the image resisting attempts of Indians to remove it, of it being placed in the temple which was now the site of the sanctuary, of the image being brought to the city in 1577, and of the cure of a

Plate 3   Title page of Luis de Cisneros, *La Santa Imagen de Nuestra Señora de los Remedios*

man falling from a mule.[41] As will be observed, these inscribed paintings offered Cisneros invaluable testimony and demonstrate how pictorial records often preceded the publication of a narrative of an image's origins.

To provide a context for his account, Cisneros quoted early Church Councils which had praised Mary as the advocate of 'all things which were arduous and difficult' and noted that Pope Innocent III had pronounced that 'Mary saved what Eve lost.' More to the point, he briefly described the miraculous origins of the chief Marian images of Spain, which was to say, Pilar, Montserrat, Guadalupe, Peña de Francia, Atocha and others, only to conclude that no documentary evidence existed for any of them, adding 'all these have been found by these miracles, not having any more known beginnings than our image of Los Remedios'. Cisneros then listed the most important images which were venerated in New Spain, noting that virtually all the great mendicant priories in Mexico City possessed a particular advocation of the Virgin which aroused devotion. He singled out Our Lady of Las Mercedes housed in his own Order's church in Mexico, which was famous for the miracles it had wrought and which 'miraculously' brought in some seventeen thousand pesos a year to the eighty friars of the Merced. By far the oldest of these images, however, was Our Lady of Guadalupe, whose miracles at Tepeyac had prompted the archbishop to rebuild its sanctuary.[42]

Citing St John Damascene's treatise, *On Holy Images*, Cisneros argued that although God had prohibited images in the Old Testament for fear of idolatry, in the epoch of Christian grace, images now served as the books of the ignorant and as such provoked great devotion, so that from the beginnings of the Church, 'God wished that always in her images are painted.' So also, all the scholastics and Church Fathers were agreed that the Virgin Mary should be approached with *hyperdulia*, a greater veneration than that accorded to the saints and angels. In the case of Our Lady of Los Remedios, Cisneros turned to scriptural typology to exalt the image. Drawing upon Torquemada's great chronicle, published but a year before he wrote, he emphasized the horrors of Aztec idolatry, where 62,000 victims had been offered during the consecration of the great temple of Huitzilopochtli, so that 'this New World was made a kingdom of darkness, where the Devil was so greatly served'. Yet Cortés had cast down the idols and placed Los Remedios in their place as a 'holy conqueror'.[43] As much as Our Lady of Pilar in the battles against the Moors, the Virgin of Los Remedios had intervened against the Indians, appearing like 'a great sign' in heaven, as chapter 12 of the Apocalypse had described the Virgin. In effect, 'the credit of the conquest and all that came from it is owed to the Most Holy Virgin'. Had not the fire of the Holy Spirit illumined 'that aqueduct of Mary', so that she became a source of light, 'the arklight'?[44] In describing the subsequent history of the image, Cisneros did not hesitate to compare it to the Ark of the Covenant and to Moses' rod. Equally important, when he narrated don Juan's return to his village after his visionary dialogue with Our Lady of Guadalupe at Tepeyac, he compared him to Moses descending Mount Sinai.[45]

Thereafter, he affirmed that it was only through the Virgin's intervention that it had been possible for the mendicants to convert so many millions of Indians. In 1576, when over 2 million Indians died of the plague, it was to the Virgin of Los Remedios that the viceroy and archbishop turned for assistance, carrying the image in public procession from its chapel to the cathedral, there to celebrate nine days of prayer and petition. Much the same assistance was again sought in 1595 when New Spain suffered from prolonged drought. Cisneros concluded: 'through her holy image of Los Remedios, the Virgin has performed heroic miracles'.[46]

By the time Cisneros wrote, the image and sanctuary of Los Remedios had become the object of such an intense cult that the sanctuary possessed some twenty-three small houses or rooms where pilgrims could stay, and a residence for the chaplain with public rooms in which to receive the viceroy and archbishop. In 1589 the Franciscans at Tlacopan had attempted to claim possession of the chapel, but despite the support of the current viceroy, they had been thwarted when the image was secretly removed to the cathedral. Citing Torquemada, Cisneros expatiated on the beauty and fertility of the surrounding Valley of Mexico, which with two thousand springs of water had supported over a million inhabitants during the days of the Emperor Xolotl. He affirmed: 'if God planted Paradise in this New World . . . the place was in this Valley of Mexico'. All this was but prelude to his ecstatic description of the sanctuary, which was lit by forty-one lamps and possessed a silver tabernacle worth over ten thousand pesos. By then the image had no fewer than sixteen crowns, together with sixteen changes in the richly decorated vestments that adorned it. It is worthy of note that above the side altar devoted to Our Lady of Las Lágrimas, there were paintings of Moses and the burning bush, and of Gideon and his fleece, both biblical figures of the Virgin.[47] But it is Cisneros' description of the Virgin's inner sanctum that attested to the emotions aroused by the richness of its decoration:

> it appears that it is a heaven, because the precious stones, which adorn all the chapel where the Virgin is, appear like celestial stars that are shining, allowing us to under-stand that what we have here is the Queen of Heaven, who has the sun for clothing, the moon for shoes and a circlet of twelve stars for a diadem. It is the most devout thing to see that sanctuary, when it is revealed, and I do not think there is a breast so frozen that the fire given off by those stones and lights does not warm and illumine, because apart from the wax candles there are always burning five lamps and on many days forty-one . . . Imagine how that Sanctuary is when the Most Holy Virgin is like this, all adorned with the little lamb of her son in her arms, dressed in clothes, the tabernacle edged with carved and golden silver, the chapel filled with a thousand pieces of gold and precious stones, in which forty-one lamps are hanging, four high candles and another six, with all the altarpiece engraved with gold. The sanctuary where the Virgin is, is surrounded by amber apples edged with gold, and on the

altarpiece suspended silver legs, hands, heads, breasts and eyes, all in a polished metal, that return the light, that receive it and duplicate it several times over: what harmony is found here? Where can the eyes rest in all that they see? How are the hearts that contemplate all this? Without exception, every time I see this sanctuary it appears to me a living portrait of glory, a firmament, that eighth sphere adorned with stars in a serene night.[48]

In these lines we encounter a faithful expression of the sentiments aroused in the pilgrims and the faithful who frequented these sanctuaries, men and women who came in search of comfort and help, and who felt themselves transported into a sphere of existence which corresponded to their expectations of heaven. At the same time, the presence of silver limbs and heads confirmed the efficacy of the Virgin, since these were the donations of those who had been cured of their physical ailments.

Written and approved in 1616, albeit published posthumously in 1621, Cisneros' account concluded with a description of the third entrance of the Virgin of Los Remedios into the city of Mexico. It was at the beginning of June 1616, when the seasonal rains had yet to arrive and maize prices had reached the exorbitant level of 5 pesos a hundredweight, that Archbishop Juan Pérez de la Serna, accompanied by the cathedral chapter and city council, sallied forth to the 'hermitage', first to celebrate mass and then to escort the image to the Franciscan convent at Tlacopan. The next day, 11 June, the image was carried in public procession through the streets of the capital and placed on the high altar of the cathedral. Such a festive occasion had never before been seen in the city, Cisneros averred, since all the bells of the churches were rung, accompanied by trumpets and flutes; the streets where the image passed were carpeted; rich tapestries hung from the balconies; and fireworks constantly exploded. The procession accompanying the Virgin was headed by the assembled array of the religious Orders, followed by no fewer than forty Indian brotherhoods and over a hundred confraternities of Spaniards and mulattos. Then came four hundred secular priests, the archbishop and cathedral canons parading before the image, which was carried under a pallium by Indian noblemen from Tlacopan. The viceroy and judges of the high court concluded the procession. The image remained in the cathedral for nine days, during which masses were celebrated and sermons preached, the ceremonies illumined by the consumption of over seven thousand pounds of wax candles. Such was the devotion elicited by the presence of the image that various members of the nobility donated jewels to the Virgin.[49] On visiting the cathedral Cisneros heard an Indian woman from Tlacopan addressing the Virgin:

Lady, what are you doing here? Why do you not go to your house? Have you not stayed here long enough? See how your children are so lonely without you and that we do not have enough to eat. Why do you not come? The crops go very badly without your presence. Return now, Lady, and do not allow us to not have our highest good.

Was not this a prayer, Cisneros added, that echoed King David in Psalm 27, verse 8, 'Your face, Lord, we seek'?[50]

The efficacy of the Virgin was manifested by an almost immediate downpour of rain, so that from the time it was brought to the cathedral until 'today, which is half way through September', it had not stopped raining, thus offering promise of abundant harvests. In gratitude, the authorities accompanied by some forty thousand persons, all carrying candles at night, escorted the image back to its sanctuary. As it drew close the Indians greeted it with *copal* incense and by 'strewing loose flowers, with which they filled their cloaks'. On witnessing this it seemed to Cisneros that the Virgin changed in her aspect and seemed to smile on receiving so much homage. But when he reviewed the entire event, Cisneros lamented that the image had been so handled and touched during its visit to the city. He recalled that Our Lady of Montserrat, the patron of Cataluña, had never left her sanctuary in six hundred years, save only to take possession of a new chapel. Surely it would be best if Los Remedios should likewise be prevented from sallying forth: after all, the Ark of the Covenant had not left the temple once it entered that sacred precinct. 'I would wish that the City, which cares so much for her increase and veneration, should make a special order that for no reason or on any occasion should the Virgin leave her sanctuary or even be placed on the altar.'[51] But this pious hope was not to be respected, since the Virgin's reputed power over rain drove the authorities on many occasions during the next two centuries to bring the image to the cathedral.

3

The Woman of the Apocalypse

In a description of the miraculous images of the Virgin Mary in Mexico City Luis Cisneros wrote:

> The oldest is that of Guadalupe, which is some leagues from this city to the North, and which is an image of great devotion and attendance, almost since this land was won, which has made and still makes miracles, and for which a distinguished church is being built, which at the order and care of the archbishop is almost completed.[1]

Consecrated in 1622 by Archbishop Juan Pérez de la Serna, the new sanctuary was in part financed by the faithful, who, in return for their donations, received an indulgence of forty days' remission of sins, their certificate printed from a copper plate designed by Samuel Stradanus on which was depicted the Virgin above her altar surrounded by eight scenes of miracles she had wrought.[2] The antiquity of the cult at Tepeyac was attested by the *True History of the Conquest of New Spain* (1632), a chronicle written in the 1560s by Bernal Díaz del Castillo, a companion of Cortés, who referred to 'Tepeaquilla, which they now call Our Lady of Guadalupe, where she works and has worked many wonderful miracles'.[3] Here was public testimony of the early origin of the devotion.

Such was the growth in the cult of this image that in 1629, Archbishop Francisco Manso y Zúñiga brought the Guadalupe to the cathedral, travelling in a canoe from the sanctuary, so as to implore the Virgin's assistance against the flood waters which then engulfed the city. Devotion obviously mounted during its stay in the cathedral and, when in 1634 after the flood had subsided, Our Lady of Guadalupe returned to her sanctuary, she was accompanied by both the viceroy and the archbishop and was carried through tapestried streets, her departure marked by fireworks and music. In verses published that year by an anonymous author, the Virgin was saluted as a Queen and as Esther, and above all, as the ark who had saved the city from destruction.[4] Moreover, in ambiguous lines, the poet not only lamented the Virgin's departure, but also appeared to suggest that the image was of heavenly origin, affirming:

Of your Sacred Image, there are diverse advocations that assure consolation for such a bitter and unhappy absence. I confess that all is one, that all are enclosed in one, and that all are derived from the first Original. But here are various, painted with human hands with the many-coloured hues that human men invent. You, Virgin, are drawn by he who made heaven and earth, whose wonder is not so much a proof, since you are the same. If you come from such hands, how much does the land weep for an absence, which needs a miracle to be absent. If you came by water, now, Virgin, you go by land, that in spite of my sin, for you God dries and cures.

The verses finished by celebrating the Virgin Mary's Nativity, on whose liturgical feast day Our Lady of Guadalupe was commemorated, and also the Virgin's Assumption, to which advocation the cathedral in Mexico was dedicated.

It was in 1640, in the prologue to a printed sermon about Felipe de Jesús, a Mexican Franciscan who had been martyred in Nagasaki in 1597 and beatified by Rome in 1627, that its author, Miguel Sánchez (1596?–1674), a well-known preacher, informed his patron, Dr Lope Altamirano y Castillo, the creole archdeacon of the cathedral in Mexico City, that 'I remain with hopes of another, larger writing: the second Eve in your sanctuary of Guadalupe, if with the favour of God and that of your lordship I can seclude myself to prepare it.' Seizing the opportunity to preach about 'the saint of our *patria*', Sánchez saluted the Franciscan as 'My Jesús of the Indies, my brave Felipe . . . the fortunate man of Mexico, the most successful of its creoles, the happiest of our country'. By way of justifying these sentiments, he cited St Jerome, who had written that 'love of the *patria* is a natural characteristic', and Hiercoles, who had averred that the *patria* is 'a second God, God's substitute'.[5] It was this blend of religion and patriotism that drove Sánchez to write the *Image of the Virgin Mary, Mother of Guadalupe. Miraculously Appeared in the City of Mexico. Celebrated in her History, with the prophecy of Chapter Twelve of the Apocalypse* (1648), where he presented the first published account of the Virgin's apparitions and the miraculous origin of her image. Handsomely printed and adorned with engravings, this small volume of 192 pages was dedicated to Dr Pedro de Barrientos Lomelín, the creole treasurer of the cathedral chapter and vicar general of the Mexican archdiocese. The story it told enthralled the creole elite of the capital and was calculated to strengthen the already fervent devotion to the Mexican Virgin.[6]

It was on a Saturday, early in December 1531, that a poor Indian named Juan Diego was passing by the hill of Guadalupe, about a league north of Mexico City, when he heard sweet music and then saw a young woman who informed him that she was the Virgin Mary, Mother of the true God, and commanded him to go and tell the bishop of Mexico that she wished to have a chapel built in her honour at Tepeyac. But, when the Indian saw Juan de Zumárraga, the bishop asked him to come back another day. On being told by the Virgin to return, Juan Diego went to see the bishop again on

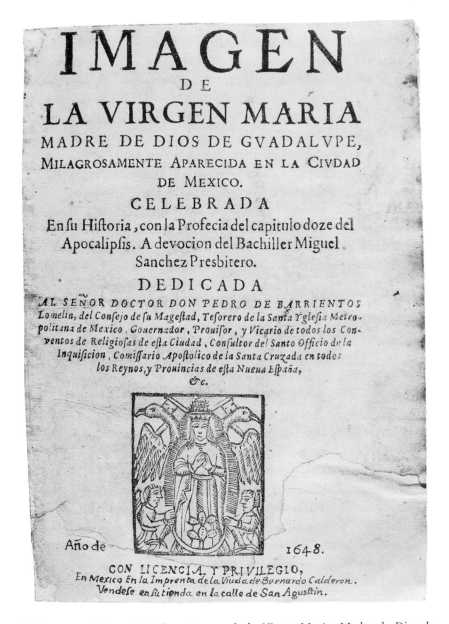

Plate 4   Title page of Miguel Sánchez, *Imagen de la Virgen María, Madre de Dios de Guadalupe*

Sunday, only to be informed that he must bring a sign that would attest to the truth of the apparitions. After being reassured by the Virgin, the Indian spent Monday at home looking after his uncle, Juan Bernardino, who was dying of the plague. On Tuesday, when he set out for Santiago Tlatelolco to find a priest for his uncle, Juan Diego was again accosted by the Virgin, who commanded him to climb the hill of Tepeyac, to collect 'roses and flowers'. After gathering these flowers in his cape, he took them to Zumárraga, only for the prelate to see that a sublime likeness of the Virgin was painted on the coarse weave of his cape. Awed by this miracle, the bishop had the image placed in the cathedral for public veneration. Meanwhile, the Virgin also appeared to Juan Bernardino, cured him of the plague, and told him that her image was to be known by the title of 'Virgin Mary of Guadalupe'. Fifteen days later, the image was carried in public procession to Tepeyac, where Zumárraga installed the painting in a new-built chapel.[7]

The impact of the *Image of the Virgin Mary* was such that its first censor, the creole chancellor of the cathedral chapter, lamented that Mexico had had to wait some 116 years for 'the superior genius, acute thought, eloquent language and fine pen' of Miguel Sánchez to read 'such a wonderful history' of God's works in the conquest of the New World. So too, the second censor, Pedro de Rozas, an Augustinian friar, praised its author, since 116 years after the apparitions 'he took up his pen, so that what we only knew from tradition without distinction, we now understand circumstantially and defined with authority and principle'.[8] Almost twenty years later, in 1665, Dr Antonio de Lara Mogrovejo, a judge in the high court of Mexico, expressed much the same opinion, when he wrote of Sánchez that 'the history of the Apparition of Guadalupe cost him a great effort', since he had been obliged to base himself on 'traditions and fragments weakened by the oblivion of time and the ancients' little curiosity'.[9]

For his part, Sánchez confessed that 'I searched for papers and writings regarding the holy image, but I did not find any, and even though I had recourse to the archives where they might have been preserved, I learnt that through the accidents of time and occasion, they had lost what they had.' Some old papers had proved helpful, but in the last resort, he relied on the testimony of 'the eldest and most trustworthy persons of the city', and 'on my side I have the common, grave and venerable right of the ancient, uniform and general tradition of that miracle'. More to the point, he drew on Cisneros' history of Los Remedios, taking comfort from that chronicler's observation that the great miraculous images of Spain, 'Pilar de Zaragoza, Montserrat, Guadalupe, Peña de Francia and Atocha', all relied on tradition rather than contemporary documents to justify their apparition narratives. Internal evidence suggests that he may also have consulted Murillo's account of Our Lady of Pilar. But Sánchez wrote to persuade 'the learned' and composed a densely argued text abounding in citations from scriptures, especially from the Book of the Apocalypse, 'to which my genius is inclined'. He also drew upon any number of theologians and Fathers of the Church, singling out St Augustine as 'my holy master'.[10] To assist him in his labours as author, he invoked the assistance of his namesake, the archangel Michael, who had fought against the Devil to protect Mary and her divine Son. Was he not himself another Michael, called upon to defend with 'his rough pen' this 'marvellous woman and holy creole', Our Lady of Guadalupe? It was with this strong sense of having been especially chosen to undertake this task that Sánchez constructed a complex chain of arguments.

II

It was on reading St Augustine's 'To Catechumens', so Miguel Sánchez averred, that he discovered that the woman described in chapter 12 of the Apocalypse represented both the Church and Mary. Recalling his excitement at this figural interpretation he exclaimed: 'How joyful did I feel at such news: without waiting I went forth in search of the Evangelist St John and I found him on the island of Patmos.' What he there encountered was of course the famous vision of 'a woman clothed with the sun and the moon at her feet, and on her head a crown of twelve stars', who was rescued from 'that old serpent called the Devil' by St Michael and his angels, and who was assisted in her flight by the 'two wings of a great eagle'. On his knees now, Sánchez implored St Augustine 'to give wings to my words and words to my concepts', since the more he pondered the matter the more he was possessed by the 'revelation' that the image seen by St John in his vision on Patmos was the self-same image revealed to Zumárraga in the island-city of Mexico. He thus invited his readers to contemplate the identity 'in the image of heaven by prophecy and, in the image of earth, the copy by miracle'.[11] Which was to say, that the likeness of the Virgin Mary imprinted on Juan Diego's cape was the self-same image that St John's visionary eye had seen prior to his writing chapter 12 of the Apocalypse. Moreover, since this image of Mary also signified the Church, it followed that 'this New World has been won and conquered by the hand of the Virgin Mary and the Church established at its head in Mexico'. As St John Damascene had argued, if man was created in the image of God, then clearly of all simply human images Mary was the most perfect. It was thus the Virgin Mary who had 'prepared, disposed and contrived her exquisite likeness in this her Mexican land, which was conquered for such a glorious purpose, won that there should appear so Mexican an image'.[12] In short, Mexico had been conquered by Spain so that Mary could found the Church through the revelation of her image, a likeness which was simultaneously intensely Mexican and yet a faithful copy of St John's prophetic vision.

What Sánchez learnt from St Augustine, as he was at pains to confess, was not merely the identification of the Guadalupe image with the Woman of the Apocalypse, but more importantly, his very method of theological interpretation. In his controversy with Julian of Erculum, the African Saint had rejected arguments taken from philosophy or literature in favour of examples found in scripture. Sánchez thus embraced typology. But as a set of meditations or *novenas* that he subsequently published demonstrated, he was also influenced by St Vicente Ferrer, known in Mexican circles as 'the angel of the Apocalypse', who had followed Joachim di Fiore in interpreting contemporary events by invocation of scriptural prophecy. In applying this method, Sánchez burdened his pages with a plethora of citations taken mainly from scripture, but with the Church Fathers and later theologians also represented. The result was a remarkably intricate, often convoluted text, which future historians were to dismiss as wearisome, but from which countless preachers were to draw inspiration. By means of his biblical citations and allusions, Sánchez composed a typological counterpoint to the narrative of events in Mexico; and thereby infused those events with an unparalleled theological significance.[13] Where else in the ardent world of Marian cults was an image of the Virgin endowed with such typological richness? And yet, despite the density of his discursive exegesis, in places Sánchez also wrote in a highly charged, deeply personal style. The result was a book brimming with devotion in which religion and patriotism were inextricably meshed, and where audacious claims were sustained by deep learning.

By way of prelude, Sánchez interpreted the conquest of Mexico as a re-enactment of the apocalyptic battle between Satan and St Michael. Moctezuma's empire thus figured as an 'imperial monarchy with seven crowns', a diabolic state based on ancient Indian kingdoms. By contrast, Hernán Cortés and his band of conquerors, somewhat oddly, 'enjoy the title of an army of angels, who destroyed the dragon and his followers, for the conversion of this New World and the foundation of its Church'. And if this conquest, which was also a birth, brought pain and sorrow, so too, the foundation of the Apostolic Church had been accompanied by martyrdom and suffering. Like Israel leaving the Egypt of idolatry, the Mexicans had suffered the assaults of the Devil in their desert exodus.[14] Indeed, thereafter 'strange pilgrims and newcomers', heretics 'without native roots in this land', had arrived, whose crimes against the faith had been discovered by the Inquisition. But these sufferings and threats were easily compensated by 'the good fortune that in the conquering of this land, the Virgin Mary was to appear in her holy image of Guadalupe'. Moreover, Mexico was ruled by the king of Spain, whom God had chosen as 'a universal sun-planet', and whom Sánchez saluted, since just as 'the sun runs, flies and circles the whole orb, so all the seas know you, venerate and offer praise'. Had not the seventh angel of the Apocalypse announced that all the kingdoms of the world would be converted? And what better prophecy of Spain's universal monarchy could be found than Psalm 89 (88), where God announced a perpetual covenant with the house of David, establishing its kingdom for ever?[15] As an island surrounded by an inland sea, Mexico was obviously governed by the moon and, as such, it offered inevitable homage to the imperial sun of the 'Catholic monarchy'. But within this context, Mexico also figured as a city which recalled the triumphant vision of the new Jerusalem described in chapter 21 of the Apocalypse, since there had appeared within its limits 'the likeness of God, the image of God, which is Mary in her holy image of our Mexican Guadalupe'. As St John Damascene had taught, every Christian is 'an image of God', engaged in battle with the Devil, but in Mexico assisted by the Virgin Mary, 'the most perfect, living and chosen image of God'.[16] As much as St Augustine and the Greek Fathers, Sánchez identified the contemporary Church as the fulfilment of biblical prophecy and thus defused the potentially subversive message of the Apocalypse.

It was in his account of the apparitions, however, that Sánchez was at his most original, since he deployed biblical typology not merely as metaphor and personification, but also as re-enactment. The scope of his vision became apparent when he recalled that St John Damascene had argued that Mary had been conceived when her mother was an old woman, a veritable skeleton, so that her birth was a miracle. And this could be taken to signify that she would be reborn by miracle in her images which performed miracles, among which none greater could be found than the painting of Guadalupe. All this was but prelude to an interpretation of the Virgin's first apparition in Mexico in early December 1531, over twelve years after Cortés and the conquerors had established the *villa* of Veracruz on Good Friday, and a hundred years before the presence of the image in the cathedral had caused the flood waters to begin to subside. It was on a Saturday that a poor Indian called Juan, with an alias or epithet of Diego, which surely signified that he was to be the St James of Mexico, was passing by the hill of Tepeyac when he heard the sweet music, not of birds, but of angels, and saw a young woman radiant with light. She asked him: 'Son Juan, where are you going?' When he replied that he was on his way to the Franciscan priory at Santiago Tlatelolco, she said:

> You should know, son, that I am the Virgin Mary, Mother of the true God. I want a house and a chapel, a church to be built for me, in which to show myself a merciful Mother to you and yours, to those devoted to me and to those who seek me in their necessities.

She then commanded the Indian to inform the bishop of Mexico of her apparition and that she wished to have a chapel built for her in the place where she had appeared. So Juan Diego went to the city where he looked for the bishop's palace so as to talk with the virtuous Juan de Zumárraga, 'a religious of our father St Francis, whose seraphic family is the primitive mother of that conversion'. At this point, Sánchez paused in his narration once more to compare Mexico City to the vision of the New Jerusalem found in the Apocalypse.[17] Had he been of an historical cast of mind, he might well have also recalled Murillo's description of the Virgin's apparition to St James at Zaragoza, where she said: 'Son Diego, I am your protector . . . build me a church in my name . . . I shall work wonderful signs, especially to help those who come in their necessity to this place.' By way of a permanent sign of her apparition in that city, the Virgin left the apostle a small wooden statue of herself, crowned and with the child Jesus in her arms, standing on a jasper column.[18]

Returning home the same day, Juan Diego reported to the Virgin at Tepeyac that Zumárraga had obviously not believed him, since he had simply asked him to return another day. He suggested that the Virgin should send someone 'of more credit', whose message would be accepted. On contemplating this scene, Sánchez cited St Luke on Christ's rejoicing in the Holy Spirit at the return of the seventy disciples who had preached the gospel, when he exclaimed: 'I thank you, O Father, Lord of heaven and earth, that thou has hid these things from the wise and prudent and hast revealed them unto babes.' So also, had not the Virgin in Mexico chosen as her messenger an Indian who was 'humble, poor and ignorant'?[19] On Sunday at Mary's command, Juan Diego attended mass at Tlatelolco, and then went to see the bishop in his palace, where Zumárraga seemed somewhat irritated by his return and told him to offer some sign attesting to the truth of the Virgin's apparition. For Sánchez, the prelate's distrust was wholly commendable. After all, the apostles had not believed Mary Magdalene when she claimed that Christ had risen from the dead: why should the bishop believe a recently converted Indian that he had been privileged to see 'the first favour, the first apparition, the first image to originate in this land'? Reflecting on this Sunday scene, where the Virgin appeared for a third time to Juan Diego at Tepeyac, Sánchez averred that the hill appeared like another Tabor where Christ had been seen transfigured in glory by his apostles. He added: 'there is not a circumstance in that miracle and most holy image of Mary that does not have the semblance of being prophesied . . . three times God called the holy patriarch Moses to the peak of Mount Sinai'. And if Moses was summoned to ascend alone on the third occasion, it was because he had to construct the tabernacle, the portable temple of the Ark of the Covenant. So also, Juan Diego had been chosen to act as 'messenger and agent of the temple and house of Guadalupe, where the true Ark, which is Mary, was to be guarded'.[20]

The next day, Juan Diego remained at home, caring for his uncle, Juan Bernardino, who was ill with the plague. On the Tuesday, the Indian set out for Tlatelolco to fetch a priest to attend to his uncle, only to be met by the Virgin at Tepeyac, who assured him that she would cure Juan Bernardino and comfort those who were ill and unfortunate. She then commanded him to climb to the hill's summit to collect 'roses and flowers' as a sign for Zumárraga. On ascending the hill, which in December should have been covered with cactus scrub, Juan Diego found 'roses inviting with their beauty, lilies offering milk, carnations blood, violets devotion, jasmin amber, rosemary hope, irises love, and broom captivity'. All these flowers he gathered in his cape, a simple mantle woven from cactus fibre, known as an *ayatl*. When the Indian presented these flowers to the Virgin, she took them in her hands, then returned them to the cape and told Juan Diego to offer them to the bishop of Mexico as a sign of her apparitions and message. At the spectacle of 'that garden of paradise', Sánchez recalled how Moses had sent spies into the Promised Land who had brought back grapes and figs, which commentators interpreted as signs of Christ and Mary. So also, he recalled chapter 2 of the Song of Songs, where, according to St Bernard, Christ was described as 'the flower of the field'. It was in the same chapter, of course, that the Virgin herself was prefigured as 'the Rose of Jericho and the lily of the valleys'.[21]

Aparición De la imagen de nuestra Sᵃ Dᵉ
guadalupe de Mexico

Plate 5   The apparition of the image of Guadalupe before Juan de Zumárraga

At the Virgin's behest, Juan Diego took the flowers in his cape to Zumárraga and let fall 'a miraculous spring, a small garden of roses, lilies, carnations, violets, jasmin, rosemary, irises, and broom'. But, when these flowers had fallen, the bishop saw painted on the Indian's coarse mantle the 'Virgin Mary, Mother of God, in her holy image which today is preserved, guarded and venerated in her sanctuary of Guadalupe of Mexico'. All present fell to their knees to venerate the image, transported by the revelation of such an incomparable image. As St Paul had written to the Corinthians: 'we all, with open face, beholding as in a glass the glory of the Lord, are changed into the same image from glory to glory even as by the Spirit of the Lord'. Earlier in the same epistle, St Paul had drawn a typological contrast between Moses, who had veiled his face before God, and the glorious revelation of Christ.[22] At this point, it occurred to Sánchez that when confronted with the 'revelation of Mary' in Mexico, St John the Evangelist might well have exclaimed, like Simeon in the Temple when the child Jesus was presented, that he too, was ready to die, since his vision on Patmos of the Woman of the Apocalypse was now materially realized in the image of the New World. As for Juan Diego, who was as transfigured by light and glory as was Moses when he descended Sinai, he might well have invoked the celebrated chapter 61 of Isaiah, cited by St Luke when Christ began to preach his gospel: 'The Spirit of the Lord is upon me, because the Lord has anointed me to preach the good news to the meek . . . to proclaim the acceptable year of the Lord.'[23] Indeed, the power of the miracle and the devotion it evoked recalled the words of St Paul in his Letter to the Romans: 'now it is time to awake out of sleep; for now is our salvation nearer than we believed'. The degree to which the apparition narrative was inspired by the Book of Exodus was confirmed when Juan Diego and Zumárraga returned to Tepeyac, there to kneel at the place of the apparitions, as if they had heard the words of God addressed to Moses when he appeared to the patriarch in the burning bush, also an image of Mary. In effect, Sánchez had conflated the dialogue in Horeb with the subsequent events at Sinai, the flowers and image replacing Moses' miraculous staff as the sign of heaven's message.[24]

However, the typological scene now changed and Sánchez compared Juan Diego and Zumárraga to Jonathan and David, the prince and the poor shepherd. In this figure, Juan Diego acted the part of Jonathan, since he entrusted his cape to Zumárraga, who, as shepherd of his flock, was thus another David. The two friends went to visit Juan Bernardino, whom they found cured by the Virgin, who had appeared to him on Tuesday morning to inform him that her image should be known as the 'Virgin Mary of Guadalupe'. The bishop invited both Indians to stay with him in the palace, where he had briefly installed the painting, acting like David when he deposited the Ark of the Covenant in the house of Obededon. But confronted with 'the true ark of God', which was Mary, Zumárraga recited Psalm 132 (131), in which David vowed to find 'an habitation for the Almighty God of Jacob', a text generally taken as a prelude to the building of the first temple on Mount Zion. Before the chapel was built at Tepeyac, however, the image was placed on the high altar in the cathedral of Mexico, where the entire population turned out to venerate it, their joy reminiscent of the shepherds who came to pay homage to the child Jesus at Bethlehem.[25]

As the crowds eventually left the cathedral, Sánchez remained on his knees, so to say, praying and pausing before engaging in a description of the image before him. He confessed: 'By writing of her I have constituted myself into the devout painter of that holy image; I have used all possible care in copying it; love of *patria* in sketching it; Christian wonder in painting it; I shall also be diligent in re-touching it.' At this point he cited Ecclesiasticus to the effect that without carpenters, potters and other work-men, the city could not be inhabited, albeit noting that although such men will not serve in high councils or act as judges, 'they will maintain the state of the world'.[26] But he openly admitted that no literary exercise could compare to the living voice of the painting, especially since it was 'another nature, a substitute of God'. At this point he cited Psalm 27 (26): 'When thou saidst, Seek ye my face, my heart said unto thee, Thy face, Lord, will I seek. Hide not thy face from me.' On approaching the task of description, he once more invoked St Augustine, 'my sacred master . . . archive of divinity, to whom I attribute the spirit, determination, and way to celebrate the miraculous apparition'. He recalled the saint's commentary on Christ's miracle of the bread and fish in the desert, where he affirmed that miracles have 'their languages, reasons and words'. It was thus necessary not merely to delight in a miracle but also to attempt to comprehend 'its sovereign height and excellent profundity'.[27]

Before continuing his narrative, Sánchez turned to describe the painting itself, first noting that the canvas was woven from the maguey cactus to form an *ayatl*, a coarse mantle used by poor Indians. It was composed of two pieces sewn together with cot-ton thread and measured about one yard across and two yards high. The image of the Virgin was of a young woman standing on a crescent moon, supported by a boyish angel with wings out-stretched, her figure enveloped in an aureoled tabernacle or niche of a hundred golden rays, her face 'silvery brown' in colour, surmounted by a crown. Her mantle, sky blue in colour, was decorated with forty-six stars and her roseate tunic ended in a roll at her feet. The surrounding space on the canvas was left bare of colour or decoration. What caused astonishment was that 'the class and quality of this painting is solely of tempora', which was to say, the kind of paint used for frescos. Despite his reverential awe, Sánchez concluded with a series of exclama-tions about the image's 'beauty, grace and loveliness' and compared his task in writing a description to that of the Greek painter Apelles, who, when he was commissioned to depict Helen of Troy, failed miserably to convey any sense of her beauty.[28]

In much the same way that God the Son had become incarnate in our human nature, so also Mary, in imitation of Christ, had chosen for her material incarnation 'a mantle which is all creole of this land, in the plant of its maguey, in its simple thread and in its humble weaving'. Moreover, as Sánchez had found when he touched the painting and inspected it closely, it had not deteriorated despite the passage of 116 years and being done in tempora. For the rest, he repeated much of what he had previously written, interpreting the hundred rays that surrounded the Virgin as signifying that she blessed a land governed by 'the Catholic monarchy of Spain, of the Philips of glorious memory, and of Philip the Great, our lord', kings he had earlier compared to the sun. So also, the moon at her feet signified Mexico, which was governed by that planet, and hence subject to the waters. Then again, the stars on her mantle referred to the conquerors, that unlikely band of angels who had conquered Lucifer in the form of Huitzilopochtli, the Mexican god of war. Finally, the angel who supported the Virgin was obviously St Michael, his wings reminiscent of the Aztec eagle which was still used as a symbol of Mexico.[29]

Furthermore, Sánchez followed St John Damascene in noting that Old Testament figures of Mary included Noah's ark, the burning bush seen by Moses, the heavenly ladder seen by Jacob at Bethel, and Gideon's fleece. But the figure which most caught his eye was Aaron's staff, which he identified with Isaiah's text that 'there shall be a rod from the root of Jesse', a link which had been first made by St Jerome. It will be recalled that when Moses called upon the twelve tribes of Israel to present their staffs, only Aaron's flowered, a sign that the tribe of Levi were destined to act as priests and he himself as first high priest. This staff had been used by Moses in Egypt and thereafter Aaron effected various miracles through it, not least dividing the waters of the Red Sea. It was later deposited, together with the Tables of the Law and an urn of manna, in the Ark of the Covenant. Appropriately enough, the staff had been made from walnut, a tree which kept its leaves in winter and flowered in that season.[30] Here was rich grist for Sánchez' exegetical mill. Had not the image of Guadalupe appeared in December, and had it not been born amidst flowers? Indeed, it was the only known image of Mary to have been born among flowers and, as such, it had claim to be recognized as superior to all other Marian images. In an extraordinary passage, which in its rhetorical form testifies to Sánchez' almost palpable excitement, he wrote:

> In my humility I call upon Christendom in all its kingdoms, cities, towns, valleys, mountains, forests, rocks, ports, seas, woods and rivers, that each one should bring the miraculous image they have of Mary, and in name of our Mexican Guadalupe, I cite, invoke, counsel, convoke, beg, supplicate, adore and await all these images, which have appeared through miracle, so that they hear, attend, argue, reply, add, contradict and reply to a well-spun syllogism.

Thus Sánchez here convoked an imaginary assembly of all miraculous images of Mary so that they could recognize the superiority of the Mexican Virgin. The syllogism on which this claim rested was strictly typological: since Aaron's staff was superior to those of the other eleven tribes because it flowered, so the image of Guadalupe was superior to other Marian images because it alone had been painted with and born amidst flowers. It followed that it thus 'has to enjoy among all the miraculous images of the Virgin Mary the supreme dignity of miracle and the primacy of the miraculous'. Devotion could go no further.[31]

With his commentary almost finished, Sánchez returned to the narrative of events to describe the solemn installation of the image in its new-built 'hermitage' or chapel at Tepeyac, some fifteen days after the apparitions, on the second day of Christmas. Accompanied by both cathedral chapter and city council, Zumárraga carried the image in public procession, accompanied by a multitude from the city, with Indians dancing, trumpets and drums sounding and choirs singing, the occasion culminating in high mass in the sanctuary. Tepeyac, which hitherto had figured as Horeb or Mount Sinai, now became the Mexican Zion, with the bishop acting as another David. But Sánchez also drew on the Book of Ecclesiasticus to describe Zumárraga as a high priest like Aaron, and added: 'To the dignity of bishop God added for that prelate the estate and patronage of the hermitage of Guadalupe, which until today his illustrious successors possess.'[32] In the same way that the flowering staff was the symbol of Aaron's priestly calling, so equally the image of Guadalupe was the pallium and crosier of the archbishops of Mexico, the symbol of their primacy. Although Abbot Guarico, not to mention Murillo, had argued that Christ gave the Church to St Peter and Mary to St John, in the Mexican case, Juan Diego, a figure of St John, gave the image to Zumárraga, in episcopal dignity the heir of St Peter, signifying that there could be no separation of Mary and the Church. Once more, Sánchez thus affirmed that the foundation and growth of the Mexican Church was based on the revelation of Mary in her image of Guadalupe.[33]

By way of conclusion, Sánchez noted that for Juan Diego, Tepeyac had become like Bethel, where Jacob had seen the ladder of angels reaching to heaven, and that in consequence he chose to assist at the sanctuary until his death sixteen years later, by then renowned for his exemplary life. His poor cape had thus become worth far more than all the splendid vestments of popes and cardinals or the robes of judges and monks. In certain measure, so Sánchez argued, his cape could be compared to the goatskin given by Rebecca to Jacob so that he might receive Isaac's blessing and thus win what should have been Esau's birthright.[34] In effect, through his mantle, Juan Diego won for himself and for 'the children of this land . . . an entailed heritage', which was 'Mary in her miraculous image'. Sánchez noted how impressed he always was to observe with what devotion and veneration the Indians approached the image of Guadalupe in its sanctuary. By the time he wrote, of course, the first chapel had been replaced by the impressive church built by Archbishop Juan Pérez de la Serna, which was illuminated by over sixty silver lamps hanging from an elaborately carved wooden roof. The high altar was graced with a retable filled with paintings and

Plate 6 Our Lady of Guadalupe in her sanctuary

sculptures, with the holy image enclosed within a silver tabernacle worth 350 silver marks, which had been recently presented by the outgoing viceroy, the Count of Salvatierra, whose consort had been devoted to the Mexican Virgin. Above the tabernacle, which had crystal windows to protect the painting, there was a silver image of God the Father, inclined with open arms, as if ready to receive the Virgin as she ascended to heaven.[35]

All that remained was for Sánchez to describe the principal miracles wrought at the sanctuary, a list of seven taken in part, no doubt, from inscribed paintings hanging on the walls of the chapel. The first was the almost instantaneous cure of an Indian who had been accidentally transfixed by an arrow during the procession when the image was installed at Tepeyac. The second occurred in 1544 when a procession of children from Tlatelolco beseeched the Virgin to cure their parents from the plague that was then raging in Mexico. Then came the cure of don Juan, the Indian nobleman who had discovered the image of Los Remedios. Other examples included a horseman saved from a bad fall, a devotee who escaped injury despite a lamp falling on him in the sanctuary, and a miraculous reignition of candles in the chapel after strong winds had extinguished their light. Finally, there occurred the decisive intervention of the Virgin when, for four years in 1629–34, she was venerated in the cathedral, her presence causing the flood waters eventually to subside.[36]

It was the cure of don Juan, however, which allowed Sánchez to define the difference between the two images of Mary to which he was so devoted. The parallels were obvious: both had been revealed to Indians called Juan, the one found under a maguey, the other painted on a maguey cloth. Both their sanctuaries were built on sites where once Aztec idols had been worshipped, with the temple at Tepeyac dedicated to 'the mother of the gods and in their language Theotlenantzi'. But the two images differed sharply in their origin and social function. For Los Remedios had been brought from Spain, whereas the Guadalupe had been born amidst flowers in Mexico. Los Remedios was regularly taken into the city to avert drought by prayers for the seasonal rains. By contrast, the Guadalupe had left its sanctuary only once, and that was to save the city from flooding. Adept as ever in finding scriptural figures to express this difference, Sánchez identified Ruth the Moabitess as a figure of Los Remedios, since she had left her country to assist her widowed mother-in-law, Noemi, in Bethlehem. By contrast, Noemi the Israelite was a figure of the Guadalupe. Sánchez declared: 'I venerate in Ruth and Noemi the two miraculous images of the Virgin Mary. In Ruth, that of Los Remedios who came from Spain accompanying the conquerors, with love of its land for its remedy, favouring them in its conquest. In Noemi, that of Guadalupe, the creole which appeared in Mexico'. Of course, Mary was but one person; but she was present in her images in different ways. Acting through her image at Guadalupe, she had cured don Juan and adjured him to build a chapel for the Los Remedios image in order to manifest the gratitude of her Mexican *patria* and satisfy its obligations to Los Remedios for the role played by that image in the conquest of Mexico and the overthrow of idolatry.[37]

Towards the close of his work, Sánchez cited the Song of Songs, where the beloved spouse, Mary, was found among the lilies. Already, he had affirmed that 'for Mary to appear among the flowers was to signalize this land as her own, not only as a possession, but as her *patria*'. But this meant that the citizens of Mexico were related to Mary in her image, 'which is re-born miraculously in the city where they were born; and the *patria*, although a common mother, is the most beloved mother'. In the same way that Mary and the Church were united in the figure of the apocalyptic woman, so Mary and the Mexican *patria* were united in the enduring miracle of the Guadalupe image. Here were more than sufficient reasons to induce the people of Mexico to visit her sanctuary, offering their joys and their sufferings. Although Mary fought the Devil through all her images, she acted most powerfully in those miraculous images which possessed their own sanctuaries, since these churches acted as spiritual fortresses where the faithful could obtain help and protection from demonic attack. All the more reason for the people of Mexico to visit Guadalupe, where they would encounter 'a new paradise, a new Adam, Juan Diego; and a new Eve, Mary'. And there they would also encounter St Michael, whose role in supporting the Virgin in the painting signified that he acted as Mexico's guardian angel.[38]

Convinced that Mary would remain in her image of Guadalupe for 'long centuries' to come, Sánchez once more turned to the difference between the painting and the written word. 'In the painting there works wonder; and in letters, understanding; the former remains in praises, the latter passes into mysteries.' Which was to say, the power of the image was such as to demand veneration and wonder, albeit without affording explanation; it was only through the written word that the miracle of the apparition could be explained. This had been the task reserved to him. But as Sánchez affirmed: 'I was not moved by the honour of gaining credit for my understanding, nor by the interest of soliciting money, and still less to inflate my life with pretensions. I was moved by the *patria* and mine own, by companions and citizens, and by all those of this New World.' He had preferred to expose himself to the charge of ignorance rather than to let the origins of 'an image so native to this land and its primitive creole' lapse into oblivion.[39]

In his concluding lines, Sánchez returned to the 'revelation' which had inspired his theological journey, the identity of the Mexican Virgin with St John's vision on Patmos. Filled with gratitude, he now sought to offer the image to that saint. But 'since in matters of importance I do not know how to act or speak other than by the hand and tongue of St Augustine', he begged the African Saint, who had first given him news of the image's prophetic original, to help him make this offering to St John. And so, in his mind's eye, he saw the saint arrive and address the evangelist, echoing the words Christ had uttered on the cross:

Behold your mother, behold here her image of Guadalupe; behold the consolation of that Christendom; behold the protector of the poor, the medicine of the ill, the relief of the afflicted, the intercessor of the sorrowful; behold the honour of the city of Mexico and glory of the faithful dwelling in the New World.

Filled with joy, St John, who at Calvary had accepted Mary as his mother, now took charge of the image of Guadalupe in perpetuity, placing it alongside 'the original image of heaven'. And on that confident note, Sánchez brought his commentary to a close.[40]

III

Some measure of the immediate impact of Sánchez' work can be obtained from the three commendations that were printed at the end of his book. The current chaplain at the 'hermitage' of Tepeyac, Lic. Luis Laso de la Vega, only recently appointed by Archbishop Juan de Mañozca, exclaimed that on reading Sánchez he felt like Adam in paradise, who on awakening found Eve at his side: 'I and all my predecessors have been like sleeping Adams, possessing this second Eve in the paradise of their Mexican Guadalupe.' He praised Sánchez as 'the most fortunate creole of all our nation', since after so many years of neglect he had deciphered both the history of the apparitions and the meaning of the painting. Speaking on behalf of the sanctuary, he now received this account of its mysteries, especially since the image formed 'entailed inheritance of merciful memory'. He concluded by expressing the hope that Sánchez would soon complete his *novenas* on the Guadalupe, since his meditations would serve all those who came to pray at Tepeyac. This confident and joyful acceptance was in contrast to the brief statement written by Francisco Bárcenas, a secular priest and an old friend of the author, who cryptically feared that Mexico was like another Nineveh which might be visited by a prophet like Jonah, sent to denounce Sánchez' 'history'.[41]

But it was Dr Francisco de Siles, at that time a young prebendary in the cathedral chapter of Mexico and a professor of theology in the university, who most clearly attested to Sánchez' influence when he confessed that since his tender years he had been a 'perpetual listener' of his sermons. Saluting Our Lady of Guadalupe as 'our sovereign creole and most sacred Mother', he praised Sánchez since 'he speaks and writes for all his *patria*, which receives this history as the executor of its greatness'. Whereas other nations possessed 'sealed charters and provisions' which established their public existence, Mexico could now rest its claims on 'a sealed history'. So too, he lauded Sánchez for a work which would certainly arouse devotion to the Virgin, but wherein also 'he writes in the style of scripture and the saints about the mysteries of the painting and the miracle, offering reasons for preachers and masters, that they should

declare and explain the glories of such a miraculous image'. So infectious was Sánchez'
scriptural mode of argument that Siles himself named the Guadalupe as 'another
Esther, our head and queen, to whom all those born in this land will ever look for
protection and patronage'.[42] It was also Siles, ever the faithful disciple, who in 1665, by
then a canon and chancellor of the university, acted as censor to Sánchez' *Novenas*,
testifying to his mastery of the pulpit and his 'rare learning'. Moreover, he once more
praised Sánchez for writing

> another book, in which he gave news of the miraculous apparition of the Virgin in
> her image of Guadalupe, forgotten with the passage of a century and in spite of that
> rescued from neglect in a short time: so profitable a book, that I do not know
> whether before it was published this miracle was well known even in our America;
> and thanks to this study the most distant kingdoms acclaim and venerate this
> marvel.[43]

Once more, the all-important role of Sánchez in defining the tradition of the
Guadalupe and its significance was clearly recognized.

After such high praise it is with some disappointment that one turns to the later
writings of Miguel Sánchez. Here is no place to dwell upon his sermon entitled 'The
Seraphic David' (1653), in which he traced the origin of Christian universities to the
epoch when 'God called the Patriarch Moses to the lofty summit of Mount Sinai in
order to graduate him as Doctor, to constitute chairs, and to give him the books of
the law written in his own hands on the two tablets of stone.' The manner in which
he connected the five stones hurled by David at Goliath to the five wounds of Christ
was not particularly persuasive, and even less so when he took them both as figures
of the five faculties of the university, Theology, Canon Law, Civil Law, Medicine and
Philosophy.[44]

It was in his *Novenas of the Virgin Mary, Mother of God, for her most devoted sanctuaries of Los Remedios and Guadalupe* (1665) that Sánchez framed a set of meditations
for nine days to be spent in either sanctuary. Taking St Augustine and St Vicente
Ferrer as his guides, he devoted a day in descending order to each of the nine angelic
orders, which was to say, to archangels, angels, virtues, powers, principalities, domina-
tions, thrones, cherubim and seraphim, a hierarchy which can be traced back to
Dionysius the Areopagite.[45] It was an arrangement that allowed him to dwell on those
biblical scenes where angels appeared. On each day there was also a contrast drawn
between the roles of Los Remedios and the Guadalupe. Once more the Spanish Virgin
was saluted as 'companion and captain of the Christian armies, the conquerors of the
New World', and was constantly named as a wanderer or pilgrim who had left her
country. By contrast, the Guadalupe again is described as 'an Eve born and formed
from a sleeping Adam, appearing for the first time among flowers'. But whereas
Sánchez had previously defined the moon as Mexico's symbol and thus subordinate

to the sun of the Catholic kings of Spain, now Los Remedios was depicted as the pillar of fire which led the Israelites by night during their exodus from Egypt, and Guadalupe as the cloud which led the Israelites by day and thus, by extension, a sun which was 'the mother of the living'.[46] As for the two Indians to whom Mary had appeared, don Juan was now surnamed *del Aguila*, which was to say, of the Eagle, and as such was compared to St John the Evangelist, whose Ezekielan symbol was the eagle. By contrast, Juan Diego, here designated simply as Juan, was described as an ox and compared to St John the Baptist, whose mother Elizabeth had acclaimed the Virgin Mary in the Visitation. The dexterity with which Sánchez shuffled his typological cards was nowhere more apparent than when, instead of identifying the two images as Ruth and Noemi, he now presented the faithful Moabitess as a common figure of Mary, asserting that as a stranger in Bethlehem Ruth was a type of Los Remedios, but once married to Booz, she became a figure of Guadalupe.[47]

Only a year after the publication of his *Novenas*, Sánchez appeared before Francisco de Siles to offer a sworn, notarized deposition about what he knew of the Guadalupe tradition, a testimony included among many others, all taken for despatch to Rome. On 18 February 1666 he declared under oath that earlier that day he had said mass and had prayed to God to give him 'a clear memory' of all that he had heard concerning 'the tradition and apparition of the Holy Virgin of Guadalupe in this her image'. By then aged over sixty, he had learnt of the apparitions to Juan Diego in 1531 'from many persons of quality, nobility and letters in past times and from fifty years until now'. About the only additional information he had to offer was that Juan Diego had come from the town of Cuautitlan and that he had gathered on Tepeyac the 'most beautiful flowers of various and singular colours and among them many of those which in Castile and New Spain are commonly called roses of Alexandria'. Once more he affirmed that his account had been based on oral tradition, transmitted by persons of age and quality. But he now recalled that he had discussed with Lic. Bartolomé García, the former vicar at Tepeyac, the reasons for the absence of any official documentation concerning the apparitions. García had suggested that the records in the archbishop's archive had been stolen owing to a shortage of paper in Mexico so soon after the conquest. More intriguing, García had informed him that he had been told by Dr Alonso Muñoz de la Torre, the former dean of the cathedral, that on visiting Archbishop Fr García de Mendoza in about 1600, he had found the prelate 'reading the decrees and proceedings of the aforesaid apparition with singular tenderness'. Finally, Sánchez emphasized how difficult it was to paint on the cloth of *ayatl* and that painters had declared that the image 'of this divine and miraculous Lady was made and formed by the angels of heaven'. How could a human painter have devised such a work which had survived for so long, despite humidity and dust, and which had not been protected by glass windows until 1647? He concluded that the image was 'a supernatural work and given and provided by the Divine Majesty of our Lord God for the general consolation of this kingdom'.[48] In effect, Sánchez thus reiterated what he had set down so elo-quently in his book.

When Miguel Sánchez died in 1674, his body was buried in the sanctuary at Tepeyac, with the dean and most of the cathedral chapter present. The diarist Antonio de Robles, a creole priest, described him as 'a master of the pulpit; he was the wonder of preaching in our America: it was the common opinion of many learned men that he knew all St Augustine by heart'. His preaching on public occasions had won him the general esteem of viceroys and archbishops, canons and judges. As a young man he had competed without success for appointment to a chair of theology in the university and thereafter on diverse occasions had served as vicar of the sanctuary at Los Remedios, and successively as chaplain to the nuns of San Jerónimo and the royal hos-pital for Indians. But despite his manifest poverty he preferred his solitude, and for some years lived as a virtual hermit at Tepeyac where he had but 'a poor room, with a crucifix, an image of Our Lady of Guadalupe, that of St Augustine and all his works'. As regards Sánchez' influence in promoting the cult of his beloved Virgin, Robles stated:

> He composed a learned book, which seems to have been the means by which devo-tion to this most holy image has extended throughout Christendom, being forgot-ten even among the citizens of Mexico until this venerable priest made it known, since in all Mexico there was not more than one image of this sovereign lady, which was in the convent of Santo Domingo, and today there is not a convent or church where it is not venerated and very rare the house or cell of a religious where there is not a copy.[49]

So high was his reputation in these years that, in a sermon preached in 1681, Fr Nicolás de Fuenlabrada, an Augustinian friar, saluted Sánchez as 'our Christian Cicero, our Catholic, Mexican Demosthenes, honour of our Nation', who wrote 'a sweet, learned, delightful history'.[50] Since in 1662 Sánchez had joined an archconfraternity of secu-lar priests known as 'the venerable union', which was later transformed into the first Oratory of St Philip Neri in Mexico, his reputation and singular achievement were perpetuated for posterity in the *Historical Memoirs of the Congregation of the Oratory of Mexico City* (1736), whose author, Julián Gutiérrez Dávila, simply reproduced with but minor alteration the entry in Robles' diary. By then, however, his books were unobtainable and had been replaced in public esteem by simpler accounts of the apparitions.

IV

These contemporary eulogies should not be misinterpreted. By the time Sánchez wrote his celebrated work the cult of Our Lady of Guadalupe was well established and obviously gathering momentum. The consecration of the new sanctuary at Tepeyac in 1622 had been followed by the transfer of the image to the cathedral in the years 1629–34. Moreover, the anonymous verses which lamented the Virgin's departure from the city suggested that the image was divine in origin. What the eulogies do demonstrate is that Sánchez took the clerical elite of Mexico by storm, his influence most powerfully manifest in the great cycle of panegyric sermons preached in honour of the Mexican Virgin in the years 1661–1766. Time and again the scriptural figures and theological doctrines he had expounded were reiterated and applied afresh. In particular, the most learned of these ecclesiastical orators turned to the Greek Fathers to elaborate a neo-platonist theology of the Guadalupe image. In effect, learned canons and erudite Jesuits vied to exalt the Virgin in sermons often preached at the sanctuary of Tepeyac before the assembled dignitaries of Church and State, their texts enlivened by bold metaphors which scaled the Great Chain of Images with audacious ingenuity.

Viewed from a secular standpoint, the cult of the Guadalupe image appears as a foundation myth. It will be recalled that in his *Monarchy of the Indies*, Juan de Torquemada had saluted Hernán Cortés as another Moses who had liberated the peoples of Anáhuac from the Devil's dominion, the Spanish conquest forming thus but a prelude to their exodus from the Egypt of idolatry into the promised land of the Christian Church. He followed Jerónimo de Mendieta in contrasting Cortés to Martin Luther, the two men both born allegedly in 1484, since, whereas in 1519, the German had led the nations of Northern Europe into heresy and damnation, the Spaniard had opened the door of salvation for the peoples of Anáhuac. The foundation of the Mexican Church thus possessed a rich spiritual significance within the divine economy of the Catholic Church: rich and arrogant Europeans betrayed the faith; poor and humble Indians embraced the gospel. At the level of symbolic discourse, myth could only be countered by myth. If the creole clergy greeted the revelations of Sánchez with enthusiasm and propagated the cult of the Guadalupe with such zeal, it was in large measure because it provided them with an autonomous, sacred foundation for their Church and *patria*. In effect, the image preserved and venerated at the holy mount of Tepeyac was the Mexican Ark of the Covenant, a sign that henceforth the Virgin Mary would act as especial protector of the Mexican people. The devotion united Indians and creoles, rich and poor, in common devotion, and served to strengthen the primacy of Mexico City and its archbishop over the far-flung dioceses of New Spain. The strength and progress of the cult derived from its inextricable intertwining of religious fervour with patriotic enthusiasm. Sharply divided by race, class, customs and even language, the inhabitants of New Spain had little to bind them together save their common identity as children and subjects of Our Lady of Guadalupe.

Despite its primordial significance for the growth of the Catholic Church in Mexico, Sánchez' work has not attracted a theological analysis comparable to the assessment of its role in the consolidation of creole patriotism. And yet Sánchez must count among the most original, learned and audacious of Mexican theologians. He wrote as if possessed of a single, blinding idea: the 'revelation' that the image of Guadalupe came from heaven and was thus divine in both origin and form. His book was 'a child of silence', the offspring of sustained meditation and prolonged contemplation of an icon in which he had come to perceive the true likeness of the Mother of God. But whereas for St Basil the Great, 'the honour given to the image is transferred to the prototype', for Miguel Sánchez all the scriptural figures generally applied to the Virgin Mary were transferred to the image of Guadalupe. Apostolic and Catholic typology was thus invoked to define the character and meaning of the Mexican Virgin. If Sánchez was so drawn to the Book of the Apocalypse, it was because it projected Old Testament figures onto the future history of the Church. But whereas St Vicente Ferrer and other medieval prophets employed scriptural prophecy to predict the imminent advent of the millennium or of the Last Judgement, by contrast, Sánchez presented the apparition of the Guadalupe image as an incarnation of Mary, albeit not in the flesh, but in the form of a material likeness. His typology was at its most original when he depicted Juan Diego as re-enacting, though in Christian fashion, the role of Moses at Horeb and Sinai. At the outset he noted that for St Augustine the Woman of the Apocalypse was a figure of both Mary and the Church, thereby indicating that in the same way that Mary brought forth Christ in the flesh, the Church brought forth Christ in the world across the centuries. Older, long-established churches might boast of an apostolic foundation, such as St James' mission in Spain; but only the Mexican Church owed its existence to the direct intervention of the Mother of God. In effect, the discovery of the New World marked a new stage not merely in the institutional life of the Catholic Church, but also in its spiritual development, since the apparition of the Guadalupe image signified that the peoples of Mexico, not to say America, had been chosen for her protection. It was in recognition of that unique distinction that it later became common to inscribe copies of the image with an epigraph taken from Psalm 147, 'Non fecit taliter omni natione', 'It was not done thus to all nations.'

4

Indian seer

I

It was in 1663 that the cathedral chapter of Mexico initiated the long campaign to persuade the Holy See to recognize the cult of Our Lady of Guadalupe. To achieve that goal, documents dealing with the apparitions had to be submitted, and if such evidence was not available testimonies as to the long-standing tradition about those events had to be compiled. In this context, the book of Miguel Sánchez did not offer much help. The cause of the Mexican Virgin, however, had already been advanced by the appearance of *Account of the Miraculous Apparition of the Holy Image of the Virgin of Guadalupe of Mexico* (1660), a concise, readable outline of the apparitions and the miracles, explicitly extracted from Sánchez, which purged the narrative of all scriptural allusions but skilfully retained the colloquies between Juan Diego and Mary. Written by Mateo de la Cruz, a Jesuit from Puebla, and first published in that city, it was reprinted in Madrid in 1662 at the instance of Pedro Gálvez, a member of the Council of the Indies.[1] In less than fourteen years after the publication of *Image of the Virgin Mary* the story of Mary's apparitions in Mexico thus became known across the Atlantic.

In addition to summarizing Sánchez, Cruz also added a commentary in which he set the cult of the Mexican Virgin within a broad Marian context. Where he scored, however, was in consulting old Church calendars, since they allowed him to establish that Mary first appeared to Juan Diego on Saturday 9 December 1531, so that the revelation of her image to Zumárraga occurred on Tuesday 12th of that month. The demands of brevity led him to reduce Sánchez' exuberant catalogue of flowers collected by Juan Diego to a succinct 'roses and flowers'. More to the point, he argued that the Guadalupe image possessed all the iconographical attributes of Mary in her Immaculate Conception, a doctrine anticipated in prophecy by St John in his description of the Woman of the Apocalypse. Cruz then followed Sánchez in contrasting the origins of Our Lady of Los Remedios and the Guadalupe, 'calling that image the conqueror

76

and *gachupina*, because it came with the conquerors from Spain, and this the *criolla*, because it appeared miraculously in this land, where it had its origin among flowers'. Since *gachupín* was the popular name for immigrants from Spain, the term emphasized the foreign character of the City of Mexico's patron. For all that, it was to Los Remedios that prayers were offered when the seasonal rains were late, whereas the power of the Guadalupe was to lower flood waters, as she had done in 1629.[2]

Not content with such domestic contrasts, Cruz concluded with a comparison with the celebrated image of Our Lady of Guadalupe in Extremadura. According to Spanish chroniclers, that image had been carved by St Luke and sent by Pope Gregory the Great to San Leandro, the archbishop of Seville, only later to be taken northwards to escape the Moors, where it was hidden. Just as in Mexico the Virgin had appeared to a poor Indian, so in Spain she appeared to a poor herdsman to reveal the whereabouts of her image and request that a chapel be built in her honour. In both cases, the images were housed in silver tabernacles in ornate sanctuaries which were visited by hosts of pilgrims. Both were named Guadalupe, an Arabic word meaning 'river of wolves', a symbol of the Virgin conquering demons and idolatry. But despite these similarities, there was one essential difference: 'that image St Luke made; this, either God painted, or the Virgin herself painted, or, at the very least, the angels painted'.[3] But if Cruz thus established the miraculous singularity of the Mexican Virgin, he made no attempt to explain why Mary should have wished to be known in Mexico as the Virgin of Guadalupe. Nor did he mention that the Spanish Virgin was a wooden statue, seated with the Christ child in her arms, whereas its Mexican counterpart was a painting of Mary either in her Assumption or as her Immaculate Conception.

In 1663 the cathedral chapter of Mexico, the Company of Jesus in New Spain and other religious Orders jointly petitioned Pope Alexander VII to transfer the feast day of Our Lady of Guadalupe from 8 September, when Mary's Nativity was commemorated, to 12 December.[4] The moment appeared favourable, since the pope had sanctioned the liturgical celebration of the Immaculate Conception in 1661 and was soon to allow the Spanish monarchy to observe the feast on 8 December.[5] Since Cruz had identified the Guadalupe as an Immaculate Conception, what could be more appropriate than that its feast should fall within the Octave of that universal cult? But the petition did not prove successful, since the cathedral did not possess in its archive any contemporary records of the apparition. It was to remedy this lack of documentation that the chapter, now joined by the city council of Mexico, commissioned Canon Francisco de Siles, assisted by Dr Antonio de Gama, to obtain notarized, sworn statements from witnesses, so as to establish the continuity of devotion from the epoch of the apparitions. After all, if Miguel Sánchez had based his account on 'the common, grave and venerable right of the ancient, uniform and general tradition of that miracle', then creditable evidence had to be offered to demonstrate the truth of that affirmation.[6] The proceedings conducted by Siles and Gama consisted of summoning witnesses who, after stating their age and civil rank, were invited to respond to seven questions about the image and its origin. They were asked to agree that the image had appeared on 12 December 1531 before Archbishop Zumárraga in his palace, when Juan Diego let fall from his cape 'most beautiful flowers of various colours and odours, and among them many roses of Alexandria, commonly called of Castile'. They then further agreed that Zumárraga had built a chapel for the image and that since that time the image had been the object of prayer and pilgrimage; that the cape on which the image was imprinted was of such a coarse material that it would have been impossible to have painted on it; and that since the colours and form of the image had been perfectly preserved for so long, it was obviously 'a supernatural work', especially since its beauty far exceeded the skill of any human painter; and finally that the humid, saline airs of the sanctuary's lakeside situation should have caused the image's deterioration if not destruction. Somewhat apart from questions, witnesses were also asked to agree that Juan Diego had been a man of mature years and of honest, Christian conduct.

It was in January 1666 that Siles and Gama went to Cuautitlan, the reputed birthplace of Juan Diego, there to ascertain by means of these standard questions what aged residents could recall about what their parents and grandparents had told them concerning the apparitions and their holy compatriot. Assisted by interpreters, they discovered seven Indians and one mestizo, whose individual ages were set down as over 80, 110, c. 112–15, 85, 78, 80, 100 and 100. Despite their excessive longevity, these witnesses proved to be both voluble and lucid, all possessed of enviable memories. The mestizo, Marcos Pacheco, who was over 80, had served as local councillor and magistrate. He testified that his aunt had told him that Juan Diego was related to her mother-in-law's family and that she had known him. Like all witnesses he agreed that the Indian's cape had been woven of the coarse thread of *ayatl*, and that owing to the saline airs of the lakes it should have decayed within twenty or thirty years.[7] Another witness, Gabriel Juárez, an Indian aged 110, recalled seeing Viceroy Luis de Velasco before he went to Peru, which was to say, in 1595, but confused him with his father of the same name, viceroy 1550–64. He described Juan Diego as 'a holy man' who was called *el peregrino*, or 'the pilgrim', adding that, when he lived close to the sanctuary in an adobe hut, natives from Cuautitlan would visit him 'to ask him to intercede with the Most Holy Virgin to give them good crops in their *milpas*'.[8] The daughter of a native nobleman recalled that her father had possessed a 'map' and writings concerning the apparitions, but lamented that they had been stolen. So too, others recalled that in the parish church there had once hung a painting of Pedro de Gante, one of the first Franciscans, flanked by Juan Diego and Juan Bernardino, only to confess that the canvas had disappeared.[9] For the rest, all agreed with the substance of the questions put to them. As regards their alleged ages and the recollections of their relatives, it may be helpful to note that the celebrated mestizo historian, Fernando de Alva Ixtlilxochitl (1578?–1650), was the great-great-grandson of Juan Diego's contemporary, Fernando

Cortés Ixtlilxochitl, the ruler of Texcoco during the Spanish Conquest and who was also baptized in 1524. Among the native peasantry the rhythm of reproduction was even more accelerated, since most Indian women were married by the time they reached sixteen.

Since in this epoch the testimony of Indians had little juridical standing, Siles and Gama also obtained statements from a number of Spaniards, which was to say, from ten priests and religious and two noblemen. In contrast to the biblical ages of the native witnesses, their years more closely fitted the normal life-span, since although the eldest were 85 and 81, the others declared their ages as 60, 55, 66, 71, 65, 66, 71, 62 and 61. The first informant was none other than Miguel Sánchez, who on 18 February 1666, stated under oath that earlier on the same day he had said mass and prayed to God to give him 'clear memory' of all that he had heard concerning 'the tradition and apparition of the Holy Virgin of Guadalupe in this her image'. By then over sixty, he had learnt of her apparitions to Juan Diego in 1531 'from many persons of quality, nobility and letters in past times, from fifty years until now'. However, as we have seen, he then affirmed that the account he published had been based on oral tradition, transmitted by persons of age and quality.[10] The absence of documents in the archbishop's archive possibly could be explained by the shortage of paper in that early epoch. For the rest, he concluded that the image was 'a supernatural work'. The remaining witnesses, who included individuals of all the leading religious orders in New Spain, unanimously agreed that they had learnt of the Guadalupe tradition during childhood and had visited the sanctuary since their earliest years, often going there on pilgrimage to offer *novenas* of prayers. Pedro de Oyanguren, a Dominican aged 85, recalled visiting the sanctuary some sixty years before, which was to say, in 1606, before the construction of the current church. All testified that they had heard of the apparitions from their parents and grandparents. Aged 61, Diego Cano Moctezuma, a Knight of the Order of Santiago, a magistrate of Mexico City, and a 'grandson' of the Emperor Moctezuma, declared that he recalled the great flood of 1629 when the Virgin had been brought by canoe from Tepeyac to the cathedral, thereby saving the city from abandonment. Like several other witnesses, he described the flowers as a mixture of lilies and roses of Alexandria.[11] The effect of these testimonies was thus to establish the existence of a tradition concerning the Guadalupe passed down across the generations, which flourished well before Sánchez wrote his book. But no witness mentioned any written source to substantiate these claims: their knowledge was based exclusively on oral tradition.

The Spanish witnesses mentioned that the current viceroy, the Marquis of Mancera, was devoted to the Guadalupe and regularly visited the sanctuary on Saturdays to offer prayer. It was no surprise, therefore, that when on 11 March 1666 the image was lowered from its tabernacle for inspection, the viceroy should have been present. The purpose of the inspection was to allow a group of seven painters to view the painting at close quarters. Their perusal led them to declare that it was not humanly possible to paint so fine an image on such a coarse canvas, so that it was undoubtedly a 'super-natural work', mysterious and miraculous, and its mode of survival known only to God, especially since the canvas did not exhibit any sign of preparatory sizing. There followed the inspection of three learned doctors, who with many citations from Galen and Hippocrates, gravely stated that although the sanctuary at Tepeyac was peculiarly humid, exposed to the nitrous airs of the lake, nevertheless, the image was uncorrupted and mysteriously preserved, leaving their minds bewildered by such a humanly incomprehensible process.[12]

By April 1666 all the enquiries conducted by Francisco de Siles were concluded and approved by the cathedral chapter, which commanded that a complete copy should be despatched to agents in Seville, who were authorised to present the matter in Rome. At the same time, the city council of Mexico wrote directly to Pope Alexander VII re-questing that he should 'canonize this Apparition as miraculous'.[13] In the event, how-ever, Mateo de Bicunia, a canon of Seville resident in Rome, proved unable to secure the transfer of the Guadalupe's feast day from 8 September to 12 December. In his *Pole Star of Mexico* (1688), Francisco de Florencia, the leading Jesuit chronicler of this epoch, who spent several years in Europe acting as the agent of the Mexican province, reported that when he visited Rome in 1670 he found that the petition had not pros-pered for a variety of reasons. Apparently Cardinal Julio Rospigliosi, later Clement IX, had complained to Dr Antonio Peralta y Castañeda, a canon of Puebla then resident in Rome, that even the Holy House of Loreto did not possess its own feast day. In any case, if the Guadalupe was an Immaculate Conception, why not transfer her feast to 8 December, when that doctrine was universally celebrated? In these objections, the measure of Mexican ambition is revealed. For the petition did not seek the transfer from one universal feast day of Mary to another, but instead envisaged the institution of a feast dedicated solely to the Guadalupe, albeit with its celebration restricted to New Spain.[14] Such a feast inevitably entailed papal approbation of the tradition and its cult.

On his visit to Rome, Florencia found the Congregation of Rites reluctant 'to open the gate to canonize miraculous images, of which there was such an abundance in Christendom', since if one gained recognition, others would soon be proposed. Oddly enough, had the Mexicans sought the canonization of a holy bishop, friar or nun, they might have been more successful. It was in 1668 that Santa Rosa of Lima was beatified and then in 1671 canonized and recognized as patron of America. To succeed in Rome, so Florencia concluded, it was necessary to have a knowledgeable person there, who could move the matter with determination and energy. 'In that way Lima obtained the canonization of Santa Rosa and the beatification of its archbishop don Toribio Mogrovejo.' As it was, all Mexico received was a papal rescript granting permission to transfer the feast to 12 September, which was to say, to move from the feast of Mary's

Nativity to that of her Most Holy Name. Obviously, for any petition to succeed, the Congregation of Rites had first to change its policy on holy images. As far as can be ascertained, the gate was at last opened in 1699, when Our Lady of Loreto, Italy's premier Marian image, was granted her own feast, with particular mass and office, on 10 December, within the Octave of the Immaculate Conception.[15]

Inserted without explanation within the 1666 statements was a paper submitted by Lic. Luis Becerra Tanco, which provided a brief account of the apparitions taken mainly from Cruz' summary and presented additional information about Juan Diego.[16] However, its author also claimed that the Indians of Mexico had not merely faithfully preserved the memory of the appearance of Mary to Juan Diego, but had also painted those scenes and thereafter had composed a narrative written in 'Mexican', which was to say, in Nahuatl. Moreover, so Becerra Tanco averred, this native account had been published by Lic. Luis Laso de la Vega, the vicar at the sanctuary, in 1649. To understand the startling character of these claims, it is first necessary to examine that text and to compare its style and content with the account found in Sánchez and summarized by Cruz.

II

Few works in Mexican history had such an enigmatic start in the world as *Huei tlamahuiçoltica . . . (The Great Happening . . .)*, a badly printed tract of thirty-six pages. Its author, Lic. Luis Laso de la Vega, who had been appointed vicar of the sanctuary at Tepeyac in 1647, was later praised by Florencia as 'a priest of great zeal as a pastor, and of singular integrity of behaviour, who later died as a most worthy prebend of Mexico'. He had rebuilt the first chapel and surrounded the spring at the site with walls, since pilgrims came to bathe there, hoping for cures of their ailments.[17] Although his merits brought Laso promotion to the cathedral chapter in 1657, little more is known about him other than that he registered for a course in canon law in the University of Mexico in 1623. As we have seen, in July 1648 he penned an enthusiastic eulogy of Sánchez' book, praising it for both revealing the history of the apparitions and explaining the significance of the image. So strong was his acknowledgement of debt that he added: 'I and all my predecessors have been like sleeping Adams, possessing this second Eve in the paradise of their Mexican Guadalupe.' However, he himself now set about with great despatch to frame an account in Nahuatl, which was approved for publication on 11 January 1649 by Dr Pedro de Barrientos Lomelín, the creole treasurer of the cathedral and vicar general of the Mexican diocese. The censor, Baltazar González, a creole Jesuit who taught the Indian nobility at the college of San Gregorio, a man renowned for his knowledge of Nahuatl, praised 'the fitting and elegant Mexican language' of the text which Laso de la Vega sought 'to give to the

HVEI
TLAMAHVIÇOLTICA
OMONEXITI IN ILHVÍCAC TLATÓCA
ÇIHVAPILLI
SANTA MARIA
TOTLAÇÒNANTZIN
GVADALVPE IN NICAN HVEI ALTEPE-
NAHVAC MEXICO ITOCAYÒCAN TEPEYACAC.

Impreſſo con licencia en MEXICO : en la Imprenta de Iuan Ruyz.
Año de **1 6 4 9.**

Plate 7   Title page of Luis Laso de la Vega, *Huei tlamahuiçoltica . . .*

presses' and commented that 'I find it agrees with what is known of the facts from tradition and the annals.' He expressed the hope that its publication might engender devotion to the Virgin among those still ignorant of the mysterious origin of 'this heavenly portrait of the Queen of Heaven'.[18] Neither González nor Laso de la Vega made any mention of the work of Miguel Sánchez.

In his brief preface, Laso de la Vega justified writing in 'Mexican' on the grounds that the Virgin had obviously spoken to Juan Diego in that language and that it was desirable that Indians should learn what the Virgin had done for them, especially since the memory of those events 'had been erased by the circumstances of time'. After all, had not St Bonaventure expressed the hope that the Virgin Mary would be praised in many tongues? Had not Christ's Crucifixion title been proclaimed in three languages? Addressing the Virgin, Laso de la Vega beseeched her, since 'with your hands you painted your image, in which you wish your sons to invoke you, especially these natives to whom you appeared'. Asserting that it had been thanks to Mary's intercession that the Holy Spirit had descended on the apostles at Pentecost, inspiring them to preach in diverse languages, Laso de la Vega begged the Virgin for a tongue of fire to descend on him, enabling him 'to write in the Mexican language the sublime miracle of your apparition to these poor natives'.[19]

There followed a text now known as the *Nican mopohua*, from its opening words, 'here is recounted', in which the story of the apparitions and colloquies between Juan Diego and Mary was told in apparently simple fashion without the intrusion of the scriptural allusions so favoured by Sánchez. In substance, which is to say, in factual detail, there was little difference between the accounts provided by Laso de la Vega and Sánchez. But in style and dramatic structure there was a profound contrast. Few peasants, let alone Indians, have ever spoken in the language placed in the mouth of Juan Diego by Miguel Sánchez. By contrast, in Laso de la Vega the Indian speaks with a simple, natural eloquence. Both texts are rhetorical; but whereas one relies on scriptural metaphors, the other draws on native oratory. The contrast, however, is not simply one of language and style; it also stems from changes in dramatic structure. Whereas in Sánchez Juan Diego's first two encounters with Zumárraga are described in retrospect, when the Indian recounts to the Virgin what had happened, in Laso de la Vega Juan Diego is presented as speaking face to face with the bishop on both those occasions. So too, when the Virgin appears to Juan Diego on the Tuesday morning, in Sánchez he merely reports his concern for the health of his uncle, whereas in Laso de la Vega the Indian speaks to the Virgin in a direct, deeply moving way. In effect, the Nahuatl version relies far more than its Spanish counterpart on dialogue and the colloquies are often skilfully developed so as to heighten the dramatic effect. At the same time, the Nahautl use of diminutives as forms of address and the poetic characterization of person and place, which obviously drew on native literary practice, infuse the text with a decidedly un-European flavour.[20]

To observe how the two accounts differ, one has only to turn to the opening first scene. In Sánchez, when Juan Diego hears the sweet music of the angelic choirs, he soon realizes that he is not hearing the song of 'nightingales or larks' or of 'the birds known to him, the chirping sparrows, peaceful linnets or the celebrated *zenzontles*', and so remains simply enchanted. In Laso de la Vega the Indian is reminded of bird song by the music he hears, only then to hear a song that surpasses 'that of the *coyoltótot* and the *tzinizcan* and of other birds', leading him to exclaim:

> Am I perchance worthy of what I hear? Am I in the earthly paradise of which our ancestors, the elders, spoke? Am I perhaps in the sky?

Then again, when he sees the Virgin, in the Spanish version he is simply filled with wonder at the beauty of the Virgin and the radiance of the light that surrounds her. But in the *Nican mopohua*, Juan Diego sees the landscape transformed:

> And when he arrived in her presence, he was filled with the greatest wonder at how her perfect beauty surpassed all things. Like the sun her clothes radiated, as if throwing out rays, and with these rays the stones and rock on which she stood were radiant with light. The earth which surrounded her appeared resplendent like precious stones, as if bathed in the light of the rainbow. And the *mezquites* and *nopales* and other bushes which were there seemed like emeralds and their foliage was like turquoises, and their trunks and branches shone like gold.

As can be observed, this aureate description is calculated to impress upon the reader the grandeur of the Virgin's heavenly presence. But the European reader is then surprised to hear the Virgin addressing the Indian as 'Juanito, Juan Dieguito' and again as 'Juanito, the youngest of my children'. In reply, the Indian addresses the Virgin as 'My Lady, My Child, My Queen'. Thus both in poetic description and in these diminutives, the Nahuatl text differs markedly from its Spanish counterpart. In places, however, the expansion of dialogue was merely reiterative, as was the case where the Virgin promised to become the mother and protector of all who seek her help. In Sánchez she says:

> Know you, son, that I am the Virgin Mary, Mother of the true God. I want a house and hermitage, a church, to be built for me, in which to show myself a merciful Mother to you and yours, to those devoted to me, and to those who seek me in their necessities.

In Laso de la Vega we read:

> Know and be certain, my son, the least of all, that I am the perfect and ever Virgin Mary, Mother of the true God, through all life, creator of men, Lord of the near and the far, Lord of the heavens and earth. I very much want and desire that in this place my church shall be built. Here I shall show myself and be manifest, I shall give all my love, compassion, help and protection, since I am your merciful mother, of you and yours, who live united in this land, and of the other kinds of persons who are my lovers, those who call upon me, those who look for me, those who trust me. Here I shall listen to their cries, their sorrow, to offer remedy, to help their many sorrows, necessities and misfortunes.

As will be observed, the meaning here is essentially the same; but the second version is more calculated to stir emotion.

After Juan Diego was rebuffed by Zumárraga for the first time, in Sánchez, he suggests to the Virgin that she should send someone else, a person 'to whom they give more credit'. In the *Nican mopohua* this plea was expanded into a moving statement, when Juan Diego says:

> I dearly beseech you, I beg you, My Lady, My Queen, My Daughter, that you charge someone from among the nobles, the well-known and esteemed and honoured, to take your message, so that he will be believed. For truly I am a little man . . . I am the tail, I am a leaf, I am of the little people, and you, my child, the youngest of my daughters, Lady, you send me to a place where I do not walk and where I cannot stop.

Here, the rhetorical resources of Nahuatl yield an utterance of genuine eloquence. It also renders the Indian's courage in returning to see Zumárraga all the more memorable. The second visit to the bishop's palace in Sánchez was described by Juan Diego to the Virgin as a terrifying occasion when he wept tears and when he was confronted by a stern, even irritated prelate, who demanded a sign that would prove the truth of his message. By contrast, in Laso de la Vega, the second encounter takes the form of a colloquy between the Indian and the bishop and less emphasis was placed on Zumárraga's annoyance. But since the occasion was thus described, there was no artistic need for Juan Diego to recount his experience to the Virgin and so Laso de la Vega sends the Indian back home without any consolation from the Virgin. This omission renders his sense of failure all the more acute. On the Tuesday morning when he goes to find a priest for his dying uncle, in Sánchez the Virgin's apparition and her promise to cure Juan Bernardino is simply described as a prelude to her injunction to climb the peak of Tepeyac and cut the flowers he will find there. By contrast, in Laso de la Vega, Juan Diego addresses the Virgin:

> My Child, the youngest of my children, My Lady, I hope you are content. How did you awake? Are you feeling well, My Lady and My Child? I shall bring pain to your face, to your heart: you should know, My Daughter, that my uncle, your servant, is very ill.

On hearing the news of his uncle's impending death, the Virgin comforts him, tells him not to be afraid, and reminds him:

> Am I not here, who am your mother? Are you not under my shadow and protection? Am I not the source of your joy? Are you not in the hollow of my mantle, in the embrace of my arms?

Once again, we can observe how pastorally effective would have been the reading of such a scene.

Oddly enough, the one episode in which Laso de la Vega was less expansive than Sánchez was in the description of Juan Diego picking the flowers on Tepeyac. Both versions contrast the cactus scrub and bushes which normally grew there with the splendid array of flowers which bloomed unseasonally on that December day. However, according to Sánchez the Indian found roses, lilies, violets, carnations, jasmin, irises, rosemary and broom, whereas in Laso de la Vega all he gathered into his cape was diverse 'flowers of Castile'. Yet the Virgin told Juan Diego that the very diversity of flowers would be a sign for Zumárraga of their heavenly origin. When Juan Diego explains to Zumárraga the Virgin's commands and what he had brought as a sign, in Sánchez he says he had brought roses, a term which in Laso de la Vega was changed once more into 'flowers of Castile'. Yet when the cape was unfolded to reveal the Virgin's image before Zumárraga, in Sánchez the diverse flowers are again listed by name. Obviously, if Laso de la Vega did not give the names of these flowers, it was because some at least were European in origin; yet by describing them all as 'Castilian', he heightened the sense that although imprinted on Juan Diego's *ayatl* cape, the image was, like the Virgin herself, derived from Spain.

In the second part of his work, the *Nican motecpana*, Laso de la Vega described fourteen miracles wrought by the Virgin at Tepeyac, a list which included the seven already inserted in Sánchez. But he devoted space to don Juan, the cacique of Totoltepec, to whom the Virgin had appeared to reveal the whereabouts of the image of Los Remedios, in order to emphasize that he went to the Guadalupe to be cured of the plague. For the rest, he noted the healing powers of the spring waters that flowed from the place where the Virgin last appeared to Juan Diego, describing the cases of two hydropic women who were so cured. But so also Pedro de Valderrama, a Franciscan, was cured of a putrid toe after visiting the sanctuary; and Luis de Castilla, a wealthy Spanish nobleman, donated a life-sized silver leg when his swollen limb was healed. Apart from the early cases mentioned by Sánchez, virtually all these additional miracles concerned Spaniards rather than Indians. The chief exception occurred in 1558 when don Francisco Quetzalmalitzin, the governor of Teotihuacan, pleaded with the Virgin to prevent his town from being transferred from the Franciscans to the Augustinian friars. Although Viceroy Luis de Velasco supported this change, the Virgin intervened on behalf of the Indians and the Franciscans returned. The prose style of the *Nican motecpana* differs notably from the narrative of the apparitions and probably consisted of translations of the inscriptions written on the paintings and tablets which hung on the sanctuary walls.[21]

Little more remained for Laso de la Vega other than to expand on the description of Juan Diego. It was Laso de la Vega, not Sánchez, who explained that the Indian came from Cuautitlan and that his wife, María Lucía, had died two years before the apparitions. But their marriage had never been consummated since they had heard a sermon of Toribio Motolinia, a famous Franciscan of the 1524 mission, who had praised chastity as especially pleasing to God. Moreover, whereas Sánchez had commented on the 'great virtue' and 'exemplary customs' of Juan Diego, who passed the years after the apparitions attending to the sanctuary, Laso de la Vega depicted him as a model of Christian sanctity, albeit cast in the mode of an ideal friar of that epoch:

> Daily he was occupied in spiritual matters and in cleaning the church. He prostrated himself before the Lady of Heaven and called upon her with fervour; he confessed frequently, took communion, fasted, did penitence, scourged himself, wore a wire cilice and hid himself in the shadows so as to give himself up alone to prayer and to call upon the Lady of Heaven.

Juan Diego thus remained a virgin all his life and before he died in 1548 at the age of 74, Mary appeared to him, as she did to Juan Bernardino, who died of the plague in 1544 aged 86. Both these Indians were buried in the chapel at Tepeyac.[22]

In a brief conclusion, Laso de la Vega once more lamented that he had remained silent on many matters, because 'time wiped them out and now no-one remembers, because the elders did not take care to write about them when they occurred'. He declared that although the Mother of the Son of God was but one person, yet she had chosen to help those in need through her holy images. Not only in Guadalupe but also in Los Remedios, in Cosamaloapan and Temazcaltzinco, she comforted the faithful, albeit it was only at Tepeyac that 'in a miraculous manner she entrusted her precious image, which no painter of the world painted, since she herself painted it, lovingly wishing to be seated there'. It was thanks to her apparition and presence in her image that idolatry was crushed in Mexico, since although the Franciscans had begun the task of overthrowing the Devil's kingdom, it was thanks to Mary that the eyes of the natives were opened and they were converted. Thus 'our precious Mother of Guadalupe' came not merely to reveal herself but to give light and help that the natives might know 'the one true God' and be saved.[23]

Badly printed, written in a language which admits diverse Spanish renderings, the *Huei tlamahuiçoltica* is a composite text, its different sections written in different styles. As we shall see, within a few years of publication, Laso de la Vega's authorship was called into question. How had he learnt to write the elegant 'Mexican' of the *Nican mopohua*? Did he have a native collaborator who polished his prose and corrected his grammar? Such collaboration had been common during the sixteenth century when the Franciscans employed their educated native disciples to assist them to frame their sermons and write their *autos*, the sacred dramas which were enacted in Nahuatl across central Mexico. Indeed, the most erudite of these Franciscans, Bernardino de Sahagún, had a team of disciples whom he thanked for helping him collect the information which filled the pages of his *History of the Things of New Spain*. Book 12 of that work, which deals with the Spanish conquest of Mexico, has a literary power which no translation can obscure. Since literary Nahuatl was the joint creation of mendicant friars and the native elite, the authorship of any particular text is not always clear. Moreover, from the 1560s onwards there were creoles and mestizos who learnt Nahuatl in childhood and who later mastered the elements of its literary style. By the seventeenth century, Indian authors emerged, most notably the historian of Chalco, Francisco de San Antín Muñón Chimalpahin. It was during the 1640s that the first Indian, an Otomí nobleman educated by the Jesuits, was ordained priest. But none of these considerations assist us in determining the authorship of the *Huei tlamahuiçoltica*, which was written in the style of Church Nahuatl which flourished from the 1550s until the 1650s.[24] As yet, we know virtually nothing about Laso de la Vega other than that he was a zealous pastor and must have known Nahuatl. By contrast, his censor, Baltazar González, was celebrated among the Company of Jesus as 'a Cicero in Mexican' and as a priest who devoted his life to the College of San Gregorio. That he described Laso de la Vega as giving his work to the presses and referred to the existence of annals was later construed to mean that he himself might well have written a history of the apparitions.[25]

But what are we to make of the relation between the texts of Sánchez and Laso de la Vega? As we have seen, the substance of the two narratives of the apparitions and colloquies is virtually identical, whereas the style and structure are patently dissimilar. There are thus only two possibilities: that one must be based on the other, or that both were based on a prior written account. The parallels are obviously too close for them to be based on a common oral tradition. Moreover, both in 1648 and in 1666 Sánchez denied seeing any written testimony. Even were it to be argued that this venerated priest was a perjured liar, it has still to be explained how he came by a Spanish version of the *Nican mopohua*, since there is no evidence that he knew 'Mexican'. In the case of Laso de la Vega, he could not have relied on oral tradition, since his narrative too closely resembles that published by Sánchez. At the same time, the *Nican mopohua* is no mere extract from Sánchez, a Nahuatl equivalent of Cruz' summary. Instead, it infuses the narration with rhetorical, indeed poetic emotion; it is designed to be read aloud; it is calculated to stir devotion and, above all, to capture the hearts and minds of native readers and listeners. It is possible that the different sections of the *Huei tlamahuiçoltica* were composed by different authors and that the *Nican mopohua* had a native author. But what still remains to be explained is the substantial similarity between that text and the account found in Sánchez.

III

Although the 1666 deposition prepared by Lic. Luis Becerra Tanco (1603–72) was published by Francisco de Siles as the *Miraculous Origin of the Sanctuary of Our Lady of Guadalupe* (1666), its original title was 'The certain grounds on which the tradition in this City of Mexico about the apparition of Our Lady the Virgin Mary and her miraculous image which is called of Guadalupe is proved to be infallible'.[26] A secular priest, qualified in canon law, who served as a parish priest before ending his career as professor of astrology and mathematics at the University of Mexico, Becerra Tanco emphasized that he had learnt 'Mexican' as a child and that in addition he read Latin, French, Italian and Portuguese and knew something of Hebrew and Greek, not to mention his fluency in Otomí, affirmations which contemporary diarists simply repeated without comment. Little more is known of his career other than that he was born in the mining camp of Taxco. What is clear, however, is that he soon became unhappy with his first attempt to justify the Guadalupe tradition, and before his death completed a second version, which was published posthumously in 1675 by Antonio de Gama under the attractive title of *Mexico's Happiness*. Although much of the original argument was retained, the second edition differs substantially from its predecessor and nowhere more so than in its translation of the *Nican mopohua*.[27] In effect, Becerra Tanco achieved a critical restatement of the Guadalupe tradition.

To start with, Becerra Tanco explained the absence of any church records about the apparitions by fixing on the anomalous position of Zumárraga, who, although acting as bishop in Mexico since 1528, did not govern a diocese with boundaries and jurisdiction. Furthermore, he returned to Spain shortly after the apparitions and did not arrive back in Mexico until 1533; nor was his diocese formally established until 9 September 1534. It was hence not surprising that the cathedral archive did not possess any documents arising from 1531. Moreover, in those years 'the creole nation was but recently born in the world', and in any case the Spaniards at that time regarded the Indians as 'beasts, incapable of reason'.[28] There was thus no hope of encountering anything from the hispanic community other than testimonies of an oral tradition and long-standing devotion to the Mexican Virgin.

The great innovation of Becerra Tanco was to assert that it was thanks to the natives, to the Indians of Mexico, that the tradition of the apparitions had been preserved. After all, Mary had appeared to an Indian, and it was essentially the Indians who remembered her intervention. But Becerra Tanco did not here refer to an oral tradition, and indeed asserted that contemporary Indians, even the most aged, did not understand the 'maps and paintings' of their ancestors and had little trustworthy information about their own history. Instead, he recalled that prior to the Spanish Conquest, the Mexica, who were 'the most polished and rational' of the peoples of the New World, had kept 'paintings' on which they recorded past events, their kings and wars, and had registered the passage of time by a remarkably accurate calendar, in which years of 365 days were divided into eighteen months of twenty days. Moreover, the 'characters' or glyphs inscribed on these 'maps and paintings' served as mnemonic devices which elicited interpretation by priests and their assistants who memorized in songs or chants the history of the events to which they referred. Had it not been for the existence and survival of these codices and the songs of their interpreters, Juan de Torquemada would not have been able to write the first volume of his *Monarchy of the Indies* (1615). How else was he able to cover five hundred years of history prior to the arrival of the Spaniards? If Torquemada had been so successful in delving into the native past, it was because the first Franciscans had established the College of Santa Cruz Tlatelolco to educate the children of the Indian nobility. It was the most talented of their pupils who became the collaborators of the friars and who taught them how to interpret the codices that survived. It was this same circle of native disciples, so Becerra Tanco argued, who first recorded the story of the apparitions of Our Lady of Guadalupe. If at first they devised 'paintings', soon they wrote down the story in Nahuatl, since within a few years of the college's existence they had learnt how to read and write, not merely in Spanish or even Latin, but also in Nahuatl, helping the first friars create a new literature in that language.[29]

After thus postulating the existence of a Nahuatl account of the apparitions written down in the sixteenth century, Becerra Tanco then asserted that he had conversed with Fernando de Alva, a man whom he described as:

> Interpreter of the Viceroy's Court of Indians in this government, a very capable and elderly man, who understood and spoke with distinction the Mexican language and had a complete knowledge of the characters and ancient paintings of the natives, being of distinguished lineage and on his mother's side a descendant of the kings of Texcoco, who had inherited many maps and historical papers.

Among Alva's papers, so Becerra Tanco affirmed, was a 'map' which covered over three hundred years of history and ended with a figure of the Virgin's apparition at Tepeyac. Equally important, 'I saw a manuscript book written in the letters of our alphabet in an Indian's hand in which were described the four apparitions of the Most Holy Virgin to the Indian Juan Diego and the fifth to his uncle Juan Bernardino.'[30]

It is fascinating to note that Becerra Tanco did not tell his readers, or did not himself know, that Fernando de Alva Ixtlilxochitl (1578?–1650) had studied at the College of Santa Cruz Tlatelolco and was the author of several unpublished chronicles dealing with his ancestors, the monarchs of Texcoco, and with the Chichimeca empire. Ixtlilxochitl had known Torquemada, whom he saluted as 'the first discoverer of the meaning of the codices and songs', and had possibly collaborated with him, since his description of Nezahualcoyotl, the philosopher-king of Texcoco, was very similar to Torquemada's account of that king. Had Becerra Tanco read Alva's description of the Olmecs, a people who settled Anáhuac well before the Toltecs and Mexica, he would have been fascinated to find mention of a bearded white sage, known as Quetzalcoatl-Huemac, who had arrived during the epoch of Christ's Incarnation to teach the natives the rules of morality and the arts of civilization.[31] At their meeting did Alva and Becerra Tanco ever discuss the possibility that St Thomas the Apostle might have preached the gospel in Mexico? As we shall see, he himself favoured that thesis.

But what was the relation between this manuscript volume in Nahuatl that Becerra Tanco saw among Alva's papers and the accounts published by Sánchez and Laso de la Vega? In his 1666 deposition, Becerra Tanco asserted that 'the tradition which Lic. Miguel Sánchez wrote was copied and transmitted from these writings and paintings' of the Indians. In particular, Alva's manuscript 'was that given to the presses in the Mexican language by order of Lic. Laso de la Vega'. Oddly enough, in that deposition Becerra Tanco himself drew little on this Indian tradition, since his account of the apparitions simply repeated the version extracted by Cruz from Sánchez. About his only innovation was that he described Juan Diego as collecting 'roses of Castile' rather than diverse flowers and roses. But he also claimed that prior to the great flood of 1629 he had heard Indian songs about the apparitions in which the Virgin addressed Juan Diego as 'my little son, my beloved, my gift', terms he had also read in the 'Mexican' account.[32] It was in *Mexico's Happiness* that Becerra Tanco effectively translated the *Nican mopohua*, albeit modifying forms of address which might seem irreverent. Here is no place to analyse the textual difference between Becerra Tanco's translation and the version printed by Laso de la Vega; but it was sufficiently close thus to introduce into the official or received Guadalupe tradition the Nahuatl account with its poetic colour and dramatic colloquies. As was to be expected, Becerra Tanco once more emphasized his own knowledge of 'Mexican' since childhood and that he had studied 'the old characters and paintings in which skilled Indians wrote the history of their ancestors and journeys'. So closely did he follow the Nahuatl version that in one place he affirmed: 'this colloquy . . . has nothing of mine, since it is the translation from the Mexican language into our Castilian tongue, phrase by phrase'. For all that, he retained his deliberate mistranslation of 'roses of Castile' and inserted a few lines recounting the Virgin's third apparition after Juan Diego's second rebuff by the bishop, which had been omitted by Laso de la Vega. But in *Mexico's Happiness*, Becerra Tanco (or his editor Gama) excised all reference to Miguel Sánchez and Luis Laso de la Vega, thus creating the impression that his translation was taken from the manuscript volume he had seen in Alva's possession rather than from the version printed by Laso de la Vega. Moreover, that manuscript was now described as written 'in the hand of an Indian, of the most learned of the college of Santa Cruz'.[33] In all this, Becerra Tanco radically modified the style in which the 'tradition of the miracle' was transcribed and justified.

Concerning Juan Diego himself, Becerra Tanco also incorporated the additional information which Laso de la Vega had first presented, only adding the rider that if the Indian came from Cuautitlan he actually lived in Tolpetlac, close to Tepeyac. Oddly enough, in what was presumably a mistranslation, he claimed that María Lucía, his hero's wife, had died two years after rather than before the apparitions. As for Juan Diego, in the years after the apparitions, not merely did he experience 'long moments of prayer and contemplation every day', but he also engaged in 'works of mortification, fasting and self-scourging'. He had been converted by Toribio Motolinia, a well-known Franciscan, and had preserved his chastity since that day. Before his death in 1548 at the age of 72, the Virgin appeared to him, as indeed she had to Juan Bernardino before his death in 1544 during the plague. These visitations were certified, Becerra Tanco affirmed, by 'the second tradition, written by natives in their language, with letters of our alphabet', which was to say, he had taken this information from the latter sections of Laso de la Vega's work, now known as the *Nican moctepan*.[34]

Not content with his new-found emphasis upon the native sources of the Guadalupe tradition, Becerra Tanco claimed that he had personally discussed the matter with Lic. Pedro Ruíz de Alarcón, a priest erudite in 'Mexican', who had served as rector of the College of San Juan Letrán and had died in 1656 at the age of 86. So also, Lic. Ponce de León, a venerable priest and a 'Demosthenes in the Mexican language', who had died aged 80 in 1626, had told him about the image of Guadalupe. But it was his uncle, Lic. Gaspar de Praves, a parish priest and a 'Cicero in the Mexican language', who informed him before his death aged over 80 in 1628 that he had learnt of the tradition from 'Juan Valeriano', a leading disciple of the Franciscans, who had been educated at the College of Santa Cruz and praised by Torquemada for teaching him Nahuatl.[35]

Since Becerra Tanco provided his readers with an accurate citation of the volume and page of the *Monarchy of the Indies* on which they could find Valeriano described, it is useful to examine this passage, especially since Valeriano also taught Fernando de Alva Ixtlilxochitl.[36]

> Don Antonio Valeriano, a native of the town of Azcaputzalco, about a league from this city, Governor of San Juan, called Tenochtitlan, who having been raised as a good Latinist, logician and philosopher, succeeded the masters named above in teaching grammar in the college for some years, and after that he was elected as Governor of Mexico and ruled for over thirty-five years, with great acceptance by the viceroys and the edification of the Spaniards. And since he was a man of great talent, the king took notice of him and wrote him a very favourable letter, offering him many graces. He died in the year 1605 and at his burial, which was in the chapel of San José of the convent of San Francisco, many people attended, both Indians and Spaniards. And the scholars of the College attended, since he had been a teacher there, and all the community of religious went out to receive the body and carried it on their shoulders from the courtyard entrance to the sepulchre since he was some-one who merited such a reception. I knew a great deal about his talent, since he had been my master for some years teaching me the Mexican language. And I was present when he died and among other things he gave me his works, worthy of his knowledge, in the Latin language as well as translations into Mexican, one being a translation of Cato, well worthy of esteem, which (if God pleases) I shall print in his name.

Since this description immediately followed a brief account of the efflorescence and decline of the college at Santa Cruz Tlatelolco, its effect was to strengthen the bonds linking the Guadalupe tradition to the circle of Indian nobles educated at that college. As we shall see, Valeriano was later to figure as the author of the *Nican mopohua*.

Despite his continuous reference to the 'tradition' of Our Lady of Guadalupe, Becerra sought to modify it in several important aspects. Although Sánchez had affirmed that Juan Diego's cape was of *ayatl*, woven from the coarse fibre of the maguey cactus, Becerra Tanco argued that there were at least three kinds of maguey plants and that the most common, from which pulque, the Indians' alcoholic drink, was drawn, yielded a fibre which was too coarse to be used for anything other than bags and cord. In fact, the cape on which the image was imprinted was woven from 'the palm known as Iczotl', a softer fibre, more like cotton, which was used by Indians of all classes for their mantles. At the conclusion of *Mexico's Happiness*, Becerra Tanco inserted a brief statement of the inspection of the image by doctors and other qualified persons in 1666, in which they concluded that the canvas was woven from the thread of the palm called *Iccoyilmatli*. Equally important, although Becerra Tanco joined his compatriots in marvelling at the way in which the image had preserved its lustre despite the passage of time, he observed that since the bread of the Eucharist decayed within a few days after its consecration, so too, the Guadalupe image might well disintegrate. What the faithful venerated, however, was not the material, but the image and likeness of the Virgin imprinted on it, and thus, were it to be destroyed by time or other physical circumstances, they would continue to venerate a copy with equal fervour.[37]

But why should Mexico's miraculous image be called by the Spanish name of Guadalupe? If the Virgin had spoken to Juan Bernardino in Nahuatl, was it likely that he could have heard or indeed pronounced the name of Guadalupe? Was it not more probable, so Becerra Tanco suggested, that what he heard was 'Tequatlauopeuh', meaning 'that which originates in the rock peak', or possibly 'Tequantlaxopeuh', signifying 'he who flees wild beasts'? After all, the place called by Indians 'Quauhnohuac' was turned by Spaniards into Cuernavaca and to the present, Indians pronounced 'Guadalupe' as 'Tequatalope'. In line with this concern was Becerra Tanco's argument that the image had been imprinted on Juan Diego's cape not before Zumárraga in the bishop's palace but on Tepeyac, when the Virgin received the roses collected by Juan Diego. It was of course close to the place where once the Aztec goddess Teotenantzin, the mother of the gods, had been worshipped. It was thus a mirror image of the Virgin as she faced the Indian, her figure illumined by the sun behind her, with the folds depicted on her mantle and tunic the result of the way he held his cape. To sustain this argument Becerra Tanco constructed a complex thesis dealing with the laws of perspective, in which he cited *Perspective communis*, written by an archbishop of Canterbury, John of Pecham (c. 1225–92), in the thirteenth century. But despite his observation that the image was painted with natural colours and gold found in

Plate 8   Apparition of Our Lady of Guadalupe at Tepeyec to Juan Diego

Mexico, he insisted that the painter was an angel and indeed none other than the guardian angel of the kingdom, whose signature was himself portrayed in the image upholding the Virgin with winged arms outstretched.[38]

Not content with these revisions, Becerra Tanco also argued that the feast day of the Guadalupe should be transferred, not to 12 December, as the 1666 petition had proposed, but to 22 December. Owing to the correction of the calendar in 1582, when Spain accepted Pope Gregory XIII's abandonment of the Julian system, in reality the Virgin had appeared in her image on the 22nd. In identifying the 12th, Cruz had simply taken existing calendars of that epoch without making allowance for the change. And yet the feast day of St Teresa of Avila had been moved from 5 to 15 October on account of that revision. In any case, what could be more appropriate than to honour the apparition of the image just before the commemoration of Christ's Nativity? Moreover, the celebration would then immediately follow the feast of St Thomas on 21 December and would serve as a reminder that the apostle had preached the gospel to the nations of of Mexico, visiting Tula or *Tollan*, 'of which I saw a painting and tradition, which cannot be applied to anyone other than the apostle, through having preserved his name *Didimus*, which is twin'. To support this thesis,

Becerra Tanco cited Juan de Solórzano's *Política Indiana* (1648), where Gregorio García was mentioned as embracing the theory of an apostolic mission to the New World. So too, he referred to Alonso Ramos Gavilán, who, in his history of the image of Our Lady of Copacabana in Peru, published in 1621, described the travels of St Thomas across South America.[39] To cap his argument, Becerra Tanco simply queried: without the presence of an apostle, how could the natives of Mexico have framed the calendar of 365 days in the year?

Nothing was more extraordinary than the confidence with which Becerra Tanco sought to restate the Guadalupe tradition. Whereas the 1666 depositions all named Zumárraga as archbishop, he noted that in 1531 the very diocese of Mexico had not been created and that the prelate was not made archbishop until 1547. So too, if the Indians of Cuautitlan all eagerly certified that Juan Diego's cape was woven from *ixtle*, he calmly obtained the agreement of the doctors who inspected the image that it was made from the palm *Iczotl*. His suggestion that the Virgin's true name was not Guadalupe did not prosper; nor was any attempt later made to adjust calendars and transfer the feast to 22 December. By contrast, his thesis of an apostolic mission in Mexico led by St Thomas aroused great interest and was to be reiterated by subsequent authors. But Becerra Tanco's paramount contribution to the tradition was his translation, no matter how modified, of the *Nican mopohua*. Since *Mexico's Happiness* was republished in Seville in 1685 and in Mexico in 1780, and was included in the two-volume collection on the Guadalupe which appeared in 1785 in Madrid, his work achieved a canonical status. However, in that version Becerra Tanco or his editor, Antonio de Gama, excised all mention of Miguel Sánchez and Luis Laso de la Vega, thus creating the impression that he had translated the colloquies in Nahuatl from a manuscript written by an Indian, whereas in fact he had obviously used the text printed by Laso de la Vega. His assertion of the existence of a written tradition in Nahuatl, first in codex, then spelt out in narrative form, clearly called into question Laso de la Vega's status as an author and indeed cast a shadow over Sánchez' assertion that he had only drawn on oral testimony. In effect, Becerra Tanco's work raised as many questions as it answered; much of what he proposed was rejected or ignored; but, when the tide of historical criticism invaded Mexico, it was to Becerra Tanco's theses that defenders of the Guadalupe tradition turned for support.

5

Presence and tradition

I

If Becerra Tanco obliquely sought to subvert the authority of Miguel Sánchez, by contrast clerical orators of the late seventeenth century zealously adopted and extended his application of scriptural typology and neo-platonic concepts to Our Lady of Guadalupe. The first sermon on the Virgin of Tepeyac to be printed, *Theory of the Prodigious Image of the Holy Virgin Mary of Guadalupe of Mexico* (1661), was preached in her sanctuary on 12 December by Dr José Vidal de Figueroa, parish priest of Tejupilco. In his prologue, he noted that a copy of the image had been sent to Pope Innocent X (1664–55) and that the feast of the Immaculate Conception had only recently been instituted in Spanish dominions, with the result that the commemoration of the Virgin's apparition in Mexico fell within the octave of that feast, which was celebrated on 8 December. After a brief comparison of Juan Diego with St John the Baptist, the one suffering the captivity of idolatry, the other the prison imposed by tyranny, he moved swiftly to announce his sermon's thesis, that God 'first painted Mary in his mind', only then to apply this dictum to the Guadalupe, affirming: 'that Image which appeared is the copy of that which God thought when he chose her for his Mother'. If Sánchez had identified the Guadalupe with the Woman of the Apocalypse, Vidal de Figueroa took the neo-platonic doctrine that God conceived ideas and pre-determinations of the universe prior to its creation, and argued that the Mexican Virgin was a direct copy of the divine idea of Mary. That he should have cited St Basil the Great, St Gregory Nazianzus and St Theodore of Studios, as well as Miguel Sánchez, indicated the degree to which the Greek theologians were read in New Spain. Enchanted by a sermon which reminded him of 'my master St Augustine', the censor, the ubiquitous Francisco de Siles, recalled that he and Vidal had both studied at the college of All Saints, 'that most ancient archive of sovereign wits'.[1] Nor was he alone in welcoming Vidal's audacious concept, since the preacher subsequently became canon and chancellor of the cathedral in Mexico City.

To justify his argument, Vidal opened his discourse by citing from the first chapter of St Paul's Letter to the Ephesians, to declare that Christ had come to reveal mysteries which had been hidden across the ages and to initiate a new succession, founded not on blood but on the Spirit. But so too, when Mary appeared to 'a barbarous Indian', she at last revealed 'a portrait image of the idea of God', which was to say, the eternal idea of Mary as the Mother of his Son. The image imprinted on Juan Diego's cape was thus 'a miracle . . . a hidden sacrament', since 'it is not known who painted it, nor can the hand be seen who drew it'. So powerful was the impact of its apparition that overnight the idols and demons worshipped by the Indians all disappeared. In the same way that Mary had used the Emperor Theodosius to crush idolatry in Egypt, so also she had inspired the Emperor Charles V to suppress paganism in Mexico. That she had chosen to appear amidst roses on Juan Diego's humble cape signified that the Virgin sought to hasten the Indians' conversion by using such a familiar, humble object. At a time when the natives of New Spain were thought to be barbarous and unfit to receive the sacraments, Mary's mode of apparition was 'a divine finesse', a sublime act of courtesy, offered to a despised people.[2]

At this point, Vidal put a question which was never again to be raised in Mexico: if the Virgin Mary appeared at Tepeyac to strengthen faith in her divine Son, why did she not appear with the Christ child in her arms? After all, in the case of Our Lady of Los Remedios, she carried her Son. The answer to his question was both abstruse and audacious:

> This image is a portrait of Mary's exemplar, when God represented her as the Mother of his Son: she thus carries in her arms, not the Word made man, but the Son of God transformed into light, which is that which illumines her hands . . . Mary appears in Mexico without the God Child in her arms, but surrounded by light; the miracle is so stupendous because the mystery is so ancient, since it takes its origin in eternity, when the Son of God was light, *erat lux vera*, and he was not made man until much later.

In effect, the Divine Word was present in the Guadalupe image in the form of the rays of the sun which surrounded the Virgin, a mode of representation which demonstrated the image's divine conception.[3]

After this vaulting claim, it was easy for Vidal to resolve the second question he put, which was: why did Mary, rather than Christ, appear in Mexico? Citing St Theodore of Studios, he argued that if Christ was made man as the image of Mary, then the best likeness of Christ's humanity was Mary. Turning to the Guadalupe, he asserted that the image was doubly blessed, since if the Virgin represented Christ as a man, the light which surrounded her represented his divinity. As can be observed, in all this line of reasoning, Vidal followed Miguel Sánchez, whose work he cited, in taking neoplatonic theological concepts from the Greek Fathers of the Church and applying them to the particular case of the Mexican Virgin. In both cases, however, the underlying premise was that the apparition of Mary in her image of Guadalupe constituted a new revelation of God's eternal plan for human redemption.

Few sermons printed in the late seventeenth century rivalled Vidal's in theological originality and generally either echoed his doctrine or turned back to the typological figures favoured by Sánchez. During these years, however, the hispanic world multiplied its devotion to the Virgin Mary and in particular plagued the papacy with petitions for recognition of the doctrine of the Virgin's Immaculate Conception. In 1661, Alexander VII pronounced in favour of both the doctrine and its liturgical celebration and in 1664 granted Spain the right to institute the feast on 8 December with its own office and mass. By this time painters such as Esteban Murillo, Francisco de Zurburán and Diego de Velásquez, to mention only the most prominent, had painted countless images in which Mary as the Immaculate Conception was depicted as the Woman of the Apocalypse, standing on a moon, surrounded by clouds or light, with a circle of twelve stars above her head, and usually assisted by angels.[4] Owing to the similarities of the images, it was an obvious step to identify the Guadalupe as a likeness of Mary in her Immaculate Conception. The effect of this identification was to provide preachers with new concepts to embellish their discourse.

On 12 December 1684, Lorenzo Benitez, a Franciscan, began his sermon on a typological note, when he compared Moses at Mount Horeb confronted by a burning bush with Juan Diego's vision of the Virgin at Mount Tepeyac. But he then elaborated a comparison of the Immaculate Conception and the Guadalupe as twin effects of the same divine idea, asserting: 'because they are so similar, this image of Guadalupe seems to have served as the Idea, so as to make the Conception of this Queen in the womb of St Anna, and the conception of that womb served as the example from which to make this Image in the cape of Juan Diego'. Taken literally, this meant that the Mexican Virgin offered a faithful likeness of how Mary appeared in the flesh in Palestine.[5] Other preachers followed the same course but often sought to discover just how the image was painted. Thus on 12 December 1672, Francisco de Mendoza, a Franciscan, after reminding his congregation at Tepeyac that they had come to a place where once the Aztec goddess Theothenantzin had been worshipped, pictured a scene in heaven, where angels used brushes and colours to paint Mary's portrait, thereby converting the divine 'idea' into an effigy of the Guadalupe.[6] A similar fancy was entertained by Luis de Santa Teresa, a Carmelite preaching at Querétaro, who after defining the Guadalupe as an Immaculate Conception, suggested that if the Holy Spirit had wielded the brushes, the actual canvas had been woven by the forty-two generations of Christ's ancestors listed in St Matthew's gospel.[7] Not all these sermons followed the same tack. In a poetic intervention, Juan Antonio Lobato, a Mercedarian preaching in 1700, acclaimed the Guadalupe as the 'Phoenix of the Indies', and saluted the Virgin as 'the bird that is particularly famous for being exempt from the general fall . . . the national Bird of our Indies . . . ever august Phoenix Empress'.[8]

On 12 December 1681, Juan de Robles, a Jesuit, preached at the consecration of the church in Querétaro built in honour of Our Lady of Guadalupe. After dutifully praising Juan Caballero, the wealthy landowner who had funded the construction, he boldly observed that although the Catholic world was filled with the miraculous images of Mary, none could compare with the Guadalupe. Had not the figures of Our Lady of Pilar at Zaragoza or of Our Lady of Loreto been sculpted or painted by St Luke, whereas the Mexican Virgin had been painted either by God or by Mary herself? Avoiding Vidal's speculations, he preferred to cite chapter 12 of the Apocalypse as a prophecy of the Guadalupe and to define the image as Mexico's Ark of the Covenant and its Tables of the Law. It was Robles who also informed his congregation that in 1678 'the distinguished artist Cornelius Galle' had inscribed 'the epigraph, or, better to say, the challenging proclamation' to serve as 'the border of a most beautiful engraving of Our Lady of Guadalupe, the words of Psalm 147 *Non fecit taliter omni natione.*' A phrase once applied to Israel, that 'it was not done thus to all nations', was now publicly attached to a likeness of the Mexican Virgin for all the world to observe and ponder. It was an epigraph, however, that was to be welcomed in New Spain and soon to be inscribed on innumerable copies of the image.[9]

A new theological interpretation of the image was introduced by Juan de San Miguel, a Jesuit who in 1671 preached at the consecration of a side chapel in the cathedral of Mexico, dedicated to Our Lady of Guadalupe. He discerned a 'rare mystery' in the sacramental character of the image, a quality which led him to compare it to the Eucharist:

> The Image of Christ in the accidents of bread, and the Image of Mary in the accidents of flowers. But with this lovable difference, that in Christ's sacrament the accidents of bread appear and not the image, and in Mary's sacrament the image appears and the accidents of flowers disappear.[10]

Here, indeed, was an audacious metaphor which was later to be echoed by several Jesuit preachers.

At the level of liturgical devotion, however, it was the biblical prefigurations favoured by Sánchez rather than the theological speculations of Vidal de Figueroa which found most favour. The charming verses composed by Felipe de Santoyo García, a Spaniard resident in Mexico, which were sung in the cathedral of Mexico during Matins on 12 December 1690, drew upon the comparison between Juan Diego and Moses and the identity of the Guadalupe image with the Woman of the Apocalypse.[11]

> The world wonders,
> Heaven, the birds, angels and men
> Suspend their echoes,
> Hold still their voices

Plate 9   Vision of St John the Evangelist on Patmos-Tenochtitlan

That in New Spain
From another John is heard
A new Apocalypse,
Although the revelations differ.

From America in the desert,
And in the crags of a hill,
Patmos of New Spain
Hides another John.

The Church, recently planted,
In its first dawn,
He saw a vision of all light
Against the gentile night.

A great Sign in the heavens
Of Guadalupe, there unfolds
A Conception in roses
Which has idols at its feet.

. . .

What is this heaven where
In a peak is discovered,
In order to be light, many roses;
And for a garden, many lights?

There the Mexican Horeb
Spreads its shining rays,
A burning bush without being consumed,
Although there are flames that encompass it.

There, see the prodigy
Of the Flower of Guadalupe.
There is no December which finishes it.
No April whose flowers do not pay homage.

There he who Moses imitates
Clearly discovers
Not only the angel in the bush,
But she who sculpts herself in flowers.

You are in the Holy Land,
Juan Diego. Go up this peak
Where not only an angel shall speak
But the Queen of the virtues.

What these lines suggest is that although preachers might well elaborate resounding interpretations of the image, liturgical celebration was more likely to fix upon the scriptural antecedents of the apparition story.

II

In the opening pages of *Polestar of Mexico* (1688), the Jesuit chronicler, Francisco de Florencia, derided an ingenious sermon which had claimed that the Guadalupe was more esteemed in Madrid than in Mexico and declared that he would not cite the 'conceptual panegyric' of sermons which barely touched 'the letter of history', since his purpose was to demonstrate that 'the constant tradition' of Our Lady of

Guadalupe's apparitions had been maintained in the city of Mexico since 1531.[12] A native of St Augustine in Florida, educated by the Jesuits in Mexico City, Florencia entered the Company of Jesus in 1643 and rose to become rector of the colleges of Espiritu Santo in Puebla and San Pedro y San Pablo in Mexico City. Acting as agent for his province, he spent the years 1669–75 in Spain and Italy, where he visited the Holy House of Loreto, 'the greatest sanctuary in Christendom', and persuaded Juan Bautista Zappa and Juan María Salvatierra to enrol for mission service in northern Mexico, assisting these Italian Jesuits to promote devotion to Our Lady of Loreto by composing a short book on her sanctuary and cult.[13] His decision to write about Our Lady of Guadalupe aroused great expectations, and indeed his censor, Canon Antonio de Gama, praised him for collecting all available evidence and thus bringing new light to bear on the subject, only then to lament that the tradition was 'received from elders, not through writing, but by words'. So too, Carlos de Sigüenza y Góngora, the great Mexican savant of this epoch, who acted as the other censor, complained that owing 'to our innate lack of care, it is not known, juridically, how we came to possess such a sovereign portent'. The measure of his trust in Florencia was revealed when he claimed that 'after so many years there is now shown to the world with sufficient clarity that which, because of the lack of particular evidence, appears to those who are simply too pusillanimous to be considered doubtful'.[14] The purpose of the *Polestar of Mexico* was thus to establish the Guadalupe tradition upon a firm historical foundation. In the event, however, Sigüenza y Góngora later expressed his dissatisfaction with its final version.

As was only to be expected, Florencia praised Sánchez as a gifted preacher whose sermons won him 'great applause and a copious spiritual fruit' and whose book, distinguished for its 'concepts and quality of its sacred and literary erudition . . . greatly enlivened the devotion of the Mexicans to the Sacred Image'. But his 'ingenious concepts' had broken the thread of the narrative of the apparitions, so that it was far preferable to read Cruz' extracted summary, which was 'the best written account which has come out'. Although Florencia commended Becerra Tanco for having drawn on 'the histories of the Indians', he commented that the 'Mexican' modes of address offended the Spanish sense of decorum and dignity since 'the words sound so excessively affectionate that they seem to be irreverent and unworthy of the Majesty of the Lady who speaks and of Juan Diego's respect when he speaks'. So obvious was Florencia's distaste for the *Nican mopohua*, even in pruned form, that when he came to describe the apparitions, he simply followed Cruz' version with very little change. Nor was he impressed by Becerra Tanco's suggestion that the Virgin's name was an ill-understood transliteration from Juan Bernardino's Nahuatl. Florencia insisted that Mary had indeed chosen to be called Guadalupe, a title signifying 'river of wolves', and thus a symbol of the Christian victory over the wolves of idolatry. In any case, the Virgin wished to 'found a Spain made new in New Spain' and to reward Hernán Cortés, who came from Medellin, close to the sanctuary of Guadalupe in Extremadura.[15] In deftly administered blows, Florencia thus dismissed both the typological interpretation of Sánchez and the Nahuatl drama of Laso de la Vega.

Anxious to justify the 'constant tradition' of the Guadalupe, Florencia was the first historian of the cult to confront the painful silence of the chief chroniclers of Mexico concerning Mary's apparitions. To be sure, he cited Becerra Tanco's observation that the diocese of Mexico had not been erected until 1534, so that there could be no question of any episcopal records until after that date. But there still remained the enigma of silence. Why had not Bernal Díaz del Castillo mentioned the apparitions, especially since in his *True History*, written in the 1560s, the aged conqueror had referred to 'the holy house of Our Lady of Tepeaquilla, which they now call Guadalupe, where she works and has worked many and wonderful miracles'? But it was the silence of the Franciscans that was most disturbing. Lamenting the loss of the twelve books written by Bernardino de Sahagún, which had been sent to Spain by Viceroy Martín Enríquez, Florencia put the question: 'can it be possible that he might have written of this miraculous apparition, as an eye-witness of it?'[16] The silence of Torquemada was yet more wounding, since he had written his *Monarchy of the Indies* while living at the Franciscan convent in Tlatelolco and at various points in his chronicle had referred to Tepeyac by its Spanish name of Guadalupe without mentioning the sanctuary or its image. Worse still, Torquemada had explained that in the pre-hispanic era Tepeyac had been one of three shrines which had attracted pilgrims from afar, in its case worshippers coming to celebrate the feast of the 'goddess called Tonan, which is to say, Our Mother'. He then noted that the friars had replaced these idols with Christian patrons and churches, dedicating the chapel 'in Tonantzin, close to Mexico, to the Most Sacred Virgin, which is Our Lady and Mother'. Since Torquemada wrote at the beginning of the seventeenth century, when the cult of the Guadalupe was well established, he thus deliberately omitted to mention the image and remained silent about Mary's apparitions.[17]

After citing this passage, Florencia drew the conclusion that the apparition narrative did not depend on written sources, but on 'the constant tradition of parents and children', adding:

> Those who believe little and trust less feel that what they want is not a constant tradition but evident certitude; the Castillos and the Torquemadas are silent about what they failed to say, be it through caution or by omission, so that for me what carries most weight is the many miracles that God has performed and every day is working through the Holy Image of Guadalupe.

Did not the Fathers of the Church and learned theologians all teach that miracles were the voice of God and could not be performed to uphold error? What value could be given to the silence of historians, even if they were canonical, when negative arguments about human testimony were surpassed by the positive evidence of 'divine support' expressed in miracles? In any case, had not Cisneros long ago argued that all the great images of Spain, not to mention Loreto, depended on tradition rather than on documentary evidence? It should be also be remembered that the sublime doctrine of Mary's Assumption was not mentioned in holy scripture. It thus followed that the Guadalupe narrative essentially depended on 'the immemorial tradition, constant and never interrupted, communicated from fathers to sons, since the beginning of this wonderful Apparition'.[18]

At this point, Florencia presented in faithful but summary form the depositions collected by Francisco de Siles in 1666, thus performing the inestimable task of bringing these manuscript testimonies into the public domain, available for future generations to scrutinize and draw upon when further initiatives in Rome were undertaken. He then inserted a brief account of the failure to obtain papal approval for the transfer of the Guadalupe's feast day to 12 December.[19]

Had Florencia left the matter there, he might have spared both himself and his readers a great deal of confusion. But, although he did not care for Becerra Tanco's translation of the *Nican mopohua*, he was obviously fascinated by the possibility of encountering Indian written sources for the Guadalupe tradition. Thus he cited Becerra Tanco's 1666 pamphlet and deposition to the effect that Fernando de Alva possessed:

> a manuscript volume written in the letters of our alphabet in very elegant Mexican style, in the hand and wit of an Indian, of those who were said to have been raised and educated in the College of Santa Cruz . . . This was that which in Mexico was brought to light in the imprint of Lic. Luis Laso de la Vega in the year 1649.

He noted that Becerra Tanco had also seen a 'map' or codex among Alva's papers, only then to admit that Sigüenza y Góngora had not located it after the historian's death. But Florencia then clouded the waters with a vengeance when he claimed to have had news of 'another writing in the form of Annals', written in the hand of an Indian, that had been in the power of Baltazar González, the Jesuit censor of Laso de la Vega. This manuscript covered the history of the Toltecs and the Mexica until 1641 and included a reference to the apparition of the Guadalupe. Florencia then added:

> Perhaps it was from this history that the manuscript volume seen by Lic. Becerra Tanco was copied and from which he translated, as a faithful interpreter, the colloquies that Juan Diego had with the Virgin and the Most Holy Virgin with Juan Diego.

In effect, Florencia here followed the trail blazed by Becerra Tanco and claimed that the Indians preserved the memory of the apparitions first in a codex or 'map', then in the form of Annals, and finally in an extended account written in Nahuatl. Oddly

Plate 10   Baltazar de Echave Orio, *Our Lady of Guadalupe*

enough, he did not here repeat the assertion attributed to him in a posthumous publication, that González himself had written 'a history of Our Lady of Guadalupe in the
most elegant style', an assertion which, since it followed insistence on González' excellence as 'the Cicero in Mexican', may well have pointed to the Jesuit as the author of
the *Nican mopohua*.[20]

If all this were not enough, Florencia now produced what he thought to be his
trump cards, which were the song of Francisco Plácido, the Lord of Acapatzalco,
addressed to Zumárraga, when the image was placed in its 'first sanctuary' and, more
important, 'a very old account, written in hand', both of which had belonged to
Fernando de Alva and which had been lent to him by their current owner, Carlos de
Sigüenza y Góngora. This manuscript account was so discoloured that he judged it to
be anywhere between seventy and a hundred years old, which was to say, written well
before the publication of the books by Sánchez and Laso de la Vega. It was a Spanish
translation from the papers of an Indian, so Sigüenza y Góngora had informed
him, written in Alva's 'own letter'. Although in the course of his discussion Florencia
promised to print this account, at the conclusion he pleaded lack of space and
refrained from burdening his already extended text. But to judge from his comments,
it would not have been worth while to print it, since it only differed from existing
accounts in minor details. The differences were these: the first apparition was given as
occurring on Saturday 8 December, not the 9th; Juan Diego was said to have scourged
himself after his first visit to Zumárraga; the last apparition of the Virgin occurred
close to the source of the spring at Tepeyac; when the image was installed in the chapel,
it was carried by Franciscans led by a bare-footed Zumárraga; the Indian wounded in
that procession, once cured by miracle, remained to serve in the sanctuary; Juan de
Tovar, the Indian nobleman who found Los Remedios, suffered from blindness and
was cured by the Guadalupe; and finally, when a hydropic woman was cured, a serpent appeared. As will be observed, these details do not occur in existing accounts and
thus demonstrate that Florencia did indeed possess a manuscript in which they were
to be found. But there is no means of knowing whether the colloquies between Juan
Diego and the Virgin were based on the Sánchez-Cruz version, which Florencia himself favoured, or on the Nahuatl-inspired version of Laso de la Vega and Becerra
Tanco.[21]

One curious feature here may prove significant. It will be recalled that Laso de la
Vega reduced Sánchez' catalogue of 'roses inviting with their beauty, lilies offering
milk, carnations blood, violets devotion, jasmin amber, rosemary hope, irises love
and broom captivity' to a simple 'flowers of Castile' which were changed by Cruz into
'diverse flowers and roses' and by Becerra Tanco into 'roses of Castile'. In the 1666
depositions most Spanish witnesses referred to 'roses of Alexandria, commonly called
of Castile, and lilies'. Yet Florencia's 'old account' mentioned 'candid lilies, alexandrine roses, purple carnations, beautiful irises, broom and jasmin'. In this important

respect, the mysterious manuscript more resembled Sánchez than it did the *Nican mopohua*. At the same time, the inclusion of 'Alexandrine roses' was reminiscent of the 1666 depositions.[22] If this document was really a translation from an Indian original, why did it differ so obviously from the version printed by Laso de la Vega and mistranslated by Becerra Tanco?

A feature of the manuscript which caught Florencia's attention was that it referred to 'our glorious seraphic St Francis' and to 'our Order of St Francis', not to mention the role of Toribio Motolinia in the conversion of Juan Diego. After discussing the matter with Agustín de Betancurt, the elderly Franciscan chronicler, he concluded: 'The author of this account (which is the same from which Lic. Miguel Sánchez and Lic. Luis Becerra took theirs) was a religious of St Francis.' And what better candidate to find than Jerónimo de Mendieta, a well-known friar whom Betancurt was later to identify as the author of a church history of Mexico which had been plagiarized without acknowledgement by Torquemada in his *Monarchy of the Indies*? In advancing this opinion, Florencia failed to note that the expressions about 'our St Francis' and 'our Order of St Francis' occur in Sánchez. By postulating his manuscript as the common source of Sánchez and Becerra Tanco he ignored the differences in style and construction that distinguished the two authors, he contradicted his earlier assertion that Sánchez had taken his account from oral tradition and thus implicitly accused that venerable priest of perjury, and he failed to realize that Becerra Tanco had simply translated Laso de la Vega's *Nican mopohua*. In short, Florencia confused himself and was to confuse generations of students and readers.[23]

If Florencia took little from Becerra Tanco's colloquies between the Virgin and Juan Diego, by contrast he incorporated virtually all the new information about the Indian's life after the apparitions that was to be found in *Mexico's Happiness*. So transformed was Juan Diego that he took a small room close to the sanctuary, 'performing the humble tasks of sweeping, carrying and bringing the things necessary for the church and the vicar's house'. So too, he devoted himself to 'works of mortification, fasting and self-scourging, and took communion three times a week by licence of the archbishop, which is an irrefutable proof of his great purity'. But Florencia corrected Becerra Tanco's mistranslation and emphasized that the Indian's wife, María Lucía, had died in 1529, thus allowing him the freedom to devote himself entirely to the Virgin. As in the case of his uncle, the Virgin appeared to him on his deathbed. Florencia concluded that 'his memory lives imprinted with indelible characters on the hearts of all Mexicans'. Curiously enough, he also included a separate 'tradition', that Juan Diego had left a son called Juan, who possessed the small, portable image of the Guadalupe that had once been owned by the Indian visionary, an image which was given by his grandson to the Jesuit, Juan de Monroy, who in turn handed it to Juan Caballero y Ocio, the wealthy benefactor of Querétaro. Florencia surmised that this son may well have been by an earlier wife than María Lucía, or have been adopted, so that there was no conflict with the account of Juan Diego's chastity after his hearing the sermon by Motolinia in 1524.[24]

As regards the miracles performed in the sanctuary by the Virgin, Florencia returned to Laso de la Vega, who, it will be recalled, had expanded Sánchez' list from the original seven to fourteen. To justify inclusion of the cure of Pedro de Valderrama, Florencia cited the account given by Baltazar de Medina in his chronicle of the Franciscan province of San Diego, but also mentioned that 'an old painting in the sanctuary attests to it, where the case is painted and explained with an inscription at its foot'. But he further claimed that 'the old account' he possessed included this miracle, which is not in Sánchez, as number six, whereas in Laso de la Vega it comes as number eleven, further evidence of its minor discrepancies with known accounts. On the image's continuing thaumaturgic powers, Florencia cited another fourteen cases, mainly of minor cures, which 'are in its church as many painted tablets'. Along with such testimonies the sanctuary was also adorned with any number of 'presentations or vows of silver, heads, eyes, hearts, arms, legs and hands of silver', which were donated by devotees who had experienced some relief to their afflictions after praying to the Virgin, their gratitude signalized by these donations. But although the Guadalupe had liberated Mexico from the onslaught of devils, her power did not extend across the Atlantic. Thus, when an Andalucian was so buffeted by devils that he fled from Spain, he was immediately cured on going to the sanctuary at Tepeyac, but when 'the love of his country, which in everyone is a powerful magnet', impelled him to return to the Peninsula, he fell victim again to the devils, so that he was obliged once more to seek relief from the Mexican Virgin.[25]

But for Florencia, 'the greatest, most ancient and most authorized miracle of Our Lady of Guadalupe is her blessed image', which like the manna in the Old Testament fed the faithful, but which, unlike its scriptural antecedent, had remained uncorrupted for 157 years. As to whether Juan Diego's cape had been woven from *ixtle* of maguey fibre as Sánchez had asserted, or from the threads of the palm *iccotilzalti* as Becerra Tanco affirmed, Florencia chose not to pronounce. Instead, he adverted that he had been present during the 1666 inspection of the image, so that 'I had the happiness of seeing it out of its tabernacle, of touching the mantle, and of looking both at its face and at the back.' Although it was obvious that the canvas had no sizing, all that could be discerned at the back was smudges of colour without any visible outline of the painting. His impression was that 'the image had been copied, not with a brush, but in the way seals are stamped'. As for the colour of the Virgin's face, it struck him as *trigueño*, which is to say, a light, golden brown, similar to the complexion of many Indians or of people in Palestine. One startling piece of information retailed by Florencia was that Francisco de Siles had informed him that in the early years of the cult the image had been surrounded by cherubim; but since these figures were additions rather than part of the original image, they had faded and were later erased.

Plate 11   Our Lady of Guadalupe with St Michael and St Gabriel

This testimony was corroborated by Juan de Casaus Cervantes, the chief accountant of the court of audit, who had heard of it from his father. What this information suggests is that at one time the image was regarded as depicting the Virgin's Assumption into heaven, the advocation of the Mexican cathedral's titular patron.[26]

As we have seen, the identity of the angel who supported the Virgin attracted a great deal of discussion in this epoch, especially since the figure was often thought to be a signature portrait of the painter of the image. But, whereas Miguel Sánchez had identified him as St Michael the Archangel, by contrast Becerra Tanco had simply defined him as the guardian angel of the kingdom. For his part, Florencia followed Cruz in defining the image as an Immaculate Conception and then argued that since it had been the archangel Gabriel who had visited Mary in Nazareth to announce the conception of Jesus, it was obviously appropriate that St Gabriel should figure as the painter of Mary, 'when she is reborn in her image and through her image in this flowery Christendom, in her new Nazareth and as Patron of the Indies'. Moreover, St Gabriel had inserted himself in the image as the angel, not merely as a signature, but to indicate that he was 'the Guardian Angel of Imperial Mexico . . . the agent of the Co-redeemer of the New World'.[27]

Florencia concluded his account by tracing recent developments in the sanctuary and in the diffusion of the cult of Guadalupe. It was during the 1670s that Francisco de Siles (sic) and Isidro de Sariñana, a canon who later became bishop of Oaxaca, made a start upon the construction of stations or oratories, built of stone, along the causeway joining Tepeyac and Mexico City, designed to commemorate the fifteen mysteries of the rosary and thus assist the prayers of pilgrims as they walked to the sanctuary.[28] In the cathedral a side chapel had been dedicated to the Guadalupe and similar altars were consecrated in the cathedrals of Puebla and Oaxaca. At Tepeyac itself a small chapel had been built at the top of the peak. By the time he wrote, the sanctuary possessed twenty-eight silver lamps, including the great central lamp, which weighed 217 marks of silver. Since the tabernacle and front-piece of the altar were all made of silver, the sanctuary possessed precious metals worth 4,325 marks, which was to say, about 36,000 pesos. Among these possessions was a life-sized silver statue of the Virgin, which had been presented by Alonso de Villaseca, the wealthy sixteenth-century miner. So popular had the cult become that there was a painter who spent all his days producing copies of the image; Florencia himself had taken three life-sized copies with him when he went to Europe. The image attracted pilgrims from far and wide, especially Indians, who on their feast day crowded into the sanctuary, coming from mountainous zones as distant as the Huasteca or Meztitlan. But Florencia lamented that they often took advantage of the festive spirit of pilgrimage to consume great quantities of pulque, so that although many displayed great devotion, others fell into drunkenness, a vice which needed to be eliminated by 'the two arms of royal and ecclesiastical justice'.[29]

Apart from great feasts, the image itself was not normally visible, since the glass windows of the tabernacle were covered by 'two rich veils or curtains' which were only drawn for 'persons of respect'. By 1688 the sanctuary maintained a vicar and six chaplains, causing Florencia to observe that were their number to be increased to twelve by generous donations, 'it might be possible to institute a college with an abbot and canons, so that they could sing the hours in the choir and perform all the offices of the cathedrals'. By way of conclusion, Florencia recalled that he visited the Holy House of Loreto, but despite its associations with Nazareth, he confessed that he was most moved by the sanctuary at Tepeyac, which seemed to exude an indescribable 'odour of sanctity that was communicated by the bodily presence of the Queen of the Angels', so that like Jacob at Bethel, he could only exclaim: 'Holy is this place!' However, he admitted that he was no doubt stirred 'by that natural affection which inclines so powerfully, often without feeling it, and moves us with even more vehemence on everything that is of the *patria*'. It was for that reason that when he commissioned medallions of Our Lady of Guadalupe to be made at Antwerp in 1678, he had them inscribed with the phrase from Psalm 147 which he had seen at Loreto, 'Non fecit taliter omni natione', 'It was not done thus to all nations.'[30]

Although Florencia acclaimed the Guadalupe as the *Polestar of Mexico*, a title first applied to the image by Pedro Rodríguez Velarde, Becerra Tanco's censor, adapting it from Camoens' *Lusiads*, he also wrote extensively about other Marian cults.[31] In 1685 he had published *The Miraculous Discovery of a Hidden Treasure*, a history of the image and sanctuary of Our Lady of Los Remedios, in which, although he drew heavily on the work of Luis Cisneros, he criticized the Mercedarian professor for filling his book with 'ingenious digressions and erudite discussions'. By contrast, he thanked Carlos de Sigüenza y Góngora for informing him that Juan de Tovar, the Indian nobleman to whom the Virgin had appeared, was an Otomí, whose family still lived in their ancestor's house. So also, he cited Baltazar de Medina, who had listed the ten occasions during the years 1639–82 when the image had been brought to the city and installed in the cathedral. Indeed, after two years of drought, in 1685 Our Lady of Los Remedios remained for over a month in the city, a clear indication that devotion to the *gachupín* image still waxed strong. Florencia noted that the sanctuary possessed a *peregrina*, a pilgrim image, which was carried across New Spain to solicit alms, its arrival generally being greeted with great rejoicing in all the leading cities.[32] Nor did Florencia restrict his attention to the capital, since in 1694 he published *Origin of the Two Celebrated Sanctuaries of New Galicia*, in which he traced the emergence of devotion to the images of Our Lady of Zapopan, just outside Guadalajara, and Our Lady of San Juan de Lagos in Jalostitlan. Both these cults had grown rapidly during the seventeenth century, attracting pilgrims and increasingly acclaimed for the miraculous cures performed in their sanctuaries, which were progressively enlarged. So too, both these images had pilgrim copies which were despatched on a wide circuit in search of alms. Indeed, Florencia averred that Our Lady of San Juan de Lagos had become so popular that the *peregrina* was more successful in eliciting pious contributions than the rival images which proceeded from the sanctuaries of Los Remedios and Guadalupe, a clear indication of the strength of regional sentiment.[33]

Despite Florencia's dismissal of the 'conceptual panegyric' of sermons, not to mention his obsessive concern to encounter native sources of the Guadalupe tradition, he also purveyed the elements of a theology of Marian images as audacious as any advanced by contemporary preachers. To start with, *Polestar of Mexico* carried a lengthy approbation written by Jerónimo de Valladolid, the current vicar at Tepeyac, who echoed Sánchez in affirming that the Guadalupe image was a copy of that seen in vision by St John on Patmos, only then to argue that if the original vision had placed a seal on the primitive Church in Asia, the copy had sealed the foundation of the primitive Church of 'our America'. However, Valladolid admitted that if the apocalyptic text enjoyed the authority of his 'evangelical secretary', by contrast 'no authentic record about this holy image has been found in the registers of this Holy Church of Mexico'. But what need was there for mere writing, when the image 'speaks for itself and testifies to its miraculous origin'? In almost contemptuous dismissal of Florencia's search for native manuscripts, Valladolid insisted that: 'In her image and through her image the Sovereign Lady speaks of the miracle . . . She herself is the writing, written in the hand and form of God himself on the membranes of our hearts.' In any case, since the peoples of Mexico had always used figures and images to record sacred events, 'this hieroglyphic writing was a letter of recommendation to her devotees, both Indians and Spaniards'. Citing Sánchez, whom he described as 'the most devout and erudite panegyrist of this miraculous effigy', Valladolid identified the image as the flowering rod of Aaron, only then to contrast it to Our Lady of Los Remedios, whose biblical figure was the rod of Moses. Recalling that the image had been born by miracle in Zumárraga's palace, he further defined it as 'a heavenly pallium' of all the archbishops of Mexico, noting that the current incumbent, Francisco de Aguiar, Seijas y Ulloa, had adopted the figure as his personal coat of arms. By contrast, Los Remedios was the patron of Mexico City and hence the emblem of the city council and its chief magistrate.[34] In these antitheses, the rods of Moses and Aaron thus served as symbols of the city and the cathedral, of the civil and the ecclesiastical powers.

It was Florencia himself, however, who defined the Guadalupe image as a Marian sacrament. In *Polestar of Mexico* he cited the *New Apocalypse*, the visionary work of Blessed Amadeus of Portugal, the fifteenth-century Franciscan to whom the Virgin Mary had confirmed the truth of her Immaculate Conception. In particular, he fixed upon the 'eighth rapture' in which Amadeus reported the Virgin's promise to the apostles that:

I will be with you until the end of the world in my images, both of brush and carving; and you will know that I am in them when you see that through them I work miracles and wonders.[35]

Although Florencia did not here refer to the source of this citation, in his *Origin of Two Celebrated Sanctuaries* he quoted the contemporary Franciscan chronicle published in 1682 by Baltazar de Medina, where the author noted that San Pedro de Alcántara, the sixteenth-century Spanish saint, had defended the orthodoxy of the *New Apocalypse*. It was in Florencia's account of the images of New Galicia that he provided the full version of the Virgin's promise, albeit interpolating Mexican examples:

> Know you my children, said the Lady, that through the grace of my Lord Jesus Christ I shall also be with you bodily until the end of the world; not in the Sacrament of the Altar, as is my Son, since that is neither convenient nor decent, but in my Images, of brush (as is that of Guadalupe of Mexico) or of sculpture (as are those of San Juan, that of Zapopan, that of Los Remedios of Mexico and others) and then you shall know that I am in them, when you see that some miracles are made through them.[36]

In this revelation the Virgin is thus reported as announcing that she will be bodily present in certain images, much in the same way that Christ was present in the Eucharist. But since her presence was demonstrated by the performance of miracles, obviously she was not present in all her representations, but only in those which attracted pilgrimage and widespread devotion. It was these miraculous 'cult' images which were destined to endure until the end of the world.

In this context, Florencia also quoted St Peter Chrysologus (c. 400–500), bishop of Ravenna, who in 1729 was to be proclaimed a Doctor of the Church, as saying:

> The Image and the Original are the same thing as regards their power, although different as regards their being. They are the same thing, because in order not to err the Catholic Religion teaches us that the Image should have the same cult and veneration as its Original.

Applying this dictum to the statue of the Virgin which attracted pilgrims to the sanctuary at San Juan de Lagos, Florencia observed that 'this Image . . . is not to be considered simply as Image, but as Mary, not only as the image of Mary, but as Mary herself, Virgin and Mother of God'.[37] Obviously, what he here implied was that in her miraculous statue Mary was sacramentally present, like Christ in the Eucharist. However, in a following passage, Florencia qualified this statement by adding:

> One should not attend so much to the images which the eyes see, as to the Original which Faith knows in them and which the Will venerates. Whoever goes to the sanctuary of San Juan, who sees Mary's miraculous image and in it adores her,

according to the devotion with which he sees her, more appears to regard the
Original, which he does not see, than the Image which the eyes see, so great is the
reverence which that holy Statue inspires.[38]

Here then, Florencia follows St Basil the Great in affirming that all devotion paid to
the image was transferred to the original. For all that, he clearly assumed that cult images differed from mere representations both in their power to awake devotion and in
performing miracles. But in this he merely followed Miguel Sánchez, who had already
declared that the sanctuaries of miraculous images formed a numinous network of
Christian fortresses wherein the faithful were protected from diabolic intrusion and
where heavenly grace was most efficacious. Since these holy figures served as visible
conduits of divine power, it was only fitting that they should be approached with the
same awe and veneration as their heavenly prototypes.

In his *Mexican Guadalupanism* (1953), Francisco de la Maza defined Sánchez, Laso
de la Vega, Becerra Tanco and Florencia as the four evangelists of the Virgin of
Tepeyac.[39] If Laso de la Vega was the St Mark and Sánchez the St John of this Mexican
revelation, Becerra Tanco was a critical St Matthew and Florencia a confused St Luke.
But by reason of its copious information and summaries of the 1666 depositions,
Polestar of Mexico was reprinted in Barcelona in 1741 and in Madrid in 1785. It is striking, however, that whereas Sánchez and Laso de la Vega were content to describe the
apparitions and to interpret their theological significance, both Becerra Tanco and
Florencia sought to confirm the tradition by postulating the existence of Indian
manuscript accounts. Was Florencia's anxiety to encounter historical authentication
the result of his visit to Rome, a city where facts rather than theories, original documents rather than theological exegesis, were required if papal recognition was to be
obtained? Or were there critics in Mexico, possibly immigrants from Spain, who questioned the reliability of the apparition narrative? If such doubts existed, no record of
them has survived: all we have is the patent anxiety of Becerra Tanco and Florencia to
encounter early native reports of these miracles. For all that, it is clear that most
creoles of this epoch, priests and preachers among them, assented to the tradition because they were moved by the spiritual power of the image. As Valladolid observed,
what need was there for historical records when the image itself was a form of writing
which 'speaks for itself and testifies to its miraculous origin'? It was precisely the heartfelt experience of being in the presence of a heavenly power that rendered Blessed
Amadeus' revelation so plausible.

III

If the part played by Carlos de Sigüenza y Góngora (1645–1700) in the formation of the
Guadalupe tradition remains enigmatic, of his profound devotion there can be no

doubt. As early as 1662 he published a long Parnassian poem, *Indian Spring*, in which he contrasted the dark heresies which overshadowed Northern Europe in the sixteenth century with the joyful apparition of Mary in Mexico, born amidst candid lilies, purple carnations, jasmin and blue irises, in a land blessed with an 'eternal spring'. Was not the presence of the Virgin at Tepeyac symbol of the ever-westward movement of the Catholic faith? In his *Glories of Querétaro* (1680), Sigüenza y Góngora commemorated the dedication of a new church to Our Lady of Guadalupe, the spiritual home of a congregation of secular priests founded in 1669 in her honour. In loving detail he described the elaborate masque staged by the governor of the local Indian community, in which figures of the city's Otomí founder, the emperors of Mexico-Tenochtitlan and Charles V, all paraded through the city streets. Commenting on the devotion to the Mexican Virgin, Sigüenza y Góngora observed that it was not until 1659 that a copy of the image had been brought to the city, adding: 'a strange case this, for Querétaro to lack the image, when the Most Holy Mary of Guadalupe is the image and gentle magnet of devoted Americans'.[40]

An ardent patriot and a speculative historian, in 1680, Sigüenza y Góngora was commissioned by the city council of Mexico to design a triumphal arch to welcome the new viceroy, the marquis of La Laguna. He loaded that classic structure with inscriptions and with statues of the twelve Mexican monarchs in the hope that 'the heroic . . . imperial virtues' of these rulers might offer models of statecraft as inspiring as any ancient Greek and Roman. In the tract he wrote on the arch, this 'Mexican priest', as he called himself, cited Enrico Farnese, an Italian humanist, who asserted that 'the citizen is he who lives not for himself but for his country'. It was to express his own commitment that Sigüenza y Góngora chose Pegasus, the winged horse of classical mythology, as his personal emblem, signifying 'a man who displays his soul always uplifted to the sublime, in service of his country'. It was heartfelt patriotism that drove Sigüenza y Góngora to draw upon Athanasius Kircher's *Oedipus Aegyptiacus* (1652–4) and conclude that the ancient Olmecs, the predecessors of the Mexica and the Toltecs, had migrated from Egypt via Atlantis, their pyramids, calendars and use of hieroglyphs a persuasive demonstration of their origin.[41]

Not content with endowing his country with an Atlantean ancestry, Sigüenza y Góngora announced in his *Western Paradise* (1684) that he later hoped to publish a work 'on the preaching of the Apostle St Thomas in this land and its primitive Christianity'. Although the work has never been located, the editor of his last, posthumous book asserted that he had indeed written *Phoenix of the West: St Thomas Found under the Name of Quetzalcoatl*. It was obviously his deep knowledge of pre-hispanic antiquities and devotion to Our Lady of Guadalupe which united Sigüenza y Góngora to Luis Becerra Tanco, 'with whom I enjoyed a close friendship for several years'.[42] Was it from the papers of Fernando de Alva Ixtlilxochitl that both these scholars came to embrace the thesis of the apostolic mission of St Thomas in Mexico? They were not alone in this belief, however, since in his *Chronicle of the Holy Province of San Diego* (1682), Baltazar de Medina (1630?–97) equally subscribed to the theory, albeit citing the Peruvian chronicler, Antonio de la Calancha as his authority. This Franciscan chronicler also propounded the theory, taken from Martín del Castillo, that the name of Mexico had a Hebrew or Syriac origin and meant 'of my Messiah'. But rather than accepting Sigüenza y Góngora's vision of an Egyptian civilization in ancient Anahuac, Medina opined that the natives of Mexico were descended from the lost ten tribes of Israel. He shared the polymath's patriotism, however, since after exclaiming that 'this court enjoys some of the qualities of paradise in its climate, freshness and beauty of roses, flowers and fruits', he declared that Mexico City was 'like an empress of this kingdom and lady of the Indian monarchy of both Americas', destined to be 'the monarch of the sceptre and crown of the true Messiah'.[43]

Virtually all the creole chroniclers of this epoch expressed impatience with Torquemada, be it because of his demon-ridden vision of ancient Mexico, or be it because of his silence over the apparitions of Our Lady of Guadalupe. Indeed, in his *Mexican Theatre* (1697–8) Agustín de Betancurt (1620–1700) accused Torquemada of having plagiarized his *Monarchy of the Indies* from the extensive manuscript left by Jerónimo de Mendieta. In his preface Betancurt thanked 'my compatriot and friend', Sigüenza y Góngora, for providing him with any number of native codices and sixteenth-century manuscripts. Nowhere did this Franciscan chronicler differ more from Torquemada than in the pages he devoted to holy images of the Virgin. He followed Baltazar de Medina, not to mention Florencia, in citing the eighth 'rapture' of Blessed Amadeus of Portugal, where the Virgin promised to be bodily present in those images through which she worked miracles. In his account of Our Lady of Los Remedios he listed the fifteen occasions when the image had been brought from its sanctuary to the cathedral, among the most notable of which were the two years spent in the city after the riots of 1692. One peculiarity of his account was that he referred to don Juan, the Indian nobleman to whom the Virgin appeared, as 'Juan Diego, called Cequauhtzin'. But Betancurt had nothing new to add to the Guadalupe tradition other than to accept Florencia's suggestion that the 'old paper', on which Sánchez and Becerra Tanco based their accounts, had been written by Jerónimo de Mendieta or by Fernando de Alva Ixtlilxochitl. Of the miracles which the Virgin of Guadalupe performed, that which drew his attention was the case related by Florencia of a Spaniard who, on coming to the sanctuary, had been liberated from the Devil's possession, only to fall once more under Satan's power once he returned to Spain, albeit to be cured finally by the import of a copy of the Virgin. Like other creoles of this epoch, Betancurt engaged in visionary rhetoric, since after observing that Mexico possessed twelve 'families' of religious, he hailed the city as 'a new Jerusalem with twelve gates through which to enter the Jerusalem of triumph, twelve precious stones . . . twelve tribes of Israel . . . which shine like stars in the crown of the Woman of the Apocalypse'.[44]

In his *Western Paradise*, Sigüenza y Góngora reproduced sacred songs composed by Nezahualcoyotl, the celebrated philosopher king of Texcoco, in which, according to his Spanish translation, that ruler addressed 'the Lord and invisible great Lord God', as a deity whose omnipotence was to be propitiated by prayer and penitence. These Christian-sounding 'hymns' came from the papers of Alva Ixtlilxochitl, 'the Cicero of the Mexican language'. It was his possession of these papers which led Sigüenza y Góngora to criticize Florencia, whom elsewhere he had praised as 'the glory of our creole nation and my most particular friend'. In a pamphlet, written and possibly published in 1689, entitled *Heroic Piety of Hernán Cortés*, he declared that he could not accept the Jesuit's assertion that the site of Zumárraga's palace, where the Guadalupe image had appeared, was occupied by houses owned by the count of Santiago, since he could adduce documents which clearly demonstrated that the original buildings had been replaced by the current palace of the archbishops and by the hospital of Amor de Dios, where he himself acted as chaplain.[45]

But it was Florencia's speculation that the 'old account' which Sigüenza y Góngora had lent him was the work of Jerónimo de Mendieta that most aroused his ire. How could the Franciscan be the author, since he had died in 1605, whereas the manuscript listed miracles which had occurred after that date? Instead, he praised the account of the apparitions found in Becerra Tanco's *Mexico's Happiness* and added that Juan Diego's name before baptism was Quauhtatoatzin. More important, he now explained the origin of the manuscript which he had lent Florencia.

> I say and swear, that I found this account among the papers of Fernando de Alva, all of which I have, and which is the same that Lic. Luis de Becerra [Tanco] in his book [page 30 of the Seville impression] affirms as having been in his possession. The original in Mexican is of the letter of don Antonio Valeriano, an Indian, who is its true author, and at the end are added some miracles in the letter of don Fernando, also in Mexican. What I lent to the Reverend Father Francisco de Florencia was a paraphrased translation that don Fernando made from one and the other, and is also in his letter.[46]

In this all-important coda to the search for Indian sources of the Guadalupe tradition, Sigüenza y Góngora here testified to the existence of a manuscript in Nahuatl dealing with the apparitions and colloquies, a work which, in his 1666 deposition and pamphlet, Becerra Tanco had already identified as the original of the version printed by Laso de la Vega and which he himself was to translate and incorporate into *Mexico's Happiness*. The contribution of Sigüenza y Góngora was to confirm the existence of this manuscript and to name Antonio Valeriano as the author of the *Nican mopohua*, the apparition narrative. He accounted for the discrepancies in style between different sections of the *Huei tlamaluiçoltica* by asserting that Alva Ixtlilxochitl had written the *Nican moctepana*, the miracle transcripts. However, as we have seen, the 'paraphrased translation' he lent Florencia differed in many small details from the version found in Laso de la Vega and Becerra Tanco, albeit almost identical in its description of Juan Diego's virtues. Its list of the flowers gathered by the Indian derived from Sánchez, with variants such as 'candid lilies, purple carnations' taken from Sigüenza y Góngora's poem, *Indian Spring*. Moreover, had this version contained the Nahuatl-inspired colloquies of the Virgin and Juan Diego, Florencia would surely have abandoned his objections to their 'childish' language and adopted them in preference for Cruz' summary.

In effect, what Sigüenza y Góngora affirmed was that Alva Ixtlilxochitl, who died in 1650 aged about seventy-two, had possessed a manuscript written in Nahuatl by Valeriano some years before his death in 1605; that Alva had written an account of the miracles in Nahuatl after 1629; and that he had translated both these accounts into Spanish, albeit in 'paraphrase' and with minor variants, including a catalogue of flowers similar to those mentioned by Sánchez in 1648. By means of these affirmations, Sigüenza y Góngora substantiated the thesis of Becerra Tanco, which was to say, he demonstrated that the Guadalupe tradition rested on a Nahuatl narrative written by Valeriano in the sixteenth century, an account based in turn on earlier native 'paintings and maps'. After all, if the key to the history of ancient Mexico lay hidden in the hieroglyphs of the codices, so also the memory of the Virgin's apparitions at Tepeyac had been preserved in similar form. It was Becerra Tanco's editor, Antonio de Gama, who described Sigüenza y Góngora as 'the best flower of the paradise of letters of our America'. The creole polymath was the central figure within the small circle of priests who delved into the Mexican past and found it populated by apostles, Israelites and Egyptians; so too, it was his possession of the Alva Ixtlilxochitl papers that allowed him to identify Valeriano as the primordial source of the Guadalupe tradition. The effect of this thesis was to oust Sánchez from his place as the first evangelist of Our Lady of Guadalupe and to relegate Laso de la Vega to the role of editor of earlier manuscripts. But although Sigüenza y Góngora's authority and prestige as a scholar commanded almost universal assent in generations to come, no documentary proof of his statements ever came to light. His great collection of manuscripts and codices was bequeathed to the Jesuit college of San Pedro y San Pablo, and thereafter was slowly dispersed or lost.[47] Neither the original account in Nahuatl by Valeriano nor the variant Spanish translation by Alva Ixtlilxochitl has ever been found or seen. All that survived was the arguments of Becerra Tanco, the confused ruminations of Florencia and the stark affirmations of Sigüenza y Góngora.

6

Patron of Mexico

I

Such was the growth of devotion to Our Lady of Guadalupe that in 1695 Archbishop Francisco de Aguiar y Seijas agreed to demolish the existing sanctuary at Tepeyac, only completed in 1622, so as to erect a more imposing church. Already Captain Pedro Ruíz de Castañeda and Lic. Ventura de Medina Picazo had respectively donated 50,000 and 80,000 pesos for that purpose. In the event, by the time it was completed in 1709, the building cost 475,000 pesos, much of which was raised by Archbishop Juan de Ortega y Montañés (1699–1710) begging on the streets of the capital for alms. The new church was a majestic, three-naved edifice, crowned with a dome and towers at its four corners, decorated in Doric style, and dominated by three great altarpieces that reached to the vaults. Above the high altar was a silver throne and tabernacle for the image weighing 3,257 marks of silver. If it be recalled that in 1647 the outgoing viceroy had donated a tabernacle worth 350 marks, then some measure of the splendour of the new sanctuary can be obtained. Its consecration in May 1709 was celebrated by a *novena*, nine days of masses and sermons, attended by dignitaries of Church and State and by crowds of the faithful.[1]

The prelate who brought the Guadalupe image to the cathedral in 1629, Archbishop Francisco Manso y Zúñiga, was later reported to have said that in New Spain the three most precious relics were 'the miraculous image of Our Lady of Guadalupe, that of Our Lady of Los Remedios, and the sacred Effigy of Our Lord Jesus Christ which is called of Ixmiquilpan'. In the years when the new church at Tepeyac was planned and built, the image of Our Lady of Los Remedios was brought from her sanctuary to the cathedral on three separate occasions with all customary pomp and devotion, and indeed, owing to the riot caused by harvest failure, she remained in the city from 24 May 1692 until 7 March 1695, at times paraded through the streets when the occasion was thought to demand her presence. But no matter how strong the devotion to Our Lady of Los Remedios remained, the creole elite turned with ever-increasing fervour to the

Mexican Virgin. In 1731 the two-hundredth anniversary of Mary's apparitions to Juan Diego was celebrated with an impressive round of festivities, which culminated in a grand procession from the city centre to the sanctuary headed by the viceroy, the high court and the city council.[2]

Present at these celebrations was Juan Antonio de Vizarrón y Eguiarreta, archbishop of Mexico 1730–47 and viceroy of New Spain 1734–40, a native of the port of Santa María in Andalucia, who was soon to become renowned for his devotion to the Virgin of Tepeyac. It was thanks to his encouragement that in 1737 the authorities of the city of Mexico proclaimed Our Lady of Guadalupe as the principal patron of the capital, an initiative that was soon echoed by city councils across the vast territories of the viceroyalty of New Spain. What impelled the creole elite to take this step was the prolonged onslaught of *matlazahuatl*, an epidemic of typhus or typhoid fever, which attacked the population with devastating force during that year. A contemporary account of the effects of this epidemic affords an unparalleled portrait of the manner in which the clergy and nobility responded to the afflictions of the populace and the degree to which Our Lady of Guadalupe came to be seen as their only true remedy.

II

It was in August 1736 that the first inroads of the epidemic were detected on the outskirts of Mexico City, the victims mainly found among Indians and the poor. By the opening months of 1737, however, the plague, as the *matlazahuatl* was called, raged across the entire city, thrusting thousands of unfortunates into an early grave. In this epoch it was still the practice to bury the faithful in churches. But as early as January the sepulchres of the cathedral and the leading churches were filled to overflowing, with the result that the air, both within these buildings and around them, was filled with 'an intolerable stench'. New cemeteries were opened and San Lázaro, a burial ground where hitherto sufferers from leprosy were interred, was used to burn the corpses of the poor, the daily funeral pyre polluting the sky for over seven months. Not until September, after nearly three months of heavy seasonal rain, did the plague finally peter out. When the death bills were finally counted, it was found that 40,157 individuals had died during the months when the epidemic haunted the city, of whom 9,787 were buried in the cathedral and the four main parish churches, and no fewer than 9,076 consigned to San Lázaro and other pauper cemeteries. Although these figures were not broken down by ethnic category, the returns from native parishes and the Royal Hospital for Indians indicate that at least 13,721 natives died within the city limits. If the fever appears to have wrought most devastation in the capital and cities such as Puebla, most of central Mexico was affected, and an early summary, obviously incomplete, estimated that over 192,000 persons died of the disease. It was thus no surprise that the capital's government should have turned to the Mexican Virgin for relief from so much suffering.³

What was a plague but an act of war waged by the Almighty against humanity as punishment for sin? Such had been the opinion of Agustín Dávila Padilla and Juan de Grijalva, chroniclers of the Dominican and Augustinian friars in New Spain, when they described the great epidemics of 1543–6 and 1576. When millions of Indians died, they interpreted these afflictions as God's punishment for the grievous sins of idolatry and the natives' failure to accept the Christian gospel. In retailing these views, Cayetano de Cabrera y Quintero (c. 1700–c. 1778), a poet and playwright, who had been appointed by Archbishop Vizarrón y Eguiarreta to write an 'historical-panegyrical account' of the events of 1737, demonstrated the scope of his literary ambition. His *Shield of Arms of Mexico* (1746) not merely recounted the ceremonies which celebrated the capital's choice of patron, but also chronicled the inroads of the plague and, above all, the selfless efforts of the clergy to help the afflicted. But he was at pains to note that 1737 was the seventeenth and one of the worst in a whole series of epidemics which had ravaged the population of New Spain since the Spanish conquest. But since it was the Indians who were always the most affected by the plague, why did God still continue to punish them? Cabrera's answer was forthright. It was because the natives were sunk in drunkenness and idolatry. Whereas before the conquest they had been governed by a rigorous moral regime, now they were free to consume as much pulque and distilled alcohol as they wanted, thus offering a lamentable contrast between 'their ancient sobriety and temperance and their present intemperance and drunkenness'. In fixing upon this issue, Cabrera drew upon the chroniclers of the late seventeenth century, Betancurt, Medina, Florencia and Sigüenza y Góngora, all of whom had insisted that the native addiction to pulque was the chief cause of their promiscuity, quarrels and idolatry. In this regard Cabrera cited the pastoral letter of Archbishop José Lanciego y Eguilez, who in 1726 had condemned the widespread worship of 'the God of harvests . . . that abominable anti-Pope whose tyrannical power, promoted with enormous offences, has undermined the whole kingdom'. Indeed, many parish priests had reported finding idols in distant caves and had denounced the Volador games, the Mexican Maypole, as inspired by the Devil, who was often to be seen present, disguised as a serpent, a lion or an Ethiopian. Here, indeed, was cause enough to provoke God's wrath.⁴

But, if the Almighty was the final cause of the 1737 plague, natural phenomena played their part. As the early seventeenth-century doctor, Juan de Barrios, had observed, Mexico City was built on a low-lying island, little better than a mudflat, which was surrounded by stagnant waters which often flooded into the foundations of its buildings. It was an obvious site for all kinds of fevers and dysentery. But social causes were equally important. Cabrera cited José de Escobar y Morales, the leading doctor of the day, who attributed native mortality to the prevalence of drunkenness, the lack of sufficient food, the difference in temperature between day and night, and the drinking of cold water. This opinion was based on Escobar's attendance at the Royal Hospital for Indians, where he himself was to die of the plague in 1737. But during that epidemic, it was found that many deaths came from neglect, since once an Indian fell ill, he was often abandoned and left to die behind closed doors. So too, many children perished once their parents were infected. Even in the hospitals it was found that 'hunger and neglect besieged innumerable individuals who were attacked by fever'. In effect, food and nursing might well have enabled many to recover from their illness.[5]

A literary man who prided himself on his knowledge of medical matters, Cabrera commented that most doctors still relied on Hippocrates for their diagnoses and observed that their medicines had proved to be ineffectual. If Dávila Padilla had complained of the inability of doctors to cure the plague of 1576, their remedies for the plague of 1737 proved to be just as ineffective. By way of demonstrating his own understanding of such matters, Cabrera inserted a dramatic description of the circulation of blood in the body, albeit without specifying his source. But he also provided an invaluable account of Mexico City's nine hospitals, tracing their foundations and describing the three religious Orders which cared for the sick. As their beds and wards became crowded with patients, so too the brothers of these orders often fell sick and died. At any time, the Royal Hospital for Indians had over 500 inmates, many of whom were soon to waste away. But Cabrera questioned the wisdom of concentrating all those suffering from the plague in these hospitals, since it extended the contagion rather than confining it. Indeed, it had been the removal of infected workers from a textile workshop, an *obraje*, which had first caused the epidemic to spread so rapidly. If Archbishop Vizarrón had set up six stations from which to distribute medicines, expending 35,372 pesos on food and remedies, he had discontinued the supply in April, disillusioned by the failure to achieve any visible result.[6]

What Cabrera was at pains to emphasize was the zeal with which so many priests ministered to the poor and afflicted. Himself a secular priest who had acted as chaplain to the archbishop's pages, he asserted that although the religious Orders had won all the credit for the conversion of the Indians, in fact many secular priests had figured in that great enterprise, and none more so that Bartolomé de Las Casas, who had been 'sent from heaven, to the old and the new world, to act as Father and Protector of the Indies and the Indians'. During the current crisis, the parish priests had suspended charging the usual fees for funerals and had expended their income and their lives in assisting those stricken by illness. Indeed, Dr Isidro de Sariñana, a member of a noble family which had numbered a bishop of Oaxaca in its ranks, himself died of the plague while ministering in his parish of Veracruz. It was an Indian nobleman and priest, Pascual de los Reyes, Cortés y Moctezuma, who took the Eucharist to workers in the textile workshops, places notorious for their unhealthy conditions. In particular, the recently established Oratory, a congregation of secular priests, had been active in visiting prisons, hospitals and homes, ministering to the sick and dying. Their *prepósito*, José Hurtado de Mendoza, arranged for alms to be distributed to the hospitals so as to feed patients and had also maintained over a thousand young Indians in the district of Atilzapan for five months at a cost of 2,694 pesos.[7]

Among the religious Orders the Jesuits took the lead, inspired by the example of Juan Martínez, who raised large sums in alms until he himself succumbed to the infection to which his labours had exposed him. In equal measure, the Franciscans of San Fernando, the new college of *propaganda fide*, distinguished themselves by their visits to the poorest cottages, their ascetic zeal a living refutation of the old canard that creoles were unable to endure hardships, since the community was composed of both American and European friars. In varying degrees all the religious Orders sought to assist sufferers from the plague and in the great enclosed convents nuns fasted and beseeched heaven to take mercy on the city. Nor were the laity found wanting in Christian compassion. The count of Santiago offered his coach to take the Eucharist to the dying and at times acted as coachman for the viaticum, thereby setting an example which was followed by other nobles. Another wealthy layman, José Vásquez, noted that the sick in hospital were often only given *atole*, a thin beverage made from maize and, to prevent them dying as much from hunger as the plague, distributed daily rations of meat, bread and soup, costing some 2,500 pesos from January to June. By multiplying these examples, Cabrera evoked a powerful image of a Christian commonwealth, a Catholic city, where both priests and laymen exposed themselves to the danger of infection in order to minister to the needs, both physical and spiritual, of the sick and the poor.[8]

But no matter how effective these measures of relief might be, everybody was convinced that, since 'the plague does not yield to natural assistance', it was necessary to seek divine help. Throughout these months the churches were filled with the faithful as the clergy called them to prayer and penitence. Above all, however, it was to its great miraculous images that the city looked for relief and intercession, for what better way could be found of approaching heaven? In the pages of Cabrera there is material enough for an entire treatise on holy images in the capital. Oddly enough, it was Our Lady of Loreto, a copy brought from Italy by the missionary Jesuits from that country, Juan Bautista Zappa and Juan María Salvatierra, which was first paraded through the streets in December 1736 before being deposited in the *casa profesa*, the main Jesuit church. But it was to its beloved patron, Our Lady of Los Remedios, that the city council then turned, that 'heavenly conqueror' who had saved Cortés and the Spaniards as they had fled from Mexico-Tenochtitlan. Never reluctant to expatiate, Cabrera recounted the history of this image, drawing upon Cisneros and Florencia, only then to cite a Spanish historian, to the effect that King Pelayo, 'the Moses' of Spain, had once owned a small image of Mary, which he had deposited in the town of Alcántara where it remained for centuries, no doubt neglected, until a dishonest priest sold it to a Spaniard from the Indies, who then took it to Mexico. What could be more obvious, Cabrera declared, than that this image was Los Remedios, brought from Cuba to New Spain by a companion of Cortés? And what better proof of its power than that in the 160 years since 1597 the image had been taken from its sanctuary in public procession to the cathedral no fewer than twenty-six times, and as much in the eighteenth as in the seventeenth century? It was thus on 9 January 1737 that Los Remedios was installed on the high altar in the cathedral, where Canon Bartolomé de Ita y Parra preached a sermon in which 'like another Pericles he unleashed the rays of his Christian eloquence against the rebellious Hydra heads of the vices'.[9]

As the plague continued to rage unabated, the city grew more desperate, so that images and relics rarely if ever seen in public were displayed and carried through the streets. Popular anxiety was heightened by the occurrence of an eclipse at the beginning of March. In particular, several confraternities took out images of Christ in his Passion, especially as *Ecce Homo*, where the Saviour was depicted with a crown of thorns and his body torn by scourging. But saints such as St Joseph and St Bernard and the much-venerated Virgins of La Piedad and Bala were also implored. In passing, Cabrera noted that the Indians of Santiago Tlatelolco sallied forth, scourging themselves and carrying an image of Santiago in which that saint held a scourge instead of a sword and was dressed as a penitent rather than as a warrior, a spectacle that disturbed many spectators. All this activity reached its climax on 28 April, when the crucified Christ of Ixmiquilpan, housed in the Carmelite convent at Cardonal, was taken out. Here was a greatly venerated image, which had been brought from Spain in 1545, only then so to deteriorate that Archbishop Juan Pérez de la Serna had ordered it to be ceremonially buried. But six years later, in 1621, the image had emerged from the grave during a hurricane, miraculously restored and all the more powerful. Such was the veneration aroused by this crucifix that it was carried in procession by priests, with the archbishop himself leading the clergy and the confraternities as they walked through the streets, church bells sounding the *miserere* as they entered the cathedral.[10]

But as early as January 1737, the city council had petitioned the archbishop for permission to bring Our Lady of Guadalupe to the cathedral, citing the great flood of 1629 as precedent. But Vizarrón refused, advising the authorities to go to Tepeyac, there to stage a *novena*, nine days of masses, prayers and sermons, to beseech the Virgin for help 'in her sanctuary of Guadalupe, as born in New Spain, the very refuge of this capital which venerates her as its Pole Star'. It was at the conclusion of these ceremonies, after preachers from the religious Orders had held forth on previous days, that on 9 February, Bartolomé de Ita y Parra delivered a sermon, entitled 'The Mother of Health', before the assembled dignitaries of Church and State. It should be noted that five years before, on 12 December 1731, Parra had addressed a similar congregation who had come to Tepeyac to celebrate the two-hundredth anniversary of the apparition of the Virgin. On that occasion, Vizarrón had but recently arrived in Mexico; whereas in 1737 he attended as both viceroy and archbishop. It was now that

Ita y Parra drew a striking contrast between Los Remedios and Guadalupe, the one a foreigner, a pilgrim Ark of the Covenant, and the other a sacred burning bush, always present in her sanctuary. He concluded his sermon by calling upon the city council and cathedral chapter to elect Our Lady of Guadalupe as 'universal patron of all this kingdom'.[11]

On 28 March 1737 the city council petitioned the archbishop that 'Our Lady the most Holy Virgin in her admirable, miraculous Image of Guadalupe' should be recognized as the principal patron both of the capital and of the kingdom, with her feast on 12 December accompanied by special prayers. Vizarrón passed the matter for consideration by the cathedral chapter, which equally voted to recognize the Mexican Virgin as patron. After taking legal advice, the archbishop pronounced that whereas it was perfectly proper for the city authorities to take such an initiative as regards the capital, it was necessary to obtain the consent of the bishops, chapters and city councils of the whole kingdom before the Virgin could be proclaimed patron of New Spain. As Cabrera argued, in Europe virtually all kingdoms, provinces and cities had their patron, as indeed did churches and ships. In any case, had not the prophet Daniel indicated that every kingdom had its own guardian angel? As regards Marian images, both Our Lady of Loreto and Our Lady of Pilar were the patrons of their respective cities and provinces.[12]

All that remained was for the city councillors, Felipe Cayetano Medina y Sarabia and José Francisco de Aguirre y Espinosa, to join with Archdeacon Alonso Moreno y Castro and Canon Bartolomé Felipe de Ita y Parra, to swear a solemn oath on behalf of their two *cabildos*, the civil and the ecclesiastical, accepting the Guadalupe as patron of the city, the ceremony held on 27 April before the archbishop in the palace chapel. It was on 24 May 1737 that the city publicly celebrated the election of its new patron by staging a great procession through the streets in which the confraternities, both Spanish and Indians, the religious communities, members of all civil institutions, both royal and municipal, and the secular clergy all accompanied a life-sized silver statue of the Mexican Virgin. In describing this scene, Cabrera averred that it reminded him of ancient times when the city fathers had acclaimed emperors, kings and military leaders as their protectors. So too the capital now solemnly took the 'Queen and Empress of Imperial Mexico, Most Holy Mary in her Image of Guadalupe', as its protector. In this scene Archbishop Vizarrón figured as 'another anointed David', dancing before the Ark of the Covenant as it entered Jerusalem. Cabrera also commented on how the Indians danced in their traditional fashion as the clergy entered the cathedral, dubbing the capital 'this Jericho and City of the Moon of Mexico'. All the buildings which lined the route of the procession were bedecked with tapestries, hangings and as many images of the Guadalupe as could be found, their omnipresence multiplied by countless mirrors, so that the whole city appeared to exhibit but one likeness. It was in the cathedral before the silver image of the Virgin on the high altar, flanked by figures

Plate 12   Baltazar Troncoso, *The City of Mexico pleads for the Intercession of Our Lady of Guadalupe during the Plague of 1737*

of Blessed Felipe de Jesús and Santa Rosa of Lima, the area resplendent with the flickering light of great candles and tapers, that the archbishop's edict was read out accepting the election 'as principal patron of this city, the Sovereign Queen of the Angels, in her admirable Image of the miraculous advocation of the Guadalupe'.[13]

Within weeks of this ceremony, city councils and cathedral chapters in Puebla, Valladolid, Oaxaca, Guadalajara and Santiago de Guatemala, not to mention lesser cities such as Guanajuato, Toluca and Querétaro, all voted to authorize the trusted delegates of the Mexican *cabildos* to initiate proceedings which would lead to the election of the Guadalupe as patron of all New Spain. On 8 June 1737 Vizarrón entrusted Cabrera with the task of writing an account of the events of that year, persuading the city council to advance the funds necessary for its publication. And yet there the matter rested for several years. It was not until 1746 that the Guadalupe was finally recognized as universal patron. Just what caused this delay is not at all clear. Did the outbreak of war with Great Britain render the communication with Spain more hazardous? Or was the project to establish a college of canons at Tepeyac to officiate in the sanctuary a cause of delay?[14] Whatever the case, the matter stalled for nearly eight years.

One possible obstacle was indicated in a pamphlet published in 1738 by Juan Pablo Zetina, master of ceremonies at the cathedral of Puebla, in which he questioned whether the prayers devised for the feast of 12 December could be used before they were approved in Rome. Here was a challenge to which Cabrera responded in *The Patronage Disputed*, a tract he published in 1741 and which he incorporated into his *Shield of Arms*. From the terms of his reply, it is clear that Zetina had extended his criticism beyond the matter of prayers to object to the choice of a patron whose miraculous apparition had yet to be approved by the papacy. In short, although the archbishop had always insisted that the Congregation of Rites had to approve the choice of feast day and the prayers assigned to it, he had assumed that the election of a patron could be undertaken without first obtaining Rome's approval of the tradition relating to that image. It was to meet Zetina's challenge that Cabrera included within his book a long review of the literature dealing with the Guadalupe. But he first cited standard works on canon law, in which he argued that patrons of kingdoms or cities were always honoured through their images, only then to cite the Council of Nicaea to the effect that images were but representations of their heavenly originals. And what was the Guadalupe but a likeness of Mary in her Immaculate Conception? For an image to be venerated, it did not need to be miraculous: it could simply be acclaimed as holy. Moreover, inscription in the Roman Breviary and Martyrology did not guarantee the certainty of faith, since knowledge of many saints and images was based on tradition handed down from parents to children. In any case, many cities in America had adopted patrons for particular purposes, without consultation with Rome, since the distances and expense were so great.[15]

It was at this point that Cabrera signalized the theological justification of the Mexican initiative when he argued that the election of a patron was 'the deliberate, spontaneous promise of the Christian People especially to reverence under sworn oath some canonized saint, in order to obtain his intercession before God'. The function of Rome was simply to confirm this action of the Christian People. Undertaken when Mexico was a Christian commonwealth, governed as much by canon law as by the laws of Castile and the Indies, the choice of a patron was thus no mere Church ceremony: the initiative lay with the city council, albeit supported by the cathedral chapter and approved by the viceroy-archbishop. Although New Spain was governed by the absolute monarchy of the Bourbon dynasty, it was still possible for the representatives of civil society to vote and acclaim the Mexican Virgin as universal patron of the kingdom of New Spain. Any notion that the country was a mere colony, bereft of legal personality, was thus implicitly rejected; as indeed was the nineteenth-century assumption that so spiritual a matter had to be determined exclusively by the clergy.[16]

In the last resort, however, Mexico still had to obtain Rome's approval for its choice of patron, especially if the feast day was officially to be transferred to 12 December and given its own accompanying prayers. But to convince the pope and the Congregation of Rites, it was necessary to demonstrate that the Virgin's apparitions had actually occurred, that they had wrought much good for the Church in New Spain and that since its apparition the image had been the object of continuous devotion. As Cabrera was quick to emphasize, the historical certainty as regards the Guadalupe rested on tradition, since no documents concerning the apparition had ever been found. He himself had searched in the archive of the archbishopric but, although papers from Zumárraga's period of office still survived, no mention was made of the Virgin. In this context, he noted that Pedro de Mexquía, a Franciscan, claimed to have seen a letter about the apparitions from Zumárraga preserved in a convent at Vitoria; but that he had taken no copy. More to the point, Cabrera echoed Florencia in lamenting the loss of Sahagún's great history, which might have presented information; and added his own lament about the disappearance of the chronicle written by the sixteenth-century Dominican, Diego Durán, a text mentioned by Dávila Padilla. Turning to the written sources of the tradition, Cabrera was cavalier to the point of disrespect:

> The Cisneros enlightened us with the Image of Our Lady of Los Remedios; which the Sánchez, Becerras and Cruzes, and then with one or the other, the Florencias imitated and exhausted; in whose histories the imitation is clear, the embellishment shines forth, and indeed even the material of the first.

About the only new item of information he adduced was that the publication of Sánchez' book had been commanded by Marcos de Torres y Rueda, bishop of Campeche and interim governor of New Spain. For the rest, he queried whether the angel supporting the Virgin was indeed St Michael as Sánchez had asserted or whether it was St Gabriel as Florencia had argued, only then himself to opt for it being the guardian angel of New Spain, adding:

Lic. Miguel Sánchez, the first historian of this prodigious Apparition, who in his panegyric of the Most Holy Mary as regards Chapter twelve of Apocalypse, left us two miracles, that of this Apparition and that of his wit. He wished that that angel should be the Archangel Michael, as if he were Michaelangelo, who instead of a signature portrayed himself at the foot of the painting.

But Cabrera did not seek to arbitrate between Sánchez and Becerra Tanco, whom he regarded as the most reliable historians of the apparitions, and although he possessed a copy of Laso de la Vega's pamphlet in 'Mexican', he failed to realize that it was the latter's chief source. In any case, the most persuasive and reliable testimony was the 1666 depositions and in particular the witnesses listed by Becerra Tanco.[17]

Although Cabrera accepted the thesis that the Indians had preserved the memory of the apparitions, first in their 'maps and paintings' and songs and later in accounts written in 'Mexican', he fixed upon Florencia's citation of 'an old account' as indicating the existence of a primary source in Spanish. Unlike most subsequent authors, he observed the peculiarity that this manuscript was closer to Sánchez than to Becerra Tanco in that it listed a great diversity of flowers picked by Juan Diego. But he himself preferred the emphasis on roses, a flower whose association with the Virgin had been confirmed by the canonization of Santa Rosa of Lima. Indeed, he quoted a Jesuit, Cristóbal de Miralles, who had compared the Guadalupe and the Peruvian saint, claiming that the Virgin 'formed from another mystical, holy Rose a second canvas and portrayed herself in her. Those roses of Mexico were the mystery of ours, which they prefigured.' But Cabrera was quick to argue that whereas the rose of Lima had soon disappeared from the face of the earth, the roses of Guadalupe still remained embodied in the Virgin's likeness after over two hundred years.[18]

Where Cabrera scored was in his citation from Sigüenza y Góngora's *Heroic Piety*, of which he possessed a rare copy, where the savant affirmed that he possessed a manuscript in 'Mexican' written by Antonio Valeriano and that the 'old account' he had given Florencia was 'a paraphrased translation' of that manuscript made by Fernando de Alva Ixtlilxochitl. But Cabrera was not impressed. After all, had not the manuscript in Nahuatl already been printed by Laso de la Vega? As for Florencia's suggestion that 'the old account' had been written by Jerónimo de Mendieta, he dismissed that possibility on the grounds that the Franciscan had only arrived in New Spain in 1554. Instead, he suggested that it had been written by Francisco Gómez, a Franciscan who came with Zumárraga to New Spain in 1533 to act as the bishop's secretary. He thus inverted the sequence favoured by Sigüenza y Góngora and declared that what Florencia had seen was the original history of the apparitions which had been written during the lifetime of both Zumárraga and Juan Diego. It followed that what Laso de la Vega published was a very old account 'in the Mexican language, in which it was printed, and is believed to have been written or translated from that which the Franciscan, whom we believe was Fray Francisco Gómez, wrote in Castilian'. This interpretation did not necessarily exclude Valeriano, but it reduced him to the level of a mere translator.[19]

After comparing the first five authors who wrote about the Guadalupe to a flight of eagles soaring to the sun, Cabrera turned to Torquemada to list every occasion when he mentioned 'Tepeyac which is now Our Lady of Guadalupe'. But he discounted the Franciscan's silence about the apparitions, since Cisneros, who wrote on Los Remedios in 1616 only a year after the publication of Torquemada's chronicle, described the Guadalupe as numbering among the oldest images in New Spain. He also rejected the assertions of both Torquemada and Grijalva that the conversion of the Indians had not been accompanied by miracles, since in fact it had been the Virgin's apparitions which were responsible for the rapidity of the evangelization. Without comment, he dutifully cited Blessed Amadeus' reporting of Mary's promise to be present in her miraculous images to the end of the world, only then to argue that the conversion of the Indians was achieved as much through sacred images as by preaching. However, he then queried a central affirmation of the tradition when he argued that Zumárraga had not installed the image in the chapel at Tepeyac two weeks after the apparitions but had waited until his return from Spain in 1533. To support his assertion, he observed that there was an old canvas hung in the sanctuary which depicted the procession when Zumárraga took the image to the chapel and where the Indian who was accidentally wounded by an arrow was miraculously cured. But this painting, which had a note on its reverse assigning it to 1653, dated the procession to 1533. Moreover, he noted the presence of another painting by the same hand in which the Virgin was shown curing Indians of the plague, albeit without any children included, so that it probably referred to 1576 rather than to the miracle of 1544. For the rest, Cabrera followed Becerra Tanco in describing the image as 'woven from palms' and agreed with that chronicler that the Virgin's name in Nahuatl was Tequatlaxopeuh, which he translated as 'she who puts to flight those who like wild beasts devour us'. How appropriate it was , he added, that the Guadalupe should be venerated where once Chalchihuitlycue, Matlatcuaye and Tonantzin, all names for the same goddess, had been worshipped. Finally, Cabrera confirmed Florencia's account that Juan Diego's grandson, also called Juan, had given the Indian's small copy of the Guadalupe to the Jesuit, Juan de Monroy, who had given it to Juan de Caballero y Ocio, who had bequeathed it to Dr José de Torres y Vergara, archdeacon of Mexico, who left it to the cathedral. In 1743 this small bronze plate was placed in the new altarpiece of the cathedral, where it attracted much devotion, especially since it was rumoured that the Virgin herself might well have painted it for her beloved Indian disciple.[20]

Shield of Arms concluded with a brief account, inserted in 1747 after most of the book had been printed, of the arrangements for the public proclamation of the

Guadalupe as patron of New Spain. But news by then had arrived of the death of Philip V. Moreover, Archbishop Vizarrón had fallen ill and was bed-ridden. In the event, public celebrations were deferred to another year and instead, on 4 December 1746, the same four deputies who had sworn the oath in 1737, which was to say, Medina, Aguirre, Moreno and Ita y Parra, entered the archbishop's bedroom and in the name of 'all the venerable ecclesiastical chapters and all the most noble cities and councils of this New Spain and those of Guatemala, New Galicia and Vizcaya' solemnly swore to take 'Our Lady the Virgin Mary in her prodigious advocation of Guadalupe' as their 'Universal and General Patron'. As Cabrera commented, what place was more appropriate for such a ceremony than the archbishop's palace, since the current edifice had been built on the site of Zumárraga's residence, where the image had first been seen by that bishop? If public celebrations were deferred, nevertheless, Ita y Parra, by then treasurer of the cathedral, preached his sermon entitled 'The Circle of Love' in the sanctuary at Tepeyac on 12 December. A month later, on 25 January 1747, Archbishop Vizarrón y Eguiarreta, who had done so much to promote devotion to the Mexican Virgin, died.[21]

In his approbation of the *Shield of Arms*, written in 1744, José de Mercado indignantly cited Manuel Martí's *Latin Letters*, which described the Indies as an intellectual desert and noted that Gregorio Mayans y Siscar had republished the earlier comments of Nicolás Antonio, the great seventeenth-century bibliographer, that 'in the Indies all merchandise is traded save books'. In his own introduction Cabrera cited Benito Jerónimo Feijoo's *Universal Critical Theatre* (1726–39) and oddly praised Dávila Padilla's chronicle for its unadorned style. He also complained of the high cost of paper and the difficulties in publishing his book. Yet *Shield of Arms* was a handsome folio volume of 522 pages and included an attractive engraving designed by José de Ibarra.[22] If ever a Mexican was given the opportunity and funds to write a memorable book it was Cayetano de Cabrera. But, although he worked valiantly to obtain information, often searching in archives, he failed to rise to the occasion. To be sure, the copious data he provided make his book an invaluable work of reference for any history of medicine or religion in New Spain. But all future readers were to be deterred by his execrable style and interminable digressions, which obscured the intrinsic interest of the events he chronicled. In his hands he had documents which might have allowed him to write an account to rival Daniel Defoe's *A Journal of the Plague Year* (1722). After all, in the previous generation, Sigüenza y Góngora had written a concise, unvarnished narrative of the great riot of 1692 in Mexico City, when the mob had invaded the viceregal palace. Nor was it simply a question of baroque culture, since it was possible to deploy literary conceits and yet write with grace. But Cabrera was diffuse and often failed to achieve the effects he attempted. Some years after his death, José Ignacio Bartolache, a Mexican scientist, wrote:

I knew the author and greatly esteemed him, for his holy character and for his varied knowledge of literature . . . it was a pity that he had not been endowed with a temperament that was less bilious, acidic and melancholic. He was extremely lively and was absorbed in conceits and wit, not always of good sense, nor indeed of benign interpretation.[23]

Nor was this a solitary judgement, since Francisco Javier Conde y Oquendo, a canon of Puebla, also complained of the difficulties caused 'by the texture of his rhetoric, by the method, manner and phrasing . . . prolix, with a thousand, allusive and importunate digressions . . . and his rough, hard, biting style'.[24]

If these negative opinions were to damn Cabrera's reputation for posterity, soon after publication he was sharply attacked by the doctors whose efficacy he had so boldly questioned. Moreover, his blunt dismissal of the Indians as a race of drunkards offended official susceptibilities. Whatever the cause, in 1748 the authorities in Madrid ordered the viceroy to withdraw the book from circulation and confiscate all the copies that had not been sold. As a result, a book which had been so lavishly produced, funded by the city council to stand as a perpetual memorial to the election of Our Lady of Guadalupe as patron of New Spain, was subjected to summary censorship and thus quietly removed from the public domain.[25] And yet were an editor to be found, blessed with courage and skill, a remarkable book could still be extracted from Cabrera's prolix pages. As regards the formation of the Guadalupe tradition, Cabrera had little new to offer other than the ingenious theory that Valeriano was merely the translator of a Spanish account written by Zumárraga's Franciscan secretary. But what his account amply confirmed was the role played by the city council of Mexico in the election of the Guadalupe as patron. In the last resort, however, his work can be read as an intensely moving account of how a Christian society reacted to the ferocious onslaught of the plague and of its anguished efforts to obtain heavenly relief.

III

It was on 13 September 1756 that the inhabitants of New Spain were formally publicly informed that Pope Benedict XIV in his bull of 25 May 1754 had approved the election of Our Lady of Guadalupe as principal patron of their kingdom and had transferred the official celebration of her feast to 12 December, with a grant of its own office, 'with double rite of the first class and octave'.[26] The capital commemorated this joyous moment with a triduum of masses and sermons held on 9–11 November of that year. It was then that Dr Cayetano de Torres, a canon of the cathedral and professor of theology in the University of Mexico, paid tribute to his former Jesuit mentor, Juan Francisco López, who had conducted the negotiations in Rome. He recounted that when the Jesuit had shown Benedict XIV a copy of the Mexican Virgin painted by Miguel Cabrera, the pope had marvelled at its beauty. If the pontiff was so impressed, then the Mexicans were indeed justified in applying to the image the phrase 'Non fecit taliter omni natione', which was cited in the mass and office conceded by the Holy See. In a note, Torres adverted that it had been Florencia who had first applied the phrase from Psalm 147 to the Guadalupe, causing it to be inscribed on a medal he had commissioned. But Torres also emphasized Mexico's good fortune, since:

> The Holy Church did for the Image of Guadalupe what it is not accustomed to do for the other innumerable miraculous images of the same Lady . . . Without doubt the privilege of a particular Mass and Office granted to our Image of Guadalupe is a most singular favour and very difficult to obtain from the Apostolic See . . . Very rare are the images which have obtained it until the present.[27]

What rendered the case extraordinary was that the Mexicans were 'without original notices or authentic documents of the Miracle and Apparition'. As it was, the 'Oracle of the Vatican' had canonized the image. Whereas the identity of the Guadalupe as a representation of the Woman of the Apocalypse had merely been a concept for preaching, now that identity was 'a solid truth'. However, Torres left it to his congregation to decide whether St John saw in his vision a 'true copy of the Original of Guadalupe' or whether Mary had given Mexico 'the most living copy of the Original of St John'.

Later accounts confirmed that Juan Francisco López, a native of Caracas but educated in Mexico, was 'an individual of high gifts, of profound knowledge of theology and of fine, polished literature'. Already in 1751 appointed by the Mexican province of the Jesuits to act as its agent in Madrid and Rome, he was entrusted with the legal powers by the archbishop, the bishop of Michoacán, and the city council of Mexico, to promote the cause of the Guadalupe in those capitals. To assist his mission, he took with him 'two copies of the Holy Image, in the hand of the celebrated painter don Miguel Cabrera', one destined for Ferdinand VI and the other for Benedict XIV.[28] In Madrid he was assisted by the prior formation in 1743 of a congregation dedicated to the Mexican Virgin in which the king was named as senior brother (*hermano mayor*). That congregation had already arranged for the republication of Becerra Tanco's *Mexico's Happiness*, thus providing court circles with access to a convenient text. Moreover, López was undoubtedly assisted by Francisco de Rávago, the king's Jesuit father-confessor, who exercised great influence in all Church affairs.[29] In Rome itself he found copies of the Mexican Virgin and also any number of Becerra Tanco's pamphlet. What he failed to encounter in the papal archive was any reference to the 1666 *Statements*. However, he then came across a rare copy of an account of the apparitions published by Atanasio Nicoselli in 1681, where reference was made both to those depositions and to Becerra Tanco's evidence.[30]

Plate 13   J. S. and J. R. Klauber, *Benedict XIV recognizes Our Lady of Guadalupe as Patron of New Spain*

If Mexico succeeded where other cities failed, it was because the moment was propitious and because its petition was supported by powerful advocacy. It was in 1699 that the Congregation of Rites abandoned its hostility to 'canonizing' holy images, when it gave Our Lady of Loreto its own feast day and office for 8 December.[31] So also, in 1723, Our Lady of Pilar at Zaragoza was given its own feast day and office for 12 October.[32] At the time these two images, both of which were thought to have been carved by St Luke, had claim to be the senior Marian images in Italy and Spain. It was thus no small achievement for the Mexican Virgin to figure in their company, especially since there was apparently no question of a similar privilege being granted to the Spanish Guadalupe. But if the petition proved successful, it was because the ground had been carefully prepared. Unlike 1663–6, when little external evidence of the diffusion of the cult was presented, in 1751–4, López could cite the construction of a majestic new sanctuary as tangible proof of the faithful's devotion. More important, his case was immeasurably strengthened by the election of the Guadalupe as patron, not merely of the city of Mexico, but of the whole kingdom of New Spain. The fact that López could rely on the influence of fellow Jesuits, both in Madrid and in Rome, obviously played its part. What is not mentioned in any account is the source or the scale of the funds he undoubtedly employed to hasten the passage of his case through the offices of the papal court.

A contributory element in these negotiations was the establishment of a college of canons to officiate at the sanctuary at Tepeyac. In 1709 Andrés de Palencia left 100,000 pesos in his will for this purpose, a sum which with accumulated interest came to 170,000 pesos in 1727. After a complicated legal battle, his executor, Pedro Ruíz de Castañeda, son of the sanctuary's previous benefactor, advanced another 125,000 pesos. After the Roman authorities first approved the project in 1727, it was not until 15 July 1746 that the matter was finally settled by the papal court. By then, with the capital standing at 527,832 pesos, income was available to support an abbot, ten canons, six prebendaries, six chaplains, and an auxiliary staff of sacristans and a *mayordomo*. But it was not until 25 October 1751 that the college was formally established, since a furious quarrel had erupted between the new abbot and the archbishop over the question of patronage and jurisdiction. Although the abbot sought to obtain exemption, the new prelate, Manuel Rubio y Salinas (1749–65), forcefully argued that the Virgin herself had given her image to Zumárraga and that thereafter Juan Pérez de la Serna and Juan de Ortega y Montañés had been responsible for completing the construction of successive churches. Such was the vigour of his arguments, not to mention his personal influence, that the college remained under the patronage of the archbishops of Mexico. By the time it was erected, the village of Guadalupe had been transformed into a *villa* (22 July 1749), and a majestic aqueduct constructed to bring fresh water to the sanctuary, running through 19,935 yards of masonry supported by no fewer than 12,287 arches, an edifice which over the years 1743–51 had cost 129,350 pesos. All these facts and figures were proudly published as evidence of public devotion and generosity.[33]

Spanish knowledge of the Mexican Virgin had been assisted by the appearance of the *Universal History of the Primitive and Miraculous Image of Guadalupe* (1743), written by Francisco de San José, the former Jeronymite prior of the 'royal and holy house' of Guadalupe in Extremadura. His purpose was both to retell the story of the finding of this image and to trace the extension of its cult across the Atlantic. What strikes a reader familiar with Mexican rhetoric is the unimpassioned fashion in which the author related the apparition of the Virgin in 1322 to an unnamed herdsman to reveal the whereabouts of an image which, according to a lead plate found along with it, had been carved by St Luke and then sent by Gregory the Great to San Leandro, archbishop of Seville, before being hidden by priests fleeing from the Moors. It was an account which entirely lacked the moving simplicity of the *Nican mopohua* or the typological erudition of Sánchez. Instead, Francisco de San José was at pains to stress the royal patronage which had given charge of the sanctuary to the Jeronymites, their monastery soon enlarged by a hospital for pilgrims and a 'palace' for regal visits. He noted that Queen Isabella the Catholic had been devoted to the image and that Hernán Cortés had come to the sanctuary to offer thanks for his victories in Mexico. Such was the vitality of the cult that copies of the image were venerated across Extremadura and in Andalucia. Equally important, copies had been taken to South America, where important cults existed in Pacasmayo in northern Peru and in the Franciscan convent at Potosí. So too, by 1600 the city of La Plata, the capital of Upper Peru, had adopted another copy for its patron. As regards the Mexican image, Francisco de San José provided a faithful narration of the Virgin's apparitions to Juan Diego together with some account of her miracles. But, although he had to admit that the painting venerated at Tepeyac differed notably from the wooden figure in Extremadura, he asserted that it had been copied from a small sculptured image of the Immaculate Conception as the Woman of the Apocalypse which had been installed in the choir of the Spanish sanctuary prior to the conquest.[34]

In his history Francisco de San José also provided a sketch of the life of Blessed Amadeus of Portugal, who had spent his early years with the Jeronymites at Guadalupe before eventually joining the Franciscans in Italy, where with papal support he founded a reformed congregation of that fissiparous Order. Like so many other authors of this epoch, he cited the Virgin's promise to Blessed Amadeus that she would remain in her miraculous images until the end of the world, only then to exclaim that the spiritual power of the Spanish Guadalupe was such that pilgrims were often overcome by sorrow for their sins, so that 'in some way we can call this holy Image a sacrament of sorrow'. It was also from the Jeronymites at Guadalupe that Juan de la Puebla sallied forth to initiate the reform of the Castilian Franciscans, thereby laying the foundation of what eventually became the province of San Gabriel, whence came the twelve friars who arrived in New Spain in 1524.[35]

Prior to the Mexican negotiations in Rome, in 1746 there appeared in Madrid *Idea of a New General History of North America*, written by Lorenzo Boturini Benaduci (1702–53), a Milanese nobleman of ancient lineage, who had travelled extensively in New Spain, where he became consumed by a passionate interest in Mexican antiquities and a deep devotion to Our Lady of Guadalupe. It was in 1735 that Boturini abandoned the imperial court of Vienna, at which he had spent several years, and travelled to Spain, where he promptly undertook a pilgrimage to Zaragoza to visit 'the first temple in Christendom, of Our Lady of Pilar'. Arriving in Mexico in 1736 he witnessed the onslaught of the plague and may well have seen the public acclamation of the Guadalupe as patron of the capital. In the years which followed he collected a great quantity of manuscripts and native codices dealing with the Mexican past, all assembled with the aim of allowing him to reinterpret that history by the application of the theories of Giambattista Vico's *New Science* (1725). But such was his devotion to Our Lady of Guadalupe that without consultation with the authorities in New Spain he communicated with his acquaintances in Rome and thanks to the intervention of Alejandro Sforza Palavicini, on 11 July 1740, obtained from the basilica of St Peter's a *breve* authorizing the coronation of the Mexican Virgin as 'the sworn, postulated, principal patron of this vast empire'. It was in 1742, when he openly solicited funds to pay for the Virgin's crown, that the viceroy learnt of his presence in New Spain and of his bold initiative. Here were ample grounds for his arrest, since not merely had he entered Mexico without obtaining the requisite licence, but he had also infringed the rights of royal patronage over the Mexican Church, under which all communications with Rome had to be approved by the Council of the Indies. In the event, the judge who investigated the matter concluded that Boturini had acted in good faith and simply recommended that his extensive papers should be confiscated and he himself deported. But on his return to Spain, the Italian attracted the attention of Gregorio Mayans y Siscar and thanks to his support not merely published his *Idea of a New General History*, but was subsequently named Chronicler of the Indies.[36]

Appended to his book was a 'Catalogue of the Historical Museum of the Indies', in which Boturini listed all the manuscripts he had acquired during his years in New Spain. By far the most important part of his collection was copies of the manuscripts which Carlos de Sigüenza y Góngora had bequeathed to the Jesuit college of San Pedro y San Pablo, many of which in turn had come from the manuscripts gathered and written by Fernando de Alva Ixtlilxochitl. But he also found a number of native 'maps', sixteenth-century codices, which came from Sigüenza's collection and from other sources. It was thanks to these materials that Boturini was able to confirm Becerra Tanco's contention that the natives of Mexico had recorded their history in 'paintings', only then to write subsequent accounts in Nahuatl and Spanish.

Moreover, such was his sympathy for the creole tradition of scholarship that he accepted the theory of an apostolic mission to ancient Mexico. Although he lamented that he had been unable to locate Sigüenza y Góngora's essay on St Thomas as Quetzalcoatl, he announced that he had found an extensive set of notes dealing with that subject and had seen a native 'map' in which a Christian apostle was depicted.[37]

It was in that section of his Catalogue which dealt with the history of the Guadalupe that Boturini most decisively intervened in the development of the Mexican tradition. For he claimed to have seen both a codex where the chapel and its image were drawn soon after the conquest and a series of native annals which described the apparitions. So too, he had found any number of documents dealing with the cult in the sixteenth century, together with testimonies of the Virgin's presence in the city during the great flood of 1629–34. He had seen a lead plate and a primitive 'map' on which the apparitions were depicted and had a copy of the account written by Fernando de Alva Ixtlilxochitl. But it was his open attack on Laso de la Vega which commanded the attention of Mexican readers. How had it been possible for the chaplain to praise Sánchez' book in terms which revealed his ignorance of the apparitions and yet six months later write such a masterful account in Nahuatl? Of the 1649 *Huei tlamahuiçoltica*, of which he had a literal translation made, Boturini concluded: 'this is not, and cannot be, by the aforesaid author'. By way of a corollary proof, he noted that among the miracles included by Laso de la Vega was the incident when the Virgin prevented the transfer of San Juan Teotihuacan from the Franciscans to the Augustinians. But this event had obviously been recorded by the natives in a primitive 'map', so he argued, which Laso de la Vega could not have understood. Citing Sigüenza y Góngora's *Heroic Piety*, which he had seen in manuscript, he arrived at a peremptory conclusion. The real author of the 1649 text in Nahuatl was Antonio Valeriano, the well-known master of Torquemada and other Franciscans. As for Laso de la Vega:

> by chance he found an old manuscript of the Indian author and did no more than print it and put his name on it, thus taking from the Indians not merely the honour of having written it but also undermining the very antiquity of the history.

In these forceful assertions, Boturini thus lent all the weight of his authority as a scholar, uniquely qualified by his research to judge on such a matter, to support and extend the thesis first advanced by Becerra Tanco and later confirmed by Sigüenza y Góngora, that the Guadalupe tradition rested firmly on the account written in Nahuatl by an Indian disciple of the Franciscans.[38]

The degree to which Boturini's contribution was immediately assimilated in Mexico can be observed in the *Mexican Library* (1755), the first volume of an ambitious bio-bibliography written in Latin, which aspired to include all Mexican authors and their works, both published and in manuscript. Its author, Juan José de Eguiara y

Eguren (1696–1763), a canon of the cathedral and professor of the university, wrote a polemical prologue in which he sharply criticized the *Latin Letters* of Manuel Martí for their dismissal of American learning. In a vigorous defence of his compatriots, Eguiara y Eguren lauded the hieroglyphics of the Mexica as a true form of writing in which they had preserved the record of their history. Among the most detailed of the entries dealing with Spanish authors was that devoted to Carlos de Sigüenza y Góngora, in which he testified not merely to that savant's knowledge of Nahuatl but also to his skill in deciphering the meaning of ancient codices and their hieroglyphics, from which he had extracted a chronology of the native past. He lamented Sigüenza's failure to use the great collection of materials he had assembled to write more extensively on Indian history, but noted that much of the information presented by Giovanni Francesco Gemelli Careri in his *Journey Around the World* had been supplied by the Mexican scholar. A friend of Cayetano de Cabrera, he praised his *Shield of Arms* and cited him as an authority concerning the publication of Sigüenza y Góngora's *Heroic Piety*, a work that he himself apparently did not possess.[39]

Eguiara y Eguren was to preach an eloquent sermon on Our Lady of Guadalupe in 1756; but he also contributed to the consolidation of her tradition when in his *Mexican Library* he inserted an entry dealing with Antonio Valeriano. He described that disciple of the Franciscans at the college of Santa Cruz as a nobleman related to the emperors of Mexico, who had acted as governor of San Juan Tenochtitlan for over thirty years. Moreover it was not only Torquemada who had praised the Indian's knowledge of Latin and Spanish, since another Franciscan, Juan Bautista, thanked him for his assistance in the preface of a collection of sermons in Nahuatl and provided the text of a letter in Latin which Valeriano had written to him at his request. But for Eguiara y Eguren, Valeriano's 'golden crown' was his narration of the apparitions of the Virgin to Juan Diego, his authorship attested not merely by Sigüenza y Góngora but now also by Boturini. Even if Cabrera had claimed that the original account was written in Spanish by a Franciscan, it was clear that Valeriano was the author of the 1649 version published by Laso de la Vega. Careful to cite by page and volume all the books in which Valeriano was mentioned, Eguiara y Eguren thus firmly established the Indian as the starting point of all written accounts in Nahuatl on the Guadalupe.[40]

IV

The cult of Our Lady of Guadalupe cannot be fully understood unless it is seen within the context of any number of other Marian images which were also often housed in splendid sanctuaries frequented by pilgrims in search of cures and relief from their infirmities. In his approbation of *Marian Zodiac* (1755) Francisco Javier Lazcano, the Jesuit preacher, compared the Guadalupe to a sun circled by planets and as the moon surrounded by the stars.[41] It was for this reason he declared that if America was the Benjamin among the continents of the world, it was first as regards the favours of the Mother of God. Although all the religious Orders encouraged devotion to Mary, in this epoch it was Jesuit authors, and in particular Francisco de Florencia, who figured most prominently in tracing the history of those miraculous images of the Virgin which were most venerated in New Spain. Never published in his lifetime, Florencia's *Marian Zodiac* (1755) was issued in a revised, augmented form by Juan Antonio de Oviedo, a former provincial of the Mexican Jesuits. But this general description was matched by the reprinting of Florencia's *Origin of the Two Celebrated Sanctuaries of New Galicia* (1694) in 1757 and again in 1766. In his approbation of this latter work, Manuel Joaquín de Eguiara y Eguren characterized the Jesuit as 'the most celebrated historian of the principal images of Our Lady, which are venerated in this kingdom, whose fame endures and will remain immortal among those who have read his writings'. It should be recalled that it was in that treatise that Florencia repeated his citation from the *Apocalypsis nova* in which the Franciscan visionary was assured by the Virgin Mary that she would be bodily present in her miraculous images until the end of the world. So too, it was here that he cited St Peter Chrysologus as asserting that 'the Image and the Original are the same thing as regards their power, although different as regards their being'. It followed that the miraculous images of Mary should be approached on the understanding that the Virgin was present in them, much as Christ was present in the Eucharist. That this theological justification of the cult of holy images was republished as late as 1766 demonstrates the cultural consensus that united the generations that stretched from Miguel Sánchez to Juan José de Eguiara y Eguren.[42]

In *Marian Zodiac* no attempt was made to diminish the importance of Our Lady of Los Remedios for Mexico City and the surrounding valley, since devotion to this Virgin remained strong and whenever the seasonal rainfall was unusually late in coming her image was still brought in public procession to the cathedral. Here is no place for any detailed analysis of its contents, since among the 106 images listed by Florencia and Oviedo were many figures which were venerated in convents or Jesuit colleges. On others the information was perfunctory. Even so, we learn that Our Lady of Izamal, the principal Virgin of Yucatán, was carved in Guatemala and installed by Diego de Landa, the sixteenth-century bishop. It was in 1648 that it was brought to Mérida to relieve that city from the plague from which it suffered. A handsome sanctuary was built to house the image and welcome the pilgrims who came in search of assistance. So too in Oaxaca, Our Lady of La Soledad was blessed with a remarkably graceful church which was completed in 1686 and to which a convent of nuns was later added. In effect, amidst this universal outpouring of prayer, a spiritual geography can be discerned in which each city, district and province came to possess a thaumaturgic image which aroused devotion within a wide circumference of territory.[43]

In summary form, *Marian Zodiac* mentioned the rise of Our Lady of Zapopan, venerated in an Indian village close to Guadalajara, and of Our Lady of San Juan de Lagos, housed in a sanctuary in Jalostitlan, close to the road to Zacatecas, cults which were more fully described in the second edition of Florencia's 1694 treatise. Both these images had identifiable origins, since Zapopan had been brought from Spain by the Franciscans and San Juan de Lagos had been made in Michoacán from maize paste. It was in the course of the seventeenth century that they had become renowned for their cures, which in one case included a resurrection from the dead. It was after 1668, when the Virgin of Zapopan was taken to the cathedral in Guadalajara to halt the plague, that work began on providing the image with an adequate sanctuary. So too, it was in 1682 that the primitive chapel at San Juan de Lagos was replaced by a church with two towers, which in turn made way for an impressive new structure that was built during the 1730s. Reflecting on the two images, Florencia suggested that in the same way that some people thought that the Guadalupe was for Indians and Los Remedios for Spaniards, so equally Zapopan attracted Indian devotion whereas the Virgin of San Juan was most venerated by Spaniards.[44] To judge from the miracles that were performed by the latter image, it figured in the frontier world of cattle-ranching, silver-mining and freight trains. By the eighteenth century, when the new sanctuary was blessed with an exquisite chamber or *camarín* behind a silver altar and throne which was worth a thousand marks, it attracted pilgrims not merely from Zacatecas and San Luis Potosí but also from Querétaro and Mexico City. In a revealing comment, Florencia noted that both these sanctuaries had *peregrinas*, pilgrim copy images, which toured a wide circuit in search of alms. So strong was devotion to the Virgin of San Juan de Lagos that her annual feast, celebrated on 12 December, attracted over 10,000 pilgrims, and when her *peregrina* sallied forth it raised more in alms than the equivalent copies of the Guadalupe and Los Remedios, even in a city like Puebla, since it was such 'a thief of hearts'.[45]

Apart from Los Remedios, no other Virgin was accorded as much space in *Marian Zodiac* as Our Lady of Ocotlán, a much-venerated image housed in a majestic sanctuary just outside Tlaxcala. In this case, Oviedo drew upon the history published in 1745 and reprinted in 1750, written by its chaplain, Manuel de Loyzaga, who had raised over 90,000 pesos to fill the church with richly carved retablos and to construct an octagonal chamber, a *camarín*, behind the altar, which excited the admiration of visiting dignitaries. Since the first chaplain at the sanctuary had only been appointed in 1670, it was perhaps not surprising that Loyzaga could not find any juridical documents or early written accounts of the Virgin's origin, and thus simply relied on tradition, arguing that words on paper were not necessary when 'news from fathers to sons abound, always uniform, never varied, which makes for human faith'. Tradition here affirmed that shortly after the conquest an Indian called Juan Diego was walking to obtain water to help the sick during a plague, when the Virgin appeared to him and on questioning him as to where he was going said:

> Come with me so that I will give you another water, which will extinguish that con-
> tagion and heal not only your relatives but all who drink of it, because my heart,
> which is always inclined to favour the helpless, will no longer allow me to see so
> many misfortunes among them without offering them a remedy.

Mary then led the Indian to a thicket of occote trees, where the trunk of one of them
opened, allowing water to flow forth. After taking the water to cure the sick, Juan
Diego told the Franciscans at Tlaxcala of the apparition, but when they approached
the occote thicket they found the tree burning with fire, albeit like the bush on Horeb,
unconsumed by the flames. The next day, when they returned, Juan Diego and the
Franciscans found an image of the Virgin in the tree and joyfully carried it to the
nearby chapel of San Lorenzo, built on a small hill. The image was soon called Our
Lady of Ocotlán, which was a corruption of the Nahuatl, meaning 'the Lady of occote
which was burning'.[46]

Although evidence existed to suggest that in the 1640s the bishop of Puebla, Juan
de Palafox y Mendoza, had encouraged the cult of this statue of Mary, it was not until
the appointment of the first chaplain in 1670 that work began on building a substantial
sanctuary. It was the second chaplain, in the years 1691–1716, who raised a retablo
dedicated to Our Lady of Guadalupe. But with the appointment of Loyzaga, the Indian
artist, Francisco Miguel, completed the *camarín* and the main altarpiece. By then the
sanctuary was visited by pilgrims in search of relief and possessed a copy, a *peregrina*,
which each year was taken through neighbouring districts in quest of alms, its attend-
ants distributing 'prints of the Lady, taken from the Original, and pieces of bread
kneaded with holy water'. By this epoch images copied from Ocotlán were venerated
in Tepeaca and Córdoba and supported by confraternities. The devotion which this
miraculous image aroused was such that in 1741 Dr Antonio de Velasco, a wealthy
cleric, arrived with a troop of companions to spend five days in the sanctuary where,
together with musicians and priests, they celebrated mass and heard sermons,
chanted the seven canonical hours, recited the rosary and sang hymns. After this liturgical banquet, Velasco gave jewels to the Virgin and alms to the poor and in 1750
funded the reprinting of Loyzaga's history. Nor did funds dry up, since subsequent
chaplains continued to extend and decorate the sanctuary until it came to number
among the most exquisite examples of churrigueresque architecture in New Spain. It
was, of course, the very obscurity of the cult's beginnings which allowed Loyzaga to
encounter the tradition of its miraculous origin, according to which 'the angels who
from the beginning had hid it in the happy bosom of the occote, had already formed it
from a piece of the tree of life'.[47]

Lest the concentration on Marian cults distort our vision of Mexican Catholicism in this epoch, it must be emphasized that each church possessed a crucifix, often
rendered realistically in life-sized figures and usually designed to exhibit Christ's

sufferings. As we have seen, in Mexico City the Christ of Ixmiquilpan was venerated almost as much as the Guadalupe and Los Remedios. So too, the Christ of Chalma had become a cult image which attracted large numbers of pilgrims and was held to perform miraculous cures. It is striking that in the closing pages of *American Thebaid* (1729–40?), the Augustinian chronicler of Michoacán, Matías de Escobar, related the mysterious appearance of no fewer than ten crucifixes which were found carved in floating logs or in the entangled roots of trees, their features often only discerned after they had been cast into a fire. Such was the origin of the famous Christ of La Piedad, whose head was 'raised' from the surrounding wood by three Indian sculptors once it had been revealed by flames. In these stories it is as if Nature herself in the New World, once so filled with hostile spirits, now gave birth to any number of holy images, be they of Christ or Mary. In most of these cases, it was these figures which acted as the spiritual patrons of the rural communities which had emerged in these newly settled lands.[48]

But in this epoch the Mexican spiritual landscape was also inhabited by a quite different image of Christ. In his *Apostolic and Seraphic Chronicle* (1746) of the colleges of *propaganda fide* established by Observant Franciscan missionaries in New Spain, Isidro Félix de Espinosa (1679–1755) wrote that Melchor López de Jesús, one of the leaders of this revival of missionary preaching, appeared as:

> a mystical cross, a living portrait of Christ crucified . . . Every Friday he sallied out to the fields, barefoot, with a heavy cross on his shoulders, a cord at his neck, and a crown of thorns pressed so tight that at times drops of blood drawn from the thorns could be seen on his venerable face.

In effect, this generation of friars who arrived from the Peninsula preached sermons which concentrated on the sufferings of Christ in his Passion and called upon the faithful to do penitence for their sins. Wherever they went, they erected Calvaries and Stations of the Cross, devotions which followed Christ as he carried his cross to the place of crucifixion. The most influential of these Franciscans, Antonio Margil de Jesús, regularly scourged himself and during one sermon quit his habit while in the pulpit and lashed his shoulders with a heavy iron chain, eliciting compassionate groans from the congregation. For these friars imitation of Christ inevitably entailed a physical mimicry of their Saviour's suffering, and such was the force of their example that they left an indelible impress upon the forms of devotion in Mexico.[49]

Nor was asceticism peculiar to friars from Spain. From the first foundation of the college of Santa Cruz at Querétaro in 1683, young creoles were attracted by the discipline and fervour of these missionary institutes. As we have seen, Cabrera commented that during the plague of 1737 Franciscans from the college of San Fernando, which had only been founded in 1731, ministered to the poor and sick in their huts, their

Plate 14   St Luke painting the Virgin of Guadalupe, flanked by St John the Evangelist, Duns Scotus and Sor María de Agreda

exemplary zeal and ascetic virtues manifest among both European and American friars. Moreover, an enquiry conducted in 1749 found that the college of Our Lady of Guadalupe in Zacatecas, founded by Margil in 1707, was almost entirely composed of creoles recruited across the territories north of Mexico City. All three colleges, it should be noted, not merely maintained mission stations on the northern frontiers, in Texas and eventually in California, but also preached missions of repentance in parishes throughout the settled zones of New Spain.[50] And nowhere was the exemplary dedication of creole friars more apparent than in the case of Isidro Félix de Espinosa himself, since not merely did he accompany Margil in the first expedition to Texas, but he also acted as first president of the college of San Fernando and, when overcome by ill-health, devoted the remainder of his life to chronicling the great achievements of these 'apostolic missionaries'. Obviously, these Franciscans all preached devotion to Mary; indeed, Margil spent hours reading María de Agreda's *Mystical City*; and obviously the creole friars at Zacatecas promoted devotion to the Guadalupe across the northern territories.[51] But at the heart of their religion was an austere emphasis upon the sufferings of Christ and the teaching that salvation could only come from repentance for sins and imitation of the Saviour. Any account of Mexican religion that concentrates on Our Lady of Guadalupe to the exclusion of her Son will gravely distort the social and spiritual realities of this epoch.

7

Divine idea

I

When Francisco de Florencia dismissed the 'conceptual panegyric' of contemporary sermons in favour of 'the letter of history' which sustained the tradition, he indicated a fundamental dichotomy in the literature dealing with Our Lady of Guadalupe. As Cabrera's monumental chronicle demonstrated, the attempt to trace the existence of sixteenth-century manuscript testimonies of the apparitions was a hazardous project and exposed to considerable controversy. By contrast, during the first six decades of the eighteenth century the preachers who officiated at the rites which commemorated the stages through which the Mexican Virgin became the patron of New Spain exhibited a joyous confidence in the revelation of her sublime presence at Tepeyac. In essence they explored, extended and deepened the affirmations of Miguel Sánchez and José Vidal de Figueroa. Unmoved by the narrative simplicities of Becerra Tanco's translation of Laso de la Vega's Nahuatl text, they elaborated a theological celebration of the Virgin which combined scriptural typology, sacramental transfiguration and the neo-platonic theory of images. To read their sermons is a rare experience, since these preachers appear to have embarked on a vertiginous ascent, scaling the heavens in a series of metaphors which challenged the very limits of orthodoxy.

Of the sermons which celebrated the consecration of the magnificent new sanctuary at Tepeyac, completed in 1709, only *The Inmarcesible Marvel and Continuous Miracle* . . . (1709) survives in printed form. The preacher, Juan de Goicoechea, a Jesuit praised by his superiors for his 'good judgement, wit and learning', saluted the Virgin Mary since she wished 'to be an *Indiana*' and to appear as a 'crowned queen' and take up residence in this 'new Jerusalem, New Spain'. As once the Ark of the Covenant had been deposited in the temple constructed by Solomon, so now the image of the Mexican Virgin, 'a mystical incorruptible ark', entered her new sanctuary. If in Jerusalem the Jews had built three temples, each greater than its predecessor, so too in New Spain three churches had been raised at Tepeyac. The first chapel, built by Archbishop Zumárraga, had lasted for ninety years before being replaced by the sanctuary completed by Archbishop Pérez de la Serna in 1622. Now the third church, planned in the 1690s by Archbishop Francisco de Aguiar y Seijas, had been completed by the viceroy duke of Alburquerque and Archbishop Juan de Ortega y Montañés, their participation expressing the union of the ecclesiastical and secular arms of the commonwealth. As the Virgin's image was brought into the church it was accompanied by the Eucharist, 'the sacramental sun'. But if Christ's symbol was the sun, Mary was best represented by the moon, and nowhere more so than at Tepeyac, since the original meaning of *Meztli*, from which Mexico took its name, was the full moon. Should not Mary in her image of Guadalupe be addressed as 'precious pearl, imperial eagle . . . rose of Jericho and moon of the Mexican sea'?[1]

Turning his attention to the majestic sanctuary, Goicoechea praised its observance of the architectural principles of Vitruvius, since its proportions were identical to those of the human body. With the towers which crowned the four corners of the edifice, and the two side entrances which replicated the design of the façade, the building exhibited an exquisite symmetry. Citing Juan de Pineda, the Spanish scriptural commentator, he recalled that Solomon's Temple was thought to have had the shape of a lion, whereas it was clear that the Mexican sanctuary had the form of an outstretched eagle. The same symmetries could be observed in the image of the Virgin, since the canvas was divided into two pieces sewn together by cotton thread; and the sun rays, the crown and the supporting angel were similarly divided between the two sides of the painting. At this point, Goicoechea could not refrain from interjecting that the angel was obviously St Michael the Archangel. Returning to his theme, he recalled that the Israelites had deposited a jar of manna in the Ark of the Covenant and thereafter, despite its insubstantiality, they had placed it in the three successive Temples of Jerusalem. Were not the flowers and roses collected by Juan Diego like manna and, despite their fragility, had they not remained imprinted on his cape in the image? Yet two successive churches had been ruined by the humid, nitrous airs and soil of Tepeyac. How could the image's survival be explained save as a 'continuous miracle'? Be it made from a crude maguey cactus fibre or from the iczotl palm, as some had averred, it was but a coarse, weak cloth that should have perished long before the 180 years it had endured. Had not the former high altar, made from fine silver, come to look like a piece of old lead? From all these considerations there emerged a triumphant conclusion: churches and temples were doomed to disappear, even the present sanctuary; but the image of Guadalupe, the 'Mexican eagle . . . the eternal Phoenix', would endure for ever.[2]

From the comparison with the manna of the Old Testament, which had always been interpreted as a prefiguration of the sacramental bread, it was but a short step to compare the image of Guadalupe to the Eucharist and for Goicoechea to describe it as a 'sacramental image and sacrament of images'. In complicated prose he emphasized:

the continuous miracle, through which she is present in her painting, according to appearances, like Christ in the Eucharist, in which with the substance of the bread destroyed the accidents remain without the support of the substance, colours of bread and wine suspended in the air, like the colours of our Marvellous Phoenix, also suspended in the air.

In all this Goicoechea cited St Basil the Great and St Gregory Nazianzus on God's creation of light, which at its inception existed as pure form without accidents or indeed subject. So too, he took from the Jesuit scriptural commentators, Benito Pereyra and Cornelius Lapierre, the observation that the Eucharist resembles light in that it maintains the accidents of bread without a subject. From which he concluded that the image of Guadalupe in some sense resembled light, since the accidents of paint were supported without a subject. All this line of reasoning was based on the Catholic doctrine of transubstantiation, according to which the sacramental bread and wine were transformed into the body and blood of Christ without any observable change in the appearance or accidents of the bread and wine. Obviously, what was important here was not the scholastic doctrine, but the virtual equivalence established between the image of Mary in the Guadalupe and Christ's Eucharist, an equivalence based on the 'eighth rapture' of Blessed Amadeus of Portugal.[3]

In conclusion, Goicoechea argued that although Christ had promised to be with his disciples until the end of the world, obviously the Eucharist, which embodied that promise, would disappear with the advent of the New Jerusalem. But he then cited the promise of the Virgin Mary, as recorded in the *New Apocalypse*, that her miraculous images would endure until the last days. From this revelation Goicoechea deduced that although the new sanctuary at Tepeyac might well crumble into ruin, the image of Guadalupe would remain for ever, 'sacramented in a cape'. Throughout his sermon he thus insisted on the equivalence of the Eucharist and the image, defining the Mexican Virgin as a living, perpetual sacrament.[4] Although he compared the Temple in Jerusalem with the sanctuary at Tepeyac and presented Old Testament manna as a prefiguration of the image, he entirely eschewed the typological approach of Miguel Sánchez and indeed was more interested in Juan Diego's cape than in the Indian himself. Nor did he refer to the high-vaulting neo-platonic doctrines of Vidal de Figueroa. Instead, all the emphasis was on establishing the sacramental character of the image.

Not all sermons of this period exhibited such a firm grasp of theological issues. The central message of *Human and Divine Image . . .* (1738), preached by Miguel Picazo, a Mercedarian, was that the Guadalupe was the best representation of Mary's Immaculate Conception. Evoking the scene of Moses and the burning bush, he not merely interpreted the bush as a figure of Mary, but affirmed that what Moses actually saw in the fire was Mary as Guadalupe. Following Goicoechea, he then argued that Mary was as much Mother of Christ in the Eucharist as in the flesh, so that 'All the Lady's Being is the Being of the Sacrament . . . because the Flesh and Blood which Mary conceived sinlessly is sacramented in the Host.' All this led to the conclusion that 'Providence has offered us the knowledge of the Being of Mary Immaculate in these two images, the Host and the Guadalupe.' In framing this sermon, Picazo cited St John Damascene and St Theodore of Studios, and his censor quoted the Seventh General Church Council held at Nicaea, which had distinguished the Catholic veneration of holy images from the pagan worship of idols.[5]

The possibility that it had been Mary rather than God who appeared to Moses in the burning bush was also entertained by José Arlegui, a Franciscan chronicler, who promptly described the Virgin as a spiritual salamander. Noting that in the ancient world cities had chosen images of pagan deities as their patrons, imagining that they had descended from heaven, he observed that Mexico was truly fortunate since the Guadalupe had come from 'the mouth of the Highest Uncreated Wisdom'. But the purpose of *Sacred Palladium of the American Orb* (1743), preached in San Luis Potosí, was to offer thanks for the victory of Spain against the British navy and to warn his congregation about the threat presented by 'the power and fleet of England . . . the Lutheran heretic', from which only the Guadalupe could protect Mexico.[6]

The role of Franciscans in promoting devotion to Our Lady of Guadalupe throughout the vast northern territories of the viceroyalty of New Spain was signalized in 1707 when the new missionary college *de propaganda fide* founded at Zacatecas by Antonio Margil de Jesús took the Mexican Virgin as its patron. Here was an institute of friars who not merely established mission stations in Texas, but who also regularly conducted 'missions' to the faithful, preaching repentance and hearing confessions. Since the Zacatecas college came to be dominated by creoles, mainly recruited in the north, its friars undoubtedly also encouraged the cult of the Guadalupe.[7] In a sermon celebrating the consecration of their church in 1721, Matías Saénz de San Antonio recalled the scene of Moses striking the rock so as to procure water, only then to define the rock as the Franciscan college, the staff as Mary's image of Guadalupe, and the waters as the Christian gospel. This figural interpretation easily led him to define the church's patron image as an Ark of the Covenant and as the flowering rod of Aaron. In any case, was not Mary the particular mother of the Franciscans who had always been distinguished by their especial devotion to the Mother of God? So here, 'the Guadalupan image guards and defends from wolves' the poor defenceless friars of this missionary college. Citing the standard biblical commentators of this epoch, Benito Pereyra and Cornelius Lapierre, he pictured Jacob's ladder to heaven up which the Franciscans climbed, thanks to their arduous works, with Mary surrounded by angels at its upper rung helping her devoted children to ascend. What this sermon illustrated was that these subordinate or secondary sanctuaries dedicated to the Guadalupe were a potent means of spreading veneration across wide territories.[8]

By far the most attractive sermon of this period was preached by José de Villa Sánchez, a Dominican, in the hospital of Amor de Dios in Mexico City in 1733. Taking as his text Psalm 45 (44), where the king's daughter is depicted as receiving gifts from Ophir and Tyre, he argued that this signified that the natives of America would receive Christ through Mary. This affirmation was supported by the thesis that both the Indians and the Spaniards were descended from the ancient Tyrians and Carthaginians, as had been demonstrated by Gregorio García in his *Origin of the Indians* (1729). In a time-honoured comparison, he asserted that whereas the Marian images venerated in Rome, and of Pilar in Zaragoza and Guadalupe in Extremadura, had all been painted or sculpted by St Luke, by contrast it had been God who had sent the Mexican Virgin to America to convert its peoples. In an unacknowledged echo of Vidal de Figueroa, Villa Sánchez asserted that God had taken his copy 'from the same beauty, from the very face of the sovereign person of Mary . . . Most Holy Mary and her Image of Guadalupe are two portraits, identical twins, drawn by the same omnipotent hand, copied from that original which God has in himself.' Oddly enough, Villa Sánchez then qualified this resounding statement by admitting that the Guadalupe image did not resemble Mary either in life or in heaven, since in the flesh she was mortal and in heaven she was seated with eyes upraised, whereas in her image she was crowned and surrounded by the sun and had the moon at her feet.[9] But Villa Sánchez remained faithful to his neo-platonic masters when he asked: 'what is that sacrosanct person of the great Mother of God but an image of the divine goodness?'.

Where Villa Sánchez drew applause was in his audacious thesis that since God had sent 'this missionary image' of Guadalupe to Mexico, he had reserved the conversion of the New World to Mary. In a bold figure, he argued that the visit of the three kings to Bethlehem, guided by a star or the Holy Spirit, signified that Christ, a winged sun, had been born to bring light to the three parts of the world represented by those kings. By contrast, Mary in her Guadalupe image was the star of America, albeit bathed in the sun, and thus 'for this sacred image of Guadalupe was reserved the mission of this New World'. And what part of America was more appropriate for her appearance than Mexico, since the original meaning of *Metzico* was 'where the moon appeared'? Where once Indians had worshipped Teonantzi, they now venerated the true Mother of God. In effect, 'the American nations' drank the milk of the gospel from the breasts of Mary. Thus a clear antithesis was drawn between the Old and the New Worlds, with America the final, the particular domain of Mary. Implicit within this contrast was the notion that whereas the Old World was converted by the Word, America accepted the gospel through the image and thus was more illumined by the moon than by the sun.[10]

Not everyone accepted Villa Sánchez' revival of Vidal de Figueroa's thesis that God painted the Guadalupe, since in a sermon preached at the Royal Mint on 19 December 1747, Antonio de Paredes, a Jesuit, argued that since on Mount Sinai the Almighty had employed an angel to inscribe the Tables of the Law, so also he had used an angel to

Plate 15   The Holy Family with Mary as Our Lady of Guadalupe

paint the Guadalupe. His censor, Dr Alonso Francisco Moreno y Castro, agreed, naming as 'the finger of God' the archangel Michael, whom he described as 'the heroic royal notary, God's government secretary'. It was thus St Michael who painted the Mexican Virgin, and by way of a signature inserted himself as the angel sustaining Mary. For his part, Paredes praised his hosts by an ingenious metaphor in which he asserted that 'the coins of the king are gold, those of God are men; on those we see the royal image, on these the Divine'. Turning to the matter of his sermon, he cited St John Damascene as describing the Hebrew ark as 'an image of the divine . . . an Ark of the Covenant' joining the wills of God and Israel. In that ark Moses had placed the Tables of the Law, the testimony authenticating the image, whereas the Guadalupe was both ark and Tables, the image and its authentication, a true *scriptura dei*, the writing of God. If David had celebrated the ark with the words of Psalm 147, 'Non fecit taliter omni natione', so also in testimony of 'an excessive love', Mary had chosen the Mexicans or *Indianos* as her especial children, giving them her image as their ark.[11]

II

In 1731 dignitaries of Church and State gathered at Tepeyac to celebrate the two-hundredth anniversary of the apparition of Our Lady of Guadalupe. Only a few years later, in 1737, the same men returned to the sanctuary to beg the Virgin to save the capital from the plague that had slain thousands of its citizens. When relief was forthcoming they proclaimed the Guadalupe the patron of Mexico City. As we have seen, other cities and dioceses in New Spain followed suit and, in 1746, delegates of the city councils and cathedral chapters of the entire viceroyalty acclaimed the Mexican Virgin as their universal patron. If these initiatives expressed the ever-rising tide of devotion, they were authorized and in part inspired by the cathedral chapter of Mexico City, a body of creole clergymen renowned for their learning and patriotism. On all these grand occasions, the preacher was Dr Bartolomé Felipe de Ita y Parra, a native of Puebla educated by the Jesuits, who was later described as 'illustrious as much for his virtue and learning as for his lineage'. The nephew of a canon of Puebla and of a well-known Jesuit, Ita y Parra entered the cathedral chapter of Mexico as a junior prebendary in 1723, became a canon in 1727 and was finally rewarded for his eloquence by appointment as treasurer in 1747. Like other canons, he lectured in theology at the University of Mexico.[12] Recognition of his ability as a preacher was evident when in 1728 he was chosen to pronounce the funeral eulogy at the burial of Archbishop José Lanciego y Eguilaz and, still more, when he represented the chapter and secular clergy of the diocese in 1729 at the celebrations which marked the canonization of St John of the Cross. In that sermon he referred to St Augustine as 'my beloved father' and praised St Teresa of Avila as another Moses who had refounded the Carmelite Order and 'whom followed the Joshua of our Juan as her son, her disciple and founder'. The preacher's fondness for typological metaphors and figures was to find expression in the four sermons that he dedicated to Our Lady of Guadalupe.

In *The Image of Guadalupe, Lady of the Ages*, preached at Tepeyac on 12 December 1731 before the viceroy, the archbishop and other dignitaries, Ita y Parra cited St John Damascene to argue that Mary had been expected since the creation of the world, her genealogy traced by St Matthew across the generations from Adam, so that she could be justly acclaimed as 'Lady of the Ages, Queen of the Centuries'. Fixing upon the 46 stars on the Virgin's mantle, the hundred rays that enveloped her, and the twelve rays of her crown, he concluded that the image 'was miraculously shaped in the office of the Omnipotent; her painter was the guardian angel of this vast empire of the Indies'. The survival of the image for two hundred years, despite the fragility of its *ayate* canvas, caused him to salute it as a 'phoenix rising from decrepitude, a rival of the eternal'. More to the point, he described it as 'a permanent column . . . to guide the *Indianos* to heaven as the Israelites were led to the Promised Land'. Citing the sermon of José Vidal de Figueroa, like himself a canon 'of this holy church of Mexico', he declared that the image was a perfect portrait of Mary which had come from eternity. Moreover, he differed from Goicoechea in asserting that the image would remain even after the world ended. Had not the Spanish Jesuit, Juan Eusebio Nieremberg, argued that the Eucharist would continue to be present after the Last Judgement, an opinion based on the writings of St John Chrysostom and St Gregory Nazianzus? If that was the case, then surely the Guadalupe image would also survive in eternity, placed on an altar in heaven alongside the sacrament, the cross and the four gospels.[13]

It was in *The Mother of Health: The Miraculous Image of Guadalupe*, preached on 7 February 1737 at Tepeyac before the Archbishop-Viceroy Vizarrón y Eguirreta and the capital's elite, that Ita y Parra besought the Virgin to rescue the city's inhabitants from the effects of the plague. He reminded the congregation that only a short while before, he had preached to them in the cathedral, when the image of Our Lady of Los Remedios had been brought from her sanctuary and placed on the high altar in a desperate plea for succour. On that occasion he had been stern, no doubt blaming the plague on the sins of the faithful. But here at Tepeyac he sought to reassure and comfort his listeners. Why was it, he queried, that whereas Los Remedios had been brought into the city, now the city had come to the Guadalupe? The reason was all important. Was not Los Remedios an image which had been brought by the conquerors from Europe, coming 'to be the Lady of all these dominions'? But if all America belonged to her, she was a perpetual pilgrim, 'without any place of her own'. By contrast, the Guadalupe had appeared in Tepeyac, and it was here that she had her palace and her throne. Reworking the typological figures favoured by Sánchez, Ita y Parra declared that 'the image of Los Remedios is the Ark of the Covenant', since it had been carved by human hand, much as had the original ark. Moreover, it was

constantly brought into the city, much as the Israelite ark had been taken from place
to place until David finally deposited it in the Temple. By contrast, 'the burning bush,
in which God appeared to Moses, is, I say, this sovereign image of Guadalupe'. It had
been 'Bishop Theodore' who had defined the bush as a figure of Mary, but although
'he talks of the burning bush of Horeb, it seems like he is talking of the *ayate* of
Guadalupe'. For if the rough branches of the bush had survived the fire, so equally the
fragile *ayate* had been preserved from the destruction wrought by the centuries. In a
more obvious reminiscence of Sánchez, Ita y Parra also declared that Los Remedios
was Ruth, and the Guadalupe Noemi, since Ruth was an immigrant Moabitess,
whereas Noemi was a native of Bethlehem. Drawing the conclusion from these
comparisons, he argued that if Los Remedios had not brought any relief from the
plague, it was because don Juan, the Indian nobleman who had discovered the image,
himself had walked to Guadalupe to be healed of his illness. After all, had not the Virgin promised Juan Diego to be a merciful mother and to help all those who sought her
in their necessities? It was for that reason that the city had come to her sanctuary. The
sermon concluded with an appeal from Ita y Parra for the city council and cathedral
chapter to unite to swear allegiance to the Guadalupe as the 'universal patron of all this
kingdom'.[14]

The third sermon of Ita y Parra, *The Image of Guadalupe, Image of Protection*,
preached at Tepeyac on 12 December 1743, was preceded by a long approbation written by José de Elizondo y Valle, the *mayordomo* of the sanctuary, who cited
Christopher Columbus and Tomás Malvenda to support his view that America was
the original site of paradise. Indeed, the hemisphere still preserved much of its original
condition, since apart from its natural abundance and fertility, it also enjoyed a perpetual spring. God had separated the New World from the rest of humanity and had
endowed it with insuperable riches. Moreover, its universities cultivated the sciences
to great effect, and saints like Santa Rosa of Lima had blessed its Church. Then again,
'Of all the monarchies of the world, that of Spain, the synonym of being Catholic, is
the most pure in faith.' If all this were not enough, no other nation on earth possessed
a holy image like the Guadalupe, which had been painted by God himself, with 'the
brush of his omnipotence', an image which was now venerated in Spain by Philip V,
who had become senior brother of the congregation of the Mexican Virgin founded in
Madrid.[15] The patriotic emotions that entered the cult of the Guadalupe can be readily
observed in the approbation written by José Torrubia, a Spanish Franciscan, who declared that all Mexico had been affronted by the recent publication of the letters of the
learned dean of Alicante, Manuel Martí. For this scholar had warned a young disciple
not to go to the Indies, since he would find few, if any, libraries and little cultivation
of letters. In this damning opinion, so Torrubia noted, Martí had simply echoed the
famous Spanish savant, Nicolás Antonio, who, in 1663, had stated that the Indies only
produced gold and silver so that 'they are only for men who want to bury themselves,

oblivious to all that is virtuous and precious in Europe'. And yet in his *History of Tobías* (1667), Antonio Peralta Castañeda, a Spaniard who became canon of Puebla, had declared that he had found as much knowledge in America as in Spain, albeit poorly rewarded and scorned in Europe. Only recently, in his *Universal Critical Theatre* (1730), Jerónimo Feijoo Montenegro, a Spanish Benedictine, had defended the talents, achievements and learning of the Americans against the vulgar prejudices of his compatriots.[16]

In his sermon Ita y Parra drew upon neo-platonic theology to exalt the image of Guadalupe before commenting on the destiny of the *Indianos*, the natives of the Indies, be they Spaniards or Indians. He began by defining the relation between the Divine Word made flesh and Mary, the Mother of God:

> Incarnating the Word, the Image came to earth and came to another Image . . . which is to say, that as the Word was the substantial image of the Father and man was created in the image of God, so an Image came to earth and came for another image . . . The Image, which came to earth incarnating the Word, appeared as the original of that other image which Mary formed, allowing it to be seen in Guadalupe.

What this piece of convoluted prose appears to mean is that the Divine Word, the image of the Father, was incarnated as man in Mary, who, like all humanity, was an image of God. At the same time, Mary appeared on earth in the flesh as the original of her image of Guadalupe, which thus could be seen as a faithful likeness of how the Virgin appeared in the Holy Land.[17] In an equally ingenious simile, Ita y Parra cited St Paul's Letter to the Hebrews, where it was written that despite his divinity, Christ had assumed the coarse cape of human nature, only then to assert that although not incarnated, Mary had appeared in the cape of Juan Diego so as to help convert the Indians. Moreover, in the same way that Christ perpetuated his Incarnation through his real presence in the Eucharist, so Mary remained unchanged in her image of Guadalupe. It was thanks to her permanent presence in her image that although mother of all humanity through Christ, Mary was in a particular degree the mother of the Indians. Only at the close of his sermon did Ita y Parra allude to contemporary polemics and Manuel Martí, when he criticized José de Acosta, the celebrated Jesuit chronicler of the sixteenth century, for denying the Indians the possibility of salvation prior to the arrival of the Spaniards. So too, the leading colonial jurist, Juan de Solórzano Pereira, had described the natives of the New World as mere savages. Why did European authors entertain such a low opinion of the natives of the New World, he exclaimed, especially since Gregorio García had pointed to the discovery of crosses in America as evidence that the apostles may well have preached the gospel to the Indians? By way of conclusion, Ita y Parra asserted that in the same way that men had been rendered superior to the angels by Christ's Incarnation, so the apparition of the Guadalupe had rendered 'the *Indianos* superior to other nations'. As will be observed, whereas Goicoechea had fixed upon the equivalence of the Eucharist and the Guadalupe image, Ita y Parra here suggested the equivalence of Christ's Incarnation and Mary's apparition in her Mexican image.[18]

Given the success of his previous sermons, it was perhaps inevitable that Ita y Parra should have been asked to preach the sermon on 12 December 1746 in which 'America Septentrional' swore to accept Mary in her image of Guadalupe as patron of all the kingdom. By now treasurer of the cathedral and loaded with lesser offices, Ita y Parra began *The Circle of Love* by citing the inscription that by then adorned many copies of the image, 'Non fecit taliter omni natione', and interpreted this line of scripture to mean that the *Indiano* now exceeded the ancient Israelite, that 'America is now super-ior to Judaea'. Citing the prophet Jeremiah and his commentator Cornelius Lapierre, he affirmed that in their idolatrous lapses the Israelites had sacrificed to the Queen of Heaven, a moon goddess taken from Egypt, whom he identified as Diana, to whom they offered bread prepared like communion hosts. Was not all this but a shadowy prophecy and figure of how the *Indianos* now came to honour Mary in her sanctuary? The sermon was preached in the presence of the Eucharist, which he alluded to as 'this sovereign host, this sacred placenta'. As for the Guadalupe image, no human artifice had shaped it; 'a Divine hand imprinted it. In the offices of the Omnipotent a copy was taken: *opus coeli* . . . this sacred copy, image of the Most Pure Conception'.[19]

Warming to his theme, Ita y Parra declared that when Christ had taken Mary as his Mother and she had taken him as her Son, they formed a sacred circle of love. But in the Guadalupe image Mary had given herself to the *Indianos* as their mother and now the '*Indiana* nation' was about to acclaim her solemnly as its perpetual patron and mother, thereby completing the circle of love. So overwhelmed was Ita y Parra by this spectacle that he affirmed: 'for the image of Mary in Guadalupe, the image of the Word came to earth . . . what in the image of the Word is not recognized, is admired'. Which was to say, that Christ's Incarnation had as its ultimate end the apparition of his Mother in the Guadalupe image. After all, as St John Chrysostom had observed, during the Incarnation, 'that celestial image of the divine, became in time an image of the human', the son of David. Once more, Ita y Parra compared Christ and Mary in Mexico. If Christ had appeared like fire, as in the burning bush on Horeb, so equally at Tepeyac 'the Moses of the Indies', Juan Diego, had been confronted with another burning bush in which Mary appeared as light, burning with the fire of the sun, the moon and the stars. And yet, what do we see in the image but 'a beautiful, modest *Indiana*? The tunic, the mantle, the dress is all of her nation', all inscribed on 'a poor, humble, coarse *ayate*, which served as her tabernacle'. If Christ had become a despised Israelite, so the Sovereign Empress of the Heavens had become a humble, despised Indian. However, Christ had not been received or acknowledged by his people, whereas in America the image of Mary was welcomed at

Plate 16   Joaquín Villegas, *God the Father painting Our Lady of Guadalupe*

once. If Mary was the best image of the Divine Word made man, it followed that
through her the *Indianos* were led to her Son. Finally, Ita y Parra argued that when
Christ on the cross asked St John to take Mary as his mother, she thereby became
the necessary and natural mother of all the faithful. But thanks to her image of
Guadalupe, Mary had also become the adopted mother of the *Indianos*, who thus were
both the natural and the adopted children of Mary.[20]

Only a year after this exuberant address, on 7 February 1747, Ita y Parra pronounced
a funeral oration in the cathedral, *Carried off by God*, in which he lamented the death
of Philip V. In his approbation, Juan Antonio de Oviedo, twice provincial of the Jesuits in this epoch, praised the preacher's many printed sermons and noted that he himself had studied philosophy with him. Citing Athanasius Kircher's *Subterranean
World* and his *Oedipus Aegyptiacus*, he briefly mentioned the art of torches, whose
flames were undying, perpetual. More to the point, the other censor, José Torrubia, a
Spanish Franciscan, praised the deceased monarch for his success in keeping the
Spanish monarchy united when its English and Dutch enemies had threatened to
divide it. As for Ita y Parra, he took as his text Psalm 135, of Israel weeping by the waters
of Babylon at the loss of their king, and referred to 'Grief-stricken America, my
illustrious, beloved *patria*'. Ingeniously, he deepened the conventional compliment
of saluting Philip V as another David by dubbing the last Habsburg, Charles II, as a
Saul. There followed mention of the battles which had preserved Spain from division.
After the piety, chastity and learning of this indolent, uxorious monarch were duly
praised, the eulogy concluded by calling upon Our Lady of Guadalupe to help the
new king, Ferdinand VI. The deep patriotism that animated devotion to the Mexican
Virgin was thus still comfortably united to a strong loyalty to the Catholic monarchy
of Spain.[21]

III

When in 1754 Benedict XIV recognized Our Lady of Guadalupe as patron of New
Spain and sanctioned the celebration of her feast day on 12 December, he assigned as
the gospel reading for the feast St Luke's account of the Visitation, which is to say,
when Mary, already expectant with Jesus, left Nazareth and went to a city of the hills of
Judaea, where she entered the house of Zacharias the priest, the husband of her cousin
Elizabeth. Once received in Mexico, the apostolic bull was greeted with festivities in
which preachers were quick to appropriate St Luke's text for the purpose of expound-
ing the sublime analogies between the Visitation and the Virgin's apparition in
Guadalupe. In a sermon delivered in the cathedral on 11 November 1756, Dr Cayetano
Antonio de Torres, a prebendary, remarked that whereas Mary had only stayed with
Elizabeth for three months, by contrast she had come to Mexico to stay for ever, 'the

gift of the copy being even more miraculous than the visit of the Original'.[22] In more fanciful strain, Pedro Herboso, a Dominican preaching at Tepeyac on 13 December 1756, pictured Mary as travelling in a carriage drawn by cherubim, only then to be welcomed by 'the child John joyfully dancing in the cloister of his mother Elizabeth', an elegant reference to the child in Elizabeth's womb, the future St John the Baptist.[23] So too, Andrés de la Santísima Trinidad, a Carmelite, cited the usual scriptural commentators, including Tomás Malvenda, to the effect that Mexico had been founded by the ten lost tribes of Israel. If this was the case, then as in the Visitation, Mary came to Mexico to be among the Jews, an argument which concluded with a resounding exordium: 'Sanctified since eternity, Mexico was that city which was chosen as a happy Zion, city of the Great King.'[24]

Among the most happy of this cycle of sermons was that preached in the cathedral on 10 November 1756 by Dr Juan José de Eguiara y Eguren (1696–1763), the celebrated author of the *Mexican Library* (1756). Taking St Luke's verses as his text, he began with a question:

> Where are you going, Most Pure Lady? Mother of the Most Holy God, where are you going? Did you leave your holy house in Nazareth for the mountains of Judaea? Or did you leave the august palace of the Empyreum to go to the Mexican Tepeyac? Are you walking to Hebron or to Mexico? Are you looking for the house of the prophet and priest Zacharias or that of the venerable pontiff Zumárraga?

Like most commentators, he accepted that Mary went to Hebron, and then drew a comparison between that hill city and Mexico, the equivalence of the Visitation and apparition confirmed by the similarity in roles of Zacharias and Zumárraga. But whereas Mary saluted Elizabeth with the canticle later known as the Magnificat, she greeted America (which should have been named after Queen Isabella the Catholic) with the image of Guadalupe. In choosing a painting, the Virgin had accommodated herself to 'the style of the country and of the Mexicans', since their books had been filled with figures, symbols and hieroglyphs. After all, had not Gregory the Great declared that paintings were the books of the ignorant? As God had inscribed the Ten Commandments on the Tables of the Law for Moses on Mount Sinai, so equally the Virgin herself had painted and coloured her image for Juan Diego, without any intercession of angels acting as artists. The effect of her apparition had been to destroy idolatry, expel demons, convert the Indians and ensure peace for 225 years. Moreover, New Spain had imitated Elizabeth in welcoming the Virgin, taking her to its heart, building churches in her honour and offering countless prayers, masses and pilgrimages as well as 'printed books, histories, sermons, poems and other ingenious writings'.[25] In drawing out the analogies between the Visitation and the apparition, Eguiara y Eguren admirably defined the prophetic character of scripture when he commented on St Luke's text:

You see a history, like all those which are, of the past; and at the same time a history, like many of the sacred, of the future: because the future event of Guadalupe was prophesied and foreseen in the past journey, visit and salutation of the great queen.[26]

In effect, the papal approval of a particular mass for 12 December was seized upon as sanction for a typological interpretation of St Luke's text, the New Testament thus offering figures of the revelation in Mexico.

If the cathedral chapter of Mexico City had taken the lead in securing Rome's approval of the cult of Our Lady of Guadalupe, so equally the Company of Jesus had played a prominent role in preaching and writing treatises devoted to the Mexican Virgin. Indeed, in his approbation of Paredes' sermon, Dr José Mariano de Elizalde, Ita y Parra, the current rector of the university, had praised the Jesuits for their angelic labours in exploring the mysteries of their country's 'sacred Hieroglyph'.[27] It comes as no surprise, therefore, to find Jesuits prominent in greeting the papal recognition of the Guadalupe as universal patron of New Spain. In his *Panegyrical Sermon*, given at Tepeyac on 12 December 1758, Francisco Javier Lazcano (1702–62), a Jesuit who taught the theology of Francisco Suárez for twenty-six years at the University of Mexico, began by praising the capital as 'our imperial court, head of Septentrional America', only then to affirm that no matter what its riches and beauties, it was most distinguished by the 'image of Mary painted by the same Lady'.[28] Like most orators of this epoch, Lazcano insisted that the most celebrated images of Mary in Italy and Spain had been painted or sculpted by St Luke and thus were of human devising. For sure, angels had brought the image of Our Lady of Pilar to Zaragoza, but 'this miracle, founded on legitimate tradition, only flatters the hearing, not the irrefutable testimony of the eyes'. By contrast, in Mexico 'we see what no other Nation has seen: 'Non fecit taliter omni natione', which was to say, that 'the Hispanic Moctezuma Nation' saw an image painted by Mary herself.

As with most sermons of these years, Lazcano compared the visitation to the apparition of Mary in the Guadalupe. If Mary had given birth to 'the Image of the Eternal Father, figure of the substance of the Divinity', in Mexico she 'portrayed to life her incarnated Jesus in the luminous mirror of her most beautiful face'. In the Old World the apostles had converted the peoples by preaching the Word, whereas in Mexico Mary had converted the Indians through her image. If at Pentecost the apostles had spoken in many tongues, in America the Guadalupe was at once understood by all peoples. When St Peter had seen a great scroll in heaven inviting him to eat all things, was it not possible that therein he had seen the Guadalupe, since the Indians were like fish – deaf, dumb and barbarous? In a series of complex metaphors, Lazcano then exalted the Mexican Virgin with audacious confidence. Although Mary had appeared in the flesh in Palestine and in vision to St John on Patmos, her apparition in

Plate 17   Antonio Baratti, *The Soul of the Virgin Mary is Our Lady of Guadalupe*. The Virgin is flanked by St John the Evangelist and St John Damascene; below are her parents, St Anne and St Joachim; and above her appears the Holy Trinity

Mexico was 'superior, not in the substance, but in the mode'. Although Mary uttered the Magnificat during her visitation, she comported herself as a passing 'guest and stranger', whereas 'she wished to be our compatriot, to be a native and as if born in Mexico; to be conqueror and first settler'. After all, was not 'to appear' much the same as 'to be born'? If this equivalence was accepted, then 'this Mary was born in Nazareth, the fruit of St Anne's womb; she appeared in Mexico as the sovereign production of her hands. In Nazareth, Mary appeared. In Mexico she was born a prodigy.' After such assertions it was only to be expected that Lazcano should have declared that 'the painting of the Apocalypse had been the copy and our Guadalupe the original'. But he surpassed other preachers when he invited his congregation to admit that were it not for the truths of the Catholic faith, they would be on their knees worshipping Mary in her Guadalupe image as the 'supreme Goddess'. His panegyric reached an imperial conclusion when, on commenting on the papal letters accepting the Guadalupe as patron of New Spain, Lazcano exclaimed: 'Mexico received the faith of Jesus Christ from Rome. Now Mexico has paid back Rome with the apostolate of the most tender love of Mary. The Sovereign Tiara bends the knee before the miraculous Mexican.'[29]

The last of these Jesuit panegyrics was preached at Tepeyac on 12 December 1765 by Juan José Ruiz de Castañeda, scion of a noble family which had lavishly contributed to the cost of the third sanctuary, who was appraised by his superiors as of 'good learning, wit and judgement'. He followed Lazcano in claiming that in scripture 'to appear' is used as a synonym of 'to be born'. He thus described Christ's Incarnation as 'the Image of the Divine Word as it appeared in the world, stamped on the coarse canvas of our human nature'. But then Mary imitated 'that apparition of the incarnate word' and appeared as 'a Mexican maiden', dressed like the natives of this kingdom so that:

> She came down from heaven to be incarnated in that *ayate*, returning as if to be conceived and be born, so as to impress that canvas with her second Conception and Birth, in imitation of the Conception and Birth of Christ.

In effect, as Christ took human nature so Mary took the likeness of the Indians and, if he was born of human flesh, she was born of roses in a second Nazareth. Not content with establishing the equivalence of Christ's Incarnation and Mary's apparition in Mexico, Castañeda then asserted that the apparition was 'in a certain way similar to the eternal generation of the Word'. After all, for over two centuries the Guadalupe had not changed, remaining perfectly illumined amidst the light of the sun, the moon and stars so that she presented a perpetual apparition, which was 'the Image of the Conception of the Lady Mary or the same Conception repeated in that Image'.[30] All that remained for Castañeda was to reiterate the common Jesuit comparison between the Guadalupe and the Eucharist, affirming that:

if in the sacrament the accidents maintain themselves without their own subject, how great is the similarity of those colours that in the painting are the accidents, conserved there by a special miracle, without their previous disposition or preparation.

At the consecration of the Eucharist priests perpetuated Christ's Incarnation; so too at all times, Mary sustained her image, which in the continuous apparition was an extension of her Conception. Thus, in the brief limits of a printed sermon, Castañeda had demonstrated that Mary in Guadalupe imitated Christ as man, as God and as sacrament. All that remained was for him to comment that whereas on Calvary Mary had silently accepted St John as her son, at Tepeyac she had spoken to Juan Diego, a sure sign of her especial love for Mexico and its peoples.[31]

No feature of all these sermons was more paradoxical than the absence of prophecy. Although preachers frequently cited biblical commentators such as Benito Pereyra and Cornelius Lapierre, who were influenced by the writings of Joachim of Fiore, all of their arguments centred on establishing the unique significance of the Guadalupe image. It was their Church's moment of foundation rather than its future destiny which caught all their attention. To this general rule, however, one striking exception can be found. In *The Transmigration of the Church to Guadalupe* (1749), Francisco Javier Carranza created a stir when he asserted that in the last days of the world the pope would abandon Rome and take up residence at Tepeyac. A later critic commented that in the congregation of Our Lady of Guadalupe in Querétaro, 'some applauded the ingenuity of the orator and others criticized his strangeness'. For all that, its Jesuit censors praised the preacher as prophet and drew elaborate comparisons between Rome and Mexico, the metropolis of the Old World as against the metropolis of the New. But not all his brethren were so impressed, since Carranza's Jesuit superiors assessed him as 'of wit and profit the best; of mediocre judgement, and in prudence barely mediocre'. And although he was reckoned to have 'talent for the ministry and preaching', the rector of the college of Espíritu Santo in Puebla refused to have him owing to 'his very childish character'.[32] Yet a sermon he gave in the cathedral in Mexico to commemorate the feast of the Epiphany in 1743 was praised by the current rector of the university, Dr Manuel de Eguiara y Eguren, as 'angelic'. Drawing upon St Peter Chrysologus and Cornelius Lapierre, Carranza had defined the three wise men as kings of Ethiopia, descendants of Solomon and the queen of Sheba, who came to Bethlehem to adore the 'Child God Pontiff', enthroned on Mary's lap. The advent of these kings symbolized the three crowns of the papal tiara and the establishment of the papacy, since with their treasures of gold, incense and myrrh they each brought a key, symbol of St Peter's office.[33]

At Querétaro on 12 December 1748, preaching in one of the first sanctuaries of the Guadalupe to be built outside Mexico City, Carranza followed a traditional tack when he insisted that, whereas all other Marian images were of human or angelic origin, the

Mexican Virgin had been drawn from life by Mary herself. But he then argued that in that sublime moment she had become 'the Chair of the Holy Spirit' and had disclosed 'the predestination of this new world'. Moreover, had she not revealed to Blessed Amadeus that her miraculous images would endure to the end of the world? If that was the case, then her chief sanctuary on earth, the Guadalupe at Tepeyac, would figure decisively in the drama of the last days. Basing himself on Cornelius Lapierre, whom he cited on three occasions, Carranza argued that the Chair of St Peter was by no means fixed at Rome, since it had spent over sixty years in Avignon. In any case, had not St Malachy prophesied that the penultimate pope would be expelled from Rome and would become a pilgrim wandering across the world? Turning to chapter 12 of the Apocalypse, Carranza interpreted it as a faithful prophecy of that final epoch when the Anti-Christ would do battle with the archangel Michael. But he declared that the great dragon would succeed in crushing the Church in the Old World and in establishing his dominion. However, since the woman described in the Apocalypse was obviously Mary in her Guadalupe image, then the Mexican Virgin, assisted by St Michael, would victoriously defend 'the two Americas' from the onslaught of Anti-Christ. At this point, the successor of St Peter would flee from Rome and fix his residence at Tepeyac, where the Church would remain until the final Judgement.[34]

In all this, so Carranza observed, Christ's parable of the workers in the vineyard would be fulfilled: the first to enter the Church, the Romans, would be the first to leave; and the last to enter, the Americans, would be those who would remain faithful. In the Old World the very celebration of the Eucharist would cease, whereas in America it would continue so that, 'when Rome will be sacrificing to Bacchus, incensing Venus and adoring Cybele, here, through the mercy of the Queen of Guadalupe, the true sacrifice of the altar will be offered'. Moreover, amidst these convulsions, the king of Spain would also flee to Mexico, since 'that universal monarchy of all the world, which the scriptures announce and which the doctors explain, is none other than the Catholic King of the Spains'. For 'the American Empress of the Angels' had conquered Mexico for the Spanish king and would maintain his monarchy until the end of the world. Any doubts as to the power of 'our Mexican Queen, Mother and Lady', were soon allayed by merely considering that in the two hundred years since her apparition, so Carranza oddly averred, 'our Eagle America' had escaped the 'wars, famines, plagues and earthquakes, which are the signs of judgement'. In effect, Mexico was thus destined to become the centre and capital of a universal Catholic monarchy, blessed with pope and king rather than archbishop and viceroy, which Our Lady of Guadalupe would protect from Satan until Christ's Second Coming. In this prophecy the messianic undertone in the cult of the Mexican Virgin at last became explicit, albeit in the familiar form of an affirmation of Mexico's singularity, although now not of Christian foundation, but of spiritual and political destiny.[35]

IV

It has been justly observed that an entire cycle of panegyrical sermons on Our Lady of Guadalupe was inspired by Miguel Sánchez.[36] Nowhere was his influence more obvious than in the application of Augustinian typology to the interpretation of the Mexican Virgin. Of the printed sermons we have considered, those by Robles, Picazo, Saénz de San Antonio and Paredes all faithfully preserved the analogy between Moses, Mount Sinai and the Ark of the Covenant and Juan Diego, Mount Tepeyac and the Guadalupe image. In the case of Goicoechea the comparison was with the Jewish Temples in Jerusalem and the sanctuaries at Tepeyac, with the jar of manna taken as a figure of the Guadalupe. Although he never cited his master's name, it was Ita y Parra who was Sánchez' most faithful disciple, since his contrasts between Los Remedios and Guadalupe as the Ark of the Covenant as against the burning bush and as Ruth and Noemi, were cast exactly in the mode favoured by his predecessor. So too, *The Circle of Love* named Juan Diego as 'the Moses of the Indies' and throughout that sermon compared the *Indianos* to the ancient Israelites. Then again, the choice of St Luke's account of the Visitation for the gospel of the mass celebrated on 12 December offered opportunity for a new range of typological exegesis, which was most vividly exploited by Eguiara y Eguren, who took that text as a prophecy of Mary's apparition in Mexico and who skilfully interpreted the Magnificat as a figure of the Guadalupe. In this he was followed by Lazcano and Castañeda, who were quick to note that whereas Mary spent but a short time as Elizabeth's guest, she came to make a permanent home for herself in New Spain. This application of Sánchez' method to new scriptural events demonstrated the fertility of his method of exegesis.

But it was Sánchez' identification of the Guadalupe image as a copy of St John's vision of the Woman of the Apocalypse which obviously inspired Vidal de Figueroa to deploy neo-platonic theological concepts to define the image as a faithful portrait of the divine idea of Mary. The other influence here was seventeenth-century iconography, which had also come to depict Mary, in her advocation of the Immaculate Conception, as the Woman of the Apocalypse. Sure enough, a contemporary of Vidal described the Guadalupe as an Immaculate Conception. But the effect of Vidal's audacious thesis was to endow the Guadalupe with a priority over any other image of Mary's Conception, since she alone was a portrait of the divine prototype. Although the implications of this argument were in part discussed by Benitez, Mendoza and Picazo, it fell to Villa Sánchez to draw the conclusion that the image was a 'twin portrait' of Mary as she appeared in the flesh in Palestine. Not everyone accepted Vidal's thesis, since Paredes still argued that the archangel Michael had painted the image, and most Jesuits thought that Mary had drawn her own portrait. But Ita y Parra cited Vidal with approval, and although at first he suggested that Mexico's guardian angel was the artist, he soon concluded that 'a Divine hand' took the copy, albeit without specifying whether it was an image of the divine idea or a portrait taken from life. In any case, Ita y Parra followed Vidal in employing the neo-platonic theology of St John Damascene and St Theodore of Studios to depict Mary in the flesh both as an image of Christ and as the original of the Guadalupe, in what was a complex set of metaphors.

A third, distinctive characterization of the Guadalupe, for which no precedent can be found in Sánchez, was its identity as a perpetual sacrament. Here was an interpretation first presented by San Miguel, strongly developed by Goicoechea, and sustained by Castañeda, with support from Picazo and a passage in Ita y Parra. This essentially Jesuit thesis applied the doctrine of transubstantiation to the Guadalupe image, arguing that in the same way as the substance of bread and wine was transformed into the body and blood of Christ in the Eucharist, so too the substance of cactus fibre and the vegetable colours of flowers were changed into the image of Mary. The possible source of this doctrine was the Virgin Mary's promise to Blessed Amadeus of Portugal, that as Christ would remain in the Eucharist until the Last Judgement, so too she would be 'bodily present' in her miraculous images until the end of the world. Here was a text cited by Florencia, Goicoechea and Carranza, albeit in the two latter cases in support of the unfailing duration of the image. However, if the comparison with the Eucharist is given full weight, then Mary was seen to be sacramentally present in the Guadalupe, her continuing apparition a perpetual miracle. Here was a theology of the image which did not derive from the Greek Fathers but drew upon Counter-Reformation worship of the Eucharist.

Nothing is more striking in the sermons of Ita y Parra, Lazcano and Castañeda than their sustained comparison between Christ and Mary, and between Mary in the flesh and Mary in Guadalupe, which led directly into a comparison of Christ and the Guadalupe. If the Divine Word was incarnated within the coarse covering of human nature, so equally the Virgin was present in the crude cape of Juan Diego, Christ appearing as a despised Israelite, she as a humble Indian. For his part, Lazcano argued that Mary's apparition in Mexico was 'superior, not in substance, but in mode', to her appearance in the flesh in Palestine or in the vision to St John on Patmos. Much the same kind of equivalence was postulated by Castañeda. Obviously behind such metaphors lay the neo-platonic theology of the image where an identity of form or likeness was seen as important as an identity of essence or substance, so that the humblest icon of Christ bore some imprint of his divine personality. But it also derived in part from the correspondence which had already been established between the Eucharist and the image of Guadalupe.

Although these sermons all aspired to sing canticles of praise, expatiating on the unique glories of the Mexican Virgin, at times they also traced the effects of the apparition. It was an article of faith, taken from Sánchez, that the conversion of the Indians was primarily due to the intervention of Mary. But this assertion was given theological and cultural force when Villa Sánchez argued that whereas the conversion of the Old

World was undertaken by Christ acting through the apostles who preached his gospel, by contrast the New World was reserved for Mary, who converted the Indians through her image of Guadalupe. It was a constant argument, from Vidal and Villa Sánchez to Ita y Parra, Eguiara y Eguren and Lazcano, that the natives of America had to be addressed in the manner they best understood, which was to say, they had to be converted through images rather than by words. It was an argument reinforced by typology when the words of the Ten Commandments inscribed on the Tables of Law or Mary's Magnificat were contrasted to the Guadalupe. If, in their eagerness to exalt the Guadalupe, the Mexican preachers suggested a virtual substitution of the words by the image, it should always be remembered that their sermons were delivered during the celebration of the sacrifice of the mass and in the presence of the Eucharist.

One feature of these panegyrics must strike any reader. Although from the outset the emphasis was on the image, slowly and more insistently as the tide of celebration mounted, the Mexican nation emerged as a participant. Once again, it was the official orator at the great occasions when the Guadalupe was chosen as patron, Ita y Parra, who most obviously invoked the 'nation', a term virtually forced upon him by his reiterated comparison with the Israelites and the citation of Psalm 147. His use of the term *Indianos*, natives of the Indies, be they Spaniards, mestizos or Indians, was decidedly ambiguous, since although he addressed his congregation of dignitaries as *Indianos*, he also lamented the scorn with which Spanish chroniclers had dismissed *Indianos* as savages. So too, he described the Virgin of Guadalupe as a modest *Indiana*, dressed in the clothes of her nation, thus obviously designating her as an Indian. Much the same ambiguity was manifest in Lazcano in his reference to 'the Hispanic Moctezuma Nation'. By contrast, Carranza adopted the term 'Americans' as the best name for his compatriots. In effect, although the preachers were all American Spaniards or creoles, they strove to encounter terms which included all the inhabitants of New Spain, no matter what their race or province.

The final emergence of the 'nation' in the discourse of these sermons, no matter how distant from any social reality, testified to the fervent patriotism which helped inspire the cult of the Guadalupe. From Sánchez onwards, religious devotion mingled with patriotic sentiment until it found expression in the prophecies of Carranza that Mexico would become the capital of the universal monarchy and home of the pope. But from the start, the inner meaning of the Apparition story was that the Mother of God had come to Mexico, and in a special way had chosen to remain in Mexico, acting as its patron. The theological doctrines which exalted the significance of the Guadalupe all emphasized the unique quality and power of this most Mexican of images. But if patriotic sentiment was so strong, it was because New Spain was a colony, a possession of Spain, whose inhabitants lived far removed from the centres of European culture and power. A canon of Cuzco in Peru, who intervened in a Spanish literary debate long after its protagonists had died, justified his tardy intervention by observing that 'we creoles live far off'.[37] The Mexican creoles also lived in cities far removed from Rome and Madrid and were ignorant of the scientific discoveries and historical scepticism that threatened the baroque forms of post-Tridentine Catholicism. But thanks to Our Lady of Guadalupe, they lived close to the Virgin Mary, convinced that the Mother of God had chosen their country and nation for her particular protection.

8

Heavenly painting

I

On 30 April 1751 the glass windows which protected the image of Our Lady of Guadalupe in the sanctuary at Tepeyac were opened so as to allow a group of painters headed by José de Ibarra (1685–1756) to scrutinize and touch the canvas. On 15 April 1752 the windows were again opened to permit Miguel Cabrera (1695–1768), assisted by José de Alcíbar and José Ventura Arnaéz, to make copies of the image, one for Archbishop Manuel Rubio y Salinas, one for Juan Francisco López to take to Rome, and the last for Cabrera himself, to serve as a model for further copies.[1] By this time, Cabrera was already recognized as the greatest painter that New Spain had produced and indeed was later described by Alcibar as 'this hero of our times'.[2] In the nineteenth century, José Bernardo Couto described him as 'the personification of the great artist and of the painter par excellence; and a century after his death the supremacy which he knew how to merit remains intact'.[3] The favourite artist of both Archbishop Rubio and the Jesuits, he was given a vast range of commissions during the last decades of his life and was celebrated for the accuracy and delicacy of his copies of the Guadalupe. A disciple of Murillo, albeit subject to certain French influences, Cabrera devoted his career almost entirely to religious scenes, turning aside only for a range of portraits of viceroys and other dignitaries of Church and State.[4] Today, he is best remembered for his portraits of three nuns, and in particular of Sor Juan Inés de la Cruz, the celebrated poet.

What could have been more appropriate, therefore, than that Cabrera should have written a brief treatise on the Guadalupe entitled *American Marvel* (1756)? Or that in his introduction Cabrera should have thanked Archbishop Rubio for his patronage, saluting the successor of Zumárraga as 'the sovereign, original and only owner' of Mexico's holy image? That it was the Jesuit preacher, Francisco Javier Lazcano, who acted as censor and used his approbation to praise the archbishop for establishing the college of canons and obtaining Benedict XIV's approval of the patronage only served to confirm the important role of Cabrera during these euphoric years. Moreover, the other censor, José González del Pinal, a canon at the sanctuary, cited Antonio Palomino, the eighteenth-century Spanish art critic, as asserting that painting was a universal, not to say, angelic language, since one canvas could express what often took a book to explain. That he concluded by comparing Cabrera to Michelangelo and Raphael spoke more for his patriotism than for his taste in art. More traditional in his reference was Cabrera's pupil José Ventura Arnaéz, since he could not resist comparing his master to his archangelic eponym, asserting that where St Michael had vanquished the Devil, the Mexican painter had dissipated the clouds of ignorance which surrounded the image of Guadalupe.[5]

The purpose of *American Marvel* was to confirm and extend the verdict of the painters who had figured in the sworn depositions of 1666. It thus represented the opinion, not merely of its author, but also of José de Ibarra (whom Cabrera recognized as 'my master') and of Juan Patricio Morelete Ruíz, Manuel Osorio and Francisco Antonio Vallejo. To start with they emphasized that the very survival of the canvas in the humid, salt-laden airs of Tepeyac for 225 years was in itself 'a special privilege'. For the cloth was made up of two pieces sewn together with a thin thread of cotton and by any general rule should have been torn apart by simple pressure, especially since the windows which protected the image were regularly opened. Cabrera testified that in 1753, 'when I was present', the image was exposed for two hours, when innumerable rosary beads were thrust at it and 'it seemed to me, about five hundred images which touched the canvas'. On the still-controverted question of the origin of the canvas, Cabrera defined it as made from 'a coarse weave of certain threads which we vulgarly call *pita*', of the kind woven by Indians from palms for their *ayatl* mantles. It thus resembled 'the rough canvas, or *bramante* of Europe, which we here call *cotense*', which was to say, a rough linen. To the touch it was soft, almost silken, and hence could not have been woven from the rough fibre of the maguey.[6] Cabrera's observations were echoed by Mariano Fernández de Echeverría y Veytia, the distinguished historian and Boturini's friend, who, in his *Bulwarks of Mexico,* testified that he had been present both in 1751 and 1752, when the painters examined the image, adding that 'on both occasions I myself touched and examined all the circumstances of the Holy Image' . He also found the material to be woven 'from the thread of palms or of cotton' and indeed asserted that it felt more like cotton than palm. He added that by this time the imprint on the canvas of the wooden bars which had sustained the image had become clearly visible and as a result they had been replaced by silver plates.[7] There was, however, a space between these plates which allowed both Cabrera and Veytia to note that the canvas lacked any sizing, since the colours showed through at the back, albeit in a smudge of yellowish hue. In all this both these distinguished observers confirmed Becerra Tanco's thesis and openly contradicted the 1666 depositions of the Indians from Cuautitlan that Juan Diego's cape had been of *ixtle* woven from maguey fibre.

Where Cabrera decisively innovated was in his assertion that the image had been painted with a highly distinctive combination of techniques. According to his expert observation, the Virgin's face and hands were done in oil, albeit without application of sizing; but her tunic, the angel and the mandorla or niche which surrounded her figure were painted in tempera, which was usually the medium used for frescoes on walls or boards. Moreover, her mantle was done in gouache, as in water-colours; and the uncoloured surround of the canvas was 'worked like tempera'. The gold dust of the sun rays was of fine powder, yet appeared to have entered the very weave of the canvas. How such a combination of techniques was possible Cabrera found hard to imagine. After all, oils needed sizing to hold them firm; tempera used gum for its colours; and gouache was usually applied to a thin white canvas; and as for 'worked like tempera' or *empastado*, this was generally applied with pallet knives rather than brushes.[8] In effect, Cabrera here testified that the elements of paint were as open to analysis as the texture of the cloth and that part of the miracle consisted in their unique combination of European and Indian techniques and materials.

The closer Cabrera scrutinized the image the more beautiful he found it, exclaiming: 'I do not know how to explain the sheer wonder that this marvel of art causes in me.' And yet academic voices had been raised to suggest that the figure of the Virgin was not perpendicular, that her hands were too small, that the left foot was too short and that the right shoulder was too prominent. But Cabrera denied all these alleged imperfections, arguing that they could all be explained by the rules of perspective. So too, the image was illumined from within by the sun's rays, so that its light did not originate from some imaginary point outside the canvas. Then again, although the Virgin's tunic was clearly drawn with 'profiles', the contours capturing its folds, by contrast its floral design, painted in gold, was drawn flat without 'profiles'. A further mystery was the colour of the Virgin's mantle, which was neither blue nor green but some pigment in between, even though the angel's wings included a clear blue. But it was the Virgin's face, painted in profile, which exhibited inimitable effects, especially since her lower lip was painted over a knot in the canvas, which thus somewhat raised it.[9] For the rest, Cabrera provided a number of measurements, noting that the canvas was two-and-a-twelfth Castilian yards high and just over one-and-a-quarter yards wide. The Virgin's crown had ten rays and she was surrounded by 129 rays of the sun and had 46 stars painted on her mantle. More important, if the Virgin's inclination was taken into account, her figure measured eight and two-thirds 'faces' in height, which was to say, somewhat less than seven 'modules'. According to the rules of portraiture, as practised by Albrecht Durer and other artists, the Virgin thus represented a girl of fourteen or fifteen years. Cabrera recalled that Becerra Tanco had described Juan Diego as addressing the Virgin as *niña*, or child, on three occasions and hence concluded: 'I conjecture that if the Divine Mother had represented herself in her image as older than fourteen or fifteen years, she would not have lacked her most Holy Son in her beautiful arms.'[10]

In conclusion, Cabrera thanked the Virgin Mary for accommodating herself to the style and usage of the Indians of Mexico, who were so accustomed to 'symbolic expressions or hieroglyphics of brush'. So too, in bequeathing this 'heavenly Marvel' to the faithful, she had paid the greatest honour possible to the art of painting, especially since all the elements of her image indicated that it was 'supernaturally and miraculously painted'.[11] Here, for the first time in over two centuries of Spanish rule, a Mexican artist expressed his opinions in public, albeit invoking all his hard-won prestige as a painter to endorse the tradition of the Guadalupe. For all that, his intervention had far-reaching implications. Whereas in 1661 José Vidal de Figueroa had explained the absence of the Christ child by defining the image as a portrait of Mary as she was conceived by the Almighty from all eternity, by contrast in 1756 Miguel Cabrera cited academic rules of portraiture to describe the Virgin as a girl too young to have borne a child. In effect, the Mexican artist subjected the image to aesthetic and 'technical' analysis, thus reducing the miracle to an inimitable combination of techniques and an incomparable rendering of the Virgin's face. What he chose not to explain was why the Virgin or the Almighty should have adopted these kinds of paint and applied them in such a fashion.

In his treatise, Cabrera inserted a brief statement by his master, José de Ibarra, who declared that although New Spain had possessed distinguished artists for over 150 years, none of these painters had succeeded in producing an accurate likeness of the Guadalupe, until 'my master Juan Correa took a profile from the image itself'. Not a great deal is known of Correa (1646–1716) other than that, like his contemporary, Cristóbal de Villalpando (1650–1714), he was influenced by Rubens and the Spanish painter, Juan de Valdés Leal. What is instructive here is that Correa took his 'profile', so Ibarra averred, by using an 'oil paper of the same size as the Lady herself, with the pointing of all her contours, lines and number of stars and rays'. Ibarra had seen this oil paper, which was itself soon copied, thus serving as an invaluable model for all artists who were commissioned to paint copies of the Guadalupe. What this testimony indicated was that the governing criterion was faithful reproduction rather than skilful interpretation.[12] However, the Virgin's face admitted no easy copying, either in its colour or in the delicacy of its downward gaze. For all that, by the eighteenth century most copies of the Guadalupe exhibited an immutable iconic likeness, no matter who the painter. Whereas portraits of Mary as the Immaculate Conception or in her Assumption, for example, admitted a considerable range of interpretation, by contrast, the Mexican Virgin presented an unchanging but distinctive face to the world.

But, if the Virgin could not be varied, the way the rest of the canvas was filled offered considerable scope for individual interpretation. In the original, Mary and the angel were enclosed in a mandorla or niche which reached in narrowed channel to the top edge of the canvas, leaving the other edges and four corners vacant. Obviously, an elaborate gilt frame was one way to overcome the impression of an unfinished canvas.

Yet, as Siles had testified, at one time angels had been painted onto the original itself, only soon to fade and be erased. But as regards the copies, it soon became common to surround the Virgin with flowers or angels and indeed to insert other figures and scenes. As yet, the chronology of these developments is by no means clear, since many surviving copies lack artists' signatures, let alone dates. However, at some point in the late seventeenth century, it became common to insert cartouches in each corner, which is to say, framed scenes, respectively depicting the Virgin's first two apparitions to Juan Diego, his offering of flowers and roses to the Virgin, and the revelation of her image by Juan Diego to Zumárraga. According to some accounts, it was Juan Correa who first inserted these scenes.[13] Whatever the case, here was a formula which was endlessly reproduced in the eighteenth century, and at no point more so than by Cabrera and his contemporaries. By then it was common to link the scenes by filling the sides with flowers or by cherubic *putti*, and to stretch their frames with rococo scrolling. In many copies of this period, the space beneath the angel was occupied by a scene of Tepeyac and its sanctuary and, either above or below the Virgin, the words from Psalm 147, 'Non fecit taliter omni natione', were inscribed. The significance of this mode of presenting the Guadalupe was that the copies thus incorporated the narrative tradition within the very frame of the Mexican icon, so that the Virgin's Apparition could not be separated from Juan Diego, her faithful Indian disciple. Jerónimo de Valladolid, the chaplain at the sanctuary who had introduced Florencia's *Pole Star of Mexico*, may well have claimed that the image 'speaks for itself and testifies to its miraculous origin', but in countless copies the apparition story was inscribed in subordinate scenes, whose meaning could be readily deciphered by the illiterate.[14]

Despite the absence of a universal catalogue, it is clear that in the seventeenth century a considerable degree of flexibility in presenting the Guadalupe still existed. There survives a charming canvas in which Juan Diego's cape is held by two angels, its folds pleated at the sides. The angel is replaced by St Michael standing and brandishing his sword. Above the Virgin, the mandorla ends with a dove, wings outstretched, the symbol of the Holy Spirit, flanked on either side by God the Father and Christ with his cross. At the sides are seven angels playing a diversity of instruments, and among them Juan Diego stands, offering his roses. Finally, below St Michael are the twelve apostles, with St Peter identified by his keys. In another painting of this epoch, there are five cartouches, all with buckled frames, with the scene below the Virgin depicting Tepeyac. Within the mandorla above the Virgin are God the Father with arms outstretched and the Holy Spirit as a dove. Around the central figures are inscribed the words: 'Most Holy Mary conceived without the stain of original sin'. What distinguishes this painting is that the face of the Virgin is more individualized than was usually the case and is deeply Mexican.[15]

Two other paintings of the late seventeenth century merit description. In one, the fifth cartouche beneath the Virgin depicts St John the Evangelist sitting with pen and

Plate 18   Baltazar Troncoso, *St Michael, surrounded by Angels and Apostles, bears Our Lady of Guadalupe*

book in hand, contemplating the Guadalupe in the sky and below her an eagle perched on a nopal cactus, the heraldic symbol of Mexico. The canvas is filled, however, by the two large, flanking figures of St Michael with helmet and standard and St Gabriel holding a strand of lilies; and above the Virgin, a dove with wings outstretched. In another painting of this epoch, the fifth cartouche depicts the Virgin curing Juan Bernardino. On one side of the Virgin is St Jacob sleeping with the ladder of angels reaching to heaven and on the other St John the Evangelist, book in hand, and an oddly placed fountain of grace. Above the Virgin, the mandorla is cut to leave space for the Holy Trinity, presented as two men, with the dove between them. Both these works thus confirm the importance of the identification made by Miguel Sánchez of the Guadalupe as the Woman of the Apocalypse.[16]

Although the eighteenth century witnessed a greater degree of standard copying, variant forms still continued to be devised. For a start, it became relatively common to insert portraits of nuns, prelates or laymen, either praying to the Virgin or simply beneath her; and in certain cases, as with Archbishop Rubio, it is the portrait rather than the Virgin who dominates the canvas. Another variant is the large fresco painted by Miguel Cabrera in the church of the college of Our Lady of Guadalupe in Zacatecas, where the Virgin is depicted as borne aloft by St Francis, surrounded by friars and a layman, who may be a self-portrait of Cabrera.[17] One curious variant depicts the Holy Family, with Mary as the Guadalupe, replete with mandorla, alongside St Joseph and the Christ child drawn in naturalistic style. Then there is an odd print which represents the Guadalupe as Mary's soul as it is assumed into heaven.[18] But the most audacious of these variant scenes are those which portray God the Father or Christ painting the Guadalupe, with brush and palette in hand. These are the pictorial equivalents of the sermons preached by Bartolomé de Ita y Parra and other theologians in much the same years. But, whereas the rhetoric rarely specified the mode of the miracle, these paintings all too realistically represent the divine artists at work, albeit usually accompanied by angels. If in the Eastern Church it was not uncommon to portray St Luke painting the Virgin Mary, it was possibly only in New Spain that the Father and the Son were so depicted.[19]

The election of the Guadalupe as patron of Mexico was also reflected in the Virgin's iconography. In a magnificent work, painted by José de Ribera y Argomanis in 1778, the Virgin occupies only the upper half of the canvas and is flanked by two figures of much the same size, one of Juan Diego offering roses and flowers, and the other of a plumed Indian representing America. Moreover, although the Virgin's first two apparitions are recorded in cartouches in the upper corners, the remaining scenes are grouped together in a highly rococo ensemble directly beneath the Virgin's angel but above a large eagle, snake in mouth, perched on a nopal which grows from an extensive lake of Mexico. From the mouth of America comes a scroll on which is inscribed 'Non fecit taliter omni natione', and at the foot of the canvas is a declaration

Plate 19   Miguel Cabrera, *St Francis Holds aloft Our Lady of Guadalupe*

Plate 20 José de Ribera y Argomanis, *Our Lady of Guadalupe as Patron of New Spain*

that the painting commemorates the swearing of the oath in 1737 when the Virgin was acclaimed as principal patron of the city of Mexico. There is a less attractive variant of this work in which the two figures flanking the Virgin represent Europe and America, the one a queen offering a crown, the other an elaborately plumed Indian. The Holy Spirit and St John the Evangelist have thus disappeared from the scene, replaced by human symbols of the public, hemispheric significance of the Mexican Virgin.[20]

For some reason, as yet unexplained, the recognition of the Guadalupe as patron of New Spain by Benedict XIV in 1754 was celebrated in an engraving done by Joseph Sebastian and Johann Baptist Klauber, whose design books had inspired a whole generation of Mexican architects and sculptors. Theirs was a whirling, crowded, rococo composition, in which the Virgin was surrounded by angels holding not merely the four Apparition scenes but another three frames depicting her miracles including, in a scene above her head, galleons at sea flanked by two rulers, one with a crown, the other with a turban, a possible reminiscence of Lepanto. The Virgin was flanked below by two figures, one of Benedict XIV holding a copy of his 1754 decree, the other of America, depicted as an Indian princess, holding a shield on which was painted the Mexican eagle and cactus. Below was a long inscription in both Spanish and Latin, telling the story of the apparitions. This design proved to be popular in New Spain, and in 1761 Juan Patricio Morelete Ruíz copied it in oil, albeit with the inscription replaced by an attractive scene of Tepeyac and the sanctuary. There is a further copy in oils, anonymous, which is even better done.[21] As in the case of Ribera y Argomanis' work, this composition demonstrated the degree to which the Mexican Virgin was now recognized by the papacy and thus played a significant role within the universal Church.

The prominent presence of Juan Diego in the Ribera y Argomanis painting exemplified the greater attention paid to the Indian in the eighteenth century. Once again, it was Miguel Cabrera who played a central role in this trend. For he copied, so he claimed, an ancient portrait of Juan Diego striding past Tepeyac, obviously hearing the songs of numerous birds and seeing from afar the Virgin in the sky. Dressed in simple cotton cloth, the Indian was portrayed as a bearded pilgrim, carrying a hat and staff. Dating from much the same epoch is an anonymous work in which Juan Diego, very similar to Cabrera's 'copy', is seen on his knees praying to the Virgin. Such freestanding portraits, however, do not appear to have been common. But in certain churches, most notably in the Santa Prisca at Taxco, the Merced at Tacuba and Santa Rosa de Viterbo in Querétaro, the elaborate Churrigueresque retables dedicated to the Guadalupe all had a simple painting of the Virgin at their centre, flanked by four large medallions in which the Apparition scenes were inserted. The effect of these enlargements was to place Juan Diego in even greater prominence as a hero worthy of veneration.[22]

Apart from his portraits of dignitaries of Church and State, the only secular themes painted by Miguel Cabrera were a series which depicted the various ethnic castes which were produced by the inter-marriage of Spaniards, Indians and blacks. The purpose of this genre is by no means clear. But it provided the opportunity for Cabrera to paint scenes from secular life and to include elaborate detail of costume, textiles and even foodstuffs. In effect, we here encounter the portrayal of the diverse social strata from which the Mexican nation was eventually to be formed, ethnic groups which were often sharply divided from each other by language and culture, and at times united only by their common devotion to Our Lady of Guadalupe. In this series Cabrera devoted all his skill to the portrayal of an Indian woman whose presence is magnified by the delicate tracery of her elaborate costume, and blessed with a daughter who looks longingly at a Spanish father, whose face, however, is turned away from both his daughter and the spectator.[23] Since Cabrera himself was an orphan of unknown parentage who was later described as an Indian, even if in legal status he counted as a Spaniard, was there here a suggestion of autobiography? Whatever the case, as with Juan Diego, this Indian woman was painted with evident sympathy. For all that, it was as the finest painter of the Guadalupe that Cabrera was most esteemed among his contemporaries.

II

The euphoria which inflamed the creole clerical elite during the 1750s was suddenly dissipated when in 1767, the Jesuits were abruptly expelled from the dominions of the Spanish monarchy. At a stroke the colleges, missions and churches of the Company of Jesus were left deserted as an entire generation of talented Mexicans were condemned to a penurious exile in the Papal States. The archbishop of Mexico who assisted the viceroy in this drastic measure was Francisco Antonio de Lorenzana y Buitrón (1766–72), a learned prelate, who expended his episcopal income on publishing editions of Cortés' *Letters*, and the Mozarab mass of Toledo. He belonged to the 'enlightened' wing of the Church and presided over the Fourth Mexican Church Council of 1771, summoned by the crown to reform the religious orders. So too, Lorenzana issued pastorals in which he expressed concern at the excesses of popular religion and summarily banned, on pain of twenty-five strokes of the lash, 'all live representations of the Passion of Christ our Redeemer, the Volador pole, the dances of Santiago . . . representations of Shepherds and Kings'. In effect, the archbishop was a member of a 'party' which questioned the value of pilgrimage, scorned astrology and oracles, and warned against popular belief in miraculous cures. It was not long before clergymen such as Lorenzana were to criticize the extravagant gilded churches built in the baroque and Churrigueresque styles and to praise the simple, unadorned lines of the neo-classic as an expression of good taste and Christian piety.

It was only to be expected, therefore, that when Lorenzana came to preach about the Lady of Guadalupe, he eschewed all reference to the Greek Fathers and their theology of images. Instead, he carefully cited the 1666 *Statements* as proof of the apparitions, and then fixed upon Miguel Cabrera's discovery that the image was painted in four different techniques as an empirical demonstration of its miraculous origin. He averred that, since the Guadalupe had been 'sent from heaven and not made on earth like those painted by St Luke', it presented the best likeness of the Virgin. Although she was depicted in her image as an Immaculate Conception, she was not shown in triumph over the Devil, since in New Spain her presence had averted the emergence of heresy. As for the angel who supported her, the archbishop refused to identify him, asserting that the cherub was merely representative of all the choirs of angels in heaven. Noting that the Virgin had a 'colour burned by the sun which is more inclined to brown', Lorenzana suggested that, like so many images in Spain, she could be described as the spouse of the Song of Songs, which was to say, 'black but lovely'. For the rest, he recalled that the Virgin had appeared in the New World to win new kingdoms for the Catholic Church at a time when Luther and Calvin had led entire nations astray. If she had chosen to be called Guadalupe, it was because that name was so cherished by the conquerors, Cortés especially, who came from Extremadura. Citing the words of Christ as reported by St Matthew, he exclaimed: 'Our Lady did not seek the rich, but the poor of St Francis and poor Indians; she did not appear to the learned, but to simple Indians; God hid his secrets from the wise and revealed them to babes.' Although he reminded the congregation that the celebrated words 'Non fecit taliter omni natione' 'are engraved at the entrance of the Holy House of Loreto', he insisted that the enduring miracle of her image of Guadalupe signified that for the Virgin, 'this America is her beloved Benjamin', which 'she cares for and protects as the most tender and beloved of her children'. In effect, Lorenzana drew on scripture, not to uncover typological comparisons, but to impart moral lessons.[24]

Testimony of the profound change in the intellectual climate of New Spain, wrought by the government of Charles III (1759–88) and his enlightened ministers, can be found in a sermon preached on 14 December 1777 by Dr José Patricio Fernández de Uribe (1742–96) in which he eschewed panegyric and warned the congregation at Tepeyac that they lived in a so-called 'century of enlightenment', which was to say, 'in a century of proud, not to say impious philosophers, who are inclined to discuss everything in order not to believe in anything'. They employed reason to attack faith and undermine devotion; they dismissed miracles as superstition; and they scorned tradition as mere ignorance. Although Uribe did not cite their names, later in Mexico it became the fashion to accuse Voltaire and Rousseau of being the instigators of this movement of philosophical scepticism. To answer this crisis in belief, Uribe had mastered the abundant literature which by then dealt with the 'immemorial tradition' of the Mexican Virgin. What he sought was to offer a demonstration of 'the truth of the Apparition of Guadalupe, solidly established and confirmed by the cult and veneration of the faithful' across two-and-a-half centuries. But in a sermon he could only provide a sketch of his case, so in the following year, 1778, he wrote a *Critical-Historical Dissertation* in which he fully expounded his arguments. However, it was not until after his death in 1801 that the sermon and dissertation were published, possibly because even to admit the challenge of incredulity in 1778 was judged harmful to belief. Soon after delivering his sermon, Uribe was promoted to become canon of the cathedral chapter of Mexico, where he distinguished himself for both his learning and his encouragement of education.[25]

By way of a start to his dissertation, he briefly listed all the authors who had written on the Guadalupe, ending with a tribute to Archbishop Lorenzana, who, after the expulsion of the Jesuits in 1767, had arranged for the manuscripts and papers of Carlos de Sigüenza y Góngora to be deposited in the archive of the University of Mexico. Uribe then inserted a brief narrative of the apparitions in which he drew more on the version extracted by Cruz from Sánchez than from Becerra Tanco's translation of the *Nican mopohua*. He then insisted that for the true Christian there could be no questioning the story, especially since both Christ's gospel and the apostles' preaching has been sustained by miracles, adding:

> there has not been a country or region, in which the heavenly seed has been planted without the irrigation of miracles; there has not been a century which has not marvelled at these portents, of which the histories and monuments of the Church are so full.

It was not surprising that Zumárraga had not written about the Virgin's apparitions, since his efforts to defend the Indians from the conquerors' exploitation had left him 'a persecuted and slandered prelate'. Moreover, the Virgin had appeared 'on the eve of his leaving for Spain', at a time when he was still 'without archive, without a secretary, and almost without priests to help him'. It was not until 1533 that he returned to Mexico, there to build his cathedral and devote all his energy to the conversion of the Indians. In any case, the failure to find any episcopal documents dealing with these events did not rule out the possibility that at some point Zumárraga may well have written a report on the apparitions.[26] Had not a Franciscan, Pedro Mezquía, once seen a letter from the bishop on this subject in a convent at Vitoria, even if this missive had later perished in a fire?

But how could one explain the silence of all the leading historians of the conquest epoch? To accept such a 'negative argument' as calling into question the veracity of the Guadalupe narrative, so Uribe warned, was to fall into the errors of Luther and Calvin, against whom Catholic theologians had defended 'the authority of unwritten traditions'. After all, if contemporary silence was invoked as an absolute criterion, then it would be necessary to reject all the images painted by St Luke as pious frauds. Instead, it was necessary to follow Benedict XIV, who on the question of silence had invoked the three rules of evidence formulated by Jean Mabillon (1632–1707), the most learned of Benedictine church historians. These rules stipulated that, before such negative arguments could be accepted, those authors who were silent had to be contemporaries living in the same country where an alleged event occurred; that there was a universal silence about the event; and that those authors who were silent wrote on subjects close to the alleged event and hence might have been expected to have written about it. Even so, as Uribe was quick to note, only two out of twelve apostles had written gospels. As for New Spain in the sixteenth century, none of the early Franciscan chroniclers, which was to say, Toribio de Benavente, alias Motolinia, Jerónimo de Mendieta and Bernardino de Sahagún, had published their works, and indeed their manuscripts had been sent to Spain, where they had disappeared from view. It was thus more than likely that their chronicles contained references to the apparitions at Tepeyac. But the chief difficulty, as Uribe readily admitted, was the silence of Juan de Torquemada. But although many Mexicans complained about the Franciscan's omissions, Uribe displayed an equable disposition in choosing to praise the immense toil that the writing of the *Monarchy of the Indies* had entailed. For all that, he rehearsed all the occasions on which the Franciscan might have written about the Guadalupe, citing the previous discussions of these texts by Florencia and Cayetano de Cabrera. Was it because the friars were so anxious to destroy idolatry that they could not accept the testimony of an Indian? But Uribe then sought comfort in the admission of the editor of the second edition of Torquemada's great work, printed in 1723, that the text was sadly marred by many errors and omissions.[27]

In the last resort, however, the infallible argument against all the attacks of heresy and scepticism was tradition. Had not Cisneros affirmed that all the most sacred images of Spain and Italy, which was to say, Pilar, Montserrat, Guadalupe and Loreto, 'had their principal support in tradition . . . immemorial, common and general to all classes of persons; constant and uninterrupted; and at the end, invariable'. In a general rejection of both Protestantism and scepticism, Uribe affirmed:

> Only an impious enemy of the true religion, or a ridiculous sceptic who degenerates into Pyrrhonism, can deny the efficacy and force of human and divine traditions. Tradition is one of the principal foundations on which the beautiful fabric of our Catholic faith rests.

After all, on what did the biblical history of Moses depend if not on tradition? And, indeed, what was the basis of the Catholic doctrines of the Immaculate Conception and Assumption of the Virgin Mary if not traditions transmitted across the centuries?[28]

As regards the Guadalupe there was abundant testimony as to the enduring strength of her cult in Mexico. Had not Cisneros testified that the image numbered among the oldest venerated in the capital? Had not Bernal Díaz attested to the miracles performed at Tepeyac? Then again, recently discovered archival material demonstrated that the archbishops who succeeded Zumárraga, Alonso de Montúfar and Pedro Moya de Contreras, had both promoted the cult, arranging for monies to be collected at the sanctuary for the dowries of female orphans. Under Montúfar the second Church Council of Mexico had been held, which decreed that all holy images had to be approved by episcopal licence, so that if the image had been painted by Indians, it would not have been accepted by the archbishop. Uribe then cited the depositions of 1666, both Indian and Spanish, and claimed that they demonstrated the long-standing devotion to the Guadalupe, adding 'the cult is a religious testimony in which the will affirms the glory and greatness, and the understanding the truth of the object to which they are directed'. In effect, there were innumerable testimonies as to the existence of the cult across two-and-a-half centuries.[29]

But Uribe did not choose to rest his case on such general arguments. At the outset of his dissertation he saluted the image, 'whose heavenly origin and miraculous apparition was maintained for over a century in the memory and reverent cult of the Americans by means of tradition'. But then, in the year 1648 Miguel Sánchez had the glory of being the first to give its narrative to the press. However, despite his manifold virtues, Sánchez was essentially 'the Orator of the Apparition', since although he had obviously consulted documents, he failed to mention them other than in the most ambiguous fashion, leading Uribe to comment that 'this respectable author would have performed a great service to posterity, if he had left us a precise notice of those documents he had used for his work'. As for Laso de la Vega, he had simply printed an old account written in 'Mexican'. As these comments indicated, it was Becerra Tanco that Uribe favoured, since not merely had he cited the testimony of venerable priests living before the great flood of 1629, but he had also affirmed having seen 'an old account', written in 'Mexican', in the possession of Fernando de Alva Ixtlilxochitl. Following Cayetano de Cabrera, Uribe then cited Sigüenza y Góngora's assertion that this account had been written by Antonio Valeriano and claimed to have seen a manuscript statement by Sigüenza preserved in the archive of the Oratory where he reiterated that what he had lent Florencia was a Spanish 'translation', written by Alva Ixtlilxochitl.[30]

All this led Uribe to the triumphant conclusion that 'it is morally certain that a very old history of the Guadalupe Apparition was written and existed for some years'. Its author was Antonio Valeriano, a talented pupil of the College of Santa Cruz Tlatelolco who, since he had become governor of San Juan Tenochtitlan in about 1570, was probably born about 1530. He thus had ample opportunity to converse not merely with the first Franciscans in Mexico, but also with both Zumárraga and Juan Diego. Valeriano thus fulfilled all the conditions demanded by Church historians and the papacy as regards contemporary testimony. In effect, Uribe skilfully combined the statements of Becerra Tanco in both his 1666 and 1675 versions and of Sigüenza y Góngora in his *Heroic Piety* to trace the history of Valeriano's 'Mexican' account:

> Lic. Luis Laso saw it, who copied it and gave it to the presses, as Luis Becerra affirms; the same Luis Becerra saw it . . . don Fernando de Alva Ixtlilxochitl saw it, in whose power it was, and who gave it to Luis Becerra to read; the most learned don Carlos de Sigüenza y Góngora saw it, and not only saw it but was its owner, among the other curious papers of don Fernando de Alva; the Reverend Father Florencia saw, if not the original Mexican history, a paraphrased translation of it composed by don Fernando de Alva.[31]

Where Cayetano de Cabrera, who had access to the same materials, had speculated that Valeriano had made a Nahuatl translation of an original account written in Spanish by a Franciscan, Uribe knitted together the scattered assertions of his predecessors into a coherent argument. At the same time he cited Boturini's catalogue as demonstrating the existence of native 'paintings' and songs, notably of don Plácido, which had preceded Valeriano in recording the apparitions.

As regards the image itself, Uribe took full advantage of Miguel Cabrera's *American Marvel* to describe in detail the four techniques of painting which entered its composition, only then to exclaim over its imponderable beauty. Had not all the painters who had studied the image in 1666 and in 1751 attested to the inimitable art which had created it? So too, all these artists had been unable to explain how such a canvas, woven from the thread of palms, had survived for so long, especially since in its first century it had been exposed to all the effects of humidity and salt-laden airs. For his part, Uribe also expressed his wonder, since:

> There is surely not a year in which on five or six occasions the glass windows are not opened so that it can be venerated close up . . . On each occasion when the glass doors are opened, the pious and, to my mind dangerous, act of touching and kissing the holy Image lasts for at least two hours. Hundreds of persons attend and place their mouths, their foreheads and even their hands on the Image; and they touch her with innumerable rosaries, medallions, prints and even paintings. And it has happened that on arriving or leaving an individual has scratched the Image, tearing off some particle of gold from the gilding.[32]

How much better it would be, so Uribe concluded, if the tabernacle enclosing the image were kept permanently closed. But the fervid devotion of these worshippers testified to the ancient, still vital hunger of the faithful to touch the material embodiment of their country's heavenly patron.

Reiterating a traditional theme, Uribe then argued that since the labours of the first Franciscans in Mexico had not been accompanied by any great miracles, it was Mary's apparition at Tepeyac which had been chiefly responsible for the sheer rapidity of the Indians' acceptance of the Christian gospel. Dismissing the hypothesis of an apostolic mission led by St Thomas as 'a pious thought' without historical foundation, Uribe insisted that it was thanks to the continued protection afforded by the Guadalupe that Mexico had remained so free from heresy and so devoted to Christ. Had not the great Franciscan missionary of the early eighteenth century, Antonio Margil de Jesús, testified that the image was God's gift to the New World, sent as 'a sacrament of his omnipotence', so as to protect the Church in America?[33]

After such arguments, all that remained for Uribe was to return to his starting point and comment that if doubts concerning the Guadalupe's miraculous origin had been raised, it was because a wave of scepticism and incredulity had swept across the world. But he then distinguished between three classes of critics. In the first place there were self-confessed atheists, deists and Protestants, scholars such as Pierre Bayle (1647–1706) and Jean Le Clerc (1657–1736), who dismissed all miracles as superstition or pious frauds and who had even dared to question the sacred authorship of holy scripture. But there was a second class of critics, who proclaimed themselves to be Catholics, yet who adopted a 'critical scepticism' about all those traditional pious beliefs and miracles which were not sustained by 'infallible authority'. Although Uribe did not name any of these individuals, he claimed that they now formed an influential 'sect' within the Church, a characterization which suggests that he had the so-called Jansenists in mind. But Uribe addressed himself to the third class of 'prudent critics', men who knew how to distinguish between 'the vulgar concerns and superstitious errors of the ignorant multitude' and 'the pure, uniform, immemorial, universal tradition of two-and-a-half centuries' which sustained belief in the miraculous Apparition of Our Lady of Guadalupe. And if all the arguments he had advanced were not enough, there still remained Benedict XIV's virtual canonization of the image when he had included in its feast-day office the epigraph 'Non fecit taliter omni natione.' And on that note Uribe concluded with a fervent *envoi*: 'Truly God was the author and sovereign artificer of this work, whose miracle and singular marvel is so evident to our eyes.'[34]

The contribution of Uribe to the consolidation of the Guadalupe tradition was all important. His achievement was to unite previous, fragmentary assertions and frame a coherent argument by postulating the existence of a primary source written in Nahuatl by Valeriano, claiming that this source lay behind Sánchez and was printed by Laso de la Vega. But Uribe was also the first voice raised in public to warn the faithful that belief in the Guadalupe apparition was now questioned by critics and indeed, dismissed by others as a superstitious fable. Although he strongly defended tradition, he sought to justify its acceptance by appeal to historical sources. In so doing he aligned himself with those Catholic scholars who strove to purge church history of fable and error, men such as Mabillon and the Benedictine congregation of St Maur. At times the findings of these historians aroused fierce controversy, as when the Jesuit Bollandists refused to accept that the Carmelite Order had been founded by the prophet Elias. It was the same community, however, who pronounced that the tradition of St James the Apostle's mission to Spain was too strong to be dismissed, even if they questioned most of the sources cited to support that belief.[35] But although Uribe distinguished between 'prudent critics' and Catholic sceptics, the line separating these two parties was by no means always clear. In any case, the Catholic cult of images and miracles was under attack, not merely from Protestants but from 'Jansenists' within the Church and more generally by the philosophers of the Enlightenment.

When Uribe distinguished between the vulgar errors and superstitions of the multitude and the learned acceptance of tradition by prudent critics, he testified to the influence of Benito Jerónimo Feijoo y Montenegro (1674–1764), who, in his *Universal Critical Theatre* (1726–39) and his *Erudite Letters* (1742–60), had roundly condemned the 'vulgar errors' that afflicted the populace in contemporary Spain. The major achievement of this Benedictine abbot was to familiarize his compatriots with the discoveries of the seventeenth-century revolution in science. To peer through a microscope or a telescope was to enter a world unknown to Aristotle. As cautious as he was orthodox, Feijoo accepted the new science of Copernicus, Descartes and Newton, but questioned the philosophies that had been inspired by these discoveries. Thanks to the Inquisition, it was not until 1751–3 that he was finally able to pronounce that Newton's mathematical physics was a true, persuasive description of the laws governing the universe. But Feijoo also devoted many essays to the criticism of popular errors.[36] At a time when prejudice in Spain questioned the talents of American Spaniards, he boldly defended their achievements, citing the poetry of Sor Juana Inés de la Cruz by way of example, a defence which earned him the thanks of José Mariano de Elizalde, Ita y Parra, the rector of the University of Mexico.[37] But although Feijoo accepted the veracity of St James' mission to Spain and numbered the image of Our Lady of Pilar among the glories of Spain, he strongly criticized popular belief in miraculous cures and questioned the value of pilgrimages.[38] So too, he condemned the practice of astrology and the fear of magical powers.

In an essay published posthumously in 1781, Feijoo defended Catholic devotion to holy images as the just mean between the opposing vices of heresy and idolatry. To start with, he admitted that it was the cult of images which most separated Protestants from Catholics, since their theological differences were often quite abstruse. Yet Luther himself had criticized Protestant iconoclasts as the followers of Mosaic Law rather than of Christian revelation and had defended the presence of crucifixes in church. Looking further back, Feijoo observed that although early Christians had accused pagans of worshipping stone and wooden idols, in fact the ancients had distinguished between the images and the heavenly reality of their deities. Where pagans differed from Catholics was not in praying to images but in their worship of false gods. For all that, Feijoo criticized popular Spanish expressions such as 'Our Lady of Guadalupe bless me', or 'Our Lady of Pilar will reward me', since they distinguished one image of Mary from another and appeared to endow them with particular powers.

Yet what were these images but representations of Mary, who alone could answer the prayers of the faithful? To identify one image as superior in power was certainly super-stitious and verged on idolatry. To support this criticism, Feijoo cited the Second Council of Nicaea and the Council of Trent, both of which defended the veneration of images by citing St Basil the Great's doctrine that all honour paid to the likeness was transferred to the original. But he also noted that some theologians affirmed that images and their heavenly prototypes should be accorded the same adoration, since the likeness participated in the very being of the prototype. But Feijoo rejected this argument as based on philosophical analogies which were all too readily misunder-stood by the populace, who needed careful instruction by parish priests if the danger of superstitious practices was to be avoided.[39]

The divergence between the Hispanic Enlightenment purveyed by Feijoo and the radical scepticism so often evident in its French and Scottish counterparts was no-where better expressed than by the Mexican Jesuits who in 1767 were despatched into an Italian exile by the arbitrary decree of Charles III. Their combination of orthodoxy and intellectual renovation was exemplified by Francisco Javier Clavijero (1731–87), who, in his *Ancient History of Mexico* (1781–2), condemned the contemporary histor-ians of America, Corneille de Pauw, Guillaume Raynal and William Robertson, as typical 'of an age in which more errors have been published than in all previous cen-turies, in which authors write with licence, lie shamelessly, and when no-one is reputed to be a philosopher who does not mock religion and adopt the language of impiety'.[40] When Clavijero came to write his history, he began with an annotated bibliography in which he drew attention to the collection of native codices and manuscripts as-sembled by Sigüenza y Góngora and Boturini and which he had consulted in the Jesuit college of San Pedro y San Pablo and in the viceregal archive, prior to his expulsion from Mexico. The purpose of this exercise was to demonstrate that Indian 'paintings' could be defined as a form of symbolic writing, the interpretation of which depended on the 'songs' carefully transmitted by priests and other record-keepers. However, once in Italy Clavijero was obliged to rely on one great source, Torquemada's *Monarchy of the Indies*, a dependence which produced more exasperation than gratitude. The Franciscan's lack of critical judgement had led him into gross inconsistencies, espe-cially as regards chronology, so that Clavijero confessed that since the chronicle had 'many valuable things for which one would search in vain in other authors, I found myself obliged to do with this history what Virgil did with Ennius: to search for pre-cious stones among the dung'. In effect, Clavijero succeeded in rewriting Torquemada from a neo-classical perspective, expunging from his narrative all mention of Satan as an historical personage, whom the Franciscan had depicted as active in guiding the Mexicans by false oracles in their journey to Anahuac. At the same time, he dismissed the possibility of St Thomas preaching the gospel in America.[41] In all this, the Jesuit proved himself to be a faithful disciple of Feijoo, combining critical judgement with Catholic orthodoxy, with Mabillon rather than Bayle the measure of historical scholarship.

Despite his enforced residence in Bologna, Clavijero succeeded in publishing in Italian a *Brief Account* (1782) of the renowned Mexican Virgin. Not only did he start by asserting that the memory of the apparitions had been preserved by the Indians in their 'paintings' and songs and thereafter written down in 'Mexican', but he also based his narrative on Becerra Tanco's translation of the *Nican mopohua*, possibly the first author to do so, since Florencia, Cabrera and Uribe had all preferred to take Cruz' version as their model. For the rest, he cited Miguel Cabrera on the artistic intricacy of the image's composition and described the joyful celebrations that had greeted the Virgin's election as principal patron of New Spain. Although the Guadalupe's greatest miracle was the conversion of the Indians, Clavijero also chose to highlight the case related by Florencia of an Andalucian possessed by devils who fled to Mexico, where the Virgin liberated him. But when he returned to Spain, he once more fell prey to the devils and had to cross the Atlantic again, where, on landing at Veracruz, he was immediately relieved of his demonic burden.[42] Was it this contrast between America and Europe, the one protected by Our Lady of Guadalupe and the other haunted by devils, that so attracted Clavijero to this story? Whatever the case, it is clear that in both his *Ancient History* and his *Brief Account* the exiled Jesuit chose to emphasize Indian codices, songs and narratives as constituting the foundation not merely of knowledge of the pre-hispanic past, but also of the Guadalupe tradition.

III

If a mere painter like Cabrera could write a treatise about the Guadalupe, surely a natural scientist could equally use his special knowledge to deepen understanding of Mexico's miraculous icon. Such a consideration clearly inspired José Ignacio Bartolache (1739–90), a doctor of medicine, a professor of mathematics at the University of Mexico, and author of several works which ranged from astronomical observations in California to instructions on how to cure smallpox. That his *Guadalupan Opuscule* (1790) had already been announced in the *Mexican Gazette*, that its cost was met by 310 subscribers whose names were printed at the back of the book, and that it was dedicated to the abbot and chapter of the sanctuary at Tepeyac all indicated the prestige of this creole polymath, not to mention the emergence of an identifiable Mexican 'public'. Moreover, it was a public in whom doubts had obviously been raised concerning the reliability of the Guadalupe tradition, since in his prologue Bartolache explained that he addressed himself to three classes of persons:

the first and greatest number of those who according to the old tradition believe in the miraculous origin of Our Lady of Guadalupe, without requesting or desiring any other proof; the second, not few in number, who no longer want to keep to that way, although it is very sure, and show their timidity and distrust; and the third, of those few who, notwithstanding their having until now walked by that sure road of tradition, would not regret having a greater abundance of other proofs.

When Bartolache named his work, a 'satisfactory manifesto', he expressed the hope that it would confirm the beliefs of the first, largest class of individuals; that it would serve as a satisfactory response for the second; and that it would console the third. For the first time in Mexico, the possibility of doubt about the Guadalupe tradition was discussed in public.[43]

In its organization, *Guadalupan Opuscule* clearly revealed its author's mathematical bent, since its 104 pages were divided into 121 numbered paragraphs and into five sections, consisting of an annotated bibliography, texts cited as evidence, the 'body of the work' or its essential argument, critical notes and an appendix. These sections were followed by another four 'pieces' of notarized depositions. That Bartolache took a group of painters to Tepeyac to inspect the image and commissioned two of these artists to paint copies using the image's original materials demonstrated that he sought to deploy the methods of observation and experiment so favoured by contemporary science. Moreover, the manner in which he set down his conclusions was as if he were resolving a geometrical problem.

In his bibliography, Bartolache listed nineteen 'Guadalupan authors', among them three Latin poets, but omitted all mention of printed sermons, thereby maintaining that peculiar separation between history and theology which Florencia had initiated. Although he admitted that Miguel Sánchez wrote an admirable panegyric, he could not excuse his deficiencies as a chronicler, exclaiming: 'if only, in place of the many texts taken from Sacred Scripture and Holy Fathers, this pious author . . . had framed a simple, historical narrative of the miracle, proven with good documents . . .'. As for Laso de la Vega, Bartolache noted Boturini's observation that a mere six months separated the chaplain's eulogy of Sánchez from the composition of his own work. But he then fixed upon a Nahuatl term used by Laso de la Vega to indicate the Virgin's height, which clearly derived from the early sixteenth century, since it was not found in subsequent dictionaries of that language. Commenting that the censor, Baltazar González, did not precisely name Laso de la Vega as author and that his name was not printed on the title page, Bartolache concluded that the chaplain had published his account in order to inform the world that he had found the papers on which Sánchez had based his version. As was to be expected, he placed Becerra Tanco 'in the first place of his class', since he demonstrated 'a perfect instruction in the language, in the maps and characters, in the usages, customs and antiquities of the Indians'. But he had not seen the 1666 edition of Becerra Tanco's pamphlet and expressed his surprise at not finding any mention of Sánchez and Laso de la Vega in the 1675 edition, albeit he noted the citation of an old, manuscript account, written in 'pure and elegant Mexican language'.[44]

If Bartolache praised the 'impartiality and good judgement' of Florencia, he doubted whether the old account he cited was in fact written by a Franciscan, and asserted that it obviously dated from the sixteenth century, with Fernando de Alva acting as a simple copyist. With considerable aplomb, he cited a manuscript in Nahuatl that he himself had found in the university library, which consisted of Tlaxcalan annals running from 1454 to 1737, copied by Marcelo de Salazar. Of Cayetano de Cabrera, he noted his bilious temperament and admitted having read his book as a student before it was withdrawn. Since Cabrera did not know Indians very well, he had failed to realize that they were quite capable of building a rudimentary chapel in a day, not to mention two weeks. Bartolache concluded by praising Luis Antonio and Cayetano Torres Tuñón, two learned brothers, 'filled with literary honours and laurels, exemplary priests', who in 1785 had arranged for the publication in Madrid of two volumes of works dealing with Our Lady of Guadalupe. If the second consisted of the third edition of Florencia's treatise, the first reprinted the works of Cruz, Nicoseli, Becerra Tanco, Miguel Cabrera, Sánchez' *novenas*, Benedict XIV's *breve* and office, and a description of the Guadalupe Congregation in Madrid written by Teobaldo Antonio de Rivera.[45] The omission in this collection of Sánchez' *Image of the Virgin Mary* demonstrated the degree to which this work was now seen as a baroque embarrassment, alien to the 'good taste' of the late eighteenth century.

Although Bartolache achieved little in this bibliography other than to arrange it systematically, he also revealed his own obsession when, on citing Nicoseli's account, he contradicted the Italian's assertion that Juan Diego's cape had been woven from the coarse fibre of the maguey cactus, observing that the actual canvas of the Guadalupe image 'in weave is not more thick, rough or loose than any of those from which sails for ships are made'. So too, he took from Florencia the description of the image made in 1666 by the painters accompanied by Becerra Tanco, who had affirmed that it was 'a canvas woven from the thread that is made from the wild palms called iczotl', from which Indians wove their capes. From his own observation, Bartolache asserted that the canvas was quite fine and that he had failed to find Indians who could weave such a cloth from palm thread. So taken was Bartolache with his discovery that he dismissed Francisco de Castro, a Latin poet, as belonging to the party of the 'magueyistas'. Although Miguel Cabrera's treatise confirmed his view, since the painter had identified the canvas as woven from a medium linen called *cotense*, Bartolache damned his work with faint praise when, although he recommended its reprinting, he added:

It was too much for a layman, without other studies than the honourable domestic easel and palette, that he should have chosen to compose an Opuscule, in which precision was united with clarity, both instructing and delighting.

As we shall see, these remarks deeply offended Cabrera's many admirers, and if Bartolache's own work was undoubtedly lucid, it failed to delight the Mexican public.[46]

Bartolache's other obsession figured prominently in the second part of his treatise, where he presented twelve texts, most of them, apart from the inevitable citation of Bernal Díaz, extracted from Torquemada's *Monarchy of the Indies*. Noting that the Franciscan claimed that he had never left the territory of his own province, he then cited passages in which Torquemada described himself as being in Michoacán and in Guatemala. More important, he cited a passage from the Franciscan preacher, Juan Bautista, in which he stated that he had given Torquemada the manuscript of the *Ecclesiastical History of the Indies* written by Jerónimo de Mendieta. Yet Torquemada had denied knowing of the whereabouts of this text, claiming that it had been sent to Spain, despite a decree issued by the General Commissary of the Franciscans in Madrid commanding that he should be given Mendieta's chronicle. In these citations Bartolache provided chapter and verse to support the charges of plagiarism that Agustín de Betancurt had levelled against Torquemada in his *Mexican Theatre*. Equally important, Bartolache cited extensively the famous passage in which the Franciscan historian noted that Tepeyac had been one of three shrines which in the pre-hispanic era had attracted pilgrims from afar, only then to explain that the idols had been replaced by Christian images, dedicating the new chapel 'in Tonantzin, close to Mexico, to the Most Sacred Virgin, who is Our Lady and Mother'. And yet at this point, Torquemada had abstained from any mention of the image of Guadalupe, thereby evading any discussion of the Virgin's apparitions. For the rest, Bartolache noted that the Nahuatl annals he had found mentioned the events of 1531 and Juan Diego's death in 1548.[47]

With his principal sources clearly set down, Bartolache then proceeded to 'the body of his work', putting the negative case first. There were five main reasons why the image of Guadalupe should not be accepted as miraculous in origin. To begin with, the miracle lacked all legal certification by Church authorities; Zumárraga had not written about the apparitions; then Torquemada had obviously suggested that the image was the work of men rather than of God; the cloth or *ayatl* was too long and narrow to have served as an Indian cape; and finally, according to the rules of art the image was defective, yet should have been perfect if formed by God. In effect, as Uribe had affirmed in an unpublished manuscript, the only sure defence was 'the constant, old and invariable tradition from fathers to sons'. Before stating the positive side of the argument, Bartolache asserted that it was first necessary to ascertain what kind of miracle was involved in the apparition of the image, especially since St Thomas Aquinas had distinguished three classes of miracles. The first class consisted of those events where there was nothing in Nature to assist their occurrence, as when in the Bible the sun was alleged to have retracted its course. In the second, power existed in Nature but without a subject endowed with the capacity to evoke it, as in the case of the resurrection from the dead. In the third class of miracle, there were a power in Nature and subjects able to employ it, with only a deficiency of time or of ordinary assistance, as in the case of rapid cures from illness without doctor or time for normal healing. Since the painters of the 1666 Inspection had declared that if it was impossible to paint an image such as the Guadalupe without sizing, then its miracle belonged to the second class. However, if it be demonstrated that the image had been painted with natural palette, brushes and sizing, then it belonged to the third class since it then derived from a rapid acceleration of natural processes, akin to a sudden cure from illness.[48]

By way of answering the negative case, Bartolache then adduced the 1666 depositions as covering the need for a legal certification of the miracle. That Zumárraga had not condemned the apparition was as important as his silence. As for Torquemada, who had obviously seen both the image and its sanctuary, 'he appears to have had some strong concern not to have spoken about the matter of the miracle'. On the size of the canvas, he noted that Indians often knotted their capes at the shoulder and that Becerra Tanco had noted that it lacked the third part of its original width. Finally, as regards alleged artistic imperfections, the image was perfect, since it admirably fulfilled God's purpose, so that it could not be judged by merely human rules.

Having thus summarized the reasons for disbelief or belief in the Guadalupe miracle, Bartolache then added 'critical notes' in which he reviewed these arguments. For a start, he confessed to not understanding why critics thought that Zumárraga should have framed legal certification of the apparitions, since in the conquest era no-one would have believed Juan Diego's account of the colloquies. Instead, the bishop had asked for a sign and the Virgin had sent him 'a credential letter, her very sacrosanct Image'. If Zumárraga had remained silent, it was because he had no reliable evidence about the Virgin's apparitions and was in any case too absorbed in preaching and in protecting the Indians at a time when the very capacity of the natives to receive the sacraments was still under debate. The argument about silence thus needed very careful handling since occurrences familiar to everyone were at times rarely if ever mentioned in writing.[49]

But it was Torquemada whom Bartolache criticized most strongly, citing a passage from his chronicle in which the Franciscan exhibited a credulous acceptance of demonic power, adding:

the author of the *Monarchy of the Indies* incurred in this celebrated work intolerable defects, such as the lack of truth, as regards the very facts and of chronology; bad faith in hiding other men's writings, for which he was responsible; and little or no critical judgement about miraculous events: all things which cannot be pardoned in an historian who merits the name.[50]

As regards the famous text about the Franciscans replacing the idol of Tonantzin with an image of Mary, Bartolache averred that everyone interpreted this to mean that Torquemada by silence implicitly denied 'the miraculous origin of this heavenly painting' of Guadalupe. But he then argued that the Franciscans, who had arrived in 1524, obviously did not wait until 1531 to install a likeness of the Mother of God at Tepeyac, and hence Torquemada had referred to an image which had preceded the installation of the Guadalupe. Moreover, Zumárraga did not arrive until 1527 or 1528, and in 1531 he entrusted the new chapel at Tepeyac to secular priests subject to the bishop. The Franciscans had never officiated at the sanctuary of Our Lady of Guadalupe. In this incisive argument, Bartolache was gratified to think that he had disposed of the Achilles of the negative arguments, 'not as invincible, but strong, robust and choleric, as the hero of Homer'. The failure of Torquemada to mention the Guadalupe could thus be dismissed as 'a violent and affected silence'.[51]

Turning to the actual canvas, Bartolache argued that the elongated shape of the original *ayatl* was caused by Juan Diego loosening the knot when he lowered his cape before Zumárraga to reveal the image imprinted amidst the flowers. As for the defects in the painting, when judged by the rules of art, he observed that Miguel Cabrera's invocation of the laws of perspective to explain these deficiencies was not utterly persuasive. However, since he was not a painter himself, Bartolache left the questions for experts to resolve and hastened to observe that contrary to what Becerra Tanco had suggested, the imprinting of the image could only have occurred in Zumárraga's palace, since had the Indian brought an already-painted image rather than mere roses and flowers, he would have been accused of being an imposter, seeking to perpetrate a fraud. But all this still left the question: what kind of miracle was performed when the image appeared imprinted on the Indian's cape? It was good theology to assume, so Bartolache argued, that God works through natural causes. One example of this mode of action was Christ's multiplication of the five loaves of bread, as reported in St John's gospel, where no commentator had ever suggested that the increased number of loaves were of better quality than the original five. Another example was the renovation of the Holy Christ of Ixmiquilpan, where the miracle consisted simply of doing rapidly all that a qualified sculptor might have done. But to apply this rule and examples to the case of the Guadalupe, so Bartolache concluded, would require the combined judgement of both painters and theologians.[52]

In the notarized depositions that were appended to his main text it was stated that on 26 December 1786 in the presence of the abbot, Bartolache and a group of painters inspected the image at Tepeyac with the windows open for two hours. The painters certified that the face and hands of the Virgin, together with the angel's face, appeared to have a certain lustre or a varnish, as if anointed with soap. Far from being a rough material, the canvas appeared to be 'like a fine linen of medium quality'. As for the thread which united its two pieces usually described as being of thin cotton, they asserted it was of the same thread as the canvas, but somewhat thicker. On a second occasion, 25 January 1787, the painters agreed that the flowers which adorned the Virgin's tunic were not painted according to the 'profiles' of its folds. So too, they found that the oil colours they had prepared for comparison obviously differed in substance from those found in the image. Unlike all previous observers, they concluded that the image had been painted with the assistance of sizing so as to bind the colours. In conclusion, they affirmed that according to the rules of their art, they considered that the image had been miraculously painted, at least in its 'primitive substance', but that 'daring hands' had executed certain lines and retouchings.[53]

Along with close observation, there went experimentation. In his appendix Bartolache declared that when he started his research on the Guadalupe, he had arranged for the leaves of the palm tree known as iczotl to be brought to the capital from over forty leagues away. But although he had commissioned Indian weavers, both Mexicans and Otomies, to weave cloth from the thread of maguey and iczotl, their work had not proved satisfactory, leading him to suppose that they no longer possessed the skills of their ancestors. Moreover, when these materials were later compared with the canvas of the image, it was found that although the palm cloth, unlike the rough weave of maguey, was soft to the touch, that of the image was finer. Undeterred, in 1787 Bartolache had Andrés López paint a copy of the Guadalupe on a cloth woven from iczotl without using any sizing, giving it to the convent of the Enseñanza. A year later, a European devotee of the Mexican Virgin commissioned Rafael Gutiérrez also to paint a copy on the same kind of cloth and arranged for it to be hung in the chapel of the Pocito at Tepeyac. However, on 24 January 1788 the painters assembled by Bartolache testified that they had inspected these two copies, only then to affirm that 'neither of the two they had seen was an identical copy of the original'. And there the matter rested.[54]

In his youth Bartolache was expelled from the Tridentine seminary of Mexico because he had derided the faded scholastic theology it still taught. A later critic wrote that although he was somewhat capricious and sharp in his criticism, 'he merits being called a genius, who like the Angel of the Waters, moved the waters of the sciences in Mexico'.[55] Yet, although his study of the Mexican Virgin caused indignation in many quarters, it must be judged something of a failure. As regards the Guadalupe, he had little to add either to the analysis of the image or to a critical revision of the tradition. Despite his condescending description of Cabrera as a 'layman', he himself failed to offer any new description of the artistic techniques and paints which were involved in the image's composition. His contribution was twofold. In the first place, he demonstrated that the original description of Juan Diego's cape as woven from maguey fibre could no longer be sustained. So devoted was Bartolache to his iczotl thesis that he even included a drawing of this wild palm tree in his treatise. In the second place, he joined Clavijero in subjecting Torquemada to trenchant criticism, reviving the old charge of plagiarism. The central importance of his work, however, lay in its open avowal that there were present in Mexico individuals who doubted the truth of the Guadalupe tradition and who judged the image to be a defective work of art. Moreover, his experiments with copies painted on palm cloth obviously suggested that it might be possible to reproduce the unique qualities of the image in a way which had eluded painters who had used ordinary canvases and oils.

The care with which Bartolache had protested his own devotion to Our Lady of Guadalupe failed to allay the anger caused by his treatise and experiments. In a letter written in 1792, José María Téllez Girón, a Franciscan friar, expressed his shock at encountering in the Pocito chapel at Tepeyac the copy by Rafael Gutiérrez, with an inscription explaining that it had been painted on a canvas woven from iczotl without sizing so as to ascertain how long it would survive uncorrupted. He then read Bartolache's treatise with mounting disquiet. He failed to understand why so much emphasis was given to the question of whether the Guadalupe canvas was woven from maguey or iczotl and noted that in many old paintings the coarse linen canvas was often well preserved. The problem here was that thanks to Voltaire and Rousseau all talk of miracles was now scorned, and such was the diffusion of impiety that even in Mexico 'antiguadalupanos' could be found. And yet the greatest Christian miracle was the Eucharist, as Becerra Tanco had argued, where the hosts soon decayed if not consumed. What did it matter if the original canvas of Guadalupe should disintegrate? The real miracle was the apparition, since the likeness of the Virgin would remain and continue to be venerated. As for Bartolache, since he had not inspected the image from the back, how could he really tell from what thread the canvas was woven and what kind of thread joined its two pieces? No-one hitherto, certainly not the painters of 1666 and 1751, had seen any evidence of the sizing that Bartolache perceived. Nor did the friar approve of the attack on Torquemada, whose 'Monarchy of the Indies is an indelible monument of the antiquities of our happy America'. Moreover, since it had been the Franciscans who had carried the Guadalupe to her sanctuary in 1531, it was obviously to her image that Torquemada had referred in his enigmatic text. In all this vigorous dissent, Téllez Girón expressed the great disquiet which Bartolache's treatise had aroused in Mexico.[56]

IV

In October 1795 Francisco Javier Conde y Oquendo (1733–99), a learned Cuban canon of Puebla, joined José de Alcíbar, a Mexican artist, to visit the sanctuary at Tepeyac. In his account of the occasion, Conde reported that Alcibar had assisted Miguel Cabrera to paint the copies of the Guadalupe that Juan Francisco López had taken to Europe to present to Benedict XIV and Ferdinand VI. A member of the group of painters who had inspected the image in 1751, Alcíbar confirmed that when it was viewed from the back, no sign of any sizing could be discerned, since the colours showed through the canvas. Moreover, although the cloth was woven from the thread of the iczotl palm, it was not as fine as Bartolache had asserted, since the weave was comparatively loose, 'with ridges and holes'. If the two men were critical of Bartolache, it was in part because on their visit they were able to verify that the creole polymath had encouraged one of his assistant painters to assault the holy image, proposing that:

> with the point of his knife he should scratch the extreme tip of the left wing of the seraphim who serves as the Most Holy Virgin's support, to see whether it had sizing. The chief sacristan, Father Domingo Garcés, who is still living, surprised him in this execrable act, and has assured me that the curious investigator had not taken more than a kind of fuzz of colour imprinted in the weave of the mantle. Thus it is, that until now the painting has remained injured and imperfect, since not without sorrow, I saw and recognized the cut on 22 October 1795, when I had the good fortune to venerate it in company of don José de Alcibar, one of the most famous painters in Mexico, through it having been lowered from the altar to the level of the presbyterium, in order to adjust the frame.[57]

Not without reason, therefore, did Alcíbar later write a letter to Conde, in which he praised Miguel Cabrera as 'this hero of our times', whose *American Marvel* was to be trusted as regards the paints and techniques employed in the composition of the Guadalupe, adding: 'I have always thought the injurious account published by Dr Bartolache to be ridiculous, false and of no value.' Moreover, the copy made by Rafael Gutiérrez which hung in the Pocito chapel was already 'totally opaque and discoloured'. So too, Conde himself reflected that although Bartolache had dismissed Cabrera as a mere 'layman', in Spain the celebrated painter, Anton Rafael Mengs, had written a book on Corregio. Was it possible, Conde queried, that Bartolache disdained Cabrera because the painter was an Indian? And yet, what could be more obvious than that 'in dealing with the glories of Most Holy Mary of Guadalupe, the Indian's brush and pen both paint and write with an angel's hand'?[58] This designation of Cabrera as an Indian was all the more significant since it was information which obviously derived from Alcíbar.

For his part, Conde remained convinced of the miraculous origin of the Guadalupe, noting that whereas Sánchez had thought St Michael to be the painter, others had attributed the painting to the Virgin herself or to God the Father. Even Bartolache had confessed that it was inimitable, and Alcíbar had simply said to him: 'one cannot explain it'. Although he noted Ibarra's testimony that it had been Juan Correa who had taken the first accurate copy, he averred that the best likeness was to be found in the church of San Francisco, a painting which had been retouched by Baltazar de Echave. As for the rules of art, how could one judge such a work by the criteria of the academy? After all, both the Chinese and the Arabs had their own kind of images, quite distinct from their European counterparts. And if their art forms could not be judged by the classical rules, why should the work of the Almighty be subjected to such demands? All this led to the conclusion that the image of Guadalupe was 'without doubt painted by the hand of God; his immortal finger has been the brush; and although its colours are natural, no-one knows from whence they have come'.[59]

Although Conde apparently completed his *Historical Dissertation* on the apparition of the Guadalupe in 1795, his work was not published until 1852, when thanks to the civil disorders that then haunted Mexico it passed relatively unnoticed. A learned man, who had spent some years in Europe before taking up his canonry in Puebla, Conde possessed what he archly called 'my small, but select library', in which were to be found many early chronicles of America.[60] Thus when he turned to review the sixteenth-century background to the apparition, he took the opportunity to rehearse the famous debate at Valladolid in 1550–1 between Bartolomé de las Casas and Juan Ginés de Sepúlveda, citing the summary written by Domingo de Soto and published in Las Casas' *Treatises* (1552), which he possessed. He praised Las Casas for framing the New Laws of 1542 which forbade the enslavement of the Indians and added: 'he bore the Indians on his shoulders, with the natural treasure of their liberty in one hand and the trophy of a decree prohibiting the printing of papers against them in the other'. So too, he printed a copy of *Sublime Deus*, the papal breve issued by Paul III in 1537, which declared the Indians to be true men, fit for baptism, and endowed with rights to freedom and property. Moreover, he possessed a rare copy of Diego Valadés' *Retórica cristiana* (1579), which discussed the Franciscans' policy of baptism and administering the Eucharist to the Indians. Yet, despite all this evidence, modern historians criticized the missionaries and dismissed the natives of the New World as barely rational, writers whom he curiously identified as 'Pa, Rainald, Robertson', which was to say, Pauw, Raynal and Robertson.[61]

But although the friars defended the Indians from the conquerors, they had burnt most of the 'paintings' of the natives. And yet, as Conde emphasized, the Indians had recorded the great events of their history on cloth 'woven from the thread of maguey or the *yezotl* palm' or cotton, and like the ancient Egyptians possessed a great range of records. With their destruction were lost 'the most precious remains of their anti-quities'. It was not until Sigüenza y Góngora and Boturini that any attempt was made to collect what remained of these codices. Even so, the Indians preserved the memory of events through their songs, and nowhere more so than in the case of the Guadalupe apparitions, since 'oral tradition lives perennially imprinted in the hearts of mortals'.[62] Conde reviewed the extensive literature dealing with the Mexican Virgin and like all commentators of this epoch complained of the 'ingenious, preachable concepts' of Miguel Sánchez, which could only be condemned for their bad taste. Although he was evidently unfamiliar with Uribe's dissertation, which had yet to be published, he reached much the same conclusions, which is to say, he accepted Sigüenza's thesis that Antonio Valeriano was the author of the version in Nahuatl which had been printed by Laso de la Vega and was later used by Becerra Tanco in his second edition. But where previous authors had treated Florencia with respect, by contrast Conde ob-served that the Jesuit 'was not a man of intelligence', adding that his reputation among critics or men of learning had dwindled, since 'he was seen to be poor and penurious in invention'. That Florencia had not printed the song of don Plácido addressed to the Guadalupe, which Sigüenza had given him, was cause for 'irremediable tears'. So too, his failure to print 'the old account', which he had cited so repeatedly, was 'a very black and indelible mark' against him. As for Torquemada, for once he agreed with Bartolache and furthermore cited Clavijero on the Franciscan, accusing the chronicler of so much prolixity while preserving an 'absolute silence' about the Guadalupe.[63]

Like his predecessors, Conde provided a description of the cluster of institutions and buildings that now served the faithful in their visits to Tepeyac. Much of what he had to say can also be found in *American Garden* (1797), a pleasing but slight book on the Guadalupe, written by Ignacio Carrillo Pérez, a functionary at the Mexican mint. Obviously, both authors rehearsed the great celebrations of the election of the Virgin as patron, and indeed Conde printed the full text of Benedict XIV's breve together with the mass and office for 12 December. In the Peninsula, so he emphasized, it was only Our Lady of Pilar, 'that of the greatest credit and celebrity in Spain', which had been granted a similar privilege, albeit as early as 1723. But as for the Guadalupe of Extremadura, its tradition was by now regarded as doubtful, and it had not been granted its own feast day. At Tepeyac, Conde deplored the subjection of its college of canons to the jurisdiction of the archbishop; as did Carrillo, who noted that it was the great creole jurist, Francisco Javier de Gamboa (1718–94), who had acted as the advoc-ate of the college against Archbishop Rubio. Both authors praised Calixto González Abencerraje, 'in Spain a soldier and retired in Veracruz', who had collected over 40,000 pesos from travellers for the construction of the Pocito chapel designed by Francisco Guerrero y Torres and completed in 1779. But it was only Carrillo who noted that the construction of the convent for Capuchin nuns, situated alongside the sanctuary, was completed in 1787 at a cost of 212,000 pesos, which was raised by

Archbishop Alonso Núñez de Haro y Peralta. So too, it was Carrillo who provided a summary description of the great gilded retables which adorned the sanctuary, only then to note that there were proposals to replace the central, Churrigueresque altarpiece with a neo-classic retable of 'white marble and jasper'.[64]

In his closing pages, Conde turned aside from his theme to praise his compatriot, the count of Revillagigedo, viceroy of New Spain 1789–94, asking 'when has there ever been, since the conquest, a viceroy who has the advantage over the second count of Revillagigedo . . . in truth none more wise in matters of government'. The American-born ruler had transformed the capital, working day and night with extraordinary energy, so that Conde simply exclaimed: 'what paving, what cleanliness of the sewers and what lighting of the streets!'. Moreover, if Viceroy Bucareli had been so devoted to the Guadalupe that he had arranged to be buried in the sanctuary, Revillagigedo had requested the king to allow him to receive his stick of office at Tepeyac. Conde commented that 'perhaps it was with the idea of receiving it from the hand of the Virgin, together with the light he needed for the success of his government, as in fact occurred, since everyone venerated him as a gift from heaven and are weeping at his retirement as the kingdom's scourge'. In these remarks we obtain some measure of the impact on public opinion of the enlightened despotism of this zealous servant of the Bourbon dynasty.[65]

Within Conde's discursive text there also lurked another, more surprising testimony to the impact of the revolutions that threatened the stability of Western Europe. For when Conde contemplated Our Lady of Guadalupe, he accepted Sánchez' identification of the image as the Woman of the Apocalypse, only then to assert that, if the Woman seen by St John in his vision was usually taken to be the symbol of the universal Church, then the Guadalupe was clearly the symbol of the Mexican Church. He then added:

> I set myself to consider America, my *patria*, as an immense country, which God has reserved since his creation, for the purpose of renovating in this new world the old world, which is now cold, sterile and tired by thousands of centuries; and that the plantation of the Catholic Faith shall flower anew in it and bear rich fruits of blessing.

Had not the persecution of the Jesuits led to the French Revolution, which had produced a universal upheaval, with countless churches and convents closed and even Rome threatened? It was amidst such tribulation that Conde recalled the prophecy set down in Isaiah, chapter 60, in which, while darkness reigned all about, Zion was once more restored and a small nation made great. He added: 'I have heard several spiritual and ecstatic persons explain this in an emphatic manner about the new American Church.' In effect, the news of the French Revolution in Europe had sparked off a wave of speculation in Mexico about the future.[66]

Indeed, Conde testified to hearing several sermons in which preachers reiterated the prophecy of Francisco Javier Carranza and cited the possibility of 'the transmigration of the Apostolic See and residence of the popes in this continent'. So too, Carrillo cited Blessed Amadeus on miracles only then to recall the sermons preached by Carranza and Juan de Villa Sánchez on the Guadalupe, adding that 'this sovereign image came not only to plant the Church in these Americas, but also to welcome her Supreme Head and her sancturary to be a safe port for the ship of St Peter at the stormy end of the centuries'. In the light of the sad plight of Europe, averred Conde, it was perfectly proper to evoke these expectations without danger to dogma or discipline. Moreover, he took from Carranza the prophecies of St Malachy, the archbishop of Armagh, especially since, after his journey to Austria, Pius VI could already be described as 'a pilgrim pope'. There was thus the possibility that the pope might well come to take up residence in Mexico.[67]

It was a sign of the menacing turmoil of these years that Conde concluded his chronicle with a strong condemnation of a scandalous sermon preached at Tepeyac in 1794, in which a Dominican theologian, 'a friar, don Fernando Mier, a creole', had argued not only that St Thomas the Apostle had preached the gospel in New Spain, but that the likeness of the Virgin of Guadalupe had been imprinted on his cape and not on that of Juan Diego. When Conde started his work with a criticism of Bartolache, only then to close his narrative with an account of Mier's arrest and 'perpetual exile' in Spain, he demonstrated the change in the cultural climate of New Spain in the closing decades of the eighteenth century.[68] The exultant confidence of the 1750s had been replaced by audacious criticism. And yet he also testified that the turmoil caused by the French Revolution did not simply hasten the inroads of scepticism, but that it also drove men to heed Carranza's prophecy, leading them to anticipate a glorious future for Mexico as the faithful bulwark of the Catholic Church. When, in 1810, Miguel Hidalgo offered his insurgent followers a copy of the Guadalupe as their banner, he thus in part used for political ends the expectations concerning the Mexican Virgin that gripped so many of the faithful in these last years of the Pax Hispanica.

9

Myth and scepticism

I

On 12 December 1794 the dignitaries of Mexico, headed by the viceroy and the archbishop, assembled in the sanctuary at Tepeyac to celebrate the feast of Our Lady of Guadalupe. The occasion was all the more moving since the church had been closed from 10 June 1791 until 11 December 1794 so as to allow the repair of the great cracks that had appeared in the vaulting. The preacher, Fray Servando Teresa de Mier, was known to many present, since only a month before, on 8 November, he had delivered to much the same congregation 'a most learned funeral oration in praise of the moral and political virtues of . . . don Fernando Cortés', a sermon which commemorated the transfer of the conqueror's bones to a new sepulchre built in the Hospital de Jesús.[1] Others present may have heard the two sermons he had preached at the behest of the former viceroy, the Count of Revillagigedo, in which he criticized the errors of Jean-Jacques Rousseau and condemned the crimes of the Jacobin regicides in France.[2] But there was nothing in these exercises to prepare them for the scandalous sermon which awaited them. To be sure, Mier began on a conventional note when he compared the consecration of the sanctuary at Tepeyac in 1709 to Solomon's dedication of the Temple in Jerusalem, exclaiming: 'there the Ark of the Covenant of the Lord with Israel and here the Image of Guadalupe, the best Ark of the Covenant of the Lord and his Mother with the truly chosen and beloved generation, with his special people, the Americans'. So too, in his notes, Mier had thought to invite the congregation to consider that although the world abounded with likenesses of Mary, it was only in America that the 'original of these images' was to be found, 'reserved since eternity for Mexico'. But he then broached a secular topic when, after noting that the king had recently called for New Spain's history to be studied, he observed that Mexican history was hidden 'in disguised traditions, in allegorical fables and national hieroglyphics', which neither Torquemada nor Boturini had succeeded in deciphering. And yet, as Alonso de Molina had affirmed, 'Mexican' was able to express truths and mysteries as sublime as anything written in Latin or Hebrew, albeit 'all figured and symbolic'.[3] The point of these enigmatic affirmations became apparent when Mier declared that the tradition of Our Lady of Guadalupe was as mysterious and symbolic as any narrative of ancient Mexico.

With his congregation's attention now aroused, Mier enunciated four audacious propositions. The first and most scandalous was that the image of Guadalupe had been imprinted on the cape of St Thomas and not on the humble *ayatl* of Juan Diego. In the second proposition he averred that the apostle had deposited the image in the hills of Tenanyuca, so that it had been venerated by the Indians over 1,750 years ago. But once the natives fell into apostasy, St Thomas had hidden it. By way of reassurance, Mier then affirmed in his third proposition that the Virgin Mary had indeed appeared to Juan Diego, but in order to reveal the whereabouts of her hidden image, so that he could take it to Zumárraga. In his last proposition, he insisted that the Guadalupe image was supernatural in origin, since the Virgin, when still living, had imprinted her likeness on the apostle's cape. As will be observed, the broad effect of these hypotheses was to raise Mexico to the level of Spain, since, where the Peninsula had gloried in the mission of St James and the appearance of the Virgin as Our Lady of Pilar, so now New Spain was endowed with the presence of St Thomas and a miraculous image which dated from that epoch. Rather than an offshoot of Spain, the Mexican Church could now boast of its own apostolic foundation.[4]

But what proofs did Mier advance to support his assertions? To start with, he referred to the ancient monuments which had been excavated in the great square of Mexico City in 1790, naming them as relics 'more precious than all those of Herculaneum and Pompeii'. They included a large, fearsome figure of the goddess Coatlicue; a circular disc later known as the stone of sacrifices; and the famous Calendar Stone. What the inscriptions on these monuments demonstrated was that St Thomas, a bearded white man known to the Indians as Quetzalcoatl, had preached the gospel in the New World. The natives of Mexico had thus been converted to Christianity soon after their Saviour's death and their religion had preserved Christian features. The very name of the goddess worshipped at Tepeyac, Teotenantzin, the Mother of the True God, indicated that in different guises Mary had always been venerated there. When St Thomas had been obliged to flee, he had left many images of Christ or Mary which were later discovered after the Spanish conquest and restored to honour. After all, as regards the Guadalupe, had not Becerra Tanco argued that Juan Diego had taken to Zumárraga a cape on which the Virgin's likeness was already imprinted? For the rest, Mier noted a strange figure of '8' inscribed on the image, which he claimed was a Syro-Chaldean letter, similar to that found on the tomb of St Thomas at Meliapor in southern India. Was not the roll of her tunic at the Virgin's feet an apostolic sign of the scrolls of holy scripture, and what was the angel but a symbol of the incorporation of Mexico into the Christian Church? By way of conclusion,

Plate 21   Juan Manuel Yllanes del Huerto, *St Thomas the Apostle as Quetzalcoatl preaching in Tlaxcala*

Mier emphasized that he had not denied the Virgin's apparitions to Juan Diego and reaffirmed the supernatural origin of the image which depicted Mary as a woman of only fourteen or fifteen years, but already expectant with the Christ child, and thus a symbol of the Incarnation. He ended with a prayer to the Virgin to protect Mexico: 'Ark, especially precious now that the Philistines of France insult and attack the people of God, do not permit that they should triumph here as they did there owing to the sins of the sons of Heli.' Among his notes was an extraordinary invocation, which he may or may not have delivered, in which he addressed Mary as 'Teotenantzin entirely Virgin, trustworthy Tonacayona . . . Flowery Coyolxauhqui, true Coatlicue de Minjó . . .'.[5]

Public reaction to this extraordinary sermon can be gauged from the indignant description in the closing pages of Conde's *Historical Dissertation*:

> The congregation were excited to such an extent, that the lord archbishop, who was celebrating the pontifical mass, had to restrain himself from silencing the preacher and ordering him to leave the pulpit, so as not to expose him to the people who might have stoned him in the midst of the church.

So too, Conde's devoted pupil, Dr José Miguel Guridi y Alcocer, commented that such was the anger aroused by 'this strange and scandalous sermon' that Mier, who 'believed he would achieve an immortal name, worked his own ruin'. Conde noted that Mier had been summarily confined to his cell after the sermon and printed the full text of the archbishop's edict of 25 March 1795 which sentenced the preacher to 'perpetual exile' in Spain, a fitting punishment, he added, for such an audacious and irreverent challenge to established tradition.[6]

In his *Apología*, written in the Inquisition prison during 1817–20, Mier recalled that he had been asked to preach the sermon only seventeen days before the event. During that interval he had been introduced to Lic. José Ignacio Borunda, an elderly lawyer, who during three or four meetings assured him that the recent excavations in the Zócalo had demonstrated the truth of the long-standing tradition that St Thomas had preached the gospel in the New World. He himself had written an entire treatise on the subject, showing that the Guadalupe image was of apostolic provenance. If these assertions concerning St Thomas were so readily accepted by Mier, it was because he was familiar with the works of Becerra Tanco and Boturini, where the apostle's presence in the New World was accepted without question. Indeed, had he visited Tlaxacala, he would have encountered a recent painting which depicted St Thomas preaching to the natives of that city. Moreover, he confessed that his faith in the traditional account of the Virgin's apparitions to Juan Diego had been shaken by Bartolache's *Guadalupan Opuscule* (1790), since although the scientist professed belief in that tradition, all his findings and arguments were designed to raise doubts. As he explained, in Borunda's theory 'I saw a system favourable to religion, I saw the *patria* assured of an apostle, a glory all nations crave and especially Spain.'[7] In any case, at no point in his sermon did he deny the Virgin's apparitions or the supernatural origin of the Guadalupe image. But Mier was utterly confounded when, after suffering confinement in the great Dominican convent in Mexico City, he at last obtained Borunda's manuscript treatise, only to find that 'it was a piece of nonsense worthy of a man who did not know theology and who, despite being an antiquarian and an etymologist, began with riddles, continued with visions and ended in madness'. In despair he offered to write and publish a retraction of his sermon. By then, however, the archbishop had ordered preachers throughout the capital to refute his wild theories and had confiscated all his papers, so that they could be scrutinized by expert theologians.[8]

Although Mier disowned Borunda so contemptuously, he was to draw upon the lawyer's theories for the remainder of his life. At first reading, the *General Key to American Hieroglyphics* is incomprehensible, since although Borunda asserted that 'the hieroglyphic writing of the Mexican nation' expressed concepts without recourse to words and thus possessed a hidden, allegorical meaning, he failed to set down any principles of interpretation or reach any clear conclusions. As a student of Nahuatl he cited Martín del Castillo, a seventeenth-century Franciscan from Puebla, who had compared Mexican to Hebrew and Syriac and asserted that the name of Mexico derived from those languages and thus meant 'of my Messiah', a resemblance more obvious in the native pronunciation of 'Mescico'.[9] Although he defended Torquemada's great work from the criticism of Bartolache, Borunda asserted that the Franciscan had failed to capture the allegorical meaning of the Indian narratives that he had collected. To assist in their interpretation, he invoked *Reflections on the Rules and Use of Criticism* (1792), a Spanish translation of a work written in 1713 by Honoré de Sainte-Marie, a French Carmelite, who had sharply questioned the critical approach of Jean Mabillon, the famous Benedictine scholar, arguing that scepticism as regards venerable miracles such as the origin of the Holy House of Loreto in Nazareth would lead to incredulity about holy scripture.[10] Borunda, who had studied at the Jesuit college of San Ildefonso and had known Francisco Javier Clavijero, 'with whom I was familar in the year 1761', was thus well aware of the debate over historical method. Unfortunately, when he came to interpret the meaning of the statue of Coatlicue he produced a mass of utterly incomprehensible notes. If he did not attempt to examine the Calendar Stone, it it was in part because in his *Historical and Chronological Description of the Two Stones* (1792), Antonio de León y Gama, a well-known savant, had employed Nahuatl manuscripts of the sixteenth century to provide the first persuasive account of the complexities of the Mexican calendrical system.[11] By contrast, even Borunda's explanation of Nahuatl led him into false etymologies, as when he associated St Thomas with Tomatlan, the place of tomatoes. Peculiarly fond of applying the term 'national' to hieroglyphics or to what he called native phraseology (*frasismos*), he was often remarkably obscure, as when he described the Guadalupe as 'the national distinctive of the symbolic veil figured in the concealment of this admirable image in the peak'. No wonder that Mier and other readers dismissed him so easily, since in many ways he was a baroque phantom lost in the age of the Enlightenment.[12]

Nowhere was Borunda's cultural allegiance more obvious than in his reliance on Gregorio García, whose *Origin of the Indians of the New World* (1607) had asserted that the natives of America were mainly descended from the ten lost tribes of Israel and that the monuments of the Incas and Mayas had been constructed by the Carthaginians. But it was the Spanish Domincan's *Preaching of the Gospel in the New World* (1625), by then a rare treatise, on which he drew most, since there the travels of St Thomas in India, China and Japan were described and his tomb located in Meliapor on the Coromandel coast. So too, García quoted Las Casas on the presence of crosses in Yucatán and Portuguese authors on St Thomas' mission in Brazil and Peru.[13] As for Mexico, Borunda cited both Becerra Tanco and Torquemada, not to mention Sigüenza y Góngora, and identified St Thomas as Quetzalcoatl, the bearded white man who had acted as high priest at Tula before being expelled by the evil lord, Huemac.[14] After the native apostasy St Thomas had buried many images which were discovered after the conquest in caves and trees, among which figures Borunda numbered both Our Lady of Los Remedios and the Christ of Chalma, noting 'the concordance between the regional monuments and Christian truths'. Referring to the famous passage in Torquemada in which the Franciscan had mentioned the three temples at Matlalcueye, Tianquizmanalco and Tepeyac where the mendicants had replaced idols with Christian images, Borunda argued that the Franciscans had simply installed or transformed ancient images. Observing that Bartolache had described the canvas of the Guadalupe as made from *iczotl* palm resembling a smooth linen, he declared that the image was obviously of the first century, painted in Syro-Chaldean style, as the figure '8' indicated, but later retouched by the Spaniards, an explanation which accounted for the diversity of paints noted by Miguel Cabrera. It was Borunda who asserted that the folded extremity of the Virgin's tunic was like 'the ancient books or scrolls of holy scripture'; that the angel signified the native reception of the gospel; and that the mandorla which encompassed the Virgin was the leaf or blade of the maguey plant. In more general terms, Borunda argued that the Indians had preserved an allegorical understanding of Christianity until the advent of the Spaniards. When the Mexicans erected a figure of their god Huitzilpochtli made from maize paste and then consumed it, did they not engage in a ceremony that recalled Christian communion? Why was the goddess worshipped at Tepeyac named Teotenantzin, 'the Mother of the Gods'? Underlying all these assertions was a theological premise: that Christ had enjoined his apostles to preach the gospel to all nations. Why, then, should America have had to wait until the advent of the Spaniards?[15]

At the archbishop's command, Mier's sermon and notes, together with Borunda's treatise, were handed to two creole canons of the cathedral, José Patricio Fernández de

Uribe, the Guadalupan scholar, and Manuel de Omana y Sotomayor. Their report was swift and merciless. They mocked Borunda's etymologies and allegories as fit to prove virtually anything, ridiculing his association of Tomatlan with the apostle by observing 'here St Thomas is converted into a tomato or the tomato into St Thomas'. More to the point, his chronology had gone sadly astray, since contrary to most other historians, he imagined that the Mexican empire dated from AD 400. As for Sigüenza's identification of St Thomas with Quetzalcoatl, they noted that his manuscript had never been found and denied that similarities in beliefs and rites between Indian religion and the Catholic faith necessarily indicated a Christian mission. And even if a missionary had arrived, why did he have to be St Thomas? In any case, Torquemada had explicitly dated the Quetzalcoatl of Tula to about AD 700. Observing that Borunda had 'an obscure character, gloomy and withdrawn', they dismissed him as 'a Mexican historical don Quijote', his mind obsessed with any number of mythical windmills. But, since he had never sought to publish his speculations without obtaining a licence, they absolved him from any responsibility for the sermon. The only punishment they recommended was that his manuscripts should be confiscated, since they were 'capable of forming a thousand chivalrous and novelistic historians'.[16]

As regards Mier, Uribe and Omana were unforgiving: 'he has deceived the people with false documents and fictions'. The young Dominican had employed the pulpit to call into question a 'venerable ecclesiastical tradition' and had thus disturbed the piety of the faithful by causing a public scandal. In particular he had advanced three false propositions: that St Thomas had preached in America; that the Guadalupe image was imprinted on his cape by Mary; and that the Virgin had been adored at Tula long before the arrival of the Spaniards. Yet the tradition of Our Lady of Guadalupe was based on a public cult that had endured for 263 years. It could be substantiated by the 1666 Testimonies and by the 'old account' which had been copied by Fernando de Alva Ixtlilxochitl from an Indian and which had served as the basis of the narratives written by Sánchez, Becerra Tanco and Florencia. It was also a tradition promoted by successive archbishops and blessed by Benedict XIV. Turning their eyes abroad, the canons observed that in Europe 'the proud erudition of the philosophical spirit' had led its exponents to 'characterize pious traditions as vulgar errors and dismiss the belief in almost all miracles as credulous superstition'. And yet in 1720 the Spanish Inquisition had condemned all questioning of the miraculous appearance of Our Lady of Pilar, leading the canons to comment on 'the similarity of the Zaragozan and Guadalupan traditions . . . the fundamentals on which they are based are almost the same'. In conclusion, they severely condemned Mier's sermon as 'a tapestry of dreams, delirium, and absurdities' and demanded that he be publicly denounced in a pastoral letter or by an episcopal edict. Their verdict was embraced by the archbishop's legal attorney, who recommended that Mier be stripped of all his sacerdotal licences and be sentenced to ten years' confinement in the Dominican convent at Caldas in Santander, a punishment designed 'to contain his proud spirit, prone to inflation and pernicious novelties'.[17]

If Mier proved so easy a victim for the archbishop's wrath, it was because the Dominican provincial was a European Spaniard who had earlier described him as a creole 'who usually views with little respect the measures of the Europeans'. Indeed, in January 1794 Mier had been involved in a public protest staged by workers of the royal tobacco manufactory, following which the provincial had characterized him as 'a young man of talent, studious and quick-witted', but also loquacious, presumptuous and seditious, and regarded as something of an oracle among the young creole Dominicans.[18] For his part, Mier bitterly complained of the prejudice exhibited by both his provincial and Archbishop Alonso Núñez de Haro, who at all points sought to advance Europeans and relegate creoles to inferior positions. Since Mier possessed excellent family connections, with distant relatives in both the Inquisition and the high court, it was Haro who condemned him for preaching false and scandalous doctrines in an edict which was subsequently published in the *Mexican Gazette* and read out in all churches throughout New Spain save in New León, where the bishop was a family friend.[19] So dangerous did Mier appear to the colonial authorities that the viceroy, the marquis of Branciforte, warned Madrid that Mier had welcomed the news of the French Revolution, so that it was advisable to keep him in Spain. Some years later, when it appeared that Mier might be absolved from his sentence, Archbishop Haro wrote to Spain observing that the Dominican was 'loose in speaking; and in sentiment and opinion is opposed to the rights of the king and Spanish government'.[20] In the light of these letters it is clear that Mier's sermon was interpreted not merely as offensive to tradition, but also as subversive of Spain's empire in Mexico, since its dominion had always been justified by appeal to the papal donation of 1493 and its Christian mission.

At Caldas, Mier found that the Spanish Dominicans were mainly recruited from the peasantry and spent their time splitting hairs over a 'few metaphysical paragraphs of Aristotle'.[21] Thanks in part to his family connections in Asturias he attracted the protection of Gaspar Melchor de Jovellanos, the distinguished author and statesman, who in 1798, acting as Minister of Justice, granted him permission to reside in Madrid. There he met Juan Bautista Muñoz, the general chronicler of the Indies, and was befriended by José de Yeregui, the Inquisitor General. Thanks to this patronage, in 1799 he appealed to the Royal Academy of History to review his case, arguing that since he had not denied either the Virgin's apparitions to Juan Diego or the Guadalupe image's heavenly origin, he had been unjustly condemned to confinement. As we shall see, by then Muñoz had presented a memorial to the Academy in which he had dismissed the Guadalupe tradition as a fable. Despite that essay, however, of the three censors appointed to consider Mier's case, one approved of Uribe's condemnation of the sermon and another described the sermon as 'a combination of historical sins, which

Plate 22   Ramón Torres, *Archbishop Alonso Núñez de Haro y Peralta and Abbot José Félix Colorado*

is to say, of fables, based on imaginary symbols', only then to add that were all preachers of miracles to be condemned, the pulpits would be depopulated.[22]

It was Dr Joaquín Traggia, a distinguished historian of the Aragonese Church, who proved most favourable to Mier, since he sharply criticized Uribe and Omana as being animated by 'fanaticism, malignity and lack of intelligence'. If Borunda's treatise was read in the light of Boturini's speculations, its attempt to decipher the hieroglyphics could not be so lightly dismissed. Although he noted that many authors had embraced the thesis of St Thomas preaching in America, he concluded that the identification of the apostle with Quetzalcoatl 'does not go beyond conjecture'. Indeed, the arguments and evidence provided by Mier and Borunda were 'insufficient to demonstrate what they were intended to prove, according to good criticism in Europe'. However, these theories might be considered to be tolerable in America, since they were designed to sustain a tradition which Bartolache had already undermined. Familiar as he was with Muñoz' memorial, Traggia himself dismissed the Guadalupe tradition, since 'it lacks the support necessary if it is to be admitted by good criticism'. It followed that there was nothing in Mier's sermon to warrant 'theological censure', especially since he had attempted to rescue 'the vulgar tradition', albeit unsuccessfully. Although Mier had been imprudent to preach about such ideas on the image's feast day, the archbishop's sentence was 'an outrage provoked by fanaticism and indiscreet zeal'.[23]

On 7 March 1800 the Royal Academy pronounced its verdict. It first cited Muñoz' memorial and then noted that when Benedict XIV granted the office to be used on 12 December, he had employed the term *fertur*, 'it seems', when referring to the Virgin's apparitions, thus indicating that there was no obligation to accept the Guadalupe tradition as a necessary part of Catholic truth. The Mexican canons, Uribe and Omana, had confused 'opinions of mere piety and devotion' with 'the universal dogmas, customs and discipline of the Church'. Borunda simply resembled Athanasius Kircher, the seventeenth-century baroque savant. As for Mier, he had been imprudent to advance new hypotheses in the pulpit, especially since he had failed to sustain them with any acceptable proofs. But he was not guilty of any real offence, since he had merely sought to rescue a tradition which had already fallen into discredit among 'educated Mexicans'. It followed that his punishment was excessive, his only fault being the substituting of a new fable for an old one; justice had not been done; nor had the rules of canon law been observed.[24]

Here is no place to follow Mier's picaresque career, which he was to describe with such gusto in his memoirs. Sufficient to say that when the Academy's verdict was ignored, in 1801 he fled to France, where he was welcomed by Henri Grégoire, the leader of the constitutionalist clergy. His subsequent travels took him to Rome, back to Spain, and then to London. His decision in 1817 to accompany the ill-fated expedition to Mexico led by Javier Mina ended in his confinement in the Inquisition prison in Mexico City from 1817 to 1820, where he wrote his memoirs and other papers. Deported to Spain in 1820, he escaped to the United States en route and eventually returned to Mexico, where he acted as deputy in the Congress. By then he had emerged as a leading advocate of independence and was well known for his *History of the Revolution of New Spain, anciently Anahuac*, which was published in London in 1813. What does concern us is that he inserted a long appendix in that work devoted to the mission of St Thomas. By then, however, his interest was less religious than political, since he claimed that his hypothesis 'gave the lie to the papal bull of donation of the Indies and thus undermined the foundation of the rights of the king over the Indies', not to mention that it denied the Spaniards the glory of having brought the gospel to America.[25]

Mier's decision to include his dissertation on St Thomas in what was the first general account of the Mexican Insurgency of 1810 indicated the strength of his attachment to his ideas. By then he had extended his reading to include any number of mendicant chroniclers, not to mention the Inca Garcilaso de la Vega, Gregorio García and Athanasius Kircher. But how did he handle the objections raised by Uribe and Omana concerning basic chronology? To start with, he observed that although both Torquemada and José de Acosta, the Jesuit historian, had noted many similarities between native religion and Christian belief and practice, they had attributed them to the Devil. But since these similarities had greatly assisted the reception of the Christian gospel once the Spaniards arrived, who was their more plausible author, the Devil or a Christian apostle? But where Mier revised his ideas was in now postulating at least two separate missions, the first by St Thomas and the second in the sixth century by a Syrian bishop from India, also called Thomas. It was this second Thomas who had figured as Quetzalcoatl at Tula and who had brought crosses and images to Mexico and who was responsible for introducing oriental vestments and monasticism. With the chronological objection overcome by this ingenious invention, Mier then inquired how Nezahualcoyotl, the lord of Texcoco, could be called an idolater, when it was clear from Torquemada that he prohibited human sacrifices and worshipped the one true God. And what was more obvious than that the Mother of the true God, Tzenteotenantzin, had been worshipped at Tepeyac, since the arrival of the first St Thomas?[26]

In the years he spent in the Inquisition prison, Mier returned to this theme, now echoing Borunda's thesis that since Christ had commanded his apostles to preach to all nations, there was no reason to suppose that America had been condemned to wait 1,600 years to adore Christ and his Mother. By then he was willing to admit the possibility of a mission by St Brendan and noted that St Bartholomew may well have visited Peru. But it was in his *Farewell Letter* (1820), written on the eve of his deportation to Spain, that he pleaded with 'my compatriots of Anahuac' to reject the Spanish Academy's orthographical decision to substitute the 'j' for the 'x' in all Mexican names. For as Martín del Castillo has argued, the meaning of Mexico was expressed in its Indian pronunciation of 'Mescico', which clearly derived from Hebrew and signified 'where the Messiah is', so that 'Mexicans are the same as Christians'. That at such a moment Mier should have pitched upon such a theme with such intensity indicated once again the strength of his emotional attachment to these ideas. It was in this letter that he claimed that the ancient Mexicans had knowledge of the entire Bible, albeit preserved in hieroglyphics. He concluded: 'What was the religion of the Mexicans but a Christianity disordered by time and by the equivocal nature of the hieroglyphics?' In all this he remained more faithful than he cared to admit to Borunda's misty speculations.[27]

II

If Traggia had so confidently dismissed the Guadalupe tradition as a pious fable, it was because he had heard or read the *Memorial on the Apparitions and Cult of Our Lady of Guadalupe of Mexico*, which the chief cosmographer of the Indies, Juan Bautista Muñoz, had presented to the Royal Academy of History in April 1794. Commissioned by Charles III in 1779 to write a general history of the Indies, Muñoz had toured the Peninsula in search of manuscripts and documents and had uncovered a wealth of material dealing with the sixteenth century. As part of his duties he supervised the establishment of the great Archive of the Indies at Seville, placing all future historians of Spanish America in his debt. A typical figure of the Spanish Enlightenment, Muñoz had taught eclectic philosophy at the University of Valencia before turning to history. When he reviewed the manuscript description of Peru written by Cosme Bueno, he demanded that the sections dealing with the mission of St Thomas in South America should be deleted as 'fables' based on 'vulgar tradition'.[28] In 1793 he finally published the first volume of his *History of the New World*, where he loftily pronounced that the Incas and Aztecs had never attained the cultural level of 'true civility'. In his judgement the natives of America were so barbaric that they proved 'incapable of overcoming the infinite distance between their mean spirits and the elevation of the conquerors'. His evident disdain provoked the furious criticism of Francisco José Iturri, a former Jesuit from Argentina, who in 1798 accused him of plagiarizing the Enlightened historians of America, William Robertson and Guillaume Raynal.[29]

Although Muñoz had encountered manuscripts dealing with Our Lady of Guadalupe as early as 1783, it was his subsequent examination of the papers of Lorenzo Boturini which apparently prompted him to write his *Memorial* on the Mexican Virgin.[30] He opened with a brief statement of principle:

> With the death of the apostles and evangelists, the canon of Holy Scripture and the deposit of our holy religion was closed. No subsequent deed or doctrine, if it is not contained or announced in the divine books or in the apostolic tradition, can ever augment the number of articles of the Christian religion.

Without doubt, many visions and 'prodigies' had occurred in the long history of the Church and some of these occurrences had proved to be of the greatest utility to the faithful. But since such prodigies did not belong to 'the constant and universal primitive tradition' and still less to the 'canonical books', they were always exposed to doubt and question. Although some 'wonders' were to be respected, even if they could not command certitude, those which lacked a historical foundation should be discarded. With this dictum, Church historians thus became judges of the authenticity of popular devotions.

After a brief outline of the Guadalupe tradition taken from Veytia, Muñoz emphasized the universal silence about the apparitions prior to the appearance of Miguel Sánchez' book in 1648. Moreover, he commented that in the course of his historical research, he had read many documents written by Zumárraga and the early mendicants in Mexico, but that he had never encountered the slightest reference to the story of Juan Diego and the Virgin. In this context, the silence of Torquemada was peculiarly instructive. By the time the Franciscan wrote his great chronicle the cult at Tepeyac was well established, so that his silence could only signify that he either knew nothing of the apparitions or rejected the story as 'a popular rumour'. Much the same could be said of Cisneros, who clearly esteemed the image. There was of course 'the old account' which Sigüenza had attributed to Fernando de Alva Ixtlilxochitl. But Alva had died in about 1650 and could not have written the account much earlier than 1600. Moreover, although Sigüenza claimed that he had seen this account, no-one had ever sought to publish it. As for the 1666 Spanish Testimonies, they were simply based on 'hearsay' evidence and at best related to the early seventeenth century. Nor were the Indian depositions more persuasive, since Becerra Tanco had explicitly warned against accepting Indian oral testimony, observing that the natives had not retained any clear memory of their history.[31] Then again, within 'this so-called tradition', important discrepancies existed regarding the precise quality of the image's canvas, the use of sizing, the very name of Guadalupe, the place where the image first appeared, and the precise date when the image was installed in its sanctuary. As regards the latter point, Muñoz criticized Cayetano de Cabrera for citing the painting which depicted Zumárraga installing the image in 1533, since the bishop was absent from New Spain from early 1532 until October 1534. Moreover, the painting bore an inscription which described Sebastián Ramírez de Fuenleal, the head of the high court, as archbishop of Santo Domingo, at a time when that see was still only a bishopric. A similar anachronism was overlooked by Boturini when he cited a document allegedly dating from the 1530s in which an Indian woman made an offering to the parish priest at Tepeyac, although the parish was only established in 1706.[32]

In all these comments Muñoz did not advance much beyond the objections that might have occurred to any critical mind in Mexico, especially after the publication of Bartolache's sceptical essay. Where he innovated decisively was in printing extracts from two early documents. The first was a letter written by Viceroy Martín Enríquez on 25 September 1575, in which he informed Philip II what he had ascertained about the foundation and financing of the 'hermitage' of Our Lady of Guadalupe.

> The foundation of the church which is there now began, so it is commonly understood, in the years 1555 or 1556, when there was a small hermitage in which was the image which is now in the church. A grazier (*ganadero*) who was there proclaimed that he had recovered his health by going to that hermitage and hence the devotion of the people began to grow. And they named the image Our Lady of Guadalupe, saying that it appeared like that of Guadalupe in Spain. And a confraternity was founded there, in which it is said there were four hundred brothers, and from the alms the church was built and all the building was made and an annuity was purchased.

The viceroy added that the site was not a convenient place for a monastery of friars; and despite the wishes of the archbishop he did not recommend the establishment of a parish either for Spaniards or Indians. All it required was for a priest to hear confessions of visitors to the church and to use the alms for the royal hospital of Indians or for orphans. At present there were two priests there, and a third might well be supported. And so, the viceroy concluded, 'it all comes down to what will feed two or three priests'.[33] Of the Virgin's apparitions and Juan Diego he wrote not a word.

The second document which Muñoz cited was a long extract from Bernardino de Sahagún's *History of the Things of New Spain*, taken from the manuscript he had found in 1783 in the Franciscan convent at Tolosa in Guipuzcoa. Renowned for his knowledge of Nahuatl, Sahagún arrived in Mexico in 1529; taught at the college of Santa Cruz Tlatelolco, and with the assistance of native disciples conducted extensive enquiries among the Indian nobility about their beliefs and rituals prior to the conquest. Completed in 1576–7, his great work had been despatched to Spain and thereafter had been lost to sight. Creole chroniclers such as Florencia had already expressed the hope that the Franciscan's manuscript would contain an early description of the Virgin's apparitions. It was thus with considerable gusto that Muñoz printed the following passage:

> Close to the mountains there are three or four places where very solemn sacrifices used to be made and people came to them from very distant lands. One of these is here in Mexico where there is a hill called Tepeyac, which the Spaniards call Tepeaquilla and now is called Our Lady of Guadalupe. In this place there was a temple dedicated to the mother of the gods, who was called Tonantzin, which is to say, our mother. There were many sacrifices made in honour of this goddess and they came from very distant lands, from over twenty leagues, from all the

surrounding region of Mexico, and they brought many offerings. Men and women, boys and girls came to these feasts; the gathering of people in those days was great; and everyone said we are going to the feast of Tonantzin. And now that there is the church of Our Lady of Guadalupe they call her Tonantzin, taking advantage that the preachers call Our Lady, the Mother of God, Tonantzin. From whence was born the foundation of this Tonantzin is not known for certain. But this we certainly know, that from its first application the word means the old Tonantzin. And it is a thing which should be remedied, because the true name of the Mother of God, Our Lady, is not Tonantzin, but Diosinantzin. It appears a satanic invention to paliate idolatry under the equivocation of this name Tonantzin. And now they come to visit this Tonantzin from afar, as distant as before. This devotion is suspicious, because in all parts there are many churches of Our Lady and they do not go to them; and they come from distant lands to this Tonantzin, as they did a long time ago.[34]

For Muñoz the conclusion to be drawn from these documents about the tradition of Our Lady of Guadalupe was decisive: 'That it was invented long after the fact is demonstrated by the incontrovertible testimonies of Father Sahagún and Viceroy Enríquez.' If that tradition was to be saved, it was incumbent upon its defenders 'to exhibit documents which are older and less suspicious than those which have been produced until now'. In a sentence the Cosmographer General of the Indies thus dismissed the intellectual labours of creole theologians and chroniclers for a century-and-a-half as radically vitiated by the absence of historical proof.

Insult was added to injury when Muñoz then proceeded to speculate that perhaps an artist had painted a scene of an Indian praying to the Virgin at Tepeyac and that from that painting the apparition narrative had been invented, since 'these are the ways in which fables are born'. As regards the period in which the story originated, Muñoz recalled that Cayetano de Cabrera had described the Indians greeting the arrival of the Guadalupe image in the city during the great flood of 1629 with dances and songs, adding: 'I suspect that it was born in the heads of Indians during the years 1629 to 1634.' After all, it was well known that the natives often had visions and indeed drank heavily to procure them. In all likelihood the story of the apparitions was invented during the drunken visions of a fanatical Indian. At no point, however, did Muñoz provide any evidence to justify these offensive speculations, and still less did he explain how such ravings could have been taken seriously by the creole clergy.[35] It was of course an Enlightenment principle that popular religion was inherently polytheistic and superstitious.

Although Muñoz rejected the Guadalupe tradition as a fable, he took care not to attack the cult itself. He had found documents which showed that devotion to the image had begun soon after the conquest and that Archbishops Alonso de Montúfar and

Pedro Moya de Conteras had both testified that the alms raised in the chapel covered the dowries of at least six female orphans. So too, Bernal Díaz del Castillo had commented on the miraculous cures performed at the chapel. He then traced the stages whereby two successive churches were built at Tepeyac, a college of canons established and the election of the Virgin as patron confirmed by Benedict XIV. But he praised the circumspection of the Holy See, commenting that in the office of the Guadalupe's feast the image was compared to the Woman of the Apocalypse, only then to add: 'in similar figure *they say* that there appeared in Mexico in the year 1531 an image of the Mother of God, wonderfully painted'. All this led to his cautious conclusion that the historical evidence demonstrated that:

> the cult given to the Virgin by means of the holy image was always given since the years soon after the conquest: a reasonable and just cult which has nothing to do with the opinion one might wish to embrace concerning the apparitions.[36]

Although radical in his historical scepticism, Muñoz had no desire to challenge the legitimacy of a cult which had been approved by both pope and king. As an enlightened Catholic, he might deplore pious fables and popular superstitions, but he had no cause to question devotion to a likeness of the Virgin Mary.

Although the particular motives which drove Muñoz to write his *Memorial* are not clear, his intervention was by no means fortuitous. In his travels in Spain, Servando de Mier found that 'no scholar in Spain believes in the preaching of Santiago' and commented that neither Traggia nor Yeregui, the Inquisitor General, accepted 'the histories of Pilar and Loreto', since these traditions had been discredited by 'the best critics'.[37] Moreover, by reason of his education in Valencia, Muñoz was obviously influenced by Gregorio Mayans y Siscar (1699–1781), a great critic, who revived the Renaissance tradition of humanist scholarship in Spain, albeit subscribing to the historical principles of the Maurists and Bollandists. But whereas Feijoo wrote essays to discredit 'vulgar errors' and to diffuse knowledge of recent scientific discoveries, Mayans devoted much energy to demolishing the false chronicles and forgeries which had proliferated in seventeenth-century Spain, some of which were designed to prove the authenticity of the Santiago mission and the apparition of Our Lady of Pilar. It was Mayans who in 1742 published the posthumous work of Nicolás Antonio, *Censure of Fabulous Histories*, in which the seventeenth-century scholar had strongly criticized Fray Román de la Higuera and other forgers of early chronicles.[38] As early as 1734 Mayans had written to José Patiño, the leading minister of Philip V, to lament:

> It is a thing most unworthy of our nation's gravity, that at the moment when elsewhere criticism has become abuse, when now more than ever scepticism and even incredulity are at their greatest strength, in Spain in general the opposite extreme of a facile credulity is found so that many writers . . . appear to be children.

A faithful Catholic, Mayans turned back to Luis de León and Cervantes for inspira-tion; disapproved of the degenerate scholasticism that still thrived in Spain; and looked to the crown to reform the excesses of popular religion.[39]

An example of the kind of religion favoured by men such as Mayans and Feijoo was set down in *Of a Well-Ordered Devotion* (1747), a widely translated and much-published work by Lodovico Antonio Muratori (1672–1750), an Italian theologian and Church historian. For Muratori argued that devotion to Christ should be at the very centre of every Christian life and expressed in faithful attendance at mass and in veneration of the Eucharist. Obviously he recommended devotion to the Virgin Mary, but warned that since only Christ was the mediator between the Almighty and humanity, it was wrong to pray to God and Mary in the same breath.[40] Although he approved of the cult of saints, he affirmed that devotion to them should lead to God through imitation of their virtues rather than be inspired by any expectation of the miracles they might perform. So too, devotion to holy images was to be encour-aged, since as St Gregory the Great had written, such paintings were the books of the ignorant. But the faithful had to bear in mind that in themselves such images had no value, since they were but physical matter, and to venerate or worship matter was to be guilty of idolatry. Saints were in heaven, not in their images. On the other hand, although crucifixes were but images, Christ was truly present in the holy Eucharist, which could thus be justly worshipped. Muratori commented that abuses in the past had provoked the iconolastic movement and that Innocent III, the great thirteenth-century pope, had condemned as superstitious the Greek idea that as regards a certain icon of the Virgin painted by St Luke, 'the Spirit of the Mother of God dwelt in it'. Indeed, the faithful had to be taught that the different advocations or images of Mary had no more power than any other, so that if an image attracted worship as if it were divine, it should be removed lest idolatry occur.[41] Although Muratori may well have read St John Damascene, he clearly had no sympathy for that saint's neo-platonic theology of images, and still less for the argument that since images had the form of their heavenly prototypes they were entitled to a similar veneration.

The degree to which popular devotion to holy images had become an affront to enlightened Catholics can be observed in the diaries of Melchor Gaspar de Jovellanos. In April 1795 he visited the chapel of the Holy Christ of Burgos, a celebrated miraculous crucifix housed in the Augustinian convent of that city. He commented with disdain on the fifty lamps which adorned the sanctuary, which were designed 'to provoke the devotion of the vulgar', and then complained of the spectacle of:

> an effigy in a very bad and horrible form . . . outside and inside the chapel and throughout the cloister cartloads of crutches, of legs and arms, breasts of wax and even of silver, vows, all testimonies of the most stupid superstition.

He added that the friar who attended the chapel sold silver crosses, medallions and prints, all at high profit. As can be observed, Jovellanos exhibited a neo-classical contempt for the image's overly realistic style; objected to the popular belief in the image's power to perform miraculous cures; and condemned the friars for profiting from an ignorant populace. In effect, the Spanish statesman here confronted a fearsome, moving figure of Christ which had been venerated since the late Middle Ages and which had inspired copies which still attract devotion throughout Spanish America. Yet all he felt was disgust. The scene thus offers a remarkable testimony to the fissure which by then separated the practices of popular religion and the aesthetic and spiritual tastes of educated Catholics.[42]

It is easy enough to describe Jovellanos, Mayans and Muñoz as Jansenists, cautious adherents of a reform movement within the Church. But in Bourbon Spain Jansenism was a complex, multi-faceted phenomenon which admits no easy definition. At its most obvious level it was profoundly Gallican, which is to say, it attacked the papal monarchy and its canon law, defining its absolutist pretensions as a medieval innovation which had undermined the rightful authority of national episcopates and Church councils. Its proponents were regalists, since they generally looked to the crown for assistance in their attempts to reform religious practice. But beyond the central question of Church government, Jansenists adopted different emphases. Obviously, most rejected the outmoded scholasticism that still haunted hispanic universities and thus criticized the religious Orders which continued to espouse this kind of theology. But they also questioned the value of asceticism and mystical prayer, favouring a simple interior piety and the performance of good works. But when they deplored the miracle-mongering, the pilgrimages and the alms-giving associated with the popular cult of holy images, Jansenists simply expressed sentiments which were broadly diffused among educated Catholics and pious clergymen. So too, when they shrank from the extravagant gilded retables of the baroque era, they exhibited a neo-classical taste which was destined soon to become almost universal.[43] In the nineteenth century, when the ultramontane clergy sought to revive the Catholic Church, they retained many of the attitudes towards popular religion already manifest among so-called Jansenists.

III

It was not until 1817 that the Royal Academy of History published Muñoz' *Memorial*, and apparently it did not reach Mexico until 1819. Although Dr Manuel Gómez Marín, a priest of the Oratory, immediately printed a reply, it was left to Dr José Miguel Guridi y Alcocer (1763–1828), a former deputy at the Cortes of Cadiz, to provide a comprehensive rebuttal in his *Apologia of the Apparition of Our Lady of Guadalupe in*

Mexico (1820). Such was his confidence that he did not hesitate to preface his work with the complete text of Muñoz' essay, so as to allow his readers to follow the debate. Like Gómez Marín, he noted that Muñoz' reputation as an historian had been sharply questioned by Francisco José Iturri, who had accused him of plagiary and error. So too, he commented that Mier's sermon had horrified public sentiment and alarmed 'the ecclesiastical jurisdiction'. More to the point, he questioned Muñoz' very premise, that Catholic revelation and the deposit of faith had been closed with the completion of the New Testament, since 'this appears to exclude the authority of the Chair of St Peter and of the Councils of the Catholic Church to define new dogmas of faith'. After all, the doctrines of the Trinity, purgatory, and the seven sacraments, not to mention the Immaculate Conception of the Virgin Mary, had all been defined or developed after the apostolic epoch.[44]

Where Guridi waxed strongest was in his denial of the criterion of silence as a reason to reject tradition. It had to be remembered, he insisted, that had Zumárraga or the early mendicants written about the Virgin's apparitions, they would not have been believed in Spain, such then was the prejudice against the Indians. And what did the silence of Torquemada actually prove? For had not Clavijero already demonstrated his contradictions and unreliability? Yet he had mentioned the sanctuary at Tepeyac no fewer than nine times in his great chronicle. In any case, although Clavijero's devotion to the Guadalupe was well attested, in his history of ancient Mexico he had omitted all mention of the Virgin. And if silence was so significant, then what weight should be given to the complete absence of all denial of the Guadalupe tradition from 1629 until 1817? With these considerations to hand, Guridi observed that Martín Enríquez' letter simply testified to the early origin of the cult; its silence about the apparitions did not signify anything. Obviously, the viceroy was misinformed about the similarity of the Mexican Virgin to its Spanish counterpart. As for the extract from Sahagún, Guridi was inclined to dismiss it as corrupt or even as apocryphal, especially since the term which Sahagún had suggested should be applied to the Virgin, Diosinantzin, was a mixture of Spanish and Nahuatl. But even if the passage was authentic, what did it indicate other than that the Franciscan was fearful of concealed idolatry? For the rest, Guridi noted that Zumárraga was consecrated bishop in May 1533 and therefore had time enough to return to Mexico by December of that year, when the image was installed in the sanctuary.[45]

Belief in the Virgin's apparitions at Tepeyac, as Guridi argued, was sustained by tradition, the cult and miracles. As regards the cult, he simply followed Muñoz in tracing its institutional development from the first chapel until the establishment of a college of canons; there was nothing here worthy of dispute. But what the Spaniard had utterly failed to address was the character of the image, whose very beauty testified to its 'heavenly origin', its preservation a perpetual miracle. How could God have allowed the cult to thrive or miraculous cures to be performed in the sanctuary if it were all based on deceit? Moreover, since the conversion of the natives of Mexico had not been accompanied by any great miracles or martyrdom, how else could its sheer rapidity and success be explained other than by the apparition of an image sent from heaven? As Fray Antonio Margil de Jesús had averred, it was Mary through the Guadalupe who had converted the Indians.[46]

For all that, 'the principal support on which the apparitions rest . . . is the tradition'. Moreover, Guridi asserted that 'a tradition does not depend on writings and for that reason their negation does not weaken it; nor are they necessary for it to subsist'. For the Jews and the early Christians, oral testimony and worship had preceded the composition of the scriptures. And if the Guadalupe lacked earlier documentation, the same was true for Pilar, Montserrat, the Spanish Guadalupe and Loreto. As for Muñoz' theory that the apparitions had been invented by some drunken Indian visionary, why on earth would the priests of that epoch have accepted such a tale? And who would have chosen to transcribe these ravings into a coherent narrative? In any case, although Muñoz had attributed 'the old account' to Fernando de Alva Ixtlilxochitl, in fact it had been written by Antonio Valeriano and printed from an old manuscript by Laso de la Vega in 1649. Guridi then inserted a long list of Guadalupan authors and documents, using the bibliographies of Boturini and Bartolache to good effect. In all this emphasis on tradition, his debt to Uribe's dissertation was manifest. He concluded by noting that if Benedict XIV had inserted the terms *fertur* and *dicitur* in the office of the Guadalupe feast, which was to say, 'it seems' and 'it is said', so also the Pilar office referred to 'a pious and ancient tradition' and the Loreto office emphasized universal veneration and 'pontifical diplomas'.[47] In raising doubts about the truth of such traditions blessed by the Church authorities, Muñoz threatened to undermine the belief of the faithful and open the way to a more general incredulity. The vigour and confidence with which Guridi conducted his defence of the apparitions gave fair warning to all sceptics, Catholics or agnostics, that the Mexican clergy were not prepared to abandon their cherished beliefs, no matter how daunting the critical onslaught might appear to be.

It was during the years 1817–20 that Servando de Mier once more intervened in the debate over the Guadalupe image and its tradition, later claiming that it was in the Inquisition prison in Mexico City that 'I reproduced the literary correspondence I had from Burgos with don Juan Bautista Muñoz'. Since he made but a passing reference to the chronicler's *Memorial*, which only became available in Mexico in 1819, it is clear that he reached his conclusions well before reading that treatise. Discussion of these six letters to Muñoz, however, is complicated by Mier's parallel composition of his *Apologia*, in which he rehearsed the events of 1794–1800, seeking to justify his sermon. The problem is compounded in both these pieces by his constant shifting of the ground of argument, since in some places he defended the propositions of his 1794 sermon, but elsewhere set down in uncompromising terms his current opinions. To explain the great change in his arguments it is necessary to recall that in Spain he had been protected by Jovellanos, Yeregui and Traggia, all of whom were identified with the so-called Jansenist party, and it was in part owing to their recommendations that he was welcomed by Henri Grégoire, who had accepted the Civil Constitution of 1791, which prescribed the election of both priests and bishops. Elected bishop of Blois, Gregoire strove to maintain 'the holy alliance between Christianity and democracy' and advocated a federal, republican doctrine of Church government. In his *Memoirs*, Mier warmly praised Grégoire and declared that 'in Europe they call Jansenist all the men who are solidly instructed in religion and who are friends of the old and legitimate discipline of the Church'. In part, the attraction of 'Jansenism' for Mier was that it allowed him to condemn the 1493 papal donation of the Indies to the Spanish kings as an illegitimate exercise of Church authority, based on the historic forgeries which had been employed to justify the papal monarchy and its canon law.[48] But as a Jansenist, Mier was also liable to adopt a critical attitude to any ecclesiastical tradition which lacked the foundation of historical documentation. It was thus his affiliations in Europe which deepened the scepticism about the Guadalupe tradition which his early reading of Bartolache had first awakened.

Like Muñoz, Mier fixed upon the universal silence about the apparitions in both chronicles and other documents until 1648 as the chief proof that the tradition was a fabrication undertaken many years after the alleged events. This silence fulfilled all the conditions stipulated by Daniel Papebroch (1628–1714), the celebrated Bollandist scholar, to question the authenticity of hagiographical accounts of saints' lives and other pious histories. In 1536 Las Casas and Julián Garcés, the bishop of Tlaxcala, had petitioned Paul III for papal declaration of the humanity and rights of the Indians; but it had not occurred to them to cite the Virgin's recent apparitions. As for Zumárraga, in Spain he had persecuted witches and in Mexico he had burnt all the native codices he found, including the great library at Texcoco, thus greatly harming 'the literary republic'. In any case, Muñoz' discovery of Enríquez' letter and Sahagún's critique of Tonantzin had demonstrated the tradition to be a fable.[49]

What then was the origin of the tradition? In devising an explanation, Mier simply ignored Muñoz' suggestion that it all started with a vision of some drunken Indian. Instead, he accepted the affirmations of Sigüenza and Uribe but cast them in polemical form, ascribing its origin to 'a Mexican manuscript of the Indian don Antonio Valeriano written eighty years after the apparition'. One possible model for Juan Diego was 'the poor shepherd', which was to say, the grazier, whom Martín Enríquez mentioned as cured in about 1555 at the sanctuary. Another possible source was that Valeriano had heard of the apparition of a woman dressed in a blue mantle to an Indian of Azcapotzalco who lay dying of the plague in 1576, a story recounted by Torquemada.[50] Whatever the source, the several anachronisms in the traditional account demonstrated that it had been written much later than the 1530s. Why was

Juan Diego walking to Tlatelolco when the convent there was only founded in 1534; and in any case, why should it have served as a parish church for Cuautitlan? Then again, how could Juan Diego have sought a priest to administer the last sacraments to his uncle, when in the 1530s the Franciscans had barely learnt Nahuatl and were only beginning to baptize the Indians, let alone administer the Eucharist or Extreme Unction to them? Why did the Virgin ask to be called Guadalupe, when the Indians notoriously could not pronounce the 'g' and the 'd'? And how could the image have been placed in the cathedral prior to its installation in the sanctuary, when that building had yet to be constructed? As for flowers being used in December as the sign of the apparition, before the conquest Mexico City enjoyed flowers across all the seasons, so that the bishop would not have been impressed by their presentation.[51]

Turning to the content of the apparition narrative, Mier first noted that the Torres brothers had not reprinted Miguel Sánchez' account, since 'it was a folio volume full of straw', a description which indicated that he had never seen that book.[52] Yet he now perceived the scriptural influence on the colloquies between the Virgin and Juan Diego and asserted that they were based on the colloquies of God with Moses and Abraham. When Mary commanded the Indian to gather flowers as a sign, this was a direct transposition of the use of Aaron's rod. Indeed, the scriptural inspiration of the colloquies was so obvious that 'the plagiary is evident, and as a consequence, the fiction'. Mier's conclusion was uncompromising: 'the Guadalupan tradition is clearly a mythological fable' similar to those dealing with Santiago and the early kings of Spain which had been invented by Fray Román de la Higuera.[53] It had all started, so Mier surmised, in the Indian college of Santa Cruz Tlatelolco:

> the history of Guadalupe is a comedy of the Indian Valeriano, forged on Aztec mythology concerning Tonantzin, so that it should be represented in Santiago, where he was a professor, by the young Indian college students, who in that time were accustomed to represent in their language the farces that they called sacramental *autos*, which were in fashion in the sixteenth century.[54]

Here, indeed, was a bold speculation which was undoubtedly more plausible than Muñoz' ascription of the story to some native visionary. Moreover, by fathering the first account on Valeriano, Mier simply reinterpreted the current Mexican consensus. As for the subsequent history of Valeriano's manuscript, he surmised that Alva Ixtlilxochitl had translated it in paraphrased form in about 1629 and that his version had been used by Miguel Sánchez, leaving the original to be printed by Laso de la Vega.[55] It is a tribute to Mier's acuity that without reading Sánchez, he had discerned the scriptural typology which had inspired that author.

But what of the image itself? In this respect it is difficult to capture the balance of Mier's thinking. It should be recalled that far from adjuring his thesis of an apostolic mission to Mexico, he continued to defend and indeed extend that doctrine. In both his letters to Muñoz and his *Apologia*, he argued that the Virgin Mary continued to be venerated at Tepeyac under the name of Tzenteotenantzin, 'the Mother of the True God', during the long centuries that elapsed between the second, Syrian St Thomas and the Spanish conquest. Her native image, so he claimed, was of a young woman dressed in a blue mantle. When Valeriano in his colloquies had Mary describe herself as the Mother of the True God, she thus identified herself as the former goddess. And indeed, when Juan Diego asked himself whether he was in the paradise of his ancestors, he clearly referred to a Christian heaven.[56] Since Mier repeated Borunda's affirmation that many of the images hidden by St Thomas in caves and woods were discovered after the conquest, he obviously still hankered after his original hypothesis that the Guadalupe image dated from a much earlier period. But he also drew on Bartolache's insistence that the canvas of the image was woven from the palm *iczotl* and so could not have been the cape of a poor Indian. Moreover, it was 'burnished' on the surface, which was to say, it was a canvas which had been smoothed and prepared for painting according to Indian techniques.[57] So too, he took from Borunda the theory that the image was painted 'within a leaf which we call the blade of maguey', an Aztec mandorla.[58] Had not Borunda called the image a 'Mexican hieroglyphic', since the black moon was a sign of native mourning for the death of Christ? For all that, after noting the similarity in the 'fables' of Los Remedios and Guadalupe, he openly declared:

> In the order of origin of both images, I believe that they came out of the workshop of painters that Fray Pedro de Gante set up for Indians alongside San Francisco, since as Torquemada says, they made as many images as there were in the retables of New Spain.

But so obvious were the artistic defects in the paintings of these native workmen that it was out of the question to describe any of them as miraculous, since how could God be the author of such imperfections?[59] Once more, Bartolache's neo-classical criteria were invoked to dismiss the heavenly claims of the Guadalupe. But what Mier did not clarify was the relation between the image painted by Gante's disciples and the image of Tzenteotenantzin which had been adored at Tepeyac prior to the conquest.

If Mier had abandoned his idea that the Guadalupe image had been imprinted on the cape of St Thomas, it was in part because he had learnt from ecclesiastical historians that the apostolic Church had not permitted paintings of Christ or the Virgin until the fourth or fifth centuries; and that statues had only appeared in the tenth century. If any Christian images had been brought to Mexico, they had been introduced by the Syrian bishop from India, also called St Thomas, in the sixth century.[60] Moreover, Mier now sharply criticized the first Spanish missionaries in Mexico for having substituted holy images for pagan idols, since the Indians were obviously incapable of distinguishing the difference between veneration of a representation and the worship of a god, and so had fallen into idolatry. It was true that Muratori had defended devotion to particular saints or images by arguing that if more miracles occurred in certain sanctuaries, it was not owing to the inherent spiritual efficacy of the image, but simply because the faithful were more fervent and filled with prayer in such churches.[61] But Mier then noted that Florencia had cited 'the certainly apocryphal authority of a Blessed Amadeus', who claimed that the Virgin had promised to be present in her images so as to perform miracles. Mier found the claim hard to stomach, since this was 'to teach idolatry and it is a blasphemy to put such a doctrine in the mouth of the Virgin'. It was a doctrine that ran contrary to the decrees of the Council of Trent, and its citation demonstrated that Florencia was not an author who merited respect.[62] Once again, Mier's discernment of the doctrines hitherto used to justify the cult of holy images in Mexico was remarkably acute. In his condemnation we can measure the gulf that separated the spiritual culture of the baroque era from the neo-classical piety of the Jansenizing clergy.

Although Mier did not greatly use Muñoz' *Memorial*, he displayed a remarkably similar approach to the Guadalupe tradition. He concluded that the image was painted by Indian artists of the middle years of the sixteenth century and that the tradition had been invented by Valeriano at least sixty years after the events it described. Like the Spaniard, he dismissed the 1666 Testimonies as mere 'hearsay', and observed that the Indians were such great liars that their evidence was never accepted in judicial cases in Mexico.[63] As a general principle, he observed that God had not granted the Church infallibility concerning 'particular histories' and indeed that in the last century a great many errors in the Roman Breviary of saints had been corrected. If it was still permitted to deny the doctrine of the Virgin's Immaculate Conception, how much more was it permitted to deny private revelations, visions and apparitions, since they did not form part of the Catholic faith. He concluded with a quotation from Richard of St-Victor, a twelfth-century French theologian, that: 'it is as much heretical to affirm something is of the faith which is not, as to deny something is of the faith which is'.[64]

After the independence of Mexico was achieved in 1821, Mier returned from exile in the United States and served as deputy in the national Congress. In July 1822 he intervened in its debates to declare that since Jesus Christ had commanded his apostles to preach to all nations, at least one of his followers had come to America. If St Thomas should be publicly acclaimed as the apostle of the New World, it was because 'the most holy Virgin did not await the passage of 1,600 years in order to be Our Lady and Mother'. Speaking in a chamber which was adorned with a copy of Our Lady of Guadalupe, Mier refrained from expounding his doubts about the image and its tradition. By contrast, he had no compunction in denouncing Rome's claim to appoint bishops as a medieval usurpation of powers which resided within every metropolitan see. When the question of opening relations with the papacy was discussed in

Congress, he confessed: 'my ideas in this matter are very liberal, since I have been a member of the constitutional clergy of France . . . Whether the Church is a monarchy as the ultramontanes claim, or whether it is a federal republic, as the university of Paris teaches, which is my opinion, is a matter for question within the Church.'[65] Admired as a patriot hero, Mier died in the national palace and was buried in the vaults of Santo Domingo. But although the dissertation on St Thomas, which had first appeared as an appendix to his history of the revolution, was soon reprinted, by contrast it was not until 1875 that his manuscript letters to Muñoz were finally published, followed in 1876 by the first edition of his *Apologia* and *Memoirs*. So valued was his role as an insurgent patriot that in his six-volume collection of documents dealing with the Insurgency, J. E. Hernández y Dávalos printed Mier's 1794 sermon, together with the judicial proceedings, Muñoz' *Memorial* and Mier's letters to Muñoz.[66] As we shall see, the publication of these works occurred in an epoch when the Liberals had ousted the Church from public life and sought to promote the diffusion of works designed to undermine clerical influence. It was thus not until then that the full extent of Mier's scepticism was revealed.

IV

When the cathedral chapter of Mexico first sought to obtain papal recognition of Our Lady of Guadalupe, it was obliged to commission Francisco de Siles to take the legal depositions of 1666, since it could not encounter any documentation of the apparitions in its archives. It was to fill this vacuum that Luis Becerra Tanco postulated the existence of an early manuscript written in Nahuatl by an Indian scholar, an individual whom Carlos de Sigüenza y Góngora later identified as Antonio Valeriano. Even so, Francisco de Florencia roundly lamented the silence of Torquemada about the apparitions and the image, only then to express the hope that the manuscripts of earlier Franciscan chroniclers might provide the historical testimony needed to substantiate the tradition. In the decades which followed, however, panegyric replaced history and Mexican theologians vied to celebrate the image with concepts taken from the Greek Fathers of the Church. Moreover, in the very years when the creole elite acclaimed the Guadalupe as their patron and won papal assent, Lorenzo Boturini confirmed the tradition by publishing a bibliography which listed both documents and early manuscript narratives dealing with Valeriano and the apparitions. This cycle reached its climax with Miguel Cabrera's marvelling at the painterly complexity of the heaven-sent image.

It was José Patricio Fernández de Uribe who in 1777 first warned the Mexican public that in the 'century of enlightenment', impious philosophers ridiculed religion and dismissed venerable devotions as mere superstition. He advanced a carefully framed defence of the Guadalupe tradition, primarily based on Valeriano's manuscript, and cited the rules of interpretation of documents formulated by Jean Mabillon, the Benedictine scholar. In 1790 José Ignacio Bartolache aspired to open the door for a critical review of that tradition. But, as Mier later remarked, if the public expected a mountain, instead they found a mouse, since Bartolache did little more than fulminate against Torquemada and establish that the canvas of the image had been woven from palm thread. By then the cycle of conceptual panegyric had expired.

The scandal caused by Servando de Mier's sermon cannot be underestimated. By suggesting that the Guadalupe image had been imprinted on St Thomas' cape, he dismissed a central feature of the standard narrative as false. In his anxiety to endow New Spain with an apostolic foundation he thus undermined the credibility of the accepted tradition. In the very same year of 1794, Juan Bautista Muñoz presented his *Memorial*. Apart from certain anachronisms, he essentially relied on the criterion of silence to dismiss the tradition as a fable. It was not simply the silence of Torquemada that now decided the matter. It was also the absence of any mention of the apparitions in the correspondence of Zumárraga and other early Franciscans. The letter of Martín Enríquez certainly testified to the existence of the cult at Tepeyac since at least the 1550s; but made no mention of the apparitions. So too, if Bernardino de Sahagún denounced the cult at Tepeyac as idolatrous, he confessed his ignorance as to its origin. But Muñoz failed to deal with the question of Valeriano's manuscript other than to attribute it to Fernando de Alva Ixtlilxochitl. Moreover, he speculated wildly when he suggested that the apparition narrative originated in visions of an Indian in the early seventeenth century, without providing the least documentation for his theory.

In his refutation of Muñoz, José Miguel Guridi y Alcocer simply denied the strength of the criterion of silence as offering sufficient grounds to deny tradition, since it was first based on oral testimony. That Muñoz had not appreciated the significance of Valeriano indicated the superficiality of his criticism. In any case, he had not explained why a priest of the early seventeenth century should have accepted the visionary discourse of an Indian about an image which had been already the object of veneration for at least seventy years. Although Servando de Mier accepted Muñoz' treatise as undermining the Guadalupe tradition, in his letter to the chronicler and in his *Apologia*, he demonstrated his close study of Becerra Tanco, Florencia, Bartolache and Uribe by naming Valeriano as the author of the original narrative. But he then characterized the account as a literary invention inspired by the biblical colloquies between God and Moses. His perception of the similarity was certainly accurate; but he did not explain why an Indian, no matter how educated, would have dared to copy scripture so closely. As regards the image, he observed that the canvas had been prepared for painting in the traditional Indian fashion and that it had originated in the workshop of native artists founded by Pedro de Gante. Writing in an Inquisition gaol, Mier did not provide any historical substantiation of his hypotheses and when liberated, turned his attention to the fate of his country.

It was a measure of Mier's perception and Jansenizing piety that he should have been so scandalized by Florencia's citation of the Virgin Mary's revelation to Blessed Amadeus of Portugal. The idea that a particular image might possess certain powers of performing miraculous cures he condemned as idolatrous. Indeed, the practice of venerating some images of Mary more than others was sharply criticized by many priests of this epoch, Jansenist or not, as implicitly leading to idolatry. It was for this reason that the tradition of the Guadalupe became as important, if not more so, than the image itself. No longer did preachers expatiate upon its portrayal of the divine idea of Mary, conceived from all eternity. Instead, they fixed upon the apparition of Mary in Mexico and the historical effect of that apparition, which is to say, the rapid conversion of the native peoples. If the tradition may have been devised to explain the heavenly nature of the image, the historical reality of that narrative was destined to become the central feature of devotion in the nineteenth and twentieth centuries.

10

The last resort

I

On 15 September 1810, Miguel Hidalgo y Costilla, the parish priest of Dolores, called out the masses of central Mexico in rebellion against Spanish dominion. For their banner he gave his followers an image of Our Lady of Guadalupe and later inscribed on their flags the slogans: 'Long live religion! Long live our most holy Mother of Guadalupe! Long live Ferdinand VII! Long live America and death to bad government!' But the Indians and mestizos who joined his movement soon simplified these war-cries into 'Long live the Virgin of Guadalupe and death to the *gachupines*', the latter term the popular name for European Spaniards. When Hidalgo approached the provincial capital of Guanajuato, he informed the intendant that the purpose of the insurrection was to recover the rights of the 'Mexican nation' and to expel the Europeans, adding that 'The present movement is great and will be still more great when it attempts to recover the holy rights conceded by God to the Mexicans and usurped by a few cruel conquerors.'[1] Whereas, in 1746, Our Lady of Guadalupe had been acclaimed as patron of the kingdom of New Spain, she was now saluted as the mother and symbol of an insurgent Mexican nation. If the moment was propitious for such a transformation, it was because by 1810 Spain had been conquered by the French armies who had installed Joseph Bonaparte on the throne, obliging Ferdinand VII, the Bourbon king, to abdicate. Only in Cadiz, a port protected by the British fleet, did an enfeebled Regency survive, albeit still claiming to govern the overseas empire.

No feature of the Mexican insurgency was more striking than the number of priests who followed Hidalgo. Some indication of their sentiments can be found in the rebel journal *The American Monitor* (1810–11), where Dr Francisco Severo Maldonado warned the 'Americans' about the atheism propagated by French revolutionary forces and invited them to defend 'the sacred rights of the altar and the *patria*'. Whereas King Joseph had dissolved the religious Orders, creoles should strive to maintain them. Was not Hidalgo a 'hero-liberator', another Washington, who after three hundred years of tyranny now sought 'the independence of a nation which has only taken up arms to recover its sacred rights and maintain intact the religion of its fathers', assisted in this noble struggle by 'our holy Mother of Guadalupe, Tutelary Numen of this empire, sworn captain of our legions'?[2] In a more exalted vein, Carlos María de Bustamante (1774–1848), editor of the *Southern American Post* (1813), asserted that, when the Virgin appeared to Juan Diego, he heard 'the authentic certificate of our liberty. "You shall call me mother and I will be yours; and you shall call upon me in your tribulations and I will hear you; you shall plead with me for liberty and I will loose your chains."'[3]

At the Congress of Chilpancingo, summoned in 1813 to frame a Declaration of Independence, José María Morelos, the country vicar who led the second, southern phase of the insurgency, delivered an opening address in which he compared the Mexicans to the people of Israel in Egypt suffering under Pharaoh. His text had been prepared for him by Bustamante and invoked the spirits of the Aztec emperors when it asserted that: 'We are about to re-establish the Mexican empire, improving its government.' However, 'the Most Holy Mary of Guadalupe' was acclaimed by Morelos as 'the patron of our liberty', whose feast day was henceforth to be celebrated as a national holiday. The Act of Independence solemnly promised to maintain the Catholic religion in all its purity and to conserve the religious Orders. The same insistence on a confessional republic can be observed in the Constitutional Decree of Apatzingan of 1814, which not merely stated that 'the Catholic, Roman and Apostolic religion is the only one to be professed in the state', but also declared that 'the status of citizen is lost through the crimes of heresy, apostasy or treason to the nation'.[4]

But the massacre of European Spaniards perpetrated by Hidalgo's followers at Guanajuato horrified many creoles, and the indiscriminate pillaging of property that accompanied the insurgency threatened the interests of the propertied classes. The bishop-elect of Michoacán, Manuel Abad y Queipo, an erstwhile friend of Hidalgo, denounced the rebel leader as another Mahomet who had profaned the Guadalupe by converting the image into the banner of a new religion which preached murder, hatred and robbery. Renowned for his liberal views, this Asturian prelate excommunicated Hidalgo and his chief associates on the grounds that they had infringed ecclesiastical immunity when they imprisoned European Carmelites at Celaya. Yet Abad y Queipo himself was soon to advocate the suspension of the immunity when he found so many priests and religious leading the insurrection, accusing them as 'those who have promoted and sustained it'.[5] The royalist journalist, Juan López de Cancelada, satirically asserted that José María Morelos had but four principles: that all Europeans should be expelled from America; that all property should be owned by the Americans; that Our Lady of Guadalupe should be obeyed in all things; and that priests should act as God's lieutenants, governing in both temporal and spiritual spheres.[6] No aspect of the Mexican insurgency more impressed foreign observers than its emphasis upon religion, and indeed Simón Bolívar paid tribute to its influence:

Happily, the leaders of the independence movement in Mexico have profited from fanaticism with the greatest skill, proclaiming the famous Virgin of Guadalupe as the queen of the patriots, invoking her name at all difficult moments, and bearing her image on their flags. With all this, political enthusiasm has formed a mixture with religion, which produced a vehement fervour for the sacred cause of liberty.[7]

Obviously, for Bolívar, a sceptic in matters of religion, the adoption of a religious symbol was more a question of astute political tactics than of genuine sentiment.

So powerful was the devotion offered to holy images in New Spain that for a bizarre moment it appeared likely that royalist and rebel armies might well fight under the opposing banners of the Virgins of Los Remedios and Guadalupe, which was to say, under the *gachupina* and the *criolla*. In both 1808 and 1809 the image of Los Remedios had been paraded through the streets of Mexico City, accompanied by the usual retinue of confraternities and religious communities, to plead for the seasonal rainfall and, sign of the times, for the victory of Spanish arms over the French invaders. Moreover, in May 1810, when a sudden storm damaged her sanctuary, the Virgin remained in the capital for seventy days, pursuing a slow peregrination of convents and churches. In the convent of San Jerónimo the nuns clothed the image with the sash of a 'Captain-General of the army' and attached a gold baton and a small sword, insignia which were retained when in August it was taken back to its sanctuary. But when Hidalgo approached Mexico City at the head of a horde of undisciplined followers, Los Remedios was hurriedly removed for fear of its falling into rebel hands. It was on 30 October, the very day the Virgin entered the cathedral, that a small royalist force defeated Hidalgo's army at Las Cruces, throwing him into precipitate retreat. The next day Viceroy Francisco Javier Venegas offered a public thanksgiving to the Virgin and later caused medallions of Los Remedios to be distributed among royalist regiments. In February 1811 a *novena* of masses was celebrated in the cathedral to thank the *gachupín* Virgin for saving the city from disaster, an occasion on which Juan Bautista Díaz Calvillo, a priest of the Oratory, praised the 800 soldiers, 'loyal and courageous sons of America', for their defeat of the 80,000 'tigers' who followed 'that bastard son of the Spanish heroes', Miguel Hidalgo.[8] But, as we shall see, similar ceremonies were also to be staged to beg Our Lady of Guadalupe to assist the royalist cause so that any danger of a war of images was soon averted.

The spectacle of Catholic priests using religious symbols for violent, political ends was not confined to Mexico. In Spain, bishops in Santander and Extremadura preached crusades against the French invaders, and throughout the Peninsula the clergy played a leading role in the resistance to Napoleon. For King Joseph not merely abolished the Inquisition, but disbanded all male religious communities and expropriated their property, thus impelling many monks and friars to join the guerrilla forces which operated across the Peninsula.[9] When Zaragoza was besieged for several months in 1808, its inhabitants were mobilized under the slogans of 'Religion, king and *patria*'. But the priests and friars who figured so prominently in the city's defence obviously called upon Our Lady of Pilar to assist them, especially since her sanctuary had been enlarged and embellished throughout the preceding century. An English traveller later reported that during the siege the defenders chanted in doggerel verse: 'The Virgin of Pilar says that she does not want to be French, that she wants to be Captain of the Aragonese people.'[10] In effect, throughout the hispanic world provincial patriotism still found expression in the invocation of traditional, religious symbols.

Although guerrilla forces across the Peninsula valiantly harassed the French armies, at Cadiz the young Liberals, who dominated the Cortes summoned by the Regency in 1810, could not resist the allure of French ideas. Many were familiar with the works of Montesquieu and Rousseau and virtually all of them had adopted Feijoo's critique of vulgar errors and prejudices. But it was the French Revolution's insistence that all men were born equal with the same rights and that 'the principle of sovereignty resides essentially in the nation' which most attracted Liberal approval. At one stroke the power of absolute monarchy had been destroyed and the corporate privileges of the nobility and clergy abolished. As regards the Church, the enlightened ministers of Charles III and Charles IV had already introduced a number of measures which curtailed ecclesiastical jurisdiction and expropriated Church property. But it was not until Joseph Bonaparte ascended the throne that feudal titles were abolished and the religious Orders dissolved. Indeed, not a few intellectuals were tempted to accept the French king, since as one dissident cleric later recalled, he could see 'no prospect of liberty behind the cloud of priests who everywhere stand foremost to take the lead of our patriots'.[11]

In the event, the Constitution of 1812 replaced absolute monarchy by the ringing statement that 'sovereignty resides essentially in the Nation', a principle which reduced the king to the status of an hereditary executive, subject to the laws and resolutions of the Cortes. If Catholicism was established as the religion of the Spanish nation, the Inquisition was abolished and in subsequent measures, religious communities were forbidden to beg for monies to rebuild the houses seized or destroyed by the French. But Liberal plans to introduce further reforms were thwarted when, in 1814, Ferdinand VII returned to Spain and promptly suspended the Constitution. However, his resumption of absolute power did not yield effective government and, in 1820, thanks to a military revolt, a new Cortes was elected. By then dominated by masonic lodges, Liberal deputies expelled the recently re-established Jesuits, halved the ecclesiastical tithe, suppressed monasteries and reduced the number of mendicant clergy. What is striking here is the degree to which hispanic intellectuals exhibited strong anti-clerical sentiments.[12] In his report on the rebellion of 1814 staged in Cuzco, the president of the high court of that city, Manuel Pardo, sharply criticized the role of priests in attacking constituted authority, both in Spain and America, and concluded that their aim was to 'leave religion with the clothing of the exterior cult, sufficient to enable their ministry to obtain from an ignorant people all the profit their avarice suggests'.[13] Whereas the Habsburg dynasty had cherished the clergy for their support of royal authority, by contrast the ministers and officers of the sovereign Spanish nation now viewed priests and religious as obstacles to the renovation of society, guilty of encouraging popular superstitions. Such attitudes were to become common in Mexico in the following generation.

If in Mexico many creoles were enthralled by the prospect of independence, others reaffirmed their identity as Spaniards and proclaimed their loyalty to the Bourbon king. Patriots could be found on either side of the ideological divide, and Our Lady of Guadalupe was acclaimed as patron by both insurgents and royalists. Indeed, the very expectations aroused in devout circles by the events in France, the hope that Mexico would emerge as a Catholic bulwark in a world subdued by Anti-Christ, still persisted. In 1809, a creole canon of the cathedral in Mexico City, José Mariano Beristain de Souza (1756–1817), preached a sermon in which he proclaimed Mexico's debt to 'the generous, invincible and Catholic Spanish Nation'. What had been Mexico before the conquest but 'a barbarous and gross people, subject to despotism', with little know-ledge of the sciences or arts, their polity a reflection of the Devil's tyranny? Observing that most of his congregation were descended from Spaniards, no matter in which generations their ancestors had migrated, Beristain affirmed that they formed part of a single Spanish nation, the lord and owner of New Spain. At the same time, he testi-fied that Americans were welcome in the Peninsula, as he himself had found during twenty-two years of residence there.[14]

But the intensity of Beristain's loyalty did not derive simply from his personal experience; it also expressed patriotic expectations of a surprising kind. It will be recalled that in 1795–6 Francisco Javier Conde reported that he had heard several preachers referring to the prophetic sermon of Francisco Javier Carranza, in which that Jesuit had argued that in the last epoch of the world Our Lady of Guadalupe would preserve Mexico from Anti-Christ's assault and thus convert New Spain into the centre of a renewed, universal Catholic monarchy. If the memory of this sermon had been revived by the outbreak of the French Revolution, it was strengthened by Napoleon's conquests in Europe. Of Carranza's sermon, Beristain wrote:

> But when I write seeing how the tyrant Napoleon Bonaparte persecutes the Roman Pontiff and the Catholic Kings, protectors of the Roman Church, and I behold that Mexico might be the safest asylum for the Pope and the Spanish monarchs from the voracity of that monster, it appears to me that Father Carranza's prophecy is not far from being verified.

But Beristain added: 'thus did I think in the past year of 1809', only then to lament that the insurrection led by Miguel Hidalgo had obliged him to abandon all such patriotic hopes.[15] For all that, here is testimony of the mood of prophetic expectation that animated many creole priests in this epoch.

His profound sense of betrayal added force to Beristain's *Patriotic Dialogues* (1810–11), where he began by exclaiming: 'What a sacrilege! To invoke the Holy Name of Our Lady of Guadalupe in order to overturn justice and to seize the goods of others . . .'. For three hundred years the Mexican Virgin had brought peace and light to New Spain, only now to see her image profaned by its inscription 'on the flags of the rebellion'. No greater scandal could be imagined than the spectacle of a parish priest leading a bloody insurrection which was already stained by the massacre of over two hundred Spanish captives in Guanajuato. Yet if Beristain once more insisted on the union of American and European Spaniards, he also now affirmed the common identity of all the inhabitants of New Spain and, in particular, deplored the use of the term 'mulatto' as divisive. 'With reason, justice and right, all of us who are born here should call ourselves Spaniards . . . we are all now equal: we are all the sons and vassals of the king of Spain.' In traditional terms he invoked the concept of 'the great body of the Spanish nation', which comprised all the territories of the monarchy, albeit with Spain still firmly identified as its head. Deploring the disruption of the economy and the attacks on property caused by the insurgents, he grandly announced that, with the Cortes now in session in Cadiz, 'the architects of our happiness are met together', engaged in the construction of a new regime based on 'religion, the sciences, the arts, true liberty, and paternal, liberal government'.[16]

In September 1811 Beristain preached at a solemn ceremony of apology offered to Our Lady of Guadalupe by the infantry battalion of 'the distinguished patriots of Ferdinand VII', in which he again inveighed against the sacrilege and blasphemy of the rebels in taking the name of the Mexican Virgin. In a peculiar interpretation of the traditional narrative, he claimed that Mary 'came down to Tepeyac to authorize this order and subordination of the Indians to Catholic Spain'. After all, her image had been revealed first to Zumárraga, before even Juan Diego had seen it. In the same way that Mary had preserved Spain from the Moors, so also she would defend 'Mexico, my holy city, where there is the Ark of the Covenant, the Ark of my covenant with the Mexicans, which is Mary of Guadalupe'.[17] There could be thus no question of royalists allowing the insurgents to monopolize Mexico's patron.

Any hopes Beristain might have entertained of the Cortes and its Constitution rapidly disappeared once their measures were published. In November 1814, he preached a *Eucharistic Discourse* at a splendid ceremony organized by the merchant guild and their militia regiment in the conventual church of San Francisco. Not merely did those assembled offer thanks for the return of Ferdinand VII to Spain, but they also celebrated his assumption of absolute power. Striking a traditional note, Beristain affirmed that the Virgin Mary had always acted as 'the patron and liberator of Spain and her kings', since not merely had she helped Santiago to found the Spanish Church, but she had also defended Spain through the ages, be it from the long invasion of the Moors or the sudden assault of Napoleon, ever active in the preservation of 'this chosen people'. In particular, it was by means of her holy images that Mary offered assistance, be it through Pilar, Montserrat and Atocha in Spain, or through Los Remedios, Ocotlán, Zapopan and Izamal in Mexico, not to mention 'this sanctuary and peak of Guadalupe', from which vantage point she protected the entire Spanish monarchy. But Beristain engaged in contemporary polemic when he deplored 'the plague of impious philosophers, strong spirits and materialistic libertines', who had demoralized the people by their denial of God, Christ and the Church. Even in Spain 'an undigested democracy' had invaded the Cortes, seeking to reduce the heir of the Catholic kings to the level of a 'Stadholder of Holland'. So too, in the last four years Mexico had been ruined by 'the newfangled spirit of a few infatuated individuals and by the political-philosophical ideas that some of our compatriots have drunk from the gilded cups of a thousand diabolical books'. It was from Europe that these evil ideas and projects had come, and they had been applied in apish imitation by a few Americans.[18]

In reward for his services to Church and State, Beristain eventually became dean of the cathedral of Mexico, knight of the Order of Charles III and Commander of the Order of Isabella the Catholic. In 1815 he served as a member of the junta of prelates and theologians who condemned José María Morelos as a heretic and handed the insurgent leader over to the secular authorities for execution. And yet, only a year before, his own brother Vicente, who had joined the insurgents in 1812, was shot in a quarrel with a fellow rebel chieftain.[19] All this was a far cry from his youth when, after studying in the Puebla seminary college, in 1773 he accompanied Bishop Francisco Fabián y Fuero to Valencia, where that prelate was installed as archbishop. After qualifying as a doctor of theology, he taught at the University of Valladolid before finally returning to New Spain in 1794 as canon in the Mexican cathedral chapter. Both the patronage of Fuero and his residence in Valencia demonstrated that Beristain belonged to that circle of enlightened, erudite clerics, many of whom were later accused of being 'Jansenists'. In an affectionate description of Fuero, he praised both the bishop's saintly generosity in alms-giving and his cultivation, adding:

> He was as much occupied in reading the Bible as Cicero; and took as much pleasure in the works of Chrysostom as those of Linneaus . . . I frequently saw those books on his table and among them Homer's *Iliad*, Pascal's *Pensées*, and the works of Luis Vives and Van Espen.

It was thanks to Fuero's support that Gregorio Mayans was able to publish the complete works of Luis Vives, the sixteenth-century Erasmian humanist. When Fuero was ousted from his see owing to political intrigue and died in obscurity, Beristain joined with other members of the bishop's 'family' in Mexico to celebrate solemn exequies in Puebla.[20]

It was in 1816, the year before his death, that Beristain published the first volume of his *Northern Hispanic American Library* (1816–21), a three-volume bio-bibliography, in which he listed over three thousand authors who had either published or written manuscripts during the three centuries of Spanish rule. In his 'Apologetic Discourse', he paid tribute to the labours of Juan José de Eguiara y Eguren, and echoed his predecessor's indignation at the disdainful manner in which Manuel Martí, the dean of Alicante, had dismissed America as an intellectual desert. But his real anger was reserved for William Robertson, Guillaume Raynal and Cornelius de Pauw, the enlightened historians of the New World, who had dismissed the Indians as barbarous, the Spanish conquerors as cruel villains, and colonial society as vegetating in sloth and superstition. In point of fact, so Beristain argued, during the sixteenth century, Spain had figured at the head of sciences and arts in Europe and its overseas possessions had participated in its thriving culture. At the same time, he admitted that amidst his listed authors there were no hidden Miltons or Newtons, since their writings could not compare with the very best European masters of recent centuries. So too, critics might well complain of the multitude of sermons, juridical opinions and theological disputations that he had included. But his *Library* was 'not select, but historical and universal', aspiring to comprise all authors and works. That admitted, Beristain affirmed that many sermons exhibited admirable examples of Christian eloquence and that the juridical opinions often took the form of legal treatises. Although the works he cited might not justify Mexicans being seated on the highest bench of European savants, nevertheless, they would easily qualify for a lower bench, an achievement which demolished the calumny that they had vegetated for centuries, with chains about their necks, fit for nothing but feeding off the fields.[21] In this defence of the talents of his compatriots, Beristain expressed his heartfelt patriotism.

If Beristain's fervid royalism led him to pen extended eulogies of Columbus and Cortés, he also praised Clavijero not merely for his superb history of ancient Mexico, but also for his attempts, when a professor in Mexico, to replace Aristotelian physics with the modern science of Newton and Descartes. As regards the Guadalupan tradition, he suggested that Sánchez might well have consulted earlier documents, and on Laso de la Vega he wrote: 'some have believed that this is the same notice of the miracle that the Indian don Antonio Valeriano wrote; but they are deceived', an assertion he did not justify by argument. He followed Eguiara y Eguren in devoting space to Valeriano, noting that he had acted as governor of San Juan Tenochtitlan for thirty years before his death in 1605. He obviously praised Sigüenza y Góngora and reported his identification of Valeriano as the author of the *Nican mopehua*, albeit also recording Cayetano de Cabrera's suggestion that the Indian had translated his account from a Spanish original. To confuse the matter, he also took from Florencia the suggestion that both Baltazar González, Laso's Jesuit censor, and Fernando de Alva Ixtlilxochitl had written accounts of the apparitions. For the rest, he defended Torquemada from

Bartolache's acerbic criticism, and commented that the scientist entertained the strange opinion that Juan Diego's cape was woven from *iczotl* palm rather than from maguey thread. As for Borunda, he dismissed him as 'exotic and capricious in his ideas and arbitrary and superficial in his interpretations'.[22] Where Beristain scored over other Guadalupan bibliographers was in his listing of a large number of sermons preached in honour of the Virgin, even if at times he mangled their titles. This apart, he added nothing to the defence or clarification of the tradition.

Ever partisan, Beristain stridently attacked Servando de Mier not merely for his 1795 sermon, which he characterized as an attempt to overturn 'the ancient and venerable tradition' of the Guadalupe, but still more for his poisonous advocacy of independence. In his introduction he had already criticized the American Spaniards, his compatriots, as the originators and leaders of the insurgency. For three hundred years, so he claimed, they had occupied leading positions in the Church and the judiciary; yet now these unnatural descendants of Spaniards had turned on their European cousins, not because they had any legitimate grievance, but merely because they had been seduced by the impious, libertine doctrines of modern philosophy. 'From a corner of the province of Michoacán and from the breast of a bad parish priest, disciple of Rousseau and Voltaire', there had emerged a movement, which like a volcano spewing forth lava, had converted 'paradises of glory into theatres of blood, horror and misery'.[23] In this denunciation of the insurgency Beristain signalized the emergence of a fissure between the upper clergy and the political forces which sustained that movement, with rebel patriots dismissed as disciples of the French Revolution. The very stridency with which this royalist priest attacked his compatriots expressed the anguish he felt at the damage done to the Church in New Spain and the betrayal of his expectation that Mexico might emerge as the bulwark of a new reinvigorated Catholic monarchy. As the huge labours on his *Library* indicated, Beristain was an ardent creole patriot who sought to defend the honour of Mexico from European slander; his recuperation of the names of three thousand authors just prior to the scattering and loss of so many of their manuscripts was an immeasurable service to all future scholars; and yet that achievement was marred by insufficient critical acumen and occasional partisan bias.

II

In February 1821 Agustín de Iturbide, a creole colonel hitherto renowned for the vigour of his campaigns against the insurgents, published his Plan de Iguala, in which, although he praised Spain as 'the most Catholic, pious, heroic and magnanimous nation', he confidently affirmed that, by reason of its wealth and population, Mexico was now ready to assume its independence. To reassure fellow royalists and the clergy, he offered three guarantees: he promised to maintain the Catholic religion; to achieve independence with a constitutional monarchy; and to preserve the peace and union of American and European Spaniards. Subordinate clauses called for the restitution of the clergy's traditional privileges and property; and offered all office-holders the right to continue, provided they accepted the Plan. If the proclamation was accorded a warm welcome, it was because conservative opinion was alarmed by the liberal, anti-clerical measures introduced by the Cortes which had swept to power in Spain a few months before. At the same time, surviving insurgents, such as Vicente Guerrero and Nicolás Bravo, at once accepted the Plan. After a campaign more characterized by negotiation than battle, in September 1821, Iturbide entered Mexico City in triumph and the dignitaries who signed the Act of Independence announced: 'The Mexican nation, which for three hundred years has had neither its own will nor free use of its voice, today leaves the oppression in which it has lived.'[24]

The exultant sentiments aroused by these events were forcefully expressed by Dr Julio García de Torres in a sermon preached in the sanctuary at Tepeyac in October 1821, when he offered thanks to Mexico's patron for 'the happy event' of the independence of North America. Present was the supreme council of the Regency, accompanied by its president, Agustín de Iturbide, 'Generalisímo of the arms of the empire, Chief and Promotor of American liberty'. If the time had come for Mexico to free itself, so Torres argued, it was because Spain, once so renowned for its devotion to the Catholic religion, was now corrupted by 'the pestilent fevers of the French contagion', which was to say, by 'the execrable maxims' of Voltaire and Rousseau, whose works had been translated into Spanish and were openly available. What was the Cortes in Madrid but 'a conventicle to attack religion', summoned to challenge the authority of the bishops and clergy? All monasteries had been closed and the novitiates of other religious Orders had been suspended. Half of the ecclesiastical tithe now went to the civil power. The Jesuits had been expelled and the three hospital Orders had been suppressed. The rights of the Holy See to intervene in the affairs of the Spanish Church had been severely limited. In a word, the Catholic piety of Charles V and Philip II was at an end; Spain was left degraded and loyal Americans were scandalized. At this juncture God had inspired Iturbide to raise the banner of 'the Mexican eagle' so that now, liberated from the claws of the Spanish lion, it might fly across the American heavens emblazoned with the emblems of Religion, Independence and Union. In the peaceful achievement of independence, Torres discerned 'the providential finger of the Eternal Being' and the intercession of 'his Mother in this advocation of Guadalupe'. The corporate, clerical interests which inspired these effusions can be discerned when, in the name of the Mexican Church, the preacher requested that Iturbide and the Regency should never interfere in questions of religion, demanding 'a blind surrender and captivity of the reason to its venerable dogmas . . . It asks of you submission and obedience to the supreme prince and universal father of believers, the Roman Pontiff.'[25]

As was to be the custom in many sermons of the nineteenth century, Torres also conducted a brief review of the Mexican past. Since the fate of all empires and states was in the hands of God, who would dare question the divine Providence that had chosen the Spain of Charles V to convert 'the most opulent empire in the world into a colony', still less to comprehend why Cortés and Pizarro, 'whose swords were cruelly reddened . . . with the blood of the peaceful Americans', should have been its instruments? However, despite the preaching of Spanish friars, it had been God Almighty and his Son, acting 'through the mediation of his august Mother, under the advocation of Guadalupe', who had singled out the Mexicans from among the nations, so that 'America will always glory in being the chosen favourite of the Lord'. Although the application of the phrase, 'Non fecit taliter omni natione,' might appear presumptuous, 'the unerring judgement of the Vatican' had certified it as 'a canonized truth'. In exultant strain, García de Torres proclaimed: 'the great day of North America, in which religion, once threatened in this vast empire, returns to recover all its rights by means of this fortunate and happy event of the Independence we so desired'. Animating this sermon was the preacher's obvious conviction that divine Providence had established Mexico as a Catholic bastion, chosen to defend the Church from the onslaughts of scepticism and despoilment. Although no reference was made to Carranza's prophecy, the underlying thesis was much the same: that Mexico was about to assume the mantle of the Catholic monarchy which Spain had discarded.[26]

When the Cortes refused to recognize Mexican independence, still less to nominate a Bourbon prince for an American throne, in 1822, Iturbide proclaimed himself constitutional emperor and to legitimize his coup created an Imperial Order of Guadalupe with himself as its Grand Master.[27] Even before his decision, a member of the Regency council, Manuel de la Bárcena (1769–1830), archdeacon of Michoacán, had advocated the establishment of 'a Mexican dynasty' on the throne, since any union with Spain was 'a political monstrosity', especially after the Cortes' attack on the Church, which he described as 'the impulsive causes of the present break'.[28] In recognition of his support, this erstwhile royalist was asked to preach the sermon on 15 December 1822 at the first annual function of the Order of Guadalupe celebrated in the Franciscan Church of San José. In origin a European Spaniard, Bárcena observed that such an illustrious assembly of personages 'had never been seen before in Anahuac' and characterized the Order as a symbol 'of the eternal memory of our covenant with the Mother of God', among whose many gifts he numbered 'the three guarantees of the Empire'.[29]

Turning to consider Mexico's foundation moment, Bárcena reminded the congregation that under the rule of Tenochtitlan, Mexicans 'groaned under the heavy weight of a barbarous paganism, sustained by errors such as horrible idols, cannibal priests, bloody sacrifices: there indeed Nature shuddered'. But then the Queen of Heaven, the Mother of God, appeared at Tepeyac like the light of dawn, piercing the shadows of night, and 'since then the faith of the Crucified began to grow and flourish mightily'. In all the fifteen centuries of Christian history there never had occurred 'an epoch so glorious for our religion' as when the Virgin pitched her sublunary residence at Tepeyac and established a new Zion, a bulwark against the heresies of Luther and Calvin which then engulfed Europe. In the last eleven years Mexico had been consumed by civil war, with both sides taking the Guadalupe as their banner, but 'if the country of Anahuac breathes liberty, we owe everything to the Virgin of Tepeyac'. As in the moment of its foundation as a Christian nation in the sixteenth century, so now, when 'the imperial eagle appears triumphant on his *nopal*', Mexico stood in opposition to Europe. If in the Old World religion was persecuted and a flood of sceptical publications fomented incredulity, by contrast Mexico had never been contaminated by heresy and indeed now figured as the most Catholic country in the world. Bárcena added:

> The holy Catholic religion . . . is the soul of this empire; yes, the faith of Jesus Christ is inseparable from it and is identified with the nation of Anahuac; and he who is not an apostolic Christian is not a citizen of ours; he is not a Mexican.

But the archdeacon struck a contemporary note when he warned the congregation that, if Mexico failed to cultivate the arts and sciences, it would repeat the experience of the sixteenth century and fall prey to foreign invaders. Above all, it was necessary to maintain patriotism and union, since 'we are all Mexicans . . . origin, language, blood and religion unite us'.[30] Disillusioned with Spain, Bárcena thus envisaged his adopted country as a Catholic redoubt in a world thrust into dissolution by scepticism and secularism.

The clerical euphoria which Iturbide's regime occasioned was soon dissipated when the emperor was forced into exile and a republic proclaimed. But even before that eclipse, on 11 March 1822, delegates from all the Mexican dioceses had met in Mexico City and concluded that, with the achievement of independence, the *patronato* granted by the papacy to the Spanish crown had lapsed, so that the Mexican State had to negotiate a new agreement with the Holy See. Without a concordat, the republic had no legal right to intervene in the internal affairs of the Church.[31] For all that, the 1824 Constitution began with the invocation 'In the name of God the Almighty, author and supreme lawgiver of society'. Article 3 declared that 'the religion of the Mexican nation is and shall be perpetually the Catholic, Apostolic and Roman. The nation protects it by wise and just laws and prohibits the practice of any other.' Furthermore, Article 110 conferred upon the president, acting with other federal authorities, the power 'to permit the passage or to retain conciliar decrees, pontifical bulls, breves and rescripts'.[32] It was not until after 1831 that the papacy moved to appoint a new bench of bishops.[33] By then the liberal government, headed by Valentín Gómez Farías, threatened to expropriate Church property and abolished the legal compulsion to pay the ecclesiastical tithe on agricultural produce. Although the republic failed to negotiate a concordat with Rome, it is clear that presidential approbation for bishops elected by the cathedral chapters and confirmed by the Holy See was still taken for granted. In effect, despite the emergence of a strong, anti-clerical party in politics, the first republic remained profoundly Catholic, with virtually all public events celebrated in cathedrals and churches and magnified by liturgical pomp and circumstance. In 1828, when Vicente Guerrero captured the flags of a French invading force, he deposited these trophies in the sanctuary at Tepeyac. So too, when the seasonal rainfall was slow to appear, the image of Our Lady of Los Remedios was still paraded through the streets of the capital before being placed on the cathedral's high altar.[34]

Despite the fulminations of Beristain and former royalist preachers, the Mexican Insurgency had been led by priests who remained loyal to their faith and who had projected a confessional republic. It was Carlos María de Bustamante, the self-appointed national chronicler, who preserved the Catholic republicanism of that movement until his death in 1848. As is notorious, Bustamante defined the Insurgency as a struggle to recover the sovereign freedom which the Mexican nation had enjoyed prior to the Spanish conquest. Whereas Bárcena dismissed Tenochtitlan as a scene of barbaric idolatry, by contrast, when Bustamante described Iturbide's triumphal march through the streets of the capital, he conjured up, in his mind's eye, the shades of the Mexican emperors rising from their tombs in Chapultepec to lead that procession.[35] Notwithstanding his fervent devotion to the Guadalupe, the insurgent chronicler never identified the apparition as the foundation moment of the Mexican nation, and still less did he condone the crimes of the conquerors. As the years passed, in successive volumes, Bustamante castigated with equable severity the anti-clerical policies of the radicals, the monarchical projects of the conservatives, and the corrupt ambitions of General Antonio López de Santa Anna, only to conclude with a despairing description of the American invasion of 1847.

In 1831, Bustamante participated in the deliberations of the 'Guadalupan Junta' which met to prepare for the celebrations of the third centenary anniversary of the Virgin's apparition to Juan Diego. He strongly supported the proposal that the image should be taken out from Tepeyac, paraded through the streets and then installed in the cathedral for three days. Had not Our Lady of Guadalupe often been the insurgents' 'only hope', during the dark days of their struggle? To take the Virgin to the cathedral would constitute a grand act of thanksgiving for all her help in the liberation of Mexico from serfdom. In any case, the image was extraordinarily resistant to being touched or to changes in air, especially since 'what God has painted, the hand of man will never erase'. In spite of his pleas, the college of canons at Tepeyac rejected the proposal on the grounds that the image had never left the sanctuary since 1629. In the event, the Junta arranged for an impressive round of celebrations that lasted for four

Plate 23   Pedro Gualdi, *The Sanctuary of Our Lady of Guadalupe*

days after Christmas, beginning in the cathedral and ending in the sanctuary at Tepeyac. On 27 December, after sermon and mass, the Junta and city council led a procession through the streets of the capital, following the route observed on the feast of Corpus Christi. Attached to the great standard was the small painting of Our Lady of Guadalupe which once had been possessed by Juan Diego and thereafter preserved in the cathedral. The following day the Junta led the way to the sanctuary, where a former insurgent priest preached the sermon, the celebrations ending with a display of fireworks at night.[36]

In his account of these proceedings, Bustamante attributed the refusal to allow the image to leave its sanctuary to the doubts about the apparition raised by Juan Bautista Muñoz. Yet in 1829 he had published the twelfth book of Bernardino de Sahagún's *General History of the Things of New Spain*, based on a copy taken by Colonel Diego Garcia Panes of the version preserved in Tolosa. His purpose in printing this native account of the conquest was 'to show the cruelties of the Spaniards'. However, he filled the text with an extended commentary and indeed inserted Servando de Mier's dissertation on St Thomas in Mexico. Observing that the Virgin had appeared when the fields were filled with the corpses of Indians slain by the plague, Bustamante argued that Sahagún had censored his account for fear of Spanish reprisals. After all, since Antonio Valeriano was 'the principal oracle whom he consulted for his history', it was obvious that he must have known of the apparitions. As for Zumárraga, the bishop had written about the event; but the country was then in uproar and the documents had gone astray. His insurgent creed was manifest in his assertion that, since the Virgin's apparition, 'for all Mexicans the idea was fixed that in Our Lady of Guadalupe they had the sacred paladin of their liberty and the emancipation they longed for'.[37]

These arguments were restated in 1840 when Bustamante published another version of Sahagún's twelfth book, written in 1585 and purchased in Madrid, explaining that 'today we possess an original manuscript, all written in his hand and letter, signed by Father Sahagún'. He seized upon the Franciscan's admission that in a previous version 'some things were put in the narration of this conquest which were badly put and other things were omitted which were wrongly omitted'. This obviously meant, so Bustamante inferred, that if Zumárraga had not mentioned the apparitions, it was because he had already been severely criticized for attempting to defend the Indians from the conquerors. As Sahagún revealed, 'in all parts and for the space of not a few years, death, hatred, devastation and slavery filled the air of America'. But when the Franciscan defined Cortés' victory as a providential miracle designed to punish the Indians for their sins, Bustamante commented that: 'heaven never punishes the men who obey the first law which heaven itself imposes on them, which is, to defend their liberty, their country and their independence against whatever aggressor'.[38]

In 1843, Bustamante finally published a systematic account of the Guadalupan tradition, but achieved little more than to repeat what had been better expressed in the dissertations of Uribe and Guridi. About the only point of divergence was that he followed Mier's suggestion that Valeriano wrote his account of the apparitions in the form of a sacramental drama or *auto*, albeit quietly suppressing the Dominican's conclusion that it was a fabrication. For the rest, he described the Virgin of Tepeyac as 'a pleasing Indian, brown, full of sweetness, humble in her attitude, very modest', adding that 'one cannot see her without the heart throbbing and the eyes filled with tears'. However, he confessed that he no longer expected to persuade all his compatriots as to the truth of the tradition, since 'I have the unhappy certainty that my voice and pen will not be more than a weak dyke against the devastating torrent of jokes and sarcasms' which had been spread abroad by 'the philosophers'. By then Bustamante was a survivor from a past age, an insurgent Catholic republican, whose patriotic creed was derided both by anti-clerical liberals and monarchical conservatives.[39]

The only serious attempt to answer Muñoz was *The Apparition of Our Lady of Guadalupe* (1849) written by Julián Tornel y Mendívil (1801–60), a professor of canon and civil law at Orizaba. At the outset, Tornel explained that he did not write to persuade those 'strong spirits' who did not believe in God or miracles; nor did he address himself to those superficial minds who dismissed all such matters so as to appear 'enlightened'. Instead, he wrote for those who believed in God and 'those who love the glories of our patria'. A careful scholar, Tornel had digested a vast amount of information, but had little new to offer save a few minor facts, noting that Muñoz had erred in his dates, since Valeriano died in 1605 and Alva Ixtlilxochitl in 1650 aged eighty. After commenting that Muñoz had relied on the negative argument of universal silence, he quoted Jean de Launoy, the Gallican theologian and Church historian, on the rules governing the employment of this criterion. Following Clavijero, he argued that in the same way that the works of Sahagún and Torquemada were based on native sources, so the apparition narrative derived from the account written by Valeriano, an account printed by Laso de la Vega and translated by Becerra Tanco. Yet Muñoz had taken no heed of this primitive account and instead had concentrated on Sánchez. As for Sahagún, whose criticism of the cult at Tepeyac Muñoz had cited to such effect, had not Bustamante shown that the Franciscan had written at least two versions of his history? In any case, why should his testimony be preferred to that of Valeriano? So too, Tornel accepted Bustamante's suggestion that, since Zumárraga had fought to defend the Indians from the conquerors, he had not judged it convenient to reveal the apparition. In the early Church there had survived 'the doctrine of the arcane', the oral tradition, which was not readily revealed. So too, in the years following the apparitions an oral tradition had preserved their memory until Valeriano wrote his account. Despite his careful erudition, Tornel exhibited himself to be the faithful pupil of Uribe and Guridi, with little new to add save the historical arguments taken from Bustamante.[40]

In the years when Tornel composed his defence of the Guadalupan tradition, the Mexican army was roundly defeated by Anglo-American expeditionary forces. The capital was occupied and, at the treaty of Guadalupe Hidalgo (1848), the vast territories which lay north of the Rio Grande were ceded to the United States. Far from uniting the country, the invasion had revealed the bitter divisions that afflicted the political elite. At the same time, most observers confessed that the population at large had been passive spectators of the war. During the very months when American forces entered Veracruz, liberals and conservatives vied for power in the capital. In an acute analysis of the ills haunting his country, Mariano Otero, a moderate Liberal, concluded that 'there is no nation' in Mexico, so that government could not rely on a 'national spirit' to mobilize support to combat foreign invasion.[41] In the last volume of his *History of Mexico* (1849–52), the conservative politician, Lucas Alamán, denounced both the insurgents and demagogic politicians for the disasters that had tormented Mexico since independence and framed an acerbic contrast between the prosperity and enlightened government of Mexico under Viceroy Revillagigedo and the desperate penury and political disorder of the Mexican republic in 1850. Apprehensive of further Anglo-American expropriations, he defined the Church as 'the only common bond which unites all Mexicans when all other ties have been broken, and the only one capable of sustaining the Spanish-American race and protecting it from the great dangers to which it is exposed'.[42]

Although sermons offered to Our Lady of Guadalupe were soon to express the ever-deepening desperation that was to afflict the Mexican Church as much as the Mexican people, in the immediate aftermath of the Anglo-American War preachers sought more to emphasize the theme of national unity. At the sanctuary at Tepeyac on 12 December 1852, Francisco Javier Miranda saluted the image as 'the ark of the eternal covenant that reconciles the Mexican people with the heavens'. Was not the sanctuary a refuge and solace for all the faithful? 'In this august church there is a place of reunion for all Mexicans, the only chain which unites their sentiments . . . the only principle of force and unity which makes us appear as a nation through whose action we can even now regenerate ourselves'.[43] So too, at much the same time, Dr Felipe Neri de Barros, a priest of the Oratory, described the Spanish conquest as an act of divine punishment for the sins of idolatry, since 'those foreigners come filled with the vengeance of God and are ministers of his justice'. But the destruction of the Devil's cult left an anguished, blood-stained solitude which was then filled by the tender voice of the Franciscans, preaching the gospel of a crucified Saviour. The Virgin Mary prayed for the Mexicans so fervently that 'The Lord signalized Mexico as her inheritance'; and thanks to her apparition her sovereign image had conquered Huizilopochtli. In her victory, there emerged 'a single people of brothers formed from the conquering and conquered race', and 'this princess of the House of David was converted into a maiden of Anahuac'.[44]

III

In 1859, at the height of the Three Years War, the Liberal cabinet headed by Benito Juárez promulgated the Reform Laws which separated Church and State, suppressed the religious Orders and confraternities, expropriated Church property, and left the clergy henceforth dependent on the voluntary offerings of the Catholic laity. In their statement justifying these measures, the radicals claimed that 'the high clergy' and the military had initiated a civil war simply to defend their privileges and wealth. It was now time to expel from the public life of the republic these remnants of 'the colonial system' which still sought to impede Mexico's incorporation into contemporary civilization. With remarkable confidence they declared that the Liberal party embodied in the government was not a political faction, but the nation itself, 'the very symbol of reason, order, justice and civilization'. Whereas the Catholic kings had once demanded that all their subjects should subscribe to the teachings of the Roman Catholic Church, now the Mexican nation decreed that religion was a matter for private conscience, albeit subject to government regulation in all its public manifestations.[45]

The Reform Laws were but the culmination of an entire set of anti-clerical measures introduced by the radicals after they seized power in 1855. In November 1855 the Juárez Law stripped the clergy of their immunity from secular jurisdiction; in June 1856 the Lerdo Law enjoined the sale and amortization of all Church property; and in April 1857 the Iglesias Law prohibited the clergy from charging the poor fees for baptisms, marriages and burials. If all this were not enough, the 1857 Constitution disestablished the Church through omission of the former Article 3; education was declared to be free of constraint; and all citizens were endowed with the right to express and publish whatever opinion or doctrine they espoused, provided they did not seek to undermine morality or public order. Not only were all private or corporate jurisdictions prohibited, but Article 27 also stated that: 'no civil or ecclesiastical corporation, no matter what its character, denomination or purpose, shall have the legal capacity to acquire property or manage real estate, with the only exception of buildings which are destined for the immediate and direct service or purpose of the institution'. Finally, Article 123 stated: 'it corresponds exclusively to the federal powers, in matters of religious cult and external discipline, to exercise the intervention which the laws prescribe'.[46] The effect of these measures was to exclude the Church from public life and convert it into a private institution, albeit denied legal personality as regards property.

The peremptory, often brutal fashion with which the Reform measures were implemented provoked fierce condemnation from the Catholic bishops and clergy. In a sermon preached at Tepeyac in February 1858 during a function organized by the diocese of Puebla, Ismael Jiménez lamented the savage, often bloody scenes that the congregation had witnessed during the last two years. Priests had been expelled, churches closed, the bishop exiled, and the charitable funds for widows and orphans expropriated. If Mary had once appeared to break the bonds of error and ignorance which had once subjugated Mexicans to 'the dark angel of hell', in the present age many men now lived as practical atheists, mocking religion and dismissing the pious practices of the people as mere superstition. In an audacious analogy he declared that since God had rescued the ancient Mexicans from barbarism 'by means of his loving Mother . . . the conversion of the Indians was in some degree rendered similar to the redemption of human kind through Jesus Christ'. When Christ was condemned to death nineteen hundred years ago, it signified 'the triumph of the cross over hell'. When Mary appeared 320 years ago and had her image of Guadalupe placed in her chapel as 'the Mother and especial protector of the Mexicans', she triumphed over Satan. Whereas Christ had shed his blood on Calvary to free all men from the sin of Adam, at Tepeyac Mary had liberated the Mexicans from idolatry. And if Christ bequeathed the Eucharist to all Christians, Mary left her image imprinted on Juan

Diego's cape for the Mexicans. But, like ancient Israel, the Mexicans had rejected their God and for the last thirty-seven years, since independence, they had engaged in civil wars, seduced by false doctrines and a corrupt education. Such was the devastation wrought that Jiménez openly speculated that Mexico might be invaded by barbarians, its people put to the sword, and the survivors expelled from the land, 'wandering without a *patria* or home, without priests or law'. As it was, the people at large still believed in the apparitions of Mary and still came on pilgrimage to the sanctuary at Tepeyac, 'the imperishable monument of our liberty'. One could only pray that, like Esther before Ahasuerus, Mary would intercede before the Almighty to save the Mexicans.[47]

The quarrel between the Liberals and the clergy was not simply a question of privileges and property: it derived from two sharply antagonistic views about the rights of the individual and the role of the Church in society. As early as 1851, when Melchor Ocampo, the former Liberal governor of Michoacán, asserted that the State authorities had the right to regulate the parochial fees charged for baptisms, marriages and burials, he was roundly condemned by an anonymous parish priest for attempting 'to usurp the Church's sovereignty, to secularize religious society and to impose the civil power over and above the divine jurisdiction of the bishops'. Ocampo had failed to realize that the Church was 'a universal society, sovereign and independent', whose bishops, its 'sovereigns', alone possessed the right to determine what charges, if any, it should make for its ministrations. Moreover, since the 1824 Constitution had recognized Roman Catholicism as the national religion, it followed that civil authorities were obliged to apply the dictates of canon law as set down by the Council of Trent. If this were not enough, the anonymous cleric informed Ocampo that 'the Church is one, States are many . . . the clergy are as independent of the State as is Mexico of England'. Undeterred by this doctrinal assault, Ocampo appealed to the authority of the German philosophers, Kant and Fichte, and affirmed that in questions of belief and morality the individual should be governed by the private judgement of his conscience, a thesis at once denounced as 'a detestable heresy' by his opponent. But Ocampo further asserted that the civil authorities had no obligation to intervene in the religious sphere and that the Church was best regarded as a voluntary association of the faithful. In the case of parochial fees, however, he argued that the Mexican republic had inherited the patronage rights of the Spanish crown over the Church, and hence could regulate the charges it levied on the citizenry.[48] When Ocampo sat down to frame the text of the Reform Laws of 1859, he may well have recalled the terms of this debate and have concluded that separation of Church and State afforded the best resolution of the problem.

The confident vigour with which a parish priest criticized the former governor of Michoacán derived from the teachings he had absorbed in the Seminary College at Morelia, where its rector during the 1840s, Clemente de Jesús Munguía

(1810–68), purveyed the intransigent, ultramontane theses of such French doctrinaires as Bonald, Maistre, Chateaubriand and Lammenais. According to these thinkers, the French Revolution was the child of the Enlightenment and had unleashed a tide of anarchic rationalism that threatened to undermine not merely the Church but all society.[49] In his treatise *On Natural Law* (1849), Munguía demonstrated, to his own satisfaction at least, that the Church constituted a sovereign society, endowed with its own laws, courts, discipline and doctrines, and concluded that there existed 'two independent powers and sovereigns in every society, the spiritual power which presides over the religious order, and the temporal power which presides over the political order'. It followed that the Church's rights to possess property, to charge fees for its operations and to exercise jurisdiction all flowed both from its divine foundation and from its status as a sovereign society.[50] As bishop of Michoacán, Munguía drew on these principles to issue a series of strongly worded pastorals in which he condemned the entire range of legislation introduced during the Liberal Reform. Other bishops echoed his arguments. So vehement was their defence that any Catholic who dealt in Church property or who swore allegiance to the 1857 Constitution was *ipso facto* excommunicated.

When General Félix Zuloaga rebelled against the Liberal government in January 1858, calling for the abrogation of the Reform legislation, Munguía warmly welcomed his initiative. As a result he remained confined to Mexico City during the Three Years War, 1858–60, and from that vantage point learnt of the confiscation of the gold, silver and jewels of the cathedral of Morelia, treasures accumulated across three centuries. In 1859 there arrived news of the expropriation of his seminary college, an ample, handsome building facing the cathedral, the institution which had nurtured his intellectual growth and whose library he had laboured to increase. By then many parishes in his diocese were without pastors, since the clergy had suffered 'fines, vexations, confiscations, attacks and banishments'.[51] Already at the beginning of his episcopate, Munguía had saluted Pius IX as a 'Pontiff-King' chosen by Providence to turn back the tide of revolution which threatened Christendom. In a pastoral issued in February 1860, he once more reiterated his defence of the temporal power of the papacy, at that time under challenge, denounced the doctrine of the rights of man as subversive of the dogmatic powers of the Church and warned of the menace of socialism.[52]

It was during these years of civil war, when Mexico City was defended by conservative forces, that Munguía preached two sermons in the sanctuary at Tepeyac that expressed both the depths of his anguish about the state of Mexico and the rocklike quality of his faith in God, the Church and Mary. On 12 March 1859 he proclaimed that all the history, character and destiny of the Mexican people was tightly bound to the Virgin Mary, since they were 'the debtors of the predestination that made our *patria* her dwelling place', even if at the present time its 'degenerate sons' had deserted their patron and brought ruin to their nation. Since the beginning of the world, of course, man had broken 'the pact of alliance with the Author of his being', falling into sins from which he could only be redeemed by 'the blood of the Man-God sacrificed for him'. From among the nations, God had chosen the Hebrews as the vehicle of his salvation and from whom would come Mary, the new Ark of the Covenant, the Mother of God. But although the Church had created a Christian civilization during the Middle Ages, philosophy had corrupted both the revival of letters and the Reformation, and both had conspired to attack the Church. At such a juncture, where else could the Church look but to the New World? 'At last there arrived your turn in the divine vocation of all the nations in the faith of the Crucified.' Thanks to divine Providence, the Spaniards discovered and conquered 'our unknown Eden' and thereafter converted 'that inconceivably barbarous and sanguinary, idolatrous people, who sought truth and sentiments, the gospel and civilization'. And yet, although the mendicant friars intervened between the conquerors and the conquered, 'calling them to a common destiny' as brothers, it was not until December 1531, when the Virgin Mary appeared at Tepeyac, that the Indians joyfully accepted the Christian gospel. What could better prove the power and motherly love of the Virgin than this extraordinary event of 'an idolatrous and barbarous nation so rapidly converted without new miracles and even without martyrs'? With the Indians flocking to accept their new faith, Our Lady of Guadalupe thus became 'the queen of happy Anáhuac, the mother of all its inhabitants, the ark of a new covenant'. When the Church incorporated the apparition 'as a pious belief, in the calendar of its solemnities', then in certain measure it suppressed the distance that separated the centuries between the birth of Christ and the appearance of Mary in Mexico, and by analogy united 'the mountains of Judaea and Tepeyac, the mother of the Baptist and the mother of our *patria*'. Munguía declared:

> Without doubt, because this is the truth and this is the faith, the tender Virgin drawn on the cape of Juan Diego is the same who, led by her love, went to lavish the infinite grace she carried in her womb on Elizabeth, her son and family. She who stood three centuries ago on this very mount of Tepeyac is the same who set out so hastily in another time for the mountains of Judaea.

For three centuries 'the sweet and suave character' of the Mexicans had been formed by Mary, and as the 'favourite child of Mary's tenderness, our *patria* figures in the history of religion as one of the peoples who have been most singularly favoured'. It was thanks to his Guadalupan vision of Mexico that Munguía could exclaim: 'O happy nation . . . You will be great, you will give to history brilliant and glorious pages, you shall be the queen of the New World.'[53]

But if the future of Mexico was full of promise, the present was desolate: 'We are sick, my brothers, sorrow has prostrated us on the death-bed . . .' Of course, there was nothing new in this progressive decline. Jerusalem had been destroyed by the Romans,

Israel scattered to the winds. Where now were the once thriving churches of Alexandria, Antioch and Constantinople? And if the countries of Northern Europe boasted of their industry, their arts and discoveries, and their 'balance of power', were they not divided into innumerable sects, each peddling false ideas, where 'interests are everything, the spirit nothing' and where 'the incessant noise of a thousand factories drowns out the cries of misery, as the unfortunate die of hunger . . .'? Protestantism had bred the sceptical philosophy of the eighteenth century which had prepared the way for 'the French Revolution, which killed the State, sacrificed the priesthood, denied God and placed the statue of Reason in his tabernacle . . .'. It had also unleashed that tide of revolution which still threatened to engulf Europe and which had driven the Vicar of Christ from Rome.[54]

And yet, in the very years when Europe was thrown into revolutionary turmoil, Mexico had remained 'firm in her beliefs, constant in her habits of order, enjoying an inalterable peace and with it all the benefits of society and civilization'. With an immense, almost painful nostalgia for a colonial Mexico he himself had never known, Munguía painted an idyllic picture of a country where magistrates acted as the fathers of their people, where vast territories were governed without any army, and where domestic morality was still animated by Catholic principles. All this was but to set off the radical decline of recent years, when a false education and a deplorable immorality haunted the Mexican nation, and where 'the government is the first of the beggars, the sovereign of the hungry'. As for the religion of most Mexicans, 'their faith is now very weak, their spiritual discernment almost extinguished, their intimacy with God barely perceptible . . .'. And yet, despite so much incredulity and sacrilege, Catholics should not despair but rather appeal to Mary: 'we are prostrate on the deathbed; but she is the mother of life'. Munguía concluded with a peroration, in which he pleaded with the Virgin Mary: 'Turn again this nation, whom you are still pleased to call your own and which will never cease to call out to you as its dear and tender Mother . . .'[55]

On 29 August 1860, Munguía returned to Tepeyac, there to lament the condition of his country and his Church, both afflicted by a terrible crisis. Speaking on behalf of the Mexican Church, he appealed to the Mother of God for assistance, citing 'the election you have made of this privileged soil for your residence, most powerful Queen, tender Mother . . .'. He echoed traditional Marian theology when he referred to 'the happy covenant between God and man, that covenant of which you are the Ark, since you carried the Mediator in your womb'. Anxious, no doubt, to reassure the congregation, he affirmed that the Church did not depend on the protection of governments and still less on the triumphs of arms: possessing the means to preserve herself, all she required was the liberty to preach the gospel and administer the sacraments. In nothing did the Church rely on human power; so that the only real injury men could inflict was to deprive her of 'external liberty'. Repeatedly emphasizing the 'dogmatic magisterium' exercised by the Church in its teachings, Munguía affirmed that the

Church possessed two characters: 'first, that of complete perfection in her formation, constitution and destiny; second, that of a constant struggle in her journey across the earth'. But he did not elaborate on this striking image of a struggling, pilgrim Church, so different from his previous insistence on hierarchical jurisdiction, but instead sought to strengthen the faith of his listeners by a fervid eulogy of the institutional Church.

> On account of the divine perfection with which Jesus Christ instituted it, the Catholic Church is one holy, Catholic, apostolic; it is infallible, indefectible, constant, perpetual, more strong than the royal crowns of warriors, more powerful than all the sovereigns of this world, more irresistible than all human influences, more prudent and understanding than all the geniuses and wise men that the centuries have produced; in sum, it is divine, it is continually assisted by Jesus Christ himself, and thinks, speaks and acts constantly under the sublime inspiration of the Holy Spirit.

Pronounced at a time when the Mexican Church was suffering grievously from Liberal attacks and was soon to suffer still more, this peroration, despite the obvious influence of classical French models, testified by the very strength of its affirmations to Munguía's inner desolation. Although his faith taught him that the Church would survive the persecution mounted by 'this bastard civilization of our times' since, while states rose and fell and doctrines waxed and waned, the Church would emerge reborn and reinvigorated, nevertheless, he could only lament the destruction wrought in Mexico.[56]

Turning to the condition of his country and people, Munguía asserted that all the strife had come from the attempt to replace God's scheme by merely human projects. 'Everyone wanted to make Mexico according to his own taste, looking for models from abroad', be they of monarchy, republic or dictatorship. Once a religious society, opulent and sweet in character, which had only needed independence to rise to the peak of prosperity and greatness, Mexico had acted like a prodigal son and through dissipation and violence had destroyed its inheritance. As in the ancient world, rationalism had undermined religion, so that anarchy and avarice, passion and tyranny, had devastated society. The result was that the *patria* was in a deplorable condition: 'it is hardly born; and already you see it faded like a beautiful flower; it is young and, nevertheless, appears like a corpse; and if it is not already in the sepulchre, it is because its agony has been very prolonged'. Like Nineveh when visited by the prophet Jonah, Mexico was in mourning at its destruction and ruin. Only if the country returned to God and formed a new covenant with Christ could its salvation be renewed. As it was, Munguía could do little more than lament like another Jeremiah: 'In all parts I can only see war, blood running in torrents, mourning, orphans, misery, tears, despair, and death.'[57]

IV

When Benito Juárez entered Mexico City, he banished the Catholic bishops who had collectively condemned the Reform Laws as 'the complete destruction of Catholicism in Mexico, the rupture of our social bonds, the prescription of all religious principles'.[58] Thereafter, the great convents of the capital were destroyed, their wealth confiscated, their paintings sold off, and their books deposited in national collections. One by one the bishops made their way to Rome, where they encountered Pelagio Antonio de Labastida, the bishop of Puebla, who had been exiled some time earlier. Pius IX had supported the Catholic hierarchy in their quarrel with the Liberal government, and he now made them welcome in Rome. In June 1862 the exiled prelates participated in the collective canonization of twenty-seven new saints, among whom was numbered Felipe de Jesús, the Mexican Franciscan who had been martyred at Nagasaki in 1597, ceremonies which 265 bishops and archbishops from across the world attended. It was in 1863 that Labastida obtained from Pius IX administrative reforms designed to reinvigorate the afflicted Mexican Church. At one stroke the dioceses of Mexico, Michoacán and Guadalajara became archbishoprics and new dioceses were created in Zamora, León, Querétaro, Zacatecas, Tulancingo, Chilapa and Veracruz. Munguía became the first archbishop of Morelia, and Labastida was named archbishop of Mexico.[59] However, in secular politics Labastida proved less adept, since he supported Napoleon III's disastrous imposition of Archduke Maximilian of Austria as emperor of Mexico. For thirty days he acted as Regent until it became clear that the French generals who then governed Mexico had no sympathy for clerical pretensions. To their horror, the Catholic bishops found that Maximilian favoured moderate Liberals rather than the conservative party and refused to countenance the return of Church property. The result of their ill-advised support was that several bishops, including Labastida and Munguía, once again had to take refuge in Rome after the collapse of the short-lived empire. In the long term, however, the separation of Church and State proved beneficial to the clergy since, provided they abstained from any public rites or pronouncements, they were left free to rebuild their churches and open schools. It was during the 1880s that the fruits of this slow, devoted renovation were to become obvious. In part, if that renewal occurred, it was because large sections of the population remained faithful Catholics, and this was especially the case among women, 'the sex which . . . with such zeal has defended religion and the Church in our domestic quarrels'.[60]

Their enforced travels and residence in Rome transformed the outlook of the Mexican bishops and the clergy who accompanied them. For the first time they became fully conscious of belonging to a universal church and of the necessity of papal support if they were to remain independent of the Mexican State. Ironically, they also learnt of the advantages of toleration, a principle which Munguía had earlier dismissed as 'necessarily pernicious for society' in a Catholic country like Mexico.[61] In his pastoral issued upon his return from exile, Pedro Espinosa, the first archbishop of Guadalajara, commented that in his travels in the United States, England and France, he had found the Catholic Church free to build churches, monasteries and colleges. The clergy enjoyed freedom in both pulpit and the press; they conducted processions in public, and were registered as owners of property. In none of these countries was the Church seen as the enemy of progress, toleration and liberty. How different was the case in Mexico, he exclaimed, where the clergy were denied the rights of association, of property and of liberty of teaching.[62] In short, the so-called Liberals in Mexico did not understand the meaning of toleration and were still engaged in the active persecution of the Church. Here were arguments which the bishops collectively adopted in 1875 when they protested against the incorporation of the Reform Laws into the Constitution. But by then they warned the laity to abstain from any public protest against the measure; and urged all Catholics to contribute alms to maintain their churches and to promote religious education.[63]

Although the ultramontane clergy dominated the upper reaches of the Mexican Church in this epoch, not all priests eschewed liberalism. That generation of insurgents who combined republicanism with Catholicism had some heirs and disciples. The union of patriotism, liberalism and the Christian gospel was nowhere better manifested than in a sermon preached by Dr Agustín de Rivera y San Román (1824–1916) in Guadalajara on 12 December 1858. Although it was delivered during the first year of civil war, the sermon numbers among the most poetic and joyful of those offered to the Virgin of Tepeyac. Taking as his text the passage from St Luke, 'And Mary arose in those days and went to the hill country in haste', he invited the congregation to imagine a scene in heaven where, at the behest of the Holy Trinity, the Virgin was about to sally forth, bound for Tepeyac. He pictured her as surrounded by millions of angels, her progress accompanied, not by the thunder and lightning which marked God's appearance at Sinai, but rather by the rays of the moon, the sign of peace and union. When the angelic choirs saw her, they asked: 'Who is this most beautiful of Virgins, whose skin is brown and whose hair is like that of the daughters of Cuauhtemoc and Moctezuma?' Not awaiting a reply, the angels begged Mary to tell them where she was going. 'Are you going to Rome, the eternal city?' they asked, or 'to Greece, the ancient home of the sciences and fine arts?' Or was she engaged in a mission to 'Jerusalem, that beautiful captive, once celebrated by David and Solomon and now with hair dishevelled and its forehead in the dust'? But the Virgin replied that she was not going to any of these renowned cities, but instead: 'I am going to an unknown corner of the world, which is called Mexico.' And she then explained how she was about to make a heavenly visitation of the native peoples of Mexico, starting with 'the simple nation of the Optatas, who live in Sonora, under tents of deer skin', and ending with the Quichés, 'who in Guatemala raised sumptuous temples, palaces, aqueducts, barracks and colleges'; but not forgetting either the Otomies, 'who do not have houses and sleep in hammocks'; the Tarascans, 'who practise mechanical arts in Michoacán'; and the Aztecs, 'who shall sing to me the praises of the New Testament in the sweetest of languages'. She concluded:

> From all these and from many other nations of diverse languages, customs, religions and governments, I am going to form a single family: a very great thing, a very holy and beloved thing, which is called a *patria*; and I shall be the protector and mother of this poor *patria*. In the pupils of my eyes I have portrayed every Mexican; I carry their sorrows in my heart and their names are written on my right hand. I come to redeem their souls from sin and their bodies from brutalization.

And since she had come to lead the Mexican peoples to Christianity, she chose to appear, not to Charles V or to Francis I, but to a poor Indian and to imprint her image on his *ayate* mantle.[64]

After this poetic, moving exordium, Rivera then affirmed that 'Every creature, every nation, has a destiny and a particular vocation.' Since no entity was ever left isolated in Nature, every human being and society was called upon to play its role in the general harmony of the world. Moreover, one by one, since Christ preached his gospel, the nations had entered the kingdom of heaven. The moment of entry was usually signalized by a specific mission, be it of St Peter in Rome, St Augustine in England, Santiago and Mary at Zaragoza, or 'the day that Our Lady of Guadalupe appeared on a hill', when Mexico found its vocation. Just why the country had been denied the gospel and the Eucharist until the sixteenth century was a mystery of 'the inscrutable will of the Most High', but since 12 December 1531 Mexico had been loyal to the faith of Jesus Christ.[65]

Turning to examine that foundation moment, Rivera invited his congregation to consider that before the conquest 'our fathers' danced around fires burning their captives; and then regaled them with a vivid description of Aztec human sacrifices and cannibalism. But God had taken pity on the native peoples, and when Mary appeared all such practices ceased. 'On the pedestal of the cruel Tonantzin was raised the image of Our Lady of Guadalupe with her hands joined at the breast, as a sign of peace and reconciliation.' Instead of human flesh, the Indians now took the holy Eucharist and at mass they offered the sacrifice of Christ, praying together with the Spaniards and the poor blacks from Africa. 'Behold the solemn proclamation of universal fraternity, of men of all races, all nations and all conditions, sons of the Father who is in heaven.' It was thanks to the apparition of the Virgin Mary that, instead of barbaric Indians, Mexico now possessed churches, convents, colleges, theatres, hospitals and factories: all this Christian civilization came from Our Lady of Guadalupe. Unlike other preachers of this epoch, however, Rivera paid tribute to the Franciscans and other religious who had dedicated their lives to the conversion of the Indians. They had learnt over

Plate 24   Ignacio Manuel Altamirano

fifty languages, they wrote the history of the country, and they 'left us grammars, dictionaries, sermons, the practice of confession and hymns'. It was the love exhibited by Bartolomé de las Casas and countless other bishops and friars that had won the hearts of the Indians. In particular the Franciscans had stained their habits with blue taken from native earth dyes, so that 'this blue habit . . . is the emblem of sacrifice and civilization'. For the civilization of Mexico did not derive from Cortés or Alvarado but from the spirit of Christianity of which Mary was an essential part. In the last resort, 'Without Our Lady of Guadalupe, the word would have died on the lips of the preacher and, taking off their sandals, the preachers would have returned disconsolate to their country and for a long time Mexico would have remained idolatrous.' As it was, Mexico's national banner was inscribed with the emblems of Christianity and civilization.[66]

The imaginative verve with which Rivera approached the Guadalupe tradition was later more than matched by the historical perceptions of Ignacio Manuel Altamirano (1834–93), a Liberal novelist and journalist, who in his radical youth at the conclusion of the Three Years War had openly lamented that 'the government has banished the bishops, instead of hanging them, as those apostles of iniquity deserved'.[67] As both deputy in Congress and soldier in the Liberal armies, he had fought against the conservatives and their French allies. But, following the execution of Maximilian, he dedicated himself to literature and eventually came to portray Mexico's Catholic tradition from a sympathetic viewpoint. In a charming essay entitled 'Holy Week in my Village', he recalled his early memories of Tixtla, when he still spoke Nahuatl. With evident nostalgia, he described the expedition of children to cut palms for Holy Week and the procession on Holy Thursday when every household sallied forth onto the streets carrying their own crucifix or image of Christ, over a thousand images illumined by the flickering torches at night. He reflected that 'religion is the good fairy of childhood'.[68] So too, in the 1880s he took advantage of the newly constructed railways to visit Texcoco, only to confess his disappointment at the desolate aspect of the town. What is striking is that Altamirano was patently more interested in the Franciscan church and its abandoned monastery than in the former glories of the court of Nezahualcoyotl, the celebrated philosopher-king of the fifteenth century. He admitted that he had been reading the chronicles of the friars published by Joaquín García Icazbalceta, which revealed how selflessly the mendicants had ministered to the Indians. In particular, he was impressed by the example of Pedro de Gante, who had taught the natives Spanish arts and crafts. Surely, he exclaimed, all Mexicans should be willing to pay homage to 'the holy memory of the first Franciscans'.[69] In an essay on the shrine of Sacromonte in Amecameca, where an image of Christ was venerated in a cave once used by Martín de Valencia, the leader of the first Franciscan mission, he praised the chronicle of Jerónimo de Mendieta for its 'easy, sweet and picturesque style' and then saluted the mendicants as 'the first friends of the Indians, the messengers of enlightenment, the true heroes of Latin American civilization'. At much the same time, he took the opportunity of a school speech to describe the college of Santa Cruz Tlatelolco as 'the first sanctuary of civilization' in Mexico.[70]

In *Landscapes and Essays* (1884), Altamirano published an extended study of the cult of Mexico's patron, admitting that 'if there is a truly old, national and universally accepted tradition in Mexico, it is that which refers to the apparition of the Virgin of Guadalupe'. As a good journalist, he began with the contemporary scene, when on 12 December, thousands of the capital's inhabitants crowded into the sanctuary at the Villa of Guadalupe. Every ten minutes a tram of twenty wagons left from the Zócalo,

the city's main square, bound for Tepeyac. So impressive did Altamirano find the vari-
egated appearance of the faithful pilgrims that he confessed:

> There are found all the races of the old colony, all the classes of our republic, all the
> castes of our democracy, all the clothes of our new civilization, all the opinions of
> our politics, all the varieties of vice and all the masks of virtue in Mexico . . . No-one
> is exceptional, no-one is distinguished: it is equality before the Virgin; it is the
> national idolatry.

Whereas many a peasant still did not know the name of the president of the republic,
virtually everyone, no matter how remote their village, had heard of Our Lady of
Guadalupe. On all political issues Mexicans were still bitterly divided and had
bloodied the land with their civil wars. Society remained profoundly stratified according to race and class. And yet all Mexicans, no matter what their party or race, venerated the Virgin of Tepeyac, and indeed it was only in her sanctuary that they all
counted as equals and set aside their differences:

> In the last extreme, in the most desperate cases, the cult of the Mexican Virgin is the
> only bond which unites them . . . It is the national idolatry, and in every Mexican
> there is always a smaller or greater dose of Juan Diego.

It was for this reason that all Mexicans sought to visit the sanctuary, so as to see the
Virgin with their own eyes.[71]

Not content with these avowals, surprising in a Liberal who elsewhere had congratulated the governor of Mexico for banning the Holy Week procession at Tacubaya
since it was 'an affront to the culture of this century', Altamirano composed a well-
informed, dispassionate account of the growth of the cult across the centuries. From
Becerra Tanco, he transcribed the account of the apparitions; he did not attempt to
disentangle the confusions of Florencia; and accepted the thesis of an original account
written in Nahuatl, albeit without fixing upon Valeriano as its author. Unlike other
authors, he provided material on the origin of the Guadalupe in Extremadura. So
too, he employed his literary skills to paint a lively description of the adventures of
Boturini and Mier. But he was at pains to insist that by the eighteenth century 'a spirit
of nationalism' influenced the cult which by then had assumed 'a patriotic character'.
Indeed, he observed that 'the cult of a national divinity in an oppressed people has
always been dangerous for foreign governors'. It was during the Insurgency of 1810
that the Virgin became 'a symbol of emergent nationality' in Mexico. Moreover, he
admitted that during the First Republic all presidents and generals had entered the
sanctuary at Tepeyac to honour Mexico's patron. Even the Liberals of the Reform,
although prevented from entering the Church by the separation of Church and State,
had respected the shrine and its cult.[72]

At the conclusion of his essay, Altamirano affirmed that in contrast to the Insurgency, devotion to the Guadalupe 'is now an exclusively religious and peaceful cult'. No-one wrote against it any more; and recent writers had found nothing new to say. In effect, Catholics venerated the Virgin because of their religion; Liberals honoured the image as the flag of 1810; and Indians adored her as 'their only goddess'. He concluded:

> The day in which the Virgin of Tepeyac is not adored in this land it is certain that there shall have disappeared, not only Mexican nationality, but also the very memory of the dwellers of Mexico today.[73]

In all this, the former radical paid homage to the religion in which he had been raised as a child; confessed the failure of Liberalism to dislodge Catholicism from its role in national life; and testified to the extraordinary power of the Guadalupe over all the classes and races of Mexico.

11

History and infallibility

I

Despite his eirenic approach to the cult of Our Lady of Guadalupe, Ignacio Manuel Altamirano cited Muñoz' sceptical dissertation and commented on the silence of early Franciscan chroniclers about the apparitions of the Virgin. So also, he noted that in his recent biography of Archbishop Zumárraga, Joaquín García Icazbalceta abstained from making any reference to the Mexican Virgin:

> In his authoritative book he does not say a single word about the apparition of the Virgin of Guadalupe of Mexico, and although such a silence only constitutes a negative argument, it merits the greatest attention, dealing as it does with so scrupulous a writer as García Icazbalceta and of such a detailed and well-founded book.

On the same page, Altamirano then revealed the existence of a document, hitherto unknown, which had been seen by persons known to him. It dealt with charges which had been brought in 1556 against Francisco de Bustamante, a Franciscan preacher who had dismissed the apparitions as a trick played by priests on the unfortunate Juan Diego, inducing him to believe that a painting done by the Indian Marcos had appeared by miracle.[1] In these brief lines, Altamirano drew attention, albeit in garbled fashion, to the causes of the furious controversy that was to divide the small world of Catholic historical scholarship in Mexico.

When Joaquín García Icazbalceta (1824–94), a wealthy landowner and a pious Catholic, published his life of Zumárraga in 1881, his aim was to free the bishop from Liberal and Protestant charges that he was 'an ignorant and fanatical friar'. In a series of essays, which exhibited critical acumen and unparalleled erudition, he demonstrated that Zumárraga and his fellow Franciscans had sought to defend the Indians from the exploitation of the conquerors and first governors of New Spain. Although he freely admitted the violence and the abuses that accompanied the conquest, he also argued that the mass of the native population had hitherto lived 'in

Plate 25   Joaquín García Icazbalceta

poverty, abjection and brutalization', subject to a 'completely despotic' regime and a religion that was 'horrible and extremely repugnant in its rites'. Once the post-conquest epoch was past, then thanks to Bartolomé de las Casas, Charles V introduced the New Laws of 1542 which regulated tribute payment and labour services, thereby eliminating the worst abuses of the Indians. Who could doubt that the mendicant friars were the 'chosen instruments' of Providence or that for the natives 'the new religion was liberty and life'? García Icazbalceta declared that although he was not indifferent to the sufferings of the Indians, he refused to condemn 'the men of my race who won and civilized the land in which I was born'.[2]

In a more general vein, he declared that 'we are tired of hearing vulgar declamations', inspired by 'the spirit of race and party', which constantly dwelt on the cruelty of the conquerors. Of such critics none was more notorious than Carlos María de Bustamante, 'the most passionate and uncritical writer our history has had the misfortune to suffer', a man who was guilty of 'all possible literary crimes'. More to the point, there could be discerned, operating across the centuries, 'a providential law', in which the conquest of the weak by the strong, no matter how cruel, constituted a political right. But Las Casas had persuaded the Spanish kings to segregate the Indian communities from the Spanish settlers and thus had prevented their absorption through 'the struggle for life'. The lamentable result was that Mexico still possessed different races and hence did not constitute a nation.[3]

Anxious to re-establish Zumárraga's reputation, García Icazbalceta noted that it was the bishop who brought the first printing press to the New World. And he then provided an expert catalogue of all books and tracts that the prelate published, echoing Beristain's complaint that the great Spanish bibliographer, Nicolás Antonio, had failed to mention these works. Moreover, he cited passages from these books, virtually all of which he possessed, where Zumárraga dismissed Aristotle as an intellectual snare for theologians and exclaimed that he should like to see all Christians, including the Indians, reading the gospels and the epistles of St Paul. From the bishop's *Brief Christian Rule* (1547), he quoted a passage which exemplified the preaching of the early mendicants in Mexico:

> Brethren, you should not give rise to the thoughts and blasphemies of the world, that tempts souls to see by wonders and miracles that which they believe by faith. These are similar to Herod, mockers of themselves who vainly and without necessity want to see visions and revelations, which is a lack of faith and is born of great pride; and thus they are paid, falling into great errors. The Redeemer of this world does not want miracles to be done now, because they are not necessary, since our faith is based on the thousands of miracles we have in the Old and New Testaments. What he asks and wants is miraculous lives, Christians who are humble, patient and charitable, because the perfect life of a Christian is a continuous miracle on earth.

It was this kind of faith which drove Zumárraga to found the hospital of Amor de Dios, where Sigüenza y Góngora was later to serve as chaplain. He also took the initiative in supporting the college of Santa Cruz at Tlatelolco, where so many of the native disciples of the Franciscans were educated, not least among them, Antonio Valeriano.[4]

No charge against his hero more angered García Icazbalceta than the accusation made by William Prescott, the New England historian of the Spanish conquest, that Zumárraga had been responsible for the wanton destruction of the native codices and the great archive at Texcoco. To be sure, he readily admitted that when the first mendicants set about destroying native temples and idols, they also probably burnt the codices which they encountered, perceiving them as devilish expressions of Indian religion. But Zumárraga had arrived in Mexico in 1528, when a great deal of such destruction had already been effected. Moreover, no chronicler mentioned a specific search for codices or ever described any great ceremony of book-burning. Indeed, the only testimony for the existence of an archive at Texcoco was offered by Fernando de Alva Ixtlilxochitl, ever prone to magnify the achievements of his native ancestors; and yet he blamed the destruction on the Tlaxcalan capture of the palace in 1520. In effect, the charges against Zumárraga originated in the insurgent declamations of Mier and Bustamante.[5] If knowledge of native history and culture survived, it was thanks to the mendicants, to men like Motolinia and Sahagún.

In his powerful defence of the friars who founded the Catholic Church in Mexico, García Icazbalceta noted the irony that the very Liberals who condemned the mendicants for burning native codices had voted in Congress to allow the free export of prehispanic sculptures and antiquities. The same men had been responsible for the destruction of the great priories and convents of Mexico City and the despoliation of their paintings and libraries. Virtually all that remained of the great cloisters of the Franciscans was the church, and that had been entrusted to Protestant clergymen, who promptly stripped its magnificent Churrigueresque façade of its statues. Commenting on the demolition of the pyramid temples, he added:

> In the fullness of the nineteenth century, when we were scandalized by the ignorance and barbarism of the missionaries, the men of the Reform of our own day did not think or act in any other way, when they threw to the ground, not just rough masses of earth, the theatre of nefarious crimes, but our churches and convents, and even the asylum of the poor, founded by Christian charity.

In this indictment, García Icazbalceta attested to that profound sense of disinheritance which afflicted Catholic intellectuals in Mexico after the Reform.[6] At the same time, the erudition and dialectical vigour of his study of Zumárraga largely succeeded, as the example of Altamirano illustrates, in reinstalling the sixteenth-century mendicants as the worthy founders of Mexican civilization.

But if García Icazbalceta impressed and even converted Liberal readers, he disturbed many Catholics by his omission of all mention of the apparitions of Our Lady of Guadalupe and Zumárraga's construction of a chapel at Tepeyac. According to later statements, apparently he had written a chapter on the subject, indicating that he had failed to find any contemporary documents dealing with these events, only then to suppress it at the entreaty of the bishop of Puebla, Francisco de Paula Verea. It was the same prelate who wrote an extraordinary letter to him on 30 September 1881:

> In respect of the publication of the biography of Zumárraga, I take this opportunity to implore you earnestly and in all confidence, not to write or to say a word about the Apparition of Our Lady of Guadalupe. The prejudice done to the piety of the people, which, as they have already informed me, saddens the prelates, you will be better able to consider than I am able to urge . . . My pastoral duty, my love of the most holy Virgin and the confidence I have in your good judgement, impels me to make this entreaty.

But if García Icazbalceta dutifully maintained a public silence about the matter, he was fiercely criticized for his discretion. In 1890, when mentioning his study of Zumárraga, he explained to Nicolás León, a fellow historian and bibliographer:

> I call that book unfortunate or unhappy, because although I made a defence of the prelate and of the honour of the Church, I was badly received for having remained silent about *that*, and thereafter I was accused to the prelate of being a heretic, so that I obtained the opposite result to what I had planned.[7]

Only two years after this letter, these criticisms were to take the form of public denunciation.

In an act of sublime imprudence, Pelagio Antonio de Labastida, the archbishop of Mexico (1861–88), requested that García Icazbalceta comment on a manuscript about the Guadalupe written by José Antonio González, a priest of Guadalajara. When the historian demurred, Labastida replied that 'I beg you as a friend and I command you as a prelate.' In a formal *Letter* to the archbishop, García Icazbalceta confessed that it was only after receiving this injunction that he resolved to break 'my firm resolution never to write a line about this matter'. But rather than dealing with González' manuscript, he chose to tell his bishop 'what history says about the apparition of Our Lady of Guadalupe to Juan Diego', adding that he presumed he was free to write as his conscience impelled him, since the traditional narrative was not 'a matter of faith'. As will be observed, in claiming to speak on behalf of 'history', García Icazbalceta clearly implied the existence of an autonomous scientific discipline which was sovereign in the sphere of historical facts and their interpretation.[8] For over thirty years he had employed his resources to purchase a remarkable collection of sixteenth-century documents and printed materials; he had funded and supervised the publication of three substantial volumes of these materials in the years 1859–70, among which were included the Franciscan chronicles of Motolinia and Mendieta; and he was well advanced in his project of writing a comprehensive bibliography of all works printed in Mexico before 1600. In all this, he was the conscious heir of Gregorio Mayans y Siscar and as such maintained the Hispanic Enlightenment's acerbic rejection of the historical falsification and mythical imaginings of the baroque era. It was thus only to be expected that he would draw on the arguments advanced by Juan Bautista Muñoz in his sceptical *Memorial*. That he was also influenced by Mier's *Letters to Juan Bautista Muñoz*, published in 1879 by J. E. Hernández in his massive collection of documents dealing with the 1810 Insurgency and by Mier's *Memoirs*, published in 1877, was more surprising, since in his study of Zumárraga he had strongly criticized the Dominican's errors. Moreover, he possessed a copy of the 1556 charges against Francisco de Bustamante, to which Altamirano referred.[9]

To start with, García Icazbalceta affirmed that the force of the negative argument, already expressed so cogently by Muñoz, had been immeasurably strengthened as more sixteenth-century documents had come to light. Any number of authors who might have been expected to comment on the apparitions had remained silent. Neither Motolinia, who wrote in 1541, nor Mendieta, who wrote in the 1590s, mentioned the events at Tepeyac, even if the latter referred to the instance of the Virgin appearing to an Indian at Xochimilco in 1576. Sahagún cited the cult, but only to criticize it as a subterfuge for idolatry; and his remarks were translated into Nahuatl by Martín de León and published in 1611 as an illustration of the dangers of superstition. Luis Cisneros merely referred to the chapel and its miracles and there was even a printed sermon of 1622, preached at Tepeyac by Juan de Cepeda, an Augustinian friar, who eulogized the Virgin Mary without reference to the image of Guadalupe. As for Zumárraga, there was not the slightest mention of either the image or the apparitions in any of his letters or works. In any case, he had written in his *Brief Christian Rule*: 'The Redeemer of the world does not want miracles to be done now, because they are not necessary, since our holy faith is based on so many thousands of miracles that we have in the Old and New Testaments.' In effect, so García Icazbalceta asserted, 'the silence of so many has increased the heavy weight of Muñoz' argument'. But the final disproof was provided by the unpublished document which contained the 1556 testimonies of Bustamante's sermon, since: 'after having read this document, no-one can remain in doubt that the apparition of the most holy Virgin in the year 1531 and her miraculous painting on the cape of Juan Diego is an invention born much later'. It was obvious, as Viceroy Martín Enriquez had informed Philip II, that the painting had been installed in the chapel during the years 1555–6. As for the image, Bernal Díaz del Castillo had described Marcos as one of several native painters who in skill rivalled the best artists in Europe.[10]

If the cult of the Mexican Virgin had started with an explosion of fervour in 1556, thereafter it declined, since in 1648 the only copy of the image known to the diarist Antonio de Robles was in the Dominican church of the capital, a sure sign that 'the devotion had completely finished'. As for Sánchez, he had found neither papers in the archives nor any written account of the apparitions, so that a surprised Laso de la Vega described himself as 'a sleeping Adam', albeit thereafter quick to extract a summary of Sánchez' account and translate it into Nahuatl. If the invention of the tradition was received so warmly, it was owing to 'the wonderful credulity of the epoch, bound to an extravagant piety'. During the seventeenth century everyone looked for miracles and the direct intervention of the Divinity in human affairs, and the most usual means of obtaining miracles was through holy images, which themselves generally had a miraculous origin. So fertile was the imagination of that epoch that Fray Roman de la Higuera composed an entire false chronicle dealing with the early history of Spain and the apparitions of the Virgin to Santiago at Zaragoza; and 'it took a great deal of time and work to cleanse the civil and ecclesiastical history of all that rubbish'.[11]

But what of the testimonies advanced by the apologists? Was there not an imposing list of documents and authors supporting the apparitions? García Icazbalceta's response was simple and direct. Despite the assertions of Sigüenza y Góngora and Becerra Tanco, no-one else had ever seen the manuscript written in Nahuatl by Valeriano or a copy of the song of don Plácido, still less the paraphrased account in Spanish prepared by Alva Ixtlilxochitl or the native annals mentioned by González. In effect, there was but one text and that was the account written in Nahuatl by Laso de la Vega, a text he had extracted and translated from Sánchez. Nor was the literary quality of the narrative any reason to doubt Laso de la Vega's authorship, since 'if the language is good, there were then for that great masters of the Mexicans, and it suffices to recall the name of Father Carochi, who in the year 1645 published his famous grammar' of Nahuatl.[12] In effect, the only reference that even hinted at the apparition prior to 1648 was to be found in the manuscript written in 1589 by Juan Suárez de Peralta, who asserted that the Virgin of Guadalupe had 'appeared among the rocks'.[13] In all this, the apologists consistently confounded evidence relating to the cult as proof of the antiquity of the tradition. As for the 1666 testimonies, they had been taken 134 years after the alleged events and thus were worthless: the dim, stereotyped recollections of a group of octogenarians could in no way counterbalance the damning force of the 1556 depositions. As regards the image itself, he noted the diversity of opinions about the quality of the canvas, since with Bartolache 'the rough *ayate* of maguey is converted into the fine mantle of *iczotl* palm'. So too, if Miguel Cabrera discerned so many different techniques of painting in the image, it was because by the eighteenth century all memory of pre-hispanic colours, paints and techniques had been forgotten. As for Florencia, his 'detestable book', *Marian zodiac*, should be put on the Roman Index of prohibited books, since it was filled with false miracles.[14]

If all this were not enough, García Icazbalceta then commented on the patent anachronisms that disfigured the apparition narrative. Why should Zumárraga have been so impressed by Juan Diego offering him flowers, when they were sold on the streets of Mexico every month of the year and could easily have been grown on the cultivated floating rafts known as *chinampas*? Even when confronted with the image, why should he have thought that he was in the presence of a heavenly artefact? In any case, no bishop of that epoch would have fallen on his knees without any attempt to ascertain the nature of such a miracle. Then again, despite Becerra Tanco's attempt to find an equivalent in Nahuatl, no-one had ever been able to understand why the Virgin chose to have her image called Guadalupe, when it was notorious that Indians could not pronounce either the 'g' or the 'd' of her name. At this point, García Icazbalceta halted his indictment and, turning to Sánchez, admitted the possibility of 'an account in Mexican' which possibly lay behind his 'insufferable book'. After all, although the Franciscans had built a small chapel at Tepeyac dedicated to the 'Mother of God', in 1555–6 the devotion had suddenly erupted, possibly the result of a miraculous cure, as Martín Enríquez had suggested. Taking his cue from Mier, García Icazbalceta then raised the possibility that Valeriano might have written a sacred drama, since the traditional narrative had all the elements of a dramatic dialogue. As for the origin of that story, might it not be found in an incident reported by Sahagún, he suggested, when in the years 1528–31 the goddess Cihuacoatl, alias Tonantzin, appeared to Martín Ecatl, the second governor of Tlatelolco?[15]

To conclude, García Icazbalceta reminded Labastida that he had written at his command; he requested the archbishop not to show his letter to anyone; and he emphasized that he wrote as an historian, since 'it is not permitted for me to enter the theological argument'. He added:

> I am a Catholic, if not a good one, Your Grace, and as far as I am able, devoted to the most Holy Virgin; I have no wish to take that devotion from anyone; the image of Guadalupe will always be the oldest, the most venerated and respected in Mexico . . . In my youth I believed, as do all Mexicans, in the truth of the miracles; I do not remember from whence came my doubts; and to rid myself of them I had recourse to the apologists: these converted my doubts into a certainty of the falsity of the fact. And I am not the only one.

As much as Muñoz before him, the Mexican historian thus had no quarrel with veneration for the Virgin of Tepeyac, accepting that image as a representation of the Mother of God; but he could not accept the truth of the apparitions and the supernatural origin of that likeness.[16]

When García Icazbalceta stated that he was not alone in doubting the Guadalupe tradition, he could easily have cited various opinions. In his *Dissertations* (1834–9), Lucas Alamán, his conservative mentor, observed: 'I have also believed that I ought to abstain from talking about all those pious traditions, which have been the object of persistent dispute among writers and which ought to be more a matter for respect than of discussion.'[17] As a young historian, García Icazbalceta had also been encouraged by José Fernando Ramírez (1804–71), a scholar with a wide knowledge of the early sources of Mexican history. In his *Additions and Corrections* to Beristain's bio-bibliography, a work which circulated in manuscript before its publication in 1898, this moderate Liberal included a letter he wrote in 1859 to Dr Basilio Arrillaga, a learned Jesuit, in which he bluntly dismissed the apparition at Tepeyac as 'an event which is not based on any historical foundation but which originates in the middle seventeenth century . . .'. In all his studies he had never found 'the slightest vestige of such a happening'. If the Franciscans had built a small hermitage to replace the temple of Tonantzin, it had been Montúfar, not Zumárraga, who built the first real church. To support this assertion, he cited three native sources, written in Nahuatl: the *Annals of Mexico* noted that 'the Virgin came down to Tepeyac' in 1556, precisely the same year assigned for the appearance of the image by the historian of Chalco, Chimalpahin. In the annals written by Juan Bautista, the year when the image became manifest was 1555. Ramírez apologized for raising the matter, however, observing that he and Bernardo Couto, the learned author of a *Dialogue on Painting in Mexico* (1872), had agreed 'not to deal with a matter where the deeper one goes the less footing one finds'.[18] It was José María de Agreda y Sánchez, a wealthy bibliophile and friend of García Icazbalceta, who had a copy of these *Corrections*, and who in the catalogue of his own extensive collection described the 1556 depositions as 'a conclusive proof against the supposed apparitions and against the supernatural origin which they have sought to give the image'.[19] In effect, in this small circle of Mexican scholars, belief in the historical veracity of the Guadalupe tradition had long since been abandoned.

In 1886 García Icazbalceta published his *Mexican Bibliography of the Sixteenth Century*, a lavishly produced work, replete with reproductions of title pages and extensive extracts from the listed works. The meticulous, erudite commentary offered a starting point for the intellectual history of New Spain in that epoch. If not the greatest work of history written by a Mexican, it is certainly the most learned, and indeed was praised by that eminent hammer of the heterodox in Spain, Marcelino Menéndez Pelayo, as 'the most perfect and excellent work in its line that any nation possesses'. Written at a time when Mexico did not even possess a university, let alone any institutes of advanced studies, the *Bibliography* embodied an immense investment of toil, intelligence and material resources.[20] Nor did García Icazbalceta rest on his hard-won laurels, since in 1886–92 he published yet another five volumes of early documents, including accounts of Texcoco and numerous letters written by Franciscans, among whom Mendieta figured prominently. Moreover, such was the effect of his example that in 1899 Vicente de Paul Andrade published his *Mexican Bibliographical Essay of the Seventeenth Century* and in 1902–8 Nicolás León printed the weighty tomes of his *Mexican Bibliography of the Eighteenth Century*. Both men were indebted to García Icazbalceta and freely acknowledged his influence. The tradition of scholarship which began in the eighteenth century with Eguiara y Eguren and found expression in Beristain's *Library* here reached its culmination.[21]

But it was in the same year of 1886 that the peremptory demands of ecclesiastical politics began to obtrude upon the erudite disquisitions of this circle of bibliographers. The three archbishops of Mexico, Guadalajara and Morelia issued a joint pastoral in which they announced that they had petitioned Rome for permission to crown the image of Guadalupe, thereby reviving the project first mounted in 1740 by Lorenzo Boturini, who had obtained a licence from the cathedral chapter of St Peter's. On 8 February 1887 the Holy See granted permission. As we shall see, the coronation was delayed, since the project soon encompassed an ambitious renovation of the sanctuary at Tepeyac, not to mention a reform of the office recited on 12 December. But at this juncture the bishop of Tamaulipas, Eduardo Sánchez Camacho, issued a pastoral criticizing the archbishops for not consulting other bishops and announcing his disapproval of the coronation. By way of answer, the archbishops obtained a ruling from the Holy Office of the Roman Inquisition, condemning Sánchez Camacho for his 'manner of acting and talking against the miracle or apparitions of the most Holy Mary of Guadalupe', a reprimand which caused him to withdraw his opposition.[22]

It was at this point, in 1888, that the bishop of Yucatán, Crescencio Carrillo y Ancona (1837–97), a well-known Church historian, published a *Letter for the Present Time*, in which he defined Sánchez Camacho's denial of the apparitions as 'a happy sin', since it had elicited the Roman Inquisitors' statement. He boldly compared the Holy Office's declaration to the papal definition of the dogma of the Immaculate Conception of the Virgin Mary. In the same way that the Church pronounced anathemas against all who opposed that doctrine, so now the Church condemned all who opposed the apparitions at Tepeyac. 'Roma locuta, causa finita', which was to say, 'Rome has spoken, the case is ended.' As befitted an historian, Carrillo admitted that certain gaps in the historical proofs still existed, but stoutly affirmed that the case for the apparitions rested on 'the unanswerable, philosophical demonstrations of tradition, history and monuments'. He then referred to 'our incomparable friend, the noble and wise don Joaquín García Icazbalceta . . . that virtuous Catholic of exemplary modesty and action, that illustrious academician, a national glory and crowned with a European reputation', only then to deplore that he had not written a word about the apparitions in his works on Zumárraga and Mendieta. His silence arose from his inability to find the letters of Zumárraga which attested to the apparitions; yet tradition taught that the memory of the archbishop's participation had been preserved in native codices. As for the Franciscan's warning against looking for miracles, that had been published as a practical moral injunction in his *Brief Christian Rule* and had nothing to do with doctrinal objections.[23]

Unwilling to become embroiled in any public dispute, García Icazbalceta replied privately to Carrillo's *Letter* on 29 December 1888, in which he expressed his reaction to the bishop's interpretation of the Roman condemnation of Sánchez Camacho:

> I believed that the reprimand referred to the manner of speaking and acting and not to the essence of the matter. But your Lordship affirms, and this suffices for me to believe it, that the matter is concluded, because *Roma locuta, causa finita*; and this being the case, it would not now be right for me to dwell on purely historical considerations. This affair can be considered on two grounds: on the theological and on the historical. The first is forbidden me by reason of obvious incompetence; and if he who is able declares that the fact is certain, we simple faithful cannot enter into the other.

In his reply, García Icazbalceta clearly reiterated his earlier decision, broken by command of Labastida, to remain silent about events for which he could find no contemporary evidence but whose historical reality had now been certified by episcopal pronouncement. For all that, only six months before his death in 1894, he wrote to Aquiles Gerste, a Belgian Jesuit: 'You know me intimately and can be sure that I would not disfigure historical truth for any worldly interest.' He thereby testified to the moral autonomy of his vocation as an historian.[24]

Before the storm broke, however, García Icazbalceta unwisely gave copies of his *Letter* to Labastida to a Carmelite priest, to José María de Agreda, and to a brilliant scholar, Francisco del Paso y Troncoso (1842–1916). It was in the latter's house that Vicente de Paul Andrade (1844–1915), a prebendary of the collegiate chapter of Tepeyac, who had spent his earlier years both as a missionary preacher and as parish priest in the capital, made a copy for his own use. According to later accounts, Andrade had 'a mischievous temperament' and a liking for 'intrigue and jokes'. More important, he was convinced that the Guadalupe tradition was an invention of Miguel Sánchez and he resolutely opposed the coronation project, submitting adverse opinions to Rome. As part of this battle, he translated García Icazbalceta's letter into Latin, enlisting Father Icaza to help him. In 1890 he published it under the title of *Exquisitio historico*; but although no author's name appeared, rumours soon circulated attributing it to García Icazbalceta.[25] It was immediately denounced by those favourable to the coronation but figured in the Roman enquiries over the reform of the office for 12 December. None of this was to the liking of García Icazbalceta, since as a friend observed: 'Don Joaquín fears that he will be subjected to reprimands and excommunion.' It was Nicolás León who later observed: 'All this anti-Guadalupan scandal was started by Canon Andrade with the collaboration of Agreda, Troncoso and the *cura* Icaza, and they smeared with mud as many as they could, both among the living and the dead.'[26]

II

In 1888 the complete text of the mysterious *Statement of 1556*, to which both Altamirano and García Icazbalceta had alluded, was finally published in Mexico, albeit under a false Madrid imprint and by anonymous editors.[27] The document turned out to consist of no more than fourteen sheets, written in diverse hands on 9 September 1556. It took the form of three unascribed denunciations to Archbishop Alonso de Montúfar of a sermon preached by Francisco de Bustamante the day before, followed by an 'interrogation' of thirteen questions about that sermon, and the sworn depositions of nine witnesses made before the prelate's apostolic notary. In effect, it was a legal testimony which might have been cited had charges been brought against the preacher. But a note at the end added: 'suspend: the case is dead'. Moreover, the depositions were so arranged that information was inserted about the sermon preached by the archbishop on Sunday, 6 September and about his visit to the sanctuary at Tepeyac on 8 September. Thus the purpose of the *Statements* was not merely to criticize Bustamante but also to defend the archbishop.

It was on the feast of the Nativity of the Virgin Mary, celebrated on 8 September in the chapel of San José in the Franciscan cloisters, that Francisco de Bustamante, the current provincial of his Order in Mexico, preached before the viceroy, the high court and other dignitaries. After a warm eulogy of the Virgin, Bustamante protested that he would never seek to diminish anyone's devotion to Mary; confessed that he himself was not sufficiently devoted; and then, with changed countenance, sharply criticized the devotion to the image of Our Lady of Guadalupe. His reason was pastoral: hitherto the Franciscans had taught the Indians not to adore images of wood and stone but rather to worship God in heaven. But all of a sudden it was bruited abroad that, if one went to pray to the image of Guadalupe, miraculous cures might occur. The danger was that the Indians might once more identify an image as God-like and fall into idolatry. Moreover, if the miracles they expected did not occur, their faith would be undermined. It was not that he condemned all devotions to the Virgin, since in the case of Our Lady of Loreto, for example, the cult was well founded. But in Mexico it was not known how devotion had come to centre on a painting done by an Indian. Since no formal enquiry had been made about the so-called miracles, anyone claiming that they had been performed should be given a hundred lashes. Then there was the question of the alms that were left in the chapel: it would be far better to give these offerings to the hospital for the poor. Such was the scandal and the damage done to the faith of the Indians that it was time for the viceroy and the high court to intervene, no matter what the archbishop might say, since 'the king has spiritual and temporal jurisdiction' which they exercised as his agents.[28]

The thirteen questions of the 'Interrogation' were designed to substantiate the criticism that the provincial had spoken in an angry fashion and had caused a public scandal by attacking a devotion that the archbishop had encouraged. At the same time, question five admirably summarized the thrust of the sermon, when witnesses were asked to agree that Bustamante had said that:

one of the most pernicious things for the good Christianity of the natives was to support the devotion of the aforesaid hermitage of Our Lady of Guadalupe, because since their conversion it had been preached to them, not to believe in images, but only in God, and that images only served to provoke devotion and now to tell them that an image painted by an Indian worked miracles would be a great confusion and undo the good that was planted in them.

In response, the three witnesses who were priests simply agreed with the questions, albeit in a non-committal way; and indeed Bachiller Puebla begged to be excused since 'this affair is a subtle matter and for lawyers'.[29] It was the two brothers, Juan and Francisco de Salazar, the first an agent of the high court and the second a lawyer, who proved of most assistance to the archbishop. Not merely did they both agree that Bustamante had appeared angry and had caused a scandal, but they also mentioned that they had heard the archbishop preach on Sunday 6 September in the cathedral. In that sermon Montúfar had compared the devotion to the Guadalupe to the cults of images of the Virgin in the cathedral of Seville, to Peña de Francia in Extremadura, to Montserrat in Cataluña and to Loreto. So also, in a carefully prepared additional 'question', Juan de Salazar testified that he had heard the archbishop citing the Fifth Lateran Council (1512–17), which had condemned anyone who brought the good name of prelates into disrepute and strictly prohibited anyone from preaching false miracles. In his sermon Montúfar claimed that the growing devotion to the Virgin of Guadalupe, in both Spanish and Indian communities, was a miracle in itself; but in no instance had he cited any miraculous cures.[30]

The scandal caused by Montúfar's sermon among the Franciscans was clearly attested by Gonzalo de Alarcón, who had come to Mexico with the archbishop. After the sermon he had gone to the Franciscan cloisters, where he heard Fray Alonso de Santiago criticize the prelate for encouraging the Indians to adore an image as if it were divine, thereby reviving idolatry. When the friar had heard that the sermon's text was 'Beati oculi', the words of Christ taken from St Luke's gospel, 'Blessed are those who have seen what you have seen', he had feared mention of the Guadalupe. At this point, Fray Alonso took out a bible and turned to chapter 13 of the Book of Deuteronomy, in which any prophet or 'dreamer of dreams' who cited signs or marvels was savagely condemned, since God alone should be loved and adored. The same friar queried why the image should be called Guadalupe, when that name referred to the figure in Spain, rather than Our Lady of Tepeaca or Tepeaquilla. This conversation with Fray Alonso was heard by another witness, Alonso Sánchez de Cisneros, who also testified that the friar had read out a passage from holy scripture.[31]

One striking feature of the testimony afforded by the Salazar brothers was that on 8 September, the day on which Bustamante preached, the archbishop had appeared in the chapel at Tepeyac. Speaking through an interpreter, he had explained to the Indians who were present that they should venerate the Mother of God who was in heaven and not the canvas, painting or sculpture which represented her. Since Montúfar had been engaged during the morning in liturgical celebration of the Virgin's Nativity in the cathedral, he had obviously rushed to Tepeyac in the afternoon, presumably in response to Bustamante's charge that he was promoting idolatry.[32]

But witnesses did not restrict their observations to the quarrel between the archbishop and the friar. Virtually all the laymen testified to the great devotion which the image evoked, commenting that many 'ladies of quality' went regularly to the sanctuary, joining the Indians who thronged there. Whereas Spanish families had often spent their Sundays in the gardens and orchards surrounding the city, now they went to Tepeyac, much in the same way as the people of Madrid visited Our Lady of Atocha. Indeed, Juan de Masseguer, a Catalan who had visited the shrine of Our Lady of Montserrat, testified that although Fray Luis Cal had sought to dissuade him from going to the chapel so as not to give a bad example to the Indians, he had taken his child there to cure her of a cough. He stressed that such was the devotion, 'all kinds of people, noble citizens and Indians', went there, even if some natives had stopped after the friars had warned them against going. He agreed that Bustamante had denounced the attribution of miracles to an 'image painted yesterday by an Indian'. In this he was corroborated by Sánchez de Cisneros, who recalled the preacher criticizing this 'new devotion' since it tempted Indians to adore 'a painting which Marcos, an Indian painter, had done'. Before it appeared, the chapel had been dedicated to 'the Mother of God'.[33]

As will be observed, the *Statements* make absolutely no reference to the apparitions of the Virgin Mary to Juan Diego, and still less did they identify the image as anything more than the work of an Indian painter. The quarrel was all about the miracles that the image was supposed to have inspired; the alms that the sanctuary attracted; and above all, the archbishop's encouragement of a devotion which might easily lead to idolatry. It is clear that these depositions were taken as much to defend the archbishop as to attack the friar. But what they equally attested was the great devotion that already existed as much, if not more, among the Spanish community in the capital as among the Indians. In effect, the settlers of New Spain had welcomed the emergence of an image of the Virgin which could be compared to the figures which they had venerated in the Peninsula. It was these pious sentiments which the archbishop sought to encourage, only to fall foul of the mendicant's defence of the austere religion the friars had preached to the Indians.

Published in 1888, a year after the Holy See had granted permission for the coronation of Our Lady of Guadalupe, the *Statements of 1556* were accompanied by a preface and notes that identified the text as a persuasive disproof of the image's tradition. They opened with a letter from José María de Agreda y Sánchez, who explained that the first mention of the document occurred in 1846 when, during a visit to Archbishop Manuel Posada y Garduño, José Fernando Ramírez raised the question of the Guadalupe. In reply the prelate pointed to papers on his table and said: 'What there is of certainty about this matter is to be found in this small file', only then to add that no-one, including Ramírez, was ever to see it. After Posada's death, the document was kept by the dignitaries of the cathedral, who allowed Agreda to read it and take an extract. It was then seen by Andrés Artola, a Jesuit priest, who described it as 'the most decisive proof against the so-called Guadalupan history'. After 1871, Archbishop Labastida took possession of it and allowed both García Icazbalceta and Jose María Andrade, a wealthy bookseller and bibliophile, to read it and presumably make copies or extracts.[34] What Agreda did not mention was that in 1884 two books with similar titles had been published in Guadalajara which summarized the 1556 *Statements*, only then to launch a furious attack on Bustamante and other Franciscans for their questioning of devotion to the image at Tepeyac. Both authors took as their premise the historical truth of the apparitions and then criticized the founders of the Mexican Church for their failure to recognize the heavenly origin of the Guadalupe.[35]

It was in this polemical context that Vicente de Paul Andrade, by then a canon at Tepeyac, inserted a preface to the *Statements of 1556*, in which he noted that, far from being condemned by Montúfar for his sermon, Bustamante was later re-elected as provincial and also became the Franciscan commissary general of New Spain. He compared the diverse reactions to his sermon and to that of Servando de Mier, a difference which could only be explained by the invention of the tradition by Miguel Sánchez in 1648. Any doubts of Sánchez' role were removed by a simple reading of the commendations of Laso de la Vega and the censors of his 1665 *Novenas*. In a crudely provocative style, Andrade referred to Juan Diego as 'the fortunate giant', on the grounds that the canvas on which the image was painted was over two yards long and hence far too long for any Indian of average height. As regards Marcos, he noted that he had been praised by Bernal Díaz del Castillo and that Betancurt in his *Mexican Theatre* had observed that 'there were painters who painted frescos with gums of trees and fine colours . . . although they had many mantles they did not use sizing'.[36]

In the notes, the editors followed García Icazbalceta in providing a list of any number of authors who might have been expected to comment on the apparitions but who had remained silent. In particular, Mendieta had commented in several places on the lack of miracles in the conversion of the Indians. They noted a new text, *Starry Heaven*, written by Juan de Alloza and published in 1654, 'which was after Miguel Sánchez and which it bettered in lies', since in this account it was the Virgin who gathered the flowers and gave them to Juan Diego, who then set them down on the bishop's table. Following Muñoz, they fixed upon silence as the great negative argument against the apparitions, and cited Daniel Papebroch, the great Bollandist scholar: 'In history silence is a proof, at times a demonstration, as when all the historians are silent.' However, Andrade then cited Sahagún's description of the apparition of the Devil in the form of a woman to Martín Ecatl, the governor of Tlatelolco, and commented that 'these apparitions without doubt gave material to the Indian Antonio Valeriano to compose a comedy with which to felicitate Zumárraga on 12 December, the anniversary of his installation as bishop', a text which had later come into the possession of Miguel Sánchez, who 'took it as a true account of an event which had never occurred'. Not content with the negative weight of universal silence, Andrade thus repeated the speculations of García Icazbalceta and Mier.[37]

This provocative edition deeply disturbed the bishops and clergy who were then engaged in promoting the coronation of the Virgin of Tepeyac. By this time Andrade hoped to halt the entire process and was soon to publish García Icazbalceta's *Letter* translated into Latin. But although fierce responses were soon published, he continued unabashed, and in 1890, using the pseudonym of Eutimio Pérez, published an ill-printed but biting attack on those authors who had sought to interpret the *Statements* in a manner favourable to the Guadalupan tradition.[38] In 1891 he obtained the support of the Minister of Justice, Joaquín Baranda, and published a second edition of the *Statements of 1556*, in which he inserted his previous critique of the 'apparitionists' and included an important account of the Indian artist, Marcos, written by Francisco del Paso y Troncoso.[39] Published in the midst of a resurgent Guadalupan cult, the second edition heaped fuel on the fires of controversy that centred on the historical veracity of the apparition narrative.

To start with, Andrade commented that 'the apparitionist belief of a most respectable priest', Fortino H. Vera, had been abused by a blatant forgery, worthy of Román de la Higuera, of a letter which purported to have been sent by the Dominican provincial to Zumárraga, congratulating him on the apparitions. But he then moved to attack *The Virgin of Tepeyac: Principal Patron of the Mexican Nation* (1884) in which Esteban Anticoli, an Italian Jesuit resident in Mexico, had argued that the 1556 *Statements* were an indictment brought by Montúfar against Bustamante and thus demonstrated the immense scandal caused by the friar's sermon and, by extension, the widespread contemporary belief in the apparition. But Andrade commented that the depositions made no mention of the supernatural origin of the image and that the statements were designed as much to defend the archbishop as to attack the preacher, since the prelate was implicitly accused of preaching both a belief in miracles and the worship of a material image. Nor did these statements add up to a legal indictment. With great glee, Andrade concluded that 'the premises presented by Father Anticoli being false, the conclusion also has to be so and the terms in which it was conceived puerile'. In any case, the archbishop did not exercise any jurisdiction over Bustamante, since as a religious he could only be tried by his ecclesiastical ordinary, the commissary general of the Franciscans in New Spain.[40]

As regards *Holy Mary of Guadalupe, Patron of the Mexicans* (1884), written by José Antonio González, a canon of Guadalajara, Andrade first fixed upon his statement that it was impossible to think of an artist painting the image, since 'what a semi-god would be the Indian Marcos'. And yet in the depositions no-one denied the allegation that it had been painted by an Indian; had Montúfar known of the apparitions he would have immediately charged Bustamante with blasphemy. Andrade then sharply questioned González' assertion that, in attacking the cult of the Guadalupe, Bustamante had profaned 'the chair of the Holy Spirit', and in criticizing Montúfar had sold himself 'for the historical thirty pieces of silver'. Why did these apparitionists seek to blacken the reputations of priests who had laboured to bring the Christian gospel to the Indians? Andrade concluded that the apparitionists formulated gratuitous and conjectural accusations and have 'stained well-founded reputations only with a view that their theories should triumph'.[41]

In a further note, Andrade returned to Anticoli, who had claimed that Benedict XIV had been the first to apply the term 'Non fecit taliter' to the image of Guadalupe, whereas in fact the contemporary sermon of Cayetano Antonio de Torres correctly attributed that application to Florencia. In any case, the phrase from Psalm 147 had been also applied to other images, such as Pilar and Loreto. Moreover, Anticoli had further exhibited 'his crass ignorance' when he took strong exception to the letter written by Martin Enríquez in which the viceroy had dismissed the cult at Tepeyac as a question of whether the chapel would support one or two clergymen, adding that such language demonstrated 'the baseness of his soul and his despicable way of judging the ministers of God and the archbishop'. For Andrade there was a sublime irony in this gratuitous attack, since all the early Jesuit chroniclers had united to praise Martin Enríquez both for his prudent government and for his assistance in helping the Company of Jesus establish itself in New Spain. He added: 'this ungrateful father . . . carried away by his apparitionist fury, has no fear in wounding the reputations of those who do not think like him on this subject'.[42]

If Andrade was an historical *franc tireur*, by contrast Francisco del Paso y Troncoso was a serious scholar with a good knowledge of Nahuatl who illumined the second edition of the *Statements of 1556* by an essay entitled 'The Indian Marcos and other Painters of the Sixteenth Century'.[43] In this seminal note he drew on the native Annals of Juan Bautista, where a painter known as Marcos Cipac was frequently mentioned. It was Pedro de Gante, the Flemish lay-brother who was 'the founder of the workshop of painting for the Mexican Indians', a school which Juan Bautista called 'the painters of San Francisco', since they all depended on the chapel of San José in the great Franciscan priory. Virtually all the Franciscan chroniclers, Motolinia, Mendieta and Torquemada, paid tribute to the skill of Indian painters. Nor was there any doubt about the eminence of Marcos, since in 1564 he was put in charge of painting the six panels of the great gilded altarpiece of San José, a project in which he was assisted by three other native artists. It was about this time that Fray Miguel Navarro, who directed many such works in the Franciscan convents, praised Marcos in effusive terms: 'it is marvellous what you do: in truth you are far superior to the Spaniards'. So too, the elderly chronicler, Bernal Díaz del Castillo, wrote that:

> There are now three Indians in the city of Mexico so outstanding in their craft of sculptors and painters, who are called Marcos de Aquino, Juan de la Cruz and Crespillo, who if they were of the time of that ancient famous Apelles or of Michaelangelo or Berruguete, who are of our time, would also be included in their number.[44]

It was thus clear to Troncoso that Marcos was indeed the artist who painted the image of Our Lady of Guadalupe. He then penned a challenge:

> It is for those who understand the art of painting to say whether Marcos was a mediocre painter or a man of genius; if the praises of Bernal Díaz and Father Navarro ought to be seen as real or as hyperbole. It would be a great honour for our country if the work was declared to be a masterpiece and that the glory of having formed it should fall upon an Indian of humble condition.[45]

Here, indeed, was a challenge: that the image of Guadalupe was the work of an inspired artist rather than the result of some heavenly intervention, and that Marcos rather than Juan Diego was the true Indian instrument of the Virgin Mary. It was not a theory, however, which was to find favour among the apparitionists. Soon after the publication of this essay, Troncoso departed for Europe, there to search for the sources of Mexican history in European archives and libraries, never to return to Mexico.

III

The degree to which Andrade's polemical edition of the 1556 *Statements* alarmed the Catholic hierarchy was expressed by Bishop Carrillo y Ancona, who called for a new edition 'with critical, historical and legal prefaces, notes and appendices in which the reader should be made to see the true sense that the document has, refuting and condemning the perverse and preposterous intention of the anonymous author of the fraudulent edition'.[46] His chosen instrument was Fortino Hipólito Vera (1834–98), vicar of Amecameca and prebendary of the collegiate chapter at Tepeyac. A leading Catholic layman described him as 'the son of parents more rich in virtue than in the fugitive goods of fortune', who was reared in rural poverty, albeit sustained by 'the holy examples of a humble and pious family'. Educated at the old college of San Juan Letrán and then in the Conciliar Seminary of Mexico, he spent over twenty years as external vicar at Amecameca, where he occupied the ruined buildings of the former Dominican priory. He had filled the cloisters with 'schools, a college, a hospice, an observatory, a printing press and workshops'. With just a room and a study for himself, Vera acted as 'a true father of the people', with a constant influx of Indians into his house, so that 'he lives like a saint and a wise man'. The truth behind this eulogy can in part be demonstrated by the range of works which this priest not only prepared for publication but also printed at Amecameca. They included three volumes of documents on Mexican Church history, not to mention the texts of proceedings of the Church Councils celebrated in New Spain. Badly printed on poor paper and often disordered in their presentation, nevertheless, these works contained an invaluable range of information and testified to Vera's devoted toil. It is notable that in 1880 he thanked both José María de Agreda and Vicente de Paul Andrade for their assistance.[47]

It was in *The Miraculous Apparition of Our Lady of Guadalupe* (1890) that Vera complied with Carrillo's injunction and presented the text of the 1556 *Statements*, taken from 'a manuscript copy' and stripped of Andrade's offensive notes. In the preceding year he had already printed for the first time the *Statements of 1666*, since Florencia had only provided a summarized version, and published his two-volume *Guadalupan Treasure* (1889), in which he commented on the ever-growing bibliography on the subject and provided a list of printed panegyrical sermons.[48] In his commentary on the events of 1556, Vera affirmed that, when Montúfar preached on Sunday, 6 September, taking as his text the lines from St Luke: 'Blessed are the eyes which see the things you see', the archbishop publicly compared the Guadalupan image with Jesus Christ, since 'as the visible image of God in our Redeemer Jesus Christ thus marvellously appeared on earth, so also the image of the Mother of God would have appeared miraculously painted on the cape of the neophyte'. Moreover, if Montúfar compared the image to its Marian counterparts in the cathedral of Seville, Peña de Francia, Montserrat and Loreto, it was because he knew that, like the Guadalupe, all these images had a miraculous origin. Had not the Holy House of Loreto been brought by angels from Nazareth in 1294, its tradition and cult blessed and honoured by popes across the centuries? By contrast, Bustamante had caused a public scandal when he claimed that veneration of the Guadalupe would lead to idolatry. For his iconoclasm ran contrary to the decrees of the Second Nicene Church Council of 787, which had defended the cult of images, since 'the honour of the original passes to the original; and he who adores the image, adores the subject which it represents'. It was thus impossible that devotion to Our Lady of Guadalupe could descend into idolatry.[49]

Where Vera scored was in providing the historical background to the quarrel between Montúfar and Bustamante, since he quoted a mendicant petition of 1526 in which the Franciscans and Dominicans united to propose that all bishops in New Spain should be elected by the religious and continue to be subject to their rule of

Plate 26   Fortino Hipólito Vera, bishop of Cuernavaca

poverty and obedience. Despite his Dominican formation Montúfar, soon after his arrival in 1554, asserted his episcopal authority and in November 1555 convoked the first Provincial Church Council in Mexico, at which the mendicants were forbidden to build new churches or priories without first obtaining their bishop's permission. Equally important, the Council decreed that 'images should not be painted without the painter and the painting being examined', so as to prevent any heterodox representations. Turning to the person of Marcos, Vera could find no more mention of him than the eulogy of Bernal Díaz and argued that the negative argument of silence applied far better to Marcos than to Valeriano, since the latter was mentioned by virtually all chroniclers of the period. It was in this context that Vera included the *Nican mopohua*, printing the text in Nahuatl, Spanish and Latin.[50] He then followed the usual trail of authorities from Becerra Tanco to Uribe. Once again, his historical knowledge was apparent when he noted that Juan Suárez de Peralta, who observed of the Guadalupe that 'she appeared among the rocks', had served as magistrate in 1556 in Cuautitlan. So also, elsewhere he emphasized that although Juan de Alloza's *Starry Heaven* had been published in 1654, it had been written in Lima in 1649, its discrepant version of the apparition narrative affording clear testimony of the author's dependence on an oral tradition which clearly preceded the publication of Sánchez' book in 1648.[51]

Following the example set by González and Anticoli, Vera concluded by launching a ferocious attack on Bustamante and his fellow Franciscans. Why had Zumárraga asserted in his *Brief Christian Rule* that there was no need for miracles in Mexico? And why had Mendieta written that: 'Our Lord God did not wish to perform for the new church and his servants in this land the miracles which were done in the primitive church'? For Motolinia confessed that many Indians were blessed with visions, writing: 'it is said that many of these converts have seen and tell of diverse revelations and visions, which, seeing the sincerity and simplicity with which they relate them, appear to be true'. If such was the case, how dare Bustamante condemn reports of miracles at Tepeyac and question the devotion? In an extraordinary passage, Vera accused Bustamante of 'profaning the chair of the Holy Spirit', in 'his rebellion against the authority of the Church in the person of the diocesan, his theological errors and his fury against those who talked of the miracles of Our Lady'. In a word, the friar was a Judas, 'sold for the historical thirty pieces of silver'. Had he not pleaded with the viceroy and the high court to correct the errors of the archbishop, thereby revealing himself to be 'more regalist than the king'? In effect, by his attack on the jurisdiction of the prelate, he had exposed the Church to the danger of schism and should have been excommunicated. Noting that Mendieta had praised Bustamante for his virtues and made no mention of his sermon, Vera concluded that the Franciscan chroniclers of this epoch were guilty of a conspiracy of silence, designed to protect the reputation of Bustamante. He concluded by querying whether the Franciscans' 'high reputation will suffer, because one of their prominent sons raised the flag of rebellion against the divine origin of the devotion of Our Lady of Guadalupe'.[52]

In his *Critical-Historical Reply* (1892) to the Latin version of García Icazbalceta's *Letter*, Vera mounted a yet more furious assault on the Franciscans. To start with, the history of the Church across the centuries had always been accompanied and illumined by miracles. Why then should Zumárraga have asserted that Christ no longer wanted miracles to be performed? So grave was his error that perhaps it might be better to place his *Brief Christian Rule* on the Roman Index of prohibited books.[53] In any case, Mendieta reported many miracles and visions among the Indians and thus obviously knew of the apparitions at Tepeyac, but chose not to mention the event for fear of bringing discredit on Bustamante and his fellow Franciscans. Turning to Sahagún and his criticism of the cult of Guadalupe, Vera noted that the chronicler had criticized the first twelve Franciscans who came to New Spain for their lack of 'serpentine wisdom', since they had failed to realize that despite ostensible conversion many Indians still remained idolaters. In this criticism Sahagún sought to defame these friars because they obviously all believed in the apparitions of the Virgin. Citing the royal rescript of 22 April 1577, which ordered Martín Enríquez to confiscate Sahagún's great chronicle, Vera gleefully interpreted this decree as a measure of the discredit which the Franciscan had incurred, since his was 'a condemned book and rightly condemned' by the patron of the Church in New Spain.[54]

Point by point, Vera sought to answer the arguments and examples advanced by García Icazbalceta, even if he refused to believe that the historian was the author of the *Exquisitio historico*. Opponents of the apparitions had always distinguished between the tradition and the cult. But in fact it was the extraordinary nature of the initial miracle which accounted for the extraordinary development of the devotion, since 'by the antiquity of the cult we prove the antiquity of the tradition'. Vera dwelt at some length on the sermon preached at Tepeyac in 1622 on the Nativity of the Virgin on 8 September, in which Juan de Cepeda had acclaimed God as a 'divine Apelles', who had 'made a creature so beautiful and finished, perfect since the moment of her Immaculate Conception'. What could this be, so he argued, but a reference to the heavenly painting before which Cepeda preached? Noting that both the Virgins of Pilar and Loreto had celebrated their feasts on 8 September, he recalled the sermon preached by Agustín de Betancurt, where the Franciscan noted that all Marian images celebrated their feast on the Virgin's Nativity, since 'to be born is to appear and to appear is to be born'. Like the Guadalupe, Loreto had shifted its feast to 10 December and Pilar to 12 October. In these equivalencies, Vera stoutly affirmed that as regards the Holy House in Italy, 'it is truly and really the house where the Divine Word was made flesh'. All these devotions were sustained by miracles, and how could God have allowed the report of such miracles to be accepted had their respective traditions not been faithful accounts of their holy origins?[55]

Once more Vera railed against Bustamante for daring to oppose Montúfar, 'the apostle and rector of the Mexican Church', and now accused him not merely of contradicting the decrees of the Second Nicene Church Council but also of adopting the Protestant iconoclasm of Martin Luther. He praised Miguel Sánchez and suggested that Florencia's *Marian Zodiac* 'merits a medal of distinction'. But it was the suggestion, taken from a passage in Sahagún, that the apparition narrative may have arisen from the experience of Martín Ecatl, governor of Tlatelolco, in 1528–31, who had been haunted by a devil in the form of the goddess Cihuacoatl, alias Tonantzin, which elicited Vera's most indignant response:

> Only a diabolically inspired spirit or a profoundly corrupted heart has been able to conceive this infamous conjecture that the marvellous Apparition of Holy Mary of Guadalupe was no more than the transformation of a demonic apparition in the shape of a woman.

This nefarious conjecture was an insult to the Mexican Church and to all its archbishops, including Labastida, not to mention 'the Immaculate Mother of the Mexicans'. Moreover, if Valeriano had fabricated his 'comedy' out of such a source, which priest or prelate would ever have accepted it?[56]

By way of conclusion, Vera asserted that the interpretation of the 1556 *Statements* all depended on whether one chose to accept the sermon of Montúfar or the sermon of Bustamante, the authority of an archbishop or the preaching of a friar. The purpose of the *Exquisitio historico* was:

> to extinguish the belief and confidence which the present generation places in the blessed Palladium of Tepeyac, the only bond of union, the only emblem of combat, the only anchor of salvation, for so hard worn a people, exhausted by so many misfortunes, disillusioned by so many deceptions, constantly attacked by hypocritical or open enemies who devour and consume it like a vulture with its prey . . .

In this bitter cry, Vera expressed that intimate union of religion and patriotism that had always characterized devotion to the Guadalupe, a devotion which led him to condemn all criticism of the tradition as a blasphemy against 'Catholicism and Mexican patriotism'. Here was the reason why he had written to defend 'the Guadalupan cause, a holy cause, beloved and blessed by religion and its high Pontiff; a sacred cause under whose standard the true sons of the Mexican Patria meet enthusiastically to realize the glorious programme of Religion, Independence and Union'. Transported by his partisan fervour, this admirable priest, who was soon to be named the first bishop of Cuernavaca, failed to realize that in blackening the reputation of the first Franciscans, Zumárraga among them, he not merely slandered the apostolic founders of the Mexican Church, but also contradicted those elements in the Guadalupan tradition which insisted on the friendship of Juan Diego and the archbishop and Motolinia's influence over the Indian's observance of chastity.[57]

Not content with Vera's appeal to the historical evidence, apologists also sought to invoke papal authority. In *The Magisterium of the Church and the Virgin of Tepeyac* (1892), the Italian Jesuit, Esteban Anticoli, cited papal encyclicals and the decrees of the First Vatican Council of 1870 to damn as bad Catholics all those who questioned the historical truth of the apparitions of the Virgin in Mexico. In particular he fixed upon the Syllabus of Errors, a schedule of propositions appended to the encyclical *Quanta Cura* (1864), in which Pius IX condemned the statement that 'the Roman Pontiff can and should reconcile himself with progress, liberalism and recent civiliza-tion'.[58] So too, he cited the declaration of the Vatican Council that there was 'a twofold order of knowledge', consisting of natural reason and divine faith. Although reason possessed its own principles and method, it could never intrude upon the sphere of revelation and could never differ substantially in its conclusions from the doctrines enunciated by revelation.[59] Equally important, the Council had reiterated the tradi-tional belief that the Church and the papacy were guided by the assistance of the Holy Spirit and then declared, as a divinely revealed dogma, that:

> The Roman Pontiff, when he speaks, *ex catedra*, that is, when exercising the office of shepherd and teacher of all Christians, in virtue of his supreme apostolic authority, he defines a doctrine concerning faith and morals to be held by the whole Church, possesses, by the divine assistance promised to him in St Peter, that infallibility which the divine Redeemer willed his Church to enjoy in defining doctrine con-cerning faith and morals.

The precise limits of papal infallibility were a matter of controversy in Europe and it soon became clear, for example, that the Syllabus of Errors did not fall into the category of infallible pronouncements.[60] For all that, what these definitions in part expressed was the intransigent resistance offered by Pius IX to the onslaught of contemporary liberalism and rationalism, a resistance rendered more intense by the loss of the papacy's temporal sovereignty, first in central Italy and then in Rome.

When confronting the arguments of Andrade and García Icazbalceta, Anticoli cited both the Syllabus of Errors and the Vatican Council to assert that 'in the natural sci-ences and philosophical studies', the Church exercised 'a directing rule'. He then boldly asserted that when the Church taught doctrines, even when they were not to be found in the original Revelation, it acted infallibly. To be more specific, when the Pope canonized a saint or condemned propositions in a book as heretical, the faithful were not at liberty to doubt the facts of the case. In Mexico, the bishops, who possessed 'an authentic magisterium', had consistently taught that the apparitions of the Virgin to Juan Diego were an 'historical fact', and when confronted with that teaching the faith-ful could only accept its truth as part of Catholic doctrine. Arguments based on silence and the lack of documents 'prove nothing against the Apparition and only express the historical falsity and theological errors' of the critics. Indeed, so Anticoli argued, 'if the Magisterium of the Church proposes to us the fact of the Apparition as real and true, it is impossible that this fact could be false or that the Apparition had not occurred'.[61] Although the apparition could not figure as a dogma of faith, since it was not part of Revelation, nevertheless, it belonged to a category of truth which was the object of 'theological faith', a category of belief which had been expertly defined by Francisco Suárez, the celebrated Spanish theologian.

> To theological faith can belong those celebrated Revelations and Apparitions of which we read in the lives of the Saints and which are commonly received in the Church through their having given rise to many feasts and devotions, be they of the universal Church or be they in ecclesiastical provinces or nations.

All this led to the conclusion that since the papacy had approved of the Virgin of Tepeyac as patron of Mexico and had established a feast day with its own mass and office, it had confirmed the historical reality of the apparition. After all, the Congregation of Rites in Rome had confirmed the authenticity of the miraculous transport of the Holy House of Nazareth to Loreto. Moreover, as Carrillo y Ancona had argued, when the Supreme Congregation of the Roman Inquisition reprimanded the bishop of Tamaulipas for opposing the coronation of the Guadalupe, they confirmed 'the historical fact' of the apparition as established by tradition. The theological status of these beliefs resembled that of the Immaculate Conception of the Virgin Mary prior to its papal definition in 1854.[62]

Turning to the role of the Catholic faithful, Anticoli insisted that they were obliged to offer 'submission of the understanding and of the will', and not what the Jansenists had called 'a respectful silence'. For the Jansenists of the seventeenth century had distinguished between questions of right principle and of fact, much as contemporary Liberal Catholics in Mexico distinguished between 'the historical aspect' and the theological aspect, in both cases asserting the rights of 'private judgement' or conscience. Since the anonymous author of the *Exquisitio historico* had not taken as his premise the historical certainty of the apparition, he had demonstrated 'religious liberalism' and a 'satanic pride' and had clearly betrayed the influence of Muñoz, who 'by all the signs was of the Jansenist brood'. Under pain of mortal sin, the faithful had to submit their judgement to the teachings of the Church, since to do otherwise would be to act as a 'schismatic or reckless Catholic Liberal'. As Carrillo had said: 'Roma locuta, causa finita.' Not for nothing had Pius IX defined religious liberalism as 'the heresy of the century'.[63]

As his citation of Suárez indicated, Anticoli was anxious to argue that the Church had always accepted private revelations and visions, and cited the cases of Pope Eugene welcoming the visions of St Hildegard, Boniface IX of St Brigid, and Gregory

XI of St Catherine of Siena. At Tepeyac there had occurred the classic trilogy of actions which characterized these events, which was to say, the apparition of the Virgin Mary, her revelation or message, and Juan Diego's vision. There was also a great resemblance to what had happened so recently at Lourdes. In both cases, the Virgin appeared in the form of the Immaculate Conception to a poor peasant, Juan Diego at Tepeyac, Bernadette at Lourdes. The only difference was that in France the local bishop made public his approbation only six years after the event, whereas in Mexico no canonical proceedings had been initiated. For all that, in 1886 the Mexican archbishops and bishops had pronounced the apparitions to be the ancient tradition of their Church and thus certified that it was 'an historical-theological fact'.[64]

Not content with this striking appeal to the infallible authority of the Church, in 1893 Anticoli published his *Defence of the Apparition of the Virgin Mary*, in which he bitterly attacked the authors of the 1891 edition of the 1556 *Statements* and then extended his critique to launch an open assault on the standing of García Icazbalceta both as an historian and as a Catholic. Since the book was dedicated to Próspero María Alarcón, the new archbishop of Mexico, 'in testimony of profound respect and gratitude', presumably that prelate had decided to unleash his Italian mastiff against Mexico's greatest scholar. At the outset, the Jesuit took care to praise Fortino Vera's 'brilliant victory' over the anonymous critics and once again affirmed the superiority of theological principles over mere history, since 'if the fact is in itself supernatural and hence theological, in the particular case you cannot avoid theological principles in the examination you make of this fact'. Noting that he himself had been criticized for asserting that Benedict XIV had been the first to apply the phrase 'Non fecit taliter' to the Guadalupe image, he employed a dialectical finesse to assert that the pope 'was the first, not by priority in time, but by priority of authority'.[65]

Turning to history, Anticoli discerned three great objections to the Guadalupe tradition, the first raised by Bustamante in 1556, the second in 1794 by 'the Jansenist Muñoz in Madrid and the extravagant Father Mier in Mexico', and now the third launched by 'religious liberalism'. That stated, he had little to say that had not been better said by Vera. After reiterating his criticism of Martín Enríquez for his 'baseness of spirit', he insisted on Valeriano as the author of the Nahuatl account from which Sánchez drew and which Laso de la Vega merely printed, since the latter, so he averred, could not possibly have written its thirty-six pages in the six months that elapsed between his excited commendation of Sánchez and the approbation of his own work. If native annals assigned the apparition to the years 1555–6, that was because these Indians had failed to master the complexities of Western chronology. As for the hypothesis that the image had been painted by an Indian, he crudely dismissed Marcos as 'this Cipac or Tic-tac', who was obviously unable to form an image which the papacy had defined as 'marvellously painted', which was to say, divine in origin. At all points the Jesuit thus judged historical facts and possibilities by appeal to Church authority.[66]

In his interpretation of the 1556 *Statements*, Anticoli simply repeated Vera's critique, insisting that these depositions amounted to a 'juridical enquiry or a canonical lawsuit'. He argued that if the apparitions had not occurred, then the image of Guadalupe was false and its cult superstitious. As for Bustamante, he defined him as a 'schismatic preacher' who had 'unleashed the iconoclastic heresy'. In calling upon the viceroy to intervene in a purely spiritual matter, he proved himself to be more regalist than the eighteenth-century exponents of that doctrine, and indeed was guilty of the Jansenist errors of the Council of Pistoia, which Pius IX had condemned in his Syllabus of Errors. The fact that after leaving office as provincial, Bustamante had retired to Cuernavaca, allegedly to perfect his 'Mexican', was obviously a sign that he had been punished for his sermon. The only point of substance that Anticoli raised took the form of a query: if devotion to Our Lady of Guadalupe was as great as the 1556 depositions claimed, how could the image have been painted by Marcos only 'yesterday'?[67]

Where Anticoli outdid Vera was in his brutal attack on García Icazbalceta, inspired, no doubt, by the well-founded suspicion that he was the author of the Spanish original of the *Exquisitio historico*. However, he confined his criticism to the biography of Zumárraga, noting that Altamirano had already commented on the absence in that work of any mention of the apparitions. It was a silence that had filled 'good Mexicans' with pain. Indeed, he quoted a letter of the bishop of Puebla, Francisco de Paula Verea, written on 6 February 1880, in which that prelate had exclaimed: 'To write the life of the Venerable Zumárraga and to omit one of the principal and most solemn facts attributed to it: what does this indicate? Bad faith, ignorance, fear of the truth, or base interest?' Anticoli concurred with this harsh judgement, ascribing the cause of the evil to the failure of García Icazbalceta to have submitted to 'the judgement of the Church on the pretext of the supposed lack of contemporary data . . . perhaps the author thinks that what is theologically true can be historically or philosophically false'. If that was indeed the case, then he stood condemned by the propositions of the Syllabus of Errors. The Jesuit concluded that in all this, García Icazbalceta 'did not conduct himself as a Catholic writer and with his silence he saddened the prelates'.[68]

Where Anticoli scored a palpable hit, however, was when he criticized the Mexican historian for his failure to discuss the campaign of the bishops to defend the Indians from the conquerors and, in particular, the petition to Rome framed by Julián Garcés, the bishop of Tlaxcala, which elicited from Paul III the papal breve which insisted on the rationality and freedom of the Indians and their right to retain their property once they accepted Christianity. García Icazbalceta had not even mentioned this intervention of 'apostolic authority', a silence which was 'inexplicable'. Moreover, Anticoli cited the passage in which García Icazbalceta referred to 'the right of conquest, that before, then and always, has been exercised by the most strong . . . the providential law manifest in accomplished facts'. Yet both Paul III and the Ecclesiastical Junta which met in Mexico in 1546, not to mention Las Casas, had all defended 'the eternal principles of justice'. It was Juan Ginés de Sepúlveda who had been 'at pains to prove the same errors which Señor Icazbalceta repeats'. Resorting to his doctrinal *vade-mecum*, Anticoli once more cited the Syllabus of Errors where Pius IX had declared that 'the successful injustice of a fact does not harm the sanctity of the right'.[69] Mere force or violence could never establish rights. In this criticism, the Jesuit undoubtedly demonstrated that García Icazbalceta had indeed been influenced by the positivism of his epoch and its Social Darwinist emphasis on the struggle for survival.

In the official history of the Jesuits in nineteenth-century Mexico, Anticoli is described as a good theologian, observant in his religious duties, and in temperament kind and humble. But he had an irascible spirit and could not abide contradiction, at times attacking his adversaries with 'injurious words'. In Mexico his books were apparently well received in Catholic circles and the bishops employed him in their efforts to change the office of the Virgin's feast. But his attempt to provide a theological justification for the apparitions was not welcomed in Rome, where in 1893 the Assistant of the Father General of the Jesuits, on referring to *The Magisterium of the Church and the Virgin of Tepeyac*, wrote: 'I did not like the book of the good Father Anticoli, either in its style or in its personal attacks, or in its anxiety to want a theological demonstration of the fact of the Apparition.'[70] In effect, the Jesuit had grossly exaggerated the reach of the Church's doctrinal authority and had ignored the moral autonomy of history as an intellectual discipline. The Syllabus of Errors did not form part of the Church's infallible teaching and had evoked widespread episcopal opposition in Europe. As an apologist, Anticoli was more notable for the vigour with which he expressed his arguments than for the accuracy of his knowledge. His attack on García Icazbalceta was deeply resented and was to elicit a crushing reproach from a prominent Mexican bishop.

IV

As a devout, conservative Catholic, García Icazbalceta was thrust into depression by the attacks on his good name, licensed by elements within the hierarchy. On reading Anticoli's book, he wrote: 'I began to read the book, but after a while I left it, irritated by so much stupidity, self-sufficiency and insolence. With such defenders there is no good cause.' He complained to Jesuits whom he knew about this Italian priest whose ignorance was only matched by his impertinence. According to José María Agreda, 'The aggression of this furious Jesuit was the cause that this worthy writer was so disheartened that he no longer wanted to continue the publication of *Documents for Our History*', despite having invaluable materials to hand. For his part, in 1893, García Icazbalceta complained that the *Codice Mendieta*, which had cost him a great deal of money and work, had not sold more than ten copies, adding: 'why should I waste my natural heat and pennies in books which no-one reads?' For their part, the apparitionists rejoiced at his discomfiture, since the bishop of Querétaro, Rafael

Camacho, wrote to Vera asking him, 'have you now read the work of Father Anticoli, printed in Puebla, in which he puts the ashes on Icazbalceta's brow?' It was thus enshrouded in depression at the outcome of his life's labour that in 1894 Mexico's leading scholar died at home.[71]

Soon after his death, at the general assembly of Vicente de Paul conferences held in the city of San Luis Potosí in December 1894, Dr Ignacio Montes de Oca y Obregón, the learned bishop of that diocese, pronounced a eulogy of Joaquín García Icazbalceta, describing him as 'an exemplary member' and president of the conferences in Mexico City, where he had encouraged many others to join him in works of charity.[72] He had also put together and printed small books of devotion which had enjoyed a wide circulation. A wealthy landowner in Morelos, a state where, as García Icazbalceta himself observed, many *hacendados* took less care of their peons than of their animals, 'he had a savings box, as he called it, for all of his employees', from which he provided 'systematic presents' for their weddings, children and illnesses, a patriarchal form of social insurance. At the intellectual level he had restored the reputation of the first missionaries in Mexico, at times himself working at the printing press, and in particular had revealed the greatness of Zumárraga. But his achievement, so Montes de Oca asserted, had aroused the envy of the world and the Devil, with the result that:

> Disguised as an angel of light, the Devil dressed himself in a religious tunic and, as envy attacks, attacked him with anger, acrimony and implacable cruelty. What he had published was interpreted badly and what he had not written was thrown in his face; and his intentions were the subject of calumny.

Despite these attacks, García Icazbalceta did not reply and indeed, 'at the indication of a prelate, he erased a chapter, an entire chapter from the most beloved of his works, a chapter which had cost him long years of study and anxiety'. On finding himself the object of criticism by ministers of the Church, of which he was an obedient son, 'he broke for ever his learned pen' and devoted his last years to compiling dictionaries and grammatical works, leaving unpublished invaluable materials for the history of the Church. The bishop concluded: 'Although a layman, he exercised on earth an apostolate which was more fertile than that of many of those called by God to the highest places.' In a note to the printed version of this eulogy, Montes de Oca emphasized that García Icazbalceta had written his *Letter* at the express command of the archbishop; he had requested that it should be not shown to others; and he had protested his Catholic belief, submitting to the authority of the prelate in all matters concerning theology. For his part, the bishop warned that although the Guadalupe tradition was not an article of the Catholic faith, it was 'an ancient, constant and universal tradition of the Mexican nation' and hence could not be contradicted by a Catholic without incurring the charge of temerity.[73]

In his preface to Vera's *Guadalupan Treasure*, José de Jesús Cuevas, a distinguished Catholic layman, lamented that 'the history of our country is an Aztec mirror of polished obsidian, which has the strange property of converting the rays of light which strike it into dark and confused waves and of turning images into shadows'.[74] During the controversies which pitted Catholic against Catholic, priest against priest, the same property seems to have invaded the cult of Our Lady of Guadalupe. At a time when the Church was excluded from public life, García Icazbalceta succeeded in resurrecting the mendicant missionaries as the founders of Mexican civilization. Whereas Mier and Bustamante had based their case for independence on the cruelties of the conquest and had not scrupled to accuse Zumárraga of the wholesale destruction of native archives and codices, he demonstrated with incomparable erudition not merely the Franciscan's defence of the Indians but also the remarkable range of his cultural achievement. The essays written by Altamirano testified to the immense change in liberal attitudes wrought by the publication of Franciscan chronicles, letters and lives. But his scholarship counted for little among the Catholic bishops who were intent on promoting the cult of the Mexican Virgin so as to re-establish the influence of the Church. For the ultramontane clergy, his questioning of the historical basis of the Guadalupe tradition was an intolerable affront both to their religion and to their patriotism. With the surfacing of the 1556 *Statements*, apologists like González, Anticoli and Vera launched an audacious attack on the early Franciscans and boldly denounced Bustamante, Sahagún and Mendieta for iconoclasm, regalism and virtual schism. When Vera suggested that Zumárraga's *Brief Christian Rule* should be put on the Roman Index, he thus dismissed Mexico's first archbishop as a virtual heretic. All these wild, ill-considered arguments derived from a passionate determination to defend the historical reality of tradition. The nineteenth century, of course, was the era in which history was viewed as the scientific discipline which was destined to reveal the mainspring of cultural progress but would also discredit the myths of past ages. When they engaged in controversy, the apologists implicitly accepted the primacy of historical method and only questioned its findings. In effect, García Icazbalceta and Vera both fixed on the origins of the cult of Guadalupe as a measure of truth and had little to say about its cultural or theological significance. No-one at this time even considered reading Miguel Sánchez with care or sympathy, and hence failed to discern the typological, scriptural character of the apparition narrative. And yet, when the apologists launched their diatribes against the Franciscans, they were inspired by patriotic sentiments similar to those which had impelled Sánchez. If the Virgin's apparition had already been widely accepted as the foundation moment of the Mexican Church, what need was there to honour the memory of those Spanish friars who had devoted their lives to the conversion of the Indians and who had preserved the memory of native culture and history?

12

The coronation

I

On 12 October 1895 the archbishops and bishops of Mexico, accompanied by prelates from Canada, the United States and the Caribbean, entered the sanctuary at Tepeyac to crown the image of Our Lady of Guadalupe. In the elaborate *Album* (1895) which commemorated the occasion, Victoriano Agüeros, the editor of the Catholic newspaper, *The Times*, described the coronation as 'the most important and transcendental event in the history of our country'. During the nineteenth century the Mexican nation had suffered more than other peoples, but it was now time to beg the Virgin for 'pardon for its past and peace for its future'. There was a great deal to ask pardon for since, although 'Mexico is but a child, with less than a century of existence, nevertheless, in its short life it has taken giant steps down the path of evil and along the rough and winding roads of crime.' Scarcely had independence been won when Mexico killed its liberator, Agustín de Iturbide, expelled all Spaniards and allowed masonic lodges to seize control of its government, only then to experience 'all the horrors of an interminable civil war, filled with hatred'. An unjust neighbour had seized half the nation's territory. And, if all this were not enough, 'an official apostasy' had unleashed a reformation comparable in its effects to the movements led by Henry VIII and Martin Luther, albeit in this case constituting an apostasy of the State, but not of the Mexican people. Such were the sufferings of those years that Agüeros asserted: 'there is no prayer more intense or more fervent than that which rises from the deep and frightful abyss of desolation'. With all his heart he marvelled at the resurrection of the Catholic devotion that was expressed so powerfully in the renewal of pilgrimage to the sanctuary at Tepeyac, with the faithful now coming, not simply from Mexico City and its environs, but from the furthest corners of the republic. When the decision to crown the image was announced in 1887, the public reaction was so enthusiastic that it was as if an electrical current had brought new life and light to the Mexican Church. In an age dominated by religious indifference, 'the Miracle Image' had once more come to fill the minds and hearts of the Mexican people.[1]

To understand these mingled sentiments of anguished memory and present joy we have only to return to 1869, two years after the collapse of Maximilian's empire, when the Catholic Society of Mexico City was informed that the sanctuary at Tepeyac no longer possessed funds sufficient to maintain its college of canons, and that its liturgy might well have to be undertaken by but one or two priests. Religion was at a low ebb and the faithful no longer offered their customary alms, so that 'little by little the cult of the Virgin Mary of Guadalupe is falling into oblivion'. Although Benito Juárez had kept 12 December as a national holiday, he had allowed his Liberal henchmen to confiscate the sanctuary's capital funds, strip the church of much of its silver and jewels, and close the adjoining convent of Capuchin nuns.[2] With Sebastián Lerdo de Tejada (1872–6) as president, the Laws of the Reform, which separated Church and State and dissolved the religious Orders, were incorporated into the Constitution. The Jesuits were once more expelled and the Sisters of Charity, a congregation devoted to the care of the sick and destitute, whom Juárez had protected, were driven into exile. As late as 1880 Tirso Rafael Córdoba preached at Tepeyac lamenting 'the desolate picture' of religious indifference in Mexico and the lack of contribution for the college of canons. Once there had been a time, he exclaimed, when Mexico had followed the teachings of Christ, when 'laws and institutions and all that ruled public life bore the seal of religion, were inspired by his spirit and applied his maxims'. The disastrous transformation wrought in Mexico had come from 'philosophism, the echo of the cry of the first revolutionary, as an impious author of our time calls Satan'. And yet, in the very land where Proudhon wrote, the Catholic Church had experienced a remarkable revival in devotion, so that France 'now overwhelms us with shame by its examples'.[3]

If that was the situation as late as 1880, whence came the explosion of devotion, the confident energy and the material resources which enabled the Mexican Church to stage the coronation of 1895 with such splendour? Part of the explanation has to be found in the still enigmatic career of Pelagio Antonio de Labastida, bishop of Puebla 1855–63, archbishop of Mexico 1863–91. It was during his years of exile that Labastida won the confidence of Pius IX and sat down with the pope in 1863 to plan the renewal of the Mexican Church through the creation of seven new dioceses and the promotion of Morelia and Guadalajara to the status of archbishoprics. The introduction of bishops in such cities as Zamora, León, Zacatecas, Tulancingo, Chilapa and Veracruz was soon followed by the establishment of diocesan seminaries and schools and the formation of congregations of nuns dedicated to education and other pious tasks. So successful did all this prove that, in the next decades, bishoprics were founded in Colima, Tamaulipas, Tabasco and Culiacán. And in 1891 in a further reorganization, Oaxaca, Durango and Linares (Monterrey) became archbishoprics and new dioceses were created in Chihuahua, Saltillo, Tepic, Tehuantepec and Cuernavaca. If the authority which introduced these changes was the Holy See, obviously the initiatives derived from the proposals of the Mexican hierarchy.[4]

After Labastida's death in 1891, Ignacio Montes de Oca, the bishop of San Luis Potosí, pronounced the funeral eulogy in which he described the archbishop as 'the leader of a conquered party and the principal actor in an unfortunate enterprise', which was to say, the French Intervention, noting that he had acted as Regent for thirty days. But, when he found that neither Maximilian nor the French generals supported the Church's demands for the return of the lands, capital and buildings seized by the Liberals, he had retired from public life, devoting himself to his pastoral ministry. After his return to Mexico in 1871 Labastida had cautioned Catholics against resorting to violent opposition to the anti-clerical measures of Lerdo de Tejada. Moreover, it was thanks to his prudence and judgement that a tacit understanding was reached with President Porfirio Díaz which had allowed the Church to renew its activities in education and build churches without suffering government intervention. Indeed, when Labastida celebrated his fiftieth anniversary as a priest in 1889, Carmen Romero Rubio, the president's wife, had attended the ceremonies in the cathedral.[5]

But the bishops and clergy would have achieved little had it not been for the contribution, both financial and social, of the Catholic laity. An exemplary figure here was José de Jesús Cuevas (1842–1901), a wealthy lawyer and landowner, who had served as the private secretary of Maximilian. After the Liberal victory, he founded Catholic Societies in the leading cities of the republic and acted as their national president. He also established three Catholic newspapers and sponsored other publications directed to Indians and children. In 1873 he was elected to Congress as deputy for Maravatio, only to be summarily expelled when he refused to swear obedience to the Reform Laws. He established a cotton mill at Xalapa, wrote a study of Sor Juana Inés de la Cruz, and composed various pieces for the theatre. Taking advantage of the railways and steam shipping, he travelled in the United States and Europe, visited the Holy Land and was received in audience by Pius IX.[6] In effect, Mexico possessed a small but influential class of wealthy, ardent Catholics who acted as the faithful coadjutors of the bishops and clergy.

To obtain an impression of the sentiments animating the educated laity at this time one has only to turn to *The Most Holy Virgin of Guadalupe* (1887), where, in the dedication to Archbishop Labastida, Cuevas expressed the fear that the projected coronation might be greeted with public blasphemy and mockery. For his part, he defiantly asserted that the only two acceptable moments in Mexico's history as an independent nation were when the country had been ruled by emperors devoted to the Guadalupe, when the people had welcomed 'the advent of Maximilian of Habsburg to the throne of Iturbide and Moctezuma'. So too, he emphasized that Morelos and other insurgent leaders had honoured Mexico's patron, not to mention the conservative heroes, Miramón, Osollo and Mejía, who had fought the Liberal Reform. Nor should it be forgotten, he added, that it was in the chapter room of the sanctuary that the Treaty of Guadalupe Hidalgo (1848) had been signed, which, although it signified a grievous loss of territory, had preserved Mexican independence. Indeed, it had been the Virgin's influence which had saved Mexico from further loss of land and had prevented the country from suffering 'the monstrous demagogueries and abominable despotisms' found so often in Central and South America. Despite these conservative opinions, Cuevas described the Spanish conquerors as 'mad wolves' who had treated the Indians as if they were animals, before the sublime intervention of the Virgin had ensured both the conversion of the natives and the humanization of the conquerors. Nevertheless, he emphasized that, when the Virgin commanded Juan Diego to present the flowers and image to Zumárraga, she had taught the Indians 'the marvellous and immutable order of Christian hierarchy', which was to say, that they should more reverence a bishop than the friars.[7]

Although Cuevas delved into the Guadalupe tradition, he had nothing new to say other than to stress an old argument which had been neglected during the controversies of the 1880s, when he affirmed that 'the most unshakeable proof of the miracle is the Image itself . . . without ceasing to be Jewish, at the same time the physiognomy of the Virgin is Aztec'. After a rehearsal of the observations of Miguel Cabrera about the complex techniques involved in the painting of the image, he observed:

> It is, so to say, the Effigy of the Most Holy Virgin transformed into an Aztec and raised to the highest point that the beauty of that race can reach . . . It has something of the old Greek and Eastern images, of the primitive paintings of the Latins and the Middle Ages . . . of the Egyptian and Aztec paintings.

So universal was its beauty, he affirmed, that it was obviously miraculous in origin and miraculous in the devotion it elicited.[8]

Despite his joy at the announced coronation, Cuevas remained despondent at the condition of his country. It had been the delusory example of 'an unjust and malevolent neighbour' which had precipitated Mexico into 'an impossible federation and a laughable democracy'. At the time he wrote, the United States had become yet more powerful and wealthy, its enterprises reaching into Mexico, so that 'in his own country the Mexican cannot be more than a labourer or a public official'. The republic did not enjoy true freedom of religion or freedom of the press; there was little work to be had and still less justice. For all that, he had the consolation that 'today Mexico is more universally, sincerely and firmly Catholic than it was thirty or forty years ago'.[9]

If the resurgence of the Mexican Church can in part be explained by the collaboration of bishops and the conservative laity, whence came the idea of the coronation of the image? To be sure, in 1740 Lorenzo Boturini had obtained a licence from the cathedral chapter of St Peter's to stage such a ceremony, but that had remained an historical curiosity. As was so often the case in late nineteenth-century Mexico, the inspiration came from Europe. In 1858, the Virgin Mary appeared to Bernadette Soubirous at Lourdes, telling her: 'I am the Immaculate Conception', which was to say, only four years after Pius IX had defined that doctrine as a divinely revealed dogma of the Catholic faith. As soon as 1862, after taking depositions and staging a formal enquiry, the local bishop accepted the apparitions as authentic and approved the construction of a small chapel. Thereafter, devotion rapidly mounted and thousands of pilgrims arrived seeking a cure for their ills. The pope blessed the cult, and such was its popular appeal that a large church was soon built. In 1876 an image of the Virgin at Lourdes was crowned in an impressive ceremony attended by 35 bishops, 3,000 priests and over 100,000 laity. By this time, the French Church was suffering the attacks of an aggressive, secularizing republicanism and it thus deployed all the new means of communication provided by the railways and the printing press to promote the cult of the Virgin at Lourdes.[10] Unlike previous devotions, however, pilgrims were more attracted by the healing powers of waters blessed by the spiritual presence of the Virgin than by the prospect of miracles wrought by a thaumaturgic image. The fame of the miraculous cures at Lourdes rapidly spread across the Catholic world, and they were interpreted as a potent sign of the Church's renewed spiritual power.

If the Mexican coronation was indebted to its French exemplar, it was because José Antonio Plancarte y Labastida (1840–98), who directed the entire project, had been educated in Europe and indeed, in 1877, went on pilgrimage to Lourdes only a year after the coronation of its image of the Immaculate Conception. The nephew of Archbishop Labastida, in 1856 he had accompanied his uncle to England, where he spent six years at St Mary's, Oscott, a seminary college near Birmingham, then attended by the young Montes de Oca. Thereafter, he completed his education at the Gregorian University at Rome and, in 1862, attended the elaborate ceremonies in St Peter's which marked the canonization of the martyrs of Nagasaki, among whom figured Felipe de Jesús, the first Mexican saint. After his ordination, he was granted a private audience with Pius IX, during which he promised that, after his return to Mexico, he would send talented students to attend the recently established Colegio Pío Latino Americano, and equally pledged 'to unite myself to the Holy See in thought, word and deed for all my life'. In effect, Plancarte was a devoted ultramontane, who was to dedicate his life to the renewal of the Mexican Church.[11]

Despite his eminent connections, Plancarte spent fifteen years as parish priest at Jacona, a small town situated close to Zamora, the birthplace of his uncle and extended family. There he founded colleges both for boys and for girls and an asylum for orphans, and even imported iron rails from England to link Jacona to Zamora with mule-drawn transport. Soon after his return he was fined and imprisoned for two months because he had dared to hold a procession in Holy Week through the

Plate 27 Silvio Capparoni, *Abbot José Antonio Plancarte y Labastida*

streets. His activism attracted the displeasure of his bishop, who, in 1876, closed the boys' college in Jacona. It was then that he led an expedition of no fewer than seventeen students to Rome, there to join another five whom he had already despatched to the Latin American College. Such was the success of this bold initiative that among these boys were several future prelates, including José María Mora y del Río, archbishop of Mexico (1909–28), Francisco Orozco y Jiménez, archbishop of Guadalajara (1913–36), Francisco Plancarte y Navarrete, archbishop of Monterrey (1912–20) and Juan Herrera y Piña, archbishop of Monterrey (1921–27), not to mention lesser dignitaries. It was in 1879 that Plancarte also obtained papal blessing for the foundation of a new congregation of nuns, known as the Daughters of the Immaculate Conception of Guadalupe, for which he had recruited teachers at the girls' college in Jacona. After an ill-fated quarrel with José María Cázares, the authoritarian bishop of Zamora, he was employed by his uncle as rector of the diocesan seminary of Mexico and became a popular preacher in the capital, raising funds to build a church dedicated to San Felipe de Jesús, where the holy sacrament was exposed for perpetual prayer offered in expiation for the sins of humanity. It was in 1885 that Plancarte joined his uncle and the archbishop of Morelia to crown the image of Our Lady of La Esperanza at Jacona, whose sanctuary he had renovated.[12]

When Plancarte came to plan the coronation, it at once became obvious to him and the archbishop that the sanctuary at Tepeyac needed a thorough renovation if it was to offer suitable surroundings for such grand proceedings. As work began in April 1887, his first priority was to remove the choir stalls of the canons, which in Spanish style had been located in the middle of the church. Then the elegant neo-classical marble and bronze altarpiece designed by Manuel Tolsa and installed in 1826–36 was demolished. However, as work continued, it was found that great cracks had opened in the vaults, so that to provide a better foundation cedar wood piles had to be sunk deep into the mud on which the church rested. To house the displaced canons a small apse was built behind the main altar, much to the displeasure of these clerics. To magnify the image a bronze baldachino, modelled on Bernini's masterpiece in St Peter's, was raised above the altar. On either side of the marble altar were placed figures of Juan Diego and Zumárraga, carved in Italy from the best Carrara marble. In the nave, immediately before the high altar, a shallow crypt was inserted, distinguished by a kneeling figure of Archbishop Labastida (by then deceased), also done in Italian marble. The walls of the sanctuary were adorned by five large paintings which respectively depicted the Franciscans converting the Indians in the presence of the Virgin of Guadalupe surrounded by angels; the procession led by Zumárraga to install the image in the first chapel; the presentation of Miguel Cabrera's copy to Benedict XIV; the four commissioners swearing the oath in 1737 before Archbishop Vizarrón; and the taking of the 1666 depositions from both Indians and Spaniards. The overall cost of this renovation is not known, since, although the *Album* printed a list of contributions broken down by diocese, which amounted to 241,800 pesos, the monies raised in the archdiocese of Mexico were not included.[13]

It was the ever-energetic Plancarte who also commissioned Edgar Morgan of Paris to design the coronation crown. To fund this operation he persuaded a select number of ladies of the wealthy families of the capital to entrust him with their favourite jewels, apparently given, so it was later alleged, in expectation that they would adorn the crown. However, Plancarte sold these stones in Paris and, with the proceeds, purchased a splendid crown which was decorated with the heraldic shields of the six archbishoprics of Mexico, below which were affixed the twenty-two medallions of the remaining dioceses. The body of the crown was surmounted by an orb, on which 'Méjico' figured prominently, and finished with an eagle bearing a cross. Since such an expensive object would soon tarnish in the humid airs of Mexico City, a silver crown adorned with local precious stones was made in the capital with the same design at a cost of 2,000 pesos, and was exhibited above the image throughout the year.[14]

If the renovation of the sanctuary took several years, the coronation was further delayed because the Mexican bishops had petitioned Rome to change the wording of the liturgical office used on the Virgin's feast. The aim of the petition was to remove the objectionable qualifying expressions 'they say' and 'it seems' from the description of the image and the apparitions. But approval was delayed because Vicente de Paul Andrade opposed the change in wording and despatched to Rome the *Exquisitio historico*, the Latin version of García Icazbalceta's *Letter*. In response, the bishops sent a fifty-page collective statement defending the Guadalupe tradition and their petition.[15] They also used a Latin translation of the *Nican mopohua* published in 1887 by Agustín de la Rosa, which was accompanied by a defence in Latin of the tradition.[16] The text of the new office was prepared by Esteban Anticoli, aided by a canon of Guadalajara and, as the Jesuit later confessed, the petition was greatly assisted by the support of three Roman Jesuits, whom he supplied with persuasive answers to all the objections raised by 'the Devil's Advocate'.[17]

The upshot of these negotiations was that in March 1894 the Congregation of Rites approved a new office in which it was stated that the Virgin Mary appeared to Juan Diego in 1531 'according to ancient and constant tradition' and that, 'in the same form in which she appeared at Tepeyac, the image of Saint Mary today is seen marvellously painted on the cape of the Indian Juan Diego'. A key agent in securing the new office was Francisco Plancarte y Navarrete, a nephew of José Antonio Plancarte, who had obtained a doctorate at the Gregorian University and was thus familiar with the Roman way of handling such matters. His uncle wrote to congratulate him, adding: 'You have deserved the gratitude of the Church, the *patria* and the family. You have indelibly engraved our name in the annals of the most holy Virgin of Guadalupe.'[18]

Although Archbishop Labastida died in 1891, his successor, Próspero María Alarcón (1891–1910), continued to support both the coronation project and its director, even if

Plate 28   Gonzalo Carrasco, SJ, *The Coronation of Our Lady of Guadalupe on 12 October 1895*

as late as April 1895 the canons of the college at Tepeyac signed a collective protest against the plan for such elaborate proceedings, arguing that 'the image should not be crowned, since God has already crowned it'.[19] But, on 8 September 1895, Plancarte was installed as abbot of the college and as bishop-elect of Constancia *in partibus infidelium*. The ceremonies he now directed could not have been more grand. Thanks to the Reform Laws it was no longer possible for the Church to stage any public processions through the streets of the capital. But the loss of public space was more than compensated by an extension in time, which was to say, the entire month of October was taken up with pilgrims arriving by train from dioceses across the republic, so that every day was marked by high mass and sermon and lesser liturgical functions. It was thus a moment when the entire Mexican Church was mobilized to pay homage to its patron, even if when it was learnt that Plancarte had invited foreign bishops to participate in the celebration, *The Guadalupan Kingdom*, a small review, protested that 'The Virgin of Guadalupe, our compatriot, our Mother and our support, does not wish to be American; she is ours and ours alone.'[20] But, on 12 October, there assembled at the sanctuary twenty-two Mexican archbishops and bishops, fourteen prelates from the United States, and another three from Quebec, Havana and Panama. The arrival of these foreign bishops created a stir in Mexico City since, rather than being lodged in hotels, they were welcomed into 'the homes of wealthy Catholics of our cultured society'. Thanks to the intervention of the bishop of Chilapa, Ramón Ibarra y González, a number of Indians were also invited to attend, albeit with the proviso that they dressed in their own costumes, so that the actual coronation was witnessed by twenty-eight natives of Cuautitlan, Juan Diego's birthplace, all dressed 'in their own clothes and with the greatest cleanliness'.[21]

At the conclusion of the celebrations, a banquet was offered in thanks to Plancarte, who took the opportunity to affirm that the magnificence of the ceremonies had demonstrated for all the world to see that 'Mexico is an eminently Catholic country' and that 'it constitutes an eminently Guadalupan people'. Was not this revival in religious sentiment a portent that Mexico might be destined at last to become 'a happy, powerful and great nation'?[22] Viewed from the immediate perspective, the coronation expressed the public resurrection of the Mexican Church after the long-drawn-out agony of the Liberal Reform and the French Intervention. During the civil war of those years the Mexican bishops had been charged with treason, with being guilty of associating with a foreign prince and his European forces. But in 1895 the bishops once again claimed to speak and act on behalf of the Mexican nation when they paid homage to the Virgin of Tepeyac. Yet, if we compare the coronation with the earlier acclamation of the Guadalupe as patron, then a striking difference is readily apparent. In 1746 it had been the city councils as well as the cathedral chapters which had commissioned the four delegates, two laymen and two priests to swear the oath accepting the Guadalupe as the principal patron of New Spain. In 1895, however, thanks to the separation of Church and State, the coronation was initiated and celebrated by the Mexican bishops without formal consultation with the laity or any civil authority. Moreover, in 1746, the constituted bodies of Catholic Mexico, both civil and ecclesiastical, had assumed the authority to elect their patron, and only after the matter was concluded did they seek the approval of Rome. By contrast, in 1886, the archbishops petitioned the Holy See for permission to proceed with the coronation. What the comparison thus reveals is the extraordinary difference between a confident Catholic society which had generated a Marian cult peculiar to New Spain and a Mexican hierarchy which paraded its dependence on Rome so as to evade political intrusion or lay influence.

II

During the entire month of October 1895 sermons were preached in the sanctuary at Tepeyac, delivered on behalf of the dioceses and religious Orders of the republic. Their texts were printed in the *Album* prepared by Victoriano Agüeros and taken together afford a remarkable conspectus of the theological doctrines, the historical experience and the patriotic sentiments evoked by the Mexican Virgin. In the opening sermon, Fortino Hipólito Vera, by then the first bishop of Cuernavaca, praised Archbishop Labastida for his courage in organizing the ceremonies where the image of Guadalupe would be crowned as queen of both a city and a nation. So too, he lauded José Antonio Plancarte as 'the providential man' who had brought the renovation of the sanctuary to a successful conclusion.[23] To gauge the depth of his sentiments, however, it is best to examine the sermon Vera preached before the image in the Capuchin chapel on 12 December 1890, since it was then that he saluted the Virgin as 'the Ark of the eternal Testament, reconciling the Mexican nation with heaven'. Was she not the Woman of the Apocalypse, engaged in a perennial battle against Satan, be it in the human form either of idolatry of modern atheism? As an historian and apologist he was at pains to emphasize that the apparition of the Miraculous Image was 'one of the Mexican ecclesiastical traditions that rests on the most solid foundations'. If no Catholic could deny the doctrines of Christ's Resurrection and the Virgin's Assumption, so equally no Catholic Mexican could deny 'the heavenly origin of this beautiful painting', which was 'the most perfect image of Mary's Immaculate Conception'. The first 'hermitage' had been built by Zumárraga, and from then on the cult rested on a 'true and unanswerable tradition'. Although missionaries such as Las Casas and Zumárraga had defended the Indians from the conquerors' exploitation, nevertheless, it was through the Virgin's intervention rather than by their efforts that Paul III pronounced in favour of the natives' rationality and freedom. Thereafter, both Spaniards and Indians came to Tepeyac so that 'this sanctuary was the meeting place where conquerors and the conquered were reconciled', out of which process was to emerge 'the present Mexican nationality'. If at one time the disorders of the nineteenth century and the influx of atheism from abroad had led many to fear that 'Mexico might be erased from the catalogue of nations', devotion to Our Lady of Guadalupe was now on the increase so that, thanks to her protection, 'Mexican nationality' and the 'Mexican *patria*' had been saved. As always, the union of religion and patriotism was an enduring feature of such sermons.[24]

It was José de Jesús Ortiz, the first bishop of Chihuahua, who exclaimed that 'when we pass under the lintels of this precinct for the first time, we who come from distant lands' experienced the same sensations as pilgrims entering the Holy Land. To walk where Christ had walked or to pray where the Virgin had appeared provided an unforgettable experience of sacred places. As Jacob said, when he saw the ladder of angels at Bethel, 'How fearsome is this place.' As a rule, so the bishop observed, the genuine works of God passed through three stages: 'humbleness and even scorn in their beginning; slowness in their development; and an admirable fertility in their results'. God sows the seed, waits patiently for the crop to grow, and finally reaps an abundant harvest. Turning to history, Ortiz declared that God had chosen Spain to bring the gospel to Mexico and had then allowed Mary to appear so as to confirm 'the providential mission of the conquering nation and with the mantle of her protection cover the conquered race'. Here in the sanctuary at Tepeyac were to be found the Tables of the Law and the Ark of the Covenant which bound Mary to Mexico, so that the celebration of her cult was a measure of 'the true progress and the enduring greatness of the *patria*'. For all that, the bishop frankly confessed that, since Independence, the country had been torn apart by civil war, public immorality and infidelity, and that virtually nothing had been done to help the Indians, Mary's 'favourite race'.[25]

Much the same note was struck by Atenógenes Silva, the bishop of Colima, who grandly announced that he had come to the Mexican Sinai to contemplate 'the bush that burns without being consumed' and 'to read the laws and destiny of my *patria*, not in tables of stone, but in the sublime monument of Guadalupan supernaturalism'. Through her apparition Mary had not merely converted the Indians, but had established 'the fundamental law of our history, the starting point and base of Mexican civilization'. Our Lady of Guadalupe should govern the social constitution of the country and give the lead in both the arts and science. When Mexicans came to Tepeyac as pilgrims, they were united in their minds and hearts, bound together by a common love so that 'the coronation is the solemn plebiscite of the religious and social kingdom of most Holy Mary in Mexico'. In effect, Silva here appears to have echoed not merely Miguel Sánchez but also Ernest Renan, who had defined a nation as a daily plebiscite.[26]

A Spanish Dominican, Rafael Menéndez, recalled that the conversion of Mexico was wrought by the glorious labours of Franciscans and Dominicans who had preached the gospel to the Indians. In an epoch when Martin Luther, that Dragon of the Apocalypse, had devastated Europe through heresy and war, Spain, 'the chosen nation', had defended the Catholic faith in Europe and had promoted its expansion into the New World. As a result, the image of Guadalupe in Mexico could now be ranked alongside the Marian images of Montserrat, Pilar, Loreto and Lourdes.[27] A similar note was struck by Manuel Díaz Rayón, a Jesuit, who recalled that both Benedict XIV and Leo XIII had applied to the image the phrase taken from Psalm 147, 'Non fecit taliter omni natione.' But this salutation could be applied to other images since 'Loreto is the *non fecit taliter* of Italy' and in France, where the doctrine of the Immaculate Conception had found such a welcome, Lourdes was its *non fecit taliter*. As for Spain, there was the celebrated image of Pilar at Zaragoza, not to mention the Guadalupe of Extremadura. He concluded with familiar scriptural figures, comparing Tepeyac and its image to Solomon's Temple and the Mexicans to the Israelites, since 'do we not also have our temple, our Ark of the Covenant, our book of the Law?'[28]

The compelling attraction of scriptural typology was illustrated by Francisco Campos, the secretary of the bishop of Tulancingo, who declared that he had come to Tepeyac to contemplate an image that St John had seen on Patmos, housed in a sanctuary that could be compared to Solomon's Temple on Mount Zion. But he came with pilgrims to celebrate the sacrifice of the mass, the commemoration of Christ's sacrifice on Calvary, albeit as on Calvary in the presence of Mary. As for her 'heavenly painting', was it not 'the Ark of the Covenant' since 'it is and will always be for Mexicans what the bush on Horeb was for Moses, which, burning without being consumed, was the mercy seat from whence God communicated with his servants'? As Moses had led the Children of Israel out of Egypt, so in 1531, Mary had led her Mexican children out from the land of idolatry. If Mary had given the Mexicans their 'Christian civilization' and national independence, her image of Guadalupe still constituted the physical sign 'of the covenant which the Nation has celebrated with heaven and the most authentic testimony that this Divine Lady will always see us as her children'.[29]

Not all sermons adopted such an exuberant tone. Speaking on behalf of the priests of Mexico City, Antonio J. Paredes asserted that, through its history, the Church had always been sustained by the blood of its martyrs and afflicted by the desertion of its unfaithful children. Despite the efforts of the mendicants, no progress on the conversion of the Indians had been achieved until the apparition since 'the very Virgin Mother of God wished to be our apostle'. What had been the experience of the Church under Spanish rule but a perpetual struggle between viceroys and bishops and between the secular and regular clergy? Moreover, from the expulsion of the Jesuits in 1767 until the Liberal Reform's seizure of Church funds and the closure of the convents, the clergy had been persecuted, so that it needed 'the harp of Jeremiah to paint the sufferings of this Martyr Church'. And yet, despite these afflictions, the Church had triumphed in its defeat and gloried in its humiliation and was now once more growing in strength with all the new dioceses and churches. Were persecution to return, the Church would survive and, through suffering, renew its growth.[30]

A further discordant note was added by José María Vilaseca, who spoke on behalf of the missions of the Josephite Fathers, since he asserted that across the republic, in both the north and the south, there were still many Indians who were sunk in idolatry, living like animals. Had not the bishop of Puebla recently admitted that, in the mountains of his diocese, 'there are savages, there are idolatrous Indians'? What was needed was prayer, but also contributions to fund the missions to such peoples as the Tarahumaras.[31] But this practical emphasis found little resonance in other preachers, who preferred to celebrate the 'Thaumaturgic Image' of Guadalupe as the 'Empress of the Mexican Church' and even cited Altamirano's essay as proof of the cult's importance for 'Mexican nationality'.[32]

It was Luis Silva, a canon of Guadalajara, who expressed the clergy's hopes for reconciliation with government. To be sure, he started on a conventional theme when he boldly compared the coronation with its assembled bishops to the Church Council at Ephesus, which had acclaimed Mary as the Mother of God. As in ancient Jerusalem, so now 'the Holy Ark of the traditional and historical grandeur of the Mexican nation' had entered the renovated sanctuary, the new Zion. Preaching on behalf of the diocese of Chiapas, he recalled that its peoples had once been inspired by the presence of 'that heavenly angel in bishop's form, Fray Bartolomé de las Casas'. But he struck a contemporary note when he argued that, thanks to the apparition of the Virgin as a 'most beautiful brown lady', not merely had idolatry been vanquished, but 'the peoples united and formed a nation and from their moral and religious progress there came the material progress that was then possible'. Had not Miguel Hidalgo, the 'great father of the *patria*', fought for independence under 'his glorious Guadalupan flag', the final achievement of which was made possible only by the fusion of races? But thereafter, the destructive influence of the French Revolution, with its wanton betrayal of the Christian principles of liberty, equality and fraternity, had thrust Mexico into civil war and the persecution of religion. And yet it was Catholicism which had created the Mexican nation and, without acknowledgement of its influence, the country could not survive. He concluded with an appeal for the progress that might come from:

> The long-awaited conciliation of our beliefs with our institutions; thus founding among us a true Christian republic, in which from the absolute union of the Mexican people there shall come the progress of religion, the prestige of our nation, the respect and veneration of public power, the enlargement of our industry, commerce and the material goods which form our legitimate grandeur; and that in harmony with our glorious past the future shall offer an era of well-being, in which tomorrow we shall be brothers, all Catholics and all happy.

In this striking conclusion can be observed the longing of so many priests for a Catholic republic in which Church and State might preside over a united Mexican nation.[33]

The task of preaching before the assembled bishops on 12 October, when the image was crowned, fell to Crescencio Carrillo y Ancona, the bishop of Yucatán and a learned Church historian. Although illness prevented his appearance, the printed version of his sermon revealed the exalted quality of his Marian rhetoric. He took as his scriptural text the verse from the Song of Songs: 'Come with me from Lebanon, my spouse, with me from Lebanon.' If it was the Vicar of God on earth, the pope, who had commanded the coronation, it was the Divine Spouse of Mary, the Holy Spirit, who now crowned her as Queen. Although only God was to be adored, Mary was the most honoured of all creation, the queen of angels and saints, the Co-redemptrix, since 'God is the Father, the Son and Spouse of Mary.' It had been the Virgin who had inspired Columbus in his determination to cross the Atlantic; she who had moved Queen Isabella to assist him; and she the patron to whom Columbus had dedicated the lands he discovered on 12 October 1492, the feast day of Our Lady of Pilar, the symbol of the Spanish Church. In her apparition in Mexico, so Carrillo y Ancona argued, Mary had identified herself as Coatlallopeuh, the Nahuatl for 'conqueror of the serpent', a title which had been assimilated to the Spanish title of Guadalupe. She had appeared to Juan Diego in the likeness of the Woman of the Apocalypse seen by St John on Patmos, a likeness imprinted on Juan Diego's cape and preserved across the centuries by means of a perpetual miracle.[34]

In a hyperbole worthy of Carlos María de Bustamante, Carrillo y Ancona suggested that the bones of all the thirty-two past archbishops of Mexico would rise from their graves to witness the coronation of 'the Queen of the Mexican People, the Celestial Empress of Christian America . . . Patron of our nationality and independence'. Acting as Mother, Mary had come to Tepeyac to end the tyranny and idolatry of the Aztecs and to halt the cruelties of the Spanish conquerors, seeking thus to unite the two races through religion so that in this way, 'the truly American race was born'. Referring to Mexico's national flag, Carrillo y Ancona declared that Our Lady of Guadalupe was 'the symbolic eagle of our heroic emblem, an eagle which tamed and destroyed the irresistible force of the serpent of perfidy against both God and the *patria*, the serpent of apostasy, division, discord and of all ruin and evil'. If the people of Israel had been led by the Ark of the Covenant to become a 'free and great nation', observing God's Law, 'so also shall we in this portentous Guadalupan Effigy, the true Ark of which the ancient was only but a shadow and a figure, an Ark which within the bosom of the true Church assures us in the presence of the Lord our possession of the promised land'. Noting that the Virgin's crown was adorned by twelve stars, symbolic of the twelve tribes, apostles and gates of the City of God, he praised its suitability for the 'Ark of the Divine Mexican Covenant'. Nowhere was this bishop's patriotism more manifest than in his conclusion, when he saluted Our Lady of Guadalupe as 'the foundation and placenta, the pedestal and coronation of our history and nation, of our Church and culture, of our Independence and of all our hopes in time and eternity'.[35]

If these coronation sermons be compared with the panegyrical orations which celebrated the Guadalupe as patron of New Spain, they reveal the complete abandonment of the neo-platonic theology of sacred images which the preachers of the baroque era had taken from the Greek Fathers. So too, there was not the slightest suggestion that Mary was present in her image in the same way that Christ was present in the Eucharist. By contrast, preachers time and again defined the image as the Mexican Ark of the Covenant, Tepeyac as a new Zion or another Sinai, and the sanctuary as the equivalent of Solomon's Temple. In effect, the typological figures which Miguel Sánchez had first applied to the Guadalupe were still enthusiastically employed. But few of these preachers had read Sánchez and, hence, did not recall that he had referred to Juan Diego as another Moses, bringing down from Tepeyac the Tables of the New Law, which was to say, the image of Guadalupe in the form of flowers. In these sermons, Juan Diego was conspicuous only by his absence. Of course, he was present in the sanctuary, shaped as a marble statue, but preachers did not dwell upon his moral qualities or indeed present him as a figure of much interest or consequence.

Where the sermons echoed earlier nineteenth-century preoccupations was in their insistence that the apparitions marked a radical disjuncture in Mexican history, in which the Virgin led the native peoples out of idolatry into the promised land of the Church. Emphasis was also put on the Virgin's role in reconciling the Spanish conquerors and the Indians and thereby promoting the emergence of the Mexican nation, based upon racial fusion. In this invocation of the nation as the ideal result of the apparitions, these bishops and priests demonstrated the degree to which they shared the assumptions of their Liberal contemporaries. But where their patriotism found clearest expression was in their conviction that Mary had chosen Mexico from among the peoples of the world for her especial protection. Although comparisons with Lourdes and, to a lesser extent, with Loreto and Pilar indicated the preachers' anxiety to enlist the Guadalupe in the contemporary efflorescence of Marian devotion in Europe, they all firmly retained the conviction that Mexico was an Elect Nation. Such had been the afflictions of the Mexican Church, however, that if Our Lady of Guadalupe was thanked for assuring the survival of Mexico as an independent nation, nowhere was it postulated that the Mexicans might play a special role in the Catholic destiny of the world. The prophecies of Carranza were long since forgotten.

In the *Album* of the coronation were printed poetic effusions and excerpts from the press. In an article published in *The Grain of Sand*, entitled 'The Great Day of our *Patria*', Santiago Ramírez framed a comparison between the events on Calvary and Tepeyac which, far more than any bishop's sermon, demonstrated the degree to which the apparitions could be interpreted in a radical fashion.

Calvary was the theatre of the Redemption of the world; Tepeyac was that of the regeneration of Mexico; Calvary stained its rocks with blood, Tepeyac pacified its rocks with flowers; Calvary immortalizes its name with the history of the death of a God, Tepeyac has the immortal history of a people; Calvary was covered with the shadows of a foreseen night so as to hide a crime, Tepeyac blushed with the rays of a foreseen dawn so as to illumine a prodigy; Calvary lent its soil for a scaffold to be raised, Tepeyac gave its soil for the construction of a sanctuary; in Calvary blasphemies were changed into praises, in Tepeyac prayers changed into consolation; in Calvary unbelievers went into ecstasy saying, 'truly this was the Son of God, in Tepeyac the unbeliever confesses that, 'truly this is the Mother of men'; Calvary saw Jesus perish, Tepeyac saw Mary appear; and this sweet, tender, divine Mary in Calvary became the Mother of all men and in Tepeyac the Mother of the Mexicans.[36]

To a careful reader there was nothing here that was specifically unorthodox; but this conjuncture of Calvary and Tepeyac was as audacious in its way as any of the speculations of the preachers of the eighteenth century and, by its very presumption of an equivalence between the crucifixion and the apparition, clearly suggested that Tepeyac had been the scene of a new revelation.

III

From 23 February 1888 until 30 September 1895 the image of Guadalupe was placed in the Capuchin chapel.[37] Only after it was installed in the sanctuary did the public become aware that the painting had suffered an alteration. The golden crown which had adorned the Virgin's brow since time immemorial had disappeared. But as early as 1887 José de Jesús Cuevas had mentioned its erasure and to interpret such a strange, inexplicable occurrence, had invited his readers to consider that in each succeeding century the Virgin had wrought a 'public and solemn miracle' which confirmed the truth of her apparition. He then speculated: 'Is this an eloquent marvel, through which the most holy Virgin shows that she accepts the piety and love with which the Mexican races would wish to crown her?' Which was to say, that it was the Virgin herself who had doffed her crown so as to allow the Mexicans to crown her anew. But Cuevas raised a further possibility when he queried: 'Does this marvel prepare the way for another miracle in which, after being crowned by her children, the crown she once had will reappear with a new brilliance?' Obviously, these sublime musings did not satisfy the Liberal press, which waxed indignant about the injury done to an ancient national monument.[38] For their part, the canons of the collegiate chapter at Tepeyac, led by Vicente de Paul Andrade, complained bitterly and accused José Antonio Plancarte of having commissioned Salomé Piña, a well-known painter involved in the sanctuary's renovation, to remove the crown. It was on 19 June 1887 that Plancarte wrote to Bishop Carrillo y Ancona that: 'the *inimicus homo*' [the name they gave Andrade] and his companions, in imitation of the soldiers at the sepulchre, have spread the news that Piña and I have erased it'. It was to counter these charges that, prior to the image being returned to the sanctuary, Plancarte assembled a number of witnesses in the Capuchin chapel, who all solemnly swore before a notary public that 'no crown existed on her and that there was no trace that it had ever been there'.[39] By then Plancarte had been installed as abbot of the college of canons and brooked no opposition.

During the sermons preached during October, it was Carrillo y Ancona who boldly admitted that, from the moment the coronation project had been launched, which was to say, since 1887, the Virgin's crown was no longer to be seen. Following Cuevas, he surmised that it was as if the Virgin had said: 'I only want your crown.' Such was her power that 'she appeared crowned through a miracle and now perhaps by another miracle she is shown without a crown, in order to bear that which her children now offer her'. Here, indeed, was a heavenly occurrence which captured the imagination of many devout priests.[40]

In his *Celestial and Terrestrial or the Two Guadalupan Crowns* (1895), Gabino Chávez admitted that the crown could not have disappeared simply through the effects of time, its gold flaking off, since there were now no traces left. At the same time, he averred that no-one would have dared to alter such a venerated image and, in any case, who could have possessed the skill to erase the crown? His conclusion was peremptory: 'if neither art nor nature has erased the crown, then the Divinity intervened . . . the hand of God' was responsible for altering the image. After all, if God continued to perform miracles at Lourdes, why should he not work a miracle in Mexico? To be sure, there had formed a monstrous alliance of 'Catholics and Protestants, masons and sceptics with Christians', who denied the original apparition, claimed that the image was painted by Marcos, alias Cipac, and who now asserted that it was mere human agency which had removed the crown. But, for Chávez, what the miracle signified was that, in a remarkable act of loving kindness and finesse, the Virgin had laid aside her celestial crown in order to allow her children to offer her a terrestrial crown. Where once the Virgin had triumphed over idolatry and demons through her apparition, she now confounded sceptics and heretics by this miracle. But if sceptics remained obdurate, as when Emile Zola visited Lourdes and failed to recognize its miraculous cures, how could true Catholics refuse to accept 'the marvel of the disappearance of the crown from the Guadalupan canvas as a confirmation of previous marvels: the painting on a rough *ayate*, the liveliness of the colours, and the preservation of the cloth across three-and-a-half centuries'? Chávez concluded by expressing the hope that the Mexican bishops would launch a formal enquiry into the matter and then proceed to 'the canonical authorization of the miracle'.[41]

In the months after the coronation, however, another kind of enquiry occupied the minds of the archbishop and the newly arrived apostolic delegate, Nicolás Averardi. For José Antonio Plancarte not merely stood accused of having arranged the erasure of the Virgin's crown, but was also denounced by the bishop of Zamora, José María Cázares (1878–1908), of improper conduct. The details of the case were wrapped in secrecy, but it was undoubtedly true that, in order to free from paternal authority a young prospective nun in Jacona, Plancarte had married her in a civil ceremony, taking the view that the proceedings had no canonical validity. It was further alleged that he had been alone for a brief time with the young woman. These charges impressed the apostolic delegate and, as a result, he asked Plancarte to resign the bishopric *in partibus infidelium* to which he had been named a year earlier. All this was based on Cázares' accusations without Plancarte being given the opportunity to defend himself, since Averardi refused to initiate a canonical enquiry.[42] After the abbot's death in 1898, Bishop Montes de Oca pronounced the eulogy, recalling that he and Plancarte had been pupils together at St Mary's College, Oscott. He praised him as the 'inspirer' of both the coronation and the renovation of the sanctuary, and paid tribute both to his eloquence as a preacher and his establishment of a congregation of nuns. But he admitted that Plancarte's many achievements had provoked 'waves of envy, calumny, resentment and rancour'. In that eulogy, however, Montes de Oca did not refer to the controversy surrounding the disappearance of the Virgin's crown.[43]

It was left to Mariano Cuevas, the Jesuit historian of the Mexican Church, to assess Plancarte's achievement at Tepeyac. Writing from a twentieth-century perspective, he lamented that Plancarte had not built a new sanctuary rather than renovating the old Church, and sharply criticized the altar and baldachino, describing the design as 'heterogeneous, exotic, lugubrious, and taken as a whole, inferior to the previous one it replaced'.[44] In the *Historical Guadalupan Album of the IV Centenary* (1930), Cuevas noted that Florencia had reported that cherubim had been added to the canvas, only later to be erased. He accepted the observations of Bartolache, plain for anyone to see, that the arabesque designs on the Virgin's tunic did not follow the folds of the cloth and concluded that they were thus later additions. So also, there was evidence that the half moon at the Virgin's feet had been retouched. In a mixture of speculation and bold admission, he added:

> We consider that when the wretched retoucher saw his brush wet with gold, he was carried away and passed from the rays of the sun to paint those arabesques on the tunic of the Virgin. He further painted an objectionable crown, very badly done, without perspective and all on the same plane. Some traces of this crown, which time had almost effaced, still remained in the year 1890. It was these, some say, which were erased by the painter Piña. If that were so, there should not be any mystery about the so-called crown: a man painted it and a man erased it, because it

ought to have been erased for being badly done. In such a case, it was imprudent to have done it secretly, when the chapter had good reasons to take such a necessary and easily understandable measure.[45]

Whereas, in an earlier period, Bartolache had been criticized for indicating the deficiencies in the artistic technique of the Guadalupan image, now the very apologists seized upon those defects as evidence of early additions and used them as a justification for removing the Virgin's crown. In later years, Rafael Aguirre, the disciple of Salomé Piña, confessed on his deathbed that Plancarte had taken the painter to remove the last traces of the crown.[46] What is rarely mentioned is that the frame which surrounded the canvas was lowered to leave almost no space above the Virgin's head, thereby obscuring the effects of the erasure. Obviously, the decision to remove rather than retouch the crown, from which the gold was doubtlessly falling, was inspired by a desire to 'modernize' the image and reinforce its similarity to the nineteenth-century images of the Immaculate Conception which were exhibited at Lourdes and elsewhere.

If Plancarte's reputation was injured by the apostolic delegate's ineptitude, Averardi's handling of the bishop of Tamaulipas, Eduardo Sánchez Camacho, led to that prelate's resignation and public separation from the Roman Church. It will be remembered that in 1886 the bishop had issued a pastoral in which he announced his opposition to the proposed coronation. But when the Roman Inquisition reprimanded him, he had withdrawn all objections, even if subsequently he did not attend the ceremonies at Tepeyac. For his part, Averardi received several secret denunciations of the bishop's personal conduct and expression of opinions. It is clear that Sánchez Camacho had no liking for Rome or its agents and had advised the priests of his diocese to respect the Constitution of 1857 and the government of Porfirio Díaz.[47] The result was that, in 1896, when Averardi called upon him to resign, he wrote a public letter which was soon printed in the Mexican press. There he noted that Carrillo y Ancona had failed to acknowledge that García Icazbalceta had not withdrawn his historical objections to the apparition narrative. Moreover, when the bishop of Yucatán invoked Rome's authority and compared the doctrine of the Immaculate Conception with the Virgin's apparition at Tepeyac, he had confused a universal dogma of the Catholic faith with a belief peculiar to Mexico, so that 'to me the comparison appears blasphemous'. Until he himself had questioned the coronation, he had received universal praise both as priest and bishop, but, since then, he had been denounced by the apparitionists to 'the Roman Inquisition' and condemned as an apostate. As for the scandal he had caused, it would not affect the Indians, who 'always have to look for their Tonantzin, the mother of Huitzilopochtli, and not the Mother of Jesus Christ'. He concluded by announcing his resignation, adding that he proposed 'to separate myself from Rome and its henchmen, so as to live alone and forgotten in some corner

or ravine in the hills and devote myself to cultivating the land, to trade and stock raising, to take care of my personal necessities'.[48] All this controversy between Catholics
was eagerly seized upon by the Liberal press.

In August 1896 the bishops assembled to deliberate in the Fifth Mexican Church
Council. Here is no place to discuss the outcome, other than to note that parish priests
were exhorted to encourage devotion to Our Lady of Guadalupe and were commanded to ensure that in every church in the republic there should be an altar and an
image of 'the patron, queen and mother' of Mexico. After setting forth the arguments
which sustained belief in the apparitions, the bishops cited both the approval of
Benedict XIV and the judgement of the Roman Inquisition in 1888, concluding:

> That the marvellous Apparition, without being a dogma of faith, as might be inter-
> preted by the simple devotion of some pious souls, is an ancient, constant and uni-
> versal tradition of the Mexican Nation, endowed with such characteristics and
> supported by such foundations, that they not only authorize Catholics to believe in
> it, but do not even permit them to contradict it with greater or lesser temerity.

In effect, any further questioning of the historical reality of the Guadalupe tradition
was ruled out of order for all committed Catholics; any discussion of the evidence had
to be based on the premise that the apparitions had occurred.[49]

In the same year of 1896, García Icazbalceta's *Letter* to Labastida was finally
published in its original, Spanish, version and was soon reproduced in Mexican newspapers. Since the Latin translation had already been savaged by Vera and Anticoli,
there was not much more to say about its arguments. However, Agustín de la Rosa
(1824–1907) published a dignified rejoinder, avoiding acrimony, in which he asserted
that without the initial apparition the devotion could never have acquired the extraordinary development it later enjoyed. As was to be expected, he emphasized certain
weaknesses in the *Letter*'s historical arguments, most notably García Icazbalceta's
claim that, prior to Sánchez' book, the devotion had virtually expired. In general,
however, Rosa's points had already been made by earlier apologists.[50] A year later,
in 1897, Esteban Anticoli published yet another book on the Virgin of Tepeyac, in
which he provided some useful information about the development of the cult
over three centuries. On this occasion he refrained from insulting the memory of
García Icazbalceta, albeit printing the text of his letter to Carrillo y Ancona, only then
to note that the historian had persisted in his error of distinguishing the theological
and historical aspects of the question, whereas 'the Apparition is a fact, supernatural
in essence and historical in its existence'.[51]

To understand the emotions of the Catholic laity in these years one has only to turn
to *The Guadalupan Cause: The Last Twenty Years 1875–1895* (1896), written by Juan
Luis Tercero (1837–1905), an obscure lawyer and novelist, resident in Tamaulipas,
who was a strong critic of Bishop Sánchez Camacho. The tone of the book was best

expressed when Tercero called himself an 'old sergeant of the Guadalupan guard' and praised José de Jesús Cuevas as 'a Mexican Bayard', a member of the 'white aristocracy' who, like a Maccabean, had defended the 'Mexican Ark of the Covenant'.[52] In effect, he wrote as an ardent partisan, asserting that the last twenty years were 'like a resurrection', when the five great apologists of the apparition, Anticoli, González, Rosa, Cuevas and Vera, had established the tradition upon immovable foundations. In particular, he praised Anticoli as a great master, who 'has made the *guadalupanos* feel that we are invincible'. Here is no place to pursue Tercero's recapitulation of the apologetics of previous years, save to note his description of Valeriano as 'the Moses of this new Pentateuch . . . the Matthew and Luke of this new Gospel', whose brief narrative he described as 'the great pyramid of the great governor of the Indians'. At the same time, he asserted that, if belief in Christ's resurrection rested on the apostles' testimony, in Mexico 'the great argument of our Guadalupe is the never fully considered marvel of its painting; here abounds the proof of God . . . the great proof is the painting itself'. Despite his fervour, however, Tercero praised García Icazbalceta's 'great book' on Zumárraga, noting that he had never wished his *Letter* to be published and had withdrawn his criticism on receiving Carrillo y Ancona's call for doctrinal submission. Indeed, he cited Montes de Oca's funeral oration and elegy, where that prelate, in elegant verse, promised to protect his memory from the insults of fools. For the rest, he commented on the role of Pedro Losa, archbishop of Guadalajara, and of Rafael Camacho, bishop of Querétaro, in providing the funds for the works of the apologists.[53]

Almost alone among the writers of this epoch, Tercero had read Miguel Sánchez and reiterated his comparison of Our Lady of Guadalupe with the Woman of the Apocalypse, arguing that 'so great a miracle as that of Tepeyac was worthy of being one of the prophetic purposes of the seer of Patmos, which is to say, of the Holy Spirit, who speaks through the prophets'. Accepting Carrillo y Ancona's suggestion that the Nahuatl version of Guadalupe was Coatlallopeuh, 'the conqueror of the serpent', he asserted that, through her apparition, the Virgin had effected the conversion of the Indians as recompense for the losses suffered by the Church in the Protestant Reformation. Since the Virgin had appeared in Tepeyac as the Immaculate Conception, then clearly the events in Mexico prepared the way for the promulgation of that dogma in the nineteenth century and the apparitions of the Virgin at Lourdes. In a remarkable historical comparison, Tercero exclaimed: 'Against Luther and Calvin, the Immaculate of Tepeyac; against Voltaire and Rousseau and the rationalists and Jacobins of today, the Immaculate of Lourdes'. In these exclamations can be observed the degree to which the cult of the Mexican Virgin had been reinforced by the Marian revival in France.[54]

Whereas the clerical apologists hurled their most furious reproaches at other priests and fellow Catholics, by contrast Tercero reserved his worst epithets for the

'Liberals' who still governed Mexico. He lamented that in Mexico 'the triumph of anti-Christian apostasy, of the infernal official atheism', had prevailed for so long, adding: 'all that the hateful Aztec Huitzilopochtli had, the Jacobin Huitzilopochtli has still more'. In theatrical style he declaimed: 'Satan, return to hell. Call yourself Huitzilopochtli or atheistical progress, the Guadalupe, a true and proven marvel, has broken your head twice over.'[55] In effect, he thus portrayed Mexican history as a dualistic struggle fought between the Devil and the Virgin, with Satan embodied both in the Aztec regime and the Liberal State. It was for this reason that he celebrated the coronation, especially since it had occurred at a moment when 'Mexico views with anguish the renovation of a regime' that was as oppressive as any it had experienced.

In Tercero's frantic outcry there can be discerned the deep hurt caused by the expulsion of committed Catholics from public life and the dualistic, almost apocalyptic manner in which they interpreted the political divisions of their country. It was this bitter sense of displacement that accounted for the sudden euphoria evoked by the coronation. If the texts of Tercero and Cuevas be taken together, they can be seen to express more general conclusions. When the bishops resisted the Liberal Reform with such intransigence, it was because they and their flock were convinced that Mexico was an essentially Catholic country. But after their hopes were betrayed and they were driven into exile, the bishops took refuge in Rome and from that vantage point made plans for the revival of religious life. Henceforth, the Mexican Church was to be distinguished by a passionate loyalty to the Vatican, and, stirred by the example set by Antonio Plancarte, despatched its ablest young clerics to be educated in Rome. But whereas the papacy constituted the principle of infallible authority, it was the French Church which offered a living example of religious renewal, and nowhere more so than at Lourdes. The apparitions of the Virgin to Bernadette and the profusion of miracles that confirmed their authenticity offered dramatic proof that the Holy Spirit was still actively present in the Catholic Church. It was the example of Lourdes, as so many sermons attested, that impelled the Mexican bishops to celebrate the coronation of Our Lady of Guadalupe with such splendour. All the doubts and polemics of previous years were set aside during the sudden outpouring of devotion elicited by this event. And if Liberals looked to France to learn how best to incorporate the Mexican republic into the civilization of the nineteenth century, the bishops and other preachers cited the French apparitions as confirmation of the privileged destiny of their country and nation, chosen by the Mother of God for her especial protection.

13

Juan Diego

I

On 12 April 1939 José de Jesús Manríquez y Zárate (1884–1951), the first
bishop of Huejutla, issued a pastoral letter in which he urged the prelates and theologians of the Mexican Church to promote the beatification of Juan Diego. He admitted
that in all the sermons and celebrations dedicated to Our Lady of Guadalupe there
was hardly any mention of 'the fortunate Indian', adding that 'one can hardly explain
the lamentable oblivion in which for over four centuries we have left Juan. It is as if this
man, for being an Indian of pure race, would not have been worthy of our attention.'
Yet were Juan Diego to be canonized eventually, his elevation to the altars would
dignify 'the native race of Mexico', so that both the Church and 'the great Mexican
family' would be immeasurably strengthened by 'the frank and friendly entrance of
these new sons' into the national community.[1] In the autumn of 1939, after his resignation as bishop, Manríquez published a small book entitled *Who was Juan Diego?*, in
which he drew upon his formation in the Gregorian University to argue that the 1666
Statements constituted 'the authentic and juridical proof of the constant tradition' of
the apparitions. If these depositions were presented together with the *Nican mopohua*,
published in 1649 by Laso de la Vega but written by Valeriano in 1544, they afforded
more than sufficient testimony for a beatification cause in the Roman Congregation
of Saints. Did they not reveal that Juan Diego was 'a predestined man' chosen by Mary
for 'the providential mission' of acting as the 'intercessor and mediator' between the
Virgin and the Mexican people? Theological scrutiny of these records demonstrated
that the Indian possessed all the virtues required for beatification, since not merely
had he faithfully responded to the Virgin's requests, but he had also passed the last
seventeen years of his life engaged in prayer and in helping all those natives who
came to seek his assistance. Once again, Manríquez argued that honouring Juan Diego
would invigorate the Church by the entrance of 3 million Indians, who would then
abandon their lingering mistrust of the clergy, born of centuries of exploitation. Since

'the Guadalupan fact' was the very basis of 'our true nationality', his eventual canonization would give 'dignity to a whole race, the establishment of a new nationality and the creation of a new *patria*'. In both his pastoral and his book, Manríquez justified opening the process in Rome by citing the comparable case of Joan of Arc, who, after five centuries of neglect, had been canonized in 1920 as the result of historical enquiry into her reputation and life.[2]

If Manríquez' imperious intervention was destined to transform the Guadalupan tradition, it was because his pastoral was a deeply meditated response to the social upheaval and bitter conflict between Church and State engendered by the Mexican Revolution of 1910–29. He wrote his pastoral in San Antonio, Texas, where he ate 'the bitter bread of exile' for no less than seventeen years, the price he paid for defiant resistance to the anti-clerical policies of Plutarco Elías Calles (1924–8) and his successors. At the height of the conflict he had publicly denounced that president as a liar and a Jacobin who sought to destroy the freedom of the Church. In a pastoral written in 1931, he had passionately lamented that the Church had become 'ugly, vilified and subjugated to the sons of darkness', suffering 'a true Babylonian captivity', protected only by the Virgin of Guadalupe, 'our liberator and defender of our faith and nationality'. A devoted bishop, who had won the affection of Indian communities by his formation of native catechists and who opened schools in the remote valleys of the Huasteca, Manríquez was honoured for his intransigence by all those priests and laymen who fought in the great Catholic rebellion of 1926–9, later known as the *Cristiada*, the crusade of Christ the King.[3]

To understand the context of that conflict it is necessary to recall that the reconciliation between Church and State, so carefully arranged by Archbishop Labastida and Porfirio Díaz, provided the bishops with the opportunity to renovate the institutions and the practices of Mexican Catholicism. The hierarchy met in national conferences to pronounce on social issues and, in the parishes, the clergy opened schools and often took the lead in organizing charitable causes. At a different level, on 24 August 1910, the hierarchy obtained from Pius X the proclamation of Our Lady of Guadalupe as patron of all Latin America.[4] So evident was the good will of Díaz that, on 17 September 1910, a banner of the Guadalupe, allegedly once used by Hidalgo's army, was paraded through the streets of Mexico City at the head of a military procession which escorted a carriage bearing the uniforms of José María Morelos, whose relics had been returned by the Spanish government. This spectacle formed part of the centenary celebration of the Insurgency of 1810. The occasion was also marked by the dedication of the imposing column of independence and the unveiling of statues of Alexander von Humboldt and Louis Pasteur, presented respectively by the German and French governments. But it was the return of the relics of Morelos which aroused the enthusiasm of the crowds, since the sight of Hidalgo's banner caused the populace to shout: 'Long live Our Lady of Guadalupe.' The *Official Chronicle* (1911) edited by

Genaro García commented that 'there was no-one who did not incline their heads before the sacred image of the first banner of independence. The religion of liberty fused all beliefs and amalgamated all consciences; the heroic past reconciled all antagonisms and love of country soared above all other loves.'[5] Had not the Mexican Virgin guided all the insurgent Fathers of the Country, not least Morelos, a mestizo and hence a 'genuine representative of Mexican nationality', assisting them in their moments of despair and assuring their victory?

Hardly had the celebrations of 1910 finished than Francisco Madero rebelled and within a few months drove Porfirio Díaz into exile, thereby unleashing social forces he proved unable to control. Here is no place to follow the cycle of civil war and struggle for power which constituted the Mexican Revolution. Suffice it to note that, in the congressional elections of 1912, a substantial Catholic party emerged, based chiefly in states such as Jalisco and Guanajuato, which actively opposed Madero's presidency, since he was more inclined to take counsel with spirits than listen to bishops.[6] There can be little doubt that some Catholics welcomed the brutal coup of General Victoriano Huerta. It was during his brief tenure of power that, on 6 January 1914, the bishops assembled in the capital's cathedral to dedicate Mexico to the Sacred Heart of Jesus, crowning an image of the Saviour, albeit with a symbolic crown of thorns. In this ceremony, which was attended by two generals, there first sounded in Mexico the cry of *Viva Cristo Rey*, 'Long live Christ the King!' Here was a devotion which had waxed strongly in nineteenth-century Europe and nowhere more so than in France, where the sanctuary of Sacré Cœur in Montmartre was built to express Catholic defiance of the secularizing policies of the Third Republic.[7]

In November 1914, after Huerta's defeat, the banner of the Guadalupe was once more carried through the streets of Mexico City, albeit on this occasion by the peasant followers of Emiliano Zapata. Moreover, many of these Indians from Morelos subsequently visited Tepeyac, where they knelt in the sanctuary before the mother of their country, venerating the Virgin as the symbol of their struggle for justice and land. But, when the capital was taken by the constitutionalist armies led by Alvaro Obregón and Venustiano Carranza, the clergy were subjected to severe harassment, since 157 priests were arrested, forty foreign clerics expelled, and a forced loan of half a million pesos demanded from those who remained. During the years of civil war, many bishops left the country or went into hiding and priests from rural districts took refuge in the cities.[8] Churches were at times desecrated and other church buildings were seized. The radical anti-clericalism of the victorious northern coalition found expression in the Constitution of 1917, which stripped all religious associations of a juridical personality and hence denied their legal right to administer property. The 'monastic Orders' were prohibited and all religious intervention in education strictly forbidden. No minister of religion could vote, still less express any opinion on public issues. Not merely was the federal government designated as the owner of all church buildings, but State authorities were given the right to regulate the number of ministers and churches in their respective jurisdictions.[9] In effect, the Constitution subjected the Catholic Church to whatever policy the revolutionary regime chose to adopt and stripped its bishops, clergy and institutions of any legal redress. Here was a system that was bound to end in violence.

With the accession of Obregón as president in 1920 a determined effort was made to restore stability and to reconcile warring factions. Any number of intellectuals, led by José Vasconcelos, enlisted in the service of the revolutionary State. Such had been the extent of popular participation in the preceding strife that it now became imperative to launch a nationalist ideology to justify both the civil wars and the authoritarian character of the regime by advocating policies such as land distribution and popular education, designed to incorporate the masses into the Mexican nation. The pre-hispanic civilizations were defined as the foundation of national history and the contemporary Indian communities were assisted by encouragement of their handicrafts and agriculture. At the same time, however, this emphasis upon the Indian basis of Mexican nationality was accompanied by a strident anti-clericalism, so that the religious rites and festivities of rural communities were condemned as obstacles to social progress. In effect, Church and State were locked in mortal combat, not merely over the role of the clergy in society but, more importantly, over the very definition and character of the Mexican nation.[10]

Under Obregón, Catholic opinion was profoundly shocked when, on 14 November 1921, a member of the presidential secretariat left a bomb to explode before the high altar of the sanctuary at Tepeyac, albeit failing to shatter the crystal frame which protected the Virgin's image. By way of defiance, in January 1923, the first stone was placed for what was destined to be a vast statue of Christ the King, built on the peak of Cubilete, which overlooks the plains of the Bajío, near the city of León, a Catholic stronghold. But it was President Calles who, on 2 July 1926, issued decrees which thrust Mexico once again into civil war. For he imposed heavy fines and terms of imprisonment on all persons who infringed the Constitution's prohibition of religious education, the maintenance of religious Orders, and the organization of Catholic trade unions. On 31 July 1926 the bishops responded to these laws by placing the republic under interdict, which is to say, they suspended all celebration of mass and other religious services and left the churches bereft of the Eucharist, Christ's absence expressed by tabernacle doors left open. Angered by this challenge to his authority, Calles exiled all bishops who could be found, leaving but a few in hiding.[11]

In the summer of 1926 bands of rural Catholics moved into rebellion, soon to carry banners of the Virgin of Guadalupe on which were inscribed the words, *Viva Cristo Rey*. They were supported by urban and middle-class Catholics organized into the League for the Defence of Religious Freedom, and it was the League which provided the insurgents with its commander, General Enrique Gorostieta. One feature of the

Plate 29   A Cristero flag, c. 1926

rebellion was the strong support offered by Catholic women who, at times, risked their lives in carrying information and supplies. If most priests fled to the cities, some joined the rebellion and a few became local leaders. For their part, in November 1926, the bishops issued a joint declaration that 'after political means are exhausted, armed defence against unjust aggression of a tyrannical power' was justified and

Plate 30   Cristero mass at Coalcomán, 12 December 1928

indeed constituted an unalienable natural right. But many prelates disapproved of
the rebellion, since it was often undisciplined and marred by brutality. The Vatican
remained silent but eventually supported those bishops who sought an accommoda-
tion with the government. In the event, it required the intervention of the American
ambassador, Dwight Morrow, not to mention Obregón's assassination by a Catholic
zealot, to effect a settlement. In June 1929, Leopoldo Ruíz y Flores, archbishop of
Morelia (1912–41) and newly appointed apostolic delegate, together with Pascual Díaz
y Barreto, the Jesuit bishop of Tabasco, negotiated with Calles and Emilio Portes Gil,
the current president, and obtained an arrangement, an *arreglo*, under which all rebels
were promised amnesty if they laid down their arms. The Constitution was left un-
modified; but, in return for the resumption of religious services, the president agreed
not to meddle with the strictly religious activities of the bishops and clergy.[12]

By this time, about 80,000 individuals had lost their lives as a consequence of the
Cristiada, roughly one Cristero for every two federal soldiers. In 1929 Gorostieta still
had about 50,000 followers, but they were poorly armed, often short of ammunition
and, despite defeating federal expeditions, unable to take any large cities. The infor-
mal settlement agreed between Ruíz y Flores and Calles dismayed both the League for
the Defence of Religious Freedom and the Cristero leaders who had led the rebellion,

and with good reason, since, once they laid down their arms, many of these leaders were assassinated. By then, Bishop Manríquez had become an ardent supporter of both the League and the Cristiada, and when he learnt of the 1929 settlement he openly confessed his dismay, observing bitterly that such a transaction with the enemies of Christ bore all the signs of apostasy. His refusal to accept the *modus vivendi* meant that he remained in exile until 1944, obliged to renounce his bishopric in 1939.[13]

In the long run, the Cristiada achieved its objectives. The willingness of so many Catholics to lay down their lives in defence of religious freedom strengthened the Church and allowed it to rebuild and extend its institutions. In years to come, new religious Orders were created, schools and even universities opened, dioceses were divided and more parishes established. Even so, much of this expansion came after 1940 when President Manuel Avila Camacho announced that he was a 'believer' and chose not to apply the anti-clerical articles of the Constitution. A steady flow of priests was assured by the foundation of the Moctezuma inter-diocesan seminary in New Mexico, 1937–72, which was mainly financed by the Catholic bishops of the United States and administered by Mexican Jesuits.[14] But with the experience of the 1895 coronation in mind, it was to the Virgin of Guadalupe that the Mexican bishops looked when they sought to re-establish the Church as the spiritual leader of the nation. Here, then, was the context in which Manríquez launched his dramatic call for the beatification of Juan Diego.

To mobilize popular support for the Church, in 1929 the new archbishop of Mexico, Pascual Díaz y Barreto (1929–36), appointed architects to renovate the sanctuary at Tepeyac which, by then, enjoyed the status of a basilica. To render it fit for the celebration of the Fourth Centenary of the apparitions, it was decided to repair the vaults, move the high altar back into the apse, eliminate the open crypt and decorate the walls and vaults with mosaics. A large new painting was commissioned which depicted Archbishop Labastida giving Plancarte the papal authorization for the coronation, surrounded by bishops and canons, with portraits of Boturini, Leo XIII and Anticoli, hung from the walls of the chamber where the ceremony took place. By then, the image itself, which had been hidden during the Cristiada and replaced by a copy, was reinstalled. To emphasize the significance of the Fourth Centenary, diocesan pilgrimages were organized throughout the preceding year culminating in a grand ceremony on 12 December 1931, which was attended by most bishops, members of the diplomatic corps and numerous Indians dressed in their traditional costumes. If all this were not enough, on 12 December 1933, Francisco Orozco y Jiménez, archbishop of Guadalajara (1913–36), presided over the much-delayed celebration of the Virgin of Tepeyac as patron of all Latin America, rites staged in St Peter's in Rome and blessed by the presence of the pope and many prelates from Central and South America. Such were the resources then available that work on the entire area of the sanctuary continued until 1938 and were estimated to have cost some 2.3 million pesos.[15]

The taste of Mexican prelates for such events was further manifested in October 1945 when Luis María Martínez, archbishop of Mexico (1936–56), presided over the commemoration of the fiftieth anniversary of the Virgin's coronation. Such was the New World's relative immunity from the ravages of the Second World War that no fewer than twenty-eight archbishops and bishops from the United States attended, accompanied by another six from Canada and eleven from Latin America. A high point in these proceedings was the voice of Pius XII, broadcast in the basilica, recalling that fifty years before, 'the noble Indian Mother of God' had been acclaimed as 'Empress of America and Queen of Mexico', a title he repeated at the close of his message. Moreover, the pope asserted that 'on the mantle of Juan Diego, as tradition records, brushes which were not of here below left painted the sweetest image that the corrosive work of the centuries would marvellously respect'. So too, despite the recent persecution in Mexico, the Catholic faith remained strong, inspired no doubt by the bravery with which men had died in its defence, uttering the cries: 'Long live Christ the King! Long live the Virgin of Guadalupe!' If these words more than satisfied expectations, it was the presence of the apostolic legate, Cardinal J. M. Rodrigo Villenueve, archbishop of Quebec, which aroused public enthusiasm. The first prince of the Church to visit Mexico, he was gratified by his warm reception and in return praised Mexicans for their heroism and their aptitude for the arts and sciences; predicted a 'brilliant destiny' for the country; and saluted Mexico City as 'the Athens of the New World'. By and large, the Mexican press lavished praise on the event, since a leading newspaper described the proceedings as an example of 'civilized and human coexistence', so that, at a time when much of Europe was governed by sectarian obscurantism, 'our country is a light, an island of civilized tolerance'.[16]

The rapidity with which the Church appeared once more on the public stage alarmed Liberal opinion, especially when a foreign cardinal was escorted by a cavalcade of cars. On 16 October 1945, Martín Luis Guzmán, the author of two celebrated novels about the Revolution, published an article entitled 'The Week of Idolatry', in which he declared that Catholicism was opposed to 'the unity of the Mexican nation', since it maintained 'absurd dogmas' and was hostile to freedom of conscience. Sceptical of the truth of the apparitions of Mary, he condemned the celebration of the image of Guadalupe as repugnant, accusing the clergy of encouraging 'the fanatical idolatry in which Mexican Christianity is submerged'. When the bishops invited prelates from abroad, greeting them with such a public reception, they violated the Constitution of 1917 and the Laws of the Reform. Indeed, 'the Francoist standard and the *Royal March* were put together with the Mexican flag and national anthem under the vaults of the basilica'. This scorching attack aroused great controversy, since Guzmán was sharply criticized in the press, albeit supported by the publication of his article as a pamphlet which sold over 50,000 copies.[17]

So aroused was the novelist by these press attacks that he wrote to Avila Camacho to denounce this threat to 'the new Mexican identity born of the Revolution'. In an interview the president reassured him, explaining that although he believed in a divine power, he was not a Catholic. He complained that the bishops had taken advantage of his desire for conciliation by enlarging the scope of the cardinal's visit. The upshot was that Guzmán was offered a banquet attended by a thousand persons, including two cabinet ministers, who patiently listened to no fewer than twenty orators expressing their fears of Catholic intolerance and the bishops' obvious sympathy for Franco, Perón and Mussolini. In response, Guzmán complained that the former ruling class still remained hostile to the Revolution and, through their control of the press, constituted a public danger. He suggested that the attorney general should investigate the leading newspapers, none of which had been willing to print his article, to ascertain whether they should be classified as 'confessional' and hence unconstitutional in their bias.[18]

Throughout the following decade, Guzmán remained alert to the threat posed by the Catholic Church. On learning in 1950 that the new American ambassador was a Catholic, he warned him that the Church was the greatest totalitarian regime known to history, worse than Fascism, Nazism or Communism, and claimed that it had provoked virtually all the civil wars in Mexico since independence. He explained that most Catholics 'live sunk in a gross and idolatrous paganism', dominated by an ignorant, corrupt clergy. In a lecture delivered at the University of Chihuahua in 1958, he contrasted 'the civic religion', which was based on science and freedom, to the reactionary obscurantism of the Church, and cited the encyclicals of Gregory XVI and the Syllabus of Errors of Pius IX as proof of the papacy's hostility to the basic freedoms of conscience, press and education that the modern epoch took for granted. Perhaps it was time, he suggested, to establish 'the Grand Order of Benito Juárez' so as to defend the principles of the Reform and Revolution. The fears expressed by Guzmán obviously derived from his fear of the Church's influence among the masses and his consciousness of being an intellectual. In his open letter to the American ambassador, he declared: 'it was a century-and-a-half ago that the Catholic Church in Mexico lost the initiative and its creative spirit, both she and the sterile masses which have listened to her at the great turning points of national history, as is demonstrated by the fact that it is the lay, enlightened and progressive minority which has positively led Mexico since the days of the great excommunicates, Hidalgo and Morelos'. In this revealing admission, Guzmán thus recognized that as much as the Liberal Reform, the revolutionary regime was the work of a minority which had imposed its policies on the recalcitrant mass of the population. It was this embattled vision that doubtless led him to defend the actions of President Gustavo Díaz Ordaz in 1968, when students were massacred at Tlatelolco.[19]

Despite his suspicions of the clergy, however, Guzmán welcomed the circular issued by Archbishop Miguel Darío Miranda (1956–77), in which the clergy were advised that on 14 September they should celebrate solemn funeral services in remembrance of the heroes of independence, and that on 16 September they should chant *Te Deums*. Issued in 1956, the circular also commanded all priests to hang the national flag on one side of the high altar and the papal flag on the other. For his part, the new archbishop offered a requiem mass in the cathedral on 14 September and, two days later, preached a sermon in which he hailed the heroes who had fought 'to forge our *patria*'; praised the virtue of 'love of country'; and called upon the faithful to respect the public authorities. The occasion ended with the national anthem. On recounting this event, Guzmán commented that at last the Catholic Church had reconciled itself to the *patria* of Hidalgo and Morelos, only then to query, when would the Church reconcile itself to the *patria* of Juárez and the Revolution? For all that, Miranda's initiative demonstrated the desire of the bishops to affirm their Mexican identity and heal the rupture with the civil power.[20]

At both the great Guadalupan ceremonies of 1931 and 1945 the preacher was Luis María Martínez, a protégé of Leopoldo Ruíz y Flores, who drew upon romantic nationalism to explain the Virgin's role in Mexico. At the fourth centenary he chose not to dwell upon the martyrdom inflicted on so many loyal Catholics; instead, he invited the congregation to enjoy 'the happiness of being Mexicans', since the current celebration 'reveals to us the unity of our country and race'. Turning back to the Garden of Eden, where God created the first man by breathing upon clay, he argued that, in much the same way, peoples were formed by 'a mysterious force', which united individuals in pursuit of a common good. 'This immaterial and fecund principle which gives unity to peoples and races we call, by analogy with our spirit, the national spirit and soul of the race.' In the same way that the Almighty had appeared on Sinai to Israel, so Mary had appeared at Tepeyac, 'to forge the soul of our *patria* and our race', mingling 'the aboriginal races with the noble hispanic race'. With the apparition of her image on Juan Diego's mantle, Mexico no longer formed 'a savage and bloodthirsty tribe', but instead became the 'favourite people of Mary' and henceforth had 'a national soul and began its history'. It was thus not the efforts of the Spanish missionaries, or even the words of the Christian gospel, that converted the Indians: it was 'this blessed image' which won their hearts. In poetic metaphor, he concluded that 'the word of heaven is crystallized in an image; that of earth was expressed in a church; the church is the shell which encloses the divine pearl which came from heaven'. Neither the image nor its church would ever disappear from earth.[21]

On 12 October 1945 Martínez welcomed both the cardinal archbishop of Quebec and a host of prelates from across America who had come to Tepeyac to celebrate the anniversary of the Virgin's coronation. After praising Antonio Plancarte, somewhat improbably, as the Juan Diego of the nineteenth century, he declared that the crown offered to the Virgin was essentially symbolic, since her true crown and temple were composed of the living souls of the faithful. But he then recalled that Pius X had named Our Lady of Guadalupe as patron of Latin America. It was thus obvious that she could no longer be restricted to Mexico, since 'today the spiritual temple of the Virgin . . . includes the American continent' all the way from Canada to Tierra del Fuego. He then reminded the congregation that 'like every individual, every nation has a providential mission to fulfil, and with even more reason, a Continent of nations, like those which compose the New World'. With Europe devastated by a terrible war, the moment of America had arrived: it was now time for her to fulfil her destiny. The empire of Our Lady of Guadalupe thus encompassed the entire hemisphere, and through her protection it was clear that 'the union of America is an unavoidable necessity'. As Pius XII affirmed in his broadcast message, the Virgin of Guadalupe was not merely the mother of Mexico, but she was also the Hope of America.[22]

The romantic reflections of Martínez were far removed from the plans for preachers offered by José Cantú Corro (1884–1951) in his *Guadalupan Sermons* (1940). Published in Huajuapan de León, where the author was a priest, it included many extracts from nineteenth-century sermons, especially from those preached at the coronation of 1895. So too, Cantú Corro included the collective pastoral issued by the Mexican bishops in October 1936 where they traced the history of the Guadalupe cult from 1737 until the Fourth Centenary. From the same year he also cited a sermon delivered by Mariano Navarro, a Dominican friar, who asserted that, although Catholics venerated the national flag with its three bands of colour, they would prefer to replace the eagle and serpent inscribed on it by the figure of the brown Virgin and Juan Diego. He exclaimed that 'we Catholic Mexicans always see our three glorious Mothers together at the same time, the Mother of Guadalupe, the Mother Country and the Mother Church. We know that these are three distinct personages; but they are so intimately united that we can never see one without seeing the other two.' Here indeed was an integral conception of Mexico. For his part, Cantú Corro recalled that when the seminary at Huajuapan de León had been closed and the bishop exiled during the years 1926–9, when masons, Liberals, Protestants and socialists had united to employ all the resources of government to persecute the Church, 'in those hours of immense tribulation, the Church raised its eyes to the sacred mount; and from the sacred mount of Tepeyac came a grace and holy joy, efficacious and consoling'.[23]

It was for preachers, so Cantú Corro counselled, to instruct their congregations that although the apparitions were not an article of the Catholic faith, 'they are religious truths, fully proven, facts which happened in reality. History and criticism join to testify to them.' The faithful should be reminded that Mexico had once been governed by the degraded, ferocious Aztecs, a people sunk in barbarism, despotism and cannibalism. And yet, although 'no other people was so unfit to receive such an immense favour as Mexico', the Virgin had appeared on Juan Diego's cape as 'an Aztec Indian'.

If Christ was the Saviour of this world, Mary was 'the co-redeemer who lived on earth, who was at the foot of the cross of the Divine Martyr and who centuries later appeared on the hill of Tepeyac'. Whereas through his Incarnation Christ had saved all humanity, the Virgin had helped to save the Mexicans, so that 'in their effects, the incarnation of the Word and the Guadalupan apparition are similar'. Here were affirmations that recalled the arguments of the Jesuit preachers of the eighteenth century.[24]

Turning to the image itself, Cantú Corro declared that although he had visited galleries and churches across Europe, he had nowhere found a painting of Mary that could equal the Virgin of Tepeyac. Mary had appeared in Lourdes in France, 'whose history is a poem of heroism'; in Italy, 'the country of saints, scholars and artists'; and in Spain, 'the nursery of Christian heroes, the country of nobles and outstanding paladins'. In all these countries there was an abundance of sculptures and paintings of the Virgin, yet they were all but representations made by human hands of fleeting apparitions. By contrast, 'the painting of Tepeyac is unique . . . here she perpetuated her apparitions; they remain imprinted in the thaumaturgic image which the Artificer of the world drew with such incomparable mastery'. Although Cantú Corro presented Juan Diego as the model of Christian virtue and cited Manríquez' theological study of the Indian seer, nevertheless, his most forceful affirmations referred to Mexico's patron, since he once again insisted that 'the only portrait of the Virgin with an authentically divine origin that the world possesses is the sacrosanct image of Guadalupe . . . it is a portrait of the eternal and glorified life of the Mother of God in her assumption'. With such a heavenly presence in Mexico, who could doubt that 'the *patria* has its foundations in the impregnable rock of Tepeyac'? In these declarations the soaring theology of the baroque era survived almost intact into the twentieth century, the insistence on the unique spiritual destiny of Mexico rendered all the more passionate by the persecution suffered by so many priests and their loyal followers.[25]

II

While bishops preached sermons and rural chieftains waged war, scholars discovered new documents and debated their significance. In his *History of the Church in Mexico* (1921–8), Mariano Cuevas (1879–1949), a Jesuit who studied in Rome and Louvain before undertaking research in Spanish archives, stated that 'the apparition of the Mother of God at Tepeyac in the year 1531 is an historical fact supported by certified documents', only then to admit that 'the most powerful reasons' for accepting these facts were the papal declarations about 'the constant and ancient tradition' of Guadalupe. Had not Mariano Rojas identified the Nahua song known as *Teponaxtli* as the very song which had been chanted by don Plácido, the Indian nobleman, to salute the image as it was installed in the first chapel? There was also Valeriano's

Nican mopohua, even if the manuscript original had been seized by General Winfield Scott in 1847 and carried off to Washington.[26] Moreover, in his *Historical Guadalupan Album* (1930), prepared for the Fourth Centenary, Cuevas printed both in Nahuatl and Spanish a summary account of the apparitions which he had discovered in manuscript. He attributed this 'primitive account', as it came to be known, to Juan de Tovar (1540–1623), a Mexican Jesuit expert in native language and history. In this version Juan Diego was not identified by name, albeit described as a poor peasant, and Mary was only named as the 'Mother of God' and as 'Child Queen'.[27] Its importance obviously lay in the possibility that the document constituted a sixteenth-century testimony of the apparition narrative.

But Cuevas also printed an extract from a description of the archbishopric of Mexico, written in 1570, in which the chaplain at the 'hermitage of Our Lady of Guadalupe Tepeaca', Antonio Freyre, stated that the church had been built by Archbishop Montúfar about fourteen years before, using alms donated by the faithful, which was to say, in 1556. He was the only priest officiating at the chapel and his duties were to say mass every Saturday and Sunday and to care for a small village of about 350 Indian adults.[28] More intriguing, however, were two letters written in 1574–5 by Diego de Santa María, a Jeronymite monk, to Philip II, which Cuevas had discovered in Seville. In the years after the conquest, so the monk averred, many alms had been bequeathed in testaments to the Holy House of Guadalupe in Extremadura, at a time when the chapel at Tepeyac bore another name. But some twelve or fourteen years ago, so he alleged, a man had come from Spain, with forged credentials from the monastery of Guadalupe and had succeeded in collecting many alms. On seeing his success, the *mayordomos* of the chapel at Tepeyac, who had collected alms for this forger, decided to change the name of their image to Guadalupe. Moreover, they then sent out *demandadores*, men who begged for alms and who usually carried a small copy of the image for which they solicited. All this was condemned by Diego de Santa María, who complained that the confraternity of Tepeyac and their collectors deliberately confused the relation between their Guadalupe and its namesake in Extremadura, thereby obtaining alms which otherwise might have been sent to Spain. To avoid future fraud, the monk demanded that the chapel at Tepeyac should be obliged to abandon the name of Guadalupe, or, if not, that the hermitage should be administered by the Jeronymites. An even better remedy might be to grant permission for the Jeronymites to establish a monastery in Mexico, preferably at Chapultepec.[29] Here, then, was an explanation of how the image and its sanctuary came to be called Guadalupe, albeit dated to the years 1560–2, whereas the 1556 *Statements* attested to an earlier use of that name.

Although Cuevas was the leading ecclesiastical historian in Mexico whose archival researches greatly advanced knowledge, not least when he printed the Spanish original of Clavijero's *Ancient History of Mexico*, he concluded his history of the Church with a passionate, partisan condemnation of the Liberal Reform led by Benito Juárez.[30] So too, in his *Album* he dismissed the anti-apparitionists as men of little learning or intelligence, an ill-advised description of García Icazbalceta. In that volume he admitted that Plancarte may have instigated Salomé Piña to erase the Virgin's crown, only then to defend this action on the grounds that the crown was but a later, unsightly addition which deserved to be erased. As for the Guadalupe's race, he commented that 'It is always said that this Virgin is an Indian; and yet this Virgin simply is not an Indian', since neither her clothes, nor her features, nor her colour were Indian. Instead, she should be seen as a prophetic likeness of the mestizo race of Mexico. As befitted his robust character, Cuevas insisted that Catholicism in Mexico did not depend on the Guadalupe and, like Becerra Tanco before him, asserted that if the image was destroyed it could always be replaced by a copy.[31]

It was in 1926 that Primo Feliciano Velásquez (1860–1946), an historian of San Luis Potosí, published a facsimile of the *Huei tlamahuiçoltica*, accompanied by a translation, and thus provided the Mexican public with the first complete Spanish version of Laso de la Vega's work. His translation revealed at first glance the great difference in style between the highly wrought, poetic style of the apparition narrative, the *Nican mopohua*, and the concise prose of the introduction, the conclusion and the account of miracles. Velásquez postulated that if Valeriano was the author of the narrative, the remainder of the text was written by Fernando de Alva Ixtlilxochitl, citing certain similarities with the prose style of that author's history of Texcoco. Ever orthodox, Velásquez followed Becerra Tanco in mistranslating the Nahuatl 'flowers of Castile' as 'roses of Castile', and inserted a small passage dealing with the Virgin's third apparition which was omitted in the Nahuatl text.[32] For all that, his translation provided a generation of students and priests with an attractive, readable version and was destined to be constantly reprinted.

In *The Apparition of Saint Mary of Guadalupe* (1931) Velásquez followed the trail blazed by Vera and Anticoli, but refrained from acrimony, and provided a relatively equable account of the sources, both native and Spanish, for the tradition and the subsequent polemics surrounding them. There was not much that was new in his account other than in its list of native annals purporting to provide early mention either of the apparitions or Juan Diego. Where he scored was in his citation of the annals of Juan Bautista, a manuscript account in Nahuatl, composed in diary form and mainly dealing with the 1560s. As we have seen, Francisco del Paso y Troncoso had already used this source in his essay on the native painters and sculptors, the pupils of Pedro de Gante, who were attached to the Franciscan priory of San José. Apparently Velásquez made a translation of these annals, but never sought to publish them. What they demonstrate, however, is that virtually all the great paintings of this epoch, which adorned the altarpieces of the mendicant churches, were done by native artists. But Velásquez was quick to point out that although Marcos Cipac, the painter whom a witness in the 1556 *Statements* described as the artist who had painted the Guadalupe, was mentioned on several occasions, he was included in long lists of native painters and was not singled out for special mention. For all that, these annals provided a remarkably intimate and vivid picture of native life in the 1560s, when these artists found their livelihood threatened by demands for tribute payment by royal visitors.[33] Preserved in the archive of the basilica at Tepeyac, it has yet to be published in either Nahuatl or Spanish, and is generally only remembered for its brief note that 'in the year 1555: at that time Saint Mary of Guadalupe appeared there on Tepeyac'.

It was Velásquez who drew attention to a puzzling reference to the Guadalupe published by Andrade in 1907, which consisted of excerpts from a manuscript poem written by Captain Luis Angel de Betancourt in 1616–22 and addressed to Our Lady of Los Remedios. The author appears to confuse the don Juan of Los Remedios with Juan Diego, or simply ignores the existence of the peasant seer. At the same time he implies that both these images were of divine origin, with God as a heavenly Apelles and Praxitles, applying himself both to the sculptured figure of Los Remedios and to the 'white mantle' of Guadalupe. The poem describes the 'devout nobleman', don Juan, as descending the valley to the waters by Tepeyac, where he found 'the precious canvas of the rose' and built a chapel of pine for the 'blessed flower' Guadalupe. What the poem suggests is that Betancourt knew nothing of the apparition narrative, yet was persuaded that the image of the Mexican Virgin was divine in origin. Apart from this new source, Velásquez had little more to offer. It was typical of his approach that he spent two pages describing the crown designed by Edgar Morgan for the coronation, but offered no explanation of how the Virgin's painted crown had disappeared so suddenly.[34]

In his *History of Nahuatl Literature* (1953–4), Angel María Garibay Kintana (1892–1967) loftily dismissed Velásquez' translation of Laso de la Vega's text as 'more literary than literal'. A leading scholar in early Nahuatl and a canon at the basilica, Garibay admirably succeeded in demonstrating the variety and poetic richness of the materials in Nahuatl which lurked in sixteenth-century manuscripts. When he came to examine the *Huei tlamahuiçoltica*, of which the basilica archive preserved a rare copy, he judged that the introduction, conclusion and account of miracles were all written in good, classical Nahuatl and that there was no good reason not to attribute them to Laso de la Vega. But the apparition narrative, the *Nican mopohua*, was written in a different style and resembled early Nahua songs, the moral colloquies known as *Huehuetlatolli*, and Sahagún's twelfth book, which dealt with the conquest, works completed by the 1570s. Citing the dialogues between the Virgin and Juan Diego, Garibay observed that 'no peasant could speak like that. It is more the fragment of a poem . . . than an historical account.' Because of its echoes, especially of the moral colloquies, he concluded that it had been written in the sixteenth century and argued that its authors 'recollected old elements which were in circulation and dressed them in literary forms which were peculiar to the elevated and elegant style of their language in accordance with idiomatic criteria. There, as elsewhere, they reconstructed a literary work on the basis of an historical nucleus, in which the style devoured the reality.' On the delicate question of whether this text afforded testimony of the apparitions 'in a rigorous historical sense', Garibay suspended judgement, leaving the matter to be decided by professional historians.[35]

As regards the authorship of the *Nican mopohua*, Garibay noted that its attribution to Valeriano depended entirely on the testimony of Sigüenza y Góngora and, after touching briefly on the confusion generated by Becerra Tanco and Florencia, concluded that Sigüenza was not a trustworthy authority. However, since stylistic analysis indicated a sixteenth-century origin, he fixed upon the native disciples of Sahagún, who were associated with the college of Santa Cruz Tlatelolco, among whom Valeriano figured, and concluded that it was a joint composition. In sibylline fashion, he then asserted than Sahagún had known of his pupils' work but had affected ignorance for reasons that Garibay knew but did not propose to divulge.[36]

In the discussion of the Nahua songs, Garibay argued that the verses known as *Teonantli*, which Cuevas had attributed to don Plácido, were essentially pre-hispanic in meaning and form, and that, despite certain Christian interpolations, they could not be applied to the Guadalupe. By contrast, however, he accepted Cuevas' discovery of a 'primitive account' in Nahuatl and innovated by suggesting that it was written by Juan González, a Spanish sixteenth-century secular priest famous for his sanctity, who, so he alleged, had acted as Zumárraga's interpreter in the dialogues with Juan Diego. Since González served as canon in the cathedral chapter before retiring to a hermitage where he devoted himself to the conversion of the Indians, it was highly likely that he had given a copy of his account to Juan de Tovar, who also acted as a canon before entering the Jesuit Order. So influential was Garibay's ascription of this fragmentary account to the early sixteenth century that it was immediately accepted as an essential testimony of the historical reality of the apparition narrative.[37] In effect, Garibay lent the weight of his authority as a scholar in Nahuatl both to question certain features of orthodoxy and, essentially, to sustain the tradition by postulating sixteenth-century origins to both the *Nican mopohua* and the 'primitive account'.

Although Juan González thus entered the Guadalupan canon of witnesses, his role was sharply challenged by Edmundo O'Gorman (1906–95), who, in his *Banishment of Shadows* (1986), launched a sarcastic attack on Garibay's scholarship. To start with, the surviving manuscript of the 'primitive account' clearly belonged to the seventeenth century and was thus coeval with Laso de la Vega's text or dependent on it. After a careful examination of the inscriptions on successive portraits of González, O'Gorman concluded that there was nothing to connect this venerable figure with the Guadalupe. It was the *Album* of the 1895 coronation which had first mentioned the existence of a portrait where the inscription described González as Zumárraga's interpreter with Juan Diego. But that painting, preserved in the chapter room of the basilica, was denounced as early as 1896 by Agustín Rivera as a nineteenth-century forgery, possibly instigated by Plancarte. Nor was there anything to connect González with Tovar, since they were canons of the chapter at quite distinct times. Having thus demolished Garibay's hypothesis, O'Gorman then suggested that a possible author of the account might have been Baltazar González, the learned censor of Laso de la Vega, but did not offer any evidence to support his speculation.[38]

By the time O'Gorman wrote *Banishment of Shadows*, he was a leading historian in Mexico, editor of the works of Alva Ixtlilxochitl and Motolinia, not to mention an edition and commentary of Servando de Mier's sermon and letters to Muñoz. The main object of his study was a close examination of the 1556 *Statements* and the controversy between Archbishop Alonso de Montúfar and the Franciscan provincial, Francisco de Bustamante. To start with, he put two questions: how, why and when did the image of Guadalupe appear in the hermitage of Tepeyac; and why, how and when was the image reckoned to be of supernatural origin? In the event he was more successful in answering the first than the second query, which was to say, the evidence certainly indicated the origin of the cult but had little or nothing to say about the origin of the tradition. The annals of Juan Bautista, the annals of the Chalco historian, Chimalpahin, the statement of Antonio Freyre, the chaplain at Tepeyac, and the letter of Viceroy Enríquez all fixed upon the years 1555–6 as the historical moment when the image of Guadalupe 'appeared' in the chapel. But, although O'Gorman presumed that Marcos de Aquino had painted the image, he chose not to follow Paso y Troncoso and examine the context in which that Indian artist flourished. Instead, he argued that the image had been first placed in the small, original chapel and, once miracles were attributed to its influence, it was transferred to the second, larger church constructed by Montúfar at this time.[39]

O'Gorman provided a meticulous reconstruction of the sermons of September 1556 and enlarged upon the significance of the controversy. Drawing upon Marcel Bataillon's *Erasmus and Spain* (1937), he asserted that Zumárraga and many of the early Franciscans in New Spain were strongly influenced by Erasmus and his critique of popular religion, and not least by his questioning of miracle-mongering, pilgrimages and the veneration of images. By contrast, Montúfar belonged to the Counter-Reformation, a movement which renewed the medieval devotion to images and questioned reliance on individual inspiration or any longing for the evangelical simplicity of the primitive Church. Indeed, in 1559, Montúfar submitted Zumárraga's *Brief Doctrine* to theological censure and had it withdrawn from circulation. It was precisely during the 1550s that in Spain the works of Erasmus were proscribed and several of his followers imprisoned by the Inquisition. But O'Gorman emphasized that the quarrel between the archbishop and the friars also centred on the payment of tithes by Indians and the authority of the prelate over the parishes, known then as *doctrinas*, which were administered by the mendicants. At issue here was whether the

Church in New Spain was to remain a missionary organization mainly directed by friars, or whether it was to be governed by the laws and structures of the universal Church and hence ruled largely by bishops and the secular clergy. When Montúfar boldly compared the chapel at Tepeyac to the great sanctuaries of Spain and welcomed the miracles performed there, he obviously sought to introduce a Counter-Reformation form of Christianity into Mexico. In effect, he questioned the value of the religion taught by the mendicants and thought that the Indians would be better served by the cult of the saints. As O'Gorman thus demonstrated, at stake in the 1556 controversy were two differing conceptions of Catholicism and the kind of religion best suited to attract Indians to Christianity.[40]

By way of conclusion, O'Gorman cited the Ordinances issued by Montúfar in 1555 to infer that the 1556 *Statements* did not constitute judicial proceedings since they lacked all the necessary prerequisites, not least the intervention of an attorney to frame charges. Contrary to what apparitionists had argued, it was a private document, procured by Montúfar as a precaution to protect himself from possible allegations that he had encouraged idolatry or recognized miracles without due enquiry. But where O'Gorman stooped to speculation was in his assertion that not merely was Valeriano the author of the *Nican mopohua*, but he had written his account in 1556. Whereas the Spaniards had imposed the name of Guadalupe on the image painted by Marcos so as to create a new Spain in America, an argument taken from Florencia, by contrast Valeriano invented the apparition narrative in order to recover the image for the natives by introducing the figure of Juan Diego. As a cultural dialectic, this hypothesis has its attractions, but it did not rest on any historical evidence. The only testimony that O'Gorman proffered was the claim of the American Jesuit, Ernest Burrus, that the New York City Library possessed a sixteenth-century manuscript version of the *Nican mopohua*. For the rest, O'Gorman provided a useful description of the manner in which the 1556 *Statements* entered the public domain in the 1880s, but failed to note that the manuscript itself disappeared for many years until 1955, when it was discovered in a trunk containing the papers of Antonio Plancarte.[41] Despite his iconoclastic pretensions, O'Gorman failed to answer his own initial questions, since he did not examine the role of Marcos, the Indian painter, and, by contrast, accepted the authority of Valeriano, which even Garibay had questioned.

In retrospect, it is clear that modern interpretation of the Guadalupe tradition began with *Mexican Guadalupanism* (1953) written by Francisco de la Maza (1913–72), a leading art historian, who boldly declared that 'Guadalupanism and baroque art are the only authentic creations of the Mexican past'. Anxious not to wound anyone's beliefs, he claimed that historical erudition could not injure the faith of a populace that could barely read a novel, and added: 'I do not attack, nor do I defend, I explain.' For all that, he began with the famous passage from Zumárraga's *Brief Christian Rule* condemning the hunger for miracles and, after a brief examination of early sources, concluded that 1555–6 was the only plausible date for the appearance of the image. If Suárez de Peralta was the only author in the sixteenth century who even hinted at the possibility of an apparition, it was because he was a creole writing in part to defend the sons of the conquerors from the charge of disloyalty. As for the poem of Betancourt written in 1622, it obviously indicated that the Guadalupe tradition was still inchoate and confused with Los Remedios.[42]

It was in his chapter on 'the four evangelists' of Our Lady of Guadalupe, which was to say, Sánchez, Laso de la Vega, Becerra Tanco and Florencia, that de la Maza opened new ground by arguing that these men were as much animated by patriotic sentiment as by religious devotion. Inspired by his sympathy for baroque culture, he provided what was the first perceptive reading of Miguel Sánchez after more than two hundred years of neo-classical and positivist disdain. With an exuberant engagement, he dwelt upon the implications of Sánchez' identification of the Guadalupe as the Woman of the Apocalypse and his patriotic portrayal of Mexico as a new Jerusalem. Only in de la Maza do we encounter any understanding of the theological originality of this Mexican priest. For the rest, he saw no reason to deny Laso de la Vega his rights as author and noted that the manuscripts of his work possessed by the New York City Library appeared to be seventeenth-century copies. As for the 1666 *Statements*, who could accept such evidence when even Becerra Tanco had dismissed native testimony about past events as worthless? Moreover, that author claimed to have seen a manuscript describing the mission of St Thomas in the New World: if that was the case, what credence could be accorded to his assertion about a similar manuscript dealing with the apparitions?[43]

Where de la Maza innovated decisively was in his careful reading of the sermons printed in the century 1661–1700 since, through carefully selected quotations from such preachers as José Vidal de Figueroa and Bartolomé de Ita y Parra, he demonstrated their doctrinal audacity and manifest patriotism. No-one could doubt, after reading these passages, that devotion to Our Lady of Guadalupe lay at the very centre of the baroque culture of New Spain. Equally important, de la Maza surveyed the iconography of the Virgin and illustrated his study by illustrations such as the painting at San Juan Tilapa which depicted God the Father and the Son holding a canvas for the Holy Spirit to paint the Virgin of Guadalupe. So too, he noted that at the Franciscan church in Zacatecas, the figure of St Luke could be observed in sculptured relief painting the Virgin. Although he did not develop Paso y Troncoso's essay on Indian artists, he indicated the Flemish stylistic antecedents of the Guadalupan image as regards both Mary's posture and the arabesques on her tunic.[44] In effect, de la Maza can be regarded as the aesthetic heir of Ignacio Manuel Altamirano, since both these authors interpreted the Guadalupan cult and tradition as a peculiarly

Mexican cultural phenomenon, in which religion and patriotism were inextricably intertwined.

Despite his originality, de la Maza had no Mexican disciples in this line of enquiry, and it was left to Jacque Lafaye in his *Quetzalcoatl and Guadalupe* (1974) to trace the role of image and myth in the formation of Mexican national consciousness. In particular, he emphasized the pre-hispanic cult of Tonantzin to account for the strength of native devotion to the Virgin. More to the point, he identified Miguel Sánchez as a creole patriot who virtually invented the Guadalupe tradition and thus affirmed that 1648, rather than 1531, was the foundation moment in the history of the cult. Indeed, he defined the acclamation of the Virgin as patron in 1737 as the ideological equivalent of the solemn oath of the Federation during the French Revolution, since both occasions marked the birth of a nation. It was left to Octavio Paz in his luminous introduction to reject Lafaye's improbable comparison and to argue that New Spain was a creole creation, a culture that was subsequently destroyed by mestizo Liberals during the nineteenth century. For the Mexican poet interpreted his country's history as broken by cataclysmic events in which one cycle of culture rejected its predecessor.[45] However, he admitted that the Virgin of Guadalupe had succeeded in capturing the minds and hearts of all Mexicans, ranging from baroque poets to nationalist intellectuals, from the insurgents who followed Hidalgo to the peasants who joined Zapata, so that 'her cult is intimate and public, regional and national. The feast of Guadalupe, 12 December, is still the central date in the emotional calendar of the Mexican people.' Indeed, he frankly admitted that 'after two centuries of experiment and failure, the Mexican people only believe in the Virgin of Guadalupe and the National Lottery'. He concluded with a remarkable exordium:

> Mother of gods and men, of stars and ants, of maize and maguey, Tonantzin/ Guadalupe was the answer of the imagination to the state of orphanage in which the conquest left the Indians. Their priests exterminated, and their idols destroyed, their links with the past and the supernatural broken, the Indians took refuge in the skirts of Tonantzin/Guadalupe, the skirts of the mother mountain, skirts of the water mother. The ambiguous situations of New Spain produced a similar reaction: the creoles searched for their true mother in the womb of Tonanztin/Guadalupe, a natural and supernatural mother, made from American earth and European theology.

In these psycho-historical reflections, Paz sought to depict the cultural contradictions of modern Mexico, admitting that neither Liberal nor revolutionary Mexico had succeeded in conceiving a symbol as powerful as that generated by the creole mind and native devotion of New Spain.[46] If Paz was entirely justified in rejecting any linear theory of Mexican history, he was equally acute in signalizing the enduring vitality of the Guadalupe cult and tradition.

III

While historians scanned the origins and intellectuals interpreted the role of the Guadalupe, devoted priests slowly transformed the tradition. To start with, the *Nican mopohua* came to be used as a kind of Mexican gospel. Whereas clerics of baroque and neo-classical culture had been irritated by its simplicity and diminutives, by contrast the romantic engagement with folk culture that characterized the revolutionary years was eventually taken up by the clergy. Equally important, the effect of the Second Vatican Council (1962–5) and the rise of Liberation Theology was to convert the text into a potent catechetical instrument, since its emphasis on a poor peasant and his willing acceptance of the Virgin's message, not to mention Zumárraga's initial disdain, responded perfectly to the new-found 'option for the poor'. All this took time to acquire a momentum, but, by the 1980s, new translations became available and a host of articles and books expounded its relevance for the contemporary era.[47]

But this concern with the *Nican mopohua* was preceded by a prolonged campaign to beatify, not to say canonize, Juan Diego. As we have seen, it was José de Jesús Manríquez y Zárate who, in 1939, both lamented the neglect of Juan Diego in most celebrations of the Virgin of Guadalupe and called for his beatification. The dramatic effect of that message was attested by Lauro López Beltrán, who later recounted that he had read the bishop's pastoral letter when attending a parochial congress of Christ the King held at San Martín Chalchicusatla, situated in a remote, mountainous corner of the Huasteca, its effect on him heightened by the coincidence that an Indian band nearby was playing an unfamiliar air called 'Juan Diego'. So enthused was López Beltrán by the bishop's call to action that, after his return to Cuernavaca, he founded a small review called *Juan Diego* which he edited for the next twenty-seven years. Moreover, when Manríquez finally abandoned his exile in 1944, he invited him to preside over a cycle of 'Guadalupan solemnities' in the cathedral of Cuernavaca, where the former bishop preached a moving sermon on 'our immortal brother, the great Juan Diego'. In the years which followed, López Beltrán offered reiterated tribute to Manríquez' role in initiating the campaign to beatify the Indian 'seer' and in 1974 published his biography, in which he included Manríquez' theological study of Juan Diego, praising him as 'the great Athanasius of the Mexican Church'.[48]

The degree to which the beatification campaign was initiated in a Cristero matrix was further demonstrated in *The Religious Persecution in Mexico* (1987), in which López Beltrán portrayed the Cristero leaders as Christian heroes and martyrs who had given their lives to prevent Calles from destroying the Church and the Christian faith. Here also, he praised Manríquez as 'the leader, the truest of Mexicans, he of the apocalyptic messages, who confronted Calles with the immortal words: "Mr President lies." ' Nor did he hesitate to reopen old wounds when he criticized Archbishops Ruíz y Flores and Pascual Díaz for surrendering to Calles at the behest of Dwight Morrow

Plate 31   Miguel Cabrera, *True Portrait of the Venerable Juan Diego*

without obtaining any real safeguards for the security of the Cristero forces, which, by 1929, so he argued, were on the verge of defeating the federal army. Indeed, he printed a long letter written to Pius XI in 1930 in which the leaders of the League for the Defence of Religious Freedom bitterly complained about the settlement of that year which had caused more injury to the Catholic faith than had the suspension of religious services in 1926. López Beltrán concluded with a detailed account, illustrated with photographs, of over fifty priests who had been martyred during the struggle, several in atrocious circumstances, and thereby testified that the memory of the epic struggle of the Cristeros was still treasured in many circles of the Mexican Church.[49]

In December 1944, López Beltrán delivered an address in the city of León in Nicaragua, where a monument of the Virgin of Guadalupe with Juan Diego was unveiled in the presence of President Anastasio Somoza. Taking heed of Agustín Rivera's famous sermon, he stressed that the Mother of God had chosen not to visit Rome or Jerusalem, but instead had come to America to converse with a poor Indian named Cuauhtatohuac, 'he who speaks like an eagle'. Evoking Sánchez' comparison of the Virgin with the Woman of the Apocalypse, he declared that 'what for St John the Evangelist was a vision, for Juan Diego was a reality'. When Mary spoke to the eagle of Tepeyac, 'she stamped her thaumaturgic image on his glorious mantle and this is the only portrait of the Mother of God which is preserved in the world'. Anxious to exalt the liberation wrought by the Virgin's appearance in Mexico, he condemned the Aztecs for their annual holocaust of 50,000 victims and claimed, somewhat improbably, that over a period of seven centuries no fewer than 70 million Mexicans had been sacrificed to Quetzalcoatl. By way of conclusion he praised the monument, since 'the Virgin of Guadalupe without Juan Diego would be like a mother without a son', adding that the definitive triumph of the Guadalupan cause would be signalized by the canonization of 'the seer, the unknown Juan Diego' since, from that moment, no-one would be able to doubt 'the divine poem of Tepeyac'.[50]

Since Juan Diego was reckoned to have been born in 1474, there was a danger that he might have been involved in the sacrificial rites of the Aztecs. At a speech at Guadalajara in October 1946, López Beltrán praised the city for being the first in Mexico to raise a monument to the Indian seer situated in the atrium of its sanctuary of Guadalupe, and referred to him as 'the mediator, spokesman and co-operator' of the Virgin. After recalling that the Aztecs had sacrificed 80,000 victims at the dedication of the great pyramid temple of Tenochtitlan in 1487, he affirmed that by contrast the inhabitants of Cuautitlan observed an austere morality, since they took but one wife, only worshipped the sun and moon as their divine parents, and offered in sacrifice animals and birds. Indeed, 'the people of Cuautitlan, faithful observers of the natural law, in not knowing the sublime law of the Gospel, resembled the children of Israel, who preserved the law of Moses in the midst of pagan and idolatrous countries'. Through a special dispensation, God had thus intervened to preserve Cuautitlan from the depravity of the Aztecs and thus enable Juan Diego to be raised in natural virtue and hence fit to be the Virgin's faithful servant. In what document or from what celestial source López Beltrán found this information he chose not to reveal.[51]

In other sermons and addresses, López Beltrán demonstrated a considerable acquaintance with the literature of the Guadalupan tradition and, for example, drew on the sermon preached by Manuel Díaz Rayón at the 1895 celebrations to salute the Guadalupe as 'our inestimable Ark of the Covenant and the Marian Sacrament of our *patria*', defining the image as 'a reliquary come down from heaven', which was an enduring testimony of 'the Covenant which, through her, God wished to celebrate with the Mexican people'. Not without reason, therefore, was the sanctuary at Tepeyac compared to Solomon's Temple. It was López Beltrán who published the first reimpression of Miguel Sánchez' *Image of God* since 1648, an edition, however, marred by the omission of the censors' approbations and the brief prologue in which the author explained how he had failed to find any written account of the apparitions. It was these omissions which caused Francisco de la Maza to dismiss the edition as 'puerile'. Although López Beltrán commented that Sánchez described Juan Diego as 'the Mexican Moses and Tepeyac as the Sinai of Anahuac', he was not tempted to develop these biblical metaphors, still less to assess their theological significance.[52]

It was in his *Guadalupan Protohistory* (1966) that López Beltrán offered his views about the historical basis of the tradition and did battle with his opponents. It was Velásquez' complete translation of Laso de la Vega's work in 1925 which had first demonstrated the difference in style between the *Nican mopohua* and the remainder of that text. He followed Velásquez in ascribing authorship of these compositions to Valeriano and Alva Ixtlilxochitl, noting that the two men must have met at the college of Santa Cruz Tlatelolco. So too, he welcomed Angel Garibay's identification of Juan González as Zumárraga's interpreter and the author of the 'primitive account'. However, he then sharply criticized the learned canon for his lofty dismissal of Velásquez' translation, and still more for his discounting the credibility of Sigüenza y Góngora, upon whom the ascription of the *Nican mopohua* to Valeriano rested. Moreover, he strongly objected to Garibay's observation that the colloquies between the Virgin and Juan Diego were written in such an elevated, poetic language that 'the style devours the reality'. In this comment Garibay verged perilously close to the errors of Mier, Muñoz and García Icazbalceta, especially since 'history without reality is not history'.[53] López Beltrán's animus against Garibay found further expression in his *Guadalupan Lyrical Homage* (1984), published after that scholar's death, where he complained that, although Mariano Cuevas and Jesús García Gutiérrez, a learned Guadalupan scholar, had concurred that the Nahuatl song uttered by don Plácido had been identified, Garibay had refused to accept that attribution. To explain his recalcitrance, López Beltrán recalled that prior to becoming a canon at Tepeyac, Garibay had been heard to deny the historicity of the apparitions. When he was named for that position, a kind friend had denounced him to the abbot as a sceptic. But Archbishop Martinez had refused to act, observing that 'the appointment is already made: it is up to the chapter to convert him'.[54] Obviously, there was something about Garibay's omniscience which profoundly irritated his contemporaries.

As a proponent of beatification, López Beltrán accepted the 1666 *Statements* as the basis of the case since, in the 1894 debate over the wording of the new office for the Virgin's feast day, Rome had accepted those documents as juridical proofs of the existence of an ancient and constant tradition about the apparitions. It was for this reason that, when a dispute arose between the parishes of Cuautitlan and Tulpetlac over which had the honour of being the site of Juan Diego's dwelling place, he favoured Cuautitlan, despite its distance from Tlatelolco. For the rest he cited recent chemical tests which had proven that the canvas of the Guadalupe image was indeed woven from the thread of maguey rather than from the *izcotl* palm, and rejected Cuevas' dismissal of the arabesques on the Virgin's tunic as later additions since, in his opinion, these lines were so finely drawn on such a rough cloth that they would have decayed or disappeared had they not been 'of supernatural origin'.[55]

It was with approval, however, that López Beltrán cited a sermon preached by Mariano Cuevas in the cathedral of Querétaro in 1931 in which the Jesuit historian argued that the Virgin had appeared without a crown and that the gold crown depicted on her image had been added later, and so badly done that it consisted of little more than ten points of gold drawn on a plane without perspective. How could such poor workmanship be attributed to the Almighty? For his part, López Beltrán observed that all the historical sources, including the office of 1754, recorded the presence of this crown and that by 1895 it had disappeared. There were only three possible explanations: it had disappeared through the effects of time or by miracle, as Gabino Chávez had argued, or it had been deliberately erased. In fact, Antonio Pompa y Pompa, a noted historian, had informed him that Rafael Aguirre, an artist who painted the copy of the Virgin exhibited in the basilica during the years 1926–9, had confessed on his deathbed that he had seen Antonio Plancarte arrive in his carriage at the Academy of San Carlos to take Salomé Pina to Tepeyac. The next day it was observed that the image had lost its crown. For all that, López Beltrán noted that Florencia had mentioned the erasure of cherubim which once had surrounded the Virgin and agreed with Cuevas that the image was all the better for the erasure of the crown. In a surprising admission he commented that, since the canvas was now obviously shorter than it once had been, it was probably doubled back at the top so as to accommodate the lowering of the frame.[56]

In the 1970s the social and institutional context within which all these debates took place changed radically. The Mexican Church now found itself not merely tolerated but even courted by politicians. A significant number of businessmen were prepared to make generous donations for the construction of churches, schools and even

Plate 32   The modern basilica of Guadalupe, 1977

universities. Behind this expansion lay the demographic explosion in which the population leapt from about 20 million in 1940 to over 80 million in 1990. A symbol of the transformation of Mexico was the construction of a new basilica at Tepeyac. By the 1970s the old sanctuary, completed in 1709, had become a crowded chaos as thousands of pilgrims poured into the building every day. Moreover, its vaults were once more cracked and the safety of visitors in such large numbers could no longer be assured. It was in 1976, thanks to the vision and initiative of Abbot Guillermo Schulenberg Prado, that a modern basilica with space sufficient to accommodate 10,000 people was dedicated, the estimated cost of 300 million pesos covered by the issue of 'Guadalupan bonds' and a substantial subsidy from President Luis Echeverría.[57] Designed by Pedro Ramírez Vásquez, the architect who had built the National Museum of Anthropology at Chapultepec, the basilica was constructed in circular form like a great raised tent, with its apex soaring above the high altar and image, bathing that area in sunlight. As Gabriel Chávez de la Mora, a Benedictine monk and an assistant architect in the project, explained, Mary had always been identified as the Ark of the Covenant of the New Testament and symbol of the pilgrim Church. And what was a church but 'a place of reunion for the people of God'? The new basilica thus expressed the liturgical renewal that had been inspired by the Second Vatican Council and was designed to welcome the thousands of pilgrims who arrived daily to pray to the Guadalupe.[58]

As part of this development of the Virgin's cult, in 1975, López Beltrán established the Centre of Guadalupan Studies, which in the following years held a series of National Encounters as a means of assembling the scholars devoted to these themes. At the second conference held at Tepeyac in December 1977, Luis Medina Ascencio, a Jesuit historian, argued that the Church had always accepted miracles as the proof of apparitions and prophecies. He recalled that Benedict XIV had approved of the revelations vouchsafed to St Hildegard, St Brigid and St Catherine of Siena, declaring that although such messages were not part of the Catholic faith, they could be accepted by 'an assent of human faith according to the norms of prudence that renders such revelations a probable and piously credible object'. Obviously, before identifying anything as supernatural, it was first necessary to establish its human reality. The truth of the apparitions, so Medina asserted, was to be found first and foremost in the image itself; but their truth was also supported by the 'primitive account' of Juan González and by Valeriano's *Nican mopohua*, which derived from oral tradition.[59]

Participants at this conference were disconcerted by the forthright arguments of Wigberto Jiménez Moreno, a leading historian, who affirmed his devotion to the Virgin, only then to assert that the image had been painted by Marcos and that Mary had appeared to Juan Diego in 1555. So too, he noted that when one of the native informants of 1666 recalled seeing Viceroy Luis de Velasco on his way to Peru, he obviously referred to an event in 1595.[60] It was left to Fidel de Jesús Chauvet, a Franciscan who had written extensively about the Virgin, to respond to these iconoclastic remarks. Without acrimony he rehearsed the traditional case, and indeed assured those present that Zumárraga had seen Juan Diego but had chosen not the initiate any canonical proceedings because that would have provoked the hostility of the conquerors, who were already aroused by the Franciscans' defence of the Indians. So too, he admitted that the Franciscan silence about the apparitions derived from 'passion and prejudice'. In more positive vein, he cited Martín Enríquez' letter, which attributed the upsurge of devotion at Tepeyac to the miraculous cure of a Spanish grazier, and identified this man as Antonio Carbajal, a city councillor and wealthy landowner, whose son had been saved after falling from his horse.[61]

It was at this conference of 1977 that Lauro López Beltrán presented a paper on 'The Historicity of Juan Diego', in which he rehearsed the argument of Bishop Manríquez that, since the 1666 *Statements* had already been accepted by Rome in 1894, they could be cited for their juridical testimony concerning the ancient tradition of Juan Diego's sanctity. These documents could be corroborated by any number of native annals, the *Nican mopohua* and Spanish sources. So persuasive was his address that Ernesto Corripio Ahumada intervened during the conference to promise that he would do all in his power to promote the beatification of the Indian peasant. At the time, he was still archbishop of Puebla, but he was soon to become a cardinal and archbishop of Mexico.[62] Moreover, the accession of a new pope was soon to effect a radical change in the rules governing the way Rome handled the applications for beatification and canonization.

In 1979 John Paul II came to Mexico and at the basilica of Tepeyac declared: 'Ever since the time that the Indian Juan Diego spoke to the sweet Lady of Tepeyac, you, Mother of Guadalupe, have entered decisively into the Christian life of the people of Mexico.' The newly elected pontiff was greeted with extraordinary manifestations of enthusiasm by millions of Mexicans, and so pervasive was his presence that he re-established the Church in the public forum by indicating so forcefully the sheer extent of its popular support. During his visit the pope constantly compared Mexico to his Polish homeland, observing: 'of my country it is customary to say Poland *semper fidelis.* I wish to be able to say: Mexico *semper fidelis,* Mexico always faithful.' Although he insisted on the necessity of prayer and faith, he also emphasized that the Church had the obligation to defend human rights. In private he obviously encouraged the Mexican bishops to adopt a more public profile and to seek reform of the anti-clerical articles of the Constitution.[63]

Two years later, in 1981, Cardinal Corripio Ahumada celebrated the 450th anniversary of the apparitions, and presided over a congress summoned to discuss the Guadalupe tradition and the beatification of Juan Diego. By then he had already appointed Monsignor Enrique Salazar as the 'postulator' of the cause, charged with the task of gathering the historical materials and framing the theological case for submission in Rome. In *The Historicity of Juan Diego* (1981), López Beltrán recycled much material he had published in early works. But he was also anxious to emphasize his own contribution in preparing the ground for the beatification process. He indicated that the first person to propose canonization was Santiago Beguerisse, a French chemist living in nineteenth-century Puebla. Moreover, Angel Vivanco Esteve, the owner of a house situated next to the basilica that was later to become the Guadalupan Museum, refused to attend the Fourth Centenary ceremonies since 'I do not find a single word of recollection or sympathy for Juan Diego'. Then there was José María Robles, a priest of León, who had written to the exiled bishop of Huejutla about the cause. For all that, López Beltrán signalized Manríquez as the true prophet who had invoked his authority as bishop to advocate the beatification.[64] Moreover, in an effort to demonstrate that Juan Diego had never been entirely forgotten, he now raked across any number of early sermons to demonstrate that Ita y Parra had named him as 'the Jacob of the Indies'; that Vidal de Figueroa had compared him to St John the Baptist; and that Lazcano had followed Sánchez in depicting him as another Moses before the burning bush at Mount Horeb. At the same time, he lamented that excavations of the dilapidated chapel built by Montúfar had failed to uncover any earthly remains

Plate 33   Ernesto Tamariz, *John Paul II*. Monumental statue in the atrium of the basilica of
Guadalupe

which could be attributed to Juan Diego. The premise on which the theological experts based their case at this time was illustrated by a pronouncement of Manuel Rangel Camacho, who affirmed that Antonio Valeriano 'had in his hands "The Gospel of the Guadalupan Apparitions", the *Nican mopohua*, written in the middle of the sixteenth century, in which, in very elegant Nahuatl language, he transmits to us all the details of the Guadalupan Fact'.[65]

The full story of how the Mexicans succeeded in persuading the Congregation of Saints in Rome to approve the beatification of Juan Diego has yet to be told, especially since the abbot of the chapter at Tepeyac, Guillermo Schulenberg Prado, opposed the measure, on the grounds that he could find no historical proof for the existence of the Indian seer.[66] But the authority of the cardinal archbishop and the Mexican episcopate carried the day. The upshot was that during his second visit to Tepeyac, John Paul II published a papal decree dated 6 May 1990, in which the Congregation of Saints recognized Juan Diego's holiness of life and the devotion he had inspired since time immemorial, reasons sufficient to justify his beatification. The decree cited both the *Nican mopohua* and the *Nican moctepana* as testifying to the Indian's ready acceptance of the Virgin's commands and to his devoted years of attendance at the first chapel. After his death he had been described as a saint; as such he had been portrayed in many paintings; and he had been venerated by the faithful in unbroken succession from the time of his death until the present day. Henceforth, in the archdiocese of Mexico it would be obligatory to commemorate his memory on 9 December, and licence was given for all other dioceses in Latin American to do likewise.[67]

In his homily delivered in the basilica on 6 May, John Paul II saluted Juan Diego, not as a seer or as a mediator, but rather as 'the confidant of the sweet Lady of Tepeyac', who could now be invoked as 'the protector and advocate of the natives' of America. His figure was inseparable from 'the Guadalupan Fact' and was always to be associated with Mary in Mexico. He added:

> In likeness of the ancient biblical personages, who were collective representations of all the people, we can say that Juan Diego represents all the natives who welcomed the Gospel of Jesus, thanks to the material assistance of Mary, always inseparable from the manifestation of her Son and the planting of the Church, as was her presence among the apostles on the day of Pentecost.[68]

In his pastoral letter announcing the beatification of Juan Diego Cuauhtlatoatzin, Corripio Ahumada described it as 'an event without precedent in the history of Mexico, because it signalizes the moment in a country when its inhabitants definitively incorporate the true roots of their nationality in perfect equilibrium'. More specifically, he declared that it signalized 'the irreplaceable part of our reality which is Indian'. The following year a costly facsimile edition of the 1666 *Statements* as recorded in 1734 was published, accompanied by a schematic analysis of Juan Diego's virtues. In a prefatory letter, Corripio Ahumada congratulated the editor for her contribution to the study of 'our Guadalupan and Juandieguin historical identity'.[69]

In the years which followed, the promoters of Juan Diego's cause expressed the hope that he would soon be canonized, which is to say, that he would be recognized as a saint by the entire Catholic Church rather than being venerated by a particular country or diocese. But when John Paul II returned to Tepeyac in March 1999, he chose to extend the Mexican Virgin's spiritual empire by recognizing Our Lady of Guadalupe as patron of America, North and South, citing an earlier declaration in which he had described 'the mestizo face of the Virgin of Tepeyac' as an example of 'perfectly inculturated evangelization'.[70] In conferring upon this image a hemispheric mission, the pope thus offered a public challenge to all those currents of thought, religious or secular, which dismissed the veneration of such representations as superstitious or puerile. Within the long history of the papacy, he joined the select company of Benedict XIV, Leo XIII and Pius X, who had endowed the Virgin with ever more ample powers, not to mention Pius XII, who had already saluted her as 'Empress of America, Queen of Mexico'. Within the Catholic Church no other Marian image has been accorded such universal honours.

By the time John Paul II visited Mexico for the last time, the situation of the Church had been transformed, since in 1992 the Mexican government opened relations with the Vatican and recognized the legal personality of all registered religious associations. In effect, the Catholic Church emerged from the shadows of unconstitutionality and was endowed by the State with the legal right to own property, administer schools and universities and organize religious events in public.[71] On the symbolic plane, it is tempting to interpret this transformation in the Church's status as the political ratification of the raising of Juan Diego to the altars. Lest this be thought too fanciful, it should be recalled that the cause of Juan Diego emerged from a Cristero matrix and was justified as the means by which the Indian peasantry would be finally incorporated into the Church. So too, Cardinal Corripio Ahumada welcomed the beatification as the public recognition of the Indian roots of Mexican nationality. Over a century before, Manuel Ignacio Altamirano had declared that 'in every Mexican there is a smaller or greater dosis of Juan Diego'. By obtaining the beatification of this native prototype of the Mexican people, the bishops and clergy who promoted his cause thus sought to affirm the essentially Catholic character of their country and nation.

14

Nican mopohua

I

If Mexican hopes for the canonization of Juan Diego were disappointed, in part Rome's reluctance may have been caused by a renewed spate of controversy and publications in 1995–6 which cast grave doubt on the 'historicity' of the Indian seer. But the polemic also revealed that the Virgin of Tepeyac and her faithful messenger had become symbols of opposing visions of the Mexican Church. If the campaign to beatify Juan Diego had issued from the ranks of former Cristeros and their clerical counsellors, by the 1980s the theologians of Liberation seized upon the Nahua *macehual* as a symbol of the Virgin's 'option for the poor'. New translations were made of the *Nican mopohua*, and the more the text was studied the more its scriptural simplicity attracted commentary and reflection. On all sides of the theological arena there was a tendency to define the apparition narrative as a Mexican, not to say, American gospel, even if no-one precisely defined the character or source of its inspiration. By contrast, the figure of Juan Diego was obscured by unfounded hypotheses about his relation with the royal family of Texcoco. So too, the image of the Guadalupe became the object of pseudo-scientific speculation concerning the configuration of the stars on her tunic and alleged reflections in her eyes. In effect, whereas theologians sought to deploy the *Nican mopohua* for catechetical and pastoral purposes, quasi-history and pseudo-science threatened to distort the tradition. In these circumstances the archbishop of Mexico intervened to defend both the historicity of the apparition narrative and the supernatural origin of the image. And yet, at much the same moment, scholars in the United States sharply questioned the native authorship of the *Nican mopohua* and failed to find any persuasive evidence of a written tradition before 1648.

To observe how traditionalists now sought to buttress their case by pseudo-science, one has only to turn to *The Guadalupan Encyclopedia* (1995), edited and largely written by Xavier Escalada, a Spanish Jesuit long resident in Mexico, whose volumes were lavishly illustrated with reproductions taken from the Guadalupan Museum, albeit in places marred by the editor's saccharine taste in contemporary art. The purpose of the work was apologetic, since it was addressed to intellectuals who doubted 'the supernatural origin' of the image. Escalada proposed to offer reasons to demonstrate 'the historicity of the apparitions' and to provide 'scientific assurance' concerning 'the presence of Mary in her "house" of Tepeyac'.[1] In pursuance of this latter aim, he printed the attractive infra-red photography of the image taken in 1946 by Jesús Cataño Wilhelmy and cited the photographer's surprise on finding that the colours of the image varied according to the degree of light to which it was exposed. So too, he printed a similar photograph taken by Philip S. Callahan in 1979, but rejected the American's conclusion that, although the Virgin's face, tunic and mantle were 'humanly inexplicable', the angel, moon, golden rays, stars, and the arabesques on the tunic were all later additions. If the American photographer had been so impressed by the core picture, it was in part because he found that the Virgin's lips were painted over a ridge caused by the coarse weave of the cloth, a 'coincidence' which created an illusion of pictorial depth. But Escalada reprinted López Beltrán's defence of the arabesques as supernatural in origin.[2] More daring, the *Encyclopedia* reproduced photographic enlargements of the Virgin's eyes which revealed the reflections of a kneeling figure. Here was a theory which had been first advanced in the 1920s, but which had been the subject of a popular book published in 1982 by Juan Benítez, a Spanish journalist. The only problem here was that with greater enlargement yet more figures were found lurking in the Virgin's pupils. For all that, Escalada was persuaded of the possibility that at least Juan Diego could be seen reflected, the image itself thus attesting to the veracity of the apparition narrative.[3] A further scientific 'proof' was provided by Juan Homero Hernández Illescas, who asserted that, if the stars on the Virgin's mantle were linked with appropriate lines, they constituted a diagram of fifteen constellations in the heavens during the solstice of 1531. This diagram was prominently reproduced by Escalada, even if he also inserted a brief note written by an engineer which warned that these stars were later additions since, where their gold had flaked, the blue of the mantle could be seen. In any case, they were painted at regular intervals unlike the clusters of stars in the heavens.[4] In presenting these scientific 'proofs', Escalada obviously sought to demonstrate that the image itself attested to its heavenly manufacture.

As regards historical proofs, Escalada admitted that 'there have always existed anti-guadalupans', intellectuals who had accused the Church of deceiving the faithful, encouraging them to venerate illusions. Following Anticoli, he rehearsed briefly the three great moments of criticism, which was to say, the attacks of Bustamante, Muñoz and García Icazbalceta, not to mention the more recent assertions of O'Gorman. As regards Miguel Sánchez, he commented that 'he is at the centre of the anti-apparitionist whirlwind, he is considered the creator of all the chimera and fables of the apparitions'. Although he had the merit of publishing the first account, he wrote little more than an extended sermon, 'full of baroque conceits and digressions in the field of Sacred Scripture'. By contrast, Escalada saluted Becerra Tanco as 'the prince of the Guadalupan historians', since he had been the first to attest to the existence of the original manuscript written by Valeriano.[5] By way of countering García Icazbalceta's assertion that Sánchez had virtually reinvented devotion to the Mexican Virgin, he reproduced the copper printing plate designed by Samuel Stradanus in 1616–22, which illustrated miracles performed by the Virgin. It was used for printing sheets offering indulgences granted by Archbishop Juan Pérez de la Serna to raise alms for the new church he was building at Tepeyac. Along with these historical proofs, the *Encyclopedia* presented any number of photographs of John Paul II, especially on his visits to Tepeyac, and included the full text of his address when he beatified Juan Diego. Anxious to demonstrate that papal approbation of the Guadalupe was no new thing, he retailed the old story that Benedict XIV had been so taken with Miguel Cabrera's likeness of the Virgin that he had exclaimed 'Non fecit taliter omni natione', a myth Andrade had demolished more than a generation before.[6]

But Escalada also testified to the new-found status of the *Nican mopohua* as a Mexican gospel and concluded his volumes by printing no fewer than six translations of the text, starting with Becerra Tanco and the literal version commissioned by Boturini, but also including those done by Velásquez and Garibay, not to mention the recent attempts by Mario Sánchez Rojas in 1978 and by Guillermo Ortiz de Montellano in 1989. For his part, he praised the account as 'the most beautiful narration that human hand has ever framed in the Continent of Mary'. More important, he affirmed that 'we believe that the mysterious action of God did not only operate in the apparitions to Juan Diego and in the imprinting of the image, but also assisted Valeriano so that he could transmit in writing with the necessary truth, the narrative of the salvific character of this history'.[7] In effect, the *Nican mopohua* was thus defined as a text which was divinely inspired.

Not content with his array of historical and scientific proofs, in his *Encyclopedia* Escalada gave notice of the recent discovery of an ancient codex, and subsequently published this new source as an appendix. Here, indeed, was a document which appeared to prove the apparition narrative. On a rough deer-skin could be observed the faint figure of Juan Diego kneeling on a hill-side before the Virgin. Their figures were the same as those depicted in the engraving of this scene done by Antonio Castro for Becerra Tanco's *Happiness of Mexico* (1675). However, the codex carried the date '1548', so it was clear, Escalada argued, that Castro had copied the scene from the deer-skin. Moreover, there was writing in Nahuatl on the codex, which twice identified Juan Diego as 'Cuatlactoastzon', stating that he had seen his 'beloved little mother' in 1531 and that he died in 1548. For good measure there was also an Aztec glyph of the period under which was written 'Anton Vareliano Judge', a reference to Valeriano's role in preparing this peculiar death certificate. To cap it all, the codex boasted of an authentic signature of Bernardino de Sahagún. Here, indeed, was a great discovery, a rare invention of modern science.[8] Within the context of the Christian tradition, it was rather like finding a picture of St Paul's vision of Christ on the road to Damascus, drawn by St Luke and signed by St Peter.

Where traditionalists mobilized the resources of modern science to demonstrate the supernatural character of the Guadalupe, theologians expatiated upon the catechetical implications of the *Nican mopohua*. In *Saint Mary Tonantzin, Virgin of Guadalupe* (1995), Richard Nebel, a German historian and theologian, displayed little interest in the image itself or in the development of its devotion. He confessed to finding the silence of the early Franciscans 'inexplicable'; remained unimpressed by Sánchez; acutely commented that Becerra Tanco had sought 'to convert tradition into history'; and found no more proof of Valeriano's authorship of the first account than Sigüenza y Góngora's assertion.[9] All his attention was given to the *Nican mopohua*, which presented the essence of the 'Guadalupan kerygma', and, indeed, he translated this gospel proclamation from Nahuatl into German for the 1992 edition of his thesis. But he drew on recent work on apparitions in late medieval Spain to demonstrate the degree to which the Mexican narrative obviously derived from hispanic 'legends', where the Virgin almost invariably appeared to a poor herdsman to reveal the whereabouts of her image and to request that a chapel be built to house it. What was not clear was the extent to which the Mexican account simply transferred these elements into a New World setting or, alternatively, drew upon disparate incidents which had been preserved in oral tradition. The actual facts about Juan Diego were 'very exiguous and fragile' and, indeed, more based on standard European hagiography than on native sources.[10] Moreover, since the colloquies between Juan Diego and the Virgin were dramatic and moving, so Nebel affirmed, they had probably been 'represented as a theatrical work', a theory first advanced by Servando de Mier. As such, the text was best read for its 'theological message' and for its 'existential truth' rather than scrutinized for any objective truth about history. In the kind of prose favoured by German theologians, Nebel concluded: 'the truth of the *Nican mopohua*, whose edifying pedagogical and parametrical functions can be so clearly observed, does not imply so much an act of historical knowledge as a Christian experience of life'. In effect, Laso de la Vega's 'interpretation of faith' grew on tradition, but probably created 'new facts'.[11]

For Nebel, the truths of theology soared far above any concern with mere historicity, since he praised the *Nican mopohua* as a sublime text whose message had endured across the centuries, since 'in the manner of an allegory or a parable, it recapitulates the story of the individual lives of Mexicans as the children of Guadalupe'. It had pastoral relevance for the contemporary Church throughout Latin America. He commented on how the proponents of the Theology of Liberation had cited the text as

Plate 34   José Luis Neyra, *Wonder Woman*

sanction for their arguments, noting that the Ecumenical Centre of Nicaragua had affirmed that 'the message of Guadalupe is that of the *Magnificat*: the poor shall be raised up and the powerful shall be dethroned'. Indeed, a Brazilian theologian had argued that the apparition narrative inverted the traditional manner of preaching the gospel since, when Mary sent Juan Diego to Zumárraga, she invested the Indian with the authority to teach the bishop, thereby anticipating the contemporary Church's 'option for the poor'.[12] What better form of 'inculturation' could be found than in the *Nican mopohua*, where the Christian gospel was expressed in language and concepts that were immediately comprehensible to the labouring masses of Latin America?

The degree to which radicals could vie with traditionalists in extravagance of interpretation was demonstrated by *Guadalupe, Mother of the New Creation* (1997), in which Virgil Elizondo, a Mexican American, boldly proclaimed that no event since Pentecost had exercised such an influence on the development of Christianity as Mary's apparition at Tepeyac, adding, 'liturgically, for us in the Americas, December 12 is as important a feast as December 25 and Easter Sunday are for the Christians of the Old World'. When still a small boy, he had been taken from Texas to Tepeyac, where in the great basilica he had felt that 'in that sacred space, I was part of the communion of earth and heaven, of present family, ancestors and generations to come'.[13] Here is no place to expound Elizondo's romantic philosophy, a mishmash of José Vasconcelos and D. H. Lawrence, in which he contrasted a Europe governed by the principles of reason and domination to pre-hispanic America which had been imbued with natural harmony and sustained by religious myth. He translated the *Nican mopohua* into English and commented that its significance lay in the Virgin telling Juan Diego 'to go to tell the chief spokesperson of God what to do'. Christian America, so he claimed, was essentially mestizo and 'in Our Lady of Guadalupe, Christ became American'. Whereas God the Father, as depicted in Europe, was a stern judge, who threatened punishment and hell-fire, by contrast at Tepeyac Mary acted as a true mother, offering a foretaste of heaven. Elizondo drew upon an ancient insight when he asserted that 'Guadalupe is an image-word that is experienced through the beauty of flower and song', the Nahua terms for divine communication. He added:

> What the written word has been for generations of biblical believers, the painted word has been for generations of believers in the New World. In Our Lady of Guadalupe at Tepeyac, God pitched a tent and came down to dwell among us. The Word became flesh of the Americas through Our Lady of Guadalupe and dwells among us truly as one of us.

In this extraordinary theological scheme, the Guadalupe image thus became the equivalent of both scripture and the Eucharist. Small wonder that Elizondo described Tepeyac as the 'Mountain of the Transfiguration of the Americas'.[14]

II

It was one thing for a German scholar to dismiss questions of history as of little interest: it was quite another for the abbot of the basilica at Tepeyac to endorse that interpretation. In his preface to Nebel's book, Guillermo Schulenberg Prado commended the German as 'a Christian theologian, completely orthodox in his faith'. Turning to the standard tradition, he dismissed Miguel Sánchez for his 'questionable scriptural interpretations saturated with Gongorisms', which was to say, with baroque conceits. With apparent approval, he observed that Nebel interpreted the dialogues of the *Nican mopohua* 'not so much as faithful transmissions of the historical truth of a real concrete fact, in the sense of modern science and historiography, but rather as devout transmissions of a beautiful Marian catechesis, full of profound human and religious significance'. Indeed, so taken was he with the venerable text that he averred that Nebel's 'profound analysis of Mexican Guadalupanism makes me think of a special divine providence' as regards the composition of the *Nican mopohua*. There was substance here for the formation of a true centre of Guadalupan studies, with 'a cultural as well as a religious projection'.[15] But any practical ambitions Schulenberg may have entertained were soon brought to an end when, soon after the centennial celebrations of the 1895 coronation had been concluded, he gave an interview to *Ixtus, Spirit and Culture*, an obscure journal published in Cuernavaca, in which he roundly declared that, owing to the lack of historical evidence for his existence, Juan Diego 'is a symbol, not a reality'. When in May 1996, the Italian journal, *30 Giorni*, reported the substance of this interview and accused the abbot of claiming that Juan Diego was but a phantom, the Mexican press erupted in full pursuit of the unwise prelate.[16]

In substance what Schulenberg affirmed was that 'the permanent miracle of Guadalupe' was the constant devotion she evoked among the Mexican people. But that devotion was based on faith in the Virgin Mary, the Mother of God, and was not inspired by any concern with the historical reality of the apparitions. In any case, what was an apparition but 'an interior phenomenon in which, by a special grace of God, a man is made to see that which no-one else sees and to hear that which no-one else hears'? At Lourdes only Bernadette saw and heard the Virgin. As for the beatification of Juan Diego, the Congregation of Saints had recognized the existence of his cult; it had not pronounced on his historical existence. Even here, Schulenberg admitted, there was a problem, since there had never been any cult in Mexico to Juan Diego and the whole process had been engineered by the archbishop and four or five priests. Were the Indian to be canonized the matter could become more serious, since at that point theologians would have to discuss the implications of an infallible pope canonizing a man of whose existence no historical proof had been found. As for the *Nican mopohua*, no-one knew who had written 'this catechetical or theatrical representation in four acts', but, although it had a certain native flavour, it was imbued with a

European character of catechesis. Turning to the image, the abbot confessed that when he first saw it close up, 'I felt that I had before me something painted by God and not by man.' However, his opinion had changed, since 'if it was the work of a native hand, which is what I believe . . . because I think it was a native hand, I respect the Indian who painted it'.[17] The effect of these declarations, once repeated by the national press, was sufficient to provoke such a public scandal that Schulenberg was obliged to resign. Abbot since 1963, he had superintended the construction of the new basilica and had welcomed John Paul II at Tepeyac both in 1979 and in 1990. For a brief moment it had appeared that he might well become bishop of a new diocese centred on the sanctuary. In the event, as with that other great renovator, Antonio Plancarte, his career ended in tears.

In May 1996 there appeared a brief pamphlet entitled *Did Juan Diego Exist?*, in which the complete text of Schulenberg's interview was reprinted, together with an introduction by José Luis Guerrero, a professor at the Pontifical University of Mexico. Published with the *imprimatur* of the new archbishop of Mexico, Norberto Rivera Carrera, it revealed that the abbot had persistently denied 'the historicity of the Guadalupan Event' and, indeed, had written to Rome opposing the beatification of Juan Diego. Although he possessed the right of conscience to act as he did, especially since there was no doubt of his devotion to the Virgin Mary, such opposition was an incongruous attitude for an abbot of the basilica. After all, most Mexicans believed in 'the objective, historical truth of her intervention in the birth of our mestizo *patria*, and in the real existence of Blessed Juan Diego'. Guerrero noted that the beatification proceedings had lasted for over five years, from 11 February 1984 to 3 April 1989, and that the Mexican case had been presented in a document of 824 pages known as the *Positio*. It was this impressive body of evidence that had persuaded the historical consultants in Rome to approve by majority vote that the historical ground for beatification was persuasive. Once this hurdle was crossed, all that remained was for the panel of theologians to reach their decision. The Congregation of Saints thus affirmed that Juan Diego was 'someone utterly real, a person of flesh and blood'. At no point did Guerrero seek to criticize Schulenberg directly and, indeed, he recognized that the abbot had zealously promoted devotion to the Mexican Virgin.[18]

The upshot of this unhappy affair was a vehement pastoral issued by the archbishop of Mexico, who, on 2 June 1996, complained that the mass media had asserted that 'the apparition of Our Most Holy Mother of Guadalupe was not real and that her peculiar presence among us by means of the miraculous image, which for our happiness we preserve, was not true'. Obviously, the matter was not a question of Catholic faith, since individuals were free in conscience to doubt the historical truth of the apparitions. But, like millions of other Mexicans, so Rivera Carrera averred, he felt wounded in his feelings as 'a son and as a Mexican'. With all the authority conferred upon him as archbishop primate of Mexico, the thirty-fourth successor of Zumárraga, he proclaimed that, as regards the Virgin of Guadalupe, 'I believe, love and profess with all my soul that she is, in a personal and most special sense, the queen and mother of our mestizo *patria*, and came in person to our soil of Mexico to ask of us a church' where she could show herself to be a compassionate mother.[19] Obviously, Mary did not come to lighten burdens, since all who follow her Son have to take up their cross and follow him, but rather she came to listen to their prayers and help cure their pains and sufferings. Although the joy and comfort experienced by the millions of pilgrims who came to Tepeyac sprang from their love and faith, the cult was based on 'tradition, the documents, the facts which constitute and adorn our history'. How could 'our Indian ancestors' have accepted Christ without her intervention, since it was she who healed the antagonism which had divided 'our Spanish and Indian parents'? In any case, 'many of the best talents of the Church, austere professionals of history and theology', had prepared the documents for the beatification of Juan Diego, and had been rewarded by the pope's approval of their cause. Moreover, in the Pontifical University, research on the subject still continued and new developments were to be expected. By way of conclusion, the archbishop cited the *Nican mopohua* to identify himself as another Juan Diego, describing himself as 'a poor commoner, a tail and wing'. Addressing the Virgin, he informed her that her people were disturbed because doubts had been raised about the reality of the apparitions, claiming that 'perhaps your miraculous presence among us is not real'. He further begged the Virgin:

> allow all my brothers to hear me, that the echo of my voice resounds in our snows and mountains, in our jungles and forests, in our lakes and deserts, proclaiming that I, your poor commoner, but also the guardian of your image and through that the spokesman of all your children, believe, and have believed since your love gave me my being through that of my parents, and with your mercy expect to defend and believe until my death your apparitions in this blessed mount, your Tepeyac, that you have now placed under my spiritual guardianship; that, together with my brothers, I believe, I love and I proclaim the apparitions as real and present as the rock peaks of our mountains, as the vastness of our seas, and yet more, much more than these, since 'they shall pass away, but your words of love shall never pass away'.[20]

The rhetorical fervour of this pastoral obviously testified to the heartfelt faith of the archbishop; yet the manner in which he appropriated the voice of Juan Diego confirmed the *Nican mopohua* as an inspired text which could be cited alongside holy scripture. At the same time, Zumárraga's successor firmly defended the supernatural origin of the image of Guadalupe and the special presence of Mary in her sanctuary at Tepeyac. Wounded by the challenge of modern criticism, he returned to the roots of the tradition and, in effect, echoed Miguel Sánchez and, indeed, Blessed Amadeus of Portugal, when he affirmed that the Virgin was spiritually present in the sanctuary where pilgrims flocked to seek help from her miraculous image. 'Non fecit taliter omni natione.' The primate thus confirmed that a particular revelation had been vouchsafed to the Mexican Church: Mary had appeared in New Spain over four hundred years ago and had bequeathed to her chosen people a supernatural image, an inspired scripture and the memory of a sanctified Indian. Obviously, Rivera Carrera was careful to preface his passionate defence of the Mexican faith by explaining that he was not about to touch on any article of Catholic belief, and that Catholics were not bound to accept the historical truths of the apparitions. But that distinction itself rendered the content of his pastoral all the more remarkable and indicated the degree to which the Mexican Church had come to cherish a distinctive Christian tradition. For the rest, it should be noted that in proclaiming himself the guardian of the image, Rivera Carrera implicitly reaffirmed Sánchez' thesis that the Guadalupe is the *pallium*, the spiritual insignia of the archbishops of Mexico.[21] And to emphasize that role, he secured the abolition of the office of abbot and adopted the basilica at Tepeyac as his second episcopal seat, especially since in these years the cathedral of the capital was threatened by collapse.

III

While prelates and theologians explored the catechetical value of the *Nican mopohua*, scholars in the universities, both in Mexico and abroad, carefully examined the historical foundations of the Guadalupe tradition and arrived at negative conclusions. In his *Guadalupan Documents* (1993), Xavier Noguez demonstrated that the array of native codices, testaments and annals cited by the hagiographers of Juan Diego all turned out to be copies taken in the eighteenth and nineteenth centuries, or had long since been lost, or were located in inaccessible private collections. There was not a single reference to the Indian seer prior to 1648. All that the research of the previous century had discovered was a range of evidence which attested to the existence of the sanctuary and its cult at Tepeyac, even if there was no unambiguous reference to the Guadalupe prior to 1555–6. For all that, Noguez followed Garibay and O'Gorman in accepting Valeriano as the author of the Nahuatl apparition account, and postulated the existence of native traditions concerning the apparitions and miracles from which that author had drawn. But, in the last resort, so he concluded, the real proof on which the tradition rested was the faith of the Mexican people, since 'historicity thus does not derive from the veracity but rather from the acceptability of the story through faith'.[22]

It was Stafford Poole, an American historian and Vincentian priest, who presented the case for the prosecution with a rigour not seen since García Icazbalceta and austerely concluded that 'Guadalupe still remains the most powerful religious and national symbol in Mexico today. The symbolism, however, does not rest on any objective historical basis.' At stake here, as his notes made clear, was the reliability of the evidence included in the *Positio*, the Mexican case for the beatification of Juan Diego. Poole had no qualms in challenging the decision of the Congregation of Saints, since he characterized the beatification as 'a benevolent response to the desires of the Mexican hierarchy, but which raises serious questions about the procedures that were followed and the historical analyses that underlay them'.[23] In *Our Lady of Guadalupe* (1995), Poole, who had already written a study of the third archbishop of Mexico, patiently reviewed all the possible sources of the sixteenth and early seventeenth centuries which referred to Our Lady of Guadalupe or which might have been expected to refer to the Virgin. After carefully eliminating the speculations, misattributions and later copies where interpolations and mistranslations were rife, he concluded that, although a number of documents indicated that the image had been installed in the chapel at Tepeyac in 1555–6, there was no mention of Juan Diego or the apparition narrative until Miguel Sánchez published his book.

Although Poole indicated that his purpose was historiographical and not sociological, he drew upon recent research to suggest that in its first century or more, the cult of Guadalupe was more creole than Indian. After all, the copper plate engraved by Stradanus in 1616–21 mainly listed miracles performed for Spaniards. On the same point, he noted that the first recorded likeness of the image was the painting done in 1605 by Baltazar de Echave Orio, where the Virgin was depicted on a mantle, with pleats falling at the sides. Unimpressed by the poem of Angel de Betancourt, he interpreted it as indicating that the apparition narrative had yet to be clarified. As for the poem of 1634, written to lament the image's departure from the city, it attested to a growing belief in the Guadalupe's heavenly origin, but made no reference to any apparitions. Finally, Poole questioned the utility of the 1666 *Statements* as evidence, since they were taken 135 years after the events to which they attested, and their purpose was to establish the existence of a tradition, not to certify the historical truth of the apparitions.[24]

Turning to the 'four evangelists', Poole took little interest in Miguel Sánchez, since 'his style must be judged baroque, meandering and highly metaphorical', capital sins these for any positivist.[25] By contrast, he employed his knowledge of Nahuatl to pronounce that Laso de la Vega's *Huei tlamahuiçoltica* was written in good Church Nahuatl of the kind which had flourished from the 1550s to the 1650s. There was no good linguistic reason to distinguish the *Nican mopohua* from the rest of the work and hence no cause to deprive Laso de la Vega of his rights as author, even if he may well have been assisted by a native scribe. Equally important, Poole examined the manuscripts located in the New York City Library and concluded that they were but later copies of the printed version.[26] So too, the manuscripts of the so-called 'primitive account', attributed by Garibay to Juan González, derived from the late seventeenth century and had no obvious author. Turning to Becerra Tanco and Sigüenza y Góngora, he observed that their claims to have seen or possessed an early manuscript account written in Nahuatl could not be substantiated, since that document had never been seen by any subsequent historian. Their ascription of this manuscript to Valeriano he dismissed as an attempt to provide 'an *imprimatur* for the authenticity of the apparitions', a manœuvre which Poole condemned sharply as 'one of the greatest single errors in the development of the Guadalupan tradition'.[27] He then noted that Florencia obviously had access to a source which contained minor variations from the accounts found in either Sánchez or Laso de la Vega. But by refraining to wield Ockham's razor, Poole then confused matters by asserting that Sigüenza y Góngora had referred to a manuscript native source which was distinguishable from the *Nican mopohua*, an hypothesis which led him to fix upon Uribe as the first scholar to identify the manuscript seen by Becerra Tanco with the text of Laso de la Vega. In his examination of the eighteenth century, Poole was less sure of his footing and for some unexplained reason he fixed upon Mariano Cuevas, the Jesuit historian, as the man responsible for converting the *Nican mopohua* into the *textus receptus* of the apparition narrative, failing to note that throughout the nineteenth century Becerra Tanco's free translation of Laso de la Vega was constantly reprinted.[28]

In his self-chosen role as historical 'detective', Poole surpassed Muñoz and García Icazbalceta and sought to destroy the case presented in the *Positio*. But his eschewal of any theological appraisal of the panegyrical sermons and his dismissal of de la Maza's brilliant hypotheses as 'unscholarly' demonstrated the limits of his historical sympathy. Moreover, when he argued that the cult was more creole than Indian, he moved beyond his self-imposed brief into speculation. For, although there is little evidence of any great geographical diffusion of devotion beyond the Valley of Mexico, the sheer rapidity with which Laso de la Vega published his account in Nahuatl indicated the existence of a native community in the capital which offered a ready audience for that work. In any case, Poole himself noted the disparity in Sánchez between the 'highly wrought interpretation and the native character of the narrative', and hence concluded that 'in a very real sense Sánchez took a cult story that should have been exclusively Indian and appropriated it for the *criollos*'. Like Muñoz and García Icazbalceta, he thus attributed the origin of the apparition narrative to native oral tradition, which was to say, to 'a vague local cult legend', on which Sánchez drew when he wrote his book.[29]

The degree to which Poole's critique disconcerted Guadalupan scholars in Mexico can be best observed in *The Nican mopohua* (1996), where José Luis Guerrero added a substantial appendix to answer the American priest. At once he noted that, in essence, Poole advanced exactly the same case as García Icazbalceta, which was to say, he relied on the argument of universal silence about the apparitions. But, as regards the early

✠

NICAN
MOPOHVA,
MOTECPANA INQVENIN
YANCVICAN HVEITLAMAHVIÇÓLTICA
MONEXITI INÇENQVIZCA ICHPOCHTLI
SANCTA MARIA DIOS YNANTZIN TOÇI-
HVAPILLATOCATZIN, IN ONCAN
TEPEYACAC MOTENEHVA
GVADALVPE.

Acattopa quimottititzino çe
maçehualtzintli itoca Iuan Diego; Auh çatepan ino-
nexiti initlaçò Ixipilatzin ynixpan yancuican Obiſpo
D. Fray Iuan de Sumarraga. Ihuan inixquich tlama-
huiçolli ye quimochihuilia.⌐

E iuh màtlac xihuitl in opehualoc in
atl in tepetl Mèxico, ynyeomoman
in mitl, in chimalli, in ye nohuian
ontlamatcamani in ahuàcan, intepe-
huàcan; in macaçan yeopeuh, yexo-
tla, ye cueponi intlaneltoquiliztli,
iniximachocatzin inipalnemohuani
nelli Teotl DIOS. In huel iquac inipan Xihuitl mill
y quinientos, y treinta y vno, quiniuh iquezquilhuioc
In metztli Diziembre mochiuh oncatca çe maçehual-
A   tzintli,

Plate 35   *Nican mopohua . . .*

Franciscans, he noted that their rigorous theology did not allow them to accept the maternal optimism of the Virgin's message. In any case, since they mainly came from a reformed province in Extremadura, they already opposed the Jeronymites of Guadalupe, so that it was no surprise that they should have chosen to remain silent. And yet their chronicles indirectly testified to the apparitions. Had not Motolinia admitted that at first their preaching elicited little enthusiasm among the Indians, only then, some ten years after the conquest, for the natives to come flocking to accept baptism and learn the elements of the new faith? It was obviously the Virgin's apparition in 1531 which had wrought this great change. If the friars barely took notice of her intervention it was because, as both Motolinia and Mendieta attested, many Indians at this time claimed to have seen visions of Mary.[30] Contrary to what Poole had argued, in those first decades, devotion to Our Lady of Guadalupe was primarily an Indian affair, since the creoles only adopted the Mexican Virgin with any enthusiasm about a century after the apparitions. For the rest, Guerrero complained of Poole's accusations that Becerra Tanco and Sigüenza y Góngora were guilty of forgery and noted that the American priest had compounded Florencia's confusion by postulating a second manuscript source in Nahuatl. By way of conclusion, he strongly objected to Poole's judgement that the symbolism of Guadalupe did not rest on 'any objective historical basis'. After all, even if the apparitions had never happened, what could be more real and objective than the Mexican people's devotion to the Virgin Mary, a devotion which derived from their faith in Christ and his Church, and which had been sustained across the centuries in the face of poverty, exploitation and persecution?[31]

The main purpose of *The Nican mopohua*, however, was to provide an exegesis of that text, and to that end Guerrero printed no fewer than twelve parallel versions, including Laso de la Vega's Nahuatl, Nebel's German, De la Rosa's Latin, Janet Barber's English, and all known Spanish translations, ranging from Becerra Tanco to the author's own interpretation, but giving pride of place to Mariano Rojas. In his introduction, Guerrero afforded a sympathetic assessment of pre-hispanic civilization in which he argued that the Mesoamericans were essentially monist in their religious philosophy, which was to say, they viewed all their gods as so many manifestations of the one divine power which animated the universe. Whereas Mariano Cuevas and countless preachers before him had dismissed the Aztecs as a barbarous tribe, guilty of such horrendous crimes as human sacrifice and cannibalism, by contrast Guerrero praised them for their 'heroic fidelity' to the dictates of natural law and, indeed, asserted that they could well be called 'a holy people'.[32] Underlying this affirmation was a dichotomy drawn between a Europe inspired by a rational, dominating civilization and a pre-hispanic America in which native society lived in harmony with nature, more attracted by poetic myth than by logical reasoning. In effect, Guerrero here attested to a sea-change in the attitudes of the Catholic clergy towards the native past, with priests now adopting the *indigenismo* of their former revolutionary opponents. From this new vantage point, Guerrero strongly criticized not merely the cruelties of the Spanish conquerors, men so inhumane that they cast off their Indian concubines and refused to recognize their mestizo offspring, but also the very friars who had laboured to defend and convert the natives. For these missionaries, no matter how devoted, had scorned Indian religion and had made no attempt to adapt the Christian gospel to the values of native culture. Indeed, as much as their secular counterparts, they treated the Indians as if they were children.[33]

In his exegesis, Guerrero gave notice of new discoveries about Juan Diego's family. Horacio Sentiel Ramírez, the chronicler of the Villa of Guadalupe, had found that two eighteenth-century Indian nuns claimed to be descendants of the Indian seer. From that starting point, he had traced the family line back to Cuatliztactzin, 'White Eagle', a prince of royal family mentioned by Alva Ixtlilxochitl in his history of Texcoco, whom he confidently identified as Juan Diego.[34] This hypothesis had already been adopted by Enrique Salazar, the official promoter of the canonization cause of the Indian seer, who in 1993 had asserted that the name of White Eagle referred to his colour of skin and that Juan Diego was of 'noble origin, a natural son of Netzahualpili', the last lord of Texcoco. So too, Salazar echoed earlier assertions of López Beltrán that in Cuautitlan, Juan Diego's clan had abandoned polytheism and human sacrifices in favour of monotheism, adoring the God of the Near and the Far.[35] In a skilful application of this hypothesis, Guerrero cited Alva Ixtlilxochitl's famous lament about the poverty to which the Spanish conquest had reduced the royal family of Texcoco, and thus described Juan Diego as 'a poor prince'. It was his noble origin that explained how the Virgin's messenger could speak such elevated Nahuatl, 'the language of the palace', and thus was able to discharge his 'diplomatic mission' to Zumárraga so well. On a polemical note he added:

> That Juan Diego is transformed for us from a poor commoner to a poor prince does not contradict history, and only those will lament who have tried to force him and the Most Holy Virgin into the categories of the Theology of Liberation.

Where once Sánchez had invoked theological typology to compare Juan Diego with Moses, these modern commentators now provided their hero with a royal genealogy.[36]

Although Guerrero derided Sánchez and Mier as creole nationalists, his close reading of the *Nican mopohua* drove him to remark that the colloquies between Juan Diego and the Virgin were as beautiful and moving as any found in holy scripture. That the Indian had been able to remember and record Mary's precise words suggested that his memory had been assisted and inspired by a 'master Artist'. So too, did not the Virgin's apparition at Tepeyac recall Christ's transfiguration at Tabor? In accordance with his suspicion of the early Franciscans, Guerrero contrasted

Zumárraga's inquisitorial suspicion of popular religion with the Virgin's request for a chapel, a request which was at once understood by the Mexicans as signifying that she wished to found a new nation under a new covenant, since for them a nation was symbolized by its temple.[37] Yet more important, when Mary commanded Juan Diego to gather flowers, she rooted the Christian gospel deep within the soil of Aztec culture, since for the Indians, flowers were both the equivalents of spiritual songs and by extension, symbols of divine life. Whereas Christ transformed the bread and wine of the Eucharist into his body and blood, the Virgin transformed the flowers into her own likeness, her image thus constituting a perpetual Mexican sacrament. Did not the choice of flowers, so Guerrero exclaimed, 'manifest the unfalsifiable hand of the divine Librettist'? Was not this transfiguration 'perhaps the most brilliant jewel of "inculturation" known to Christian history, which is not to be wondered at, being the Author who he is'?[38] In these comments, Guerrero clearly identified the *Nican mopohua* as a divinely inspired text, a Mexican gospel, which marked the foundation of a new nation. When the Virgin sent Juan Diego to Zumárraga, she united Spaniards and Indians, and thus created 'the Church of Mexico and Mexico itself', especially since in her image she could be seen with 'an unmistakably mestizo face'. If the bishop was converted into 'the lord of the Image . . . the lord of the codex of the Mexican people', Juan Diego could only be venerated as another Moses, as 'the Father of the *Patria*, the true Founder of Mexico'.[39]

In his anxiety to emphasize the Indian origin and character of the Guadalupe tradition Guerrero poured scorn on Miguel Sánchez, arguing that if his book had created a sensation in seventeenth-century Mexico, it was because he had identified the Virgin as the Woman of the Apocalypse. He dismissed this typological argument by observing that 'today we would die laughing at such an idea'.[40] Yet he himself did not hesitate to compare Moses' rod with Juan Diego's flowers, and Mary's apparition with Christ's transfiguration, types which could be found in Sánchez. But, since Guerrero's whole purpose was to identify the *Nican mopohua* as the primordial text of the Guadalupe tradition, he could not afford to recognize the quality of the creole priest's theology. At the same time, his acceptance of Juan Diego as a poor prince had the advantage of answering Garibay's query as to how a peasant could have spoken such fine language, and his upbringing in a palace reinforced the resemblance to Moses. In Guerrero we thus encounter the culmination of some sixty or more years of reflection in which Mexico was finally seen to be blessed, not merely by an image of supernatural origin in which Mary remained miraculously present, but also by an Indian Moses, a poor prince who led his people out of Egypt into the promised land of the Christian Church and, still more, by the possession of an apparition narrative, the *Nican mopohua*, the scriptural power and simplicity of which clearly revealed the assistance of 'the divine Librettist'.

IV

In 1998, Lisa Sousa, Stafford Poole and James Lockhart published a slim volume entitled *The Story of Guadalupe*, in which they printed the Nahuatl text of Laso de la Vega's *Huei tlamahuiçoltica*, accompanied by an English translation and commentary. In his study of the Nahuas after the Spanish conquest, a work based on profound knowledge of the development of colonial Nahuatl, Lockhart had already commented on the linguistic excellence of this work.[41] To understand the significance of their commentary, it should be recalled that, from 1926, when Velásquez published the first complete Spanish translation of the *Huei tlamahuiçoltica*, Mexican scholars had emphasized the differences in style which distinguished the *Nican mopohua* from other sections of this work. Moreover, Garibay had lent all the weight of his scholarship to this argument, affirming that the apparition narrative had been written in the 1560s by a group of Sahagún's pupils at Tlatelolco. The combined effect of these observations was to reinforce the tradition that Laso de la Vega had copied the *Nican mopohua* from a native manuscript source.

But Souza, Poole and Lockhart now concluded that, although obvious differences in style between the various sections of the *Huei tlamahuiçoltica* could be observed, those differences derived from the varying nature and content of the sections. The dialogues between the Virgin and Juan Diego were certainly written in a different way from the relatively brief accounts of miracles. Yet careful scrutiny of the choice of words, verbal constructions, incorporation of Spanish loan words, and spelling variations revealed identical patterns throughout the work. No matter what their origin, all sections had been written or rewritten by the same author. In their linguistic analysis, the American scholars found that the *Huei tlamahuiçoltica* was written in standard Church Nahuatl of Stage Two, which flourished from the 1550s until the 1650s, a form which was more conservative than its 'mundane' counterpart, and hence preserved the literary forms which could be found in Sahagún and other clerical authors of the sixteenth century. Subject to certain modifications, the orthography resembled that used by Horacio Carochi, the Jesuit author of *The Art of the Mexican Language* (1645). However, the text contained features which indicated that the author was a Spaniard, since there were certain errors in verbal constructions, inexplicable variations in the spelling of the same word, and a conscious attempt to avoid using Spanish loan words which, by then, had been incorporated into standard Nahuatl. If the general conclusion was that Laso de la Vega was the author, it was also likely that he had been assisted by one or more native scribes, and there still remained the mystery of how he came to write such generally excellent Nahuatl.[42] In reaching this conclusion, these scholars thus concurred with John Bierhorst, the translator of Aztec 'ghost-songs' who, after examining the *Nican mopohua*, concluded that 'although composed in Nahuatl, the account is clearly the invention of a European mind'.[43]

But on what source did Laso de la Vega base himself? Did he work from an oral tradition or were there traces of an earlier account? The answer to these often-raised questions was peremptory. As regards the apparition narrative, Laso de la Vega based himself on Miguel Sánchez. The American scholars extracted from Sánchez the bare outline of the apparition narrative and showed that Laso de la Vega converted reported speech into dialogues and engaged in rhetorical, often poetic enlargement without significant change to the content of the story. There was an identity in substance between the two accounts, save that Laso de la Vega omitted the third apparition. If that was the case, then it was clear that one author borrowed from the other, or both borrowed from a common source. But, apart from his choice of an Indian as protagonist, there was nothing in Sánchez to suggest any Nahuatl influence. By contrast, in Laso de la Vega there were a few obscure constructions, the meaning of which became readily apparent by scrutiny of the equivalent passage in Sánchez. Here was direct linguistic proof of dependence on the Spanish version. Thus, for example, in the *Nican moctepana*, the record of miracles, there occurs a strange phrase which literally means 'here two people', but which the context indicates should be understood as 'two here-people, two indigenous people'. At the corresponding point in his account, Sánchez simply has 'two Indians'.[44]

As regards the list of miracles, fourteen in Laso de la Vega as against six in Sánchez, these American scholars suggest that the source of the additional miracles was mainly to be found in the copper plate engraved by Stradanus in about 1615, a source which Stafford Poole had previously studied with great care. However, it should be noted that Francisco de Florencia commented on the number of tablets and paintings of miracles which hung in the sanctuary, most of which were adorned with inscriptions telling the story of the scenes depicted.[45] In effect, Stradanus copied his miracles from the sanctuary walls and Laso de la Vega may well have done likewise when he came to relate the marvels listed in the *Nican moctepana*.

In a few precise pages Sousa, Poole and Lockhart have launched a devastating criticism of the received linguistic and textual foundation of the tradition of Our Lady of Guadalupe. In the late seventeenth century, Luis Becerra Tanco first postulated the existence of a primordial manuscript written in Nahuatl which related the story of the Virgin's apparitions to Juan Diego. It was a text, so he admitted in 1666, which had been printed by Laso de la Vega. It was Carlos Sigüenza y Góngora who identified the author of the manuscript as Antonio Valeriano, the most celebrated native disciple of the Franciscans. In the eighteenth century, thanks to Lorenzo Boturini, Juan José de Eguiara y Eguren and Patricio Fernández de Uribe, this version became the orthodox account. Despite bouts of fierce controversy, the defenders of the Guadalupan tradition in the nineteenth century did little more than defend this hypothesis. From the time of Sigüenza y Góngora, however, it was customary to distinguish the authorship of the *Nican mopohua* from the authorship of the remainder of the *Huei tlamahuiçoltica*. When in 1926 Primo Feliciano Velásquez printed a facsimile of the entire text, together with a Spanish translation, the poetic style of the apparition narrative could clearly be distinguished from the concise prose of the miracles and other sections. Here was a distinction which was further emphasized by Angel María Garibay Kintana, who, if he saw no good reason to deny that Laso de la Vega was the author of the introduction, conclusion and miracles, was at pains to define the *Nican mopohua* as the work of Sahagún's native disciples and hence written in the sixteenth century at the college of Santa Cruz Tlatelolco. It is this Mexican tradition, sustained and developed over three hundred years, which has now been sharply controverted by a group of American scholars, all expert in colonial Nahuatl. They argue that the entire *Huei tlamahuiçoltica* was written by Laso de la Vega and that he took the apparition narrative from Miguel Sánchez, albeit employing dialogue and poetic embellishment to transform it. In effect, the attempt to by-pass Sánchez and base the Guadalupan tradition upon a native foundation now appears to have been fundamentally misconceived.

In all this there is a poignant irony. At the very time when the *Nican mopohua* had come to be seen as an inspired text, a Mexican gospel, its true authors have been identified as two creole priests. Yet, apart from Francisco de la Maza, virtually all modern scholars and theologians have united to dismiss the *Image of the Virgin Mary, Mother of Guadalupe, Miraculously Appeared in the City of Mexico* (1648) as an insufferable example of baroque conceits and extravagant applications of scripture. Moreover, the hunt for native sources of the apparition narrative has led to the complete neglect of Miguel Sánchez and Luis Laso de la Vega, the first evangelists and true founders of the Guadalupe tradition. As yet we know little about these men. What were their parentage and education? How did Sánchez come to frame such a profound theology of the image? Where did Laso de la Vega learn such excellent Nahuatl? What were the relations between these two priests? Here are questions enough for more than another book.

15

Epiphany and revelation

In the very years when devotion to Our Lady of Guadalupe was magnified by the beatification of Juan Diego and her recognition as patron of all America, the historical foundations of the tradition were thus seen to be unstable. To be sure, the research and arguments of scholars had little influence over the ardent faith of the millions of pilgrims who entered the sanctuary at Tepeyac. Nor, indeed, did these findings demand a radical revision of the apparition narrative since, if need be, that account could always be defended by appeal to an oral rather than a written tradition. So too, devotion could be justified by the obvious affirmation that the Guadalupe is a Mexican portrait of the Virgin Mary and, as such, should command all due veneration. In effect, the current controversy which surrounds the image derives from a nineteenth-century concern with 'historicity' and is animated on both sides of the debate by a latter-day positivism which impels apparitionists to insist on 'the Guadalupan Fact', and their opponents to hint at forgery and condemn error. What is absent is a theological interpretation of the image and its tradition which takes recent research into account. In these circumstances, all that an historian can do is to consult the principal declarations of the Catholic Church and see how they bear, if at all, on Our Lady of Guadalupe and her first evangelist, Miguel Sánchez.

The constitutions and decrees of the Second Vatican Council (1962–5), however, have little to say about holy images other than to exhort the faithful to 'carefully observe what has been laid down in the past concerning the cult of images of Christ, of the blessed Virgin and of the saints'. This recommendation is supported by reference to the Second Council of Nicaea (787) and the Council of Trent (1545–63).[1] That sixteenth-century assembly, it will be recalled, defended the veneration offered to holy paintings and sculptures by silently appropriating the famous dictum of St Basil the Great (330–79) when it declared that 'due honour and reverence is owed to them, not because of some divinity or power that is believed to reside in them . . . but because the honour showed to them is referred to the original which they represent'.[2] So too, the *Catechism of the Catholic Church*, approved by John Paul II in 1992, includes this devotion within the context of liturgical celebration and justifies the presence of holy images in churches as witnesses of Christ's Incarnation and as aids to prayer. The four articles on the subject cite the Second Council of Nicaea and St John Damascene's treatise on images, without mention of any veneration which these paintings and sculptures might attract.[3] In effect, the modern Catholic Church carefully eschews any official theological pronouncement about the cult of images, but implicitly endorses the arguments of the Greek Fathers.

To comprehend the significance of the Guadalupe it is thus necessary to consult the theology of the Orthodox Church, especially since, by reason of the iconoclastic crisis, the veneration and style of icons were so carefully regulated. It was St Basil the Great, so Orthodox theologians claim, who proposed an equivalence between images and the gospels when he wrote: 'What the word transmits through the eye, that painting silently shows through the image . . . by these two means mutually accompanying one another . . . we receive knowledge of the one and same thing.' To this day, these theologians teach that 'the holy image, just like Holy Scripture, transmits not human ideas and conceptions of truth, but truth itself – the divine revelation'. Through contemplation of icons, the faithful strengthen and deepen the truths imparted by the gospels, a veneration in which the learned as much as the ignorant participate. There is no question here of paintings being regarded as the Bible of the illiterate. It follows from this equivalence of image and scripture that the great iconographers were as much inspired by the Holy Spirit as were the evangelists, with the consequence that their portrayals of Christ and the Virgin Mary were regarded as authoritative by their disciples. There was no room for individual originality in sacred art. On the other hand, there was always the possibility of new inspiration. It was in fifteenth-century Russia, for example, that Andrew Rublev depicted the Holy Trinity in the form of the three angels who visited Abraham. In a memorable reflection, St Ignatius of Antioch (c. 35–c. 107) wrote to the Ephesians: 'He who possesses in truth the word of Jesus can hear even its silence.'[4] In much the same words a patriarch of Constantinople, Nicephorus (758–828), defended the veneration of icons on the grounds that 'they are expressive of the silence of God, exhibiting in themselves the ineffability of a mystery that transcends being'.[5]

If the decrees of the Second Vatican Council and the modern *Catechism* are reviewed from the perspective of Eastern theology, nowhere is there greater agreement than in their constant invocation of the Holy Spirit. In *Lumen gentium* the Church is defined as a mystical body, with Christ as its head and the Holy Spirit as its soul, since, as St Thomas Aquinas wrote: 'as one body is constituted by the unity of the soul, so is the Church by the unity of the Spirit'.[6] In these decrees and in its *Catechism*, the Catholic Church affirms that it was the Holy Spirit who inspired the authors of holy scripture; who guides popes and bishops in their teaching of the gospel; who consecrates the Eucharist and sacraments; and who animates individual prayer and conscience. Moreover, in *Lumen gentium* the Virgin Mary is described as the 'shrine of the Holy Spirit', as the first and super-eminent Christian, and as 'the type of the Church'. In the same way that, through the Holy Spirit, Mary conceived and brought forth Christ into the world, so also, by the power of the Holy Spirit, the Church strives through its members to incarnate Christ across the centuries and among all nations.[7] It obviously follows from these principles that, as in the Eastern Churches, holy images in the Catholic Church are to be seen as the work of the Holy Spirit, with the most venerable endowed with a sacred charisma, silently offering pilgrims the occasion to renew their prayer and deepen their faith.

The implicit conclusion to be drawn from the official pronouncements of the Vatican is that the image of Our Lady of Guadalupe must number among the most potent expressions of the Holy Spirit in the long history of the Catholic Church. Why else has the image been recognized by the Holy See as the patron, not merely of Mexico, but of the entire New World? Like the great, primordial icons of the Orthodox Church, the Guadalupe was thus the inspired work of the Holy Spirit, and so powerful was that inspiration that for three centuries Mexican painters sedulously reproduced the image, not daring to modify even the slightest detail of its figure, their originality confined to the margins and corners of the canvas. From the time that the Guadalupe was first seen until the present day, the image has evoked the devotion and strengthened the faith of countless Mexicans. Instinctively saluted as 'Our Mother of Guadalupe' and even, in Mexican style, as 'the little mother', the Virgin of Tepeyac acts like a magnet, as Sigüenza y Góngora affirmed, silently generating a power which attracts millions of pilgrims to a sanctuary where the Eucharist is daily offered for their benefit.[8] At the same time, the Virgin has acted as a symbol of the Mexican Church and has been invoked in all moments of trial and persecution. And as Mexicans now settle in the United States, so they take their devotion with them, thus extending the range of the Virgin's realm. In all this, if we are to believe the official pronouncements of the Catholic Church, the influence of the Holy Spirit is manifest.

Although Miguel Sánchez has been much derided for his baroque conceits, his identification of the Guadalupe as the Woman of the Apocalypse was an application of St Augustine's teaching and an anticipation of the Second Vatican Council. The vision of St John was always interpreted as a type of both Mary and the Church and hence, as Sánchez himself noted, the Guadalupe was thus the type and symbol of the Mexican Church. Applying the evangelist's cosmic drama to New Spain, he presented the Spanish conquest as a battle between the angels of light led by Cortés and the legions of Huitzilopochtli. From that struggle there came a new Jerusalem, the Guadalupe born amidst the flowers of paradise, symbol, as always, of the Church which worshipped the Lamb. So too, when Sánchez described the image as the equivalent of Aaron's flowering staff, he recalled that the same staff had been used by Moses as a sign to impress Pharaoh, and that it was eventually to be preserved in the Ark of the Covenant.

Plate 36   Our Lady of Guadalupe

Since the image had been offered to Zumárraga as a sign of the Virgin's presence, it could be defined as the bishop's *pallium*, his insignia of office, and a clear symbol of the archbishop's primacy in New Spain. Moreover, when Sánchez described the image as the Ark of the Covenant, he implicitly invoked the Holy Spirit who 'overshadowed' the Israelite original, not to mention the operation of his power in Christ's conception. The appearance of the image thus marked the foundation of the Mexican Church.[9] Although Sánchez' typological mode of reasoning at first sight appears obscure, in essence he drew upon St Augustine to frame a profound theology of the birth of the Church in Mexico.

But, within the cult of images as it developed in New Spain, there is a stumbling block, what scriptural scholars call an *aporia*, a difficulty or doubt. Sánchez drew a clear distinction between miraculous images and mere representations, and declared that the sanctuaries of miraculous images were like spiritual fortresses where the faithful were protected from the assaults of Satan. As we have seen, Blessed Amadeus of Portugal reported in his *New Apocalypse* that the Virgin Mary had promised him that 'I shall also be with you bodily until the end of the world . . . in my images of brush or of carving and then you shall know that I am in them, when you see that some miracles are done through them.' It was this text which inspired colonial preachers, especially Jesuits, to compare the image of Guadalupe to the sacrament of the Eucharist, arguing that, in a mode similar to the Eucharistic transubstantiation of bread and wine into the body and blood of Christ, the flowers of Tepeyac had been transformed into paint and colour and then transfigured into a heavenly likeness of the Virgin.[10] Such an interpretation, however, appears to run counter to the declaration of the Council of Trent, when it denied that a divine power dwelt in any holy image. But whatever the theological reasoning, it is clear that cult images do indeed differ from mere representations. To this day, there are a select number of images, mainly, but not invariably, of the Virgin, which attract pilgrims; figure as patrons of cities, provinces and nations; and elicit fervent devotion. In a word, they possess a charisma and a presence which exert a power over the faithful. What is the theological explanation of their power? Once again, about the only acceptable alternative to Blessed Amadeus' revelation is to invoke the power of the Holy Spirit, which impels the faithful to turn to those images which he inspired.

The equivalence of word and image advanced by Orthodox theologians was echoed in New Spain, when Jerónimo de Valladolid lamented the absence of documents certifying the appearance of the Guadalupe, only then to declare that the image did not require written proof, since 'it speaks for itself and testifies to its miraculous origin . . . In her image and through her image the Sovereign Lady speaks of the miracle . . . She herself is the writing in the hand and form of God on the membranes of our hearts.' What could be more appropriate than this 'hieroglyphic writing', since the natives of Mexico had always used figures and images to record the sacred events of their history and religion?[11] As much as any icon, the Virgin of Tepeyac silently taught the truths of revelation as effectively as scripture since, like the gospels, the image was conceived through the inspiration of the Holy Spirit. But this equivalence raises questions. After all, in framing the gospels God employed human authors who, despite their inspiration, retained the full use of their faculties and who could in no sense be seen as mere puppets used by a divine ventriloquist. Such is the teaching of the Second Vatican Council. Indeed, theologians had already criticized the doctrine of direct verbal inspiration as a form of docetism, since it denied the humanity of the prophets and evangelists.[12] If that be the case, is there any real reason to suppose that when the Holy Spirit conceived the idea of the Guadalupe, he refrained from employing a human agent to implement that design? Why should this particular image be thought to have been created through the transfiguration of flowers without human intervention? It is surely more theologically appropriate to presume that the Holy Spirit worked through a human agent, which is to say, through an Indian artist, possibly the painter known as Marcos de Aquino. Such an origin in no way derogates from the character of the Guadalupe as a pre-eminent manifestation of the Holy Spirit's inspiration.

But, if a native artist was the inspired painter of the Guadalupe image, does this mean that the apparition narrative now has to be discarded as a figment of Sánchez' baroque imagination? As we have seen, the *Nican mopohua* was but a dramatic enlargement of the account found in Sánchez, embellished with all the rhetorical resources of Church Nahuatl. Before addressing that question, however, it is useful to ascertain what the *Catechism of the Catholic Church* has to say about such matters.

> Throughout the ages, there have been so-called 'private' revelations, some of which have been recognized by the authority of the Church. They do not belong, however, to the deposit of the faith. It is not their role to improve or complete Christ's definitive Revelation, but to help live more fully by it in a certain period of history. Guided by the Magisterium of the Church, the *sensus fidelium* knows how to discern and welcome in these revelations whatever constitutes an authentic call of Christ or his saints to the Church.[13]

Since the apparition narrative of Our Lady of Guadalupe has been welcomed so warmly by the faithful and accepted so authoritatively by popes and bishops, there can be no question of Catholics rejecting the truths it teaches. What needs to be ascertained, however, is the character of those truths.

Since a growing number of churchmen have concluded that in some sense, not clearly defined, the *Nican mopohua* is an inspired text, it is advisable to turn to *Dei verbum*, in which the Second Vatican Council addresses the question of biblical inspiration. It declares that: 'God chose and employed human agents, using their own powers and faculties in such a way that they wrote as authors in the true sense, and yet

God acted in and through them, directing the content solely and entirely as he willed.' Interpretation of scripture has to take into account literary *genre*, since 'truth is presented and expressed differently in historical, prophetic, or poetic texts, or in other styles of speech'.[14] The application of these principles has allowed Catholic commentators to admit that the Infancy narratives of St Matthew and St Luke are more inspired by theological purpose than by any concern for biographical detail. The flight of the Holy Family to Egypt was in part modelled on Moses' infancy and in part on the Joseph of Genesis. So too, St John the Baptist's tardy conception corresponded to Sarah's equally late conception of Isaac. In the Magnificat the Virgin Mary uttered the words once sung by Hannah in thanksgiving for the birth of Samuel. In effect, the evangelists composed their narratives in order to demonstrate that the birth of Christ, Messiah and Lord, fulfilled scriptural prophecy and initiated a new covenant between God and humanity. As a leading biblical commentator has noted: 'it is now clear in Roman Catholic thought that inspiration of the Scriptures does not guarantee historicity', always provided that the theological truth of the narrative is respected.[15]

If these principles of interpretation be applied to the apparition narrative composed by Sánchez, then it is clear that his primary purpose was theological and that historical facts were of little concern to him. The starting point, the conclusion and the whole purpose of his work were to exalt, define and explain the heaven-sent image of Guadalupe. To this end he filled his text with citations from scripture, the Church Fathers and later theologians. In accordance with the cultural climate of New Spain, he wrote within a well-established *genre* of narratives about miraculous images and the Virgin's apparitions and, in particular, drew on Cisneros' account of Los Remedios and, in all likelihood, on Murillo's history of Our Lady of Pilar. But he transformed their conventional approach by modelling his story on the biblical accounts of Moses' encounters with God at Horeb and on Mount Sinai. His deployment of typology was thus not a question of metaphor, a mere comparison of Juan Diego with the Patriarch, but took the form of a re-enactment in which Juan Diego acted like Moses, with the image of Guadalupe not merely identified as the staff used both by Moses and Aaron to impress Pharaoh, but also as the Ark of the Covenant with the Tables of the Law. In devising this 'theologoumen', Sánchez sought to provide his country and Church with a theological foundation based on a primordial covenant celebrated between the Virgin Mary in her image of Guadalupe and the Mexican people. So profound was his prophetic revelation that the Mexican Church has spent almost four centuries developing its implications.

But did Juan Diego really exist? There seems no good reason to deny the possibility that there may well have been an Indian called Juan who lived close to Tepeyac at some point in the sixteenth century, and who was renowned for his devoted service in the sanctuary. Such a man may well have claimed to have spoken with the Virgin. In this context, Florencia reported that a small copy of the Guadalupe once owned by Juan

Diego was given by his grandson to a well-known Jesuit. It is possible that the Indian seer at times may well have acted as a *demandante*, which is to say, he solicited alms for the sanctuary at Tepeyac, since it was common for these men to carry a copy of the image on whose behalf they begged.[16] So too, Sánchez may well have heard reports and reminiscences of so devoted a servant of Our Lady of Guadalupe. But all these suppositions are but hypotheses, since no written historical evidence of the existence of such a man has survived. In any case, Juan Diego, the Santiago of Mexico, is a personage far removed from any Indian who lived in the sixteenth century, since his dialogues with the Virgin and his subsequent actions were designed by Sánchez so as to portray him as a symbolic Mexican Moses.

When John Paul II went to Tepeyac in 1990 to beatify Juan Diego, he declared that 'In the likeness of the ancient biblical personages, who were collective representations of all the people, we can say that Juan Diego represents all the natives who welcomed the Gospel of Jesus, thanks to the maternal assistance of Mary.' In the same way that Mary is the type of the Church, so Juan Diego is the type, the symbolic, representative figure, of all the Indians whose devotion to Our Lady of Guadalupe brought them into the Mexican Church.[17] Controversy over ill-judged questions about historicity can only obscure the theological truths imparted both by the image of Guadalupe and by the *Nican mopohua*. That human hands and minds intervened, as much in the painting of the image as in the framing of the apparition narrative, does not alter the conclusion that, in the eyes of the Catholic Church, the Guadalupe is an inspired work of the Holy Spirit and the *Nican mopohua* a revelation which depicts the spiritual foundation of the Mexican Church.

Notes

Abbreviations

Colección de obras	*Colección de obras y opúsculos pertenecientes a la milagrosa aparición de la bellísima imagen de Nuestra Señora de Guadalupe, que se venera en su santuario extramuros de México*, 2 (unnumbered) vols. (Madrid, 1785)
Sermonario mexicano	*Sermonario mexicano*, ed. Narciso Bassols, 3 vols. (Mexico, 1889)
Testimonios históricos	*Testimonios históricos guadalupanos*, ed. Ernesto de la Torre Villar and Ramiro Navarro de Anda (Mexico, 1982)

Introduction

1 Richard Hakluyt, *The Principal Navigations, Voiages and Discoveries of the English Nation* (London, 1589), 8 vols., Everyman edn (London, n.d.), VI, 256–9.

2 The text of this dispute is reprinted in *Testimonios históricos*, pp. 36–141.

3 Hakluyt, *Voiages*, VI, 314–15.

4 For St Ignatius and Labre see *The Oxford Dictionary of the Christian Church*, ed. F. L. Cross and E. A. Livingstone, 3rd edn (Oxford, 1997), pp. 818–19, 940. For Loreto, see Michel de Montaigne, *The Complete Works*, trans. Donald M. Frame (Stanford, 1948), pp. 970–4.

5 Herbert Thurston, 'Santa Casa di Loreto', *The Catholic Encyclopedia*, ed. Charles Herberman *et al.*, 16 vols. (New York, 1907), XIII, 454–6; Rafael Chiribay Calvo, 'Apuntes para una cronología sobre el temple de Nuestra Señora del Pilar', in Eduardo Torra de Arana *et al.*, *El Pilar es la Columna: historia de una devoción. Ensayos* (Zaragoza, 1995), pp. 195–201. Note also Esteban Anticoli, *Historia de la aparición de la Santísima Virgen María de Guadalupe en México*, 2 vols. (Mexico, 1897), II, 89, where it is stated that Loreto received its office on 16 September 1699, Pilar on 7 August 1723 and Guadalupe of Mexico on 25 May 1754.

6 Hans Belting, *Likeness and Presence: A History of the Image before the Era of Art*, trans. Edmund Jephcott (Chicago, 1994), pp. 458–9, 471–4.

7   Antonio de la Calancha, *Crónica moralizada del orden de San Agustín en el Perú*, ed. Ignacio Prado Pastor, 6 vols. (Lima, 1974), II, 623–5, 642–4.

8   On Amadeus see *Prophetic Rome in the High Renaissance Period: Essays*, ed. Marjorie Reeves (Oxford, 1992), pp. 129–83.

9   Here begins a summary of the book; consult the relevant chapters for references.

10   The best introduction to Sánchez is still Francisco de la Maza, *El guadalupanismo mexicano*, 3rd edn (Mexico, 1984), pp. 48–73; see also D. A. Brading, *The First America: The Spanish Monarchy, Creole Patriots and the Liberal State, 1492–1867* (Cambridge, 1991), pp. 343–61.

11   See Peter Brown, *The Cult of the Saints* (London, 1981), pp. 13–18; David Hume, 'The Natural History of Religion', in *Hume on Religion*, ed. Richard Wollheim (London, 1963), pp. 31–98.

12   Owen Chadwick, *The Popes and the European Revolution* (Oxford, 1981), pp. 456–7.

13   Richard Ford, *A Hand-Book for Travellers in Spain and Readers at Home*, ed. Ian Robertson, 3 vols. with continuous pagination (Carbondole, Ill., 1966), III, 1425.

14   Ruth Harris, *Lourdes: Body and Spirit in the Secular Age* (London, 1999), *passim*.

15   *The Education of Henry Adams: An Autobiography* (Boston and New York, 1918), pp. 384–5; see also Henry Adams, *Mont-Saint-Michel and Chartres* (Boston and New York, 1933), pp. 87–103.

1   **Image and typology**

1   Jaroslav Pelikan, *Imago Dei: The Byzantine Apologia for Icons* (New Haven, 1990), pp. 72–3.

2   Moshe Barasche, *Icon: Studies in the History of an Idea* (New York, 1992), pp. 111–21; Edwyn Bevan, *Holy Images* (London, 1945), pp. 87–93.

3   Exodus 20.4–5; Deuteronomy 5.4–5.

4   Romans 1.22–3; Bevan in *Holy Images* lists the Old Testament texts which denounce idolatry, pp. 18–19.

5   Belting, *Likeness and Presence*, pp. 80–107.

6   Pelikan, *Imago Dei*, pp. 65–6; St Theodore the Studite, *On the Holy Icons*, trans. Catherine P. Roth (Crestwood, N.Y., 1981), p. 53.

7   Belting, *Likeness and Presence*, pp. 49–53, 62, 208–23.

8   *Ibid.*, pp. 47–9, 62, 84–95; see also Jaroslav Pelikan, *The Christian Tradition: A History of the Development of Doctrine*, 5 vols. (Chicago, 1971–89), II, *The Spirit of Eastern Christendom 600–1700*, in 91–145.

9   Pelikan, *Imago Dei*, pp. 74–8; Belting, *Likeness and Presence*, pp. 144–54.

10   *Decrees of the Ecumenical Councils*, ed. Norman P. Tanner, 2 vols. (London, 1990), I, 135–6.

11   St John of Damascus, *On the Divine Images*, trans. David Anderson (Crestwood, N.Y., 1980), pp. 15, 21–31.

12   *Ibid.*, pp. 27, 80; Hebrews 9.4.

13   St John of Damascus, *On the Divine Images*, p. 98.

14   *Ibid.*, pp. 25, 73.

15   *Ibid.*, pp. 16–17, 52–3.

16   *Ibid.*, pp. 73–4; for the concept of the Great Chain of Images see Pelikan, *Imago Dei*, pp. 159–76; and Barasche, *Icon*, pp. 221–30.

17   St John of Damascus, *On the Divine Images*, pp. 27, 46, 75–80. See also David Freedberg, *The Power of Images: Studies in the History and Theory of Response* (Chicago, 1989), pp. 378–407.

18   St Theodore the Studite, *On the Holy Icons*, pp. 47, 100–3, 110.

19   Belting, *Likeness and Presence*, pp. 173–83, 225–55.

20   *Ibid.*, p. 213.

21   Barasche, *Icon*, p. 202.

22   Belting, *Likeness and Presence*, pp. 314, 342–53.

23   St Augustine, *City of God*, ed. David Knowles (London, 1972), Bk XXII, chap. 8, pp. 1033–48.

24   Peter Brown, *The Cult of the Saints, passim*.

25   Américo Castro, *España en su historia: cristianos, moros y judíos*, 2nd edn (Madrid, 1983), pp. 104–35; T. D. Kendrick, *St James in Spain* (London, 1960), pp. 13, 38–40, 63.

26   Benedicta Ward, *Miracles and the Medieval Mind: Theory, Record and Event 1000–1215* (Aldershot, 1987), pp. 36–42.

27   Belting, *Likeness and Presence*, pp. 298–308.

28   Peter Linehan, *History and Historians of Medieval Spain* (Oxford, 1993), pp. 592–9.

29   Miri Rubin, *Corpus Christi: The Eucharist in Late Medieval Culture* (Cambridge, 1991), pp. 176–95.

30   On typology see G. W. H. Lampe and K. J. Woollcombe, *Essays in Typology* (London, 1957), *passim*; and Leonhard Goppelt, *Typos: The Typological Interpretation of the Old Testament in the New*, trans. Donald H. Madorig (Grand Rapids, Mich., 1982), pp. 108–31.

31   For a lucid interpretation of this difficult text see Richard Bauckham, *The Theology of the Book of Revelation* (Cambridge, 1993), *passim*.

32   St John of Damascus, *On the Divine Images*, p. 78; Lampe and Woollcombe, *Essays in Typology*, pp. 31–2.

33   D. S. Wallace-Hadrill, *Eusebius of Caesarea* (London, 1960), pp. 169–78.

34   St Augustine, 'On the Catechising of the Uninstructed', *The Works of Aurelius Augustine*, ed. Marcus Dods (Edinburgh, 1831), IX, 312–33.

35   St Augustine, *City of God*, pp. 593–9, 643, 687.

36   *Ibid.*, pp. 873–8, 860–2; on chronology see p. 213.

37   R. A. Markus, *Saeculum: History and Society in the Theology of St Augustine* (Cambridge, 1970), pp. 20–3, 52–5.

38 Marjorie Reeves, *The Influence of Prophecy in the Later Middle Ages: A Study of Joachimism* (Oxford, 1969), *passim*; also Delmo C. West and Sandra Zimdars-Swartz, *Joachim of Fiore* (Bloomington, 1983), *passim*.

39 Reeves, *The Influence of Prophecy*, pp. 176–228; on the medieval use of typology see Erich Auerbach, *Scenes from the Drama of European Literature* (Manchester, 1984), pp. 11–76.

40 Reeves, The *Influence of Prophecy*, pp. 171–4, 275–6, 279–80; also San Vicente Ferrer, *Biografía y escritos*, ed. José María de Garganta and Vicente Forcada (Madrid, 1946), pp. 37–49, 460–2.

41 St John of Damascus, *On the Divine Images*, pp. 31–2, 71–2.

42 Luke 1.35, 46–55; Exodus 40.34; see Raymond E. Brown, *The Birth of the Messiah: A Commentary on the Infancy Narratives in Gospels of Matthew and Luke*, 2nd edn (New York, 1993), pp. 311–28, 357–65.

43 St Irenaeus, *Proof of the Apostolic Preaching*, trans. Joseph P. Smith (London, 1952), pp. 69–72.

44 *Decrees of the Ecumenical Councils*, I, 70.

45 Thomas Livius, *The Blessed Virgin in the Fathers of the First Six Centuries* (London, 1893), pp. 273–7.

46 Revelation 12.1–3, 7, 13–14.

47 Livius, *The Blessed Virgin*, p. 341.

48 St John Damascene, *On Holy Images followed by Three Sermons on the Assumption*, trans. Mary H. Allies (London, 1898), pp. 158–60, 168–73.

49 *The Catholic Encyclopedia*, XIII, 454–6; see also Kathleen Weil-Garris, *The Santa Casa di Loreto: Problems in Cinquecento Sculpture*, 2 vols. (New York, 1977), *passim*.

50 Ana Morisi-Guerra, 'The *Apocalypsis Nova*: A Plan for Reform', in *Prophetic Rome*, ed. Reeves, pp. 27–50; Ramón Mujica Pinilla, *Angeles apócrifos en la América virreinal*, 2nd edn (Lima, 1996), pp. 55–79.

51 Desiderius Erasmus, 'The Handbook of the Militant Christian', in *The Essential Erasmus*, ed. John P. Dolan (New York, 1964), pp. 61–2, 66–9.

52 Carlos M. N. Eire, *War against the Idols: The Reformation of Worship from Erasmus to Calvin* (Cambridge, 1986), pp. 16–17, 58–62, 75–5, 151; Richard Bauckham, *Tudor Apocalypse* (the Sutton Courtenay Press, 1978), pp. 41–54, 126–49; Thomas H. Luxon, *Figures: Puritan Allegory and the Reformation Crisis in Representation* (Chicago, 1995), pp. 34–75.

53 *Decrees of the Ecumenical Councils*, II, 774–6.

54 Examine the printed catalogues of the British Library and the Cambridge University Library.

55 *Decrees of the Ecumenical Councils*, II, session 22, pp. 732–4.

56 *Ibid.*, II, 733.

57 Belting, *Likeness and Presence*, pp. 458–72; also Hugh Trevor-Roper, *Renaissance Essays* (London, 1985), pp. 223–38.

58 *The Spiritual Exercises of Saint Ignatius of Loyola*, trans. W. H. Longridge (London, 1919), pp. 100–8, 198–9; also H. Outram Evenett, *The Spirit of the Counter-Reformation*, ed. with postscript by John Bossy (Cambridge, 1968), pp. 43–66.

59 Joscelyn Godwin, *Athanasius Kircher: A Renaissance Man and the Quest for Lost Knowledge* (London, 1979), pp. 18–23, 56; R. J. W. Evans, *The Making of the Habsburg Monarchy 1500–1700* (Oxford, 1979), pp. 433–42.

2   Myth and history

1   Juan de Salazar, *Política española*, ed. Miguel Herrero García (Madrid, 1945), pp. 43, 73–82, 223.

2   *Ibid.*, pp. 49–51, 64, 151–76, 199–219, 224–31.

3   Robert B. Tate, *Ensayos sobre la historiografía peninsular del siglo XV* (Madrid, 1970), pp. 75–99, 289–94.

4   Hernando de Acuña, *Varias poesías*, ed. E. Catena de Vindel (Madrid, 1954), p. 342.

5   Francisco López de Gómara, *Historia general de las Indias*, ed. Jorge Gurría Lacroix (Caracas, 1979), pp. 7–8, 118–19, 319.

6   Juan Caramuel Lobkowitz, *Architectura civil recta y obliqua* (Vegeren, 1678), pp. 25–6.

7   Juan Antonio Ramírez et al., *Dios arquitecto: J. B. Villalpando y el templo de Salomón* (Madrid, 1996), pp. 32–3, 169–74, 208–9.

8   Fernando Chueca Goitia, *Casas reales en monasterios y conventos españoles* (Bilbao, 1982), pp. 143–56.

9   Eusebius of Caesarea, *The Church History and Other Writings* (New York, 1890, facs. edn, 1979), pp. 586–7.

10 Juan de Palafox y Mendoza, *Obras*, 13 vols. (Madrid, 1762), I, 650–5; V, 324.

11 Juan de la Puente, *Tomo primero de la conveniencia de las dos monarquías católicas, la de la Iglesia Romana y la del Imperio Español, y defensa de la precedencia de los Reyes Católicos de España de todos los reyes del mundo* (Madrid, 1612), pp. 9–11, 201–3, 245–8.

12 Juan Miguel González Gómez and José Roda Peña, *Imaginería procesional de la Semana Santa de Sevilla* (Seville, 1992), *passim*; Susan Verdi Webster, *Art and Ritual in Golden Age Spain* (Princeton, 1998), pp. 57–61.

13 Peter Linehan, 'The Beginnings of Santa María de Guadalupe and the Direction of 14th Century Castile,' *Journal of Ecclesiastical History*, 36 (1985), pp. 284–304.

14 William A. Christian Jr, *Apparitions in Late Medieval and Renaissance Spain* (Princeton, 1981), pp. 688–95; Chueca Goitia, *Casas reales*, pp. 117–19, 127–33.

15 Diego Murillo, *De la excelencias de la insigne y noblísima ciudad de Zaragoza* (Barcelona, 1616), pp. 1–3, 8–15, 32.

16 Diego Murillo, *Fundación milagrosa de la capilla angélica y apostólica de la Madre de Dios del Pilar* (Barcelona, 1616), pp. 1–13, 23–5, 277.

17   *Ibid.*, pp. 61–5.

18   *Ibid.*, pp. 67–9, 258, 272–3.

19   *Ibid.*, pp. 65, 95–9, 106–11, 127–36, 273; citations on pp. 133, 273.

20   Sor María de Agreda, *Mística Ciudad de Dios*, 3 vols. (Antwerp, 1694), III, 122–38.

21   *Ibid.*, I, unpaginated approbation by Miguel de Escortia, bishop of Tarazona, 6 May 1667.

22   *Ibid.*, I, 'prólogo galeato', i–xvii, lxv.

23   Gonzalo Fernández de Oviedo, *Historia general y natural de las Indias*, ed. Juan Pérez de Tudela, 5 vols. (Madrid, 1959), IV, 228–9.

24   Francisco López de Gómara, *Historia de la conquista de México*, ed. Jorge Gurría Lacroix (Caracas, 1979), pp. 164–5.

25   Juan de Torquemada, *Los veinte y un libros rituales y monarquía indiana*, ed. Miguel León-Portilla *et al.*, 7 vols. (Mexico, 1975–83), II, 9–10, 39, 326–30; Brading, *The First America*, pp. 102–27, 272–92.

26   Jerónimo de Mendieta, *Historia eclesiástica indiana*, ed. Joaquín García Icazbalceta (Mexico, 1870, fasc. edn, 1971), pp. 15–17, 175–6, 210–11; Torquemada, *Monarquía indiana*, II, 9–10.

27   Torquemada, *Monarquía indiana*, I, 132–5, 283–4, 314–15, 396–7.

28   *Ibid.*, V, 339–40, 344, 355; *Códice Mendieta: documentos franciscanos siglos XVI y XVII*, ed. Joaquín García Icazbalceta, 2 vols. (Mexico, 1892, facs. edn, 1971), II, 172–5.

29   Torquemada, *Monarquía indiana*, III, 357–8.

30   Mendieta, *Historia eclesiástica*, pp. 220–2, 448; on Pedro de Gante and native painters see Guillermo Tovar de Teresa, *Pintura y escultura en Nueva España 1557–1640* (Mexico, 1992), pp. 43–7; Joaquín García Icazbalceta, *Bibliografía mexicana del siglo XVI*, ed. Agustín Millares Carlo, 2nd end (Mexico, 1954), pp. 474–8; Torquemada, *Monarquía indiana*, V, 174–8.

31   Torquemada, *Monarquía indiana*, I, 408–15, 418–21.

32   Juan de Grijalva, *Crónica de la orden de N. P. S. Agustín en las provincias de la Nueva España* (Mexico, 1624), p. 42.

33   *Documentos inéditos del siglo XVI para la historia de México*, ed. Mariano Cuevas (Mexico, 1914, facs. edn, 1975), p. 299; Bernardino de Sahagún, *Historia de las cosas de Nueva España*, ed. Angel María Garibay K., 4 vols. (Mexico, 1956), III, 160.

34   Grijalva, *Crónica*, pp. 21–2.

35   *Ibid.*, pp. 71–5.

36   *Ibid.*, pp. 82–5.

37   Luis de Cisneros, *Historia del principio y origen, progresos venidas a México y milagros de la santa imagen de Nuestra Señora de los Remedios, extramuros de México* (Mexico, 1621), pp. 26–37.

38   *Ibid.*, pp. 39–44.

39   *Ibid.*, unpaginated introduction.

40   *Ibid.*, p. 25.

41   *Ibid.*, pp. 49–63.

42   *Ibid.*, pp. 2–4, 15–22.

43   *Ibid.*, pp. 11–13, 24–9, 45–6, 139.

44   *Ibid.*, pp. 7–11.

45   *Ibid.*, p. 39.

46   *Ibid.*, pp. 80–98, 137.

47   *Ibid.*, pp. 48–79.

48   *Ibid.*, p. 48.

49   *Ibid.*, pp. 99–127.

50   *Ibid.*, pp. 46–7.

51   *Ibid.*, pp. 124–28.

3   The Woman of the Apocalypse

1   Cisneros, *Historia*, p. 20.

2   Stafford Poole, *Our Lady of Guadalupe: The Origins and Sources of a Mexican National Symbol, 1531–1797* (Tucson, 1995), pp. 122–4.

3   Bernal Díaz del Castillo, *Historia verdadera de la conquista de la Nueva España*, ed. Joaquín Ramírez Cabañas, 2 vols. (Mexico, 1968), II, 17; see also II, 365.

4   *Coplas a la partida, que la soberana Virgen de Guadalupe hizo de esta Ciudad de México, para su hermita, compuesta de un devoto suyo* (Mexico, 1634, re-edition, Mexico, c. 1683–94); unpaginated. There is a copy of this rare pamphlet in the John Carter Brown Library, Providence, Rhode Island; it is quoted extensively in *Album conmemorativo del 450 aniversario de las apariciones de Nuestra Señora de Guadalupe* (Mexico, 1981), pp. 46–51, 233–5.

5   Miguel Sánchez, *Sermón de San Felipe de Jesús* (Mexico, 1640), unpaginated introduction, pp. 1, 13.

6   Miguel Sánchez, *Imagen de la Virgen María, Madre de Dios de Guadalupe. Milagrosamente aparecida en la ciudad de México. Celebrada en su historia, con la profecía del capítulo doce del Apocalipsis* (Mexico, 1648). All references are to *Testimonios históricos*, pp. 152–276, which provides the first complete re-edition of the original text. I have consulted copies of the 1648 edition in both the British Library and Condumex.

7   *Ibid.*, pp. 178–97, 236–8.

8   *Ibid.*, pp. 153–5.

9   Miguel Sánchez, *Novenas de la Virgen María, Madre de Dios, para sus dos devotísimos santuarios, de los Remedios y Guadalupe* (Mexico, 1665), reprinted in *Colección de obras*, I, 64. Note that Mogrovejo compared Sánchez to 'our Spaniard Flavio Dextro, forgotten in antiquity, but now restored'.

10   Sánchez, *Imagen de la Virgen María*, pp. 158–9.

11   *Ibid.*, pp. 158–62; Sánchez also cited the sermon *De sanctis*, at that time attributed, albeit wrongly, to St Augustine.

12   *Ibid.*, pp. 162–4.

13   *Ibid.*, pp. 162–3; on St Vicente Ferrer, see Sánchez, *Novenas*, p. 71.

14   Sánchez, *Imagen de la Virgen*, pp. 167–74.

15   *Ibid.*, pp. 165–77.

16   *Ibid.*, pp. 177–8.

17   *Ibid.*, pp. 177–81. Note that Sánchez described 'Diego' as Juan's 'sobrenombre', which could mean an epithet, a title or a surname.

18   Murillo, *Fundación milagrosa*, pp. 68–9, 272–3.

19   Sánchez, *Imagen de la Virgen*, p. 182.

20   *Ibid.*, pp. 183–6.

21   *Ibid.*, pp. 186–9.

22   *Ibid.*, pp. 190–1; see 2 Corinthians 3.18.

23   Sánchez, *Imagen de la Virgen*, pp. 192–3; see Isaiah 61.1; Luke 4.18.

24   Sánchez, *Imagen de la Virgen*, pp. 194–5; Romans 13.11.

25   Sánchez, *Imagen de la Virgen*, pp. 193–6; Psalm 132.5.

26   Sánchez, *Imagen de la Virgen*, pp. 196–7; Ecclesiasticus 38.28–36.

27   Sánchez, *Imagen de la Virgen*, pp. 196–8; Psalm 27.8.

28   Sánchez, *Imagen de la Virgen*, pp. 199–201.

29   *Ibid.*, pp. 201, 211–12, 221, 229, 233.

30   *Ibid.*, pp. 203–9; for Aaron's rod see Numbers 17.8; Hebrews 9.4.

31   Sánchez, *Imagen de la Virgen*, pp. 205–7.

32   *Ibid.*, pp. 236–7; Ecclesiasticus 45.7–31.

33   Sánchez, *Imagen de la Virgen*, pp. 215–6; see also Murillo, *Fundación milagrosa*, p. 51.

34   Sánchez, *Imagen de la Virgen*, pp. 241–3.

35   *Ibid.*, pp. 238–44.

36   *Ibid.*, pp. 246–52.

37   *Ibid.*, pp. 238–40, 247–9.

38   *Ibid.*, pp. 229–33, 248–56. See also Serge Gruzinski, *La guerra de las imágenes: de Cristóbal Colón a 'Blade Runner' (1492–2019)* (Mexico, 1994), pp. 132–3.

39   Sánchez, *Imagen de la Virgen*, pp. 255–8.

40   *Ibid.*, pp. 259–60.

41   *Ibid.*, pp. 263–6; Laso de la Vega's opinion was dated 2 July 1648; that of Bárcenas, 16 July 1648.

42   *Ibid.*, pp. 260–3.

43   Sánchez, *Novenas*, p. 69.

44   Miguel Sánchez, *El David seráphico* (Mexico, 1653), pp. 2–7.

45   Sánchez, *Novenas*, p. 81; see also St Dionysius the Areopagite, *The Mystical Theology and the Celestial Hierarchies* (Fintry, Surrey, 1949), pp. 32–49.

46   Sánchez, *Novenas*, pp. 79, 170.

47   *Ibid.*, pp. 101–3, 225, 259–64, 282–6.

48   *Informaciones sobre la milagrosa aparición de la Santísima Virgen de Guadalupe recibidas en 1666 y 1723*, ed. Fortino Hipólito Vera (Amecameca, 1889), pp. 66–72.

49   Antonio de Robles, *Diario de sucesos notables (1665–1703)*, ed. Antonio Castro Leal, 3 vols. (Mexico, 1946), I, 144–6.

50   Nicolás de Fuenlabrada, *Oración evangélica y panegyrica . . . a María Santísima en su milagrosísima imagen del español Guadalupe en la Estremadura* (Mexico, 1681), p. 15; Julián Gutiérrez Dávila, *Memorias históricas de la congregación del Oratorio de la ciudad de México* (Mexico, 1736), pp. 253–5.

4   Indian seer

1   Mateo de la Cruz, *Relación de la milagrosa aparición de la santa imagen de la Virgen de Guadalupe, sacado de la historia que compuso Br. Miguel Sánchez* (Mexico, 1660), reprinted in *Testimonios históricos*, pp. 267–81; José Mariano Beristain de Souza, *Biblioteca hispano-americana septentrional*, 3rd edn, 5 vols. (Mexico, 1957), II, 174–5.

2   De la Cruz, *Relación*, pp. 279–80.

3   *Ibid.*, p. 281. There is a facsimile reproduction of the manuscripts of these statements in *Las Informaciones jurídicas de 1666 y el beato Juan Diego*, ed. Ana María Sada Lambretón (Mexico, 1991), pp. 110–426.

4   *Diccionario bio-bibliográfico de la Compañía de Jesús de México*, ed. Francisco Zambrano and José Gutiérrez Casillas, 16 vols. (Mexico, 1961–77), VII, 310; *Informaciones de 1666*, pp. 130–1, 186–9.

5   Susanne L. Stratton, *The Immaculate Conception in Spanish Art* (Cambridge, 1994), pp. 103–4.

6   *Informaciones de 1666*, pp. 1–4; Sánchez, *Imagen de la Virgen María*, in *Testimonios históricos*, p. 158.

7   *Informaciones de 1666*, pp. 16–19.

8   *Ibid.*, pp. 24–7.

9   *Ibid.*, pp. 21, 52–9; Fernando de Alva Ixtlilxóchitl, *Obras históricas*, ed. Edmundo O'Gorman, 2 vols. (Mexico, 1975), pp. 9–36.

10   *Informaciones de 1666*, pp. 66–73.

11   *Ibid.*, pp. 73–130.

12   *Ibid.*, pp. 133–8, 172–83.

13   *Ibid.*, pp. 187–9.

14   Francisco de Florencia, *La Estrella del Norte de México* (Mexico, 1688, reprinted as 2nd vol. of *Colección de obras*), pp. 281–93; Florencia summarized the Statements of 1666, pp. 216–78.

15   *Ibid.*, pp. 290–3; on Loreto see *The Catholic Encyclopedia*, III, 454–6.

16   *Informaciones de 1666*, pp. 138–67.

17   The translation by Primo Feliciano Velásquez (Mexico, 1826) is reprinted in *Testimonios históricos*, pp. 282–308; see also Florencia, *La Estrella del Norte*, p. 91; Cruz also praises him, *Testimonios históricos*, pp. 268–9.

18   *Testimonios históricos*, p. 266; on González see *Diccionario*, VII, 298–313. There is now a translation in English accompanied by a transcription of the Nahuatl original in: *The Story of Guadalupe: Luis Laso de la Vega's 'Huei tlamahuiçoltica' of 1649*, ed. and trans. Lisa Sousa, Stafford Poole and James Lockhart (Stanford, 1998).

19   *Testimonios históricos*, pp. 289–90.

20   See Jesús Galera Lamadrid, *Nican mopohua: breve análisis literario e histórico* (Mexico, 1991), which together with the Nahuatl original prints in parallel columns the translations by Luis Becerra Tanco (1675), Primo Feliciano Velásquez (1926), Angel María Garibay (1978) and Mario Rojas Sánchez (1978). See the commentaries by Stafford Poole, *Our Lady of Guadalupe*, pp. 110–26; and James Lockhart, *The Nahuas after the Conquest: A Social and Cultural History of the Indians of Central Mexico, Sixteenth through Eighteenth Centuries* (Stanford, 1992), pp. 247–50. Although this chapter was written before the appearance of *The Story of Guadalupe*, I see no reason to modify its conclusions; for a discussion of that work see chapter 14.

21   *Testimonios históricos*, pp. 179–90; for miracles see pp. 245–51, 298–304; Galera Lamadrid, *Nican mopohua*, pp. 134–7. Quotations pp. 135–7, 140–7, 158–9, 186–9.

22   *Testimonios históricos*, pp. 275–6, 304–5.

23   *Ibid.*, pp. 305–7.

24   See Poole, *Our Lady of Guadalupe*, pp. 112–14; Lockhart, *The Nahuas after the Conquest*, pp. 246–50, 387–90, 402.

25   *Diccionario*, VII, 298; Francisco de Florencia, *Menologio de los varones más señalados en perfección religiosa de la provincia de Jesús de Nueva España, nuevamente añadido por Juan Antonio de Oviedo* (Mexico, 1747), pp. 115–16, where González is described as the author of a history of Our Lady of Guadalupe.

26   Luis Becerra Tanco, *Origen milagroso del santuario de Nuestra Señora de Guadalupe, extramuros de la ciudad de México* (Mexico, 1666). For a description of this rare work see José Toribio Medina, *La imprenta en México (1539–1821)*, 8 vols. (Santiago de Chile, 1912, facs. edn, Mexico, 1989), II, 381–2. Note that this text was inserted as 'a paper' in the *Informaciones de 1666*, pp. 138–67.

27   Luis Becerra Tanco, *Felicidad de México en el principio y milagroso origen que tuvo el santuario de la Virgen María Nuestra Señora de Guadalupe, extramuros: en la aparición admirable de esta soberana Señora y de su prodigiosa imagen*, 2nd edn, ed. Antonio de Gama (Mexico, 1675); see Beristain, *Biblioteca*, I, 237–40.

28   Becerra Tanco, *Felicidad de México*, pp. 10–11, 18, 28–30; *Informaciones de 1666*, p. 139.

29   *Ibid.*, pp. 11–13.

30   *Ibid.*, pp. 13–14; *Informaciones de 1666*, pp. 149–50.

31   Alva Ixtlilxóchitl, *Obras históricas*, I, 418–25; II, 7–9, 137.

32   *Informaciones de 1666*, pp. 149–51; Becerra Tanco failed to note that Laso de la Vega had omitted the third of the four apparitions; on the authorship of Laso de la Vega's book see Medina, *La imprenta en Mexico*, II, 269–73; and Sousa, Poole and Lockhart, *The Story of Guadalupe, passim.*

33   Becerra Tanco, *Felicidad de México*, pp. 1, 3, 7, 14.

34   *Ibid.*, pp. 15, 18–19.

35   *Ibid.*, pp. 16–18.

36   Torquemada, *Monarquía indiana*, v, 176–7.

37   Becerra Tanco, *Felicidad de México*, pp. 16, 31.

38   *Ibid.*, pp. 9–10, 14, 20–4; on guardian angel, p. 25.

39   *Ibid.*, pp. 26–8; Alonso Ramos Gavilán, *Historia del célebre santuario de Nuestra Señora de Copacabana y sus milagros e invención de la Cruz de Carabuco* (Lima, 1621), pp. 30–53, 164.

5   Presence and tradition

1   José Vidal de Figueroa, *Teórica de la prodigiosa imagen de la Virgen Santa María de Guadalupe de México* (Mexico, 1661), p. 3; on Vidal see Beristain, *Biblioteca*, v, 146. Note that this edition of Beristain incorporates José Fernando Ramírez, *Adiciones y correcciones* (Mexico, 1898); see chapter 11, n. 18.

2   Vidal de Figueroa, *Teórica*, pp. 5–7.

3   *Ibid.*, pp. 8–9.

4   Stratton, *The Immaculate Conception*, pp. 58–65, 98–104.

5   Lorenzo Benítez, *Sermón panegyrico que en la solemne fiesta con que celebra la aparición de Nuestra Señora de Guadalupe de México, su ilustre archicofradía* (Mexico, 1685), pp. 4–10.

6   Francisco de Mendoza, *Sermón que en el día de la aparición de la imagen de Guadalupe, doce de diciembre de 1672 predicó* (Mexico, 1673), pp. 2–9.

7   Luis de Santa Teresa, *Sermón que predicó . . . a la milagrosa aparición de su sacratísima y prodigiosa imagen* (Mexico, 1683), p. 8.

8   Juan Antonio Lobato, *El fénix de las Indias único por inmaculado floreciendo en una tilma de palma, María en su Concepción Purísima aparecida en Guadalupe* (Mexico, 1700), pp. 5, 14–15.

9   Juan de Robles, *Sermón que predicó . . . el día doce de Diciembre de 1681 en la iglesia de Nuestra Señora de Guadalupe de Querétaro, su patria* (Mexico, 1682), pp. 2, 4–8.

10   Juan de San Miguel, *Sermón . . . a nacimiento de Nuestra Señora y dedicación de su capilla de Guadalupe en la santa iglesia catedral . . .* (Mexico, 1671), pp. 1–15.

11   *Flor y canto de poesía guadalupana siglo XVII*, ed. Joaquín Antonio Peñalosa (Mexico, 1987), pp. 219–24.

12   Florencia, *La Estrella del Norte*, p. 59.

13   *Diccionario*, VI, 703–66; Beristain, *Biblioteca*, II, 273–4; Florencia, *La Estrella del Norte*, p. 161; Francisco de Florencia, *Origen de los dos célebres santuarios de la Nueva Galicia, obispado de Guadalajara en la América Septentrional*, 3rd edn (Mexico, 1766), p. 49.

14   Florencia, *La Estrella del Norte*, pp. 44, 51.

15   *Ibid.*, pp. 356–8, 373, 132–3, 390–405.

16   *Ibid.*, pp. 192–4, 576–7.

17   *Ibid.*, pp. 195–204; see Torquemada, *Monarquía indiana*, III, 357–8.

18   *Ibid.*, pp. 187–215.

19   *Ibid.*, pp. 216–78; these statements were not published in full until 1889.

20   *Ibid.*, pp. 383–9; Florencia, *Menologio*, pp. 115–16.

21   Florencia, *La Estrella del Norte*, pp. 299–336.

22   *Ibid.*, p. 325; *Testimonios históricos*, p. 187.

23   Florencia, *La Estrella del Norte*, p. 316; Agustín de Betancurt, 'Menologio franciscano', pp. 45–6, published with separate pagination in his *Teatro mexicano* (Mexico, 1697–98, facs. edn, Mexico, 1971).

24   Florencia, *La Estrella del Norte*, pp. 416–33.

25   *Ibid.*, pp. 439–86, 533–73, 682; miracle cure of Andalusian, p. 484.

26   *Ibid.*, pp. 163–9, 503–23.

27   *Ibid.*, pp. 591–604.

28   *Ibid.*, pp. 148–53.

29   *Ibid.*, pp. 619–38, 661–2, 674–82; Villaseca's silver statue, p. 650.

30   *Ibid.*, pp. 157–61, 497, 666–7.

31   For Camoen's 'Estrella del Norte' (Polestar) see Rodríguez Velarde's unpaginated approbation of Becerra Tanco's *Felicidad de México*.

32   Francisco de Florencia, *La milagrosa invención de un tesoro escondido . . .* , 2nd edn (Seville, 1745), pp. 1–3, 86–91, 123.

33   Francisco de Florencia, *Dos célebres santuarios*, pp. 130–6, 149.

34   Florencia, *La Estrella del Norte*, pp. 5–12, 17–18, 28.

35   *Ibid.*, pp. 486–9.

36   Baltazar de Medina, *Crónica de la santa provincia de San Diego de México de religiosos descalzos de N. S. P. Francisco de la Nueva España* (Mexico, 1682), p. 123; Florencia, *Dos célebres santuarios*, p. 150.

37   Florencia, *Dos célebres santuarios*, p. 49.

38   *Ibid.*, p. 49. See also Gruzinski, *La guerra de las imágenes*, pp. 118–42, 189–90.

39   Francisco de la Maza, 'Los evangelistas de Guadalupe y el nacionalismo mexicano', *Cuadernos Americanos*, 6 (December 1949), pp. 163–88, reprinted in his *El guadalupanismo mexicano*, pp. 54–97; see also Vicente de Paul Andrade, *Ensayo bibliográfico mexicano del siglo XVII* (Mexico, 1899, facs. edn, Mexico, 1971), pp. 559–60.

40   On Sigüenza y Góngora, see Andrade, *Ensayo bibliográfico*, pp. 716–28; Brading, *The First America*, pp. 362–72; Carlos Sigüenza y Góngora, *Primavera indiana. Poema sacro-histórico. Idea de María Santísima de Guadalupe de México, copiada de flores* (Mexico, 1662), reprinted in *Testimonios históricos*, pp. 334–58; Also Carlos de Sigüenza y Góngora, *Glorias de Querétaro* (Mexico, 1680, reprinted Mexico, 1945), pp. 10, 53–4.

41   Carlos de Sigüenza y Góngora, 'Teatro de virtudes políticas', in *Obras históricas*, ed. José Rojas Garcidueñas (Mexico, 1960), pp. 230–8, 240–1, 254–5.

42   Carlos de Sigüenza y Góngora, *Paraíso occidental* (Mexico, 1684), unpaginated prologue; Carlos de Sigüenza y Góngora, *Piedad heróica de don Fernando Cortés*, ed. Jaime Delgado (Madrid, 1960), p. 64.

43   Medina, *Crónica*, pp. 222–3, 226–7, 230–5; for Calancha see Brading, *The First America*, pp. 322–34.

44   Betancurt, *Teatro mexicano*, unpaginated prologue, where he lists Sigüenza y Góngora's works. See also Agustín de Betancurt, *Crónica de la provincia del santo evangelio de México: quarta parte del Teatro Mexicano* (Mexico, 1697), pp. 127–32; and his 'Menologio franciscano', pp. 45–6. All these works are reprinted in facs. edn in one vol. (Mexico, 1971).

45   Sigüenza y Góngora, *Paraíso occidental*, pp. 3–5; *Piedad heróica*, pp. 58–61; and Carlos de Sigüenza y Góngora, *Libra astronómica y filosófica* (Mexico, 1690; reprinted Mexico, 1959), p. 4.

46   Sigüenza y Góngora, *Piedad heróica*, p. 65.

47   Florencia, *La Estrella del Norte*, unpaginated approbation; Elías Trabulse, *Los manuscritos perdidos de Sigüenza y Góngora* (Mexico, 1988), *passim*.

6   Patron of Mexico

1   Cayetano de Cabrera y Quintero, *Escudo de armas de México* (Mexico, 1746), facs. edn, introduction by Victor M. Ruiz Naufal (Mexico, 1981), pp. 35–7, 499–513.

2   *Ibid.*, pp. 51–8, 60–8, 71–9.

3   *Ibid.*, pp. 33–44, 68–71, 221–8.

4   *Ibid.*, pp. 38–42, 79–95, 396–412.

5   *Ibid.*, pp. 214–26, 237–50.

6   *Ibid.*, pp. 206–13, 228–33.

7   *Ibid.*, pp. 96–126.

8   *Ibid.*, pp. 148–71, 450–5; see also Juan Ignacio María de Castorena, Ursúa y Goyeneche and Juan Francisco Sahagún de Arévelo y Ladrón de Guevara, *Gacetas de México* (Mexico, 1722–42), facs. edn, 3 vols. (Mexico, 1988), III, 876–7, 884–5, 901–8.

9   Cabrera, *Escudo de armas*, p. 132; Bartolomé Felipe de Ita y Parra, *La Madre de la salud: la milagrosa imagen de Guadalupe* (Mexico, 1739), pp. 5–9, 17.

10   Cabrera, *Escudo de armas*, pp. 268–79.

11   *Ibid.*, pp. 392–4, 465–83; *Gacetas de México*, II, 908–10.

12   Cabrera, *Escudo de armas*, pp. 490–6.

13   *Ibid.*, pp. 285–98.

14   *Ibid.*, pp. 299–306.

15   *Ibid.*, pp. vii, xxxv, 7–8, 319–35, 367; citations on pp. xxvi, 17.

16   *Ibid.*, pp. 314–16, 331–3.

17   *Ibid.*, pp. 314–7, 331–5; citation on p. 337.

18   *Ibid.*, pp. 341–7; Amadeus cited pp. 340; 353–7; Juan Diego's image of Guadalupe, p. 520.

19   *Ibid.*, pp. 520–1.

20   *Ibid.*, pp. 366–82.

21   *Ibid.*, pp. 516–19; see also Antonio Pompa y Pompa, *El gran acontecimiento guadalupano* (Mexico, 1967), pp. 86–7.

22   Cabrera, *Escudo de armas*, approbation, pp. xxiv, xxxviii.

23   José Ignacio Bartolache, *Manifiesto satisfactorio: opúsculo guadalupano* (Mexico, 1790), pp. 44–7.

24   Francisco Javier Conde y Oquendo, *Disertación histórica sobre la aparición de la portentosa imagen de María Santísima de Guadalupe de Mexico*, 2 vols. (Mexico, 1852), I, 102; II, 177.

25   Medina, *La imprenta en México*, v, 21–2; see Victor M. Ruiz Naufal, introduction to facs. edn, Cabrera, *Escudo de armas*, pp. xli–clii.

26   Francisco de Florencia, *Zodiaco mariano*, ed. and augmented by Juan Antonio de Oviedo (Mexico, 1755), facs. edn, with introduction by Antonio Rubial García (Mexico, 1995), p. 39.

27   Cayetano Antonio de Torres, *Sermón de la Santísima Virgen de Guadalupe . . .* (Mexico, 1757), pp. 23, 32; on Florencia's application of Psalm 147 to the Guadalupe see p. 34, n. 34; for citations, pp. 15–18, 21.

28   Conde, *Disertación*, II, 420–1.

29   John Lynch, *Bourbon Spain 1700–1808* (London, 1989), pp. 160–3, 187–92. See also Teobaldo Antonio de Ribera, *Relación y estado del culto, lustre, progresos y utilidad de la real congregación sita en la Iglesia de San Felipe el Real . . .* (Madrid, 1740, 1757), reprinted in *Colección de obras*, I, 725–804. See Beristain, *Biblioteca*, IV, 222–8 on Ribera; v, 41–2, 47–8 for Torres.

30   José Mariano Dávila y Arrillaga, *Continuación de la historia de la Compañía de Jesús en Nueva España de P. Francisco Javier Alegre*, 2 vols. (Puebla, 1888) I, 106–18.

31   *The Catholic Encyclopedia*, XIII, 454–6.

32   Eduardo Torra de Arana *et al., El Pilar es la Columna*, pp. 195–201.

33   Florencia, *Zodiaco mariano*, pp. 111–15; Conde, *Disertación*, II, 399–410; see also Ignacio Carrillo y Pérez, *Pensil americano florido en el origen del invierno, la imagen de María Santísima de Guadalupe* (Mexico, 1797), pp. 53–64.

34   Francisco de San José, *Historia universal de la primitiva y milagrosa imagen de Nuestra Señora de Guadalupe* (Madrid, 1743), pp. 9–23, 49, 74–84, 128, 168–85; on Mexican image, pp. 140–67.

35   *Ibid.*, pp. 88, 239–53.

36   Lorenzo Boturini Benaduci, *Idea de una nueva historia general de la América Septentrional*, ed. Miguel León-Portilla (Mexico, 1974), p. xiii; see also Archivo de Indias, Mexico 1337, Count of Fuenclara to Madrid, 28 February 1743.

37   Boturini, *Idea*, pp. 128, 131; Trabulse, *Los manuscritos perdidos*, pp. 29–50.

38   Boturini, *Idea*, pp. 143–5.

39   Juan José de Eguiara y Eguren, *Biblioteca mexicana*, ed. Ernesto de la Torre Villar and Ramiro Navarro de Anda, Spanish trans. Benjamín Fernández Valenzuela (Mexico, 1982), pp. 704–10 on Cabrera; pp. 720–36 on Sigüenza y Góngora. See also Juan José de Eguiara y Eguren, *Prólogos a la Biblioteca mexicana*, ed. Agustín Millares Carlo (Mexico, 1944), *passim*.

40   Eguiara y Eguren, *Biblioteca mexicana*, pp. 516–21 on Valeriano.

41   Florencia, *Zodiaco mariano*, pp. 38–41.

42   Florencia, *Dos célebres santuarios*, unpaginated approbation, pp. 49, 150.

43   Florencia, *Zodiaco mariano*, pp. 53–73, 116–23, 272–4; see also Thomas Calvo, 'El zodiaco de la Nueva Eva: el culto mariano en la América septentrional hacía 1700', in *Manifestaciones religiosas en el mundo colonial americano*, ed. Clara García Ayluardo and Manuel Ramos Medina, 2nd edn (Mexico, 1997), pp. 267–82.

44   Florencia, *Dos célebres santuarios*, pp. 50, 138–40, 200–12.

45   *Ibid.*, pp. 83–5, 130–6, 149, 199.

46   Manuel de Loyzaga, *Historia de la milagrosísma imagen de Nuestra Señora de Ocotlan que se venera extramuros de la ciudad de Tlaxcala* (Puebla, 1745), pp. 1, 7–31.

47   *Ibid.*, pp. 40–4, 60–78; on *demandantes*, pp. 103–7; for Velasco's visit, see Loyzaga, *Historia*, 2nd edn (Mexico, 1750), pp. 80–3.

48   Matías de Escobar, *Americana thebaida*, 2nd edn, ed. Nicolás P. Navarrete (Morelia, 1970), pp. 468–9.

49   Isidro Félix de Espinosa, *Crónica apostólica y seráphica de todos los colegios de propaganda fide de la Nueva España de los misioneros franciscanos observantes*, ed. Lino G. Canedo (Washington, 1964), pp. 533, 570, 608–9, 633.

50   Cabrera, *Escudo de armas*, pp. 212–13.

51   Brading, *Church and State in Bourbon Mexico: The Diocese of Michoacán 1749–1810* (Cambridge, 1994), pp. 32–40.

7   Divine idea

1   Juan de Goicoechea, *La maravilla inmarcesible y milagro continuado de Santísima Señora Nuestra en su prodigiosa imagen de Guadalupe de México* (Mexico, 1709), pp. 1–5. On Goicoechea see *Diccionario*, xv, 682.

2   Goicoechea, *Maravilla inmarcesible*, pp. 6–22.

3   *Ibid.*, pp. 23–6.

4   *Ibid.*, pp. 27–8.

5   Miguel Picazo, *Imagen humana y divina de la Purísima Concepción* (Mexico, 1738), pp. 13–15.

6   José Arlegui, *Sagrado paladión del americano orbe . . .* (Mexico, 1743), pp. 13, 15–16.

7   Brading, *Church and State in Bourbon Mexico*, pp. 36–8.

8   Matías Saénz de San Antonio, *Conveniencia relativa entre el término de un templo apostólico, sujeto, que se dedican y la imagen Guadalupe, predicada, que se coloca* (Mexico, 1721), pp. 1–20.

9   Juan de Villa Sánchez, *Sermón de la milagrosa imagen de Nuestra Señora de Guadalupe* (Mexico, 1734), pp. 4–10; on Gregorio García see Brading, *The First America*, pp. 195–200, 382.

10 Villa Sánchez, *Sermón*, pp. 17–23.

11 Antonio de Paredes, *La auténtica del patronato que en nombre de todo el reino votó la caesarea, nobilísima ciudad de México a Santísima Virgen María Señora Nuestra en su imagen maravillosa de Guadalupe* (Mexico, 1748), pp. 2–12; on Paredes, see Beristain, *Biblioteca*, IV, 102–3.

12 See Beristain, *Biblioteca*, III, 41, entered under 'Hita y Parra'. Bartolomé Felipe de Ita y Parra, 'Sermón panegyrico', *Canonización en vida de San Juan de la Cruz* (Mexico, 1729), pp. 286–309.

13 Bartolomé Felipe de Ita y Parra, *La imagen de Guadalupe, Señora de los tiempos* (Mexico, 1732), pp. 1–18.

14 Bartolomé Felipe de Ita y Parra, *Madre de la salud* pp. 1–16.

15 Bartolomé Felipe de Ita y Parra, *La imagen de Guadalupe: imagen de patrocinio* (Mexico, 1744), unpaginated approbation by José de Elizardo y Valle.

16 *Ibid.*, unpaginated approbation by José Torrubia; see also Benito Jerónimo Feijoo Montenegro, *Teatro crítico universal* (1726–39), 8th edn, 8 vols. (Madrid, 1753–5), III, 110–25.

17 Ita y Parra, *La imagen de Guadalupe: imagen de patrocinio*, pp. 6–8.

18 *Ibid.*, pp. 12–26.

19 Bartolomé Felipe de Ita y Parra, *El círculo del amor formado por la América Septentrional jurando Maria Santísima en su imagen de Guadalupe, la imagen del patrocinio de todo su reino* (Mexico, 1747), pp. 3–7. Note that Ita y Parra's sermons on the Guadalupe were reprinted in facs. edn in *Siete sermones guadalupanos 1709–1765*, ed. David A. Brading (Mexico, 1994), together with sermons by Goicoechea, Carranza, Ruiz Castañeda and Lazcano.

20 Ita y Parra, *Círculo del amor*, pp. 11–27.

21 Bartolomé Felipe de Ita y Parra, *El arrebatado de Dios: el Señor D. Felipe V. Oración fúnebre* (Mexico, 1747), unpaginated approbation, pp. 1–15.

22 Torres, *Sermón de la Santísima Virgen*, p. 2.

23 Pedro Herboso, *Sermón panegyrico . . . a la milagrosa imagen de Nuestra Señora de Guadalupe de México* (Mexico, 1757), p. 5.

24 Andrés de la Santísima Trinidad, *La venerada y glorificada en todas las naciones por haberse aparecida en estos reinos . . .* (Mexico, 1759), pp. 22–4.

25 Juan José de Eguiara y Eguren, *María Santísima pintándose milagrosamente en su bellísima imagen de Guadalupe de México, saluda a la Nueva España y se constituye su patrona: Panegyrico* (Mexico, 1757), pp. 1–25; this sermon is reprinted in *Testimonios históricos*, pp. 480–93.

26 *Ibid.*, p. 2.

27 Paredes, *La auténtica del patronato*, unpaginated approbation.

28 Francisco Javier Lazcano, *Sermón panegyrico al inclito patronato de María Señora Nuestra en su milagrosísima imagen de Guadalupe sobre la universal Septentrional América* (Mexico, 1759), pp. 3–6. On Lazcano see Beristain, *Biblioteca*, III, 107–8; and *Diccionario*, XVI, 42–4.

29 Lazcano, *Sermón panegyrico*, pp. 8–26.

30 Juan José Ruiz de Castañeda, *Sermón panegyrico en glorias de María Santísima bajo el título de Guadalupe* (Mexico, 1766), pp. 2–13; see *Diccionario*, XV, 458.

31 Castañeda, *Sermón panegyrico*, pp. 14–17.

32 Francisco Javier Carranza, *La transmigración de la Iglesia a Guadalupe* (Mexico, 1749), *passim*. Beristain, *Biblioteca* II, 52–3; *Diccionario*, XV, 424–5. This sermon is reproduced in *Siete sermones guadalupanos*, pp. 198–222.

33 Francisco Javier Carranza, *Sermón de la adoración de los Reyes . . .* (Mexico, 1743), pp. 1–13.

34 Carranza, *La transmigración*, pp. 1–18.

35 *Ibid.*, pp. 20–7.

36 De la Maza, *El guadalupanismo mexicano*, pp. 131–2.

37 Juan de Espinosa Medrano, *Apologético en favor de D. Luis de Góngora* (Lima, 1662), unpaginated prologue.

8 Heavenly painting

1 Miguel Cabrera, *Maravilla americana y conjunto de varias maravillas observadas con la dirección de las reglas del arte de la pintura en la prodigiosa imagen de Nuestra Señora de Guadalupe de México* (Mexico, 1756, facs. edn, Mexico, 1977), unpaginated approbation by José Ventura Arnaez; p. 1.

2 Conde, *Disertación*, I, 342; according to Conde, López took to Europe two copies painted by Cabrera, one for Ferdinand VI and the other for Benedict XIV.

3 José Bernardo Couto, *Diálogo sobre la historia de la pintura en México*, ed. Manuel Toussaint (Mexico, 1947), pp. 92–108.

4   Guillermo Tovar de Teresa, *Miguel Cabrera, pintor de camarín de la reina celestial* (Mexico, 1995), pp. 87–9, 101–10, 187–96.

5   Cabrera, *Maravilla americana*, unpaginated dedication and approbations.

6   *Ibid.*, pp. 1–5.

7   Mariano Fernández de Echeverría y Veytia, *Baluartes de México. Descripción de las cuatro milagrosas imágenes de Nuestra Señora que se veneran en la muy noble, leal e imperial ciudad de México* (Mexico, 1820, fasc. edn, 1967), pp. 30–7.

8   Cabrera, *Maravilla americana*, pp. 12–17.

9   *Ibid.*, pp. 6, 17–24.

10 *Ibid.*, pp. 7–9, 25–7.

11 *Ibid.*, pp. 28–9.

12 *Ibid.*, pp. 9–11.

13 José Ignacio Conde and María Teresa Cervantes de Conde, 'Nuestra Señora de Guadalupe en el arte', *Album conmemorativo del 450 aniversario de la aparición de Nuestra Señora de Guadalupe* (Mexico, 1981), pp. 121–4. Here is a splendid collection of reproductions of eighteenth-century paintings of the Virgin, many of which are in the Basilica Museum at Tepeyac.

14 Florencia, *La Estrella del Norte*, pp. 7–9.

15 Reproduced in Rodrigo Rivero Lake, *La visión de un anticuario* (Mexico, 1997), pp. 178–81.

16 Conde and Conde, *Album conmemorativo del 450 aniversario*, p. 145; Jaime Cuadriello, 'Visiones en Patmos Tenochtitlan: la Mujer águila', *Artes de México*, 29 (1995), pp. 12–23.

17 Tovar de Teresa, *Cabrera*, p. 195.

18 Cuadriello, 'Visiones', p. 46; Jaime Genaro Cuadriello, 'Los pinceles de Dios Padre', *Maravilla americana, variantes de la iconografía guadalupana siglos XVII–XIX* (Mexico, 1989), p. 66.

19 Conde and Conde, *Album conmemorativo del 450 aniversario*, pp. 174–5; *Guadalupe. Maravilla americana. Homenaje a Monseñor Guillermo Schulenburg Prado*, ed. Manuel Olimón Nolasco (Mexico, 1998), pp. 6–7; Jaime Cuadriello *et al.*, *Juegos de ingenio y agudeza: la pintura emblemática de la Nueva España* (Mexico, 1994), p. 83.

20 Conde and Conde, *Album conmemorativo del 450 aniversario*, pp. 159–61; Cuadriello, 'Visiones', pp. 20–1, 52.

21 Cuadriello *et al.*, *Juegos de ingenio*, pp. 109, 387.

22 Tovar de Teresa, *Cabrera*, pp. 102–4, 42–3, 238–9; Conde and Conde, *Album conmemorativo del 450 aniversario*, pp. 19, 152–3, 155.

23 Tovar de Teresa, *Cabrera*, pp. 240–7.

24 Francisco Antonio del Lorenzana, *Oración de Nuestra Señora de Guadalupe* (Mexico, 1770), reprinted in *Sermonario mexicano*, III, 322–4, 330, 335–7. On Lorenzana in Mexico see Brading, *The First America*, pp. 495–501.

25   José Patricio Fernández de Uribe, *Sermón de Nuestra Señora de México* (1777), to
     which was appended his *Disertación histórico-crítica en que el autor . . . sostiene
     la celestial imagen de Nuestra Señora de Guadalupe de México milagrosamente
     aparecida al humilde neófito Juan Diego* (1778), published together with separate
     pagination (Mexico, 1801), pp. 4–5.

26   Uribe, *Disertación*, pp. 18–23.

27   *Ibid.*, pp. 25–40; on Mabillon see David Knowles, *Great Historical Enterprises*
     (London, 1962), pp. 34–62.

28   Uribe, *Disertación*, pp. 42–6.

29   *Ibid.*, pp. 56–65.

30   *Ibid.*, pp. 1, 70–7.

31   *Ibid.*, pp. 78–89.

32   *Ibid.*, pp. 92–111.

33   *Ibid.*, pp. 117–20; on Bayle in Mexico see Elías Trabulse, *Ciencia y religión en el siglo
     XVII* (Mexico, 1974), pp. 37–44.

34   Uribe, *Disertación*, pp. 126–9.

35   Knowles, *Great Historical Enterprises*, pp. 1–62; T. D. Kendrick, *St. James in Spain*
     (London, 1961), pp. 144–7, 150–67.

36   On Feijoo see Giovanni Stiffoni, 'Intelectuales, sociedad y estado', in *Historia de
     España*, ed. José María Jover Zamora, vol. xxix (Madrid, 1988), ii, pp. 119–49.

37   Feijoo, *Teatro crítico*, iv, 109–24.

38   *Ibid.*, v, 348–462.

39   Feijoo, 'Sobre la recta devoción y adoración de los imágenes': this essay was pub-
     lished posthumously in *Adiciones a las obras del muy ilustre y reverendísimo padre
     maestro Benito Jerónimo Feijoo y Montenegro* (Madrid, 1783), pp. 1–17.

40   Francisco Javier Clavijero, *Historia antígua de México*, ed. Mariano Cuevas
     (Mexico, 1964), pp. xviii, xxi.

41   *Ibid.*, pp. xvii, xxx; on Clavijero see Brading, *The First America*, pp. 450–62.

42   Francisco Javier Clavijero, 'Breve noticia sobre la prodigiosa y renombrada imagen
     de Nuestra Señora de Guadalupe', in *Testimonios históricos*, pp. 578–96.

43   José Ignacio Bartolache, *Manifiesto satisfactorio: opúsculo guadalupano* (Mexico,
     1790), unpaginated prologue.

44   *Ibid.*, pp. 1–12.

45   *Ibid.*, pp. 19–31, 44–7, 54–6.

46   *Ibid.*, pp. 15–16, 21–2, 49–52.

47   *Ibid.*, pp. 59–69.

48   *Ibid.*, pp. 70–3.

49   *Ibid.*, pp. 73–9.

50   *Ibid.*, pp. 82–3.

51   *Ibid.*, pp. 83–91.

52   *Ibid.*, pp. 91–9.

53   *Ibid.*, appendix, pp. 1–10.

54   *Ibid.*, pp. 98–105; appendix, 13–14.

55   Beristain, *Biblioteca*, I, 225–6.

56   José María Téllez Girón, 'Impugnación al manifiesto satisfactorio del Dr. José Ignacio Bartolache', *Testimonios históricos*, pp. 651–88.

57   Conde, I, 160, 170–5.

58   *Ibid.*, I, 341–4; II, 186–8.

59   *Ibid.*, I, 257–8, 274–80; II, 333–4.

60   *Ibid.*, II, 34; see Beristain, *Biblioteca*, II, 136–7, where the honours Conde received in Europe are noted.

61   *Ibid.*, II, 50–69.

62   *Ibid.*, II, 71–96, 268.

63   *Ibid.*, II, 89, 158, 115–47, 218–43.

64   *Ibid.*, II, 279–90, 303–5, 399–414; see also Carrillo, *Pensil americano*, pp. 30–6, 56–64, 75–80.

65   Conde, *Disertación*, II, 347–8, 394–5.

66   *Ibid.*, I, 358–65.

67   *Ibid.*, I, 365–9; Carrillo, *Pensil americano*, pp. 117–19.

68   Conde, *Disertación*, I, 85–8; II, 516–19.

9   Myth and scepticism

1   Carrillo, *Pensil americano*, p. iii, gives the dates of the image's stay in the chapel of the Capuchin convent, situated adjacent to the sanctuary. For the sermon on Cortés see *Gaceta de México*, VI, (1794), pp. 647–8.

2   Servando Teresa de Mier, *Memorias*, ed. Antonio Castro Leal, 2 vols., (Mexico, 1946) I, 218.

3   Servando Teresa de Mier, *Obras completas: el heterodoxo guadalupano*, ed. Edmundo O'Gorman, 3 vols. (Mexico, 1981), I, 233–55. These volumes comprise the original texts and the editor's extended commentary. On Mier see also D. A. Brading, *The Origins of Mexican Nationalism* (Cambridge, 1985), pp. 24–65.

4   Mier, *Obras*, I, 238–9.

5   *Ibid.*, I, 241–52; citations on p. 254.

6   Conde, *Disertación*, I, 86–7; II, 516–19; see also José Miguel Guridi y Alcocer, *Apuntes* (Mexico, 1984), pp. 78–9.

7   Mier, *Memorias*, I, 5–10.

8   *Ibid.*, I, 91; for the painting of St Thomas preaching in Tlaxcala, see Cuadriello *et al.*, *Juegos de ingenio*, p. 391.

9   José Ignacio Borunda, 'Clave general de jeroglíficos americanos', in Nicolás León, *Bibliografía mexicana del siglo XVIII*, 5 vols. (Mexico, 1902–8), III, 222–4, 240. On Borunda see Mier, *Obras*, I, 29–30, 206–7; II, 63–107.

10 León, *Bibliografía*, III, 320–3. On Honoré de Sainte-Marie see Owen Chadwick, *From Bossuet to Newman* (Cambridge, 1957), pp. 63–5; a translation of his work was published in Mexico in 1792 by Francisco de San Cirilo, a fellow Carmelite.

11 León, *Bibliografía*, III, 224; see Antonio León y Gama, *Descripción histórica y cronológica de las piedras que se hallaron en la plaza principal de México* (Mexico, 1792), *passim*.

12 León, *Bibliografía*, III, 242–57.

13 Gregorio García, *Predicación del evangelio en el Nuevo Mundo viviendo los apóstoles* (Baeza, 1625), pp. 44–8, 169, 178–222. On García see Brading, *The First America*, pp. 195–200, 382.

14 See Jacques Lafaye, *Quetzalcoatl y Guadalupe: la formación de la conciencia nacional en México* (Mexico, 1977), pp. 205–94.

15 León, *Bibliografía*, III, 277–96.

16 Mier, *Obras*, II, 119–21, 129, 140, 166–7.

17 *Ibid.*, II, 151–76.

18 *Ibid.*, I, 197–210.

19 Mier, *Memorias*, I, 100–14.

20 Archivo General de Indias, Mexico, 1894. Branciforte wrote in 1795 and Haro on 24 February 1798.

21 Mier, *Memorias*, I, 233; Mier, *Obras*, III, 101.

22 Mier, *Memorias*, I, 235–42; Mier, *Obras*, II, 212–14, 244–7.

23 Mier, *Obras*, II, 224–41, Joaquín Traggia, 2 November 1799.

24 *Ibid.*, II, 249–54.

25 *Ibid.*, III, 18; see also Brading, *The First America*, pp. 583–602.

26 This dissertation was appended to José Guerra (Servando de Mier), *Historia de la revolución de Nueva España, antiguamente Anahuac* (London, 1813) and is reprinted in Mier, *Obras*, III, 18–56.

27 Servando Teresa de Mier, 'Carta de despedida' (1820), in Mier, *Escritos y memorias*, ed. Edmundo O'Gorman (Mexico, 1945), pp. 33–52.

28 See the articles by A. Ballesteros-Beretta: 'Juan Bautista Muñoz: dos facetas científicas', *Revista de Indias*, 2 (1941), pp. 5–38; 'Juan Bautista Muñoz: la creación del archivo de Indias', *Revista de Indias*, 2 (1941), pp. 55–95; 'Juan Bautista Muñoz: la historia del Nuevo Mundo', *Revista de Indias*, 3 (1943), pp. 589–660.

29 Juan Bautista Muñoz, *Historia del Nuevo Mundo* (Madrid, 1793), pp. 12, 18; see also Francisco Iturri, *Carta crítica sobre la Historia de América del Señor d. Juan Bautista Muñoz* (Madrid, 1797, reprinted Buenos Aires, 1818), pp. 3, 37, 72.

30 Juan Bautista Muñoz, 'Memoria sobre las apariciones y el culto de Nuestra Señora de Guadalupe de México' (1794), reprinted in *Testimonios históricos*, pp. 688–91.

31 *Ibid.*, pp. 692–9.

32 *Ibid.*, p. 692.

33 *Ibid.*, pp. 694–5.

34 *Ibid.*, pp. 694–6; see also Sahagún, *Historia*, iii, 352.

35 *Ibid.*, pp. 698–9.

36 *Ibid.*, pp. 699–701.

37 Mier, *Memorias*, i, 136–8; Mier, *Obras*, iii, 136.

38 Gregorio Mayans y Siscar, 'Censura de historias fabulosas', *Obras completas*, ed. Antonio Mestre Sánchez (Valencia, 1983), i, 265–305. See also Julio Caro Baroja, *Las falsificaciones de la Historia (en relación con la de España)* (Barcelona, 1992), *passim*.

39 Mier, *Memorias*, i, 256.

40 Lodovico Antonio Muratori, *The Science of Rational Devotion*, trans. Alexander Kenny (Dublin, 1789), pp. 9–11, 152–7; see also Chadwick, *The Popes and the European Revolution*, pp. 399–402.

41 Muratori, *The Science of Rational Devotion*, pp. 177–81, 211–14.

42 Gaspar Melchor de Jovellanos, *Obras completas*, ed. Miguel Artola, 5 vols. (Madrid, 1956), iii, 256.

43 On Spanish Jansenism see Joel Saugnieux, *Les jansénistes et le renouveau de la prédication dans l'Espagne de la seconde moitié du XVIIIe siècle* (Lyons, 1976), *passim*.

44 Manuel Gómez Marín, *Defensa guadalupana contra la disertación de don Juan Bautista Muñoz* (Mexico, 1819), p. 35; José Miguel Guridi Alcocer, *Apología de la aparición de Nuestra Señora de Guadalupe de México* (Mexico, 1820), pp. 28–9, 151, 181–2.

45 Guridi, *Apología*, pp. 34–55, 80–98, 117.

46 *Ibid.*, pp. 152–75, 192.

47 *Ibid.*, pp. 58–74, 160–4, 139, 125–31.

48 For the dating of Mier's 'Cartas a Juan Bautista Muñoz' see O'Gorman's discussion in Mier, *Obras*, iii, 59–88, especially p. 64.

49 Mier, *Obras*, iii, 105, 125, 164.

50 *Ibid.*, iii, 106, 135, 178–9.

51 *Ibid.*, iii, 155–9, 165–74.

52 *Ibid.*, iii, 141. Sánchez' book was published in quarto, not folio.

53 *Ibid.*, iii, 179–81; Mier, *Memorias*, i, 81–5.

54 Mier, *Obras*, iii, 212.

55 *Ibid.*, iii, 122, 137–41.

56 *Ibid.*, iii, 205–9; Mier, *Memorias*, i, 19–42.

57 Mier, *Obras*, iii, 125, 169–71, 187; Mier, *Memorias*, i, 43–9.

58 Mier, *Obras*, iii, 126, 187; Mier, *Memorias*, i, 157.

59 Mier, *Memorias*, i, 164.

60 Mier, *Obras*, iii, 205–12.

61 Mier, *Memorias*, i, 136–8, 158.

62 On Amadeus see Mier, *Obras* iii, 147; Mier, *Memorias*, i, 140–1.

63 Mier, *Memorias*, i, 72.

64 Mier, *Obras*, III, 219–21.

65 Cited in Carlos María de Bustamante, *Continuación del cuadro histórico de la revolución mexicana*, ed. Jorge Gurría Lacroix, 4 vols. (Mexico, 1953–63), I, 92–3; Servando Teresa de Mier, *Pensamiento político del padre Mier*, ed. Edmundo O'Gorman (Mexico, 1945), p. 83.

66 *Colección de documentos para la historia de la guerra de independencia de México desde 1808 hasta 1821*, ed. Juan E. Hernández y Dávalos, 6 vols. (Mexico, 1877; facs. edn, Mexico, 1985), III, 5–222.

10   The last resort

1 Lucas Alamán, *Historia de Méjico*, 5 vols. (4th edn, Mexico, 1968), pp. 243–5; *Historia documental de México*, ed. Ernesto de la Torre Villar *et al.*, 2 vols. (Mexico, 1964), II, 40–9.

2 Francisco Severo Maldonado, 'El Despertador Americano', *Periodismo Insurgente*, facs. edn without continuous pagination, 2 vols. (Mexico, 1976), I, 4–5, 17–28, 40–3.

3 Carlos María de Bustamante, 'Correo Americano del Sur', *Periodismo insurgente*, facs. edn without continuous pagination, 2 vols. (Mexico, 1976), II, 194–5.

4 Ernesto Lemoine Villicaña, *Morelos* (Mexico, 1965), pp. 365–79; Felipe Tena Ramírez, *Leyes fundamentales de México 1808–1967* (Mexico, 1967), pp. 31–5.

5 Manuel Abad y Queipo, *Cartas pastorales* (Mexico, 1811–13), 'Edicto instructivo', 30 September 1810; *Carta pastoral* (Mexico, 1813), pp. 2, 34, 49–52, 73–81.

6 Juan López de Cancelada, *El Telégrafo Mexicano* (Cadiz, 1813), p. 254.

7 Simón Bolívar, *Obras completas*, ed. Vicente Lecuna, 3 vols. (Caracas, 1964), I, 174.

8 Juan Bautista Díaz Calvillo, *Sermón que en el aniversario solemne a María Santísima de los Remedios celebrado en esta iglesia catedral el día 30 de Octubre de 1811 por la victoria del Monte de las Cruces* (Mexico, 1811), pp. 8–29, 89–103, 116–22.

9 Gabriel H. Lovett, *Napoleon and the Birth of Modern Spain*, 2 vols. (New York, 1965), II, 216–21; Elizabeth, Lady Holland, *The Spanish Journal*, ed. The Earl of Ilchester (London, 1910), pp. 140–1.

10 Lovett, *Napoleon and Spain*, I, 233–84; Ford, *A Hand-Book for Travellers in Spain and Readers at Home*, III, 1423–36.

11 Joseph Blanco White (Leucadio Doblado pseud.) *Letters from Spain* (London, 1822), pp. 40–2.

12 François Xavier Guerra, *Modernidad e independencias: ensayos sobre las revoluciones hispánicas* (Mexico, 1993), pp. 336–55.

13 Manuel Jesús Aparicio Vega (ed.), *La revolución del Cuzco de 1814, Colección documental de la independencia del Perú*, III. *Conspiraciones y rebeliones en el siglo XIX*, vol. VII (Lima, 1974), pp. 529, 547–54.

14 José Mariano Beristain de Souza, *Discurso político-moral y cristiano . . .* (Mexico, 1809), pp. 5–8, 15, 21.

15 Beristain, *Biblioteca*, II, 52–3.

16 José Mariano Beristain de Souza, *Diálogos patrióticos* (Mexico, 1810–11), pp. 1, 5–6, 54–5, 98–107, 120–2.

17 José Mariano Beristain de Souza, *Declamación cristiana que en la solemne función de desagravios a María Santísima de Guadalupe . . .* (Mexico, 1811), pp. 16, 23.

18 José Mariano Beristain de Souza, *Discurso eucarístico que en la muy solemne acción de gracias celebrada . . . por la libertad y restitución a su trono a Fernando Séptimo, soberano monarca de España e Indias* (Mexico, 1814), pp. ii–vi, ix–xii.

19 Beristain, *Biblioteca*, I, 251–3; Medina, *La imprenta en México*, VIII, 90–1.

20 Beristain, *Biblioteca*, II, 312–18. In Valencia Beristain met Mayans; see Agustín Millares Carlo, *Cuatro estudios biobibliográficos mexicanos* (Mexico, 1986), p. 344.

21 Beristain, *Bibliotheca*, I, 15–33.

22 Ibid., I, 126–7, 280; II, 8–9, 119–21, 371–2; III, 106; IV, 343–54; V, 37–8, 83–5.

23 Ibid., III, 246–7; I, 22.

24 Tena Ramírez, *Leyes fundamentales*, pp. 113–19, 122–3.

25 José Julio García de Torres, *Sermón de acción de gracias a María Santísima de Guadalupe por el venturoso suceso de la independencia de la América Septentrional* (Mexico, 1821), pp. 11–30.

26 Ibid., pp. 1–11.

27 Alamán, *Historia de Méjico*, V, 396–8.

28 Manuel de la Bárcena, *Manifiesto al mundo: la justicia y la necesidad de la independencia de la Nueva España* (Mexico, 1821), pp. 4, 14–15.

29 Manuel de la Bárcena, *Sermón exhortatorio que en la solemne función anual, que hace la imperial orden de Guadalupe a su celestial patrona* (Mexico, 1823), pp. 2–3.

30 Ibid., pp. 4–15.

31 Brading, *Church and State*, pp. 250–1.

32 Tena Ramírez, *Leyes fundamentales*, pp. 167–8, 184.

33 Roberto Gómez Ciriza, *México ante la diplomacia vaticana* (Mexico, 1977), *passim*.

34 Annick Lempérière, '¿Nación moderna o república barroca? México 1823–1857', in *Imaginar la nación*, ed. François-Xavier Guerra and Mónica Quijada (Munster, 1994), pp. 135–78.

35 Carlos María de Bustamante, *Cuadro de la revolución mexicana*, ed. Jorge Gurría Lacroix, 3 vols. (Mexico, 1961), III, 332; on Bustamante see Brading, *The First America*, pp. 634–46.

36 Carlos María de Bustamante, *Manifiesto de la junta guadalupana a los mexicanos y disertación histórico-crítica de Nuestra Señora en Tepeyac* (Mexico, 1831), pp. 2–28; appended *Disertación*, separate pagination, pp. 10–15.

37 Bernardino de Sahagún, *Historia general de las cosas de la Nueva España*, ed. Carlos María de Bustamante, 3 vols. (Mexico, 1829–30). Mier's dissertation was printed without pagination between, pp. 277–9, vol. I.

38 Carlos María de Bustamante, *La aparición de Nuestra Señora de Guadalupe* (Mexico, 1840), pp. vi, 7.

39 Carlos María de Bustamante, *La aparición guadalupana de México* (Mexico, 1843), pp. 21, 61.

40 Julián Tornel y Mendivil, *La aparición de Nuestra Señora de Guadalupe de México*, 2 vols. (Orizaba, 1849), I, 4, 42–62; II, 8–9, 59, 182–205.

41 Mariano Otero, *Obras*, ed. Jesús Reyes Heroles, 2 vols. (Mexico, 1967), I, 99, 124–7.

42 Lucas Alamán, *Historia de Méjico*, v, 568.

43 Francisco Javier Miranda, 'Sermón panegyrico de Santa María de Guadalupe', *Sermonario mexicano*, III, 244–9.

44 Felipe Neri de Barros, 'Sermón predicado . . . a su patrona, María Santísima de Guadalupe . . .', *Sermonario mexicano*, III, 456–70.

45 Tena Ramírez, *Leyes fundamentales*, pp. 634–41, citation on p. 637; see also Edmundo O'Gorman, *La supervivencia política novo-hispana* (Mexico, 1969), pp. 60–1.

46 Tena Ramírez, *Leyes fundamentales*, pp. 491–2, 607, 610, 626.

47 Ismael Jiménez, 'Sermón predicada en la colegiata . . .', *Sermonario mexicano*, III, 187–97.

48 Melchor Ocampo, *Obras completas*, ed. Angel Pola, 3 vols. (Mexico, 1978), I, 32–6, 90–1, 106, 144, 152.

49 José Bravo Ugarte, *Mungía, obispo y arzobispo de Michoacán (1810–1868): su vida y su obra* (Mexico, 1967), *passim*; but see also the invaluable but uncompleted Miguel Martínez, *Monseñor Munguía y sus escritos* (Mexico, 1879), which deals with the bishop's intellectual formation; and D. A. Brading, 'Clemente de Jesús Munguía: intransigencia ultramontana y la reforma mexicana', *Historia de la Iglesia en el siglo XIX*, ed. Manuel Ramos Medina (Mexico, 1998), pp. 13–46.

50 Clemente de Jesús Munguía, *Del derecho natural en sus principios comunes y en sus diversas ramificaciones . . .* , 3 vols. (Mexico, 1849), III, 207–89.

51 Clemente de Jesús Munguía, *Defensa eclesiástica en el obispado de Michoacán desde fines de 1855 hasta principios de 1858*, 2 vols. (Mexico, 1858), I, 534–40; II, 165–71, 176–8.

52 Clemente de Jesús Munguía, *Dos cartas pastorales* (Mexico, 1860), pp. 24, 49, 52–3, 71.

53 Clemente de Jesús Munguía, *Sermón de Nuestra Señora de Guadalupe predicado en la insigne y nacional colegiata, el 12 de Marzo de 1859* (Mexico, 1860), pp. 8–13.

54 *Ibid.*, pp. 47–61.

55 *Ibid.*, pp. 66–9, 72, 80–1.

56 Clemente de Jesús Munguía, *Sermón que predicó en la insigne y nacional colegiata de Guadalupe, el 28 de Agosto de 1860* (Mexico, 1860), pp. 7–8, 11, 14–16; the long citation is from p. 16.

57 *Ibid.*, pp. 31–40, 61–5.

58 *Episcopado y gobierno en México: cartas pastorales colectivas del episcopado mexicano 1859–1870*, ed. Alfonso Alcalá and Manuel Olimón (Mexico, 1989), pp. 21–2.

59 Pedro Espinosa, *Pastoral del Illmo. Señor Arzobispo de Guadalajara a la vuelta de su destierro* (Guadalajara, 1864), pp. 18–22; Ignacio Montes de Oca y Obregón, 'Elogio fúnebre del Illmo. y Excmo. Señor Dr. D. Pelagio Antonio de Labastida y Dávalos', *Oraciones fúnebres* (Madrid, 1901), pp. 185–203.

60 *Episcopado y gobierno*, pp. 128–40, 213–50; José Guadalupe Romero, 'Sermón de Nuestra Señora de Guadalupe', *Sermonario mexicano*, III, 135.

61 Munguía, *Derecho natural*, III, 333–7.

62 Espinosa, *Pastoral*, pp. 4–7, 14.

63 *Episcopado y gobierno*, pp. 298–331.

64 Agustín Rivera y San Román, 'Sermón de la Santísima Virgen de Guadalupe', *Sermonario mexicano*, III, 473–80.

65 *Ibid.*, III, 477–9.

66 *Ibid.*, III, 480–9.

67 Ignacio Manuel Altamirano, *Discursos* (Paris, 1982), p. 32.

68 Ignacio Manuel Altamirano, *Paisajes y leyendas*, First Series (Mexico, 1974), pp. 9–19.

69 Ignacio Manuel Altamirano, *Paisajes y leyendas*, Second Series (Mexico, 1949), pp. 172–84, 192–4, 235.

70 Altamirano, *Paisajes y leyendas* (1974), pp. 4–7; *Discursos*, p. 364; on Altamirano see Brading, *The First America*, pp. 710–28.

71 Ignacio Manuel Altamirano, 'La fiesta de Guadalupe' (1884), reprinted in *Testimonios históricos*, pp. 1127–33.

72 Altamirano, *Paisajes y leyendas* (1949), p. 228; *Testimonios históricos*, pp. 1133–1208.

73 Altamirano, *Testimonios históricos*, pp. 1259–60.

11 **History and infallibility**

1 Altamirano, 'La fiesta de Guadalupe', *Testimonios históricos*, pp. 1140–5, 1156–7.

2 Joaquín García Icazbalceta, *Don fray Juan de Zumárraga, primer obispo y arzobispo de México*, 2nd edn, ed. Rafael Aguayo Spencer and Antonio Castro Leal, 4 vols. (Mexico, 1947), I, 4–9, 89–156, 221–9.

3 *Ibid.*, I, 221–32; II, 120; see also *Correspondencia de Adolfo F. Bandelier*, ed. Leslie A. White and Ignacio Bernal (Mexico, 1960), p. 115.

4 García Icazbalceta, *Zumárraga*, II, 1–85.

5 *Ibid.*, II, 88–162.

6 *Ibid.*, II, 129, 162.

7 Joaquín García Icazbalceta, *Cartas*, ed. Felipe Teixidor (Mexico, 1937), pp. 202, 251.

8 Joaquín García Icazbalceta, 'Carta acerca del origen de la imagen de Nuestra Señora de Guadalupe' (1883), *Testimonios históricos*, which reprints text and introduction of the 1896 first edition; see pp. 1092–6.

9 Manuel Guillermo Martínez, *Don Joaquín García Icazbalceta: su lugar en la historiografía mexicana*, trans. Luis García Pimental y Elguero (Mexico, 1950), for list of publications, pp. 147–53.

10 García Icazbalceta, 'Carta', *Testimonios históricos*, pp. 1096–1108.

11 *Ibid.*, pp. 1109–10.

12 *Ibid.*, pp. 1112–15.

13 *Ibid.*, p. 1112.

14 *Ibid.*, pp. 1117–21.

15 *Ibid.*, pp. 1121–4.

16 *Ibid.*, pp. 1125–6.

17 Lucas Alamán, *Disertaciones*, 3 vols. (Mexico, 1969), II, 157.

18 José Mariano Beristain de Souza, *Biblioteca hispano-americana septentrional. Adiciones y correcciones que a su fallecimiento dejó manuscritas el Sr. Lic. d. José Fernando Ramírez*, ed. Victoriano Agüeros and Nicolás León (Mexico, 1898), pp. 422–34. Note that these additions were inserted in the third, 1957 edn; see Beristain, *Biblioteca*, III, 157–62.

19 José María Agreda y Sánchez, *Catálogo*, no date or place, pp. 553–4.

20 Joaquín García Icazbalceta, *Bibliografía mexicana del siglo XVI*, 2nd edn, ed. Agustín Millares Carlo (Mexico, 1954), *passim*; Martínez, *García Icazbalceta*, pp. 61–2.

21 Andrade, *Ensayo bibliográfico*; León, *Bibliografía*; and in our own days, Guillermo Tovar de Teresa, *Bibliografía novohispana de arte*, 2 vols. (Mexico, 1988).

22 Próspero María Alarcón y Sánchez de la Barquera, *Carta pastoral del Illmo: Señor Arzobispo de México* (Mexico, 1895), p. 21; Esteban Anticoli, *Historia de la aparición*, II, 310.

23 Crescensio Carrillo y Ancona, *Carta de actualidad sobre el milagro de la aparición guadalupana en 1531* (Mexico, 1888), pp. 2–10.

24 García Icazbalceta, *Cartas*, p. 328; García Icazbalceta, *Zumárraga*, 'prólogo', I, xiv.

25 Alberto María Carreño, 'Noticias biográficas', *Sesión celebrada por la Sociedad Mexicana de Geografía y Estadística en memoria del socio honorario Sr. Lic. Canónigo don Vicente de Paul Andrade* (Mexico, 1915), pp. 23–7.

26 García Icazbalceta, *Cartas*, pp. 182–4; see also Jesús Amaya, *Génesis e historia de Nuestra Señora de Guadalupe, Madre de Dios* (Mexico, 1931), pp. 301–33.

27 *Información que el arzobispo de México don Fray Alonso de Montúfar mandó practicar . . .* , 2nd edn (Mexico, 1891), reprinted with notes and introduction under the title 'Información por el sermón de 1556' in *Testimonios históricos*, pp. 36–141.

28 *Testimonios históricos*, pp. 43–4.

29 *Ibid.*, pp. 45, 55.

30 *Ibid.*, pp. 48–53, 57–69.

31 *Ibid.*, pp. 60–5.

32 *Ibid.*, pp. 52–3, 59–60.

33 *Ibid.*, pp. 63, 69–71.

34 *Ibid.*, pp. 38–40.

35 These two books are often confused since their titles are similar and both were published anonymously. Note: Esteban Anticoli, *La Virgen del Tepeyac patrona principal de la nación mexicana* (Guadalajara, 1884); José Antonio González (pseudonym 'X'), *Santa María de Guadalupe, patrona de los mexicanos* (Guadalajara, 1884); see Gloria Grajales and Ernest J. Burrus, *Bibliografía guadalupana 1531–1984* (Washington, 1986), p. 96.

36 *Testimonios históricos*, pp. 39–42, 73–5, 93.

37 *Ibid.*, pp. 82, 89, 99.

38 Eutemio Pérez (Vicente de Paul Andrade), *Ciertas aparicionistas, obrando de mala fe, inventan algunos episodios* (Cuilpam, 1890). This was included in the 1891 edition; see *Testimonios históricos*, pp. 109–20.

39 Andrade named Baranda as his 'Maecenas' in the prologue to his *Ensayo bibliográfico*, p. vii.

40 See above, n. 35; *Testimonios históricos*, pp. 109–12; Juan de Alloza, *Cielo estrellado . . .* (Madrid, 1654).

41 *Testimonios históricos*, pp. 113–20; González, *Santa María de Guadalupe*, pp. 324–31.

42 *Testimonios históricos*, pp. 120–9.

43 Francisco del Paso y Troncoso, 'Noticias del indio Marcos y de otros pintores del siglo XVI', *Testimonios históricos*, pp. 129–41.

44 *Ibid.*, pp. 130–4; Díaz del Castillo, *Historia verdadera*, I, 275.

45 *Testimonios históricos*, p. 135; on Troncoso's European mission see Silvio Zavala, *Francisco del Paso y Troncoso: su misión en Europa 1892–1916* (Mexico, 1938), *passim*.

46 García Icazbalceta, *Cartas*, pp. 184–6.

47 Fortino Hipólito Vera, *Tesoro guadalupano: notícias de los libros, documentos, inscripciones etc. que tratan, mencionan o aluden a la aparición y devoción de Nuestra Señora de Guadalupe*, 2 vols. (Amecameca, 1887), prologue by José de Jesús Cuevas, I, i–vii; see also Fortino H. Vera, *Colección de documentos eclesiásticos de México*, 3 vols. (Amecameca, 1887).

48 Fortino Hipólito Vera, *La milagrosa aparición de Nuestra Señora de Guadalupe comprobada por una información levantada en el siglo XVI contra los enemigos de tan asombroso acontecimiento* (Amecameca, 1890). Vera also published the full text of the 1666 Statements in 1889.

49 Vera, *La milagrosa aparición*, pp. 67–103; Luke 10.21–4.

50 Vera, *La milagrosa aparición*, pp. 3–12, 106–16; text of *Nican mopohua*, pp. 155–63, 178–9.

51 Vera, *La milagrosa aparición*, p. 171; also Vera, *Tesoro guadalupano*, II, 46–9.

52 Vera, *La milagrosa aparición*, pp. 81, 141, 189–91, 228–9, 330–41.

53 Fortino Hipólito Vera, *Contestación histórico-crítica en defensa de la maravillosa aparición de la Santísima Virgen de Guadalupe* (Querétaro, 1892), pp. 37–9.

54 *Ibid.*, pp. 117–36.

55 *Ibid.*, pp. 188–92, 215–20, 663; see also Juan de Cepeda, *Sermón de la Natividad de la Virgen María Señora Nuestra, predicado en la ermita de Guadalupe, extramuros de México en la fiesta de la misma iglesia* (Mexico, 1622), pp. 6–7.

56 Vera, *Contestación*, pp. 305–9, 398, 580, 647–8.

57 *Ibid.*, pp. 648–50, 677.

58 Esteban Anticoli, *El magisterio de la Iglesia y la Virgen del Tepeyac* (Querétaro, 1892), pp. 27–30. For *Quanta Cura* and the Syllabus of Errors see Owen Chadwick, *A History of the Popes 1830–1914* (Oxford, 1998), pp. 168–80.

59 Norman P. Tanner, *Decrees of the Ecumenical Councils*, 2 vols. (London, 1990), II, 808–9.

60 *Ibid.*, II, 816; Chadwick, *A History of the Popes*, pp. 180–214, 220–4.

61 Anticoli, *El magisterio de la Iglesia*, pp. 3–4, 24–37.

62 *Ibid.*, pp. 45, 100–18.

63 *Ibid.*, pp. 4–5, 56–8, 137.

64 *Ibid.*, pp. 100–28.

65 Esteban Anticoli, *Defensa de la aparición de la Virgen María en el Tepeyac . . . contra un libro impreso en México el año de 1891* (Puebla, 1893), pp. 11, 16, 26–7.

66 *Ibid.*, pp. 40–2, 49, 69–74, 89; on Marcos, pp. 156–7.

67 *Ibid.*, pp. 189, 205–36, 255–60, 297.

68 *Ibid.*, pp. 119–22.

69 *Ibid.*, pp. 126–32; see García Icazbalceta, *Zumárraga*, I, 222.

70 José Gutiérrez Casillas, *Jesuitas en México durante el siglo XIX* (Mexico, 1977), pp. 252–8.

71 García Icazbalceta, *Cartas*, pp. 249–55.

72 Ignacio Montes de Oca y Obregón, 'Breve elogio de don Joaquín García Icazbalceta', *Oraciones fúnebres*, pp. 349–57.

73 *Ibid.*, pp. 352–4.

74 Vera, *Tesoro guadalupano*, I, i.

12 The coronation

1 *Album de la coronación*, pp. 9–15; part 2, p. 2. See also Manuel Ceballos Ramírez, 'Siglo XIX y guadalupanismo: de la polémica a la coronación y de la devoción a la política', in *Historia de la Iglesia en el siglo XIX*, ed. Manuel Ramos Medina (Mexico, 1998).

2   *La Revista Eclesiástica*, 44 (Puebla, 1864), pp. 221–2, 323–5.

3   Tirso Rafael Córdoba, 'Sermón en honor de Nuestra Señora de Guadalupe', *Sermonario mexicano*, III, 265–76; see also the Mexican bishop's collective pastoral, 19 March 1875, *Episcopado y gobierno*, pp. 298–331.

4   José Gutiérrez Casillas, *Historia de la Iglesia en México* (Mexico, 1974), pp. 333–45; an invaluable guide is José Bravo Ugarte, *Diócesis y obispos de la Iglesia mexicana 1519–1965* (Mexico, 1965), *passim*.

5   Montes de Oca, *Oraciones fúnebres*, pp. 157–61, 190–212. The bishop observed that in 1861 Labastida 'had become leader of the monarchical party, which in that moment was identified as the Catholic party'.

6   José de Jesús Cuevas, 'Noticias biográficas del autor', *Obras*, ed. Victoriano Agüeros (Mexico, 1898), I, ii–xiii; Mariano Cuevas, *Historia de la Iglesia en México*, 5th edn, 5 vols. (Mexico, 1947), V, 417–18, 421–8.

7   José de Jesús Cuevas, *La Santísima Virgen de Guadalupe* (Mexico, 1887), pp. 3–11, 65–7, 174–7.

8   *Ibid.*, pp. 116–21.

9   *Ibid.*, pp. 92–3, 178–81.

10   Joseph Deery, *Our Lady of Lourdes* (Dublin, 1958), pp. 31–42; coronation, p. 96; see also the excellent recent study, Harris, *Lourdes*, *passim*.

11   Aureliano Tapia Méndez, *El siervo de Dios. José Antonio Plancarte y Labastida. Profeta y mártir*, 2nd edn (Mexico, 1987), pp. 65–6, 95, 135–6.

12   *Ibid.*, pp. 109–17, 123–32; for their appointments see Bravo Ugarte, *Diócesis y obispos*, pp. 138–9, 181–7, 194–8. On this generation of bishops see Laura O'Dogherty, 'El ascenso de una jerarquía eclesial intransigente, 1890–1914', *Historia de la Iglesia en el siglo XIX*, ed. Manuel Ramos Medina (Mexico, 1998).

13   The renovation of the sanctuary is described by Agüeros in *Album de la coronación*, pp. 106–18; also Anticoli, *Historia de la aparición*, II, 171–4, 419–30.

14   Agüeros, *Album*, p. 120; Anticoli, *Historia de la aparición*, II, 449–52.

15   Anticoli, *Historia de la aparición*, II, 391–7.

16   Agustín de la Rosa, *Disertatio historico-theologia de apparitione B.M.V. de Guadalupe* (Guadalajara, 1887), *passim*.

17   Anticoli, *Historia de la aparición*, II, 399–407.

18   Tapia Méndez, *El siervo de Dios*, pp. 208–10.

19   *Ibid.*, pp. 212–21.

20   José C. Valadés, *El porfirismo, historia de un régimen*, 2 vols. (Mexico, 1948), II, 208.

21   Agüeros, *Album de la coronación*, part 2, separate pagination, describes the ceremonies; for list of bishops, see pp. 33–4; for Indians, pp. 8, 84; see also Anticoli, *Historia de la aparición*, II, 453–4.

22   Agüeros, *Album de la coronación*, part 2, pp. 172–90.

23   For these sermons see *ibid.*, appendix to part 2, with separate pagination. The sermons are not given individual titles.

24   Fortino H. Vera, *Sermón pronunciado en el templo de Capuchinas, residencia actual de la imagen guadalupana* (Querétaro, 1890), pp. 4–8, 13.

25   Agüeros, *Album de la coronación*, part 2, appendix, with separate pagination, José de Jesús Ortiz, 11 October 1895, pp. 18–20.

26   *Ibid.*, Atenógenes Silva, 7 October 1895, pp. 3–4.

27   *Ibid.*, Rafael F. Menéndez, 21 October 1896, pp. 45–6.

28   *Ibid.*, Manuel Díaz Rayón, 27 October 1895, pp. 72–5.

29   *Ibid.*, Francisco Campos, 15 October 1895, pp. 47–51.

30   *Ibid.*, Antonio Paredes, 20 October 1896, pp. 30–1.

31   *Ibid.*, José María Vilaseca, 28 October 1895, pp. 32–4.

32   *Ibid.*, Pedro Romero, 10 October 1895, pp. 39–40, who cited Altamirano as 'the impartial author'.

33   *Ibid.*, Luis Silva, 4 October 1895, pp. 64–6.

34   *Ibid.*, Crescencio Carrillo y Ancona, 12 October 1895, pp. 10–14.

35   *Ibid.*, pp. 14–17; For some reason the sermon is assigned to 10 October in the *Album*; but see Anticoli, *Historia de la aparición*, II, 443–4.

36   See Agüeros, *Album de la coronación*, part 2, p. 123.

37   Anticoli, *Historia de la aparición*, II, 421.

38   Cuevas, *La Santísima Virgen*, pp. 149–52.

39   Tapia Méndez, *El siervo de Dios*, pp. 221–5; Gabino Chávez, *Celeste y terrestre o las dos coronas guadalupanas: reflexiones acerca de la desaparición de la corona en la imagen de Nuestra Señora de Guadalupe* (Mexico, 1895), pp. 8–10.

40   Agüeros, *Album de la coronación*, part 2, appendix, pp. 16–17.

41   Chávez, *Celeste y terrestre*, pp. 7–20, 32–3.

42   Tapia Méndez, *El siervo de Dios*, pp. 144–52, 239–61. On Averardi see José Miguel Romero de Solís, *El aguijón del espíritu: historia contemporánea de la Iglesia en México (1895–1990)* (Mexico, 1994), pp. 41–5.

43   Montes de Oca, 'Elogio fúnebre del Ilustrísimo Señor don Antonio Plancarte y Labastida, Abad de Guadalupe', *Oraciones fúnebres*, pp. 227–33, 242–5, 252.

44   Mariano Cuevas, *Historia de la Iglesia*, v, 452.

45   Mariano Cuevas, *Album histórico guadalupano del IV Centenario* (Mexico, 1930), pp. 206–7, 262–3.

46   Tapia Méndez, *El siervo de Dios*, pp. 224–5.

47   José Miguel Romero de Solís, 'Apostasía episcopal en Tamaulipas, 1896', *Historia Mexicana*, 37 (1987), pp. 239–81.

48   Sánchez Camacho's letter, 23 August 1896, first appeared in *La Voz de México*, and was later reprinted with García Icazbalceta's *Carta acerca del origen de la imagen de Nuestra Señora de Guadalupe de México* (Mexico, 1896), pp. 55–60; it is also printed in *Testimonios históricos*, pp. 1280–6.

49   Esteban Anticoli, *Novena triduo y deprecaciones a Nuestra Señora de Guadalupe*, 3rd edn (Puebla, 1902), pp. 85–9.

50 Agustín de la Rosa, *Defensa de la aparición de Nuestra Señora de Guadalupe* (Mexico, 1896), reprinted in *Testimonios históricos*, pp. 1222–79.

51 Anticoli, *Historia de la aparición*, I, 2.

52 Juan Luis Tercero, *La causa guadalupana: los últimos veinte años (1875–1895)* (Ciudad Victoria, Tamaulipas, 1896), pp. 15–16, 94–102.

53 *Ibid.*, on Anticoli, pp. 27, 51; on Moses, p. 42; the painting, p. 45; and García Icazbalceta, pp. 24, 126–34.

54 *Ibid.*, pp. 137–9, 66.

55 *Ibid.*, pp. 53–4, 89, 118, 124.

13   Juan Diego

1   For the text of this pastoral see Lauro López Beltrán, *Manríquez y Zárate. Primer obispo de Huejutla. Sublimador de Juan Diego. Heróico defensor de la Fe* (Mexico, 1974), pp. 40–7.

2   José de Jesús Manríquez y Zárate, '¿Quien fue Juan Diego?' (1939), reprinted in López Beltrán, *Manríquez y Zárate*, pp. 24, 77–84, 155–61; on Joan of Arc, p. 152.

3   *Ibid.*, pp. 173–87, 233–7, 258.

4   Lauro López Beltrán, *Patronatos guadalupanos* (Mexico, 1982), pp. 134–41. In 1910 the bishops of the United States did not wish to accept the Guadalupe as their patron.

5   *Crónica oficial de la fiesta del primer centenario de la independencia de México*, ed. Genaro García (Mexico, 1911, fasc. edn, 1991), pp. 70–6.

6   Enrique Krauze, *Mexico: Biography of Power 1810–1996*, trans. Hank Heifetz (New York, 1997), pp. 239–73; on the Catholic party see Gutiérrez Casillas, *Historia de la Iglesia*, pp. 278–84.

7   Lauro López Beltrán, *La persecución religiosa en México*, 2nd edn (Mexico, 1991), p. 51; see also Jean Meyer, *The Cristero Rebellion: The Mexican People between Church and State 1926–29* (Cambridge, 1976), pp. 9–12.

8   Pompa y Pompa, *El gran acontecimiento guadalupano*, pp. 120–2; López Beltrán, *Persecución religiosa*, p. 37.

9   Tena Ramírez, *Leyes fundamentales*, pp. 875–7.

10 See D. A. Brading, *Prophecy and Myth in Mexican History* (Cambridge, 1984), pp. 59–80; and D. A. Brading, 'Manuel Gamio and Official Indigenismo in Mexico', *Bulletin of Latin American Research*, 7 (1988), pp. 75–89.

11 López Beltrán, *Persecución religiosa*, pp. 29, 40–1, 47–51; Meyer, *The Cristero Rebellion*, pp. 33–44.

12 For an outline of events see Meyer, *The Cristero Rebellion*, pp. 44–66; for a strong criticism of the 1929 agreement see López Beltrán, *Persecución religiosa*, pp. 23, 137–55.

13 López Beltrán, *Persecución religiosa*, pp. 76–87, 142–55, 175–9; Meyer, *The Cristero Rebellion*, pp. 178–9.

NOTES TO PAGES 317–26

14   Gutiérrez Casillas, *Historia de la Iglesia*, pp. 431–8.

15   Pedro J. Sánchez, *La basílica guadalupana y las fiestas del IV centenario de las apariciones de Nuestra Señora* (Mexico, 1935), pp. 17–35, 109–35; José Bravo Ugarte, *Cuestiones históricas guadalupanas* (Mexico, 1940), pp. 86–97.

16   José Cantú Corro, *Album de las bodas de oro de la coronación guadalupana* (Cuernavaca, 1946), pp. 29–35, 72–5, 106–7, 112–24.

17   Martín Luis Guzmán, *Obras completas*, 2 vols. (Mexico, 1985), II, 917–22.

18   *Ibid.*, II, 924–60.

19   *Ibid.*, II, 896–917, 999–1000; see Fernando Curiel, *La querella de Martín Luis Guzmán* (Mexico, 1993), pp. 24–40, 180–203.

20   Guzmán, *Obras*, II, 980–94.

21   The sermon of 12 December 1931 is reprinted in Pompa y Pompa, *El gran acontecimiento guadalupano*, pp. 149–56.

22   The sermon of 12 October 1945 is reprinted in Cantú Corro, *Album de las bodas de oro*, pp. 79–88; it is also included in Luis M. Martínez, *María de Guadalupe*, 7th edn (Mexico, 1991), pp. 121–9.

23   José Cantú Corro, *Sermones guadalupanos (esquemas)* (Huajuapan de León, 1940), pp. 56, 193–202, 218.

24   *Ibid.*, pp. 86–91, 135, 174.

25   *Ibid.*, pp. 134, 153, 175, 232.

26   Cuevas, *Historia de la Iglesia*, I, 304–15.

27   The 'primitive account', attributed to Tovar, is reprinted in *Testimonios históricos*, pp. 24–5; see also Cuevas, *Album histórico guadalupano*, pp. 275–94.

28   *Documentos inéditos del siglo XV*, pp. 287–8.

29   Cuevas, *Historia de la Iglesia*, II, appendix, pp. 531–4.

30   *Ibid.*, V, 335–406.

31   Cuevas, *Album histórico guadalupano*, pp. 9–10, 211–14.

32   Primo Feliciano Velásquez, *La aparición de Santa María de Guadalupe* (Mexico, 1931), facs. edn with introduction by J. Jesús Jiménez López (Mexico, 1981), pp. 115–40; the translation is on pp. 142–83.

33   On Marcos and Annals see *ibid.*, pp. 52–8; and other native sources, pp. 60–92.

34   *Ibid.*, pp. 58–9.

35   Angel María Garibay Kintana, *Historia de la literatura nahuatl*, 2 vols. (Mexico, 1953–4), II, 256–65.

36   *Ibid.*, II, 264–5.

37   See Garibay's article in *The New Catholic Encyclopedia*, 16 vols. (Washington, 1967), VI, 821–2, where Juan González was identified as the author of the 'primitive account'. For the song of don Plácido see Xavier Noguez, *Documentos guadalupanos: un estudio sobre las fuentes de información tempranas en torno a las mariofanías en el Tepeyac* (Mexico, 1993), pp. 33–44.

38   Edmundo O'Gorman, *Destierro de sombras: luz en el origen de la imagen y culto de Nuestra Señora de Guadalupe del Tepeyac* (Mexico, 1986), pp. 161–212; for attack on Garibay, see pp. 199–206.

39   *Ibid.*, pp. 1–40.

40   *Ibid.*, pp. 115–41; Marcel Bataillon, *Erasmo y España*, trans. Antonio Alatorre, 2 vols. (Mexico, 1950), II, 445–54.

41   O'Gorman, *Destierro de sombras*, pp. 43–61, 232–7, 265–76; Jesús García Gutiérrez, 'Un documento guadalupano del siglo XVI: la información contra el padre Bustamante', *Memorias de la Academia Mexicana de la Historia*, 14 (1955), pp. 313–30.

42   Francisco de la Maza, *El guadalupanismo mexicano* (Mexico, 1953, 2nd edn, 1981), pp. 101–1, 14–17, 26, 41–2.

43   *Ibid.*, pp. 48–106.

44   *Ibid.*, pp. 119–51, 182–6.

45   Lafaye, *Quetzalcoatl y Guadalupe*, pp. 336–48; see Octavio Paz, 'Prefacio: entre Orfandad y Legitimidad', pp. 13–14, 24; this preface was republished in Octavio Paz, *El ogro filantrópico: historia y política 1971–1978* (Mexico, 1979), pp. 38–52.

46   *Ibid.*, pp. 13, 21–2.

47   See chapter 14.

48   López Beltrán, *Manríquez y Zárate*, pp. 53–60, 258–61.

49   López Beltrán, *Persecución religiosa*, pp. 77, 108–55, 484, 552–7, 591–3.

50   López Beltrán, *Conferencias guadalupanas*, pp. 174–83.

51   *Ibid.*, pp. 251–60.

52   *Ibid.*, p. 143; López Beltrán, *La primera historia guadalupana*, pp. 21, 36. In this re-impression of his 1952 edition of Miguel Sánchez, López Beltrán described de la Maza as 'this little Borunda of the twentieth century'; see de la Maza, *El guadalupanismo mexicano* (Mexico, 1953), pp. 55–6, where he referred to that edition as 'infantile'.

53   Lauro López Beltrán, *La protohistoria guadalupana* (Mexico, 1966), pp. 38, 67, 92–6, 106–16, 124.

54   Lauro López Beltrán, *Homenaje lírico guadalupano* (Mexico, 1984), pp. 169–80.

55   López Beltrán, *La protohistoria guadalupana*, pp. 203, 224–9, 237.

56   *Ibid.*, pp. 232, 244–52, 264; he noted that vestiges of the crown were reappearing.

57   Roberto Blancarte, *Historia de la Iglesia católica en México* (Mexico, 1992), pp. 302–6.

58   Gabriel Chávez de la Mora, 'La Nueva Basílica', *Primer Encuentro Nacional Guadalupano*, Centro de Estudios Guadalupanos (Mexico, 1978), pp. 113–39.

59   Luis Medina Ascencio, 'Las apariciones como un hecho histórico', *Segundo Encuentro Nacional Guadalupano*, Centro de Estudios Guadalupanos (Mexico, 1979), pp. 25–30.

60   Fidel de Jesús Chauvet, 'Las apariciones guadalupanas del Tepeyac', *Primer Encuentro Nacional Guadalupano*, pp. 25–48. Note that Chauvet amended his 1976 paper in order to respond to Wigberto Jiménez Moreno's 1977 paper, which,

however, did not appear in the published version of the *Segundo Encuentro*. Notice of Jiménez Moreno's theory had already appeared in Rodolfo Usigli, *Corona de Luz* (Mexico, 1965), pp. 75–81.

61 *Ibid.*, pp. 25–48.

62 Lauro López Beltrán, 'La historicidad de Juan Diego', *Segundo Encuentro Nacional Guadalupano*, pp. 55–70; see also Lauro López Beltrán, *La historicidad de Juan Diego y su posible canonización* (Mexico, 1981), pp. 7–9.

63 Blancarte, *Historia de la Iglesia*, pp. 375–6; *Las informaciones jurídicas*, p. 18.

64 López Beltrán, *La historicidad de Juan Diego*, on predecessors and his own role, pp. 7, 12–45; on Salazar, pp. 142–7, 185–97.

65 *Ibid.*, pp. 167, 180–2.

66 José Luis Guerrero, *¿Existió Juan Diego?* (Mexico, 1996), p. 5.

67 For the text of the decree in Latin and Spanish see *Las informaciones jurídicas de 1666 y el beato indio Juan Diego*, pp. 156–71.

68 *Ibid.*, p. 21.

69 *Ibid.*, pp. 13, 22.

70 Juan Pablo II (John Paul II), *La Iglesia en América: exhortación apostólica postsinodal* (Mexico, 1999), pp. 20–2.

71 Marta Eugenia García Ugarte, *La nueva relación Iglesia–Estado en México* (Mexico, 1993), *passim*.

14   *Nican mopohua*

1 Xavier Escalada, *Enciclopedia guadalupana*, 4 vols. bound in 2, continuous pagination (Mexico, 1995), prologue.

2 *Ibid.*, pp. 358, 384–6; see Jody Brant Smith, *The Image of the Guadalupe*, 2nd edn (Macon, Ga., 1994), for Callahan's findings, pp. 61–70.

3 Escalada, *Enciclopedia guadalupana*, pp. 643–4; Juan J. Benítez, *El misterio de la Virgen de Guadalupe* (Mexico, 1982), pp. 165–212.

4 Escalada, *Enciclopedia guadalupana*, pp. 263, 355–6, 520–1, 643–4.

5 *Ibid.*, pp. 42–50, 632, 670–1.

6 *Ibid.*, pp. 191–3, 131. See the striking photographs between pp. 192 and 193 and 483 and 487.

7 *Ibid.*, pp. 50, 740–1.

8 *Ibid.*, 455–7; Xavier Escalada, *Enciclopedia guadalupana. Apéndice Códice 1548. Estudio científico de su autenticidad* (Mexico, 1997), *passim*.

9 Richard Nebel, *Santa María Tonantzin Virgen de Guadalupe: Continuidad y transformación religiosa en México*, trans. Carlos Warnholtz Bustillos (Mexico, 1995), pp. 143–53.

10 *Ibid.*, p. 169. Nebel translated the *Nican mopohua* into German; here he provides a Spanish version and a facsimile and transcription of Laso de la Vega's Nahuatl text, pp. 339–67; see also pp. 226–7.

11   *Ibid.*, pp. 235–47.

12   *Ibid.*, pp. 263, 288–9, 292–4, 302–4.

13   Virgil Elizondo, *Guadalupe: Mother of the New Creation* (New York, 1997), pp. x, 93.

14   *Ibid.*, pp. 47–53, 67–9, 113–18, 129–35.

15   Guillermo Schulenberg, prologue, Nebel, *Santa María Tonantzin*, pp. 9–11.

16   The full text of these interviews is reprinted in Guerrero, *¿Existió Juan Diego?*, p. 18.

17   *Ibid.*, pp. 13, 18, 20–4; see the tribute of Pedro Ramírez Vásquez, in *Guadalupe. Maravilla americana*, pp. 13–14.

18   Guerrero, *¿Existió Juan Diego?*, pp. 3–9.

19   Norberto Rivera Carrera, *¿No estoy yo aquí que soy tu Madre?* (Mexico, 1996), pp. 1–2.

20   *Ibid.*, pp. 4–7.

21   Sánchez, *Imagen de la Virgen María*, in *Testimonios históricos*, p. 237.

22   Noguez, *Documentos guadalupanos*, p. 189.

23   Poole, *Our Lady of Guadalupe*, pp. 12, 225.

24   *Ibid.*, pp. 95–9, 122–42.

25   *Ibid.*, p. 102.

26   *Ibid.*, pp. 42–3, 115–18.

27   *Ibid.*, pp. 147–61, 169.

28   *Ibid.*, p. 118; see Gloria Grajales and Ernest J. Burrus, *Bibliografía guadalupana 1531–1984* (Washington, 1986), where nine editions of Becerra's work are listed for the nineteenth century.

29   Poole, *Our Lady of Guadalupe*, pp. 7, 10–11, 107, 223. He describes his work as 'a species of detective work' on p. 14; for his dismissal of Sánchez see p. 107. As regards the limited extension of the cult among Indians, Poole follows William Taylor, 'The Virgin of Guadalupe: An Inquiry into the Social History of Marian Devotion', *American Ethnologist*, 20 (1986), pp. 9–33.

30   José Luis Guerrero, *El nican mopohua: un intento de exégesis* (Mexico, 1996), pp. 467–8, 497–512, 525, 614.

31   *Ibid.*, pp. 497, 533, 546–65, 624.

32   *Ibid.*, pp. 44–9.

33   *Ibid.*, pp. 53–61.

34   *Ibid.*, p. 98.

35   Enrique Roberto Salazar, 'El beato Juan Diego, modelo e intercesor de los indígenas', *Encuentro Nacional Indígena* (Mexico, 1993), pp. 127–34.

36   Guerrero, *El nican mopohua*, pp. 102–3; note that Guerrero dismisses Escalada's recently discovered *Códice de 1548* as too good to be true, p. 495.

37   *Ibid.*, pp. 152–65, 173–7, 188.

38   *Ibid.*, pp. 330–3.

39   *Ibid.*, pp. 360, 405, 414, 456.

40 *Ibid.*, pp. 71, 243, 614.

41 Sousa, Poole and Lockhart, *The Story of Guadalupe*; see also Lockhart, *The Nahuas after the Conquest*, pp. 247–50; and Poole, *Our Lady of Guadalupe*, pp. 113–14.

42 Sousa, Poole and Lockhart, *The Story of Guadalupe*, pp. 19–22, 30–1, 45–7.

43 John Bierhorst, *Cantares mexicanos: Songs of the Aztecs* (Stanford, 1985), p. 61.

44 Sousa, Poole and Lockhart, *The Story of Guadalupe*, pp. 8–12, 18; on the miracle sequences, pp. 12–17.

45 Florencia, *La Estrella del Norte*, p. 464, where a miracle, not in Sánchez, is accepted, since 'an old painting in the sanctuary testifies to it, where the case is painted and explained with an inscription at its foot'.

15 Epiphany and revelation

1   Tanner, *Decrees of the Ecumenical Councils*, ii, 'Lumen gentium', p. 897.

2   *Ibid.*, ii, session 25, p. 775.

3   *Catechism of the Catholic Church* (London, 1994), articles 1159–62, pp. 265–6.

4   Cited in Leonid Ouspensky and Vladimir Lossky, *The Meaning of Icons* (Crestwood, N.Y., 1982), p. 30; see also pp. 41–8, 15.

5   Pelikan, *The Christian Tradition*, ii, 133.

6   Tanner, *Decrees of the Ecumenical Councils*, ii, 850–4.

7   *Ibid.*, pp. 865, 890–8.

8   Sigüenza y Góngora, *Glorias de Querétaro*, pp. 10–11.

9   Exodus 40.35; Numbers 9.18, 22; Luke 1.35.

10 Florencia, *Dos célebres santuarios*, pp. 150–1.

11 Jerónimo de Valladolid, prologue to Florencia , *La Estrella del Norte*, p. 8.

12 James Tunstead Burtchaell, *Catholic Theories of Biblical Inspiration* (Cambridge, 1969), pp. 232, 261–3.

13 *Catechism of the Catholic Church*, article 67, pp. 22–3; see also Karl Rahner, *Visions and Prophecies* (New York, 1963), p. 55: 'The history of Christianity would be unthinkable without prophetic and visionary elements.'

14 Tanner, *Decrees of the Ecumenical Councils*, ii, 'Dei verbum', p. 976.

15 Raymond E. Brown, *The Birth of the Messiah: A Commentary on the Infancy Narratives in the Gospels of Matthew and Luke*, new edn (New York, 1997), pp. 37–8, 113–15; citation on p. 245; pp. 269, 258–9.

16 Florencia, *Dos célebres santuarios*, pp. 130, 134; on the early *demandantes* of Guadalupe see Noguez, *Documentos guadalupanos*, p. 232.

17 *Las informaciones jurídicas de 1666*, p. 21.

Bibliography

This bibliography lists the works cited in the text and notes and generally refers to the editions used by the author. Where works are discussed the date of the original edition is given in the text or the relevant note. Authors are here listed under their most commonly used name, e.g., Veytia rather than Fernández de Echeverría y Veytia. Unless stated otherwise, all facsimile editions were printed in Mexico.

Abad y Queipo, Manuel. *Carta pastoral* (Mexico, 1813)

    Cartas pastorales (Mexico, 1811–13)

Acuña, Hernando de. *Varias poesías*, ed. E. Catena de Vindel (Madrid, 1954)

Adams, Henry. *Mont-Saint-Michel and Chartres* (Boston and New York, 1933)

    The Education of Henry Adams: An Autobiography (Boston and New York, 1918)

Agreda, Sor María de. *Mística Ciudad de Dios*, 3 vols. (Antwerp, 1694)

Agreda y Sánchez, José María. *Catálogo* (n.p., n.d.)

Alamán, Lucas. *Disertaciones*, 3 vols. (Mexico, 1969)

    Historia de Méjico, 4th edn, 5 vols. (Mexico, 1968–9)

Alarcón y Sánchez de la Barquera, Próspero María. *Carta pastoral del Illmo. Señor Arzobispo de México* (Mexico, 1895)

Album conmemorativo del 450 aniversario de las apariciones de Nuestra Señora de Guadalupe (Mexico, 1981)

Album de la coronación de la Santísima Virgen de Guadalupe, ed. Victoriano Agüeros (*El Tiempo*, Mexico, 1895)

Alloza, Juan de. *Cielo. estrellado . . .* (Madrid, 1654)

Altamirano, Ignacio Manuel. *Discursos* (Paris, 1982)

    Obras completas, 22 vols. (Mexico, 1986–92)

    Paisajes y leyendas, First Series (Mexico, 1974)

    Paisajes y leyendas, Second Series (Mexico, 1949)

Alva Ixtlilxóchitl, Fernando de. *Obras históricas*, ed. Edmundo O'Gorman, 2 vols. (Mexico, 1975)

Amaya, Jesús. *Génesis e historia de Nuestra Señora de Guadalupe, Madre de Dios* (Mexico, 1931)

Andrade, Vicente de Paul. *Ensayo bibliográfico mexicano del siglo XVII* (Mexico, 1899, facs. edn, 1971)

    Estudio histórico sobre la leyenda guadalupana (Mexico, 1908), reprinted in *Testimonios históricos*, pp. 1287–1337

Anticoli, Esteban. *Defensa de la aparición de la Virgen María en el Tepeyac . . . contra un libro impreso en Mexico el año de 1891* (Puebla, 1893)

    El magisterio de la Iglesia y la Virgen del Tepeyac (Querétaro, 1892)

    Historia de la aparición de la Santísima Virgen María de Guadalupe en México, 2 vols. (Mexico, 1897)

    La Virgen del Tepeyac patrona principal de la nación mexicana (Guadalajara, 1884)

    Novena triduo y deprecaciones a Nuestra Señora de Guadalupe, 3rd edn (Puebla, 1902)

Aparicio Vega, Manuel Jesús (ed.). 'La revolución del Cuzco de 1814', *Colección documental de la independencia del Perú, III. Conspiraciones y rebeliones en el siglo XIX*, vol. VII (Lima, 1974)

Arlegui, José. *Sagrado paladión del americano orbe . . .* (Mexico, 1743)

Auerbach, Erich. *Scenes from the Drama of European Literature* (Manchester, 1984)

Augustine, Saint. *City of God*, ed. David Knowles (London, 1972)

    The Works of Aurelius Augustine, ed. Marcus Dods (Edinburgh, 1831)

Ballesteros-Beretta, A. 'Juan Bautista Muñoz: dos facetas científicas', *Revista de Indias*, 2 (1941), pp. 5–38

    'Juan Bautista Muñoz: la creación del archivo de Indias', *Revista de Indias*, 2 (1941), pp. 55–95

    Juan Bautista Muñoz: la historia del Nuevo Mundo', *Revista de Indias*, 3 (1943), pp. 589–660

Bandelier, Adolfo F. *Correspondencia*, ed. Leslie A. White and Ignacio Bernal (Mexico, 1960)

Barasche, Moshe. *Icon: Studies in the History of an Idea* (New York, 1992)

Bárcena, Manuel de la. *Manifiesto al mundo: la justicia y la necesidad de la independencia de la Nueva España* (Mexico, 1821)

    Sermón exhortatorio que en la solemne función anual que hace de la imperial orden de Guadalupe a su celestial patrona (Mexico, 1823)

Barros, Felipe Neri de. 'Sermón predicado . . . a su patrona, María Santísima de Guadalupe . . .', *Sermonario mexicano*, III, pp. 465–71

Bartolache, José Ignacio. *Manifiesto satisfactorio: opúsculo guadalupano* (Mexico, 1790)

Bataillon, Marcel. *Erasmo y España*, trans. Antonio Alatorre, 2 vols. (Mexico, 1950)

Bauckham, Richard. *The Theology of the Book of Revelation* (Cambridge, 1993)

    Tudor Apocalypse (The Sutton Courtenay Press, 1978)

Becerra Tanco, Luis. *Felicidad de México en el principio y milagroso origen que tuvo el santuario de la Virgen María Nuestra Señora de Guadalupe, extramuros: en la aparición admirable de esta soberana Señora y de su prodigiosa imagen*, 2nd edn, ed. Antonio de Gama (Mexico, 1675)

Origen milagroso del santuario de Nuestra Señora de Guadalupe, extramuros de la ciudad de México (Mexico, 1666)

Belting, Hans. *Likeness and Presence: A History of the Image before the Era of Art*, trans. Edmund Jephcott (Chicago, 1994)

Benítez, Juan J. *El misterio de la Virgen de Guadalupe* (Mexico, 1982)

Benítez, Lorenzo. *Sermón panegyrico que en la solemne fiesta con que celebra la aparición de Nuestra Señora de Guadalupe de México, su ilustre archicofradía* (Mexico, 1685)

Beristain de Souza, José Mariano. *Biblioteca hispano-americana septentrional*, 3rd edn, 5 vols. (Mexico, 1957)

Declamación cristiana que en la solemne función de desagravios a María Santísima de Guadalupe . . . (Mexico, 1811)

Diálogos patrióticos (Mexico, 1810–11)

Discurso eucarístico que en la muy solemne acción de gracias celebrada . . . por la libertad y restitución a su trono a Fernando Séptimo, soberano monarca de España e Indias (Mexico, 1814)

Discurso político-moral y cristiano . . . (Mexico, 1809)

Betancurt, Agustín de. *Teatro mexicano* (Mexico, 1697–8, facs. edn, 1971)

Bevan, Edwyn. *Holy Images* (London, 1945)

Bierhorst, John. *Cantares mexicanos: Songs of the Aztecs* (Stanford, 1985)

Blancarte, Roberto. *Historia de la Iglesia católica en México* (Mexico, 1992)

Blanco White, Joseph (Leucadio Doblado pseud.). *Letters from Spain* (London, 1822)

Bolívar, Simón. *Obras completas*, ed. Vicente Lecuna, 3 vols. (Caracas, 1964)

Borunda, José Ignacio. 'Clave general de jeroglíficos americanos', in Nicolás León, *Bibliografía mexicana del siglo XVIII*, 5 vols. (Mexico, 1902–8), III, 195–324

Boturini Benaduci, Lorenzo. *Idea de una nueva historia general de la América Septentrional*, ed. Miguel León-Portilla (Mexico, 1974)

Brading, D. A. *Church and State in Bourbon Mexico: The Diocese of Michoacán 1749–1810* (Cambridge, 1994)

'Clemente de Jesús Munguía: intransigencia ultramontana y la reforma mexicana', in *Historia de la Iglesia en el siglo XIX*, ed. Manuel Ramos Medina (Mexico, 1998), pp. 13–46

'Manuel Gamio and Official Indigenismo in Mexico', *Bulletin of Latin American Research*, 7 (1988), pp. 75–89

Prophecy and Myth in Mexican History (Cambridge, 1984)

The First America: The Spanish Monarchy, Creole Patriots and the Liberal State, 1492–1867 (Cambridge, 1991)

The Origins of Mexican Nationalism (Cambridge, 1985)

Bravo Ugarte, José. *Cuestiones históricas guadalupanas* (Mexico, 1940)

Diócesis y obispos de la Iglesia mexicana 1519–1965 (Mexico, 1965)

Munguía, obispo y arzobispo de Michoacán (1810–1868): su vida y su obra (Mexico, 1967)

Brown, Peter. *Society and the Holy in Late Antiquity* (London, 1982)

The Cult of the Saints (London, 1981)

Brown, Raymond E. *The Birth of the Messiah: A Commentary on the Infancy Narratives in the Gospels of Matthew and Luke*, 2nd edn (New York, 1993)

Burtchaell, James Tunstead. *Catholic Theories of Biblical Inspiration* (Cambridge, 1969)

Bustamante, Carlos María. *Continuación del cuadro histórico de la revolución mexicana*, ed. Jorge Gurría Lacroix, 4 vols. (Mexico, 1953–63)

'Correo Americano del Sur', *Periodismo insurgente*, facs. edn without continuous pagination, 2 vols (Mexico, 1976), II

Cuadro de la revolución mexicana, ed. Jorge Gurría Lacroix, 3 vols. (Mexico, 1961)

La aparición de Nuestra Señora de Guadalupe (Mexico, 1840)

La aparición guadalupana de México (Mexico, 1843)

Manifiesto de la junta guadalupana a los mexicanos y disertación histórico-crítica de Nuestra Señora en Tepeyac (Mexico, 1831)

Cabrera, Miguel. *Maravilla americana y conjunto de varias maravillas observadas con la dirección de las reglas del arte de la pintura en la prodigiosa imagen de Nuestra Señora de Guadalupe de México* (Mexico, 1756, facs. edn, 1977)

Cabrera y Quintero, Cayetano de. *Escudo de armas de México* (Mexico, 1746, facs. edn, 1981)

Calancha, Antonio de la. *Crónica moralizada del orden de San Agustín en el Perú*, ed. Ignacio Prado Pastor, 6 vols. (Lima, 1974)

Calvo, Thomas. 'El zodiaco de la Nueva Eva: el culto mariano en la América septentrional hacia 1700', *Manifestaciones religiosas en el mundo americano*, ed. Clara García Ayluardo and Manuel Ramos Medina, 2nd edn (Mexico, 1997)

Cantú Corro, José. *Album de las bodas de oro de la coronación guadalupana* (Cuernavaca, 1946)

Sermones guadalupanos (esquemas) (Huajuapan de León, 1940)

Caramuel Lobkowitz, Juan. *Architectura civil recta y obliqua* (Vergeren, 1678)

Caro Baroja, Julio. *Las falsificaciones de Historia en relación con la de España* (Barcelona, 1992)

Carranza, Francisco Javier. *La transmigración de la Iglesia a Guadalupe* (Mexico, 1749)

Sermón de la adoración de los Reyes . . . (Mexico, 1743)

Carreño, Alberto María, 'Noticias biográficas', *Sesión celebrada por la Sociedad Mexicana de Geografía y Estadística en memoria del socio honorario Sr. Lic. Canónigo don Vicente de Paul Andrade* (Mexico, 1915)

Carrillo y Ancona, Crescencio. *Carta de actualidad sobre el milagro de la aparición guadalupana en 1531* (Mexico, 1888)

Carrillo y Pérez, Ignacio. *Pensil americano florido en el origen del invierno, la imagen de María Santísima de Guadalupe* (Mexico, 1797)

Castañeda, Juan José Ruíz de. *Sermón panegyrico en glorias de María Santísima bajo el título de Guadalupe* (Mexico, 1766)

Castorena, Ursúa y Goyeneche, Juan Ignacio María de, and Juan Francisco Sahagún de Arévelo y Ladrón de Guevara. *Gacetas de México* (Mexico, 1722–42, facs. edn, 3 vols., 1988)

Castro, Américo. *España en su historia: cristianos, moros y judíos*, 2nd edn (Madrid, 1983)

Catechism of the Catholic Church (London, 1994)

Catholic Encyclopedia, The, ed. Charles Herberman *et al.*, 16 vols. (New York, 1907)

Ceballos Ramírez, Manuel. 'Siglo XIX y guadalupanismo: de la polémica a la coronación y de la devoción a la política', *Historia de la Iglesia en el siglo XIX*, ed. Manuel Ramos Medina (Mexico, 1998)

Cepeda, Juan de. *Sermón de la Natividad de la Virgen María Señora Nuestra, predicado en la ermita de Guadalupe, extramuros de México en la fiesta de la misma iglesia* (Mexico, 1622)

Chadwick, Owen. *A History of the Popes, 1830–1914* (Oxford, 1998)

    From Bossuet to Newman (Cambridge, 1957)

    The Popes and the European Revolution (Oxford, 1981)

Chauvet, Fidel de Jesús. 'Las apariciones guadalupanas del Tepeyac', *Primer Encuentro Nacional Guadalupano* (Mexico, 1978), pp. 25–48

Chávez, Gabino. *Celeste y terrestre o las dos coronas guadalupanas: reflexiones acerca de la desaparición de la corona en la imagen de Nuestra Señora de Guadalupe* (Mexico, 1895)

Chávez de la Mora, Gabriel. 'La Nueva Basílica', *Primer Encuentro Nacional Guadalupano*, Centro de Estudios Guadalupanos (Mexico, 1978), pp. 113–39

Christian, William A., Jr. *Apparitions in Late Medieval and Renaissance Spain* (Princeton, 1981)

Chueca Goitia, Fernando. *Casas reales en monasterios y conventos españoles* (Bilbao, 1982)

Cisneros, Luis de. *Historia del principio y origen, progresos venidas a México y milagros de la santa imagen de Nuestra Señora de los Remedios, extramuros de México* (Mexico, 1621)

Clavijero, Francisco Javier. 'Breve noticia sobre la prodigiosa y renombrada imagen de Nuestra Señora de Guadalupe', in *Testimonios históricos*, pp. 578–96

    Historia antigua de México, ed. Mariano Cuevas (Mexico, 1964)

Códice Mendieta: documentos franciscanos siglos XVI y XVII, ed. Joaquín García Icazbalceta, 2 vols. (Mexico, 1892, facs. edn, 1971)

Colección de documentos eclesiásticos de México, ed. Fortino Hipólito Vera, 3 vols. (Amecameca, 1887)

Colección de documentos para la historia de la guerra de independencia de México desde 1808 hasta 1821, ed. Juan E. Hernández y Dávalos, 6 vols. (Mexico, 1877; facs. edn, 1985)

Colección de obras y opúsculos pertenecientes a la milagrosa aparición de la bellísima imagen de Nuestra Señora de Guadalupe que se venera en su santuario extramuros de México, 2 (unnumbered) vols. (Madrid, 1785)

Conde, José Ignacio and María Teresa Cervantes de Conde, 'Nuestra Señora de Guadalupe en el arte', *Album conmemorativo del 450 aniversario de la aparición de Nuestra Señora de Guadalupe* (Mexico, 1981), pp. 121–223

Conde y Oquendo, Francisco Javier. *Disertación histórica sobre la aparición de la portentosa imagen de María Santísima de Guadalupe de México*, 2 vols. (Mexico, 1852)

Coplas a la partida, que la soberana Virgen de Guadalupe hizo de esta Ciudad de México, para su hermita, compuesta de un devoto suyo (Mexico, 1634, re-edition, Mexico, c. 1683–94)

Córdoba, Tirso Rafael, 'Sermón en honor de Nuestra Señora de Guadalupe', *Sermonario mexicano*, III, 265–76

Couto, José Bernardo, *Diálogo sobre la historia de la pintura en México*, ed. Manuel Toussaint (Mexico, 1947)

Crónica oficial de la fiesta del primer centenario de la independencia de México, ed. Genaro García (Mexico, 1911, facs. edn, 1991)

Cross, F. L. and E. A. Livingstone, *The Oxford Dictionary of the Christian Church*, 3rd edn (Oxford, 1997)

Cruz, Mateo de la. '*Relación de la milagrosa aparición de la santa imagen de la Virgen de Guadalupe, sacado de la historia que compusó Br. Miguel Sánchez* (Mexico, 1660), reprinted in *Testimonios históricos*, pp. 267–81

Cuadriello, Jaime Genaro. 'Los pinceles de Dios Padre', *Maravilla americana, variantes de la iconografía guadalupana siglos XVII–XIX* (Mexico, 1989)

'Visiones en Patmos Tenochtitlan: la Mujer águila', *Artes de México*, 29 (1995), pp. 1–80.

Cuadriello, Jaime *et al. Juegos de ingenio y agudeza: la pintura emblemática de la Nueva España* (Mexico, 1994)

Cuevas, José de Jesús, *La Santísima Virgen de Guadalupe* (Mexico, 1887)

Obras, ed. Victoriano Agüeros (Mexico, 1898)

Cuevas, Mariano. *Album histórico guadalupano del IV Centenario* (Mexico, 1930)

Historia de la Iglesia en México, 5th edn, 5 vols. (Mexico, 1947)

Curiel, Fernando, *La querella de Martín Luis Guzmán* (Mexico, 1993)

Dávila y Arriliaga, José Mariano. *Continuación de la historia de la Compañía de Jesús en Nueva España de P. Francisco Javier Alegre*, 2 vols. (Puebla, 1888)

Decrees of the Ecumenical Councils, ed. Norman P. Tanner, 2 vols. (London, 1990)

Deery, Joseph. *Our Lady of Lourdes* (Dublin, 1958)

Díaz Calvillo, Juan Bautista. *Sermón que en el aniversario solemne a María Santísima de los Remedios celebrado en esta iglesia catedral el día 30 de Octubre de 1811 por la victoria del Monte de las Cruces* (Mexico, 1811)

Díaz del Castillo, Bernal. *Historia verdadera de la conquista de la Nueva España*, ed. Joaquín Ramírez Cabañas, 2 vols. (Mexico, 1968)

Diccionario bio-bibliográfico de la Compañía de Jesús de México, ed. Francisco Zambrano and José Gutiérrez Casillas, 16 vols. (Mexico, 1961–77)

Dionysius the Areopagite, Saint. *The Mystical Theology and the Celestial Hierarchies* (Fintry, Surrey, 1949)

Documentos inéditos del siglo XVI para la historia de México, ed. Mariano Cuevas (Mexico, 1914, facs. edn, 1975)

Eguiara y Eguren, Juan José de. *Biblioteca mexicana*, ed. Ernesto de la Torre Villar and Ramiro Navarro de Anda, Spanish trans. Benjamín Fernández Valenzuela (Mexico, 1982)

María Santísima pintándose milagrosamente en su bellísima imagen de Guadalupe de México, saluda a la Nueva España y se constituye su patrona. Panegyrico (Mexico, 1757)

Prólogos a la Biblioteca mexicana, ed. Agustín Millares Carlo (Mexico, 1944)

Eire, Carlos M. N. *War against the Idols: The Reformation of Worship from Erasmus to Calvin* (Cambridge, 1986)

Elizondo, Virgil. *Guadalupe: Mother of the New Creation* (New York, 1997)

Episcopado y gobierno en México: cartas pastorales colectivas del episcopado mexicano 1859–1870, ed. Alfonso Alcalá and Manuel Olimón (Mexico, 1989)

Erasmus, Desiderius. 'The Handbook of the Militant Christian', in *The Essential Erasmus*, ed. John P. Dolan (New York, 1964)

Escalada, Xavier. *Enciclopedia guadalupana*, 4 vols. bound in 2, continuous pagination (Mexico, 1995)

Enciclopedia guadalupana. Apéndice códice 1548. Estudio científico de su autenticidad (Mexico, 1997)

Escobar, Matías de. *Americana thebaida*, 2nd edn, ed. Nicolás P. Navarrete (Morelia, 1970)

Espinosa, Isidro Félix de. *Crónica apostólica y seráphica de todos los colegios de propaganda fide de la Nueva España de los missioneros franciscanos observantes*, ed. Lino G. Canedo (Washington, 1964)

Espinosa, Pedro. *Pastoral del Illmo: Señor Arzobispo de Guadalajara a la vuelta de su destierro* (Guadalajara, 1864)

Espinosa Medrano, Juan de. *Apologético en favor de D. Luis de Góngora* (Lima, 1662)

Eusebius of Caesarea. *The Church History and other writings* (New York, 1890, facs. edn, 1979)

Evans, R. J. W. *The Making of the Habsburg Monarchy 1500–1700* (Oxford, 1979)

Evenett, H. Outram. *The Spirit of the Counter-Reformation*, ed. with postscript by John Bossy (Cambridge, 1968)

Feijoo Montenegro, Benito Jerónimo. *Adiciones a las obras del muy ilustre y reverendísimo padre maestro Benito Jerónimo Feijoo y Montenegro* (Madrid, 1783)

Teatro crítico universal (1726–39), 8th edn, 8 vols. (Madrid, 1753–5)

Ferrer, San Vicente. *Biografía y escritos*, ed. José María de Garganta and Vicente Forcada (Madrid, 1946)

Flor y canto de poesía guadalupana siglo XVII, ed. Joaquín Antonio Peñalosa (Mexico, 1987)

Florencia, Francisco de. *La Estrella del Norte de México* (Mexico, 1688, reprinted as second (unnumbered) vol. of *Colección de obras*)

La milagrosa invención de un tesoro escondido . . . , 2nd edn (Seville, 1745)

Menologio de los varones más señalados en perfección religiosa de la provincia de Jesús de Nueva España, nuevamente añadido por Juan Antonio de Oviedo (Mexico, 1747)

Origen de los dos célebres santuarios de la Nueva Galicia, obispado de Guadalajara en la América Septentrional, 3rd edn (Mexico, 1766)

Zodiaco mariano, ed. and augmented by Juan Antonio de Oviedo (Mexico, 1755; facs. edn with introduction by Antonio Rubial García, 1995)

Ford, Richard. *A Hand-Book for Travellers in Spain and Readers at Home*, ed. Ian Robertson, 3 vols with continuous pagination (Carbondale, Ill., 1966)

Freedberg, David. *The Power of Images: Studies in the History and Theory of Response* (Chicago, 1989)

Fuenlabrada, Nicolás de. *Oración evangélica y panegyrica . . . a María Santísima en su milagrosísima imagen del español Guadalupe en la Estremadura* (Mexico, 1681)

Galera Lamadrid, Jesús. *Nican mopohua: breve análisis literario e histórico* (Mexico, 1991)

García, Gregorio. *Predicación del evangelio en el Nuevo Mundo viviendo los apóstoles* (Baeza, 1625)

García Gutiérrez, Jesús. 'Un documento guadalupano del siglo XVI: la información contra el padre Bustamante', *Memorias de la Academia Mexicana de la Historia*, 14 (1955), pp. 313–30

García Icazbalceta, Joaquín. *Bibliografía mexicana del siglo XVI*, 2nd edn, ed. Agustín Millares Carlo (Mexico, 1954)

'Carta acerca del origen de la imagen de Nuestra Señora de Guadalupe' (Mexico, 1896), reprinted in *Testimonios históricos*, pp. 1092–1126

Cartas, ed. Felipe Teixidor (Mexico, 1937)

Don fray Juan de Zumárraga, primer obispo y arzobispo de México, 2nd edn, ed. Rafael Aguayo Spencer and Antonio Castro Leal, 4 vols (Mexico, 1947)

García de Torres, José Julio. *Sermón de acción de gracias a María Santísima de Guadalupe por el venturoso suceso de la independencia de la América Septentrional* (Mexico, 1821)

García Ugarte, Marta Eugenia. *La nueva relación Iglesia–Estado en México* (Mexico, 1993)

Garibay Kintana, Angel María. *Historia de la literatura nahuatl*, 2 vols. (Mexico, 1953–4)

'Our Lady of Guadalupe', *The New Catholic Encyclopedia*, 16 vols (Washington, 1967) VI, 821–2

Godwin, Joscelyn. *Athanasius Kircher: A Renaissance Man and the Quest for Lost Knowledge* (London, 1979)

Goicoechea, Juan de. *La maravilla inmarcesible y milagro continuado de Santísima Señora Nuestra en su prodigiosa imagen de Guadalupe de México* (Mexico, 1709)

Gómara, Francisco López de. *Historia de la conquista de México*, ed. Jorge Gurría Lacroix (Caracas, 1979)

Historia general de las Indias, ed. Jorge Gurría Lacroix (Caracas, 1979)

Gómez Ciriza, Roberto. *México ante la diplomacia vaticana* (Mexico, 1977)

Gómez Marín, Manuel. *Defensa guadalupana contra la disertación de don Juan Bautista Muñoz* (Mexico, 1819)

González, José Antonio (pseud. 'X'). *Santa María de Guadalupe, patrona de los mexicanos* (Guadalajara, 1884)

González Gómez, Juan Miguel and José Roda Peña. *Imaginería procesional de la Semana Santa de Sevilla* (Seville, 1992)

Goppelt, Leonhard. *Typos: The Typological Interpretation of the Old Testament in the New*, trans. Donald H. Madorig (Grand Rapids, Mich., 1982)

Grajales, Gloria and Ernest J. Burrus, *Bibliografía guadalupana 1531–1984* (Washington, 1986)

Grijalva, Juan de. *Crónica de la orden de N. P. S. Agustín en las provincias de la Nueva España* (Mexico, 1624, 2nd edn, 1985)

Gruzinski, Serge. *La guerra de las imágenes: de Cristóbal Colón a 'Blade Runner' (1492–2019)* (Mexico, 1994)

Guadalupe. Maravilla americana. Homenaje a Monseñor Guillermo Schulenburg Prado, ed. Manuel Olimón Nolasco (Mexico, 1998)

Guerra, François Xavier. *Modernidad e independencias: ensayos sobre las revoluciones hispánicas* (Mexico, 1993)

Guerrero, José Luis. *El nican mopohua: un intento de exégesis* (Mexico, 1996)

¿Existió Juan Diego? (Mexico, 1996)

Guridi Alcocer, José Miguel. *Apología del aparición de Nuestra Señora de Guadalupe de México* (Mexico, 1820)

Apuntes (Mexico, 1884)

Gutiérrez Casillas, José. *Historia de la Iglesia en México* (Mexico, 1974)

Jesuitas en México durante el siglo XIX (Mexico, 1977)

Gutiérrez Dávila, Julián. *Memorias históricas de la congregación del Oratorio de la ciudad de México* (Mexico, 1736)

Guzmán, Martín Luis. *Obras completas*, 2 vols. (Mexico, 1985)

Hakluyt, Richard. *The Principal Navigations, Voiages and Discoveries of the English Nation*, Everyman edn, 8 vols. (London, n.d.)

Harris, Ruth. *Lourdes: Body and Spirit in the Secular Age* (London, 1999)

Herboso, Pedro. *Sermón panegyrico . . . la milagrosa imagen de Nuestra Señora de Guadalupe de México* (Mexico, 1737)

Historia de la Iglesia en el siglo XIX, ed. Manuel Ramos Medina (Mexico, 1998)

Historia documental de México, ed. Ernesto de la Torre Villar *et al.*, 2 vols. (Mexico, 1964)

Holland, Lady Elizabeth. *The Spanish Journal*, ed. The Earl of Ilchester (London, 1910)

Hume, David. 'The Natural History of Religion', in *Hume on Religion*, ed. Richard Wollheim (London, 1963)

Ignatius Loyola, Saint. *The Spiritual Exercises of Saint Ignatius of Loyola*, trans. W. H. Longridge (London, 1919)

Información que el arzobispo de México don Fray Alonso de Montúfar mandó practicar . . . , 2nd. edn (Mexico, 1891, reprinted in *Testimonios históricos*, pp. 36–141)

Informaciones jurídicas de 1666 y el beato indio Juan Diego, Las, facs. edn of mss., ed. Ana María
 Sada Lambretón (1991)

*Informaciones sobre la milagrosa aparición de la Santísima Virgen de Guadalupe recibidas en 1666
 y 1723,* ed. Fortino Hipólito Vera (Amecameca, 1889)

Irenaeus, Saint. *Proof of the Apostolic Preaching,* trans. Joseph P. Smith (London, 1952)

Ita y Parra, Bartolomé Felipe de. *El arrebatado de Dios: el Señor D. Felipe V. Oración fúnebre*
 (Mexico, 1747)

 *El círculo del amor formado por la América Septentrional jurando María Santísima en su
 imagen de Guadalupe, la imagen del patrocinio de todo su reino* (Mexico, 1747)

 La imagen de Guadalupe: imagen de patrocinio (Mexico, 1744)

 La imagen de Guadalupe, Señora de los tiempos (Mexico, 1732)

 La Madre de la salud: la milagrosa imagen de Guadalupe (Mexico, 1739)

 'Sermón panegyrico', *Canonización en vida de San Juan de la Cruz* (Mexico, 1729)

Iturri, Francisco. *Carta crítica sobre la Historia de América del Señor d. Juan Bautista Muñoz*
 (Madrid, 1797, reprinted Buenos Aires, 1818)

Jiménez, Ismael. 'Sermón predicado en la colegiata . . .', *Sermonario mexicano,* III, 187–97

John of Damascus, Saint. *On the Divine Images,* trans. David Anderson (Crestwood, N.Y., 1980)

 On Holy Images followed by Three Sermons on the Assumption, trans. Mary H. Allies (London,
 1898)

Jovellanos, Gaspar Melchor de. *Obras completas,* ed. Miguel Artola, 5 vols. (Madrid, 1956)

Juan Pablo II (John Paul II). *La Iglesia en América: exhortación apostólica postsinodal* (Mexico,
 1999)

Kendrick, T. D. *St James in Spain* (London, 1961)

Knowles, David. *Great Historical Enterprises* (London, 1962)

Krauze, Enrique. *Mexico: Biography of Power 1810–1996,* trans. Hank Heifetz (New York, 1997)

Lafaye, Jacques. *Quetzalcoatl y Guadalupe: la formación de la conciencia nacional en México*
 (Mexico, 1977)

Lampe, G. W. H. and K. J. Woollcombe. *Essays in Typology* (London, 1957)

Lazcano, Francisco Javier. *Sermón panegyrico al inclito patronato de María Señora Nuestra en su
 milagrosísima imagen de Guadalupe sobre la universal Septentrional América*
 (Mexico, 1759)

Lemoine Villicaña, Ernesto. *Morelos* (Mexico, 1965)

Lempérière, Annick, '¿Nacion moderna o república barroca? México 1823–1857', in *Imaginar la
 nación,* ed. François-Xavier Guerra and Mónica Quijada (Munster, 1994)

León, Nicolás. *Bibliografía mexicana del siglo XVIII,* 5 vols. (Mexico, 1902–8)

León y Gama, Antonio. *Descripción histórica y cronológica de las piedras que se hallaron en la
 plaza principal de México* (Mexico, 1792)

Linehan, Peter. *History and Historians of Medieval Spain* (Oxford, 1993)

'The Beginnings of Santa María de Guadalupe and the Direction of 14th Century Castile', *Journal of Ecclesiastical History*, 36 (1985), pp. 284–304

Livius, Thomas. *The Blessed Virgin in the Fathers of the First Six Centuries* (London, 1893)

Lobato, Juan Antonio. *El fénix de las Indias único por inmaculado floreciendo en una tilma de palma, María en su Concepción Purísima aparecida en Guadalupe* (Mexico, 1700)

Lockhart, James. *The Nahuas after the Conquest: A Social and Cultural History of the Indians of Central Mexico, Sixteenth through Eighteenth Centuries* (Stanford, 1992)

López Beltrán, Lauro. *Conferencias guadalupanas* (Mexico, 1957)

Homenaje lírico guadalupano (Mexico, 1984)

'La historicidad de Juan Diego', *Segundo Encuentro Nacional Guadalupano* (Mexico, 1979)

La historicidad de Juan Diego y su posible canonización (Mexico, 1981)

La persecución religiosa en México, 2nd edn (Mexico, 1991)

La primera historia guadalupana (Mexico, 1981)

La protohistoria guadalupana (Mexico, 1966)

Manríquez y Zárate. Primer obispo de Huejutla. Sublimador de Juan Diego. Heróico defensor de la Fe (Mexico, 1974)

Patronatos guadalupanos (Mexico, 1982)

López de Cancelada, Juan. *El Telégrafo Mexicano* (Cadiz, 1813)

Lovett, Gabriel H. *Napoleon and the Birth of Modern Spain*, 2 vols. (New York, 1965)

Loyzaga, Manuel de. *Historia de la milagrosísima imagen de Nuestra Señora de Ocotlan que se venera extramuros de la ciudad de Tlaxcala* (Puebla, 1745)

Luxon, Thomas H. *Figures: Puritan Allegory and the Reformation Crisis in Representation* (Chicago, 1995)

Lynch, John. *Bourbon Spain 1700–1808* (London, 1989)

Maldonado, Francisco Severo. 'El Despertador Americano', *Periodismo Insurgente*, facs. edn, 2 vols. (Mexico, 1976), I, 1–43

Manríquez y Zárate, José de Jesús. '¿Quien fue Juan Diego?' (1939), reprinted in Lauro López Beltran, *Manríquez y Zárate: primer obispo de Hue jutla* (Mexico, 1974)

Markus, R. A. *Saeculum: History and Society in the Theology of St Augustine* (Cambridge, 1970)

Martínez, Luis M. *María de Guadalupe*, 7th edn (Mexico, 1996)

Martínez, Manuel Guillermo. *Don Joaquín García Icazbalceta: su lugar en la historiografía mexicana*, trans. Luis García Pimentel y Elguero (Mexico, 1950)

Martínez, Miguel. *Monseñor Munguía y sus escritos* (Mexico, 1979)

Mayans y Siscar, Gregorio. 'Censura de historias fabulosas', *Obras completas*, ed. Antonio Mestre Sánchez (Valencia, 1983), I, 265–305

Maza, Francisco de la. *El guadalupanismo mexicano*, 3rd edn (Mexico, 1984)

'Los evangelistas de Guadalupe y el nacionalismo mexicano', *Cuadernos Americanos*, 6 (1949), pp. 163–88

Medina, Baltazar de, *Crónica de la santa provincia de San Diego de México de religiosos descalzos de N. S. P. Francisco de la Nueva España* (Mexico, 1682)

Medina, José Toribio. *La imprenta en México (1539–1821)*, 8 vols. (Santiago de Chile, 1912, facs. edn, Mexico, 1989)

Medina Ascenio, Luis. 'Las apariciones como un hecho histórico', *Segundo Encuentro Nacional Guadalupano*, Centro de Estudios Guadalupanos (Mexico, 1978)

Mendieta, Jerónimo de. *Historia eclesiástica indiana*, ed. Joaquín García Icazbalceta (Mexico, 1870, facs. edn, 1971)

Mendoza, Francisco de. *Sermón que en el día de la aparición de la imagen de Guadalupe, doce de diciembre de 1672 predicó . . .* (Mexico, 1673)

Meyer, Jean. *The Cristero Rebellion: The Mexican People between Church and State, 1926–29* (Cambridge, 1976)

Mier, Servando Teresa de. *Escritos y memorias,* ed. Edmundo O'Gorman (Mexico, 1945)

  Historia de la revolución de Nueva España, antiguamente Anahuac (London, 1813, facs. edn, Mexico, 1986)

  Memorias, ed. Antonio Castro Leal, 2 vols. (Mexico, 1946)

  Obras completas: el heterodoxo guadalupano, ed. Edmundo O'Gorman, 3 vols. (Mexico, 1981)

  Pensamiento político del padre Mier, ed. Edmundo O'Gorman (Mexico, 1945)

Millares Carlo, Agustín. *Cuatro estudios biobibliográficos mexicanos* (Mexico, 1986)

Miranda, Francisco Javier. 'Sermón panegyrico de Santa María de Guadalupe', *Sermonario mexicano*, III, 244–55

Montaigne, Michel de. *The Complete Works*, trans. Donald M. Frame (Stanford, 1948)

Montes de Oca y Obregón, Ignacio. *Oraciones fúnebres* (Madrid, 1901)

Morisi-Guerra, Ana. 'The *Apocalypsis Nova*: A Plan for Reform', in *Prophetic Rome in the High Renaissance Period. Essays*, ed. Marjorie Reeves (Oxford, 1992)

Mujica Pinilla, Ramón. *Angeles apócrifos en la América virreinal*, 2nd. edn (Lima, 1996)

Munguía, Clemente de Jesús. *Defensa eclesiástica en el obispado de Michoacán desde fines de 1855 hasta principios de 1858*, 2 vols. (Mexico, 1858)

  Del derecho natural en sus principios comunes y en sus diversas ramificaciones . . . , 3 vols. (Mexico, 1849)

  Dos cartas pastorales (Mexico, 1860)

  Sermón de Nuestra Señora de Guadalupe predicado en la insigne y nacional colegiata, el 12 de Marzo de 1859 (Mexico, 1860)

  Sermón que predicó en la insigne y nacional colegiata de Guadalupe, el 28 de Agosto de 1860 (Mexico, 1860)

Muñoz, Juan Bautista. *Historia del Nuevo Mundo* (Madrid, 1793)

  'Memoria sobre las apariciones y el culto de Nuestra Señora de Guadalupe de México' (1794), reprinted in *Testimonios históricos*, pp. 688–701

Muratori, Lodovico Antonio. *The Science of Rational Devotion*, trans. Alexander Kenny (Dublin, 1789)

Murillo, Diego. *De las excelencias de la insigne y nobilísima ciudad de Zaragoza* (Barcelona, 1616) *Fundación milagrosa de la capilla angélica y apostólica de la Madre del Dios de Pilar* (Barcelona, 1616)

Nebel, Richard. *Santa María Tonantzin Virgen de Guadalupe: Continuidad y transformación religiosa en México*, trans. Carlos Warnholtz Bustillos (Mexico, 1995)

New Catholic Encyclopedia, The, 16 vols. (Washington, 1967)

Noguez, Xavier. *Documentos guadalupanos: un estudio sobre las fuentes de información tempranas en torno a las mariofanías en el Tepeyac* (Mexico, 1993)

Ocampo, Melchor. *Obras completas*, ed. Angel Pola, 3 vols. (Mexico, 1978)

O'Dogherty, Laura, 'El ascenso de una jerarquía eclesial intransigente, 1890–1914', in *Historia de la Iglesia en el siglo XIX*, ed. Manuel Ramos Medina (Mexico, 1998)

O'Gorman, Edmundo. *Destierro de sombras: luz en el origen de la imagen y culto de Nuestra Señora de Guadalupe del Tepeyac* (Mexico, 1986)

La supervivencia política novo-hispana (Mexico, 1969)

(ed.) *Obras completas de Servando de Mier: el heterodoxo guadalupano*, 3 vols. (Mexico, 1981)

Otero, Mariano. *Obras*, ed. Jesús Reyes Heroles, 2 vols. (Mexico, 1967)

Ouspensky, Leonid and Vladimir Lossky. *The Meaning of Icons* (Crestwood, N.Y., 1982)

Oviedo, Gonzalo Fernández de. *Historia general y natural de las Indias*, ed. Juan Pérez de Tudela, 5 vols. (Madrid, 1959)

Oxford Dictionary of the Christian Church, The, ed. F. L. Cross and E. A. Livingstone, 3rd edn (Oxford, 1997)

Palafox y Mendoza, Juan de. *Obras*, 13 vols. (Madrid, 1762)

Paredes, Antonio de. *La auténtica del patronato que en nombre de todo el reino votó la caesarea, nobilísima ciudad de México a Santísima Virgen María Señora Nuestra en su imagen maravillosa de Guadalupe* (Mexico, 1748)

Paso y Troncoso, Francisco del. 'Noticias del indio Marcos y de otros pintores del siglo XVI', *Información que el arzobispo de México don Fray Alonso de Montúfar mandó practicar*, 2nd edn (Mexico, 1891), pp. 167–88, reprinted in *Testimonios históricos*, pp. 129–41

Paz, Octavio. *El ogro filantrópico: historia y política 1971–1978* (Mexico, 1979)

Pelikan, Jaroslav. *Imago Dei: The Byzantine Apologia for Icons* (New Haven, 1990)

The Christian Tradition: A History of the Development of Doctrine, 5 vols. (Chicago, 1971–89)

Pérez, Eutemio (Vicente de Paul Andrade), *Ciertas aparicionistas, obrando de mala fe, inventan algunos episodios* (Cuilpam, 1890)

Picazo, Miguel. *Imagen humana y divina de la Purísima Concepción . . .* (Mexico, 1738)

Pompa y Pompa, Antonio. *El gran acontecimiento guadalupano* (Mexico, 1967)

Poole, Stafford. *Our Lady of Guadalupe: The Origins and Sources of a Mexican National Symbol, 1531–1797* (Tucson, 1995)

Puente, Juan de la. *Tomo primero de la conveniencia de las dos monarquías católicas, la de la Iglesia Romana y la del Imperio Español, y defensa de la precedencia de los Reyes Católicos de España de todos los reyes del mundo* (Madrid, 1612)

Rahner, Karl. *Visions and Prophecies* (New York, 1963)

Ramírez, Juan Antonio *et al. Dios arquitecto: J. B. Villalpando y el templo de Salomón* (Madrid, 1996)

Ramos Gavilán, Alonso. *Historia del célebre santuario de Nuestra Señora de Copacabana y sus milagros e invención de la Cruz de Carabuco* (Lima, 1621)

Reeves, Marjorie. *The Influence of Prophecy in the Later Middle Ages: A Study of Joachimism* (Oxford, 1969)

(ed.) *Prophetic Rome in the High Renaissance Period: Essays* (Oxford, 1992)

Revista Eclesiástica, La (Puebla, 1864)

Ribera, Teobaldo Antonio de. *Relación y estado del culto, lustre, progresos y utilidad de la real congregación sita en la Iglesia de San Felipe el Real* . . . (Madrid, 1740, reprinted in *Colección de obras*), I, 723–804

Rivera Carrera, Norberto. *¿No estoy yo aqui que soy tu Madre?* (Mexico, 1996)

Rivera y San Román, Agustín. 'Sermón de la Santísima Virgen de Guadalupe', *Sermonario mexicano*, III, 473–80

Rivero Lake, Rodrigo. *La visión de un anticuario* (Mexico, 1997)

Robles, Antonio de. *Diario de sucesos notables (1665–1703)*, ed. Antonio Castro Leal, 3 vols. (Mexico, 1946)

Robles, Juan de. *Sermón que predicó* . . . *el día doce de Diciembre de 1681 en la iglesia de Nuestra Señora de Guadalupe de Querétaro, su patria* (Mexico, 1682)

Romero, José Guadalupe. 'Sermón de Nuestra Señora de Guadalupe', *Sermonario mexicano* III, 125–36

Romero de Solís, José Miguel. 'Apostasía episcopal en Tamaulipas, 1896', *Historia Mexicana*, 37 (1987), pp. 239–81

El aguijón del espíritu: historia contemporánea de la Iglesia en México (1895–1990) (Mexico, 1994)

Rosa, Agustín de la. *Defensa de la aparición de Nuestra Señora de Guadalupe* (Mexico, 1896), reprinted in *Testimonios históricos*, pp. 1222–79

Disertatio historico-theologia de aparitione B. M. V. de Guadalupe (Guadalajara, 1887)

Rubin, Miri. *Corpus Christi: The Eucharist in Late Medieval Culture* (Cambridge, 1991)

Saénz de San Antonio, Matías. *Conveniencia relativa entre el término de un templo apostólico, sujeto, que se dedican y la imagen Guadalupe, predicada, que se coloca* (Mexico, 1721)

Sahagún, Bernardino de. *Historia de las cosas de Nueva España*, ed. Angel María Garibay K., 4 vols. (Mexico, 1956)

Historia general de las cosas de la Nueva España, ed. Carlos María de Bustamante, 3 vols. (Mexico, 1829–30)

Sahagún de Arévalo Ladrón de Guevara, Juan Francisco. *Gacetas de México*, 3 vols. (Mexico, 1722–42, facs. edn, 1986)

Salazar, Enrique Roberto. 'El beato Juan Diego, modelo e intercesor de los indígenas', *Encuentro Nacional Indígena* (Mexico, 1993), pp. 127–34

Salazar, Juan de. *Política española*, ed. Miguel Herrero García (Madrid, 1945)

Sánchez, Miguel. *El David seráphico* (Mexico, 1653)

   Imagen de la Virgen María, Madre de Dios de Guadalupe. Milagrosamente aparecida en la ciudad de México. Celebrada en su historia, con la profecía del capítulo doce del Apocalipsis (Mexico, 1648), reprinted in *Testimonios históricos*, pp. 152–275

   Novenas de la Virgen María, Madre de Dios, para sus dos devotísimos santuarios, de los Remedios y Guadalupe (Mexico, 1665), reprinted in *Colección de obras* I, 61–309

   Sermón de San Felipe de Jesús (Mexico, 1640)

Sánchez, Pedro J. *La basilica guadalupana y las fiestas del IV centenario de las apariciones de Nuestra Señora* (Mexico, 1935)

San José, Francisco de. *Historia universal de la primitiva y milagrosa imagen de Nuestra Señora de Guadalupe* (Madrid, 1743)

San Miguel, Juan de. *Sermón . . . a nacimiento de Nuestra Señora y dedicación de su capilla de Guadalupe en la santa iglesia catedral . . .* (Mexico, 1671)

Santa Teresa, Luis de. *Sermón que predicó . . . a la milagrosa aparición de su sacratísima y prodigiosa imagen* (Mexico, 1683)

Santísima Trinidad, Andrés de la. *La venerada y glorificada en todas las naciones por haberse aparecida en estos reinos . . .* (Mexico, 1759)

Saugnieaux, Joel. *Les jansénistes et le renouveau de la prédication dans l'Espagne de la seconde moitié du XVIIIe siècle* (Lyons, 1976)

Sermonario mexicano, ed. Narciso Bassols, 3 vols. (Mexico, 1889)

Siete sermones guadalupanos 1709–1765, ed. David A. Brading (facs. edn, 1994)

Sigüenza y Góngora, Carlos de. *Glorias de Querétaro* (Mexico, 1680, reprinted, 1945)

   Libra astronómica y filosófica (Mexico, 1690, reprinted 1959)

   Paraíso occidental (Mexico, 1684, facs. edn, 1995)

   Piedad heróica de don Fernando Cortés, ed. Jaime Delgado (Madrid, 1960)

   Primavera indiana. Poema sacro-histórico. Idea de María Santísima de Guadalupe de México, copiada de flores (Mexico, 1662), reprinted in *Testimonios históricos*, pp. 334–58

   Obras históricas, ed. José Rojas Garcidueñas (Mexico, 1960)

Smith, Jody Brant. *The Image of Guadalupe*, 2nd edn (Macon, Ga., 1994)

Sousa, Lisa, Stafford Poole and James Lockhart, ed. and trans. *The Story of Guadalupe: Luis Laso de la Vega's 'Huei tlamahuiçoltica' of 1649* (Stanford, 1998)

Stiffoni, Giovanni. 'Intelectuales, sociedad y estado', in *Historia de España*, ed. José María Jover Zamora, vol. XXIX (Madrid, 1988), ii, 119–49.

Stratton, Susanne L. *The Immaculate Conception in Spanish Art* (Cambridge, 1994)

Tanner, Norman P. *Decrees of the Ecumenical Councils*, 2 vols. (London, 1990)

Tapia Méndez, Aureliano. *El siervo de Dios. José Antonio Plancarte y Labastida. Profeta y mártir*, 2nd edn (Mexico, 1987)

Tate, Robert B. *Ensayos sobre la historiografía peninsular del siglo XV* (Madrid, 1970)

Taylor, William. 'The Virgin of Guadalupe: An Inquiry into the Social History of Marian Devotion', *American Ethnologist*, 20 (1986), pp. 9–33

Tellez Girón, José María. 'Impugnación al manifiesto satisfactorio del Dr José Ignacio Bartolache', *Testimonios historicos*, pp. 651–88

Tena Ramírez, Felipe. *Leyes fundamentales de México 1808–1967* (Mexico, 1967)

Tercero, Juan Luis. *La causa guadalupana: los últimos veinte años (1875–1895)* (Ciudad Victoria, Tamaulipas, 1896)

Testimonios históricos guadalupanos, ed. Ernesto de la Torre Villar and Ramiro Navarro de Anda (Mexico, 1982)

Theodore the Studite, St. *On the Holy Icons*, trans. Catherine P. Roth (Crestwood, N.Y., 1981)

Tornel y Mendivil, Julián. *La aparición de Nuestra Señora de Guadalupe de México*, 2 vols. (Orizaba, 1849)

Torquemada, Juan de. *Los veinte y un libros rituales y monarquía indiana*, ed. Miguel León-Portilla *et al.*, 7 vols. (Mexico, 1975–83)

Torra de Arana, Eduardo, *et al. El Pilar es la Columna: historia de una devoción. Ensayos* (Zaragoza, 1995)

Torres, Cayetano Antonio de. *Sermón de la Santísima Virgen de Guadalupe . . .* (Mexico, 1757)

Tovar de Teresa, Guillermo. *Bibliografía novohispana de arte*, 2 vols. (Mexico, 1988)
    Miguel Cabrera, pintor de camarín de la reina celestial (Mexico, 1995)
    Pintura y escultura en Nueva España 1557–1640 (Mexico, 1992)

Trabulse, Elías. *Ciencia y religión en el siglo XVII* (Mexico, 1974)
    Los manuscritos perdidos de Sigüenza y Góngora (Mexico, 1988)

Trevor-Roper, Hugh. *Renaissance Essays* (London, 1985)

Uribe, José Patricio Fernández de. *Sermón de Nuestra Señora de Guadalupe de México (1777). Disertación histórico-crítico en que el autor . . . sostiene la celestial imagen de Nuestra Señora de Guadalupe de México milagrosamente aparecida al humilde neófito Juan Diego* (1778) (Mexico, 1801)

Usigli, Rodolfo. *Corona de Luz* (Mexico, 1965)

Valadés, José C. *El porfirismo, historia de un régimen*, 2 vols. (Mexico, 1948)

Velásquez, Primo Feliciano. *La aparición de Santa María de Guadalupe* (Mexico, 1931, facs. edn with introduction by J. Jesús Jiménez López, 1981)

Vera, Fortino Hipólito. *Colección de documentos eclesiásticos de México*, 3 vols. (Amecameca, 1887)

Contestación histórico-crítico en defensa de la maravillosa aparición de la Santísima Virgen de Guadalupe (Querétaro, 1892)

La milagrosa aparición de Nuestra Señora de Guadalupe comprobada por una información levantada en el siglo XVI contra los enemigos de tan asombroso acontecimiento (Amecameca, 1890)

Sermón pronunciado en el templo de Capuchinas, residencia actual de la imagen guadalupana (Querétaro, 1890)

Tesoro guadalupano. Noticias de los libros, documentos, inscripciones etc. que tratan, mencionan o aluden a la aparición y devoción de Nuestra Señora de Guadalupe, 2 vols. (Amecameca, 1887)

Veytia, Mariano Fernández de Echeverría y. *Descripción de las cuatro milagrosas imagenes de Nuestra Señora que se veneran en la muy noble, leal e imperial ciudad de México* (Mexico, 1820, fasc. edn, 1967)

Vidal de Figueroa, José. *Teórica de la prodigiosa imagen de la Virgen Santa María de Guadalupe de México* (Mexico, 1661)

Villa Sánchez, Juan de. *Sermón de la milagrosa imagen de Nuestra Señora de Guadalupe* (Mexico, 1734)

Wallace-Hadrill, D. S. *Eusebius of Caesarea* (London, 1960)

Ward, Benedicta. *Miracles and the Medieval Mind: Theory, Record and Event 1000–1215* (Aldershot, 1987)

Webster, Susan Verdi. *Art and Ritual in Golden Age Spain* (Princeton, 1998)

Weil-Garris, Kathleen. *The Santa Casa di Loreto: Problems in Cinquecento Sculpture*, 2 vols. (New York, 1997)

West, Delmo C. and Sandra Zimidars-Swartz, *Joachim of Fiore* (Bloomington, 1983)

Zavala, Silvio. *Francisco del Paso y Troncoso: su misión en Europa 1892–1916* (Mexico, 1938)

Index